Gateway to American Civics and Government

The Bridge to Success on Florida's EOC Test

Mark Jarrett, Ph.D. ▪ Robert Yahng, J.D.

Florida Transformative Education

Florida Transformative Education
10 Folin Lane
Lafayette, CA 94549
Tel: (925) 906-9742 Fax: (925) 939-6557 www.floridasocialstudies.com

Florida Transformative Education and its logo are registered trademarks.

Printed in the United States of America

Our books are printed on long-lasting acid-free paper. When it is available, we choose paper that has been manufactured by environmentally responsible processes. These may include using trees grown in sustainable forests, incorporating recycled paper, minimizing chlorine in bleaching, or recycling the energy produced at the paper mill.

ISBN 978-0-9894845-9-6

Revised Edition

27 27 26 25 24 23 10 9 8 7 6 5 4 3 2 1

About the Authors

Mark Jarrett studied at Columbia University (B.A.), the London School of Economics (M.A. in international history), Stanford University (Ph.D. in history), and the University of California at Berkeley, where he received a law degree with honors (Order of the Coif). He was an editor of the school's law review and received the American Jurisprudence Award for Comparative Legal History. He studied constitutional law with Robert Post, now dean of the Yale Law School. Mark has taught at Hofstra University, at the Mander Portman School in London, and in the New York City Public Schools. He has served as a test writer for the New York State Board of Regents, and practiced law at Baker & McKenzie, the world's largest law firm. He is the co-author of more than thirty test preparation books and textbooks. James Sheehan, past President of the American Historical Association, describes Mark's book, *The Congress of Vienna and its Legacy* (London: I. B. Tauris, 2013), as "beautifully written" and providing "a fine sense of political structures without losing the human element," while Robert Jervis, past president of the American Political Science Association, calls his book a "model treatment." In 2021, Dr. Jarrett was the recipient of the Dr. Randy Felton Outstanding Citizen Award of the Florida Association of Social Studies Supervisors (FASSS).

Robert Yahng has taught Honors U.S. Government and Honors Micro and Macroeconomics at Salesian High School in Richmond, California, for the past sixteen years. He has been the school's Chairman of the Board of Directors from 2003 to 2013. Robert earned a B.A. in History at Berea College in Kentucky, the South's first interracial college, where his grandfather, father and mother were professors. He received his Juris Doctor degree from the University of Kentucky School of Law. Robert was a partner in the law firm of Baker & McKenzie for twenty-one years. He was the Managing Partner of its San Francisco and Palo Alto offices in the 1990s, and also founded its Taipei office. From 1999 to 2002, he served as a Public Governor on the Board of Governors of the Pacific Stock Exchange. He has been a member of the Board of Trustees of Berea College since 2003 and was Chairman of the Board from 2018 to 2021. From 1997 to 2014, he has been Chairman of American Bridge Company, which constructed the Bob Graham Sunshine Skyway Bridge, and the new Bay Bridge in San Francisco, as well as many other national landmarks, including the Chrysler Building in New York City. From 1967 to 1972, Robert served in the USAF and was honorably discharged with the rank of captain. In 2019, Mr. Yahng was inducted into the Hall of Fame of the University of Kentucky Law School

The Cover

The cover shows the Arlington Memorial Bridge, Washington Monument, and Lincoln Memorial in Washington, D.C.

Contents

Dedications

To Małgorzata, Alexander, and Julia Jarrett

—Mark Jarrett

To my family, Tina, Christopher, and Kacie

—Robert Yahng

Acknowledgments

The authors wish to thank Social Studies supervisors and teachers across the State of Florida, too numerous to name, for their invaluable suggestions and generous comments on earlier editions of this book.

The authors would also like to thank Mr. Alex Jarrett, Ms. Julia Jarrett, Ms. Krisanne Snider, Ms. Julia Soloveva and Ms. Małgorzata Jarrett, for a multitude of services in the preparation of this book, from finding images and typing to writing initial drafts of some study cards. Thank you also to Ms. Nina Tyksinski for her proofreading skills and to artist Jerianne Van Dijk for her wonderful illustrations. Finally, we would like to thank Jonathan Peck and Joan Keyes of Dovetail Publishing Services for their creativity in the design and layout of this book.

This is not to be taken as an endorsement of this product by any of the individuals or their organizations listed above. In fact, in some cases we were not able to follow all of their recommendations. Any remaining errors are therefore our own. Nevetheless we have endeavored to remain as doggedly close as possible to Florida's statewide standards for Civics and Government. Everything mentioned in those standards is, we truly believe, clearly and comprehensively explained in this book. We hope you enjoy reading and using this book as much as we enjoyed writing it.

Preface

"We Want You!" America's Future and Your Citizenship Skills

Welcome to civics! Civics is the study of government and citizenship.

Why is it so important for you to study civics?

The answer lies in the fact that you are either an American citizen or may someday become one. For the future prosperity and success of our nation, we depend on you to perform your obligations and responsibilities as a citizen—to vote, to obey laws, to pay taxes, and to serve on a jury if summoned. Perhaps you may even run for political office or serve in the armed forces in our nation's defense. Look around your classroom. Maybe you or one of your classmates will be a future mayor, district court judge, U.S. Senator, or even President of the United States.

You will also want to receive the rights and benefits of citizenship, including freedom of speech, freedom of religion, security of property, the right to expect others to follow the law, and the right to help choose our leaders and to shape our nation's policies.

All this lies within your grasp! That is because the United States has a democratic government and we live under the rule of law.

In fact, the United States was the first large nation in modern history to adopt the democratic system of government. In a democratic government, people are the ultimate source of governmental power. Instead of being ruled by all-powerful kings or dictators, we elect our leaders to fixed terms in office. We give them only limited powers, carefully defined in our Constitution and other laws. This type of democratic government with elected representatives is known as a republic.

What is Government?

Much of this book describes the American system of government. You may be wondering: what, exactly, is government?

Government is the organization that makes up rules for the community, settles disputes, and protects the community from outsiders. It not only makes these rules, but also has the power to enforce them.

The word *govern* comes from a Greek word, *kubernan*, which means to steer a ship. Just as sailors steer a ship, our government steers our society in the right direction.

What is Citizenship?

Not everyone living in the United States can participate in government by voting, holding political office or serving on juries. To fully participate in our democratic system of government, one must be an American citizen. A **citizen** is a legally recognized member of a community.

The ancient Greeks were the first to develop the concept of citizenship, just as they were the first to develop the system of democracy. In fact, the two concepts often go hand in hand. However, for Greeks the concept of citizenship was very limited. It did not include foreigners, women, children or slaves.

The ancient Romans expanded the concept of citizenship into a legal category. Citizens of the Roman Empire were entitled to certain rights. The Romans strengthened their empire by granting the rights and benefits of Roman citizenship to conquered peoples who promised to obey their laws. In fact, our word "citizen" comes from *civis*, the ancient Roman word for citizen, and from *civitas*, the Roman word for city. A Roman citizen was, in effect, a member of the imperial city of Rome.

Today, the world is divided into almost 200 independent countries. Each country has its own rules for citizenship. Citizenship—legal recognition of being the member of a country—gives a person the right to live in that country and to carry its passport when traveling to other countries.

In the United States, citizens are entitled to special rights but also bear special obligations and responsibilities. Our system of democratic government relies on the active participation of its citizens to succeed. As you know, American citizens are expected to vote, to obey laws, to pay taxes, and to serve on juries. Young men must also register for possible future military service. Americans also have the right to express their opinions, to complain to their government leaders, and to run for public office.

To fulfill their obligations and responsibilities, and to enjoy their rights, our citizens should be informed, be active, and respect the rights of others. Voting becomes a meaningless exercise if we don't know the major issues, listen to the chief arguments on each side, check what we are told against known facts, and come to our own conclusions. Active participation in the political process is just as important as being informed. Democratic government would quickly collapse if everyone left volunteer efforts, the support of candidates, and running for public office to someone else.

The lessons of history teach us, again and again, that terrible things can happen to a society when its citizens are uninformed, misinformed, or not actively engaged in their government.

So, as you read this book, keep this message in mind: we are all depending on **you**!

How Does One Become an American Citizen?

Everyone born in the United States, or born from American parents (even when abroad), is automatically an American citizen. This is known as **birthright citizenship**.

Not everyone living in the United States today, however, is a citizen. Some people are visitors or **lawful permanent residents** (*foreign nationals who are authorized to live and work in the United States permanently*).

A foreign national can become an American citizen by being "**naturalized**." To be naturalized, a person must: (1) be at least 18 years old, (2) be a lawful permanent resident, and (3) have lived in the United States for five years before applying. Applicants must also (4) be of "good character," (5) have a working knowledge of English, and (6) pass a brief test on American history and government. Finally, the applicant must (7) swear an oath of loyalty to the United States. You will learn more about the naturalization process later in this book.

What You Will Learn in this Book

Gateway to American Civics and Government explains everything you need to know to become an informed and active citizen.

This book begins by examining the roots of our system of representative government in the ancient world and later in England and its colonies. You will learn how English traditions and new ideas in Europe in the 17th and 18th centuries led people to develop more democratic forms of government. The English colonies, far from European rulers, provided fertile ground for these new ideas to take shape.

Then you will learn about the American Revolution, the Declaration of Independence, and the U.S. Constitution. American colonists first struggled with the question of whether to become independent. Afterwards, they had the problem of designing a new system of government that would be effective but that would still respect individual rights. To make sure our national government was strong enough but not oppressive, the authors of the U.S. Constitution introduced the separation of powers, checks and balances, limited powers, individual rights, and federalism. The result was the system of government we still have today—with its separate legislative, executive and judicial branches, and its division of power between our national government and the state governments.

After learning how our system of government came into being, you will then explore how it works today. First, you will look at Congress, our national law-making body. Who sits in Congress? How are its members selected? How is Congress organized? How does it make our laws? Next, you will look at the Presidency. How is the President of the United States elected? What are the President's powers under the Constitution? How is the President assisted by administrative agencies?

After that, you will consider the judicial branch—the U.S. Supreme Court and other federal courts. You will learn how the Supreme Court established its power of "judicial review"—the ability to declare a state or federal law "unconstitutional" if the Court determines it conflicts with the U.S. Constitution. You will also learn what laws are, what courts do, and the differences between state and federal laws, civil and criminal laws, and statutory and common law (*laws passed by legislatures and those based on prior court decisions*).

Next, you will look at the Bill of Rights and later amendments to the U.S. Constitution that expanded the rights of individuals. You will also review several important Supreme Court decisions that interpreted and expanded individual rights.

From here, you will move to state governments—especially the government of Florida—and examine the complex relationship between our national and state governments known as "federalism."

After this, you will look at the obligations, responsibilities and rights of citizenship, and how citizens participate in politics and government to determine public policy—the decisions that our government actually makes. You will review what citizenship is and how foreign nationals can become American citizens. Then you will see how citizens can participate in political decision-making by attending civic meetings, petitioning government leaders, peacefully protesting, joining political parties, participating in election campaigns, and voting in elections. You will also see how public opinion is shaped by political advertisements, paid lobbyists and the "media"—newspapers, magazines, television, radio and the Internet. And you will see how people monitor, influence and hold government officials accountable.

Finally, you will look at the different types of governments and economic systems around the world, and consider how the United States relates to the rest of the international community through its foreign policy.

Through the study of civics and government, you will learn how government affects your life now and in the future, and how you can influence government through the exercise of informed, active and responsible citizenship.

Florida's Civics End-Of-Course Assessment

This year you will be studying civics and government. You will also be taking Florida's End-of-Course Assessment. The assessment tests your knowledge of 39 Benchmarks.

Florida's 39 Civics and Government Benchmarks

SS.7.CG.1.1 Analyze the influences of ancient Greece, ancient Rome, and the Judeo-Christian tradition on America's constitutional republic.

SS.7.CG.1.2 Trace the principles underlying America's founding ideas on law and government.

SS.7.CG.1.3 Trace the impact that the Magna Carta, Mayflower Compact, English Bill of Rights, and Thomas Paine's Common Sense had on colonists' views of government.

SS.7.CG.1.4 Analyze how Enlightenment ideas, including Montesquieu's view of separation of powers and John Locke's theories related to natural law and Locke's social contract, influenced the Founding.

SS.7.CG.1.5 Describe how British policies and responses to colonial concerns led to the writing of the Declaration of Independence.

SS.7.CG.1.6 Analyze the ideas and grievances set forth in the Declaration of Independence.

SS.7.CG.1.7 Explain how the weaknesses of the Articles of Confederation led to the writing of the U.S. Constitution.

SS.7.CG.1.8 Explain the purpose of the Preamble to the U.S. Constitution.

SS.7.CG.1.9 Describe how the U.S. Constitution limits the powers of government through separation of powers, checks and balances, individual rights, rule of law, and due process of law.

SS.7.CG.1.10 Compare the viewpoints of the Federalists and the Anti-Federalists regarding ratification of the U.S. Constitution and including a bill of rights.

SS.7.CG.1.11 Define the rule of law and recognize its influence on the development of legal, political, and governmental systems in the United States.

SS.7.CG.2.1 Define the term "citizen," and explain the constitutional means of becoming a U.S. citizen.

SS.7.CG.2.2 Differentiate between obligations and responsibilities of U.S. citizenship, and evaluate their impact on society.

SS.7.CG.2.3 Identify and apply the rights contained in the Bill of Rights and other amendments to the U.S. Constitution.

SS.7.CG.2.4 Explain how the U.S. Constitution and the Bill of Rights safeguard individual rights.

SS.7.CG.2.5 Describe the trial process and the role of juries in the administration of justice at the state and federal levels.

SS.7.CG.2.6 Examine the election and voting process at the local, state, and national levels.

SS.7.CG.2.7 Identify the constitutional qualifications required to hold state and national office.

SS.7.CG.2.8 Examine the impact of media, individuals, and interest groups on monitoring and influencing government.

SS.7.CG.2.9 Analyze media and political communications and identify examples of bias, symbolism, and propaganda.

SS.7.CG.2.10 Explain the process for citizens to address a state or local problem by researching public policy alternatives, identifying appropriate government agencies to address the issue and determining a course of action.

SS.7.CG.3.1 Analyze the advantages of the United States' constitutional republic over other forms of government in safeguarding liberty, freedom, and a representative government.

SS.7.CG.3.2 Explain the advantages of a federal system of government over other systems in balancing local sovereignty with national unity and protecting against authoritarianism.

SS.7.CG.3.3 Describe the structure and function of the three branches of government established in the U.S. Constitution.

SS.7.CG.3.4 Explain the relationship between state and national governments as written in Article IV of the U.S. Constitution and the 10th Amendment.

SS.7.CG.3.5 Explain the amendment process outlined in Article V of the U.S. Constitution.

SS.7.CG.3.6 Analyze how the 13th, 14th, 15th, 19th, 24th, and 26th Amendments broadened participation in the political process.

SS.7.CG.3.7 Explain the structure, functions, and processes of the legislative branch of government.

SS.7.CG.3.8 Explain the structure, functions, and processes of the executive branch of government.

SS.7.CG.3.9 Explain the structure, functions, and processes of the judicial branch of government.

SS.7.CG.3.10 Identify sources and types of law.

SS.7.CG.3.11 Analyze the effects of landmark Supreme Court decisions on law, liberty, and the interpretation of the U.S. Constitution.

SS.7.CG.3.12 Compare the U.S. and Florida constitutions.

SS.7.CG.3.13 Explain government obligations to its citizens and the services provided at the local, state, and national levels.

SS.7.CG.3.14 Explain the purpose and function of the Electoral College in electing the President of the United States.

SS.7.CG.3.15 Analyze the advantages of capitalism and the free market in the United States over government-controlled economic systems (e.g., socialism and communism) in regard to economic freedom and raising the standard of living for citizens.

SS.7.CG.4.1 Explain the relationship between U.S. foreign and domestic policy.

SS.7.CG.4.2 Describe the United States' and citizen participation in international organizations.

SS.7.CG.4.3 Describe examples of the United States' actions and reactions in international conflicts.

Special Features of *Gateway to American Civics and Government*

▸ We usually learn best when we have a general idea of what we are about to learn in advance. Every chapter in this book begins with information that tells you what the chapter is about. First, there is the **title of the chapter**, which describes its topic. This is followed by a **list of Florida Social Studies Standards** that are covered in the chapter. These standards are the Benchmarks listed on pages viii and ix.

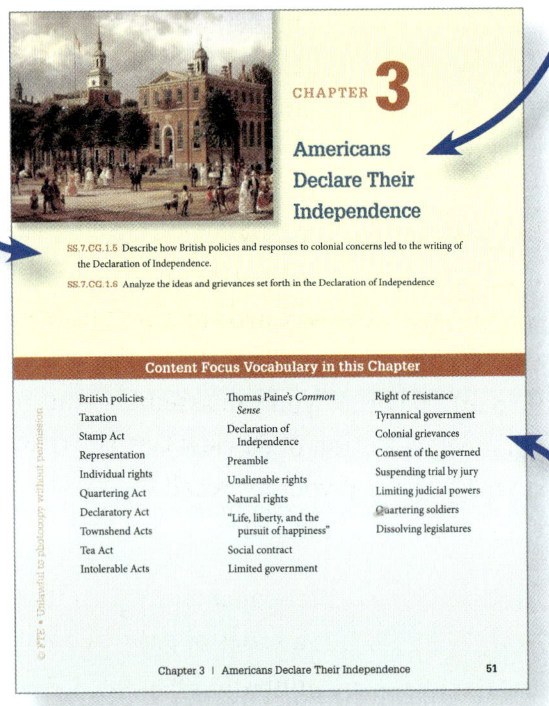

CHAPTER 3

Americans Declare Their Independence

SS.7.CG.1.5 Describe how British policies and responses to colonial concerns led to the writing of the Declaration of Independence.

SS.7.CG.1.6 Analyze the ideas and grievances set forth in the Declaration of Independence

Content Focus Vocabulary in this Chapter

British policies	Thomas Paine's *Common Sense*	Right of resistance
Taxation	Declaration of Independence	Tyrannical government
Stamp Act	Preamble	Colonial grievances
Representation	Unalienable rights	Consent of the governed
Individual rights	Natural rights	Suspending trial by jury
Quartering Act	"Life, liberty, and the pursuit of happiness"	Limiting judicial powers
Declaratory Act	Social contract	Quartering soldiers
Townshend Acts	Limited government	Dissolving legislatures
Tea Act		
Intolerable Acts		

Chapter 3 | Americans Declare Their Independence 51

▸ At the bottom of the first page of each chapter is a list of **Concept Focus Vocabulary in This Chapter.** You can use this list to guide your way through the chapter. Most of these terms are either listed in the Benchmarks or in the "Item Specifications" guide provided to those teachers who are writing your test.

Florida "Keys" to Learning

1. After the French and Indian War, the British government was deeply in debt. It had borrowed large sums of money to pay for the war. This led to new British policies (*actions by government*). Parliament passed a series of laws to tax the colonists. It made no attempt to obtain the colonists' consent (*approval; agreement*) to this taxation. There was a causal relationship between British colonial polices (*policies towards the colonies*) and colonial concerns (*things that upset the colonists*). A causal relationship exists when one event or development leads to another—it causes the second event to occur. In this case, British policies led to colonial concerns.

2. The first of the new British taxes was the Stamp Act. This law required colonists to put government stamps on all court documents, licenses, newspapers, and other documents. Because the colonies were not represented in Parliament, the colonists objected that there should be no taxation without representation. Colonial assemblies sent petitions to Parliament to change the law, and many colonists boycotted (*refused to buy*) British goods. Parliament finally repealed (*set aside; cancelled*) the Stamp Act after widespread colonial protests.

3. Although it repealed the Stamp Act, Parliament also passed the Declaratory Act. This act stated that Parliament had the right to pass laws for the colonies, including taxes. Parliament then passed the Townshend Acts. These laws placed new taxes on glass and other household goods in the colonies.

4. To prevent colonial unrest, the British government sent more troops to North America. Parliament passed the Quartering Act, which required the colonists to feed and house some of the British troops in their barns and homes. Despite these steps, the colonists loudly protested against the Townshend Acts.

5. Parliament eventually repealed the Townshend Acts. However, Parliament next passed the Tea Act. This act placed a tax on tea brought from India to the colonies. Again, it was passed without the colonists' consent.

6. The "Boston Tea Party" was a protest against the Tea Act. A group of colonists boarded British ships at night and threw chests of tea into Boston Harbor. The British government was greatly angered by this destruction of property. It passed the "Intolerable Acts," which closed Boston Harbor, suspended (*temporarily dissolved*) the colonial legislature of Massachusetts, and allowed judges instead of juries to try cases. The colonists believed the British government was threatening their individual rights (*the rights to which they were entitled under both English law and natural law.*)

7. British troops and armed colonists fired on each other in April 1775, starting the American Revolution. Delegates from the colonies met in two Continental Congresses.

8. In January 1776, Thomas Paine's *Common Sense* was published. It urged the colonists to seek independence. In June 1776, a majority of the Second Continental Congress agreed to support independence. A special committee was formed to write a declaration that would explain this decision.

9. The Preamble (*introduction*) to the Declaration of Independence announced the American theory of government: (1) that people have certain "unalienable rights" (*rights that cannot be separated*), which include the rights to "life, liberty, and the pursuit of happiness" (*our right to live freely and to seek our own goals*). These are natural rights that we are born with: people are endowed by their Creator (*given by God*) with these rights, which cannot be rightfully taken away; (2) that governments are created as part of a social contract (*agreement among the members of a society*) to protect these rights and exist with the consent of the governed (*approval of the people they rule*); (3) that when a government tries to take away these rights, its people have the right to change that government, by force if necessary; and (4) that people should not change their government lightly (*easily*).

10. Much of the Declaration is taken up by its list of colonial grievances (*complaints from the*

52 Chapter 3 | Americans Declare Their Independence

▸ This is followed by **Florida "Keys" to Learning**. No, these aren't the real Florida Keys at the southern end of the state! They are the keys to what you should know for the test. This section provides a summary of the most important ideas and facts, forming the backbone to the chapter. You might look at these before you read the chapter to see just how many of these "Keys" you already know. The rest of the chapter simply expands on these key ideas and facts. Once you have finished the chapter, you can read through the "Keys" again as a form of review. If you don't understand or remember one of these "Keys," you might want to look back at the more detailed discussion in the chapter. Finally, you may want to review all 18 **Florida "Keys" to Learning** sections (one for each chapter) just before you take the Civics End-of-Course Assessment.

▸ The "Keys" are followed by the main text of the chapter. Each chapter is divided into sections. The text is accompanied by illustrations, diagrams, graphs and maps. Information in each chapter is organized around core concepts to make it easier to learn.

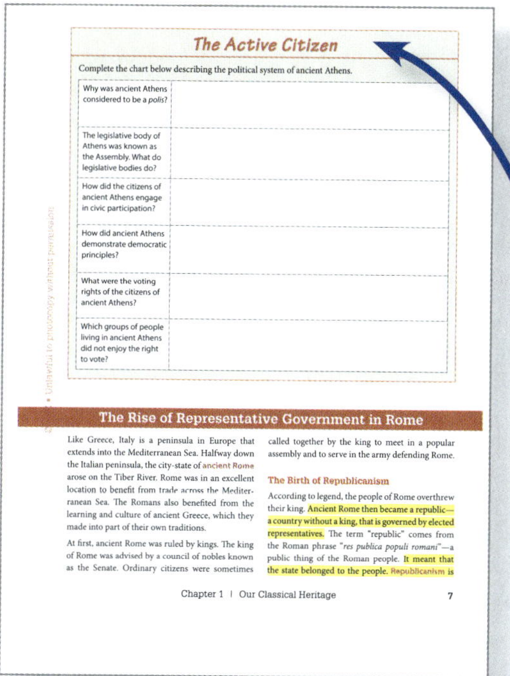

The Active Citizen

Complete the chart below describing the political system of ancient Athens.

Why was ancient Athens considered to be a *polis*?	
The legislative body of Athens was known as the Assembly. What do legislative bodies do?	
How did the citizens of ancient Athens engage in civic participation?	
How did ancient Athens demonstrate democratic principles?	
What were the voting rights of the citizens of ancient Athens?	
Which groups of people living in ancient Athens did not enjoy the right to vote?	

The Rise of Representative Government in Rome

Like Greece, Italy is a peninsula in Europe that extends into the Mediterranean Sea. Halfway down the Italian peninsula, the city-state of ancient Rome arose on the Tiber River. Rome was in an excellent location to benefit from trade across the Mediterranean Sea. The Romans also benefited from the learning and culture of ancient Greece, which they made into part of their own traditions.

At first, ancient Rome was ruled by kings. The king of Rome was advised by a council of nobles known as the Senate. Ordinary citizens were sometimes called together by the king to meet in a popular assembly and to serve in the army defending Rome.

The Birth of Republicanism

According to legend, the people of Rome overthrew their king. Ancient Rome then became a republic—a country without a king, that is governed by elected representatives. The term "republic" comes from the Roman phrase "*res publica populi romani*"—a public thing of the Roman people. It meant that the state belonged to the people. Republicanism is

Chapter 1 | Our Classical Heritage 7

- Throughout the text, you will find **The Active Citizen**. This feature recommends activities for you and your classmates to complete under the supervision of your teacher. In these activities, you may be asked to conduct research, to interpret a historical document, to role-play, or to participate in government and politics.

- At the end of each chapter, there are several additional features to help you review concepts in the chapter, reinforce your understanding, and check your knowledge. First, there is a **Concept Map**. This map provides an overview showing how all the developments in the chapter are related.

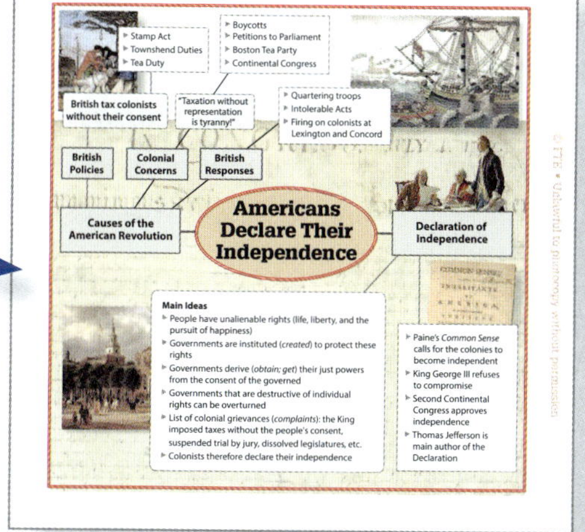

- This is followed by a series of **Review Cards**.

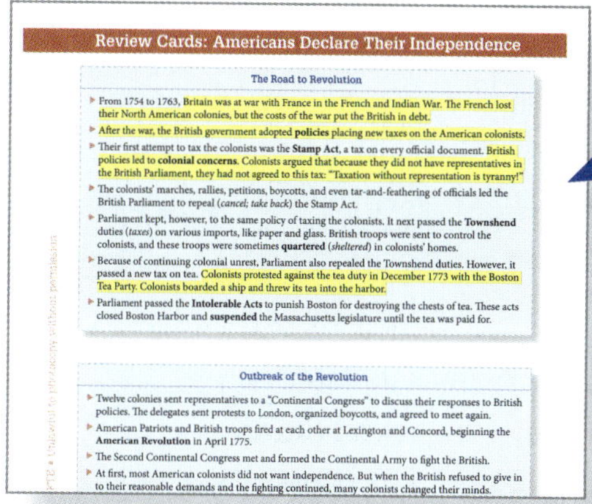

Review Cards: Americans Declare Their Independence

The Road to Revolution

- From 1754 to 1763, Britain was at war with France in the French and Indian War. The French lost their North American colonies, but the costs of the war put the British in debt.
- After the war, the British government adopted **policies** placing new taxes on the American colonists.
- Their first attempt to tax the colonists was the **Stamp Act**, a tax on every official document. British policies led to **colonial concerns**. Colonists argued that because they did not have representatives in the British Parliament, they had not agreed to this tax: "Taxation without representation is tyranny!"
- The colonists' marches, rallies, petitions, boycotts, and even tar-and-feathering of officials led the British Parliament to repeal (*cancel; take back*) the Stamp Act.
- Parliament kept, however, to the same policy of taxing the colonists. It next passed the **Townshend** duties (*taxes*) on various imports, like paper and glass. British troops were sent to control the colonists, and these troops were sometimes **quartered** (*sheltered*) in colonists' homes.
- Because of continuing colonial unrest, Parliament also repealed the Townshend duties. However, it passed a new tax on tea. Colonists protested against the tea duty in December 1773 with the Boston Tea Party. Colonists boarded a ship and threw its tea into the harbor.
- Parliament passed the **Intolerable Acts** to punish Boston for destroying the chests of tea. These acts closed Boston Harbor and **suspended** the Massachusetts legislature until the tea was paid for.

Outbreak of the Revolution

- Twelve colonies sent representatives to a "Continental Congress" to discuss their responses to British policies. The delegates sent protests to London, organized boycotts, and agreed to meet again.
- American Patriots and British troops fired at each other at Lexington and Concord, beginning the **American Revolution** in April 1775.
- The Second Continental Congress met and formed the Continental Army to fight the British.
- At first, most American colonists did not want independence. But when the British refused to give in to their reasonable demands and the fighting continued, many colonists changed their minds.

These cards summarize the most important information in the chapter, which may appear on Florida's End-of-Course Assessment. You can use these **Review Cards** in a variety of ways. You might cover part of a **Review Card** and check if you can recall the information you have covered. You might make your own pictures to illustrate a **Review Card** or add further information. You can also use **Review Cards** to test your friends, or to make sample test questions. As you read through the book, you can assemble your own personal collection of **Review Cards**. Scramble them up to see if you can recall their contents when they are not in order.

- Each content chapter concludes with **What Do You Know?** This is a series of practice multiple-choice questions, similar in format to the assessment items on Florida's End-of-Course Assessment.

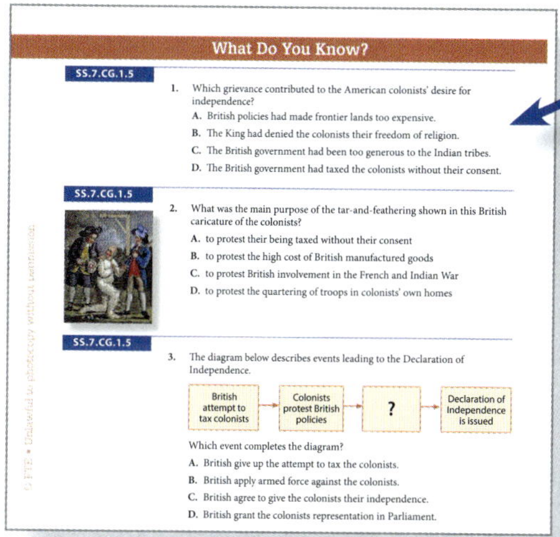

What Do You Know?

SS.7.CG.1.5

1. Which grievance contributed to the American colonists' desire for independence?
   A. British policies had made frontier lands too expensive.
   B. The King had denied the colonists their freedom of religion.
   C. The British government had been too generous to the Indian tribes.
   D. The British government had taxed the colonists without their consent.

SS.7.CG.1.5

2. What was the main purpose of the tar-and-feathering shown in this British caricature of the colonists?
   A. to protest their being taxed without their consent
   B. to protest the high cost of British manufactured goods
   C. to protest British involvement in the French and Indian War
   D. to protest the quartering of troops in colonists' own homes

SS.7.CG.1.5

3. The diagram below describes events leading to the Declaration of Independence.

   British attempt to tax colonists → Colonists protest British policies → ? → Declaration of Independence is issued

   Which event completes the diagram?
   A. British give up the attempt to tax the colonists.
   B. British apply armed force against the colonists.
   C. British agree to give the colonists their independence.
   D. British grant the colonists representation in Parliament.

The last chapter of the book provides **a final practice test** covering all of the Benchmarks in the book. The questions on this test follow the same specifications as the actual Florida Civics and Government End-of-Course Assessment. By taking this test and reviewing any errors you make, you can be sure you have prepared your very best for the test!

There are many ways to use this book. You may want to use it as your main resource. It covers everything you need to know for the test.

You may also want to use this book for a final review in the weeks just before the test. With its many special learning features, reading through this book should be a great way for you to recall everything you have studied to prepare for the test.

How to Answer a Multiple-Choice Question

Besides knowing what is being tested, you also have to be a good test-taker to do your best on this or any test. Here are three steps we recommend for answering multiple-choice questions on Florida's Civics and Government End-of-Course Assessment. These same steps can be used, in fact, to answer multiple-choice questions on almost any test:

1. Understand the Question

Make sure you read the question carefully. Take special care to examine any graph, picture, document or other information that appears as part of the question itself.

Make sure you understand what the question asks for. Questions on the End-of-Course Assessment will most likely ask you one of the following:

- to identify the **cause** of something: *what made it happen?*
- to identify the **effect** or **impact** of something: *how did it change things?*
- to **explain** or **describe** an event or development: *how did it happen? what is it like?*
- to **identify** or **define** something: *what is it?*
- to **compare** two or more things: *what are their* **similarities** *and* **differences?**
- to **sequence** events: *in what order did they occur? which was first or last?*
- to **interpret** a document, an illustration, a cartoon, a map, a table, or a graph
- to make a **generalization** or to draw a **conclusion**
- to provide an **example** of something: *which best illustrates this principle?*
- to make a **prediction**: *what is most likely to happen next?*

2. Think about What You Know

Here comes the hardest part. Many students wish to rush ahead: they want to finish the test early. To do your best, however, you have to take your time. Once you have read and understood the question, take a moment to think about the topic it asks about.

For example, suppose a question asks you how colonial concerns led to the writing of the Declaration of Independence. You should think about what you can remember about the causes of the American Revolution and how those events led the colonists to declare independence. You might recall the Stamp Act, "taxation without representation," the Boston Tea Party, the Intolerable Acts, the violence at Lexington and Concord, and the meeting of the Second Continental Congress. You might also remember how the members of the Continental Congress debated whether to seek independence, and how Thomas Jefferson wrote the first draft of the Declaration.

Then you might try to answer the question in your mind *without looking at the answer choices.*

3. Answer the Question

Now you are actually ready to answer the question. Look carefully again at the question itself. Then look at all four answer choices. Eliminate any answer choices that are obviously wrong or irrelevant (*not related to the question or its topic*). Then choose the ***best*** of the remaining answer choices, based on your knowledge and understanding.

If you have extra time after you have finished the test, be sure to check your work again to eliminate any careless mistakes.

Special Types of Questions

Many questions on Florida's End-of-Course Assessment will ask about a "graphic" that is a part of the question. It is important for you to be able to interpret these different types of graphics, including maps, graphs, charts, tables, political cartoons, illustrations, photographs, and timelines. Each of these is simply another way of presenting or displaying information.

Questions may ask what the graphic shows, or they may ask you to make an inference or draw a conclusion about the graphic. You might also be asked to identify the causes or effects of a situation or event described by the picture, timeline, photograph or other graphic. Often you will have to apply your knowledge of civics to answer the question.

The rest of this chapter looks at six of the most important types of graphics that may appear on the test.

Maps

A map shows geographical information. It may show the boundaries between states, the locations of cities, or election districts. A *key* or *legend* will often explain any symbols on the map. Maps may also have a *scale* to show what their dimensions represent in real life, and a *compass* (or *direction indicator*).

- What does this map show?
- Based on the map, how many states gave their electoral votes to Donald Trump in the 2016 presidential election?
- Based on the map, how many electoral votes did Florida have in the 2016 election?

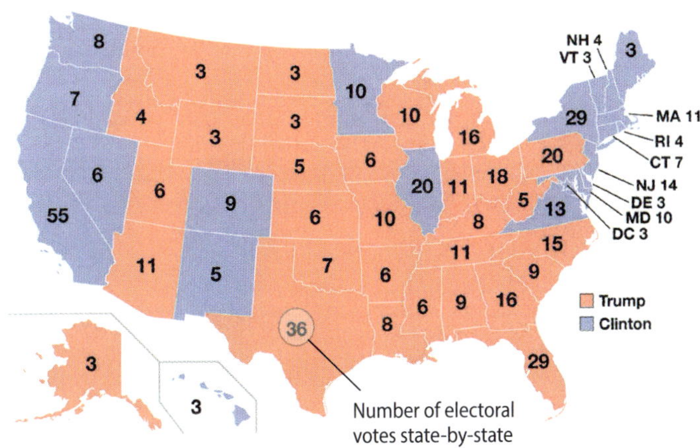

- What conclusions can you draw from this map?

Graphs

Graphs are used to display quantitative information. A *bar graph* has bars representing different amounts. Often it is used to compare things, such as the number of Representatives different states have in the House of Representatives, or the number of federal judges.

- Based on the graph, which group of federal judges is the largest? Why?

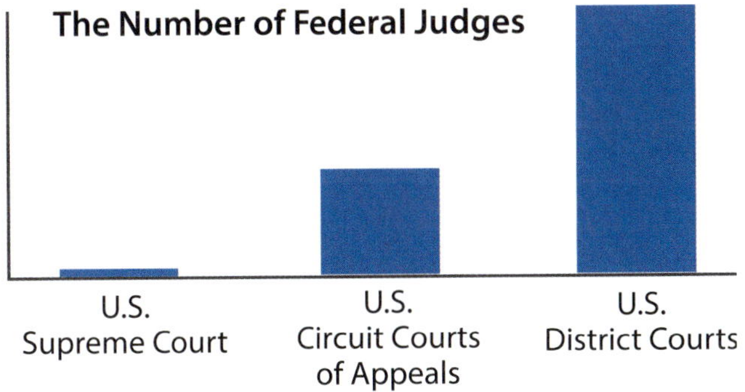

Line graphs show how the number or size of something has changed over time. For example, a line graph might show the number of federal employees from 1865 to today. Or it could show annual federal government revenues from 1900 to 2000. To interpret a line graph, be sure to understand both the "Y-axis" on its left side and the "X-axis" on its bottom. Usually the Y-axis is a "yard stick," providing the numbers for measuring, while the X-axis indicates the passage of time.

- Based on the graph, which five-year period saw the least increase in salary for a U.S. District Court Judge?

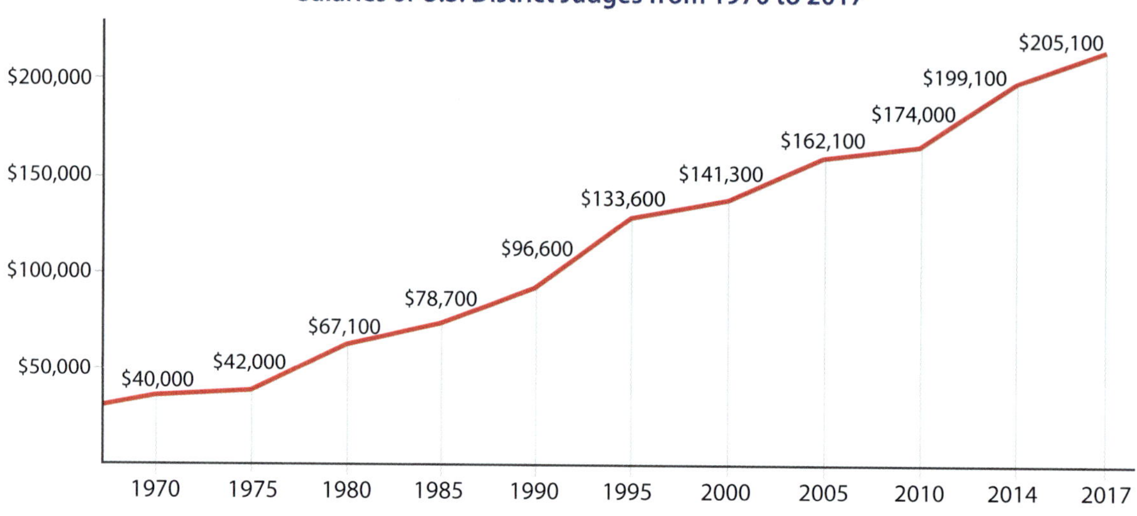

Charts and Tables

Charts and tables often present information in rows and columns. This format makes it easy to locate particular facts or numbers. The top row usually provides headings, telling the reader what each column stands for. The left column lists the individual items the chart or table describes.

Year	Florida Circuit Court Judge Salary	U.S. District Court Judge Salary
2001	$130,000	$145,100
2002	$133,250	$150,000
2003	$134,650	$154,700
2004	$134,650	$158,100
2005	$139,497	$162,100
2006	$145,080	$165,200
2007	$146,080	$165,200
2008	$145,080	$169,300
2009	$142,178	$174,000
2010	$142,178	$174,000

Sources: Office of State Courts Administrator and Administrative Office of the U.S. Courts

- Which judicial officer was more highly paid in 2010: a U.S. District Court Judge or a Florida Circuit Court Judge?
- In which years was the difference in salary between federal and Florida trial judges the greatest? The least?
- Have salaries for judges always increased with the passage of time? Explain your answer.
- What conclusions can you draw from this table?

Political Cartoons

A political cartoon is a drawing by an artist commenting on current affairs, social conditions or events. Political cartoons often challenge authority or expose corruption. Cartoonists may use satire, exaggerated features, or comparisons to make their point.

When looking at a political cartoon, be sure to understand what it shows. What is the time period of the cartoon? Who is represented? What are the people in the cartoon doing? Are there any special symbols or references? Think about the key issues of the time period if it is a political cartoon from the past. Finally, what is the cartoonist's message?

This cartoon makes a statement about what politicians were expecting from Wall Street and corporate interests ("trust interests") in 1904. Thomas Taggart, on the left, was born in Ireland but immigrated to the United States as a young boy. He was Chairman of the Democratic National Committee from 1904 to 1908. George B. Cortelyou, on the right, was born in New York City. He was with President McKinley when the latter was shot in 1901. He was a close friend of President Theodore Roosevelt's. He was Secretary of Commerce as well as Chairman of the Republican National Committee in 1904, when this cartoon was made.

- Describe what the cartoon shows.
- Which features are exaggerated or distorted in this cartoon?
- What is the cartoonist's view of the relationship between the two major political parties and the corporations on Wall Street?
- Explain your interpretation using evidence from the cartoon

Photographs and Illustrations

A photograph or an artist's illustration (a drawing or painting) can show us what a place is like, how a person looks, or what happened at an event. To interpret a photograph or illustration, you have to be a good detective. What details does the picture show? Consider the faces and clothing of any people in the photograph or picture. Also, consider the setting or background. What can you learn from it?

Think of the photograph or illustration as a piece of evidence. A photograph might be used, for example, to show the activities of a congressional committee. From the photograph, you can see where the committee meets, how many members are on the committee, and how energetic or tired the members seem. You can also see the members' ages, their gender, and their cultural diversity. You can further get a sense of the attitudes and relationships between members of the committee and the public. Questions on a photograph or illustration may ask you what the picture shows or to draw conclusions from it. The photograph above is from a special Senate Committee investigating a break-in into Democratic headquarters at the Watergate hotel and office complex in June 1972. The committee hearings took place almost a year later and were nationally televised.

- Based on the photograph, what was the atmosphere during the committee hearings?
- How diverse was the committee's membership? Would you expect to see greater diversity today? Explain your answer.
- What conclusions can you draw from this photograph?

Timelines

A timeline shows a series of events arranged along a line in the order, or sequence, in which they occurred. Usually, the left side of the timeline marks the beginning of the time period it shows, and the right side marks the end. As dates move from left to right, they move closer to the present. A timeline usually shows a series of related events. It is useful because we can see exactly when they occurred and how they relate to each other. Questions on timelines may ask about how the events on the timeline are related, or they may ask you to make an inference or draw a conclusion about the events that are shown.

- What other events might be placed on this timeline?
- What were some of the consequences of the events shown on the timeline?
- Make your own timeline showing how you spent today.

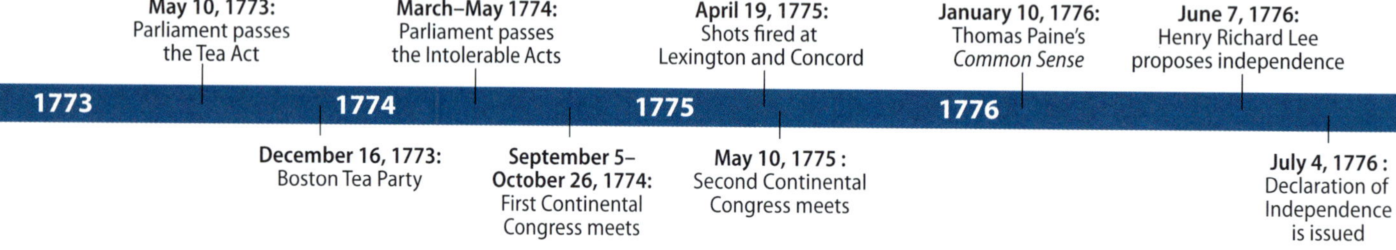

CHAPTER 1

Our Classical Heritage

SS.7.CG.1.1 Analyze the influences of ancient Greece, ancient Rome and the Judeo-Christian tradition on America's constitutional republic.

Every chapter of this book has a section called "Content Focus Vocabulary in This Chapter." In these sections, circle or highlight any names or terms that are unfamiliar to you. These are the essential terms for mastering the benchmarks for the EOC.

Content Focus Vocabulary in This Chapter

Constitutional republic
Ancient Greece
Polis
Democratic principles
Civic participation
Legislative bodies
Voting rights
Written Constitution
Ancient Rome
Republicanism
Representative government
Rule of law
Separation of powers
Judeo-Christian tradition
Ethical ideas of justice
Individual worth
Personal responsibility

Florida Keys to Learning

1. In 1776, American colonists declared their independence and established a **constitutional republic**, which is a country with a written constitution and governed by elected representatives. The founders who created the American constitutional republic were greatly influenced by ancient Greece, ancient Rome and the Judeo-Christian tradition.

2. **Ancient Greece** was a civilization on the Mediterranean Sea. Separated by mountains and the sea, the communities of ancient Greece developed into independent city-states. A Greek city-state was known as a **polis** (plural: *poleis*). Each *polis* was a self-governing community consisting of a town or city and its surrounding territory. Sometimes a *polis* even developed its own **written constitution**. A constitution is a plan of government.

3. Athens was the largest and wealthiest *polis*, or city-state. It became the world's first known democracy. This meant its government was placed in the hands of ordinary citizens. The word "democracy" actually comes from the ancient Greek for "rule by the people." All adult male Athenian citizens had the right to attend meetings of the "Assembly," Athens' **legislative body** (*law-making part of government*). Each citizen who attended had the right to vote and address the assembly. This was an early example of **civic participation**, in which citizens were engaged in government. Children, enslaved people, women, and foreigners were not considered citizens and did not participate.

4. The Athenian Assembly decided important public issues by giving its members **voting rights** (*the right to vote*). The view of the majority (*more than half*) of those present was followed by the Assembly. The **democratic principles** of ancient Athens, which were civic participation, voting rights, and decisions by the majority, had a great influence on the founders of the American constitutional republic.

5. **Ancient Rome** began as a city-state on the peninsula of Italy. At first, Rome was ruled by kings. Later, Romans overthrew their king, and Rome became a republic—a country with a **representative government**, made of representatives elected by its citizens.

6. The government of ancient Rome had a **separation of powers**. This meant all power was not held by any one branch or part of the government. Each part of the government had different powers. This separation of powers made it more difficult for any one person or group to become too powerful and take over the government.

7. Romans also lived under the **rule of law**. This meant all citizens had to obey the same set of rules, with no exceptions. These laws were made public.

8. The later collapse of the Roman republic had a great impact on the founders of the United States. They wanted to create a constitutional republic that would not fall under the control of a powerful leader. The founders wanted to create a representative government like the Roman republic, based on the idea of **republicanism** (*support for government by elected representatives*), the rule of law, and the separation of powers.

9. Both ancient Greece and ancient Rome had **democratic principles**. In Athens, citizens participated in legislative bodies and decided issues directly. In Rome, citizens elected representatives to decide issues. In the United States, citizens participate in government and elect representatives to decide issues.

10. The **Judeo-Christian tradition**, based on Jewish and Christian beliefs and practices, also influenced the founders of the United States. The ancient Jews had **ethical ideas of justice**. They believed that laws should punish wrongdoers and reward those who are good. According to the Judeo-Christian tradition, each person rich or poor, has **individual worth**, or value as a human being. Each individual also has a **personal responsibility**. They should follow the law and be good to others.

In 1776, Americans declared their independence and established **a constitutional republic**—a form of government based on a set of written rules in which the people hold power through their elected representatives.

Americans continue today to benefit from this form of government. All citizens have the right to participate in our government. They have the right to make their views known through free speech and a free press. They enjoy the right to demonstrate in public, the ability to vote in elections, and even the right to run for public office. Voters elect their representatives as well as many other government officials. Citizens in many other countries do not enjoy these same rights.

You may be asking yourself: how did such a system arise? In this chapter, you will learn how the origins of our form of government can actually be traced back thousands of years to ancient Greece, ancient Rome, and the Judeo-Christian tradition.

The Birth of Democratic Principles in Ancient Greece

Ancient Greece consisted of a mountainous peninsula and nearby islands. Mountains and the sea separated the areas where different groups of ancient Greeks once lived. Because of its hilly geography and separate islands, many different independent city-states arose. "*Polis*" was the ancient Greek word for a city-state. Each ancient Greek *polis* was a self-governing community, made up of a town or city and its surrounding countryside, used for farmland or grazing.

At one time, all the ancient Greek city-states, or *poleis* (plural of *polis*), were ruled by kings. Later, wealthy noble families took over many of the city-states. As the number of people increased, it became difficult to grow enough food. Some poor Greeks even sold themselves into slavery to pay off their debts (*money that they owed to others*). Poor families began to resent the wealth and power of those few noble families who owned most of the land and controlled the government.

Athens was the largest and wealthiest *polis* in ancient Greece. Conflicts between the rich and poor in Athens finally ended when all citizens, poor as well as rich, were given the right to participate in the meetings of the Assembly, the body that governed the

This map shows the location of the major city-states (*poleis*) in ancient Greece.

Athens was the largest and most important *polis* in ancient Greece. It was the birthplace of our democratic principles.

city-state. Eventually, all male citizens of the age of 18 or older, even if they owned no property, were allowed to attend the Assembly. The Assembly became a large meeting of citizens, which met on a hill just outside the city at least ten times a year. As many as 5,000 citizens usually attended its meetings. Members of the Assembly were paid a small fee for their attendance, so that even the poorest citizens could participate.

In the United States today, someone has to be elected to be a member of a state legislature or Congress. In the *polis* of Athens in ancient Greece, every qualified citizen could attend the Assembly. Members did not need to be elected.

The Assembly was the main **legislative body** of Athens. It made the laws for the *polis*. Every participant of the Assembly had **voting rights** (*the right to vote*). Voting was done by a show of hands or by making a mark on a piece of broken pottery. Those who came to the Assembly voted directly on such matters as whether the *polis* should pass a new law or go to war. The view of the majority (*more than half*) of the Assembly would be followed. Any citizen present had the right to address the Assembly to express his point of view. Every important decision of the *polis* had to be approved by this legislative body. Today, we can only imagine how lively and noisy these meetings must have been.

The Active Citizen

In ancient Greece, members of the Assembly of Athens voted through a show of hands or by making a mark on a piece of broken pottery. How do Americans exercise their voting rights today?

Only about one in five Athenians was actually a citizen with voting rights. Women, children, and enslaved people could not vote. Foreign residents of the *polis* also had no right to vote. Even so, the number of people qualified to participate in government—more than 50,000 citizens—was a much larger share of the general population than had ever occurred in any society before.

This new system of government in which ordinary citizens held power is known as a democracy. The Assembly passed its laws on behalf of the *demos*—the people. Our word "democracy" is actually made up of two ancient Greek words: *demos* ("people") and *kratia* ("rule" or "power"). Democracy actually means "rule by the people."

Democratic principles are the basic ideas and rules of democracy. They include civic participation, voting rights, and decisions by the majority. As we have seen, these democratic principles were first established in ancient Greece more than 2,500 years ago.

Civic Participation in Ancient Greece

The Athenian Assembly in ancient Greece provided an important example of **civic participation**—the involvement of citizens in government processes. If ordinary citizens did not volunteer to attend the meetings of the Assembly, the system would not have worked. The same is true of our government today.

Ancient Greeks also engaged in civic participation in other ways. Athens had a system of written laws. Athenians believed these laws helped to protect the poor from the actions of the rich. A person accused of a crime would be tried by an Athenian court. Ordinary Athenian citizens participated directly in the legal system by serving as jurors. Athenian juries were much larger than the juries we have today. A court might even have 200 or more jurors, all chosen by lot. Serving on juries was an important form of **civic participation**.

Throughout ancient Greece, citizens volunteered for military service. Each volunteer provided his own

Democratic Principles and Civic Participation in Ancient Greece Compared to the United States Today

- All of the people living in the *polis* were subject to its laws.

  In the United States today, all citizens, residents and visitors are also subject to the rule of law—the idea that we must all follow the same set of rules.

- In ancient Athens, the Assembly served as the **legislative body** of the *polis*, making laws and other decisions. This body was a large meeting of citizens that met on a hillside several times a year.

  How does this compare to legislative bodies in the United States today, such as Congress?

- All free, adult male citizens could attend the Assembly.

  Who can attend our legislative bodies today?

- All members of the Assembly had **voting rights**. They voted by a show of hands or by marking pieces of broken pottery.

  How do Americans exercise their voting rights today?

- All free, adult male citizens in ancient Athens could serve as jurors.

  In a later chapter, you will learn how jury service is an important obligation of U.S. citizenship today.

- All free, adult male citizens in ancient Athens could volunteer for military service.

  In a later chapter, you will learn how registering for Selective Service is an important obligation of U.S. citizenship.

clothing and weapons. The citizen-soldier—with his helmet, shield, sword, and armor on his chest and legs—provided the backbone of the Athenian army. Military service in defense of the *polis* was another important form of **civic participation**.

Aristotle Collects the Constitutions of the City-States

The development of democracy encouraged Greek thinkers to ask new questions, such as: "What is the best form of government?" One famous thinker, Aristotle, collected the constitutions of several different Greek city-states to find an answer. A constitution is the plan of a government. It defines how a government is organized and establishes its basic rules.

The United States has a **written constitution**. This means that the basic rules of our government are written down in a document that everyone can read and that government officials must obey. In later chapters, you will learn about both the Constitution of the United States and the Constitution of the State of Florida.

Enrichment

The Influence of Ancient Greece on the American Constitutional Republic

As young students, many of the American colonists read the writings of the ancient Greeks. The history of ancient Greece helped to shape their ideas about government. They especially admired the democratic principles of ancient Athens.

The colonists quoted the ancient Greeks in their speeches and writings, both before and during the American Revolution. Two years before the Constitutional Convention of 1787 (*the meeting of delegates who wrote our Constitution*), James Madison undertook an extensive investigation of the Greek city-states. Thomas Jefferson sent him dozens of history books from Paris. Madison wanted to understand why the Greek city-states had failed so that the Americans could avoid their mistakes. Madison concluded that the league (*association*) of Greek city-states had been too weak. He became convinced it was necessary to strengthen the association of American states to avoid the same fate.

For the EOC, be sure to know these influences

How the Founders of the American Constitutional Republic were Influenced by Ancient Greece

The founders of the American constitutional republic were greatly influenced by the model provided by the ancient Greeks, especially the democratic *polis* of Athens.

Polis

Athens and the other city-states of Greece were self-governing communities. Each one had a separate government. In our constitutional republic today, citizens form their own city and county governments, while all Americans live under a self-governing national government.

Civic Participation

Athens extended the right to participate in government to all its citizens. They voted in the Assembly, served as jurors, and volunteered for military service. These were seen as obligations of citizenship. In our constitutional republic today, citizens also participate in government.

Legislative Bodies

Athens was governed by the "Assembly," which had the power to make laws. For the first time in history, ordinary citizens participated in their country's highest legislative body. All adult male citizens could attend meetings of the Assembly. They had the right to propose and vote on new laws. Today, our constitutional republic also has legislative bodies. We have our state legislatures and Congress as our national legislature.

Voting Rights

All Athenian citizens had the right to vote in the Assembly. However, not all Athenians were citizens. Women, children, slaves and foreigners had no right to vote. In the United States, voting rights were also limited in the early years of our history, but they have gradually expanded. Now all adult citizens have the right to vote.

Written Constitutions

Several Greek city-states developed their own written constitution, or plan of government. Americans later adopted written constitutions for both their state and national governments. Today, Americans live in a constitutional republic with a written constitution.

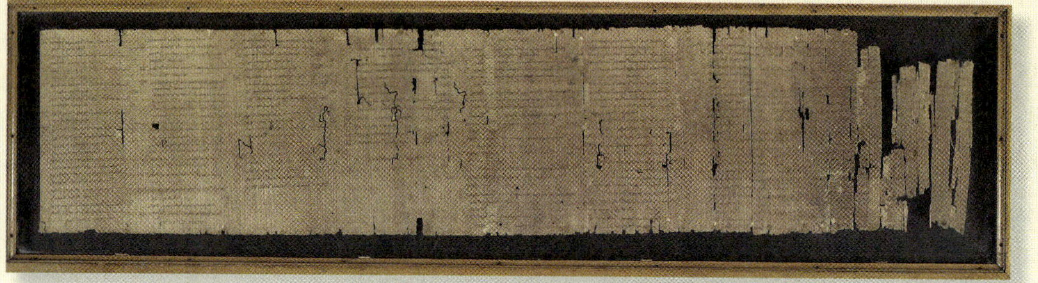

Aristotle's "Constitution of Athens," discovered in 1891

The Active Citizen

Complete the chart below describing the political system of ancient Athens.

Why was ancient Athens considered to be a *polis*?	
The legislative body of Athens was known as the Assembly. What do legislative bodies do?	
How did the citizens of ancient Athens engage in civic participation?	
How did ancient Athens demonstrate democratic principles?	
What were the voting rights of the citizens of ancient Athens?	
Which groups of people living in ancient Athens did not enjoy the right to vote?	

The Rise of Representative Government in Rome

Like Greece, Italy is a peninsula in Europe that extends into the Mediterranean Sea. Halfway down the Italian peninsula, the city-state of **ancient Rome** arose on the Tiber River. Rome was in an excellent location to benefit from trade across the Mediterranean Sea. The Romans also benefited from the learning and culture of ancient Greece, which they made into part of their own traditions.

At first, ancient Rome was ruled by kings. The king of Rome was advised by a council of nobles known as the Senate. Ordinary citizens were sometimes called together by the king to meet in a popular assembly and to serve in the army defending Rome.

The Birth of Republicanism

According to legend, the people of Rome overthrew their king. Ancient Rome then became a republic—a country without a king, that is governed by elected representatives. The term "republic" comes from the Roman phrase "*res publica populi romani*"—a public thing of the Roman people. It meant that the state belonged to the people. **Republicanism** is

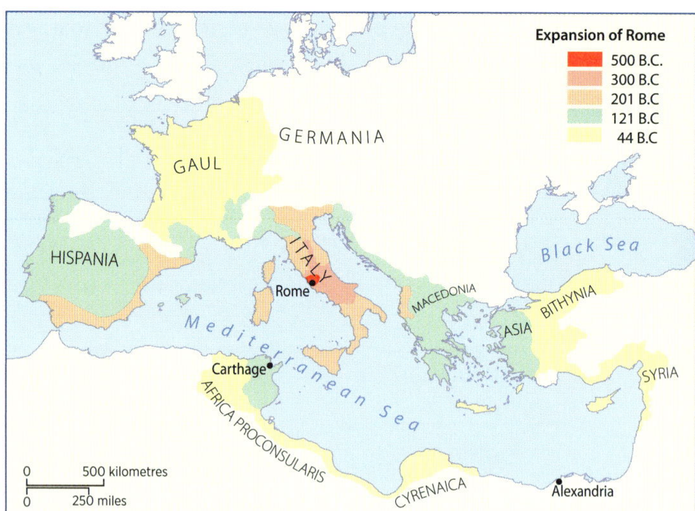

The expansion of the Roman Republic from 201 B.C. to 44 B.C.

The Senate of ancient Rome once met in this building. Which part of our government today has the same name?

support for the republican form of government—a government by elected representatives.

Article IV of the U.S. Constitution guarantees every state "a Republican Form of Government." You will learn more about the Constitution in Chapter 5.

After overthrowing their king, Romans were governed by the Senate and two consuls—officials who were elected for one year and took the place of the king. Each consul had the right to *veto*, or reject, decisions taken by the other consul. The two consuls therefore had to agree before any action could be taken.

The Roman republic tried to balance different interests in its government. The Senate was supposed to represent the wisdom and experience of Rome's oldest and wealthiest citizens. Our word "Senate" actually comes from the ancient Roman word "senex," or old man. Roman Senators were originally wealthy noblemen. Later, the Roman Senate included former consuls and other retired officials with government or military experience. Senators in ancient Rome served for life.

The Active Citizen

Today, our American constitutional republic also has a Senate. You will learn more about this legislative body in Chapter 6. The minimum age for becoming a U.S. Senator is older than the minimum age for becoming a member of the House of Representatives, the other part of Congress. There are fewer Senators than members of the House of Representatives. Senators also serve for longer terms. What evidence of the legacy of ancient Rome can you see in these characteristics of the Senate?

In addition to having two consuls and the Senate, Romans also had several popular assemblies. Not just the rich and the powerful, but all Roman citizens could attend their meetings. The most important of these assemblies met on an open field, where it elected the consuls and made other important decisions.

Ancient Rome was frequently at war with its neighbors. Rome's leaders needed the support of ordinary citizens to fill their armies. So they granted the common people important rights. The common people gained the right to elect their own special representatives, known as tribunes. Each tribune had the right to veto any proposed action by the government.

The Rule of Law

The common people insisted that Rome should have written laws so that wealthy landowners could not take

The ruins of the Roman Forum, where the Twelve Tables were once displayed, guaranteeing the rule of law to all Romans.

unfair advantage of them. A special committee was formed to write down Rome's laws on "Twelve Tables." The tables were displayed in public for all to see.

Romans thus enjoyed the "**rule of law**." This is the principle that all members of society should obey the same set of rules, without exception. The rules should be fair and reasonable, and they should be publicly available.

The Birth of Representative Government

Unlike the citizens who voted in the Athenian assembly, the citizens of ancient Rome did not decide all issues directly. Instead, their popular assemblies elected officials, such as the consuls and tribunes. Rome's most important decisions were made by its elected officials, acting with the advice of the Senate.

Government by elected representatives is known as **representative government**. In this form of government, decisions are made by elected representatives rather than directly by the people themselves. Like ancient Rome, Americans today are also governed by elected representatives. Like ancient Rome, we have a representative government.

The Separation of Powers

Instead of one part of the government holding all the power, the government of the Roman republic had several parts. Each part had a different function. This created a **separation of powers**.

The three main parts of the government of the Roman republic were: (1) the consuls and other government officials; (2) the Senate; and (3) the popular assemblies. Each of these parts of the government had different powers. In some cases, one part could check —or stop—the actions of another part. For example, each consul could veto (*reject*) action by the other consul.

Because the different parts of the Roman government had to work together, general agreement was needed for the government to take action. The separation of powers also made it more difficult for one part of the government to seize absolute power. This safeguard helped the Roman republic to survive for 500 years. In a later chapter, you will learn how our constitutional republic today also has a separation of powers and a system of checks and balances.

See Chapter 5 for how our government today has a separation of powers and checks and balances

Enrichment

Other Influences of Ancient Rome on the American Constitutional Republic

Roman values were key to the success of the republic. Civic virtue—placing the interests of the republic above personal interests—was the most important Roman value. Dozens of Roman myths told of heroes who had sacrificed their lives for Rome. Self-sacrifice was necessary for the survival of a city-state often at war. This quality of ancient Rome later influenced the founders of the American constitutional republic.

Around 100 B.C., Rome introduced important military reforms. Rome needed a larger and more professional army than the citizen soldiers who had defended the city in the past. These reforms greatly improved the strength of the Roman army. However, Rome's soldiers became more loyal to their generals than to Rome itself. During the last fifty years of the republic, Rome was frequently threatened by generals trying to seize power. One of them, Julius Caesar, broke with tradition when he brought his army into the city of Rome. A group of 20 Senators, fearing

For the EOC, be sure to know these influences

How the Founders of the American Constitutional Republic were Influenced by Ancient Rome

The founders of the American constitutional republic were greatly influenced by the ancient Romans, especially the final years of the Roman republic.

Civic Participation

Like the ancient Greeks, the ancient Romans had a strong tradition of civic participation. Wealthy Romans participated in the Senate. Other citizens participated in the popular assemblies. Male citizens with enough money to buy weapons were expected to provide military service. Romans honored those who sacrificed their own interests for the good of the community. Men like George Washington and John Adams were inspired by the example of Romans who gave their lives to preserve the republican form of government.

Republicanism

According to legend, the Romans overthrew their king and turned Rome into a republic—a government made up of elected representatives. The United States also is a republic, in which the government belongs to "We the People." We elect representatives and officials to govern us. Republicanism refers to support for the republican form of government.

Representative Government

Citizens cannot always decide important issues directly, as they did in ancient Athens. Ancient Rome adopted the representative form of government. Qualified citizens elected officials who made many decisions for them. Republican Rome was governed by two consuls, elected by a popular assembly. An assembly of commoners elected the tribunes. In the United States today, we also have a system of elected officials and representatives. American citizens elect members of the House of Representatives, Senators, and the President. They also elect their state and local officials.

Rule of Law

At one time, Roman laws were oral and only fully known to nobles and government officials. Those in power might change the rules at will. The common people demanded that the laws be written down. Roman laws were written onto twelve tablets and placed in the Roman Forum for all to see. That way, everyone knew the rules. They could also see that everyone else, including government officials and the very rich, was following the same set of rules without exception. This is known as the "rule of law." Today, Americans similarly rely on the rule of law. We all follow the same rules, which are fair and reasonable, which are written down, and which are publicly available. No one is above the law.

Separation of Powers

During the period of the republic, power was not held by just one part of the government. Instead, it was divided between: (1) elected consuls and other officials, (2) the Senate, and (3) the popular assemblies. Later writers were greatly impressed by Rome's separation of powers and its use of checks and balances to protect the republican form of government, which lasted 500 years. The founders of the American constitutional republic introduced the separation of powers by dividing government powers between the legislative (*law-making*), executive (*enforcing*) and judicial branches.

Caesar would make himself king, murdered him on the floor of the Senate. Caesar's adopted son later avenged his death and became Rome's first Emperor, ending the republic.

The memory of these struggles had a great impact on the "Founding Fathers" who established America's constitutional republic two thousand years later. The last years of the Roman republic was the period that most fascinated them. They especially admired the bravery of those trying to preserve the republican form of government. George Washington ordered that a play about ancient Rome be performed in front of his soldiers during the American Revolution, while John Adams modeled his career as a lawyer and political leader after a famous ancient Roman legislator. Americans regretted the collapse of the Roman republic, and they wanted to take steps to avoid the same fate.

A statue of Julius Caesar, the successful general who threatened the republican government of ancient Rome

The Active Citizen

- Why do you think the separation of powers failed to preserve the republican form of government in ancient Rome?
- If you were designing a new government, what steps would you take to ensure that a strong military leader did not take over the government?

The Ethical Ideals of the Judeo-Christian Tradition

The colonists who declared their independence from Great Britain in 1776 and who wrote the Constitution in 1787 were also greatly influenced by the **Judeo-Christian tradition**—the beliefs and practices of those following the Jewish and Christian religions.

Like the Romans, the ancient Jews depended on written laws. These laws were based on principles of morality and justice. They included such basic rules as: do not steal; do not kill; and show respect towards one's parents.

According to Judeo-Christian tradition, the laws that a society follows should be based on **ethical ideas of justice**. This means they should reward those who perform good deeds, while they punish wrongdoers. They should promote justice, based on our most basic ideas of right and wrong. Ethics teaches us to be kind to others and not to hurt them. Ethical laws require that we take **personal responsibility** for our actions. This means we have control over what we do, and we are responsible for our own conduct. When we commit wrongful actions, we should expect to be punished.

According to Judeo-Christian teachings, each person has **individual worth** or value as a human being. Every person is important and deserving of basic rights. These ideals inspired the later founders of the United States. In the Declaration of Independence, Thomas Jefferson proudly proclaimed that "all men are created equal."

You will learn more about the Declaration of Independence in Chapter 3

For the EOC, be sure to know these influences

How the Founders of the American Constitutional Republic were Influenced by the Judeo-Christian Tradition

The founders of the American constitutional republic were greatly influenced by the Judeo-Christian tradition.

Ethical Ideas of Justice

The Judeo-Christian tradition introduced ethical ideas of justice. Jewish and Christian teachings emphasized acting justly and performing good deeds. Bad deeds were to be punished while good deeds were to be rewarded. The colonists were deeply influenced by these beliefs. They attempted to establish laws that were ethical and just for their communities.

Individual Worth

According to Judeo-Christian teachings, each person has value as a human being. The colonists were outraged when British policies did not seem to value their lives or welfare. You will learn more about these developments in Chapter 3.

Personal Responsibility

According to Judeo-Christian tradition, each of us is personally responsible for our actions. American colonists, such as the Pilgrims and Puritans, followed this principle closely. Their belief in personal responsibility encouraged the colonists to work hard and to act independently.

The Rule of law

According to Judeo-Christian tradition, people are subject to the law. In founding their own constitutional republic, the former colonists attempted to establish a system of just laws based on the Judeo-Christian tradition.

Name ______________________________

Democracy is a form of government in which ordinary citizens hold power. In some democracies, citizens meet and make decisions directly. In others, citizens elect representatives who make decisions for them. Fill in the chart below comparing the "democratic principles" of ancient Greece, ancient Rome, and the United States today. Use your background knowledge of our modern government to fill in the last column. You may want to return to this page after learning more about our current government in later chapters of this book.

Comparing Ancient and Modern Democratic Governments

	Democratic Principles of Ancient Greece (Polis of Athens)	Democratic Principles of Ancient Rome (Republican Period)	Democratic Principles of the U.S. Government Today
Who qualifies as a citizen?			
What are the main legislative bodies?			
Do citizens decide issues directly or elect representatives to make major decisions for them?			
How do citizens and/or legislators exercise their voting rights?			
Is there "majority rule" (decisions by the majority)?			
Is there a "separation of powers" (a separate legislative, executive and/or judicial branch)?			
What other ways can citizens participate in government?			
Is there the "rule of law"?			

Name ________________________________ Teacher ________________________________

Enriching Your Understanding

The two charts on page 15 show the governments of Athens, the largest *polis* in ancient Greece, and Rome in greater detail. Compare the two charts. You will not have to remember the details on these charts, but they will help you to understand how these ancient governments actually worked and how they influenced the founders of the American constitutional republic.

1. Identify one similarity between these two systems of government.

2. Identify one difference between these two systems of government.

3. Based on the charts, describe one way in which either the ancient Greek or ancient Roman system of government still influences us today.

The Government of Athens, a *Polis* in Ancient Greece, (around 450 B.C.)

Council of 500
(chosen by lot from members of the Assembly)
Prepared business for the Assembly; the council also had a leadership role when the Assembly was not meeting, such as commanding Athens' warships.

Assembly
All adult male citizens could attend and vote on issues (about 50,000 Athenians were eligible to attend)

Courts
(Jurors were chosen by lot from the Assembly)

Excluded from citizenship: women, children, slaves, former slaves, and "foreign" residents (about 200,000 Athenians)

The Government of the Roman Republic (around 50 B.C.)

Legislative Bodies (Popular Assemblies)

Assembly of Centuries
Assembly of citizens/soldiers divided into 193 groups; mainly for military purposes and to elect the highest government officials

Assembly of Tribes
Assembly of citizens divided into 35 groups, mainly for non-miltary purposes and to elect lower officials

Council of Commoners ("Plebeians")
Assembly of commoners that elects tribunes; enacts laws for commoners; tries cases between commoners

Executive

Two Consuls

Other High Government Officials

Lower Government Officials

Tribunes
Officials who can veto proposed government actions

Senate

Senate
Men with high-level government or military experience, who advise the consuls; Senators serve for life.

Democratic Principles

Both ancient Greece and ancient Rome had democratic principles—the basic rules and ideas of democracy.

- Civic participation: citizens participate in government processes
- Voting: citizens express their choices by voting on issues or for representatives
- Decisions by the majority: the government follows the decisions of the majority (*more than half*)

Our Classical Heritage

Ancient Greece

Polis: A self-governing city-state in ancient Greece

Democratic principles: Athens became the first democracy (rule of the people). It followed the democratic principles of civic participation, voting rights, and decisions by the majority.

Legislative bodies: Athens was ruled by the Assembly, a large meeting of thousands of citizens, which made laws and other decisions

Voting rights: All citizens could vote in the Assembly; however, not all Athenians were citizens

Civic participation: Ordinary citizens participated in government; ancient Greeks volunteered for the army, served as jurors, and in Athens sat in the Assembly

Written constitution: Some of the Greek city-states had written a plan of government

Ancient Rome

Civic participation: Roman citizens participated in government. They served in the army, sat in the popular assemblies, and volunteered for government service

Republicanism: Romans supported the idea of republican government—rule by elected representatives without a king

Representative government: Romans elected representatives to decide issues and provide government

Rule of law: All Romans were subject to the same laws, displayed on the Twelve Tables in the Roman Forum

Separation of powers: Instead of one part of the government holding all power, power was divided among different parts of the government. In some cases these different parts could check each other

Judeo-Christian Tradition

Rule of law: As human beings, we are all subject to the same laws

Ethical ideas of justice: The belief that our most important laws are based on ethics and justice: rewarding the good and punishing the bad

Individual worth: Each person has great value

Personal responsibility: We are responsible for our actions

Review Cards: Our Classical Heritage

The American Constitutional Republic

- During the period 1776–1787, the founders of the United States established the American **constitutional republic**. This was a government by elected representatives based on a written constitution.
- The founders were greatly influenced by ancient Greece, ancient Rome, and the Judeo-Christian tradition.

Ancient Greece: The Rise of the *Polis*

Ancient Greece was a civilization along the Mediterranean Sea about 2,500 years ago. Its ideas and practices had a great impact on the founders who established our form of democratic government.

- Because of its hilly geography and separate islands, many different independent city-states arose in ancient Greece. "***Polis***" was the ancient Greek word for a city-state.
- Each ancient Greek polis was a self-governing community, made up of a town or city and its surrounding countryside.

Legislative Bodies: The Assembly of Athens

- Athens was the largest and wealthiest polis in ancient Greece. The Assembly was the main **legislative body** of Athens. A legislative body makes laws. The Athenian Assembly made laws for the polis of Athens.
- Conflicts between the rich and poor in Athens ended when ordinary citizens were given the right to participate in the meetings of the Assembly. Eventually, all male citizens of the age of 18, even those who owned no property, were allowed to attend the Assembly. Every qualified citizen could attend the Assembly. Any citizen present had the right to address the Assembly to express his point of view.
- Only about one in five Athenians was actually a citizen with the right to attend the Assembly. Women, children, and enslaved people could not attend the Assembly. Foreign residents of the polis also had no right to attend the Assembly.

Ancient Greece: Voting Rights

- Every participant of the Athenian Assembly had **voting rights** (*the right to vote in the Assembly*). Voting was done by a show of hands or by making a mark on a piece of broken pottery.
- Members of the Assembly voted directly on such matters as whether the polis should pass a new law or go to war.
- The view of the majority (*more than half*) of the Assembly was followed.

Ancient Greece: Democratic Principles

- This new form of government, in which citizens held power, is known as a democracy. Our word "democracy" is actually made up of two ancient Greek words: demos ("people") and kratia ("rule" or "power"). Democracy means "rule by the people."
- **Democratic principles** are the basic ideas and rules of democracy. They include civic participation, voting rights, and decisions by the majority (*more than half*).

Ancient Greece: Civic Participation

- The Athenian Assembly in ancient Greece provided an important example of **civic participation**—the involvement of citizens in the government of their community.
- Athenian citizens also participated directly in the legal system by serving as jurors. Serving on juries was another important form of civic participation.
- Throughout ancient Greece, citizens volunteered for military service. Military service in defense of the polis was yet another important form of civic participation.

Ancient Greece: Written Constitutions

- A **written constitution** is a written document that defines how a government is organized and establishes its basic rules. Some Greek poleis (plural of polis) had written constitutions. Their basic rules of government were written down, so that citizens and government officials knew their rights and powers.
- The United States today has a written constitution.

The Legacy of Ancient Rome

Ancient Rome, especially during the period of the Roman republic, also greatly influenced the founders who established the American constitutional republic.

The Rise of Rome

- Like Greece, Italy is a peninsula that extends into the Mediterranean Sea.
- At first, ancient Rome was ruled by kings. The king of Rome was advised by a council of nobles known as the Senate.

Ancient Rome: Representative Government and Republicanism

- The people of ancient Rome overthrew their king and Rome became a republic—a country without a king, governed by elected representatives. The term "republic" comes from a Roman phrase meaning a "public thing." It meant that the state belonged to the people.
- **Republicanism** is support for the republican form of government—a government by elected representatives.
- After overthrowing their king, Romans were governed by the Senate and two consuls—officials who were elected for one year and took the place of the king. The Senate represented the wisdom and experience of Rome's oldest and wealthiest citizens. Ancient Rome also had several popular assemblies. Roman citizens could attend their meetings.
- The United States also is a republic, in which the government belongs to "We the People." We elect representatives and officials to govern us. Article IV of the U.S. Constitution guarantees the "republican form of government" in each state.

Ancient Rome: Civic Participation

- Like the ancient Greeks, the ancient Romans had a strong tradition of **civic participation** (*citizens participating in government*).
- Wealthy Romans participated in the Senate. Other Roman citizens participated in the popular assemblies. Male citizens were expected to provide military service. Romans honored those who sacrificed their own interests for the good of the state.

Ancient Rome: The Rule of Law

- The common people insisted that Rome have written laws so that wealthy landowners could not take unfair advantage of them. A special committee was formed to write down Rome's laws on "Twelve Tables." The tables were displayed in public for all to see.
- Romans thus enjoyed the "**rule of law**"—the principle that all members of society must obey the same set of rules, without exception. This included government officials and the very rich as well as the poor. These rules should be publicly available for all to see.

Ancient Rome: Representative Government

- The citizens of ancient Rome did not decide all issues directly. Instead, their elected officials made important decisions for them.
- This form of government is known as **representative government**. In this form of government, decisions are made by elected representatives rather than by the people themselves. Like ancient Rome, Americans today are governed by elected representatives.

The Separation of Powers

- Instead of all power being held by one part of the government, the Roman republic had a **separation of powers**. Different parts of the government held different powers and performed different functions.
- The three main parts of the republican government of Rome were: (1) the consuls and other government officials; (2) the Senate; and (3) the popular assemblies. In many cases, one part of the government could check (or stop) the actions of another part.
- Because different parts of the Roman government had to work together, general agreement was needed for the government to take action. The separation of powers made it more difficult for one leader or group to seize total control over the government.

The Ethical Ideals of the Judeo-Christian Tradition

The colonists who declared their independence and established our system of government were also greatly influenced by the **Judeo-Christian tradition**—the beliefs and practices of those following the Jewish and Christian religions.

The Rule of Law

- Ancient Jews and Christians obeyed written laws based on principles of morality and justice. They included such basic rules as: do not steal; do not kill; and show respect towards one's parents.

Ethical Ideas of Justice

- According to Judeo-Christian tradition, the laws that a society follows should be based on **ethical ideas of justice**. Ethical laws reward those who perform good deeds, while they punish wrongdoers.

Personal Responsibility

- Ethical laws require us to take **personal responsibility** for our actions. If we commit wrongful actions, we can expect to be punished.

Belief in Individual worth

- According to Judeo-Christian teachings, each person has **individual worth**—value as a human being.

Democratic Principles

Ancient Greece and Rome shared the **democratic principles** of civic participation, voting rights and decisions by the majority.

- In the ***polis*** of Athens in ancient Greece, citizens decided issues directly.
- In ancient Rome, citizens elected representatives and officials.

In the United States today, citizens elect representatives and officials and can participate in government.

What Do You Know?

SS.7.CG.1.1

1. Which statement identifies an important influence of ancient Greece on the founders of the American constitutional republic?
   A. The founders adopted democratic principles.
   B. The founders based their laws on ethical ideas of justice.
   C. The founders established a representative form of government.
   D. The founders created a government with a separation of powers.

SS.7.CG.1.1

2. In ancient Athens, all adult male citizens were able to vote in the Assembly, the legislative body that decided on important issues facing the *polis*. What did this practice illustrate?
   A. the separation of powers
   B. representative government
   C. the rise of democratic principles
   D. the protection of individual rights

SS.7.CG.1.1

3. Which characteristic did the government of the city-state of Athens in ancient Greece share with the government of ancient Rome?
   A. republicanism
   B. civic participation
   C. separation of powers
   D. representative government

SS.7.CG.1.1

4. The diagram below shows the impact of an important tradition.

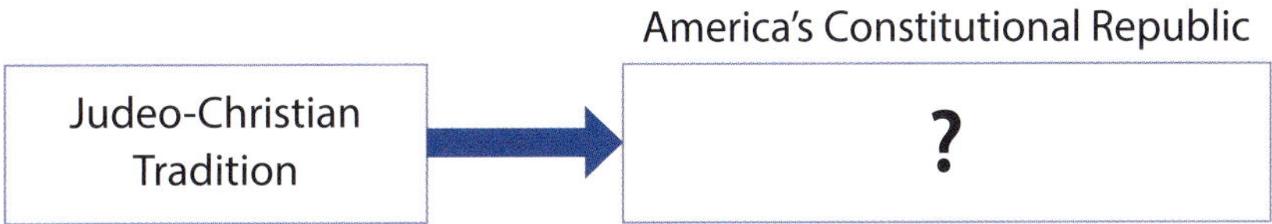

   Which phrase completes the diagram?
   A. Voting rights
   B. Republicanism
   C. Separation of powers
   D. Ethical ideas of justice

SS.7.CG.1.1

5. The statement below was made in a speech by Pericles, the leader of Athens, around 430 B.C.

> Our government does not copy the laws of our neighbors. Instead, it serves as an example to them. We are called a democracy because our government is in the hands of the many and not of the few . . .

How did the example mentioned in this speech influence the founders of the American constitutional republic, 2,500 years later?

A. They designed a system of checks and balances.
B. They gave political power to an all-powerful ruler.
C. They created a government of elected representatives.
D. They placed the final power of government in ordinary citizens.

SS.7.CG.1.1

6. The passage below was written by John Adams in his book *Defence of the Constitutions of Government of the United States of America* (1787).

> The republic of Athens, the school mistress of the whole civilized world, for more than a thousand years in arts, eloquence and philosophy . . . was for a short period . . . the most democratical commonwealth in Greece.

Based on this passage, with which statement about ancient Athens would Adams have agreed?

A. Its government protected individual rights.
B. Its government was based on majority rule.
C. Its government was based on ethical ideas of justice.
D. Its government was controlled by an all-powerful dictator.

SS.7.CG.1.1

7. The statement below was sent by George Washington to John Burgoyne, a leading British general, during the American Revolution.

> The associated armies in America act from the noblest motives, liberty. These same principles [inspired] the arms of Rome in the days of her glory . . .

Which conclusion can be drawn from this statement?

A. The ancient Romans believed all individuals were equal in the eyes of God.
B. Washington hoped to make himself as powerful as the emperors of ancient Rome.
C. Washington was inspired by the example of ancient Romans who defended republicanism.
D. The Romans created a separation of powers to protect their form of republican government.

SS.7.CG.1.1

8. The table below shows a comparison of two different systems of government.

Comparison of Ancient Greek and Roman Governments

The *Polis* of Athens in Ancient Greece	Rome during the Republic Period
All adult male citizens attend the Assembly.	Citizens can attend the popular assemblies.
The Assembly makes important decisions for the *polis*.	?

Which information completes the table?

A. The popular assemblies include women, slaves and foreign residents.
B. The popular assemblies make the most important decisions in Rome.
C. The popular assemblies claim that human laws come directly from God.
D. The popular assemblies elect consuls and other officials to make decisions.

SS.7.CG.1.1

9. Which institution today is most similar to a *polis* in ancient Greece?

A. a self-governing city
B. a federal system of government
C. an association of independent nations
D. a state legislature of elected representatives

SS.7.CG.1.1

10. The chart below shows the influence of certain democratic principles.

Which sentence completes the chart?

A. A king or queen inherits power.
B. Citizens elect their own representatives.
C. Judges are appointed for to serve for life.
D. An all-powerful President controls the government.

SS.7.CG.1.1

11. Which is an important difference between the democratic principles of ancient Greece and those of the United States today?

A. In the United States, citizens serve as jurors.
B. In the United States, citizens participate in government.
C. In the United States, citizens are guaranteed their individual rights.
D. In the United States, government decisions are based on the rule of the majority.

SS.7.CG.1.1

12. The chart below shows some of the influences of ancient Rome on America's constitutional republic.

Influence	Description
Civic Participation	Ordinary citizens voted in the popular assemblies, served in the army, and served as jurors
Republicanism	Romans supported the republican form of government—by elected representatives instead of by a king.
Representative Government	Rome's popular assemblies elected consults, tribunes and other officials.
Rule of Law	**?**
Separation of Powers	Roman government was divided between the consuls and other officials; the Senate; and the popular assemblies.

Which sentence completes the chart?

A. Most city-states at this time had their own written constitutions.

B. Rules of conduct were based on ethical ideas of justice about right and wrong.

C. All citizens were subject to the same rules, displayed in public on twelve bronze tablets.

D. Women, children, foreign residents, and enslaved individuals had no rights since they were not considered as citizens.

SS.7.CG.1.1

13. How did the government of ancient Rome differ from that of Athens, a *polis* in ancient Greece?

A. The government of the Roman republic had a separation of powers.

B. The government of the Roman republic guaranteed individual rights.

C. The government of the Roman republic had no elected representatives.

D. The government of the Roman republic relied on citizens serving in its army.

SS.7.CG.1.1

14. Which characteristic was shared by ancient Rome and the Judeo-Christian tradition?

A. respect for the rule of law

B. government based on majority vote

C. a separation of powers in government

D. willingness to sacrifice one's life for the city-state

CHAPTER 2

English Rights and Enlightenment Ideas

SS.7.CG.1.2 Trace the principles underlying America's founding ideas on law and government. (*This chapter describes these underlying principles; to trace how these principles influenced America's founding documents, see Chapters 3–5 and 10.*)

SS.7.CG.1.3 Trace the impact that the Magna Carta, Mayflower Compact, English Bill of Rights and Thomas Paine's *Common Sense* had on colonists' views of government.

SS.7.CG.1.4 Analyze how Enlightenment ideas, including Montesquieu's view of separation of powers and John Locke's theories related to natural law and Locke's social contract, influenced the Founding.

Content Focus Vocabulary in This Chapter

Magna Carta
Right to justice
Right to a fair trial
Due process of law
Limitation of government power
Limited monarchy
Mayflower Compact
Consent of the governed
Self-government
English Bill of Rights
Right to life, liberty, and property
No taxation without representation
Right to a speedy and fair jury trial
No excessive punishments
Thomas Paine
Common Sense
Representative self-government
Enlightenment ideas
John Locke
Natural law
Social contract
Montesquieu
Separation of powers
Equality of mankind
Limited government
Natural rights
Individual liberties/rights
Rule of law
Religious liberty
Protected right
Founding/Founders/Founding Fathers
Founding Ideas
Founding Documents
For Government, see Preface, page v

Florida "Keys" to Learning

1. In addition to being influenced by ancient Greece, ancient Rome and the Judeo-Christian tradition, the colonists benefited from their English past.

2. Centuries earlier, King John of England had been forced by his nobles to sign a document known as **Magna Carta**. This document promised that no free man could be imprisoned or have his property taken away except after a trial by a jury of his peers (*equals*), following the laws of the land. Magna Carta also promised that no new taxes would be raised without the consent of the nobles. The importance of Magna Carta was that it established the **right to justice** (*the king offered to punish crimes and resolve disputes*), the **right to a fair trial** (*a fair hearing, based on evidence and the law*), the right to the "**due process" of law** (*a person cannot have his or her life, liberty, or property taken away without a fair process like a trial*), and a **limitation of government power** (*the government had limits on what it could do*). Magna Carta turned England into a **limited monarchy** (*the king's powers were limited*).

3. In 1620, the Pilgrims signed the **Mayflower Compact.** In this document, they agreed to create their own government for their colony and to obey its rules. The importance of the Mayflower Compact was that it gave birth to **self-government** in the colonies. This was the idea that people should govern themselves. The Compact also showed the need for the **consent of the governed** (*the approval of the people who lived under that government*).

4. Later English kings did not always respect their people's rights. In the 17th century, the king and Parliament (the English law-making body) entered into a series of conflicts. In 1688, the English king was overthrown. England's new rulers promised to respect many **individual rights/liberties** (*the rights of the people to do certain things*) in the **English Bill of Rights** in 1689. This document promised the **right to life, liberty and property** (*people could not be executed, imprisoned, or lose their belongings except as punishment for crimes*); **no taxation without representation** (*no taxes would be collected without the approval of Parliament*); accused citizens would be given a **speedy and fair jury trial** (*a trial by a group of fellow citizens*); and **no excessive punishments** (*unfairly harsh punishments*) would be imposed.

5. The colonists were further influenced by **Enlightenment ideas.** These ideas applied human reason and scientific thinking to improve society instead of just following tradition. The Enlightenment took place in Europe and America in the late 17th and 18th centuries.

6. **John Locke** was an important Enlightenment thinker. He believed in **natural law**—that there were certain rules, or "laws," found in nature itself. Locke believed these laws established **natural rights**— basic rights that all human beings are born with and should enjoy. Among these rights were the **right to life, liberty, and property.** Locke further wrote that people entered into a **social contract**, or agreement, with one another when they formed a community. As part of this social contract, members of the community agreed to obey their ruler. The ruler, in turn, promised to protect the individual rights of his (or her) subjects. If a ruler broke his promises, Locke argued, the people had the right to rebel and overthrow him.

7. Another Enlightenment thinker, Baron de **Montesquieu**, felt that societies work best when there is a **separation of powers.** This occurs when the powers of the government are divided among separate legislative, executive, and judicial branches. The legislative branch makes the laws. The executive branch carries out or enforces the laws. Finally, the judicial branch interprets how the laws are applied to specific situations. This separation makes it difficult for one person or group to seize control.

8. In the 1770s, American colonists came into conflict with the British government. Early in 1776, **Thomas Paine** published ***Common Sense***. In this pamphlet, Paine argued it was only "common sense" for the

colonists to break away from Britain and establish their own independent republic without a king. Paine favored a system of **representative self-government** in which people elected their own representatives to govern them.

9. The colonists established **religious liberty** (*the freedom to follow one's own religious beliefs*) as a **protected right** (*a right that is established and protected by law*). This religious freedom prevented wars over religious beliefs such as those in Europe.

10. From these experiences, the **Founding Fathers** (or **Founders**) who established our nation developed **America's Founding Ideas.** These were a set of basic beliefs and principles that guided their actions at the time of the **Founding** (*when our nation was established*). They believed in: the importance of **the rule of law** (*that all citizens must obey the same rules*); the existence of **natural rights** (*that we are all born with certain basic rights, such as the right to life, liberty and property*); **limited government** (*that the powers of government should have limits*); **due process of law** (*that citizens should not have their lives, liberty, or property taken away without a fair process like a trial*); and the **equality of mankind** (*that all individuals have value as human beings and are entitled to certain basic rights*). You will learn how these principles influenced America's **Founding Documents**, like the Declaration of Independence and Constitution, in later chapters.

Our English Heritage

The people living in the thirteen colonies were greatly influenced by their English heritage. Because England has a protected island location, the English developed traditions different from the rest of Europe. They had rights that people living on the Continent of Europe did not share.

Magna Carta

Back in the early 1200s, King John of England wanted to increase his power so that he could fight his wars in France. John introduced new taxes and forced some of his subjects to give him loans that he never planned to pay back. The King's leading nobles—known as the barons—joined with Church leaders and England's largest towns in an armed rebellion against the King. To end the rebellion, John met with his unhappy barons on the field of Runnymede in 1215. A charter is a document that gives a person or group special rights. John signed a charter of rights that he granted to his subjects, which became known as **Magna Carta**, or "Great Charter."

Although his main enemies were the barons, King John granted these rights to all free Englishmen. Some of the most important rights were these:

1. The king would not imprison or take away the property of his subjects without a trial by a jury of peers (*equals*) based on the laws of the land. In a trial by jury, a group of ordinary citizens sit together to hear the evidence and decide the case. All free subjects thus had the **right to a fair trial**.

2. The **right to justice**: the king would give "justice" to his people. He would help them to resolve their disputes and would punish crimes.

3. The king would not impose new taxes without the approval of a committee of 25 barons.

By guaranteeing these rights to his subjects, John was actually placing limitations (*limits*) on his own power. Later English kings agreed to respect the rights granted by King John in Magna Carta. These rights belonged to all free Englishmen and became an important part of English law.

Magna Carta helped establish four important principles:

- **The right to justice:** Citizens have the right to expect just treatment and the help of the government in pursuing justice from others.

- **The right to a fair trial:** Citizens accused of a crime have the right to a fair trial by a jury.
- **The right to due process of law:** The government cannot take away a person's life, liberty, or property without a fair process, such as a trial by jury.
- **The limitation of government power:** There are limits on what the government can do. The government should not imprison citizens unjustly, take away their property, or tax them without their agreement. England became a **limited monarchy**, in which the King's power was not absolute.

The Active Citizen

Clause 12. No [special taxes] shall be imposed on our kingdom, unless by common counsel (*consent*) of our kingdom . . .

Clause 14. For obtaining the common counsel of the kingdom . . . we will cause to be summoned (*called*) the archbishops, bishops, abbots, earls, and greater barons, severally by our letters . . .

Clause 39. No freemen shall be taken or imprisoned or [have his property taken] or exiled (*sent away*) or in any way destroyed, nor will we go upon him nor send upon him, except by the lawful judgment of his peers (*equals*) or by the law of the land.

Clause 40. To no one . . . will we refuse or delay right or justice.

—King John of England, Magna Carta (1215)

- Which of these rights do you think was most important? Why?
- How did Magna Carta place limitations on the king's government?
- Which of the rights above do American citizens enjoy today?

Parliament

Because of Magna Carta, English kings began calling together assemblies of nobles whenever they needed more money. They also began inviting representatives from counties and towns to participate. These assemblies became known as Parliaments. To *parley* means "to talk."

Parliament developed into two houses. English nobles (*wealthy landowners who inherited their property and position*) sat in the House of Lords. Elected representatives from the towns and counties sat in the House of Commons. Parliament became England's legislative (*law-making*) body.

The Mayflower Compact

In 1620, a group of Pilgrims sailed across the Atlantic to establish a colony where they could worship God in their own way. The Pilgrims landed at Plymouth Rock, Massachusetts. Before leaving their ship, the *Mayflower*, all the men on board agreed to a set of rules to govern themselves.

The agreement the Pilgrims signed is known as the **Mayflower Compact**.

Sometimes the language of the past can be difficult to understand. In this document, the colonists agreed to "combine" themselves into "a body politic"—or a political body—in order to pass their own laws. The signers of the Mayflower Compact further promised to obey all such laws of the community.

With this document, we can see the beginnings of a strong tradition of colonial self-government. The basic idea of **self-government** is that people can govern themselves. The Mayflower Compact equally asserted the principle of the **consent of the governed**: that the laws of a community must be passed with the agreement of its members.

The Mayflower Compact

In the name of God. We whose names are underwritten, the loyal subjects of King James, of Great Britain, France and Ireland having undertaken for the glory of God, and advancement of the Christian faith, and honor of our country, a voyage to plant the first colony in the Northern parts of Virginia, do [agree] and combine ourselves together into a body politic (a government made by the community), *for our better order and preservation and . . . to enact and frame just and equal laws, ordinances, acts, and constitutions from time to time, as shall be thought most convenient for the general good of the colony, unto which we promise all due submission and obedience.*

—In witness whereof we sign our names at Cape Cod, 11th of November [1620]

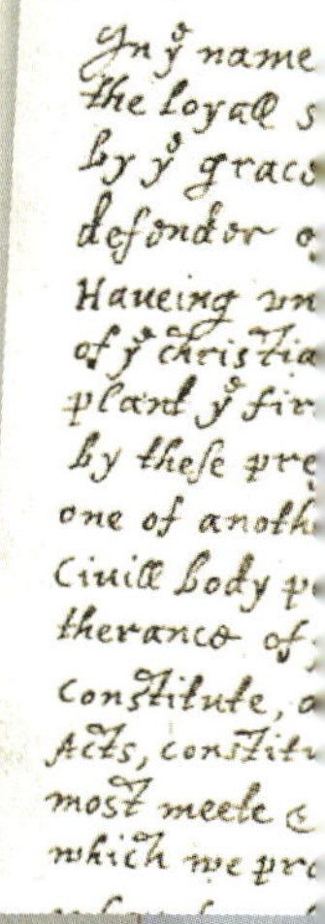

The Active Citizen

- Imagine you were about to land in a new place in an unfamiliar land. What rules do you think you and your companions would make?
- How do your rules compare to those of the Mayflower Compact?
- In the document above, circle or highlight the section of the Mayflower Compact that establishes the principle of self-government. Then circle the section of the document that establishes the "consent of the governed."

The English Bill of Rights

Back in England, King Charles I attempted to increase his royal power. He began collecting new taxes and forced loans. Some people felt these actions violated (*went against*) Magna Carta and other English laws. In 1642, a civil war broke out between Parliament and the King. Parliament won the contest and executed King Charles I in 1649. A military leader took control of the English government. When this leader died, Charles II (the son of Charles I) was restored to the throne. Charles II was a very popular ruler.

While he was king, Parliament passed the Habeas Corpus Act of 1679. This act gave people the right to challenge an imprisonment as unlawful. The jailer was ordered to bring the prisoner to court so that the court could determine if the imprisonment was lawful. In effect, this act gave prisoners the right to appeal to the court for a review of their case.

After the death of Charles II, his younger brother James did not cooperate with Parliament. James II was overthrown by Parliamentary leaders in the Glorious Revolution of 1688. James II fled to France.

To safeguard their rights from royal interference, Parliament passed the **English Bill of Rights** in December 1689. This important document limited the powers of the king or queen. It firmly established the supreme power of Parliament over the monarchy. The English Bill of Rights also introduced many specific safeguards for individual liberty. A century later, many of the same safeguards were placed in the U.S. Constitution and the Bill of Rights.

The English Bill of Rights stated that:

- The king could not collect new taxes without the approval of Parliament. There could be "no taxation without representation."
- People had the right to bear arms to defend themselves.
- Any subject could petition the government. (*To petition is to write to the government for a redress of grievances.*)
- An accused person was entitled to a speedy and fair jury trial (*a trial by a group of fellow citizens*). There also could be no excessive punishments (*unfairly harsh punishments*).

In summary, English people had the right to life, liberty and property (*people could not be executed, imprisoned, or lose their belongings except as punishment for a crime*).

The founders of our nation were affected by many influences. You have previously learned about the impact of ancient civilizations and our nation's English heritage. In this next section, you will learn about the impact of **Enlightenment ideas**, especially the writings of John Locke, Baron Montesquieu, and Thomas Paine. By now you may be wondering, what was the "Enlightenment" and what were "Enlightenment ideas"?

What was the Enlightenment?

By the late 1600s, the people of Europe and America became very impressed by the discoveries of science. For example, the Englishman Sir Isaac Newton had discovered the "laws" of gravity. With these laws, Newton was able to predict the speed at which a ball fell to the ground. He could also predict the movements of the planets in space.

People were amazed by these discoveries. European thinkers began to apply this same scientific approach in order to understand human society and make it better. They believed that there were **natural laws** that explained how people behaved, just as the laws of gravity could explain how objects moved. Some saw these laws as the work of God.

Sir Isaac Newton

Because these thinkers brought the light of reason to everything they studied, their movement became known as the Enlightenment. Enlightened thinkers applied human reason to understand the world. They refused to blindly follow tradition, authority, or superstition. **Enlightenment ideas** applied human reason and scientific thinking to improve society and make the world a better place. This period became known as the Age of Reason.

You should know Locke's ideas on the social contract for the EOC.

John Locke and the Social Contract

One of the earliest Enlightenment thinkers was another Englishman, **John Locke**. Locke believed that we are all like blank sheets of paper at birth. Later experiences and education then shape each of us as a person. Differences develop from differences in our experiences and education, and not because one of us is better or nobler than another at birth.

John Locke

Enlightened thinkers like Locke began to question social relationships. They questioned the special position that nobles and the Church held in most European countries at the time. (Nobles were landowners with special privileges.) These thinkers also questioned the power of kings. Most kings claimed to hold their power directly from God, but was this claim reasonable?

John Locke didn't think so. He rejected the idea that rulers receive their powers from God. Instead, Locke said that rulers receive their powers from the people whom they govern. A group of people makes an agreement, known as the **social contract**, to form a community. This community then makes an agreement with a ruler. The members of the community promise to obey the ruler. The ruler, in turn, promises to protect their **individual rights**. These are rights that each of us has as a human being. The whole purpose of this **social contract**, Locke wrote, was to protect these individual rights.

The ruler forms a government—a body that protects the community, provides laws and settles disputes between members.

Like most Enlightened thinkers, Locke believed in **natural law.** These were not laws passed by governments, but rules that all societies must follow, just as nature followed the laws of gravity. They were based on reason and common sense, such as the belief that killing or stealing is wrong. These laws applied to all societies at all times. Some believed, based on the Judeo-Christian tradition, that **natural laws** were based on God's commands.

Locke believed that natural law guaranteed each of us our **natural rights**. These rights included the **right to life, liberty, and property**. Locke saw these as natural rights that we are born with. Locke believed that no government should be able to take them away.

If a king or government made a law that went against our natural rights, Locke said this law was unjust. Locke thought that people should not obey such unjust laws. If a ruler repeatedly violated our natural rights, then his subjects even had the right to overthrow him.

This in fact happened at the very time that Locke was writing. As you know, King James II of England was very unpopular. He threatened many traditional rights. In 1688, leading members of the English Parliament overthrew him. The following year, Locke wrote a book to justify their actions. Locke explained that the government was established by a **social contract** between a ruler and his people. If a ruler, like King James II, repeatedly violated (*broke*) this contract, then the people had the right to overthrow him.

Divine Right Theory

Many kings claimed that their powers came from God. Therefore, their powers were unlimited.

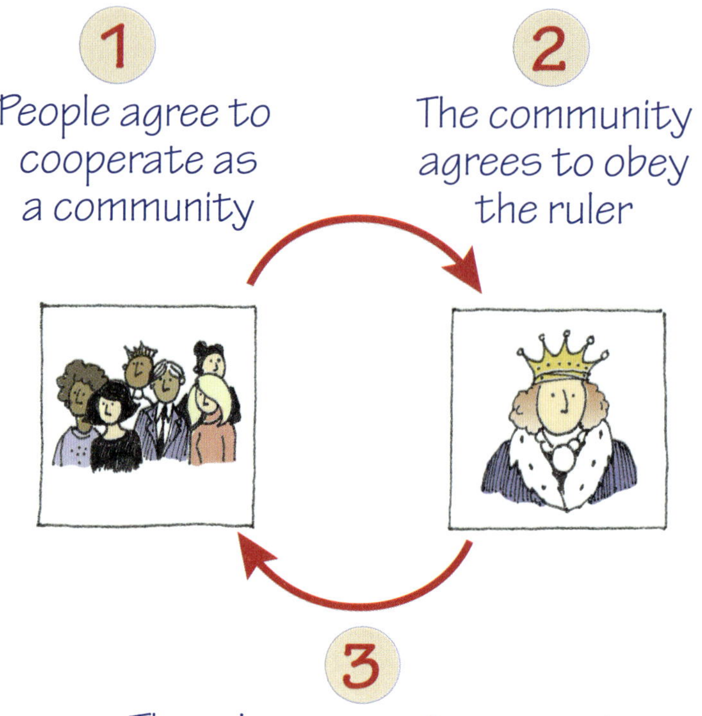

Locke's Theory of Social Contract

Locke claimed that rulers received their power from the people. The people therefore had the right to overthrow an unjust King.

The Active Citizen

Imagine you are an American colonist in 1689. You have just read some of Locke's writings. Write a short letter to a friend explaining why you agree or disagree with his views.

Your letter should have these parts:

(1) A greeting:

Dear ______________________,

(2) A statement of your point of view: I agree/disagree with Locke's views on the social contract.

(3) A short summary of Locke's views:

Locke says that rulers do not get their powers from God. Instead, their powers come from the people they rule. People promise to obey their ruler. The ruler, in turn, promises to protect and help his/her people. Locke calls this the "social contract." If the ruler breaks his/her promise, then the people have the right to change the ruler.

(4) A brief statement of why you agree or disagree with Locke:

I think Locke must be right/wrong because . . .

(5) a closing:

Your friend, ________________________

Montesquieu and the Separation of Powers

You should know about Montesquieu and the separation of powers for the EOC

Baron de Montesquieu

Another Enlightenment thinker who wrote about government was a French nobleman, Charles de Secondat, **Baron de Montesquieu**. Montesquieu studied governments in several countries and drew comparisons. He thought, for example, that different systems of government worked better in different countries because of their size. Switzerland was so small it could be a democracy in which every citizen helped make decisions. Russia was so large that all power had to be placed in the hands of a single absolute ruler.

Montesquieu also studied the ancient Roman republic. From these studies, he came up with the idea of the **separation of powers**. Montesquieu thought the government of England was especially successful because one body, the Parliament, made the laws. A second "branch" of government, the king, enforced those laws. A third "branch," the courts, interpreted and applied the laws.

> *"When the legislative and executive powers are united in the same person, or in the same group of officials, there is no liberty because we have fear that this monarch or Senate might pass tyrannical laws and execute them in a tyrannical manner."*
>
> —Montesquieu, *Spirit of the Laws*, Book XI, Chapter 6

Montesquieu concluded that it was best to divide the powers of government into three parts. He called this the **separation of powers**:

- The legislative branch makes the laws.
- The executive branch executes (*carries out*) the laws.
- The judicial branch interprets the laws and rules on their application to specific situations. For example, a court may have to decide if a person did a crime. The court not only looks at the actions of the accused but also what the law means in that situation.

Montesquieu thought that this separation of powers was good. It kept government leaders from becoming too powerful or trying to boss everyone else around. Having a separation of powers made it harder for government leaders to abuse their power. Each branch needed the cooperation of the other branches to do its work. If one person or a small group from one branch tried to seize power, the other branches would resist.

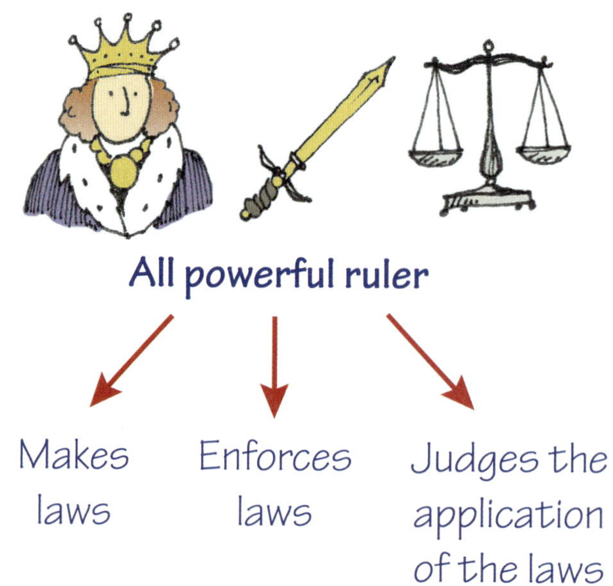

All powerful ruler

Makes laws

Enforces laws

Judges the application of the laws

Unitary Power

In this system, a single ruler holds all power.

Legislative branch

Makes laws

Executive branch

Enforces laws

Judicial branch

Judges the application of the laws

Montesquieu's Separation of Powers

In this system, the powers of government are divided among three separate branches.

The American Revolution and Thomas Paine's *Common Sense*

In the 1760s, the British Parliament decided to place new taxes on the American colonists to help pay for their defense. The colonists felt that these new taxes were being placed on them unfairly without their consent (*agreement*). A new cry was heard throughout the colonies: "**no taxation without representation!**" The colonists had clearly been influenced by English tradition and by John Locke's **social contract** theory.

Parliament, however, felt the colonists were too far away to ask their permission. They tried several different types of taxes, but each one led to even greater protests from the American colonists. By 1775, fighting broke out between the colonists and Britain. The American Revolution had begun!

You will learn more about the Revolution in the next chapter. Here, we want to focus on how these developments affected a famous writer and his views on government. In January 1776, **Thomas Paine**, an English visitor to the colonies, published an influential pamphlet. Paine called his pamphlet ***Common Sense***. Based on Enlightenment ideas, Paine argued that there was something very foolish about the monarchical form of government that existed in Britain and Europe. Rulers inherited their power from their parents–but there was no guarantee that any child would be as talented or as good a ruler as his or her parent. In fact, since kings and queens led sheltered lives, Paine felt they were usually "out-of-touch" with their own people and the rest of the world. Therefore, they often made the worst leaders. Instead of rule by kings, Paine favored **representative self-government**: people should elect their own representatives to govern them.

Thomas Paine

Paine further said it was ridiculous for the colonies, in the vast continent of North America, to be governed by a distant, tiny island. He saw no advantages for the colonists in this arrangement. Paine recommended that they break from Britain and establish their own representative government.

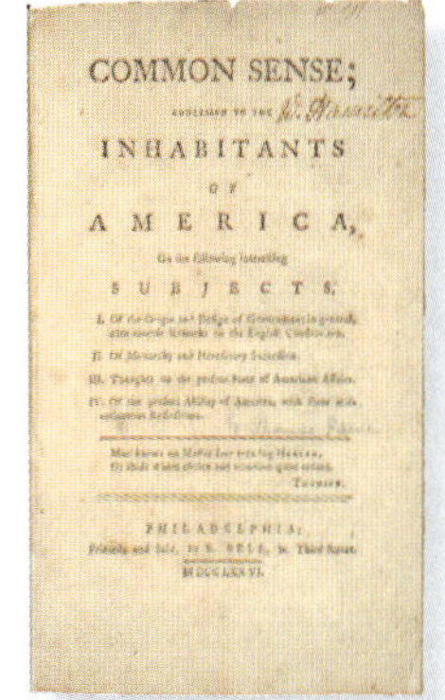

COMMON SENSE;

INHABITANTS

OF

AMERICA,

SUBJECTS.

PHILADELPHIA;

The Active Citizen

- How were Paine's ideas influenced by John Locke and the Enlightenment?

The Birth of Religious Liberty

Another important principle that inspired the founders of the United States was the protection of **religious liberty**—the right to follow your own religious beliefs.

At the time that the English colonies in North America were founded, Europeans with different religious beliefs were often at war. Protestants and Catholics fought against each other, and different groups of Protestants were in frequent disagreement. Colonists who came to practice religion in their own way—such as the Pilgrims and Puritans—did not always tolerate (*permit*) those of other religious beliefs.

Roger Williams, a minister in Massachusetts Bay Colony, thought that fighting in the name of religion was wrong. He believed no one could know with certainty which religious practices were correct. Williams was forced to leave Puritan Massachusetts and established his own new colony at

Providence, Rhode Island. His new colony was based on the principle of **religious liberty**—that people of all beliefs should be able to practice their religions openly and live peaceably together. He urged religious toleration: the permitting of other religions. In 1663, Rhode Island received a special royal charter, granting its colonists "full liberty in religious [matters]."

Other colonies also promoted religious toleration for people of all faiths: Lord Baltimore, a wealthy English nobleman, founded the colony of Maryland to serve as a home for Britain's persecuted Catholics. To protect Catholic settlers from Protestant colonists, Baltimore introduced the Edict of Toleration, a law that guaranteed religious liberty for Christians throughout the colony.

Further north, the Dutch permitted Jewish settlers to settle in New Netherland in 1656. Ten years later, the Dutch colony was conquered by England and became New York. The English colony of New York continued to permit religious liberty for people of all faiths.

The English philosopher John Locke published a popular book in England also in favor of religious liberty. In 1688, the English Parliament passed the Act of Toleration, granting religious liberty to all Protestants.

Thomas Jefferson, one of America's "Founding Fathers" and the main author of the Declaration of Independence (see Chapter 3), was greatly influenced by the ideal of religious liberty. Jefferson wrote Virginia's "Statute for Religious Freedom." Jefferson argued that it was wrong for the government to push people to accept particular religious beliefs. Religious truth, Jefferson said, was powerful enough by itself. It did not need the help of government to win supporters. Instead, people should enjoy freedom of choice in religion, which Jefferson saw as a basic individual right.

Today, Americans enjoy **religious liberty** as a **protected right**. As you will learn in a later chapter, the First Amendment protects religious liberty. Our government protects our religious freedom so that Americans of different beliefs can live together peacefully. By protecting our right to religious liberty, the United States has avoided the bitter wars of religion that have too often caused destruction in other countries.

The Impact of English Rights and Enlightenment Ideas on Colonial America

Each of the documents and beliefs described in this chapter influenced the colonists' views on government, including the "**Founding Fathers**" (*the men who established the American system of government*) at the time of the **Founding** (*the period when our nation was established*).

- Because of **Magna Carta**, the English colonists enjoyed a system of trial by jury. They were also protected against new taxation by the king without the approval of Parliament. Magna Carta thus established our **right to justice** and **right to due process** while placing **limitations on government power** (see page 28 earlier in this chapter).
- The **Mayflower Compact** established a strong tradition of colonial **self-government** and **consent of the governed**. While some issues, such as defense of the colonies from France or Spain, were decided in Great Britain, many local issues were left to the colonists themselves to decide (see page 28).
- Each of the 13 colonies eventually established its own colonial legislature. In most of the colonies, the king appointed a royal governor and the landowners of the colony elected the members of the colonial legislature.

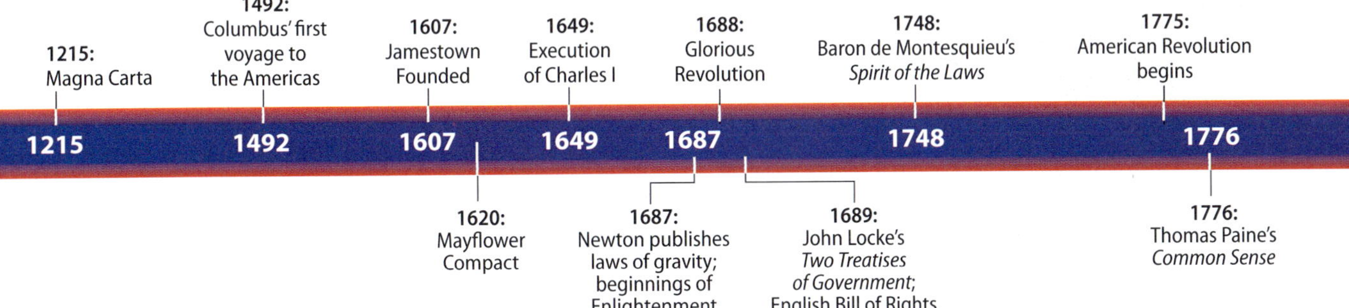

- Because of the **English Bill of Rights**, the English colonists felt they should have all the rights of freeborn Englishmen. This meant **no taxation without representation**, they had the right to a **speedy and fair jury trial**, they were permitted to carry arms to protect themselves, and there could be **no excessive punishments** (see page 29).
- John Locke's theory of the **social contract** gave the colonists the idea that the powers of government were based on their own consent (see pages 30–32). This theory especially influenced the American Revolution and the "**Founding Fathers**" who wrote our nation's **Founding Documents**, such as the Declaration of Independence and the Constitution. You will learn more about these documents in the next chapter.
- Montesquieu's ideas on the **separation of powers** were based on ancient Roman and later English methods of government. In England, power was divided between the king, Parliament, and the courts of law. In each of the colonies, power was divided between the royal governor, the colonial legislature and the courts of law. Montesquieu believed that this separation of powers was beneficial (see pages 33–34). His ideas on the separation of powers greatly influenced the authors of the U.S. Constitution. They created a government with three separate branches, just as Montesquieu had proposed. You will learn more about the Constitution in later chapters.
- **Thomas Paine's *Common Sense*** encouraged the colonists to declare their independence and adopt the republican form of government during the American Revolution (see page 35).
- Colonists and Enlightenment thinkers like John Locke promoted **religious liberty** to avoid wars of religion (see pages 35–36).

John Locke (1632–1704)

Baron de Montesquieu (1689–1755)

The Principles Underlying America's Founding Ideas

Be sure to know these principles for the EOC.

In Chapters 1 and 2, you traced the origins of the basic principles that influenced the **Founding Fathers** who established the American constitutional republic. All of these principles were reflected at the **Founding** in America's **Founding Documents**—the Declaration of Independence, Articles of Confederation, Constitution and Bill of Rights. These important principles and their origins can be summarized as follows:

Principle	Sources	Explanation
Rule of Law	Ancient Rome; Judeo-Christian Tradition (see Chapter 1); Magna Carta	We are all subject to the same rules, without exception. Even government officials and wealthy citizens must obey these laws. Because we live under the rule of law, we are safe from arbitrary actions by our government. No one is above the law.
Natural Rights	Judeo-Christian Tradition (see Chapter 1); John Locke and the Enlightenment	There are certain basic rights that every person is born with. These rights apply to all societies and should not be taken away. They include the right to life, liberty and property. In the next chapter, you will learn how the colonists demanded independence when the British government threatened these rights.
Limited Government	Magna Carta; English Bill of Rights; John Locke	We give our government certain powers over us, but the powers of our government are not unlimited. There are limits on what government officials can do. These limits prevent our government from becoming too strong and threatening our individual rights.
Due Process of Law	Ancient Rome (see Chapter 1); Magna Carta; English Bill of Rights	We are entitled to a speedy and fair trial by jury or some other public hearing before our lives, liberty or property can be taken away. At this trial or hearing, we have the right to defend ourselves, to present evidence, to see any evidence against us, and to have the case decided by an impartial judge, jury or decision-maker. Our due process rights protect us from arbitrary actions by government officials.
Equality of Mankind	Judeo-Christian Tradition (see Chapter 1)	We each have individual worth, and we are all equal as human beings. Each of us is entitled to the same rights. In the next chapter, you will learn how this belief in equality was expressed in the Declaration of Independence.
Protection of Religious Liberty	Colonial charters; English Bill of Rights; John Locke and the Enlightenment	There is no official religion in the United States, and everyone has the freedom to practice his or her own religious beliefs without fear of discrimination or persecution. Because of this protection of religious liberty, Americans have avoided wars over religious beliefs.

In later chapters, you will see how these six principles are contained in America's **Founding Documents**.

Name ______________________________

Fill in the last two columns in the chart below.

Document	Date	Author	Main Ideas	Importance
Magna Carta	1215	King John		
Mayflower Compact	1620	Pilgrims		
Writings on the social contract	1689	John Locke		
English Bill of Rights	1689	English Parliament		
Writings on the separation of powers	1748	Montesquieu		
Common Sense	1776	Thomas Paine		

Explain the following concepts in your own words.

Concept	Explanation
Natural Law	
Self-government	
Separation of Powers	
Religious Liberty	

Name ______________________________

When learning about historic documents, it is important to remember:

- Who wrote the document
- When and where it was written
- Why it was written
- The main ideas of the document
- Its impact (*effects*)

Fill in the charts below.

Magna Carta (1215)	
What rights did the Magna Carta give to "free Englishmen"?	How did this document influence the colonists?

Mayflower Compact (1620)	
Describe this document.	How did this document influence the colonists?
How were the ideas in this document similar to John Locke's later idea of a social contract?	

Name ________________________________

Fill in the charts below.

English Bill of Rights	
Which rights did the English Bill of Rights grant to English subjects (*citizens under rule of a monarch*)?	How did these rights influence the colonists?

John Locke's *Social Contract* (1689)	
Describe John Locke's "Social Contract."	How did this theory differ from the view that God gave kings their power?
How did Locke's ideas influence the colonists?	

Name ______________________________

1. Imagine it is 1215 and you are King John of England. Write a short declaration to your subjects explaining the new rights you have granted (*given*) them in Magna Carta.

2. Imagine you are a Pilgrim colonist in 1620. Write a paragraph to a friend in England describing the Mayflower Compact and why you decided to sign it.

Name ______________________________

3. Complete the paragraph frame below.

The Enlightenment

The Enlightenment took place in Europe in the 17th and 18th centuries. People were very impressed by the achievements of science. Sir Isaac Newton, for example, had discovered the "laws" of gravity. From these discoveries, many people concluded that natural laws also controlled how people as well as nature behaved. A natural law is ____.

Two influential Enlightenment thinkers were John Locke and the Baron de Montesquieu. John Locke rejected the idea that kings received their powers from God. Instead, he argued that each person had certain natural rights. These natural rights included ______________________________.

Locke wrote that each group of people living together made an agreement known as a social contract. In each social contract, people agreed to form a community and to give all of their power to a monarch (a king or queen). In this contract, the job of the monarch was to ____. The job of the people was to ____.

Locke said that if the monarch didn't carry out his or her job, then the people had the right to ____.

Locke wrote just after the Glorious Revolution in England (1688). He justified Parliament's actions in overthrowing King James II. Locke's ideas had a great influence on the American colonists. They would later help inspire the American Revolution.

A second important Enlightenment thinker was the Baron de Montesquieu. He was a French nobleman. Montesquieu wrote in favor of the separation of ____________________. In this system, the powers of government are separated. An assembly, like the English Parliament, has the ________________ power. This is the power to ______________________. An individual, like the king or queen, has the ____________________ power. This is the power to ____________________________. A court system, like the English courts, has the ______________________________ power. This is the power to ______________________________.

Montesquieu realized that when power is separated into three different branches, no one individual or group ____. Montesquieu's ideas also greatly influenced the "Founding Fathers"—the men who established the American government.

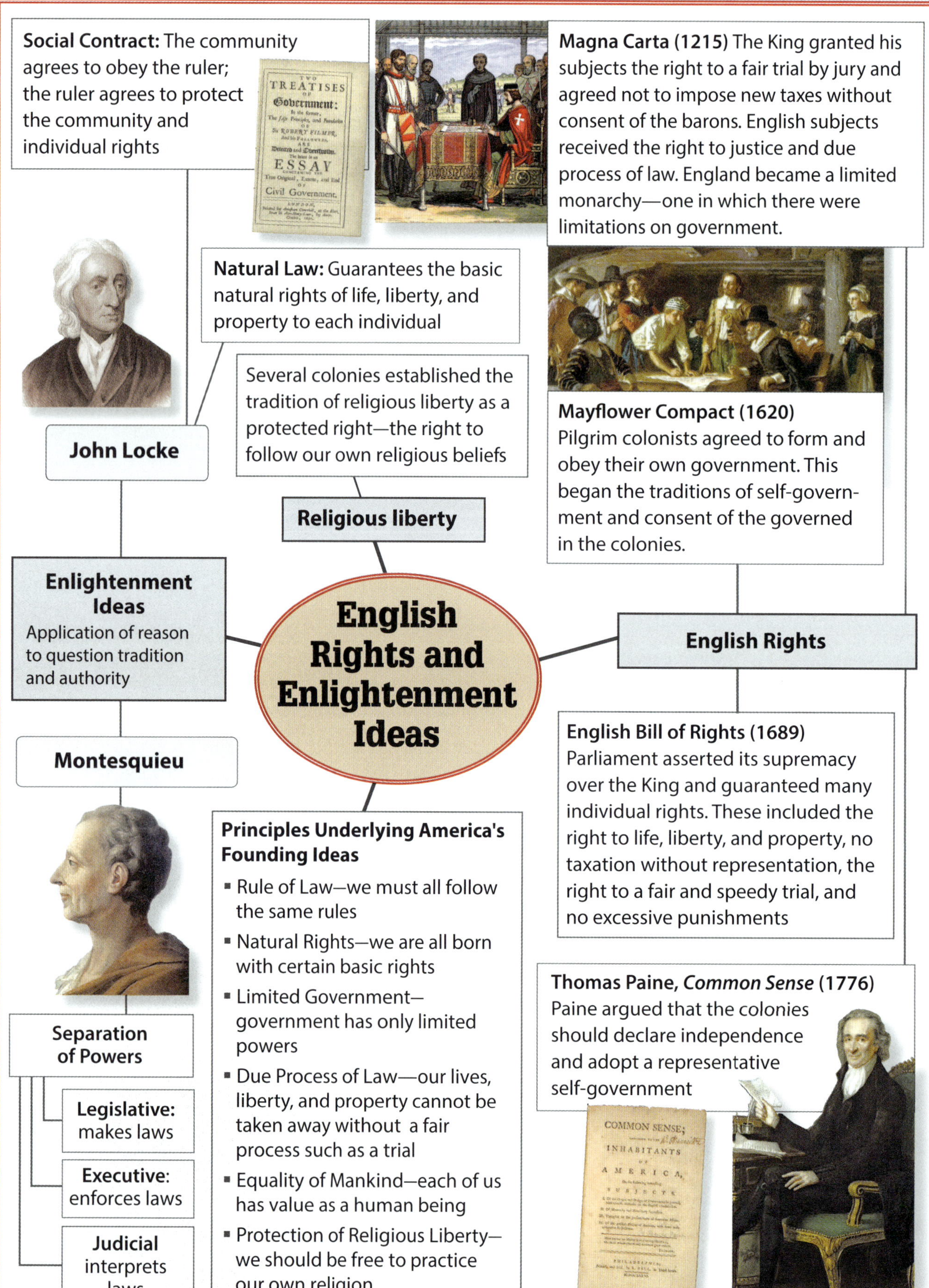
English Rights and Enlightenment Ideas
Social Contract: The community agrees to obey the ruler; the ruler agrees to protect the community and individual rights
Magna Carta (1215) The King granted his subjects the right to a fair trial by jury and agreed not to impose new taxes without consent of the barons. English subjects received the right to justice and due process of law. England became a limited monarchy—one in which there were limitations on government.
Natural Law: Guarantees the basic natural rights of life, liberty, and property to each individual
Several colonies established the tradition of religious liberty as a protected right—the right to follow our own religious beliefs
John Locke
Religious liberty
Mayflower Compact (1620) Pilgrim colonists agreed to form and obey their own government. This began the traditions of self-government and consent of the governed in the colonies.
Enlightenment Ideas
Application of reason to question tradition and authority
English Rights
Montesquieu
English Bill of Rights (1689) Parliament asserted its supremacy over the King and guaranteed many individual rights. These included the right to life, liberty, and property, no taxation without representation, the right to a fair and speedy trial, and no excessive punishments
Principles Underlying America's Founding Ideas
▪ Rule of Law—we must all follow the same rules
▪ Natural Rights—we are all born with certain basic rights
▪ Limited Government—government has only limited powers
▪ Due Process of Law—our lives, liberty, and property cannot be taken away without a fair process such as a trial
▪ Equality of Mankind—each of us has value as a human being
▪ Protection of Religious Liberty—we should be free to practice our own religion
Separation of Powers
Legislative: makes laws
Executive: enforces laws
Judicial interprets laws
Thomas Paine, Common Sense (1776)
Paine argued that the colonies should declare independence and adopt a representative self-government
COMMON SENSE;
INHABITANTS
AMERICA,

Review Cards: The Origins of American Government

Magna Carta (1215)

- **Magna Carta** was a document forced on King John of England by his barons (*nobles*). It established important rights that were later enjoyed by all free Englishmen.
- Magna Carta promised the **right to justice** (*punishment of crimes and fair resolution of disputes*). It also promised that new taxes or loans would not be imposed without the consent of a committee of barons.
- Magna Carta also promised that no freeman would be imprisoned or lose his property or be otherwise punished except after a trial by jury based on the law of the land. This established the **right to a fair trial** (*a fair hearing in a court*) and the **right to due process** (*citizens could not have their lives, libertiy or property taken away without a fair process like a trial*).
- Magna Carta created a **limitation of government power**. Under Magna Carta, the King could not impose new taxes without the consent of his subjects. Every freeborn Englishman was also entitled to a trial by jury when accused of a crime.

Mayflower Compact (1620)

- The Pilgrims sailed to North America to start their own colony where they could worship God in their own way.
- Before leaving the ship, they signed an agreement to form their own community and to obey its rules. The **Mayflower Compact** established the principle of **self-government** in the colonies. This was the idea that on many matters, the colonists could govern themselves. The colonists also agreed to obey their own laws. This indicated that a government's laws are based on the **consent of the governed**.

The English Bill of Rights (1689)

- King James II tried to increase his royal powers. He was overthrown in the Glorious Revolution in 1688.
- Parliament passed the **English Bill of Rights** in 1689, shortly after James II was overthrown.
- The English Bill of Rights promised to protect many **individual rights/liberties**. It promised that that there would be **no taxation without representation** (*no taxes would be collected without the approval of the people's representatives in Parliament*), that citizens could petition (*make requests to*) the government, and that **no excessive punishments** would be imposed. It guaranteed individuals the right to **life, liberty and property** (*these could not be taken away except as punishment for a crime*), and to a **speedy and fair jury trial** (*a trial by a group of fellow citizens*).

The Enlightenment

- The Enlightenment was a movement of ideas in Europe and America in the late 17th and 18th centuries.
- **Enlightenment ideas** were based on applying human reason and scientific thinking, instead of following tradition, to understand and improve society and government.
- Two of the most important Enlightenment thinkers were John Locke and Montesquieu.

John Locke on Natural Law and the Social Contract

- **Locke** believed that people enjoyed certain **individual rights** under **natural law**. These "**natural rights**" include the **right to life, liberty, and property**. They are rights that each of us is born with. No government has the right to take away these natural rights.
- Locke wrote that people joined together in a **social contract** (*an agreement*) to form a community to protect themselves and their individual rights.
- As part of this social contract, the community gives its power to a ruler, whom it promises to obey.
- If the king (or queen) breaks his or her promise to respect the rights of his individual subjects, then the people have the right to rebel against their ruler.

Montesquieu's Separation of Powers

A French nobleman, **Montesquieu** believed that the powers of government should be separated among three branches:

- **Legislative** branch has the power to make laws;
- **Executive** branch has the power to carry out and enforce the laws; and
- **Judicial** branch has the power to interpret and apply the law to particular cases.

Montesquieu's idea of dividing up legislative, executive, and judicial powers is known as the **separation of powers.** He believed that this would prevent government leaders from abusing their power. No one person could seize power because the other branches would resist.

Thomas Paine's *Common Sense*

- In the 1770s, American colonists came into conflict with the British government. Fighting broke out in 1775. Early in 1776, **Thomas Paine** published ***Common Sense***.
- Paine poked fun at rule by hereditary kings and queens. He recommended that the colonists declare their independence and establish a **representative self-government**.

Principles Underlying America's Founding Ideas

These ideas influenced the **Founding Fathers** who established the American constitutional republic, at the **Founding** (*the period when our nation was established*). Their **Founding Ideas** are reflected in the **Founding Documents**, such as the Declaration of Independence and Constitution, which you will study in later chapters.

- **Rule of Law** All people are subject to the same set of rules, without exception. No one is above the law.
- **Natural Rights** All people are born with certain basic individual rights, such as the right to life, liberty, and property.
- **Limited Government** There are limits on the powers that government has over us and on what government can do.
- **Due Process of Law** Government cannot take away our life, liberty or property without a fair process, such as a trial by impartial jurors.
- **Equality of Mankind** Each of us has indivdual worth and we are all equal as human beings. All citizens are equal in the eyes of the law, entitled to the same rights.
- **Protection of Religious Liberty** Each of us has the right to practice our own religion freely.

What Do You Know?

SS.7.CG.1.4

1. According to John Locke, which agreement did individuals enter into when forming their own society?

   A. constitution

   B. social contract

   C. Mayflower Compact

   D. English Bill of Rights

SS.7.CG.1.4

2. According to John Locke, which rights were guaranteed by natural law?

   A. freedom of worship and the right to petition

   B. trial by jury and no cruel punishments

   C. freedom of speech and of the press

   D. life, liberty and property

SS.7.CG.1.3

3. The statement below is an excerpt from Magna Carta (1215).

> No freeman shall be taken or imprisoned or disseised or outlawed or exiled or any way destroyed, nor will we go upon him nor send upon him, except by the lawful judgment of his peers or by the law of the land.

   Which right was guaranteed in this excerpt from Magna Carta?

   A. no taxation without representation

   B. freedom of the press

   C. freedom of religion

   D. trial by jury

SS.7.CG.1.4

4. Which example illustrates Montesquieu's idea of the separation of powers?

   A. Citizens of the United States choose many of their public officials in elections.

   B. The state government of Florida has a governor, state legislature and state court system.

   C. Individual rights to life, liberty and property are guaranteed by natural law.

   D. People have the right to overthrow an unjust government.

SS.7.CG.1.4

5. How was Locke's social contract theory related to his belief in natural law?
   - **A.** He argued subjects had the right to rebel against a ruler who acted against natural law.
   - **B.** He argued that whatever the king did was good according to natural law.
   - **C.** He argued that natural law required the colonists to be given their independence.
   - **D.** He argued that God had especially chosen kings to rule over their subjects as part of natural law.

SS.7.CG.1.3

6. Which describes an impact of Magna Carta on the American colonists in the 1770s?
   - **A.** They believed they could not be taxed without their consent.
   - **B.** They believed they could not be governed by a far-away island.
   - **C.** They thought they had the right to overthrow a king who did not protect their rights.
   - **D.** They favored a separation of the powers of government into different branches.

SS.7.CG.1.4

7. What most attracted the Founding Fathers to Montesquieu's idea of the separation of powers?
   - **A.** It could prevent the central government from becoming tyrannical and oppressive.
   - **B.** It could protect the rights of the nobility from the actions of the king.
   - **C.** It could preserve the privileges of the monarch and nobles from popular attack.
   - **D.** It could raise judicial power to a level of equality with legislative and executive power.

SS.7.CG.1.3

8. Which right was established by Magna Carta in 1215?
   - **A.** the right to vote in elections
   - **B.** the right to choose the monarch
   - **C.** the right to freedom of speech
   - **D.** the right to a trial by jury

SS.7.CG.1.3

9. Which document confirmed the rights of English subjects after the overthrow of James II in the Glorious Revolution?
   - **A.** Magna Carta
   - **B.** Mayflower Compact
   - **C.** English Bill of Rights
   - **D.** Montesquieu's *Spirit of the Laws*

SS.7.CG.1.4

10. Which of the following were most similar?

A. the Mayflower Compact and John Locke's social contract theory

B. the English Bill of Rights and Thomas Paine's *Common Sense*

C. Magna Carta and Montesquieu's separation of powers

D. the Mayflower Compact and Montesquieu's separation of powers

SS.7.CG.1.3

11. The diagram below indicates that the colonists based some of their political views on historic documents.

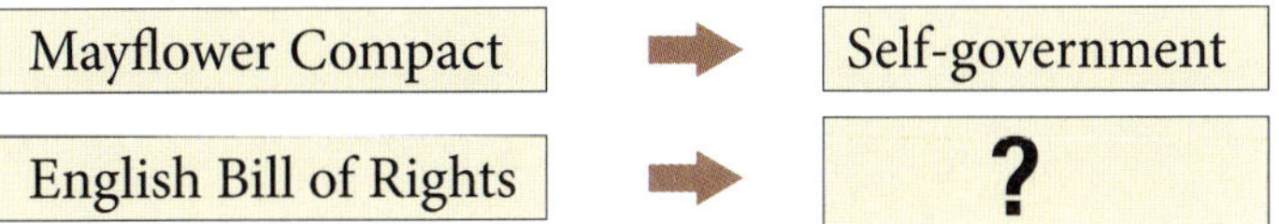

Which phrase completes the diagram?

A. Natural law

B. Separation of powers

C. Divine Right of Kings

D. Guarantees of individual rights

SS.7.CG.1.3

12. The statements below are from the 1776 Virginia Declaration of Rights.

> 1) That in all capital or criminal prosecutions a man hath a right to demand . . . evidence in his favor, and to a speedy trial by an impartial jury . . .
> 2) That the legislative, executive, and judiciary department shall be separate and distinct . . .
> 3) That the freedom of the press is one of the great bulwarks of liberty, and can never be restrained . . .
> 4) That a well-regulated militia, composed of the body of the people, trained to arms, is the proper, natural, and safe defense of a free state . . .

Which statement guarantees a right first granted by Magna Carta?

A. 1

B. 2

C. 3

D. 4

SS.7.CG.1.3

13. The statements below are from three of the first amendments to the U.S. Constitution.

> *"Congress shall make no law . . . prohibiting . . . the right of the people . . . to petition the government for a redress of grievances."*
>
> —First Amendment
>
> *"[T]he right of the people to keep and bear arms shall not be infringed"*
>
> —Second Amendment
>
> *"[No] cruel and unusual punishments [shall be] inflicted"*
>
> —Eighth Amendment

Which earlier document contained similar rights?

A. Magna Carta (1215)

B. The Mayflower Compact (1620)

C. The English Bill of Rights (1689)

D. Montesquieu's *Spirit of the Laws* (1748)

SS.7.CG.1.4

14. Which statement describes the influence of natural-law beliefs on John Locke and other Enlightenment thinkers?

A. They argued it was natural for subjects to obey established governments.

B. They questioned any practices that seemed to go against reason and natural law.

C. They believed that royal power was natural because it was based on divine right.

D. They claimed church teachings should not be challenged since they rested on natural law.

The ideas of Locke and Montesquieu were read and discussed in Europe and the colonies during the Enlightenment.

CHAPTER 3

Americans Declare Their Independence

SS.7.CG.1.5 Describe how British policies and responses to colonial concerns led to the writing of the Declaration of Independence.

SS.7.CG.1.6 Analyze the ideas and grievances set forth in the Declaration of Independence.

Content Focus Vocabulary in This Chapter

British policies/colonial policies
Colonial concerns
Causal relationship
Taxation
Stamp Act
Representation
Individual rights
Quartering Act
Declaratory Act
Townshend Acts
Tea Act
Intolerable Acts
Declaration of Independence
Preamble
Unalienable rights
Natural rights
Endowed by their Creator
"Life, liberty, and the pursuit of happiness"
Social contract
Limited government
Right of resistance to tyrannical government
Colonial grievances
Consent of the governed
Imposing taxes without consent
Suspending trial by jury
Limiting judicial powers
Quartering soldiers
Dissolving legislatures

Florida "Keys" to Learning

1. After the French and Indian War, the British government was deeply in debt. It had borrowed large sums of money to pay for the war. This led to new **British policies** (*actions by government*). Parliament passed a series of laws to tax the colonists. It made no attempt to obtain the colonists' consent (*approval; agreement*) to this **taxation**. There was a **causal relationship** between **British colonial polices** (*policies towards the colonies*) and **colonial concerns** (*things that upset the colonists*). A causal relationship exists when one event or development leads to another—it causes the second event to occur. In this case, British policies led to colonial concerns.

2. The first of the new British taxes was the **Stamp Act**. This law required colonists to put government stamps on all court documents, licenses, newspapers, and other documents. Because the colonies were not represented in Parliament, the colonists objected that there should be no taxation without **representation**. Colonial assemblies sent petitions to Parliament to change the law, and many colonists boycotted (*refused to buy*) British goods. Parliament finally repealed (*set aside; cancelled*) the Stamp Act after widespread colonial protests.

3. Although it repealed the Stamp Act, Parliament also passed the **Declaratory Act**. This act stated that Parliament had the right to pass laws for the colonies, including taxes. Parliament then passed the **Townshend Acts**. These laws placed new taxes on glass and other household goods in the colonies.

4. To prevent colonial unrest, the British government sent more troops to North America. Parliament passed the **Quartering Act**, which required the colonists to feed and house some of the British troops in their barns and homes. Despite these steps, the colonists loudly protested against the Townshend Acts.

5. Parliament eventually repealed the Townshend Acts. However, Parliament next passed the **Tea Act.** This act placed a tax on tea brought from India to the colonies. Again, it was passed without the colonists' consent.

6. The "Boston Tea Party" was a protest against the Tea Act. A group of colonists boarded British ships at night and threw chests of tea into Boston Harbor. The British government was greatly angered by this destruction of property. It passed the "**Intolerable Acts**," which closed Boston Harbor, suspended (*temporarily dissolved*) the colonial legislature of Massachusetts, and allowed judges instead of juries to try cases. The colonists believed the British government was threatening their **individual rights** (*the rights to which they were entitled under both English law and natural law.*)

7. British troops and armed colonists fired on each other in April 1775, starting the American Revolution. Delegates from the colonies met in two Continental Congresses.

8. In January 1776, Thomas Paine's *Common Sense* was published. It urged the colonists to seek independence. In June 1776, a majority of the Second Continental Congress agreed to support independence. A special committee was formed to write a declaration that would explain this decision.

9. The **Preamble** (*introduction*) to the **Declaration of Independence** announced the American theory of government: (1) that people have certain "**unalienable rights**" (*rights that cannot be separated*), which include the rights to "**life, liberty, and the pursuit of happiness**" (*our right to live freely and to seek our own goals*). These are **natural rights** that we are born with: people are **endowed by their Creator** (*given by God*) with these rights, which cannot be rightfully taken away; (2) that governments are created as part of a **social contract** (*agreement among the members of a society*) to protect these rights and exist with the consent of the governed (*approval of the people they rule*); (3) that when a government tries to take away these rights, its people have the right to change that government, by force if necessary; and (4) that people should not change their government lightly (*easily*).

10. Much of the Declaration is taken up by its list of **colonial grievances** (*complaints from the*

colonists) against King George III. These complaints justified the colonists' decision to declare independence. Colonial grievances included **imposing taxes without consent** (*such as the Tea Act*), **suspending trial by jury** (*temporarily taking away this right*), **limiting judicial powers** (*limiting the powers of colonial courts to try cases*), **quartering soldiers** (*putting British troops in colonial barns and homes*), and **dissolving legislatures** (*ordering colonial legislatures to shut down*). The King also cut colonial trade and waged war on the colonists.

11. The colonists therefore claimed the **right of resistance to a tyrannical government.** This was the right to resist and even to overthrow a government that was harsh and controlling, and that used force against its own citizens. Instead of obeying such a government, the colonists declared their independence. They intended to create a **limited government** (*a government with limited powers*).

In the last chapter, you learned how England established thirteen colonies in North America. These colonists enjoyed the same rights as people in Great Britain. The colonists also enjoyed some unique powers of self-government. Each colony had its own legislature, which resolved many local problems.

The French and Indian War

In 1754, Britain went to war with France. This conflict became known in America as the French and Indian War. France lost the war and was forced to surrender its colonies in North America. Canada and the Ohio River Valley came under British rule. The American colonists were pleased with this outcome. They no longer had to worry about defending themselves against the French and their Indian allies. On the other hand, the British government found itself deeply in debt. It had borrowed large sums of money to pay for the war.

For the EOC, you should know that colonial responses to British policies after the French and Indian War began the process of separation between the colonies and Great Britain.

British Policies and Colonial Reactions: Taxation without Representation

People living in Britain were already paying more in taxes than the colonists in North America. The British government therefore decided that the colonists should pay more towards their own defense. It adopted new **British policies.** A policy is a course of action or series of steps taken by a government or other decision maker. Parliament passed a series of laws to tax the colonists. Since the colonies were so far from London, no attempt was made to obtain their consent (*approval; agreement*) to this **taxation.**

The first of these new British policies was the **Stamp Act.** It was passed in 1765. This act required every official document, newspaper, or pamphlet in the colonies to have an expensive government stamp. Everything from college diplomas to playing cards needed a stamp. The colonists were greatly angered by the Stamp Act. They objected (*complained*) that this was imposing taxes without consent of the people. Colonists held marches and rallies against the Stamp Act. Colonial assemblies sent petitions (*formal requests*) to Parliament to change the law. Colonists boycotted (*refused to buy*) British goods. Protestors held a special "Stamp Act Congress" in New York City. Some angry colonists even captured government tax collectors and poured hot tar and placed feathers on them.

Colonists harrassing a British tax collector

The British government was taken by surprise by the number of protests against the Stamp Act. Parliament acted quickly to repeal (*cancel; withdraw*) the Stamp Act. At the same time, Parliament passed the **Declaratory Act**. In this act, Parliament insisted on its right to pass laws that applied to the colonies without obtaining their consent (*approval*).

The British government still needed to collect money from the colonists. Parliament therefore tried a different type of tax. It passed the **Townshend Acts**. These acts placed taxes on paper, paint, glass, lead, and tea. These common goods were shipped to the colonies from Britain.

Once again, Parliament passed these taxes without the consent of the colonists. Members of Parliament still felt that the colonists were too far away to consult (*discuss or check*) with them.

Could the colonists have sent their own representatives to Parliament? At a time when crossing the Atlantic was slow, any colonial representatives in London would soon have been out of touch with the colonists in America. Most colonial leaders did not want to have representatives in Parliament. Instead, they wanted to make their own laws in their own colonial assemblies. Such laws would include any new taxes.

The colonists formed special committees to protest against the Townshend Acts. To prevent unrest, the British government sent 4,000 soldiers to Boston, where discontent was greatest. The **Quartering Act**, passed in 1765, gave the government the right to quarter some of these troops in colonists' barns and homes. To "quarter" means to send soldiers to live on private citizens' properties. The homeowner was expected to provide food and lodging (*a place to stay*) for each soldier, for which they would be paid.

Colonists dressed as Indians throw tea into Boston Harbor

Parliament finally repealed (*canceled or withdrew*) the hated Townshend Acts. However, it kept to its general policy by passing the **Tea Act**, a new tax on tea. The act allowed tea to be shipped directly from India to the American colonies, so the final price of the tea was actually less than previously, despite the tax. The colonists still complained that the tax was passed without their consent.

British ships carrying tea arrived in Boston Harbor in December 1773. A group of colonists, dressed as American Indians, boarded the ships at night and threw their chests of tea into the harbor in protest. This event became known as the "Boston Tea Party."

The British government was greatly angered by this destruction of property. Parliament passed the **Intolerable Acts**. These closed Boston Harbor and dissolved (*shut down*) the Massachusetts legislature. The Intolerable Acts also said the British

The Active Citizen

In your own words, summarize the British policies that annoyed colonists in the years after the French and Indian War. Then describe colonial responses to those policies.

British Policies	Colonial Responses

government would appoint all officials in Massachusetts until the tea was paid for. Finally, these acts suspended (*temporarily ended*) many jury trials. Royal officials would no longer be put on trial by jury (*a panel of local citizens*) in the colonies, but would instead be tried by judges in Great Britain. The Intolerable Acts **limited the judicial powers** of colonial courts by allowing the British government to move the trials of colonists as well as of royal officials to a different colony or to Great Britain, where a judge appointed by the King would decide the case.

The Outbreak of the Revolution

You can see that the colonists were very concerned about the issues of **taxation** and **representation**. If they were going to be taxed, they felt they had the right to be represented. They felt their **individual rights** were being threatened. There was a clear **causal relationship** between **British colonial policies** (*policies towards the colonies*) and **colonial concerns**. In other words, these policies created colonial concerns.

In response to British policies, the colonies sent representatives to Philadelphia to meet as a "Continental Congress" in September 1774. The Congress assembled, sent protests to Britain, and agreed to a boycott (*refusal to buy*) of British goods. Its members also decided that a second Continental Congress should be held.

Meanwhile, American colonists organized in Boston. They collected guns and ammunition (*bullets and gunpowder*). The Royal Governor of Massachusetts sent soldiers to seize colonial leaders and arms just outside Boston. British troops and armed colonists fired on the colonists in April 1775. This exchange of gunfire started the American Revolution.

The Second Continental Congress was about to meet. Many of its delegates were already on their way to Philadelphia. The Second Continental Congress began its meetings in May 1775. Most of the delegates from the other colonies strongly supported the decision of Massachusetts to resist the British. They encouraged the other colonies to join in the struggle.

The Continental Congress then formed its own army and chose George Washington, a Virginian, to command it.

The Question of American Independence

Even after the outbreak of fighting, many colonists still wanted to remain under British rule. They saw themselves as loyal subjects of the King.

In July 1775, the Continental Congress issued a declaration (*public statement*) explaining why the colonists were resisting the British government. The declaration contained a long list of complaints. But it also emphasized that the colonists were not seeking independence. Two days later, the Continental Congress sent a petition to George III, the King of Great Britian. The colonists asked the King for peace and reconciliation.

King George III refused to receive the colonists' petition. Instead, he told Parliament that the colonies were in open rebellion. Parliament passed an act forbidding all trade with the colonists until the rebellion was crushed. The King declared the rebellious colonists to be outside of the scope of his protection. All American ships, ports and sailors became subject to capture.

The King also sent more troops to America to fight the colonists. His forces included foreign mercenaries (*hired soldiers*) from Germany. These steps greatly angered the colonists.

In January 1776, Thomas Paine published his pamphlet, *Common Sense*. As you learned in Chapter 2, Paine argued that the colonists received little benefit from their connection with Great Britain. Paine urged the colonists to seek independence.

COMMON SENSE;
INHABITANTS
OF
AMERICA,
SUBJECTS.
PHILADELPHIA;
MDCCLXXVI.

In March 1776, General Washington and his troops drove the British out of Boston. Washington then moved his army to New York City. However, the British also landed a large force there. He lost battles on Long Island and in New York City that summer and fall. Washington was forced to retreat across the Delaware River.

Most colonists now felt that Britain had treated them badly. They disliked British taxes, placed on them without their consent (*approval; agreement*). They were angry at the dissolution of their legislatures and the suspension of their right to a trial by jury. Even more, they resented the use of armed force. More and more colonists agreed with Thomas Paine that they should end their connection with Great Britain. They wanted to free themselves from British rule.

Colonial leaders also realized that they could not obtain allies (*friendly countries that would act with them*) so long as they remained subjects of the British King. Only by becoming independent could they ever hope to conclude alliances with foreign powers, like France and Spain. They needed the help of these foreign powers to win the Revolutionary War.

The Second Continental Congress began debating the question of American independence early in 1776.

John Adams, a lawyer from Massachusetts, was one of the strongest voices for independence. Adams persuaded many of the other delegates to vote in favor of separating from England.

John Adams

In June 1776, Richard Henry Lee, a Virginian, introduced a resolution proposing independence:

> *Resolved, That these United Colonies are, and of right ought to be, free and independent States, that they are absolved from all allegiance to the British Crown, and that all political connection between them and the State of Great Britain is, and ought to be, totally dissolved.*

Word Helper

absolve = to release or set free
allegiance = loyalty to a superior
British Crown = the King
connection = a link or formal association
dissolved = ended or eliminated

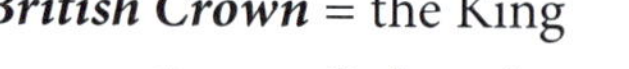

A special committee of five members was formed to write a declaration explaining this decision to other colonists and to the rest of the world. A young Virginian, Thomas Jefferson, was the main author of the Declaration. Two other important members of the committee were John Adams and Benjamin Franklin. Jefferson wrote the first draft (*written version*) of the Declaration. The Declaration was later revised by the committee and then by the Continental Congress itself.

The Active Citizen

Imagine it is early in 1776. Your class should divide into different groups, representing the different colonies at the Second Continental Congress. Hold a discussion on whether or not the colonies should declare their independence from Great Britain. Groups representing different colonies should present the most important arguments either for or against independence. For example, "We, the representatives of the Colony of Virginia, favor independence because . . ." After your discussion, take a class vote.

For the EOC test , you should be sure to know the main ideas of the Declaration of Independence.

The Declaration of Independence

You probably have already heard of the Declaration of Independence. It was signed on July 4th—still our national holiday. Every year we celebrate the signing of the Declaration with parades, speeches and fireworks. But what makes this document so very special to Americans?

The Declaration of Independence actually accomplished five things:

1. It declared American independence. It boldly stated that the colonies were no longer part of the British Empire. The former colonists were no longer subjects of King George III.
2. It announced a theory of government based on natural law and the protection of **individual rights** (*rights each of us should have*).
3. It listed the **colonial grievances** (*complaints of the colonists*) against King George III and the British government.
4. It justified the conduct of the colonists, both to their fellow countrymen and to the rest of the world.
5. It announced the arrival of the United States as an independent and equal member of the international community, able to wage war and to make alliances. This cleared the way for the former colonies to conclude alliances with France and Spain.

It can be difficult to understand a document that was written more than 200 years ago. But the Declaration of Independence has been so influential, both in the United States and other countries, that it is important to read some of this original document for yourself.

1. The first part of the Declaration is known as the **Preamble** (*introduction*). You will see that the first paragraph of the Preamble states that it sometimes becomes necessary for a people to end the ties that once joined them to others. When they do, they should explain their reasons for doing so to the rest of the world.

The Declaration states that people have unalienable rights and that governments should protect those rights

2. The next section is the most famous part of the Declaration. It states the American theory of government. This theory is based on a belief in **natural rights** and John Locke's **social contract**. It begins by stating that all people enjoy certain "**unalienable rights**" under natural law. People are **endowed by their Creator** (*given by God*) with these rights, which should not be taken away. Among these rights are "**life, liberty and the pursuit of happiness**." In other words, we should be able to conduct our lives freely without the government trying to control us.
3. The Declaration next explains that people institute (*create, establish*) governments to protect these rights. It is the role, or purpose, of government to protect these rights. The Declaration thus favors **limited government**—the idea that the government should be limited to specific powers and purposes. When a government acts to restrict these rights, its citizens have the right to abolish (*end*) that government and to create a new one.

   The Declaration recognizes that people should not change their government lightly (*quickly or easily*). Disagreement with a few government decisions does not justify changing an entire system of government. But when there has been a long pattern of abuses (*harmful actions*), showing that the government has become oppressive (*harsh and unfair*), then the people clearly have the **right of resistance to a tyrannical government**—the right to resist and to change a government that has become harsh and controlling.
4. Such has been the case, the Declaration argues, for the American colonists. The British government has made repeated injuries against them. The Declaration lists many of these

For the EOC test, you should know the main colonial grievances.

specific abuses. This list of **colonial grievances**, or complaints, is actually the longest section of the Declaration. These include:

- refusing to approve necessary laws
- **imposing taxes without consent** of the colonists
- **quartering soldiers** in colonists' homes
- **suspending trial by jury** in many cases by letting judges instead of juries decide the case
- **limiting judicial powers** by making judges dependent on the King's will
- sending royal officials and colonists for trial in Britain instead of in the colonies
- suspending or **dissolving legislatures** in the colonies

To **dissolve** a legislature is to end its meetings, dismiss its members, and send its members home. To **suspend** a legislature is to stop its meetings temporarily.

The Declaration works up to the most serious grievances at the very end of the list:

- The King has cut off the colonists' trade.
- He has made war on the colonists.
- He has hired foreign mercenaries to fight against them.
- He has ordered the burning down of towns.
- He has even stirred up neighboring American Indians to attack them.

5. The final paragraphs of the Declaration explain that the colonists have tried to settle their disagreements with Britain peacefully, but that all of their attempts have failed. The time has therefore come for the colonists to declare their independence.

The last paragraph of the Declaration actually contains the same wording as the resolution for independence already proposed in the Continental Congress: the former colonies are and of right should be free and independent states. The colonists therefore no longer consider themselves to be subjects of the King. They further claim the right to wage war and to make alliances on their own behalf.

Can you find the phrase "Declaration of Independence" in the document? Curiously, it does not appear there, although people began referring to it as the "Declaration of Independence" almost as soon as it was signed.

Benjamin Franklin, John Adams, and Thomas Jefferson

Now try reading the Declaration of Independence for yourself. Some of its more difficult words are defined to the right of each section. Then rewrite each section of the Declaration in your own words below.

In CONGRESS, July 4, 1776.

The unanimous Declaration of the thirteen United States of America.

Preamble: The Purpose of the Declaration

When in the course of human events, it becomes necessary for one people to dissolve the political bands which have connected them with another, and to assume among the Powers of the Earth the separate and equal station to which the Laws of Nature . . . entitle them, a decent respect to the opinions of mankind requires that they should declare the causes which impel them to the separation.

dissolve = to make disappear; to end

political bands = ties that bind together

connect = to join together

Powers = independent countries or states with military strength

separate and equal station = independent and equal position

entitle = to give a right to something

impel = to force

separation = a division of something into separate parts

▶ Explain what this section says in your own words: ______

______

______

______

______

______

▶ What was the purpose of this introduction?

______

______

______

______

______

______

The next two sections are the most important part of the Declaration. Be sure to know these sections for the EOC test.

Preamble: A Theory of Government Based on Natural Law and Individual Rights

> *We hold these truths to be self-evident, that all men are created equal, that they are endowed by their Creator with certain unalienable Rights, that among these are Life, Liberty, and the pursuit of Happiness.*

self-evident = obvious, clear

endowed = given

Creator = God

unalienable = not capable of being taken away (usually spelled "inalienable")

In this important paragraph, the Declaration explains that we all enjoy certain "unalienable rights" that should never be taken away. These include the right to life, liberty and the pursuit of happiness—that is, the right to be alive, the right to enjoy our lives in freedom without government leaders telling us what to do, and the right to seek happiness in our own individual way. According to the Declaration, we are created by God with these rights. Because we all enjoy these same basic rights, the Declaration says we are all created equal.

▶ What is meant by "unalienable rights" in this part of the Preamble?

▶ Which "unalienable rights" are specifically expressed in this part of the Preamble?

▶ If you had to explain this paragraph to a third grader, what would you say?

That to secure these rights, Governments are instituted among Men, deriving their just powers from the consent of the governed[.] That whenever any Form of Government becomes destructive of these ends, it is the Right of the People to alter or to abolish it, and to institute new Government . . . organizing its powers in such form, as to them shall seem most likely to effect their Safety and Happiness.

secure = to obtain
instituted = created
derive = to obtain from; to get from
consent = agreement
alter = to change
ends = purposes
abolish = to end; to get rid of
institute = to start; to create
organize = arrange in order
effect = to bring about

▶ Explain what this part of the Preamble means in your own words: ______

▶ According to this paragraph, from where do governments derive (obtain) their "just powers"?

▶ How does this paragraph establish the existence of a social contract?

▶ According to the Declaration, how can the government violate (*break*) the social contract?

▶ Which philosopher did you study in Chapter 2 whose ideas are applied here? ______

Prudence, indeed, will dictate that Governments long established should not be changed for light and transient causes . . . But when a long train of abuses and usurpations, pursuing invariably the same object evinces a design to reduce them under absolute Despotism, it is their right, it is their duty, to throw off such Government, and to provide new Guards for their future security.

prudence = cautious and careful judgment
dictate = to demand; to determine
transient = temporary; not important
long train = long chain or series of events
usurpation = a wrongful taking of someone else's rights
pursue = to chase after something in order to obtain it
invariably = always, without change
object = goal
evince = to provide evidence of
design = a plan; a purpose
absolute = total; complete
despotism = a harsh and controlling government with absolute power that does not listen to its people

▶ Explain what this section says in your own words: ______________________

▶ Where does this paragraph express the right of resistance to tyrannical government?

▶ Do you agree that citizens should overthrow a government whose actions reveal a plan to establish an "absolute Despotism" (*a harsh and controlling government*)? Why or why not?

Such has been the patient sufferance of these Colonies; and such is now the necessity which constrains them to alter their former Systems of Government. The history of the present King of Great Britain is a history of repeated injuries and usurpations, all having in direct object the establishment of an absolute Tyranny over these States. To prove this, let Facts be submitted to a candid world.

patient = willing to accept delays without becoming annoyed

sufferance = suffering

constrain = to force; to restrict or limit

alter = to change

usurpation = a wrongful taking of someone's rights

tyranny = a cruel and oppressive government; a power exercised without legal right

submit = to present or give to another

candid = truthful; straightforward; frank

▸ Explain what this section says in your own words: ______

▸ Why did the colonists believe they needed to explain their theory of government to justify their decision to declare independence?

▸ How did this section of the Declaration reflect the views of Thomas Paine?

▸ Would the Declaration of Independence have been just as effective without these sections explaining the colonists' theory of government? Give one or more reasons in support of your answer.

IN CONGRESS, JULY 4, 1776.

The unanimous Declaration of the thirteen united States of America

The List of Colonial Grievances

In this next section, the Declaration lists the grievances (*complaints*) that the colonists had against King George III and the British government.

> *He has refused his Assent to Laws, the most wholesome and necessary for the public good. . . .*
>
> *He has **dissolved** Representative Houses repeatedly . . . .*
>
> *He has made Judges dependent on his Will alone for the tenure of their offices, and the amount and payment of their salaries . . .*
>
> *He has kept among us, in times of peace, Standing Armies without the Consent of our legislatures . . .*
>
> *For **quartering** large bodies of armed troops among us . . .*
>
> *For cutting off our Trade with all parts of the world:*
>
> *For **imposing Taxes on us without our Consent:***
>
> *For depriving us in many cases, of the benefit of Trial by Jury. . .*
>
> *For **suspending** our own Legislatures . . . .*
>
> *He has plundered our seas, ravaged our coasts, burnt our towns, and destroyed the lives of our people.*
>
> *He is at this time transporting large Armies of foreign Mercenaries to complete the works of death, desolation, and tyranny, already begun. . . .*

assent = approval; agreement

wholesome = beneficial

public good = what is good for the community

dissolve = to dismiss; to close; to end

dependent = to depend upon; to be based upon

will = the part of the mind that determines what a person wants or desires

tenure = period in which they hold their offices

standing army = an army of soldiers ready to fight

consent = agreement; approval

quarter = to shelter troops in private homes

impose = to force on someone

deprive = to take away

transport = to carry from one place to another

suspend = to temporarily stop

plunder = to steal; to rob

transport = take or carry from one place to another

mercenary = a soldier who fights for money; a hired troop

desolation = complete destruction

tyranny = a cruel and oppressive government; a power exercised without legal right

▶ Explain what this section says in your own words: ______________________

____

____

____

____

____

____

▸ Which of of the following grievances do you think were violations of the colonists' natural rights? Justify your answer with evidence.

☐ Imposing taxes without consent

☐ Suspending trial by jury

☐ Limiting judicial powers

☐ Quartering soldiers

☐ Dissolving legislatures

▸ Based on the grievances listed above, how did the underlying themes of British colonial policies on taxation, representation and individual rights form the basis for the American colonists' desire for independence?

King George III has Refused the Colonists' Attempts at Compromise

In every stage of these Oppressions We have Petitioned for Redress in the most humble terms: Our repeated Petitions have been answered only by repeated injury. A Prince, whose character is thus marked by every act which may define a Tyrant, is unfit to be the ruler of a free people. . . .

oppression = harsh and unjust treatment

petition = (*verb*) to send a formal written request to an official or government body; (*noun*) a formal written request to a government or legislature

redress = a remedy; something to correct or make right a problem or an injustice

tyrant = despot; a dictator; someone who seizes or uses power unjustly

▶ Explain what this section says in your own words: ______

▶ Why did the colonists feel it was important to show that they had attempted to obtain a peaceful "redress" of their grievances?

▶ A tyrannical government is one that rules harshly and unjustly. Do you believe King George III was a tyrant? What evidence did the Declaration provide to show that the British had established a "tyranny" over the colonists?

English King George III

Colonists Therefore Declare Their Independence

We, therefore, the Representatives of the United States of America, in General Congress, Assembled, . . . do, in the Name, and by Authority of the good People of these Colonies, solemnly publish and declare, That these united Colonies are, and of Right ought to be Free and Independent States; that they are Absolved from all Allegiance to the British Crown, and that all political connection between them and the State of Great Britain, is and ought to be totally dissolved; and that as Free and Independent States, they have full Power to levy War, conclude Peace, contract Alliances, establish Commerce, and to do all other Acts and Things which Independent States may of right do. . . .

solemn = formal; sincere; serious

publish = make publicly known

absolve = to release or set free

allegiance = loyalty to a superior

British Crown = the King

connection = a link or formal association

dissolved = ended or eliminated

commerce = trade

levy war = make war

contract Alliances = sign treaties of alliance with other countries

▶ Explain what this section says in your own words:

▶ What was the causal relationship between the British responses to the grievances of the colonists and the writing of the the Declaration of Independence? (A causal relationship is when one thing leads another to happen.)

▶ What was the importance of this phrase at the end of the Declaration of Independence: "that as Free and Independent States, they have full Power to levy War, conclude Peace, contract Alliances . . ."

▶ If you had been a colonist in 1776, would the Declaration of Independence have persuaded you to support the independence of the colonies? Why or why not?

Enrichment

The Impact of the Declaration of Independence

The Declaration had an immediate effect on the colonists. It allowed them to open talks with France and Spain to conclude military alliances. It also helped them to win support from other Americans for the Revolutionary War.

The Declaration was actually the first time that a group of colonists made a public announcement while breaking away from imperial rule. This example was soon followed by other countries. It helped lead to the outbreak of a revolution in France in 1789 and to later revolutions throughout Latin America. According to Harvard historian David Armitage, more than a hundred countries later copied the example of the American Declaration of Independence. Many of these countries actually borrowed some of the wording of the American Declaration.

The Declaration had other effects, even within the United States itself. The colonists did more than declare their independence from Britain. The Declaration of Independence proclaimed (*announced publicly*) a new theory of government based on equality and individual rights. It announced that all men were created equal and enjoyed certain unalienable rights that could not be taken away. While American society was far from equal at the time, the Declaration laid the seeds for further change and later demands for equality. President Lincoln was thus able to breathe new life into the Declaration 86 years later when he abolished slavery. Since then, the Declaration has been used in support of voting rights for women, the Civil Rights Movement, and movements for equality for women, minority groups, and Americans with disabilities.

The Active Citizen

1. Did you know that Thomas Jefferson originally had a paragraph in the Declaration condemning George III for promoting the slave trade? This paragraph was taken out of the Declaration to win the support of South Carolina and other slave-holding states. Was it wrong for slave-holding states to support a declaration in the name of freedom and equality?

2. In 1848, women reformers met in Seneca Falls, New York. They adopted the following Declaration of Sentiments:

> *"We hold these truths to be self-evident: that all men and women are created equal; that they are endowed by their Creator with certain inalienable rights; that among these are life, liberty, and the pursuit of happiness; that to secure these rights governments are instituted, deriving their just powers from the consent of the governed. . . . The history of mankind is a history of repeated injuries and usurpations on the part of man toward woman, having in direct object the establishment of an absolute tyranny over her."*

- What did this statement owe to the Declaration of Independence of 1776?
- Why do you think the American Declaration of Independence has been so influential?

Name ______________________________

Define each word or phrase and then make up a sentence using that word or phrase.

Word/Phrase	Definition	Sentence
Imposing taxes without consent		
Stamp Act		
Quartering Act		
Declaratory Act		
Townshend Acts		
Intolerable Acts		
Suspending trial by jury/ limiting judicial powers		
Dissolving legislatures		
Unalienable rights		
"Life, liberty and the pursuit of happiness"		
Right of resistance to tyrannical government		

Name ________________________________

The Story of the Declaration of Independence

After several years of disagreement over taxation and representation, fighting finally broke out between the colonists and Great Britain in April 1775. The colonies sent representatives to Philadelphia, where they formed the Second Continental Congress. The Second Continental Congress established a colonial army to oppose the British.

In January 1776, Thomas Paine published a popular pamphlet, *Common Sense*. Paine argued that it made no sense for a large area like the American colonies to be governed by a small and distant island. Paine therefore argued that the colonies should ________________________________.

Paine's arguments persuaded many colonists.

After a year of fighting, the members of the Continental Congress finally decided to declare __________.

They appointed Thomas Jefferson and others to write a declaration explaining their decision to the rest of the world.

Jefferson was the main author of the Declaration of Independence. He began this famous document by explaining the colonists' theory of government. This part of the Declaration was based on John Locke's ________________ theory.

The Declaration states that all men are created________________________. The Declaration further states that all men have certain *unalienable*, or natural, rights. Among these natural rights are the rights to

____

____.

The Declaration then explains that governments are actually created by people to *protect* these rights. When a government continually attacks these rights instead of protecting them, the people therefore have the right of ________________________________ to a tyrannical government.

Such has been the case, the Declaration argues, for the colonists.

The next part of the Declaration lists the grievances that the colonists have against King George III of Great Britain and his government. (A grievance is a ____________________________.) Some of the grievances that the Declaration mentions are the following:

The King has ____.

He has ____.

He has ____.

He has ____.

Because of these grievances, the Declaration concludes that the colonists no longer owe the King their allegiance (*loyalty and obedience*).

Instead, the colonies now declare themselves to be free and ______________________________ states.

They further claim the right to form their own alliances, to engage in trade, to make war, and to conclude peace, just as any other nation would do.

The signing of the Declaration of Independence on July 4, 1776, marked the birth of our nation—the United States of America. The event is still celebrated by Americans each year on the holiday known as the Fourth of July, or Independence Day.

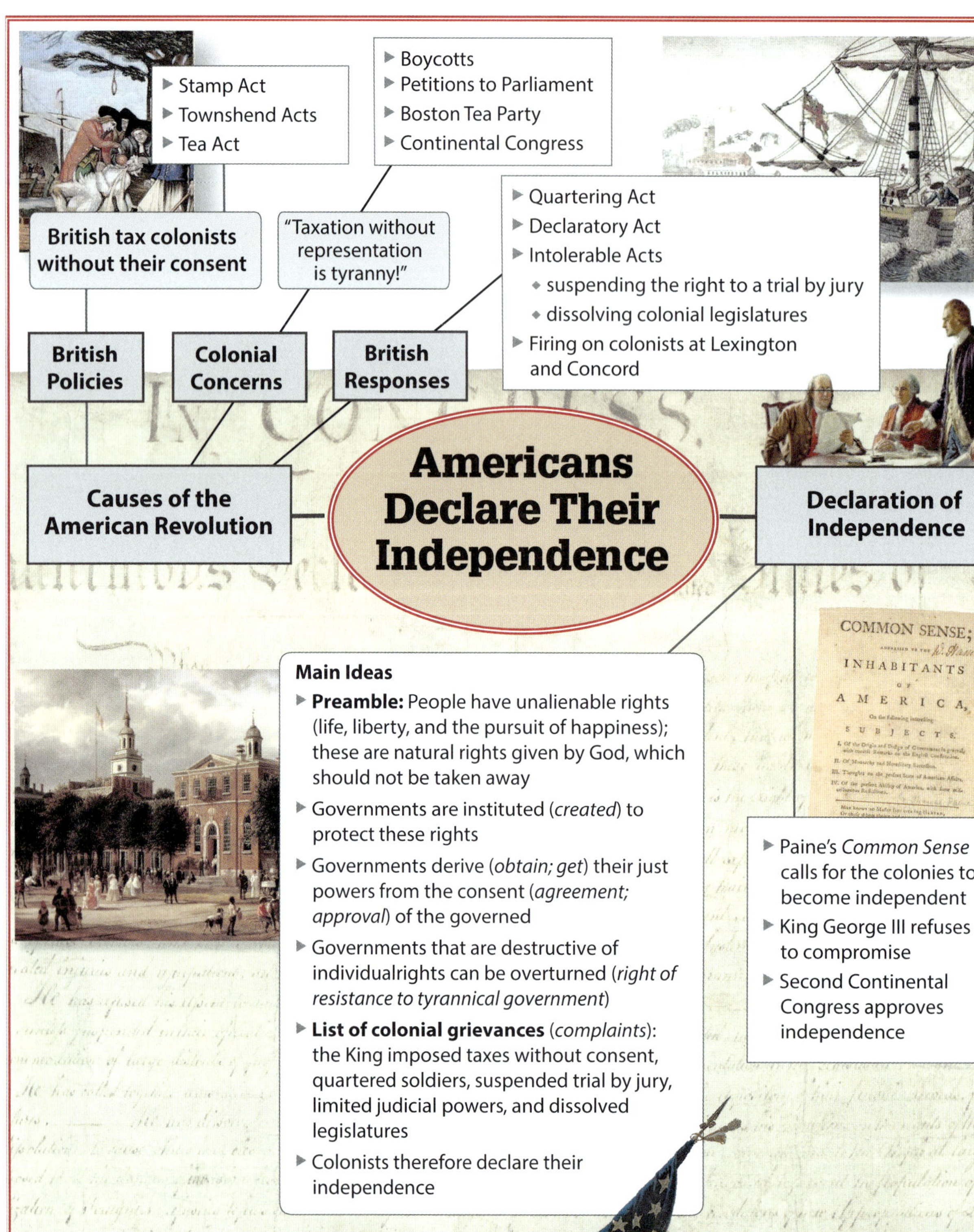
Americans Declare Their Independence
Causes of the American Revolution
British Policies
British tax colonists without their consent
▶ Stamp Act
▶ Townshend Acts
▶ Tea Act
Colonial Concerns
"Taxation without representation is tyranny!"
▶ Boycotts
▶ Petitions to Parliament
▶ Boston Tea Party
▶ Continental Congress
British Responses
▶ Quartering Act
▶ Declaratory Act
▶ Intolerable Acts
◆ suspending the right to a trial by jury
◆ dissolving colonial legislatures
▶ Firing on colonists at Lexington and Concord
Declaration of Independence
Main Ideas
▶ Preamble: People have unalienable rights (life, liberty, and the pursuit of happiness); these are natural rights given by God, which should not be taken away
▶ Governments are instituted (created) to protect these rights
▶ Governments derive (obtain; get) their just powers from the consent (agreement; approval) of the governed
▶ Governments that are destructive of individualrights can be overturned (right of resistance to tyrannical government)
▶ List of colonial grievances (complaints): the King imposed taxes without consent, quartered soldiers, suspended trial by jury, limited judicial powers, and dissolved legislatures
▶ Colonists therefore declare their independence
▶ Paine's Common Sense calls for the colonies to become independent
▶ King George III refuses to compromise
▶ Second Continental Congress approves independence
COMMON SENSE;
INHABITANTS
OF
AMERICA,
SUBJECTS.

Review Cards: Americans Declare Their Independence

The Road to Revolution

- From 1754 to 1763, Britain was at war with France in the French and Indian War. The French lost their North American colonies, but the costs of the war put the British in debt.
- After the war, **British policies** (*actions by government*) placed new taxes on the American colonists.
- Their first attempt to tax the colonists was the **Stamp Act**, a tax on every official document. These new British policies led to colonial concerns. There was a **causal relationship** (*cause-and-effect*) between **British colonial policies** (*policies towards the colonies*) and colonial unrest. A causal relationship occurs when one event leads another to happen. Colonists argued that because they did not have representatives in the British Parliament, they had not agreed to this tax . The British were **imposing taxes without consent**: "**Taxation** without **representation** is tyranny!"
- The colonists' marches, rallies, petitions, boycotts, and even tar-and-feathering of officials led the British Parliament to repeal (*cancel; take back*) the Stamp Act.
- Parliament kept, however, to the same policy of taxing the colonists. The **Declaratory Act** stated that Parliament had the right to pass laws for the colonies, including taxes without their consent. Parliament next passed the **Townshend Acts**, placing duties (*taxes*) on various imports, like paper and glass. British troops were sent to control the colonists. Under the **Quartering Act**, these troops were sometimes quartered (*housed*) in colonists' barns and homes.
- Because of continuing colonial unrest, Parliament also repealed the Townshend Acts. It then passed the **Tea Act**, placing a new tax on tea. Colonists protested against the tea duty in December 1773 with the Boston Tea Party. Colonists boarded a ship and threw its tea into the harbor.
- Parliament passed the **Intolerable Acts** to punish Boston for destroying the chests of tea. These acts closed Boston Harbor and suspended the Massachusetts legislature until the tea was paid for. They gave the British government to move trials to different colonies or even to Great Britain. The Intolerable Acts thus **suspended the right to a trial by jury** and **limited judicial powers**.

Outbreak of the Revolution

- Twelve colonies sent representatives to a "Continental Congress" to discuss their responses to British policies. The delegates sent protests to London, organized boycotts, and agreed to meet again.
- American colonists and British troops fired at each other in April 1775, beginning the American Revolution.
- The Second Continental Congress met and formed the Continental Army to fight the British.
- At first, most American colonists did not want independence. But when the British refused to give in to their reasonable demands and the fighting continued, many colonists changed their minds.

The Declaration of Independence

- By 1776, many colonists came to agree with Thomas Paine's pamphlet *Common Sense*, which urged the colonies to seek independence and create a republican form of government without a king or queen. Paine recommended representative self-government.
- In June 1776, a resolution was introduced in the Second Continental Congress, proposing independence.
- A special committee wrote the **Declaration of Independence**. Thomas Jefferson was the main author. The document was approved by the Second Continental Congress on July 4, 1776. The colonies became independent states.

Main Ideas of the Declaration

- The Declaration announced American independence and explained this decision to the rest of the world. It presented a new theory of government, listed the colonists' grievances against the British, and established the United States as a new and independent nation.
- The **Preamble** (*introduction*) to the Declaration explained that all people had certain "**unalienable rights**." People were **endowed by their Creator** (*given by God*) with these **natural rights**, to which everyone was entitled. Among these rights were the right to "**life, liberty, and the pursuit of happiness**" (*the ability to conduct our lives without being controlled by the government*). Governments were "instituted" (*formed*) to protect those rights.
- The Declaration was based on the ideas of John Locke. It stated that governments "derive (*obtain; get*) their just powers from the consent (*agreement*) of the governed." This meant that governments receive their power from the people. as part of the **social contract**.
- People therefore had the **right of resistance to tyrannical government**—the right to overthrow any government that was harsh and controlling, and that did not protect their natural rights.
- The Declaration claimed that Britain's government had become tyrannical (*one that oppresses the people*).The Declaration included a list of **colonial grievances** (*complaints*) to prove it. The King was responsible for **imposing taxes without consent** (*without the agreement of the colonists*), **suspending trial by jury** (*having judges decide cases instead of juries*), **limiting judicial powers** (*sending some cases to be decided in Britain*), **quartering soldiers** (*placing soldiers in people's barns and homes*), **dissolving legislatures** (*ending their sessions*), and sending troops to burn down the colonists' towns and destroy their lives. The Declaration claimed that the colonists had a **right of resistance** against such a tyrannical government. Because of these British actions, the colonists were declaring independence.
- The Declaration thus introduced a new theory of government based on liberty and equality. Its language has been used by many later social movements in the United States, especially those on behalf of women and minorities.

What Do You Know?

SS.7.CG.1.5

1. Which grievance contributed to the American colonists' desire for independence?
   A. British policies had made frontier lands too expensive.
   B. The King had denied the colonists their freedom of religion.
   C. The British government had been too generous to the Indian tribes.
   D. The British government had taxed the colonists without their consent.

SS.7.CG.1.5

2. What was the main purpose of the tar-and-feathering shown in this British caricature of the colonists?
   A. to protest their being taxed without their consent
   B. to protest the high cost of British manufactured goods
   C. to protest British involvement in the French and Indian War
   D. to protest the quartering of troops in colonists' own homes

SS.7.CG.1.5

3. The diagram below describes causal relationships leading to the Declaration of Independence.

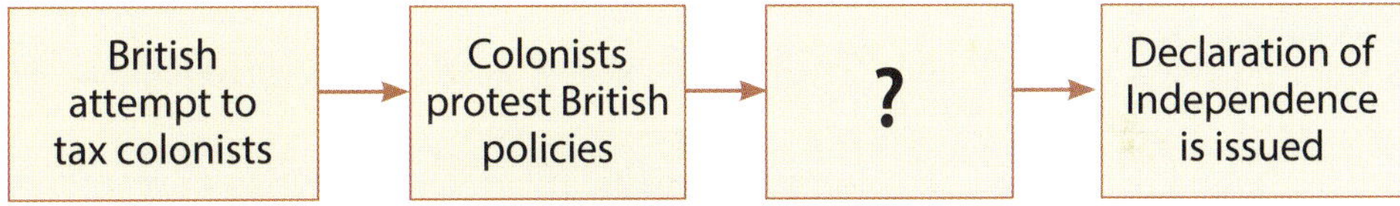

   Which event completes the diagram?
   A. British give up the attempt to tax the colonists.
   B. British apply armed force against the colonists.
   C. British agree to give the colonists their independence.
   D. British grant the colonists representation in Parliament.

SS.7.CG.1.5

4. In the 1760s and 1770s, the British Parliament passed the Stamp Act, Townshend Acts, Tea Act, and Intolerable Acts. What was the impact of these British colonial policies?
   A. Indian tribes were able to keep their lands.
   B. Colonists began to think of becoming independent.
   C. The British government was able to pay off its debts.
   D. The French were defeated in the French and Indian War.

SS.7.CG.1.6

5. Which complaint against King George III was stated in the Declaration of Independence?
   A. He had quartered his troops among the colonists.
   B. He had forced the colonists to accept the practice of slavery.
   C. He had required the colonists to trade with French merchants.
   D. He had failed to defend the colonists in the French and Indian War.

SS.7.CG.1.6

6. Which source publicized the concept of "natural rights," later found in the Declaration of Independence?
   A. Magna Carta
   B. the English Bill of Rights
   C. the Mayflower Compact
   D. John Locke on the social contract

SS.7.CG.1.6

7. According to the Declaration of Independence, what was an "unalienable right" that all governments should protect?
   A. the right to social equality
   B. the right to personal liberty
   C. the right to religious equality
   D. the right to elect government officials

SS.7.CG.1.6

8. The passage below comes from the Declaration of Independence (1776).

   > *"He has kept among us, in times of peace, Standing Armies without the Consent of our legislatures . . ."*

   Which section of the Declaration contained this passage?
   A. its list of colonial grievances
   B. its justification of the conduct of the colonists
   C. its theory of government based on a social contract
   D. its announcement of American independence from Britain

SS.7.CG.1.6

9. Which statement best describes the role of government according to the Declaration of Independence?
   A. "The main purpose of government is to expand and glorify the state."
   B. "The main purpose of government is to protect the unalienable rights of individuals."
   C. "The main purpose of government is to protect the rights and privileges of His Majesty, the King."
   D. "The main purpose of government is to promote the general welfare of the community by taking steps toward social equality."

SS.7.CG.1.6

10. The passage below comes from the Declaration of Independence.

"We hold these truths to be self-evident, that all men are created equal, that they are endowed by their Creator with certain unalienable Rights, that among these are Life, Liberty and the pursuit of Happiness. That to secure these rights, Governments are instituted among Men, deriving their just powers from the consent of the governed."

According to this passage, what is the principal role of government?

A. to promote greater social equality

B. to protect the natural rights of citizens

C. to glorify the ruler in the eyes of the Creator

D. to help individuals cooperate against the forces of nature

SS.7.CG.1.6

11. The diagram below summarizes ideas from the Declaration of Independence.

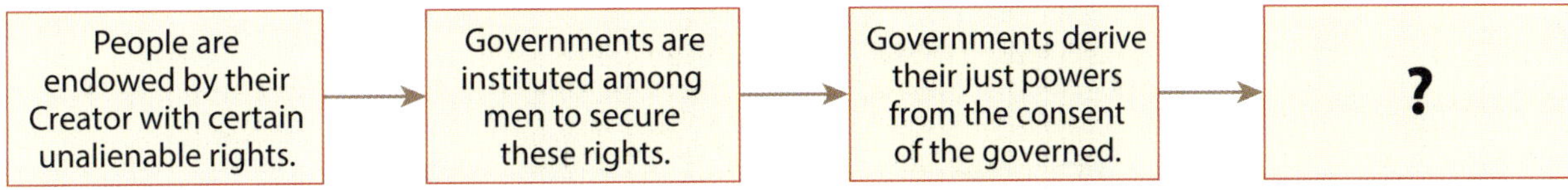

Which statement completes the diagram?

A. Because governments derive their just powers from the consent of the governed, they are incapable of acting against the people.

B. Whenever any form of government becomes destructive of these ends, it is the right of the people to take peaceful measures to alter those policies.

C. Whenever any form of government becomes destructive of these ends, it is the right of the people to alter or abolish it, and to institute new government.

D. Because governments derive their powers from the consent of the governed, it is the obligation of the people to obey their government whatever it commands.

SS.7.CG.1.6

12. Based on the Declaration of Independence, which is a natural right?

A. the right to vote

B. the right to bear arms

C. the right to pursue happiness

D. the right to equal protection of the laws

George Washington entering New York at the end of the Revolutionary War.

CHAPTER 4

The Story of Our Constitution

SS.7.CG.1.7 Explain how the weaknesses of the Articles of Confederation led to the writing of the U.S. Constitution.

SS.7.CG.3.3 Describe the structure and function of the three branches of government established in the U.S. Constitution. (*This chapter provides the historical background to the U.S. Constitution; for an overview of the Constitution, see Chapter 5; for specific branches of our national government, see Chapters 6–8.*)

Content Focus Vocabulary in This Chapter

Articles of Confederation
Strengths of the Articles
Weaknesses of the Articles
Power to tax
Power to regulate trade
Power to enforce laws
National government
National court system
Central leadership

National armed forces
Unanimous consent
Debt
U.S. Government
Three branches of government
U.S. Constitution
Article I
Legislative branch
Congress

House of Representatives
Senate
Article II
Executive branch
President of the United States
Article III
Judicial branch
Supreme Court

Florida "Keys" to Learning

1. After independence was declared, each former colony became a new state with its own state constitution. Members of the Second Continental Congress agreed to a document known as the **Articles of Confederation**. It created a form of association between the states. A confederation is a group of states that decide to act together. In a confederation, most of the powers of government remain with the member states.

2. The Articles of Confederation created a very weak central government. The new central government consisted of a "Congress" made up of representatives from the states. The state governments remained "sovereign" (*supreme in power*) except for those powers they gave to Congress.

3. **Strengths of the Articles**: The Articles created our first national government. This government had the power to declare war, to exchange ambassadors with foreign nations, to enter into treaties and alliances, to resolve disputes between states, to regulate (*set rules for; control*) relations with certain Indian tribes, to borrow money, to build a navy, and to direct an army.

4. **Weaknesses of the Articles**: The government under the Articles had many weaknesses (*disadvantages; things it was missing*). It had no **central leadership** (*executive branch*) with the **power to enforce laws** (*carry them out*). It had no **national court system** (*judicial branch*). It had no **national armed forces** (*army and navy*) and had no **power to tax**. Congress had no **power to regulate trade** (*set rules for trade between states*). Any new law needed to be approved by nine states. All thirteen states had to agree to any changes in the Articles of Confederation, known as "**unanimous consent**".

5. Because the national government was weak, foreign nations could threaten American property and interests. American trade between states suffered, not enough money was printed, and the government threatened not to pay off its **debt** (*money it owed*).

6. In Massachusetts, the state government raised taxes and seized the farms of poor men who could not pay their debts. Daniel Shays helped lead a rebellion in protest. The state militia (*part-time, local troops*) eventually ended Shays' Rebellion. There was no national army to put down the rebellion if it spread to other states. This opened the eyes of many Americans to the **weaknesses of the Articles** of Confederation.

7. In May 1787, delegates gathered in Philadelphia to revise the Articles of Confederation. The delegates quickly decided it would be better to write a whole new constitution—a plan of basic rules for government. Their assembly became known as the Constitutional Convention. They wrote the **U.S. Constitution.**

8. The members of the Constitutional Convention agreed that the country needed a stronger national government with **three branches**, or parts: legislative, executive and judicial.

9. **Article I** of the new Constitution created the **legislative branch** (*law-making body*), known as **Congress**. It would have two parts or "houses": the **House of Representatives** and the **Senate**.

10. The number of members each state would have in the House of Representatives would be based on its population, while in the Senate, every state would have two Senators.

11. **Article II** created the **executive branch**, which would enforce the laws. The head of the new executive branch would be the **President of the United States**.

12. **Article III** created the new **judicial branch** (*part of government applying the law to individual cases*). It consisted of the **Supreme Court**.

The Articles of Confederation

After independence was declared, each colony became a separate and independent state.

A state is a territory with its own government.

When the Second Continental Congress appointed a committee to write the Declaration of Independence, it also appointed a second committee to decide how the thirteen new states should cooperate. This committee drafted (*wrote*) a document known as the **Articles of Confederation**. The Articles were debated for almost an entire year in the Continental Congress. Then they were sent to the state legislatures. The Articles of Confederation were finally approved by all thirteen states in 1781.

A confederation is an association—an organization of separate states that cooperate together.

The Articles of Confederation created a "league of friendship," to which all thirteen states belonged.

After their experiences with Great Britain, most Americans feared giving too much power to the central government. They did not want a remote authority taxing them or threatening their rights, as the British government had done.

The Articles of Confederation therefore left most governmental powers in the hands of the states. The Articles set up a loose association in which the thirteen states could cooperate, especially in dealing with foreign affairs (*relations with other countries*). This association had a "Congress," which was the only branch of the national government. There was no national executive or national court system.

The Confederation Congress, the new body created by the Articles, was actually a council made up of the representatives of thirteen powerful, independent states. Each state had one vote in Congress.

Page 1 from the Articles of Confederation

For the EOC test, you should know the main provisions of the Articles of Confederation and the weaknesses of the government it created.

Provisions of the Articles of Confederation

1. The new Confederation was to be known as the "United States of America."
2. Each state was to remain generally sovereign (*to have final authority*). The states kept all governing powers except those few given exclusively (*only*) to the Confederation Congress.
3. The Congress of the Confederation was to meet every year. Each state was to send from two to seven delegates to the Congress. Each state had one vote in Congress. All states, whatever their size, thus had equal representation.
4. Congress was given the exclusive power to declare war, to exchange ambassadors with foreign states, to enter into treaties and alliances, to set weights and measurements, to resolve disputes between states, to establish post offices, and to regulate (*set rules for; control*) relations with Indian tribes not found within one state. An exclusive power is one that is not shared with others. These powers could only be exercised by Congress and not by the states.
5. Congress could also borrow money, and build and equip a navy.
6. Congress had the power to direct its own army. However, it could not raise its own troops: these were contributed by the states.
7. All the expenses of the Confederation were to be paid from a general fund. State legislatures

contributed to this fund. Congress could not directly tax citizens on its own.

8. The approval of nine states was needed to pass any new law in Congress.
9. All thirteen states had to agree to any changes in the Articles of Confederation. Changes to the Articles required **unanimous consent** (*complete agreement by everyone*).

Strengths of the Articles: The Articles created a national government to which all the states belonged. This government held important powers. However, individual state governments remained more powerful than the central government. For example, states could print their own money. They could tax goods brought from other states. Only the state governments could collect taxes and raise troops. The Congress of the Confederation relied on contributions from the states to pay its expenses, yet had no power to force states to contribute. Could such a government work?

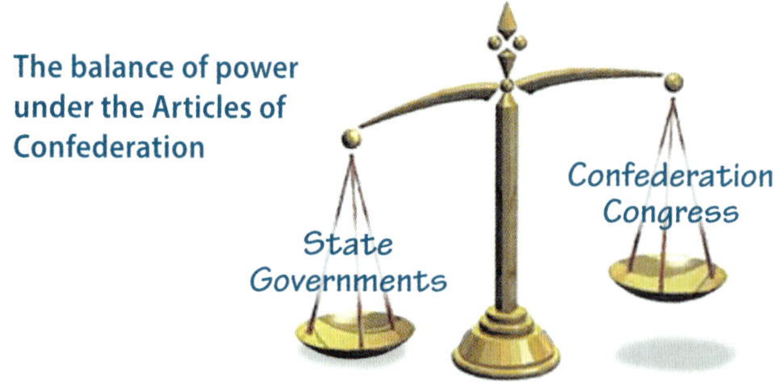

The balance of power under the Articles of Confederation

Weaknesses of the Articles of Confederation

The Articles of Confederation had many **weaknesses** (*things it was missing; things that made the government weak*). The most important ones are listed below.

1. Congress had no **power to tax**.
2. Congress had no **power to regulate trade** (*set rules for trade between states*).
3. Congress had no **power to enforce its laws**. There was no separate branch that enforced (*carried out*) the laws passed by Congress. Congress had no way to force the states to obey it.
4. There was no **national court system**.
5. The national government lacked **central leadership**. There was no executive who could lead the national government.
6. There were **no national armed forces** (*army and navy*).
7. Changes to the Articles required **unanimous consent** (*complete agreement by all 13 states*).

The Active Citizen

- Imagine a family with two children. One child is given allowance money to spend each week. The second child is told to ask the first child for money. Which child is likely to become more powerful in this relationship? How is this situation similar to the relationship between the central government and the states under the Articles of Confederation?
- How did the experience of British rule affect the authors of the Articles of Confederation?
- What in your opinion was the greatest weakness of the Articles of Confederation? Explain your answer in a well-written paragraph.

America under the Articles of Confederation

Once the Articles of Confederation were approved in 1781, the Continental Congress was replaced by the Confederation Congress. The members, however, stayed the same. These were critical years when it was unclear whether the former colonies would survive as independent, democratic states.

Under the Articles of Confederation, Congress had several major accomplishments. It sent delegates to negotiate the peace treaty with Great Britain that ended the American Revolution. (To "negotiate" is to discuss issues and settle on terms.) The Congress also created an orderly procedure for new territories to be admitted into the United States as states.

Congress under the Articles of Confederation

State Governments

Nevertheless, serious problems soon arose. First, there were problems with foreign nations. The British refused to abandon several of their forts in the Northwest despite the terms of the peace treaty ending the Revolutionary War. Spain challenged the borders of the new United States to the southwest. In far away North Africa, pirates attacked American ships once protected by the British navy. Without a strong national government, there was no one to watch over American interests.

Then there were growing economic difficulties at home. Despite winning the Revolution, many Americans faced hard times. To raise revenues, states taxed one another's goods. This hurt trade. There was a general shortage of money. Some state governments refused to honor their debts or to pay overseas lenders. Under the Confederation, Congress lacked money, even though it owed back pay to veterans who had fought in the American Revolution. The national government threatened not to pay off its **debt** (*money it owed*).

A growing number of Americans believed that the state governments were becoming tyrannical and corrupt. Some state governments threatened freedom of religion; others failed to respect private property rights. George Washington feared that the jealousies and divisions of the states would prevent the development of a genuine national spirit. James Madison feared the "tyranny of the majority"—that state governments would not respect the rights of minorities, including property-owners.

Shays' Rebellion

In Massachusetts, an economic crisis led the state government to raise taxes and increase its efforts to collect its debts (*amounts of money owed to others*). It sent debtors (*those who owed money*) to prison and foreclosed on farms.

What is foreclosure? Often people borrow money to buy property. The property serves as security that the borrower will repay the debt. If the borrower cannot pay, the lender has the right to seize the property, known as foreclosure. In Massachusetts, lenders were taking the homes and lands of poor farmers who could not make the payments on their debts.

Many of these struggling farmers had fought as soldiers in the Revolution. Poor farmers protested. Demonstrators shut down courts trying to collect taxes and debts. They demanded that Massachusetts print cheap paper money, as nearby Rhode Island had done. This would have raised the prices paid for crops and made the farmers' debts easier to repay.

Daniel Shays, a Massachusetts farmer, had served as a captain during the American Revolution. Shays led a group of angry farmers and debtors who attacked one of the state's courthouses. They demanded freedom for debtors, cheap paper money, and lower taxes. Shays' Rebellion created a wave of fear among wealthy landowners and merchants across the country. There was no national army to put down the rebellion if Massachusetts was unable to stop its spread.

The only known picture of Daniel Shays

For the EOC test, you should know that the weaknesses of the Articles of Confederation and the fears excited by Shays' Rebellion led to the meeting of the Constitutional Convention.

A Call to Revise the Articles

In the end, the Massachusetts militia (*citizens' military force*) was able to crush Shays' Rebellion. But with all the other problems facing the country under the Articles of Confederation, many Americans began to think that it was time for a change. Merchants feared the loss of trade; army officers feared the loss of their back pay; lenders feared the loss of their loans to the government.

In 1786, a meeting was held in Annapolis, Maryland, to discuss trade between the states. Five states sent representatives. The members called for a meeting to be held in Philadelphia the following year. Its purpose would be to revise the Articles of Confederation. All thirteen states were invited to send representatives.

The Maryland State House, where the Annapolis meeting took place

"Miracle at Philadelphia"— The Constitutional Convention

Fifty-five delegates gathered at the state house in Philadelphia in May 1787. It was the same building where eight of them had signed the Declaration of Independence 11 years earlier.

Back in 1776, the colonists had cut their ties to Britain in the name of liberty. The challenge now was to construct a central authority strong enough to defend the nation and promote its well-being, yet not so strong that it would threaten individual liberties.

Every state except Rhode Island sent representatives to Philadelphia to revise the Articles. All of the delegates were men who owned property. More than half of them had trained as lawyers. One third of these men had fought in the Revolution.

The delegates immediately elected George Washington to preside over their proceedings. Just as quickly, they voted to keep their discussions secret from the public, in order to encourage a freer exchange of ideas.

Next, the delegates took a surprising step. They decided to replace the Articles of Confederation rather than just to revise them. The delegates set about writing a new constitution—a plan of basic rules for government. Their assembly became known as the Constitutional Convention because they wrote the **U.S. Constitution**, the document that still governs us today.

The Active Citizen

Imagine that your class is about to form its own government. You must answer a series of questions to do so:

- Who should make the class rules?
- Who should make sure those rules are obeyed?
- Who should settle disputes between class members?
- Who should pay for class expenses?

Make a chart or outline showing your ideas for a plan of government for your class.

A constitution generally provides a framework for government. It limits government authority and protects the rights of the people. A government created by a written constitution is known as a constitutional government. Because we have a written constitution, we live under a constitutional government.

What the Delegates Agreed on

The delegates who met in Philadelphia in 1787 generally agreed that the government created by the Articles of Confederation was too weak. But how would they remedy (*fix*) this?

George Washington presiding over the Constitutional Convention

This speech identified some of the weaknesses of the Articles of Confederation.

The Active Citizen

In his address opening the Convention, the Governor of Virginia pointed to the following weaknesses in the Articles of Confederation:

Edmund Randolph, the Governor of Virginia

"(1) the Confederation produced no security against foreign invasion . . .

(2) the [Confederation] government could not check the quarrels between states nor a rebellion in any . . .

(3) there were many advantages which the United States might acquire (*get*), which were not attainable under the Confederation, such as a productive impost (*a tax on goods coming from other countries*)—counteraction of the commercial regulations of other nations—pushing of commerce (*trade*). . .

(4) the [Confederation] government could not defend itself against the encroachments (*improper advances*) from the states . . ."

—James Madison's *Notes of the Constitutional Convention*, for May 29, 1787

Continues ▸

▸ Which weaknesses of the Articles of Confederation identified in this speech do you feel were the most important? Explain your answer.

___

___

___

___

___

___

___

___

___

▸ Imagine that you are a delegate at the Constitutional Convention. Complete this letter to your family from Philadelphia by explaining how the weaknesses of the Articles of Confederation have led the delegates to decide to write a whole new constitution.

Philadelphia, May 1787

Dear ___

We are meeting here in Philadelphia. We are sworn to secrecy, but I will tell you a little about what is going on if you promise not to tell anyone else. All of the delegates agree that the government created by the Articles of Confederation is too weak. Some of its major weaknesses are ___

___

___

___

___

___

No one can see any good way to save the Articles of Confederation, so we have agreed to write a whole new constitution in their place.

Your loving ___

The members of the Constitutional Convention quickly decided that the new national government, which would replace the Articles of Confederation, should have **three branches**, or parts: a **legislative branch** to make the laws, an **executive branch** to enforce the laws, and a **judicial branch** to apply the laws.

They felt the new national government should also have a separation of powers between these three independent branches. This was just what Montesquieu had recommended. It was also what most of the state constitutions already had.

The members of the Constitutional Convention further agreed that the new **legislative branch** (*law-making body*) should have two houses, similar to the British Parliament:

- The first house, to be known as the **House of Representatives**, would represent the people. Its members would be elected directly by the people.
- The second house, to be known as the **Senate**, would represent the wisdom, wealth and property of America. As one delegate put it, the Senate should have "the most distinguished characters by rank and property." Senators would serve for longer terms than members of the House of Representatives. This way they would not be subject to the same popular pressures.

The delegates equally recognized the need for a national **executive branch** to provide **central leadership** and to carry out the laws. But should this national executive be a single person or a small group? After some debate, the members of the Constitutional Convention decided that the national executive should be one individual, known as the **President of the United States**. They further decided that the President should be given the power to veto (*deny or refuse*) new laws passed by Congress. However, to make sure the President was not too powerful, the delegates decided that two-thirds of both houses of Congress should be able to override the President's veto.

Finally, they decided on the need for a national **judicial branch** to interpret the laws.

You do not need to know about this disagreement for the EOC test, but it explains why the two houses of Congress are organized differently.

Enrichment

Large against Small

Of course, the delegates did not agree on everything. Their most important disagreement was over representation in the new houses of Congress.

Here, the larger states opposed the smaller ones. The larger states felt it was unfair for smaller states to have an equal voice in Congress when they had fewer people. The smaller states feared that the larger states would abuse their power if they were given more representatives because of their larger populations.

Virginia—then the most populous state in the nation—proposed that the representation of each state in Congress should be in proportion to its population. That is, the number of each state's representatives should be based on the size of its population. The delegates from Virginia wished to apply this principle to *both* houses of Congress. Since Virginia, Massachusetts and Pennsylvania had the largest populations, they would therefore hold the most seats in both the House of Representatives and the Senate.

New Jersey, one of the smallest states, suggested just the opposite. Its delegates even changed their minds about having two houses. They argued that representation in the legislature should remain as it had been under the Articles of Confederation. Each state should have an equal number of representatives in just one house. At the heart of this disagreement were conflicting views on the role of states in the future national government.

The Active Citizen

William Paterson

Mr. William Paterson (*New Jersey*): "Give the large states an influence in proportion to their [size], and what will be the consequence? Their ambition will be proportionally increased, and the small states will have everything to fear. New Jersey will never [agree]. She would be swallowed up. He had rather submit to a monarch, to a despot, than submit to such a fate. . . ."

James Wilson

Mr. James Wilson (*Pennsylvania*): "[A]s all authority was derived from the people, equal numbers of people ought to have an equal number of representatives, and different numbers of people different numbers of representatives. This principle had been improperly violated in the Confederation, owing to the urgent circumstances of the time . . . If small states will not [agree] to this plan, Pennsylvania . . . would not [agree] to any other . . ."

—James Madison's *Notes of the Constitutional Convention*, for June 9, 1787

- Explain in your own words why Paterson opposes letting the larger states have more representatives in Congress.

- Explain in your own words why Wilson argues larger states should be permitted to have more representatives in Congress.

- Which speaker would you have supported—Paterson or Wilson? Explain your answer.

- Imagine that you are a delegate to the Constitutional Convention in 1787. Using a separate sheet of paper, prepare a short speech (1–2 paragraphs) to the other delegates at the Constitutional Convention in which you address the disagreement between the large and small states.

The Two Houses of Congress

You will learn more about Congress in Chapter 6.

A compromise occurs when each side in a dispute gives up something in order to reach a solution that both sides can accept. The delegates to the Constitutional Convention made an important compromise that still affects us today. They decided that the two houses of Congress should be formed differently.

- States were given proportional representation in the **House of Representatives**. States with larger populations would therefore have more representatives there. This would benefit the larger states by giving them greater influence in the House.
- Each state would have an equal number of Senators in the **Senate**, regardless of its size. Each state would have two Senators. This would benefit the smaller states , which would have just as much power in the Senate as the larger states.

This compromise explains the organization of the two houses of Congress that we still have today.

The Executive Branch

You will learn more about the Presidency and the Electoral College in Chapter 7.

Article II of the Constitution created the **executive branch**—the part of government that enforces the laws. The absence of an executive branch was one of the weaknesses of the Articles of Confederation. As you know, the new executive branch consisted of the **President of the United States** and the Vice President.

The delegates had to decide how the new President should be chosen. Many of the delegates did not trust the people enough to permit them to elect the President directly. In an age before radio or television, most citizens would have no direct contact or even much familiarity with those individuals who wanted to become President. The delegates eventually decided that the President should be chosen by a group of special "electors," known together as the Electoral College. To become President, a candidate would need the support of a majority of these electors. If no candidate won a majority, then the election would be decided by the House of Representatives.

The Judicial Branch

You will learn more about the judicial branch in Chapter 8.

Finally, the delegates at the Constitutional Convention also agreed to create a **national court system**. You will recall that the lack of a national court system was a weakness of the Articles of Confederation. **Article III** of the Constitution created the U.S. **Supreme Court** to decide disputes between the states themselves, and cases involving foreign countries. The Supreme Court could also hear appeals from state courts regarding the U.S. Constitution or laws passed by Congress. The Constitution left it up to Congress to decide later whether or not to create additional federal courts below the Supreme Court to decide cases involving federal law. Federal judges were to be appointed for life to protect their impartiality.

In the next chapter, you will look more closely at the Constitution. You will learn about the organization of our national government and about the most important principles of our Constitution.

The Active Citizen

1. How did the structure of Congress under the Constitution differ from that of Congress under the Articles of Confederation?

2. Benjamin Franklin was one of those few men at the Constitutional Convention who had also been a member of the Second Continental Congress. He signed both the Declaration of Independence in 1776 and the Constitution in 1787. Pretend that you are Benjamin Franklin in 1787. On a separate piece of paper, write a letter to a friend comparing the discussions on declaring independence with the discussions leading to the new Constitution. Be sure to give Franklin's views on both sets of events.

Comparing Two Structures of National Government

Articles of Confederation	U.S. Constitution
One Branch	**Three Separate Branches**
Congress of the Confederation	Article I. Legislative Branch (makes the laws)

Articles of Confederation

One Branch

Congress of the Confederation

States

Each state sends several delegates but has only one vote in the Congress.

U.S. Constitution

Three Separate Branches

Article I. Legislative Branch

(makes the laws)

Congress

House of Representatives

Representatives elected by the people; states represented according to population

Senate

Two Senators from each state

Article II. Executive Branch

(enforces the laws; heads the government; controls the armed forces; directs foreign policy)

President

Vice-President

- Chosen by the Electoral College

Article III. Judicial Branch

(interprets and applies the laws)

Supreme Court

- Justices appointed by the President
- Lifetime tenure (term in office)

Changing (amending) the Articles or the Constitution

Articles of Confederation	U.S. Constitution
Unanimous consent (agreement by all the states)	2/3 of each house of Congress + 3/4 of the states (See Chapter 10 for the amendment process)

Weaknesses	Powers
• No power to tax	• Congress has power to tax
• No power to raise its own army	• Congress has power to raise an army
• No power to regulate trade	• Congress has power to regulate trade
• No power to enforce its own laws	• President has power to enforce laws

Name ______________________________

Complete the concept ladder below by adding your own descriptions and explanations.

The Articles of Confederation (1781)

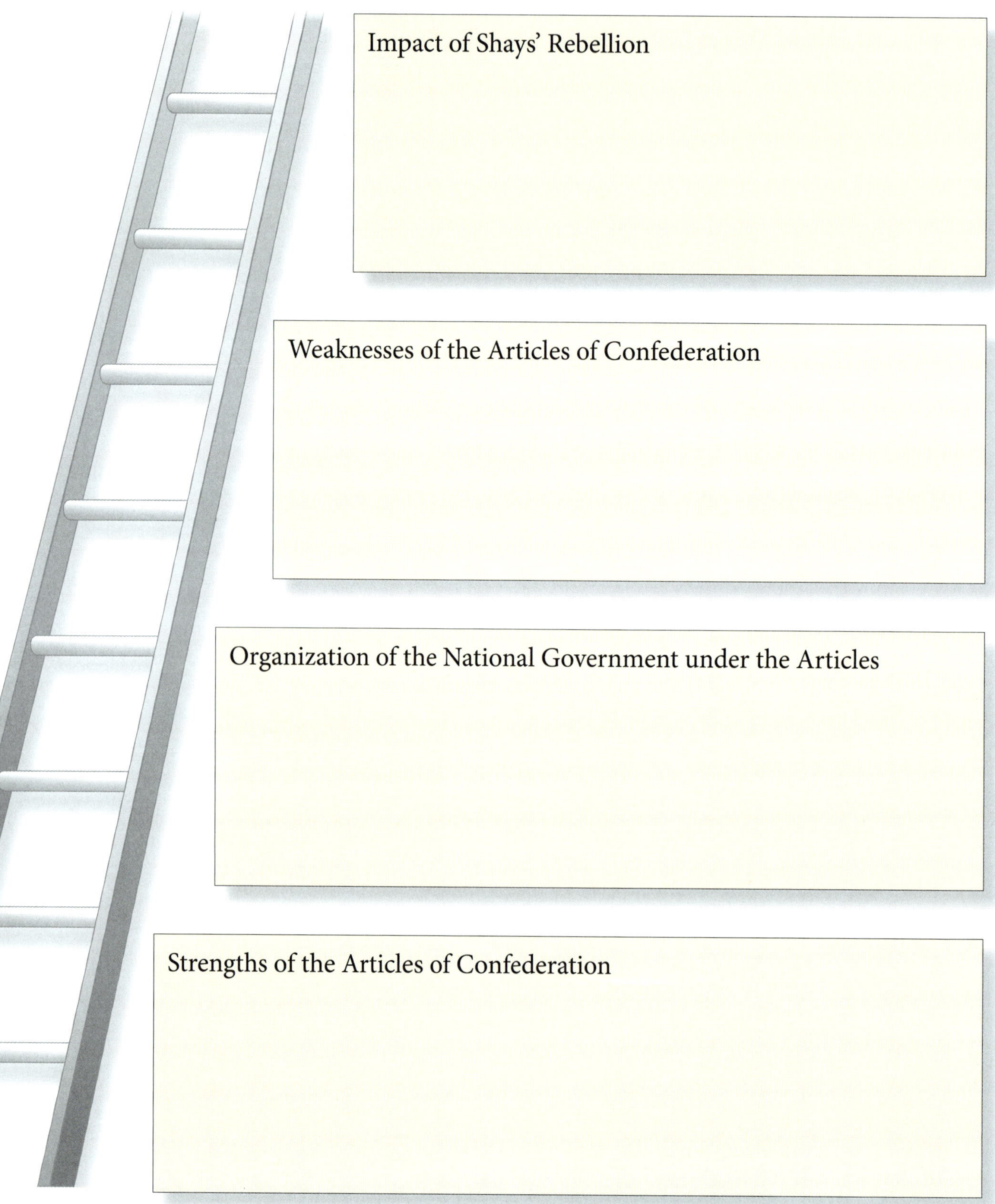

Name ____

Complete the concept ladder below by adding your own descriptions and explanations.

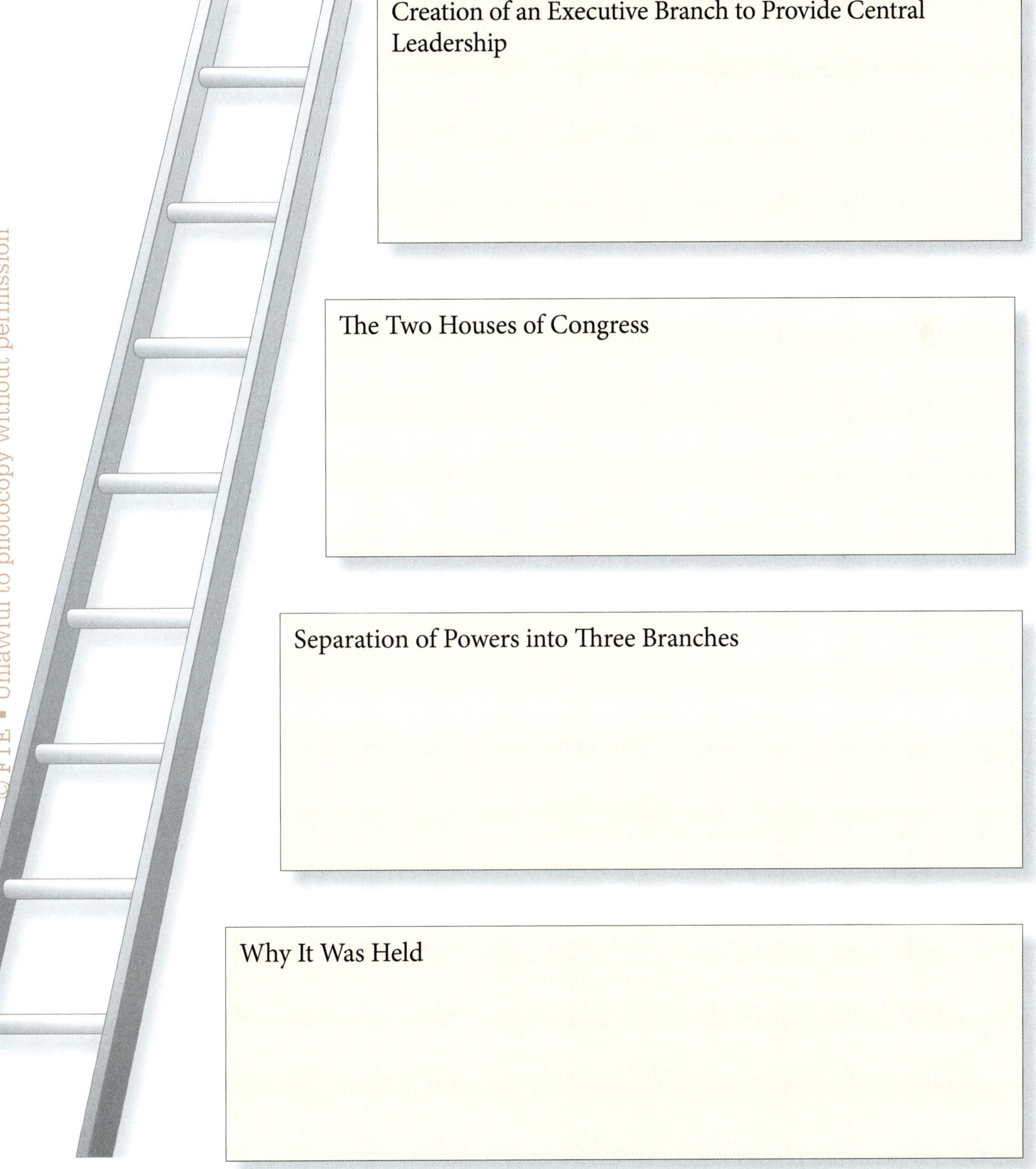

Name ____

Enrichment

Pretend you are a member of the Constitutional Convention. Write a note to another member of the Convention giving your views on the most important issues facing the Convention.

To Mr. ____________________, representative from the State of ____________________________

My dear Sir,

In my humble view, the main weaknesses of our Articles of the Confederation are _______________

____

____

____

Therefore, I think we should forget about trying to revise the Articles. Instead, we should write a whole new Constitution.

It is very clear to me that our national government needs to have its own separate executive, legislative, and judicial branches.

Some people wonder whether the head of our new national executive should be one person or a small group. I believe ____

____

____

____.

I do not believe that the common people can know our leaders well enough or watch them closely enough to decide who should be chosen as President. Therefore, I believe the President should be chosen by ____

____

____

____.

As you know, we have had plenty of debate over our new legislature, known as Congress. Should each state have the same number of representatives, or should larger states have more representatives?

I believe ____

____

____

____.

This is because ____

____

____

____

____.

We have agreed on creating a national court system. Article III of the Constitution creates the Supreme Court, but we cannot agree on whether to create other, lower federal courts. To avoid any more disagreements, this issue has been left to our future Congress. I hope they decide to ____________

____

____

____.

There are those who fear that our new government will be too strong. They say it might abuse and oppress ordinary citizens. But I say that we need a stronger government to protect us from foreign countries and unrest at home.

I believe the Constitution can establish a strong and stable government while also protecting our individual liberties.

Yours sincerely with utmost respect,

Your very humble servant,

____

Using as many of the names and terms from this chapter as you can, write two paragraphs on a separate sheet of paper explaining how the weaknesses of the Articles of Confederation led to the writing of the Constitution.

Review Cards: The Story of Our Constitution

The Articles of Confederation: Relationship to the States

After independence was declared, members of the Second Continental Congress reached an agreement known as the **Articles of Confederation**. A confederation is an association of states. In a confederation, most of the powers of government remain with the individual member states. The most important **strength of the Articles** was that this document provided the former colonies with their first national government.

- The Articles of Confederation established a "league of friendship" between the 13 states.
- After their experiences under British rule, the members of the Second Continental Congress did not want to make a central government that was too strong. The Articles created a very weak central government, consisting of a "Congress" of delegates from the states.
- Most power remained with the states themselves, which had their own state constitutions. The state governments remained sovereign (*supreme; the highest authority*) except for those powers given to Congress by the Articles of Confederation.

The Articles of Confederation and its Weaknesses

Each state had only one vote in the Congress of the Confederation.

The Confederation Congress—the only body of national government created by the Articles of Confederation—had these powers:

- Its main power was over foreign affairs: it could declare war, exchange ambassadors with foreign nations, and enter into treaties and alliances.
- It could also resolve disputes between states and regulate relations with certain Indian tribes.
- The Congress could borrow money, build a navy, and "direct" an army.

The national government created by the Articles of Confederation had several important **weaknesses** (*things it was missing; disadvantages*):

- The Confederation had no **power to tax**. It could not tax citizens; instead, it relied on the states to contribute money.
- The Confederation had no **power to regulate trade** (*make rules for trade*).
- The Confederation had no **executive branch** with the **power to enforce laws** or to provide **central leadership**.
- There was no **national court system** to interpret the laws and decide how they should be applied to specific cases.
- Nine states were needed to approve any new law, and all thirteen states had to agree to any changes in the Articles (**unanimous consent**).

Weaknesses of the Articles of Confederation Bring Problems

Under the Articles of Confederation, the nation had many problems, in both foreign and economic affairs.

- Because their national government was so weak, many Americans feared that foreign nations might take advantage of them.
- American trade suffered when states began to tax each other's goods, did not print enough money, and refused to pay their debts.
- During Shays' Rebellion, Massachusetts farmers rebelled when the state began to foreclose on their farms to collect debts. Daniel Shays, a former captain in the Revolution, led these protestors in attacking courthouses. There was no national army to put down the rebellion if it spread. The state militia eventually ended the rebellion.
- Events like Shays' Rebellion made many Americans realize the **weaknesses of the Articles**. The rebellion led many Americans to desire a stronger central government. In 1786, representatives from several states called for the Articles of Confederation to be revised.

The Constitutional Convention Creates a National Government with Three Branches

- In 1787, fifty-five delegates, headed by George Washington, met in Philadelphia to revise the Articles of Confederation. They decided to get rid of the Articles altogether and write a whole new constitution (*plan of government*). Their meeting became known as the Constitutional Convention. They wrote the **U.S. Constitution**, giving the United States the system of constitutional government (*government based on a constitution*) that we still have today.
- The members of the Constitutional Convention agreed that the country needed a stronger national government with **three branches**: the legislative, executive, and judicial branches.
  - **Article I** created the new **legislative branch**. It would have two houses: the **House of Representatives** and the **Senate**.
  - The number of representatives that a state had in the House of Representatives would be based on its population. That meant larger states would have more representatives. In the Senate, every state would have two Senators. Small and large states would thus have the same number of Senators.
  - **Article II** of the new Constitution created the **executive branch**, to enforce the laws. The head of the new executive branch would be the **President of the United States**. The President would have the power to veto laws passed by Congress, but such vetoes could be overridden by a two-thirds majority of each house of Congress. This new executive branch provided the **central leadership** that had been lacking under the Articles of Confederation.
  - **Article III** of the new Constitution created the **judicial branch**, the part of government that would interpret the laws and apply them to specific situations. The judicial branch of the new national government would consist of the **Supreme Court**. This created the **national court system** that had been missing from the Articles of Confederation.

The Constitutional Convention: Disagreement and Compromise

- The delegates to the Convention disagreed over the structure of the new Congress. Larger states wanted representation in Congress to be proportional to each state's population. Smaller states wanted all states to have equal representation. The issue was finally resolved by establishing each house of Congress on a different basis: the number of members each state had in the **House of Representatives** would be based on its population, while in the **Senate**, every state, regardless of size, would have two Senators. (See Chapter 6.)

The Story of Our Constitution

Articles of Confederation

- Each state had one vote in the new national government created by the Articles of Confederation
- The national government had to ask states for revenue (*money*) and soldiers
- The national government could direct an army and maintain a navy
- The national government conducted the nation's foreign relations and could declare war

Weaknesses of the Articles of Confederation

- No power to tax or enforce laws
- No national armed forces
- No central leadership (executive branch)
- No national court system
- No power to regulate interstate trade
- Unanimous consent (*approval by all*) needed to change Articles

Problems under the Articles of Confederation

- The national government was too weak to resist foreign nations
- States taxed one another's goods
- Shays' Rebellion posed a threat, creating a desire for stronger government
- Call to revise the Articles of Confederation

Constitutional Convention (1787)

- Delegates agreed to get rid of the weak Articles of Confederation and to write a whole new constitution, the U.S. Constitution
- They adopted Montesquieu's separation of powers by creating a national government with three branches
- Article I created the legislative branch, with the power to tax, to regulate trade, and to raise an army. The new Congress would have two houses, each formed on a different basis:
  - Senate: States were represented equally with 2 Senators each
  - House of Representatives: Number of members each state had in the House would be based on its population
- Article II created the executive branch, headed by the President, providing central leadership
- Article III created the new judicial branch, the U.S. Supreme Court, introducing a national court system

What Do You Know?

SS.7.CG.1.7

1. The postage stamp on the left shows a committee of the Second Continental Congress drafting the Articles of Confederation.

Why did this committee create a weak central government?

A. to encourage more trade between states

B. to preserve the powers of the individual states

C. to promote national security against foreign invasion

D. to permit the taxation of citizens to pay the nation's debts

SS.7.CG.1.7

2. How did Americans' experience under British rule influence the form of government they established under the Articles of Confederation?

A. The new legislature had two houses, just like the British Parliament.

B. The states were sovereign, just as the colonies had been under British rule.

C. The new central government was not given any power to direct the military.

D. The new central government was not able to tax citizens as the British government had tried to do.

SS.7.CG.1.7

3. Why did the members of the Constitutional Convention decide to create a national government with three separate branches?

A. This system made it easier for government officials to specialize.

B. This was as a compromise since some delegates wanted four branches.

C. Having separate branches gave the government greater flexibility in wartime.

D. This structure would prevent any one branch of government from becoming too strong.

SS.7.CG.1.7

4. By 1786, why did many merchants want the Articles of Confederation to be replaced?

A. Several states were taxing the activities of the Confederation.

B. States were discouraging trade by taxing one another's goods.

C. Congress was forcing the states to contribute to its general fund.

D. The national government had printed so much money that it lost its value.

SS.7.CG.1.7

5. How did the U.S. Constitution solve a problem created by a weakness of the Articles of Confederation?

A. It stopped the national government from imposing taxes.

B. It gave the national government the power to raise an army.

C. It required unanimous consent of the states to pass amendments

D. It prevented acts of piracy against American ships off the coast of Africa.

SS.7.CG.1.7

6. The illustration on the left, from a popular almanac in 1787, shows Captain Daniel Shays.

Why did his rebellion send a wave of fear among wealthy merchants and landowners?

A. Officers worried about losing their back pay.

B. Shays planned to take money from the rich and give it to the poor.

C. There was no national army to put down domestic unrest if it spread.

D. Bankers and other lenders feared the loss of their loans to the national government.

SS.7.CG.1.7

7. Which weakness of the Articles of Confederation was addressed by the Constitution?

A. the continuation of slavery

B. the lack of a national court system

C. the absence of a balanced budget

D. the need to strengthen the power of the states

SS.7.CG.3.3

8. Below are two opposing views expressed at the Constitutional Convention.

1	2
As delegates from small states, we insist on a national legislature in which each state receives equal representation.	As delegates from large states, we believe that representation should be based on population. States with more people should have more representatives.

Which feature of American government today was the outcome of this disagreement at the Constitutional Convention?

A. A Bill of Rights was added to the Constitution to protect individual rights.

B. Each state can decide how its own representation in Congress is determined.

C. Representation in both our federal and state legislatures is now based on population.

D. States have equal representation in one house of Congress and representation based on their population size in the other.

CHAPTER 5

A Quick Tour of the Constitution

SS.7.CG.1.8 Explain the purpose of the Preamble to the U.S. Constitution.

SS.7.CG.1.9 Describe how the U.S. Constitution limits the powers of government through separation of powers, checks and balances, individual rights, rule of law and due process of law.

SS.7.CG.1.10 Compare the viewpoints of the Federalists and the Anti-Federalists regarding ratification of the U.S. Constitution and including a bill of rights.

SS.7.CG.3.3 Describe the structure and function of the three branches of government established in the U.S. Constitution. (*This chapter provides an overview of the U.S. Constitution. For specific branches of our national government, see Chapters 6–8.*)

Content Focus Vocabulary in This Chapter

U.S. Constitution
Preamble
"We the People"
Form a more perfect Union
Establish justice
Ensure domestic tranquility
Provide for the common defense
Promote the general welfare
Secure the blessings of liberty
Posterity

National government
Government power
Article I
Legislative branch
Article II
Executive branch
Article III
Judicial branch
Limited government
Constitutional government

Separation of powers
Checks and balances
Individual rights
Rule of law
Due process of law
Ratification
Federalists
Anti-Federalists
Bill of Rights
Influence on other governments

Florida "Keys" to Learning

1. The **U.S. Constitution** was finally approved by the delegates to the Constitutional Convention in 1787. It established the **constitutional government** that still governs the United States, more than two hundred years later. The "Founders" wanted to create a **national government** with enough **government power** to protect the nation and to promote greater cooperation, while not so strong that it would oppress the people.

2. The first part of the new Constitution was its **Preamble**. The Preamble began with "**We the People**," emphasizing that our government depends on the American people for its power and exists to serve them.

3. The **Preamble** identified the goals and purposes of the new national government that the Constitution was establishing: to "**form a more perfect Union**" (*bring the states closer together into one country*), to "**establish justice**" (*protect citizens from crime and injury*), to "**insure domestic tranquility**" (*peace within the country*), to "**provide for the common defense**" (*defend the nation from foreign enemies*), to "**promote the general welfare** (*well-being*), and to "**secure the blessings of liberty**" (*protect individual freedom*) for **posterity** (*future generations*). To meet these goals, the people of the United States ordained (*ordered; established*) the new Constitution.

4. The Constitution has seven articles. **Article I** established the **legislative branch**, known as Congress, for making the laws. Congress has two "houses": the Senate and the House of Representatives. In the Senate, each state is represented by two Senators. In the House of Representatives, each state is represented in proportion to its population. Article I further defines the powers of Congress, such as the power to tax.

5. **Article II** established the **executive branch** for enforcing the laws, headed by the President and Vice President. The President enforces federal laws, serves as Commander in Chief of the armed forces, makes appointments, and delivers a "State of the Union" Address.

6. **Article III** established the **judicial branch** for interpreting the laws. The Supreme Court was established as the highest court in the land. The Constitution gave Congress the power to create lower federal courts.

7. Articles IV–VII concerned relations with the states and established procedures for ratifying (*approving*) and amending (*changing or adding to*) the new Constitution.

8. The U.S. Constitution limited the powers of government in several key ways including the **separation of powers** (*government power was divided among three branches*), the system of **checks and balances** (*the branches could check one another*), and by establishing **individual rights** (*rights each of us has as persons*), **rule of law** (*we are all subject to the same rules*), and **due process of law** (*the right to a fair process before losing one's life, liberty or property*). These principles created a **limited government** (*a government with limited powers*). Because of the separation of powers, each branch of government has a different and specific function. Because of checks and balances, each branch can check the others.

9. The **Anti-Federalists** opposed **ratification** (*approval of the new Constitution*). They felt the new federal government would threaten individual rights and liberties. They also demanded that a "**bill of rights**" (*a guarantee of certain individual rights*) be added to the Constitution for it to be ratified.

10. The **Federalists** supported ratification. They believed the country needed a stronger government. They argued that the federal government would not grow too powerful because power

would be divided among three branches and each branch would be able to check the others. Three leading Federalists published essays, known as *The Federalist Papers*, in favor of ratification. At first, the Federalists thought a bill of rights was unnecessary; later, most agreed to add it in order to get the Constitution ratified.

11. The U.S. Constitution has had an **influence on other governments**. Other countries, such as France and Mexico, have copied the example of a written constitution with special rules for ratification and amendment. Many governments also have a separation of powers, a President, and a bill of rights.

A Quick Tour of the Constitution

In the last chapter, you learned about the Articles of Confederation and the Constitutional Convention. By August 1787, the delegates in Philadelphia had completed the first draft (*written version*) of the new constitution. The final document was approved by the Convention just over one month later. It consisted of a preamble and seven articles. The same document still governs us today, more than two centuries later. This chapter will give you an overview of the main provisions of the Constitution.

Be sure to know the purposes of government stated in the Preamble for the EOC test.

The Preamble

The first part of the Constitution is the **Preamble**, an introductory statement. The Preamble serves as an introduction to the U.S. Constitution. It states the intentions (*aims*) of its authors. The Preamble explains the goals of the Constitution, which remain the goals and purposes of our national government today:

We the People of the United States, in order to form a more perfect Union, establish justice, insure domestic tranquility, provide for the common defense, promote the general welfare, and secure the blessings of liberty to ourselves and our posterity, do ordain and establish this Constitution for the United States of America.

"We the People" = the citizens of the United States
More perfect = more complete; better than before
Union = a group of states united under one government
Establish justice = to enforce laws fairly; to protect citizens from crime and injury
Tranquility = calm and peacefulness
Domestic tranquility = peace and calm inside the country
Common defense = defense of the entire community
General welfare = well-being (happiness, health and good fortune) of the entire community
Posterity = all future generations; those who will live after us
Ordain = order or decree

Explain what each phrase of the Preamble means in your own words:

"We the People"____

____

"in order to form a more perfect Union," ____________________________

____

"establish justice," ____

"ensure domestic tranquility,"

"provide for the common defense,"

"promote the general welfare,"

"and secure the blessings of liberty to ourselves and our posterity,"

"do ordain and establish this Constitution for the United States of America."

The Active Citizen

- Why did the Preamble begin with the words, "We the People"?
- Explain in your own words how the Preamble served as an introduction to the U.S. Constitution. Do you think it was necessary?

The very first words of the Constitution are "We the People." This phrase expresses the fact that under our system of government, the people are the final source of all political power. The government depends on the people for its power and exists to serve them.

The American people first expressed their will by ratifying the Constitution in 1789. They continue to express their will today by electing representatives and government officials, and by amending (*changing or adding to*) the Constitution from time to time.

The Active Citizen

- Did the Constitution "form a more perfect Union" than the Articles of Confederation? Discuss this question with a partner and then share your views with the class.

- The Preamble to the Constitution is generally viewed as a statement of the goals and purposes of our national government. Which ***two*** goals do you think are the most important ones?

  - ☐ form a more perfect Union
  - ☐ establish justice
  - ☐ ensure domestic tranquility
  - ☐ provide for the common defense
  - ☐ promote the general welfare
  - ☐ secure the blessings of liberty

Explain your selections (*choices*): ____________________

____

____

____

____

- Which of these goals do you think can best be met by our national government? Mark these with "N." Which of these goals can best be met by state governments? Mark these with "S."

  - ____ form a more perfect Union
  - ____ establish justice
  - ____ ensure domestic tranquility
  - ____ provide for the common defense
  - ____ promote the general welfare
  - ____ secure the blessings of liberty

Explain your selections: ____________________

____

____

____

____

The Organization of our National Government

The first three articles (*an article is a separate paragraph or section of a legal document*) of the Constitution established the basic structure of our **national government** (*government for the entire nation*)—also known as the "federal government." These articles created three separate branches of government with different powers and responsibilities. You will look at each branch in more detail in later chapters:

Article I. The Legislative Branch: Congress

- This first article, **Article I**, established the **legislative branch**, known as Congress (*law-making part of government*).
- Congress has two "houses": the Senate and the House of Representatives.
- In the Senate, each state is represented by two Senators.
- In the House of Representatives, each state is represented by a number of members in proportion to its population.
- Members of the House of Representatives are elected for two-year terms.
- Senators are elected for six-year terms. (In the original Constitution, they were chosen by their state legislatures, but since 1913, Senators have been elected.)
- Article I gives Congress very specific powers (sometimes known as the "enumerated powers"). These include the power to declare war, to lay and collect taxes, to raise and support an army and navy, to coin money, to borrow money, to regulate trade between states, to establish post offices, to grant patents and copyrights, and to create lower courts. Patents and copyrights give inventors and authors sole ownership rights over their works for a limited period.

- Congress was also given the power to pass any law "necessary and proper" for carrying out the powers listed above. The clause granting this power has become known as the Elastic Clause.
- A bill must pass both houses of Congress and must be signed by the President in order to become a law. The President can veto (*reject*) a bill by refusing to sign it. A two-thirds majority in each house can pass a bill without the President's signature. This is known as "overriding a veto."

You will learn more about Congress and the law-making process in Chapter 6.

The Active Citizen

- List two important rules about Congress found in Article I of the Constitution.

Article II. The Executive Branch: the Presidency

- Article II established the offices of President and Vice President, forming the executive branch.
- The President must be a natural-born citizen who is at least 35 years old. The President is chosen by the Electoral College. After being elected, the President serves for a four-year term.
- The President enforces our federal laws, serves as the Commander in Chief of our armed forces, appoints and receives ambassadors, negotiates treaties, gives a "State of the Union" Address, and appoints judges and other federal officials.
- Congress can remove the President from office for misconduct by impeachment.

You will learn more about the Presidency in Chapter 7.

The Active Citizen

- List two important rules about the President found in Article II of the Constitution.

Article III. The Judicial Branch: the Supreme Court

- Article III established the the judicial branch. It created the U. S. Supreme Court as the highest court in the land.
- The Supreme Court decides all disputes between states or concerning foreign ambassadors. The Supreme Court can also hear appeals of other cases.
- Federal judges hold office for life, during "good behavior." They can be impeached for misconduct.
- The Constitution did not create any lower federal courts. However, it gave Congress the power to create lower federal courts in the future.

You will learn more about the Supreme Court and other federal courts in Chapter 8.

The Active Citizen

- List two important rules about the judicial branch found in Article III of the Constitution.

Other Articles of the Constitution

Later articles of the Constitution concerned the following matters:

Article IV	Established rules concerning the states. (See Chapter 12)
Article V	Established procedures for amending (*changing or adding to*) the Constitution. (See Chapter 10)
Article VI	Stated that federal law was the "supreme law of the land"—superior to state laws. (See Chapter 12)
Article VII	Established a process for ratifying (*approving*) the new Constitution.

Comparing the Three Branches of Government

Imagine you had to compare the three branches of our national government. What do you see as their similarities? What do you see as their differences?

Similarities	Differences
▸ Each branch is part of our national government. ▸ Each branch has specific powers defined by the U.S. Constitution. ▸ Each branch has authority over one part of the governing process. ▸ Each branch has the authority to make decisions with the force of law. ▸ Each branch has some powers to check the actions of the other branches. ▸ Each branch owes its authority to the consent of the people.	▸ The number of people in each branch differs. The Presidency consists of one person. Congress has a large number of members. The Supreme Court consists of a panel of a few judges. ▸ How the members of each branch are chosen differs. Members of Congress are elected by the people. The President is chosen by the Electoral College, which is based on the choices voters make in each state. The Justices of the U.S. Supreme Court are appointed by the President. ▸ The length of time in office for the members of each branch differs. Members of Congress serve 2 or 6-year terms and there are no limits on the number of terms. The President serves for a 4-year term and can only serve two elected terms. Justices of the U.S. Supreme Court are appointed for life. ▸ The areas over which each branch exercises its main responsibilities differ. Congress controls lawmaking; the President enforces the law, represents the United States, and is Commander in Chief of the armed forces; the Supreme Court interprets and applies the laws.

The Active Citizen

▸ How did the new Constitution remedy the major weaknesses of our national government under the Articles of Confederation? Use information from Chapters 4 and 5 to complete the chart below.

Weaknesses under the Articles of Confederation	How the Constitution Remedied this Weakness
Congress had no power to tax.	Article I gave Congress the power to lay and collect taxes.
Congress had no power to raise its own troops.	
Congress had no power to regulate trade.	
Congress had no power to enforce its laws.	
There was no national court system.	
There was no national executive to provide central leadership.	

For the EOC, you should know how the Constitution limits the powers of government.

How the Constitution Limits the Powers of Government

The delegates to the Constitutional Convention struggled with one central problem. They wanted to create a central government strong enough to protect them and to promote greater cooperation, while not so strong that it would oppress (*mistreat or abuse*) them.

The solution they came up with was to create a central government with important powers, such as the power to tax, to raise a national army, and to regulate trade. At the same time, they introduced several features that limited the powers of the central government:

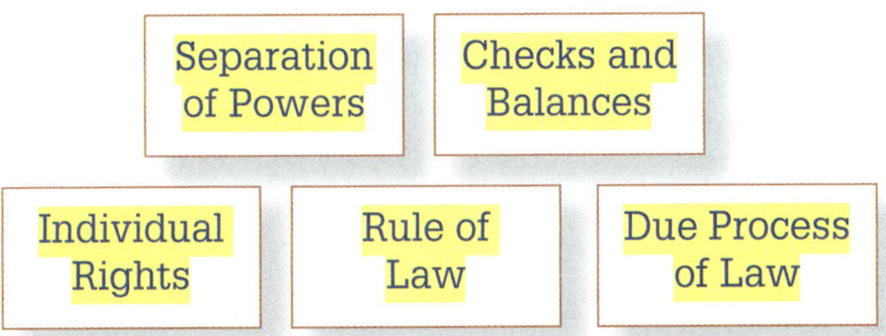

One of the main reasons for having a constitutional government (*a government based on a written constitution*) is that the constitution defines and limits the powers of government over its citizens. The U.S. Constitution established a much stronger national government. But this government was still only given limited powers. It had only those powers specifically listed in the Constitution (especially in Article I). These powers were granted to it by the people.

All other powers, not listed in the Constitution, were left to the state governments and the people.

This should be compared to conditions in many other countries at the time. Many rulers enjoyed absolute power. There were no limits on what these rulers could do. The Tsar of Russia, for instance, could imprison his subjects and take away their property at will. Every person owed the Tsar absolute obedience. In the United States, neither Congress nor any state government has the power to take away someone's property or liberty without just cause and fair procedures. A government with limited powers is known as a **limited government**.

Now let's look more closely at each of the ways central power was limited.

Separation of Powers

In our national government, power is limited through the **separation of powers**. The Constitutional Convention created a national government with three separate branches: legislative, executive and judicial. Each branch exercises its own separate power:

- **Legislative Power**—the power to make federal laws—is exercised by Congress.
- **Executive Power**—the power to carry out and enforce federal laws—is exercised by the President.
- **Judicial Power**—the power to hear and decide cases by applying national law to specific situations—is exercised by the Supreme Court.

This separation of powers was based on the ideas of Baron de Montesquieu, whom you read about in Chapter 2. In fact, by 1787 each state already had a separation of powers in its own state constitution.

The authors of the Constitution saw the separation of powers as a way of making sure that the national government did not become too strong.

In an absolute monarchy, a king or queen holds all of the powers of government. The monarch makes the laws, enforces the laws, and decides if the laws have been correctly applied. It is impossible for ordinary citizens to challenge anything that the king or queen has done. (You will learn more about monarchies and autocracies in Chapter 17.)

With the separation of powers, it becomes more difficult for the government to commit arbitrary (*unreasonable*) and unfair acts. Once the legislature makes a law, it is left to an independent executive to enforce that law in a fair and reasonable manner. A separate judiciary then decides if the application of the law was fair and just.

Each branch further acts to monitor and watch over the others. Each branch makes sure that the other branches do not grow too strong. "Ambition," James Madison explained, thus curbs (*limits*) "ambition."

The separation of powers and system of checks and balances (about which you will read below) limit the power of our national government so that it does not threaten our individual liberties.

Checks and Balances

Closely related to the separation of powers was the creation of a system of **checks and balances**. Each branch was given several specific powers to "check"—or *stop*—the other two. The overall aim of these checks and balances was to prevent any one branch of the federal government from becoming too strong.

The system of checks and balances also created an incentive for the different branches to cooperate.

Checks on Congress

- Each house of Congress checks the other house: the approval of both houses is needed to pass any new law.
- To pass a bill into law, Congress requires the signature of the President. The President can check Congress by vetoing its proposed legislation (*refusing to sign the bill*), although two-thirds of each house can override the veto.
- The Supreme Court can check Congress by ruling that a federal law is unconstitutional (*violates some aspect of the Constitution*).

Checks on the President

- The President appoints Justices to the Supreme Court, ambassadors and other officials, but these appointments must be approved by a majority of the Senate.

Examples of Checks and Balances

- The President negotiates treaties with foreign nations, but these treaties must be approved by two-thirds of the Senate.
- The President controls foreign policy and acts as the Commander in Chief of the armed forces, but only Congress can declare war.
- The President establishes programs, but Congress can refuse to provide money for these programs.
- Congress can impeach the President.
- The Supreme Court can check the President by ruling that an executive order or Presidential action is unconstitutional.

Checks on the Supreme Court

- Congress can override decisions of the Supreme Court on federal law by passing a new law.
- Congress and the states can override the Supreme Court's interpretation of the Constitution by amending the Constitution.
- The President can influence the composition of the Supreme Court through judicial appointments.
- Congress can impeach federal judges, as civil officers, for treason, bribery or other crimes.
- The President can grant a pardon to someone convicted of a federal crime.

The Active Citizen

- Which of these situations illustrate the separation of powers and which illustrate checks and balances?

	Separation of Powers	Checks and Balances
Congress passes a bill limiting carbon dioxide emissions. The President vetoes the bill. It never passes into law.		
Congress declares war on a foreign country that has attacked the United States. Acting as Commander in Chief, the President orders U.S. armed forces to attack that country.		
Congress passes a law against printing counterfeit money. Jocelyn Smith is put on trial in federal court for violating this law by counterfeiting.		
A Supreme Court Justice secretly accepts money from a company in a case the Court is about to review. The payment becomes known and Congress impeaches the Justice.		

Individual Rights

The Declaration of Independence stated that the purpose of government was to protect our "unalienable rights." The Preamble to the Constitution announced that one of its purposes was to "secure the blessings of liberty." The Constitution, and later the Bill of Rights, established **individual rights** that the government is required to respect. This limits the power of our government, which cannot take steps that deny these rights.

For example, the Constitution says that Congress cannot pass an *ex post facto* law. This is any law that penalizes someone for an act that was not against the law at the time it was committed. The Constitution says that the government cannot pass such a law. This prevents government officials from taking such a step.

The Bill of Rights are the first ten amendments to our Constitution. They guarantee our freedom of religion, freedom of the press, freedom of speech and other individual rights. These individual rights limit the power of our government, which cannot pass any laws that unreasonably restrict (*limit*) those rights.

Rule of Law

Another way in which the U.S. Constitution limits the powers of our government is by maintaining the **rule of law**. As you know, the "rule of law" goes back to ancient times. It refers to a society in which average citizens, rich and powerful individuals, and government officials are all subject to the same set of laws, without exception. We all must obey the same rules. These rules should be fair and reasonable. They also should be written down and easily available for everyone to see.

The Constitution established federal law—the laws created by our national government—as the supreme (*or highest*) law of the land. Federal laws must, above all, follow the U.S. Constitution, which is our fundamental (*most basic*) law. Our government officials are required to follow these laws. If the government takes an action that violates the Constitution, this action will be struck down by our courts.

Due Process of Law

The Fifth Amendment to the U.S. Constitution states that: "No person shall . . . be deprived of life, liberty or property without due process of law . . ."

"**Due Process of law**" here refers to a very important individual right. It means that the government cannot take away our life, liberty, or property without conducting some process or procedure. This process must be fair and reasonable. We are entitled to the process that is "due," based on what is at stake.

In general, this means we should be given a public trial or a public hearing with a chance to defend ourselves and our position. We should be able to

present evidence and witnesses on our behalf. We should also be able to see any evidence or hear any witnesses against us. We have the right to obtain expert advice—such as the help of a lawyer—both before and during the trial or hearing. We are entitled to be given enough time to prepare our case. Finally, the trial or hearing should be conducted before an impartial decision maker, such as a jury of our "peers" (*equals*). Our "due process" rights limit the powers of government officials to take arbitrary and abusive actions against us.

The Active Citizen

- Which of these constitutional limits on government power do you think are the most effective ones? Why? ____

  ____
- Make a Venn diagram or chart comparing the principles of separation of powers and checks and balances. How are these principles alike? How are they different?

For the EOC, you should know the main arguments of the Federalists and Anti-Federalists over ratification.

The Debate over Ratification

Our Constitution begins with these stirring words: "We the People." But did the American people truly support the new Constitution when it was proposed?

Patrick Henry, a popular patriotic leader, loudly questioned the claim: "What right had they to say, 'We, the people?' . . . Who authorized (*gave permission to*) them to speak the language of, 'We, the people,' instead of, 'We, the states?' . . .The people gave them no power to use their name. That they exceeded (*went beyond*) their power is perfectly clear."

Article VII of the new Constitution set forth a procedure for its official adoption. The Constitution would come into force once it was ratified (*officially approved*) by nine states. To decide on **ratification**, each state held a special ratifying convention.

Federalists against Anti-Federalists

Debates now sprang up in all thirteen states to decide whether the Constitution should be ratified. Those who favored the new constitution called themselves **Federalists**. They took their name from the new federal system.

Opponents of the new constitution became known as **Anti-Federalists**. Many of the Anti-Federalists had been leading patriots during the American Revolution. They feared that the proposed Constitution would establish a central government just as oppressive as the British government had been. The Anti-Federalists were convinced that this new government would threaten personal liberties.What, for example, would stop the President from seizing greater power? As one leading Anti-Federalist warned: "If your American [President] be a man of ambition and abilities, how easy is it for him to render himself absolute! . . . What will become then of you and your rights?"

The Federalists, however, argued that if a stronger central government were not soon adopted, the country might split apart or be invaded by foreign powers. They further insisted that the new central government would never become despotic or oppressive because of the several safeguards built into the Constitution itself such as the separation of powers and system of checks and balances.

Enrichment

The most important Federalist arguments were published in a series of articles known as *The Federalist Papers*.

The purpose of *The Federalist Papers* was to persuade the ratifying convention in New York to approve the Constitution. *The Federalist Papers* argued that a stronger government was badly needed, while the separation of powers and checks and balances would protect the liberty of every citizen.

> *"Ambition must be made to counteract ambition. . . . It may be a reflection on human nature, that such devices should be necessary to control the abuses of government. But what is government itself, but the greatest of all reflections on human nature? If men were angels, no government would be necessary. If angels were to govern men, [no] controls on government would be necessary.*
>
> *In framing a government which is to be administered by men over men, the great difficulty lies in this: you must first enable the government to control the governed; and in the next place oblige it to control itself. . . ."*
>
> —James Madison, *Federalist No. 51*, February 6, 1788

Word Helper

ambition = strong desire to do something

counteract = act against

reflection = a thought; also something that bounces back

framing = making; designing

administered = managed or run by

oblige = require

▶ Why does Madison believe that different "devices" are needed to prevent the potential abuses of government?

▶ How did the new Constitution use "ambition" to counteract "ambition"? What steps did it take to make the government control itself?

Because the Federalists published *The Federalist Papers*, many historians refer to the writings of the Anti-Federalists as the "*Anti-Federalist Papers.*" This name simply refers to the best essays and pamphlets written by those against ratification of the Constitution.

Clashing Viewpoints on a Bill of Rights

For the EOC, you should know that the Anti-Federalists insisted that a bill of rights be added to the Constitution.

A **bill of rights** is a list of rights guaranteed to individuals, such as freedom of religion or freedom of speech. In Chapter 2, you learned how King John had granted his subjects certain rights in 1215, and how Parliament issued the English Bill of Rights in 1689.

After the American colonies achieved their independence, most states included a bill of rights in their state constitutions. However, the idea of a bill of rights was hardly discussed at all at the Constitutional Convention, where it was quickly dismissed.

The **Anti-Federalists** strongly criticized the absence (*lack*) of a bill of rights in the new Constitution. They felt that this revealed that the true aim of the authors of the Constitution was actually to rob the people of their liberties. For this reason, they would not support the new Constitution unless a bill of rights was added.

Federalists argued that, while a bill of rights might be helpful in a monarchy, it was quite unnecessary in a government formed by the people themselves. This was because government power was already in the hands of the people.

Even so, to win support for the Constitution in the state ratifying conventions, the Federalists finally promised to add a bill of rights. This helped persuade several states to ratify the Constitution.

After the Constitution was adopted, the Federalists kept their word. The first Congress proposed a bill of rights in the form of several amendments in 1789.

Ten proposed amendments were quickly ratified by the states and became part of the Constitution by 1791. These first ten amendments became known as the **"Bill of Rights."** The First Amendment may be the most famous one. It guarantees freedom of speech, freedom of the press, the right to assemble, the right to petition the government, and freedom of religion. You will learn more about this and the other amendments in the Bill of Rights in Chapter 10.

Pretend you are a Federalist who supports ratification of the Constitution. Write a letter to a friend giving your views.

It is clear that we need a stronger national government. But many fear that the new federal government under the proposed Constitution will oppress us. I disagree. We will be protected by several important constitutional principles.

The separation of powers will protect us by ______________________________

______________________________.

The system of checks and balances will protect us by ______________________________

______________________________.

For these reasons, I believe you should support ratification of the Constitution.

The Active Citizen

- How were the "Founding Fathers" (*those who framed our system of government*) influenced by the ideas of Locke and Montesquieu, which you studied in Chapter 2?
- Imagine that your class is a state convention in 1788, deciding whether or not to ratify the new Constitution. Some members of the class should pretend to be Federalists. Others should pretend to be Anti-Federalists. Your "convention" should then debate the question of ratification. Be sure to consider the absence of a bill of rights as part of the debate. After the debate is over, your class should take a vote on whether the Constitution should be ratified.
- Imagine it is 1788. Write your own newspaper article for or against ratification of the Constitution. Also make your own political cartoon to accompany your article.

THE
New-England Courant.

Add your cartoon below.

Name ______________________________

Make a question relating to each box of words and phrases. Then exchange questions with a classrooom partner and answer them.

Constitution
Preamble
"We the People"
Posterity
Ordain

More perfect Union
Justice
Domestic tranquility
Common defense
General welfare
Blessings of liberty

Article I
Congress
House of Representatives
Senate
Senator

Article II
President
Vice President
Execute the laws
Commander in Chief

Article III
Judicial Branch
National court system
Supreme Court
Supreme Court Justice

The Global Impact of the U.S. Constitution

For the EOC, you should know how the U.S. Constitution has influenced other countries.

Not surprisingly, the U.S. Constitution has had a direct influence on the development of other nations' governments. The British believed they had an "unwritten constitution," which developed over centuries. Thomas Paine said there really could be no such thing. He pointed out that a constitution was something that had to be written down before a government was established. Paine concluded: "The constitution of a country is not the acts of its government, but of the people constituting its government."

What was new about the U.S. Constitution was that it was a single written document that provided all the basic rules for the government and its powers, as well as the rights of citizens. The ways in which it was written and adopted were also new. These helped ensure that the constitution expressed the will of the people.

The U.S. Constitution has had a direct **influence on other governments**. Several of its features have often been copied by other countries in their own constitutions:

- Beginning with a preamble that identifies the people as the source of all political power.
- Establishing a system of federalism in which power is divided between the national government and the state governments.
- Calling the head of the executive branch the "President."
- Making the constitution superior to all other laws.
- Having special rules for amending the constitution that differ from the rules for passing an ordinary law.
- Holding a convention to write the constitution and having a special ratifying process to approve it.
- Including a bill of rights.

There were fifteen new written constitutions in Europe between 1787 and 1800. Many of these showed the influence of the United States. Belgium's constitution of 1787, for example, named the country the "United States of Belgium." The Polish Constitution of 1791 borrowed much of its preamble from the U.S. Constitution. France adopted several constitutions during the years of the French Revolution.

In the nineteenth century, many of the newly independent countries of Latin America were influenced by the U.S. Constitution. Once they gained their independence, these countries chose to become republics like the United States, rather than constitutional monarchies. Following the United States, many of them adopted a federal system and called their head of state the "President." In the late twentieth century, many former colonies in Africa and Asia were influenced by the U.S. Constitution when they became independent. The countries of Eastern Europe were influenced by the American example when they rewrote their constitutions at the end of the Cold War (1945–1991).

Today, many countries continue to have constitutions that share features with the U.S. Constitution. Australia, Canada, Germany, Switzerland, Mexico, Brazil and Nigeria all have federal systems like the United States, where power is divided between the national and regional governments. More than 40 countries, including Mexico, Argentina, Indonesia, and Nigeria, have presidents as their head of state. Others, including France, have a mixed system with both a president and a prime minister. Almost all constitutions now have a special process for amendment and a bill of rights. All these examples demonstrate the enduring influence of the U.S. Constitution and later Bill of Rights on the governments of other countries.

Comparing the First and Final Drafts of the Preamble

Enrichment

The Constitution that was passed by the Constitutional Convention and later ratified by the states went through more than one draft (*written version*). The first draft of the Constitution was submitted to the Constitutional Convention on August 6, 1787. It began with this Preamble:

> *"We the people of the States of New Hampshire, Massachusetts, Rhode Island and Providence Plantations, Connecticut, New York, New Jersey, Pennsylvania, Delaware, Maryland, Virginia, North Carolina, South Carolina, and Georgia do ordain, declare, and establish the following Constitution for the Government of Ourselves and our Posterity."*

A later draft of the Constitution was finally approved by the Constitutional Convention on September 17, 1787. Its Preamble stated:

> *"We the People of the United States, in order to form a more perfect Union, establish justice, insure domestic tranquility, provide for the common defense, promote the general welfare, and secure the blessings of liberty to ourselves and our posterity, do ordain and establish this Constitution for the United States of America."*

Look at the two versions of the Preamble above. Compare the first draft of the Preamble to the Constitution with the final version.

- What changes do you see? ______________________________

____

- What do these changes tell us about the purpose of the Preamble? ______________

____

Fill in the chart below.

Separation of Powers	
Define this constitutional principle:	How does the separation of powers differ from other constitutional principles?
Give an example of something in the Constitution illustrating the separation of powers:	Give an example ***not*** illustrating the separation of powers:

Name ____________________________________

Fill in the chart below.

Checks and Balances	
Define this constitutional principle:	How do checks and balances differ from other constitutional principles?
Give an example of something in the Constitution illustrating checks and balances:	Give an example ***not*** illustrating checks and balances:

▸ How does the separation of powers differ from checks and balances?

Think about what characteristics they have in common. For example, both are important principles of the U.S. Constitution. Then think about what characteristics each principle has that are not shared with the other principle. Finally, complete the Venn shown here.

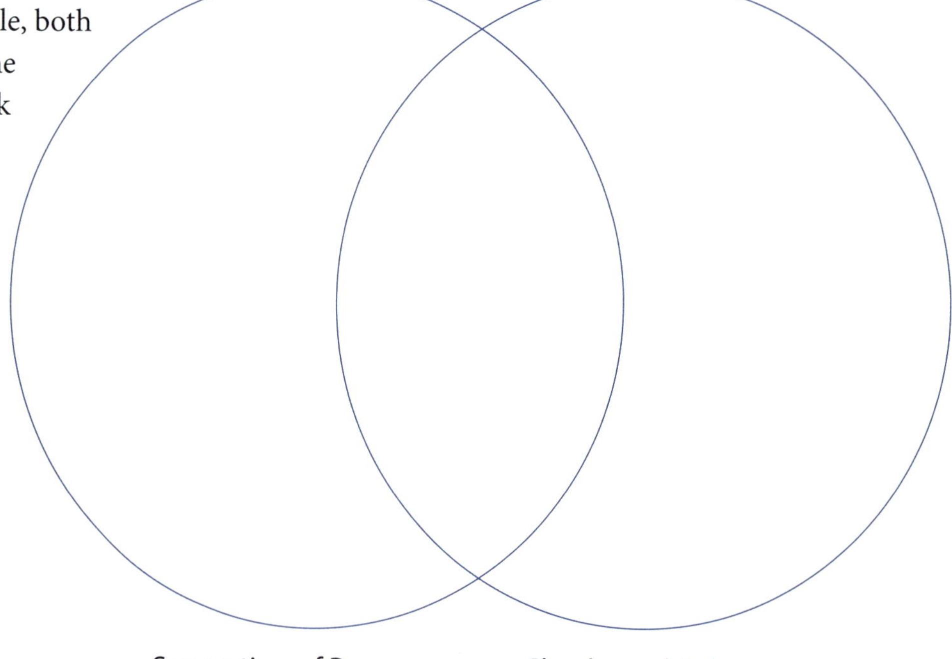

Name ______________________________

Fill in the chart below.

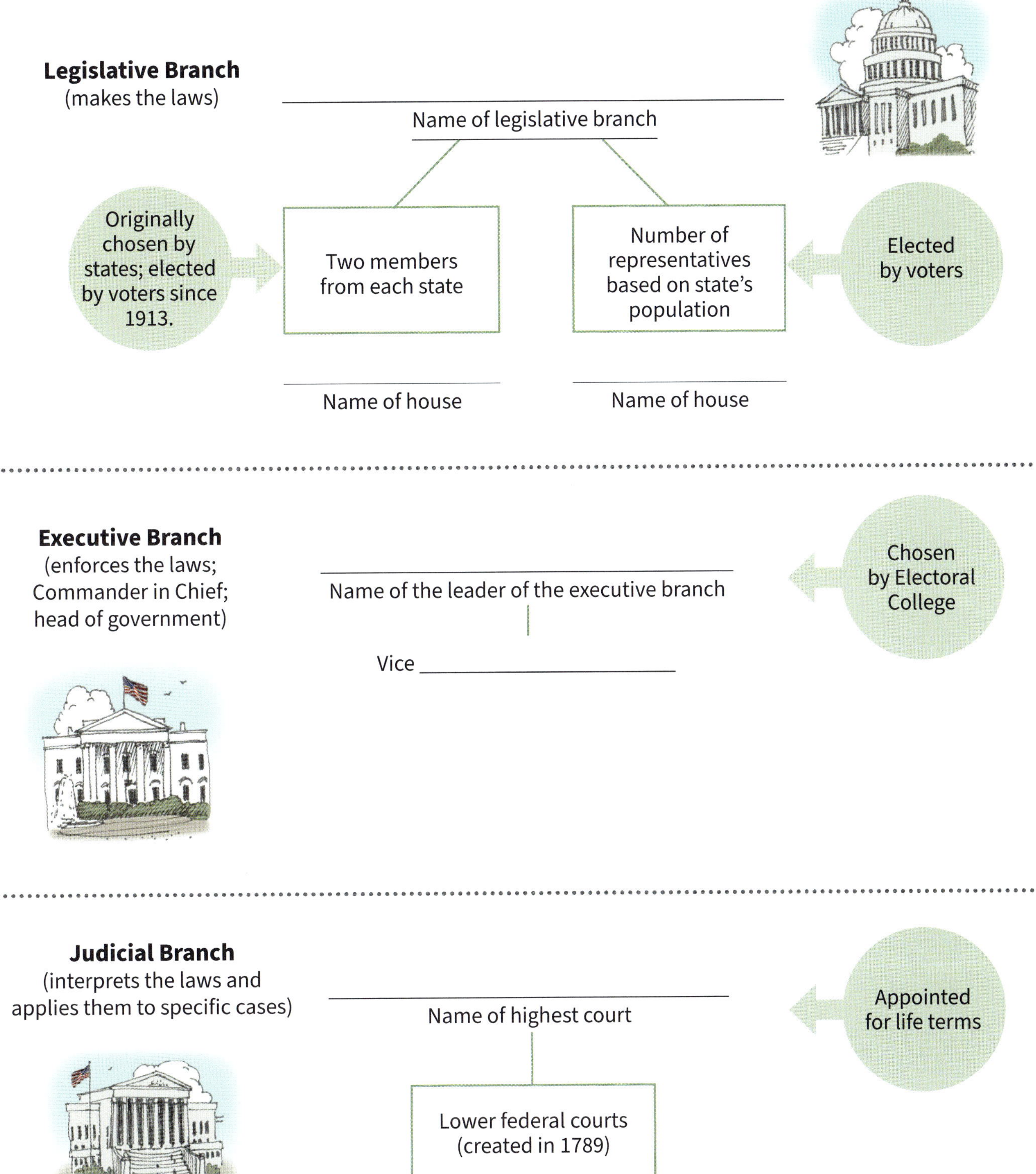

Checks and Balances

- Why did the authors of the Constitution create this system of checks and balances?
- Does the Constitution have too many checks?

Review Cards: A Quick Tour of the Constitution

The Preamble

The **U.S. Constitution** established our system of government more than 200 years ago. The first section of the Constitution is the **Preamble**, or introduction. It begins with the words "**We the People,**" indicating that the Constitution is the work of the American people. The government it created depends on the people for its power and exists to serve them. The Preamble serves as an introduction to the Constitution. It states six goals and purposes (*reasons*) for establishing our **national government**:

(1) To "**form a more perfect Union**": The new national government would be stronger and more unified than the government under the Articles of Confederation. Under the Articles of Confederation, for example, states had taxed one another's goods, hurting the national economy. Under the new government, which would unite the country, Americans would act together. Congress would regulate trade between the states.

(2) To "**establish justice**": This is one of the roles of governments generally. Unlike the Articles of Confederation, this new government would have a national court system.

(3) To "**ensure domestic tranquility**" (*peace at home*): Shays' Rebellion had demonstrated that the national government needed greater resources to insure peace and to maintain order.

(4) To "**provide for the common defense**": Several potential threats had shown the need for a stronger national government to defend American interests against foreign powers.

(5) To "**promote the general welfare**": The new national government would promote the "general welfare"—the general well-being of all its citizens.

(6) To "**secure the blessings of liberty**": "Liberty" (*individual freedom*) was one of the "unalienable" rights mentioned in the Declaration of Independence. Only by being strong, however, could the new national government protect liberty and other individual rights.

The Structure of Our Constitution: Article I

Article I: Congress: the **legislative branch**—makes the laws.

- Two houses: Senate and House of Representatives.
- Every state has two Senators.
- Each state is represented in the House of Representatives in proportion to its population.
- "Enumerated" Powers: the specific powers of Congress listed in the Constitution, such as to coin money and declare war.
- Necessary and Proper Clause, also known as the Elastic Clause: Congress has whatever other powers it needs to carry out its enumerated powers.
- A bill must pass both houses of Congress and be approved by the President to become a law. Two-thirds of each house of Congress can override the President's veto.
- You will learn more about Congress in Chapter 6.

The Structure of Our Constitution: Article II

Article II: The President—the **executive branch**—carries out the laws.

- The President enforces our federal laws.
- The President also acts as Commander in Chief of our armed forces.
- The President must be a natural-born citizen and be at least 35 years old.
- The President can be impeached and removed by Congress for misconduct.
- You will learn more about the Presidency in Chapter 7.

The Structure of Our Constitution: Article III

Article III: The Supreme Court: the **judicial branch**—interprets and applies the laws.

- The Supreme Court is the highest court in the land.
- Federal judges hold their offices for life during "good behavior."
- Congress was given the power to create lower federal courts.
- You will learn more about the Supreme Court in Chapter 8.

The Structure of Our Constitution: Other Articles

Other articles (Articles IV–VII) of the Constitution concerned relations with the states, how to ratify (*approve and adopt*) the new Constitution, and how to amend (*change or add to*) the Constitution. You will learn more about these articles in Chapters 10 and 12.

The Ratification Debate

Based on Article VII, the proposed Constitution had to be ratified (*approved*) by special state conventions. At least 9 states had to ratify it for adoption. A lively debate took place in each state over ratification—whether the new Constitution should be adopted.

- **Anti-Federalists:** The **Anti-Federalists** opposed ratification. They felt the new national government, proposed by the Constitution, would be too strong and would threaten individual rights and liberties. They also demanded that a "**bill of rights**" be included in the Constitution. Their demand for a bill of rights became the most important difference between the Federalists and the Anti-Federalists.
- **The Federalists:** The **Federalists** supported ratification of the new Constitution. They believed the country needed a stronger government for defense against foreign powers and to ensure tranquility (*calm*) at home. They argued that the national government created by the Constitution would not become too powerful because power would be divided among the three separate branches of the national government, and each branch would check the other branches.

How the Constitution Limits the Government's Powers

Limited government: The Constitution gave the new national government only limited powers.

Separation of Powers: The powers of the national government are divided among three branches: the legislative, executive, and judicial. Each branch has its own function.

Checks and Balances: Each branch of the national government has specific powers to check the other branches; for example, the President can veto legislation; the Senate can refuse to confirm a nomination or to ratify a treaty; the Supreme Court can decide that a law is unconstitutional. This was to prevent any one branch from becoming too strong.

Individual Rights: The Constitution and Bill of Rights guarantee many individual rights that government cannot take away.

Rule of Law: We are all subject to the same rules. Government officials must act according to the law.

Due Process of Law: The government cannot take away our life, liberty or property without a fair, reasonable and public process or procedure.

Illustrate with Quotations How the Constitution Limits Government

Your teacher will divide your class into five groups. Each group will be assigned one of the constitutional principles limiting government power on the chart on the next page. Your group should (1) identify the articles where your assigned principle is found in the Constitution, and (2) illustrate that principle with a quotation from one of the "Founders" who attended the Constitutional Convention. Your group should look at the back of this book for a copy of the Constitution to identify the articles where the principle is found. They can find quotations by the Founders in Chapters 3 and 4 of this book, or on the Internet. The members of your group should place their answers in the chart on the next page. Then they should fill in the rest of the chart using the information and examples found by other groups.

For example, for the system of checks and balances a group might use this quotation, which can be found in Madison's writings online:

> *"Place three individuals in a situation [in which] the interest of each depends on the voice of the others, and give to two of them an interest opposed to the rights of the third. Will the latter be secure?"*
>
> —James Madison, 1821

- What is Madison saying in this quotation about the power of two branches of government to check the actions of a third branch?

The quotation in the Enrichment section on page 116 might also be used to illustrate the concept of checks and balances.

Name ________________________________

Fill in the chart below.

Constitutional Principles Limiting Government Power

	Article(s)	Quotation
Separation of Powers		
Checks and Balances		
Individual Rights		
Rule of Law		
Due Process of Law		

Name ___________________________

Complete the following text.

The Story of Our Constitution

The 55 members of the Constitutional Convention assembled in Philadelphia on May 25, 1787. They continued their meetings until late September. They met in the same building where the members of the Second Continental Congress had signed the ___________________________ eleven years earlier.

In 1787, the delegates were sent to Philadelphia to revise the ____________________. They quickly decided to replace them with a whole new constitution and a stronger national government. They generally agreed that the new national government should have three separate branches, including an __________________ branch and a __________________ branch, as well as a legislative branch.

The new legislature was to be known as Congress. Most of the delegates believed that Congress should have two houses, like the British Parliament. Delegates from larger states, such as Virginia, proposed that the number of representatives each state had in Congress should be based on ______________ ______________. Members from smaller states, such as New Jersey, disagreed. They argued that in Congress, the number of representatives that each state had should be ____________________ ___________________________________.

This dispute over representation in Congress was only finally resolved when the representatives from Connecticut proposed a skillful compromise. They proposed that the two houses of Congress should be organized differently. In the Senate, each state would have ________________. In the House of Representatives, each state would have ___________________________________.

This "Great Compromise" explains the way in which our Congress is still organized today.

The members of the Constitutional Congress also discussed how the President, the head of the new executive branch, should be chosen. Many delegates feared that average citizens did not know individual leaders well enough to choose the President themselves. So they decided that the President would be selected by the ____________________. Each state would have a number of electors equal to the number of that state's Senators and ______________ in Congress.

The members of the Constitutional Convention further set up a process for approval of the Constitution by the people. Before it could be adopted, the new Constitution had to be ______________ by at least nine of the thirteen states. Those who favored adopting the new Constitution became known as the ______________________. Those who opposed the new Constitution became known as the ______________________. One of their strongest criticisms was that the proposed Constitution lacked a ___________________________. By June 1788, enough states had approved the Constitution for it to go into effect. Some of the largest states, like Virginia and New York, actually approved the Constitution after this date. George Washington became our first President in 1789. We are still governed by the same Constitution more than 200 years later.

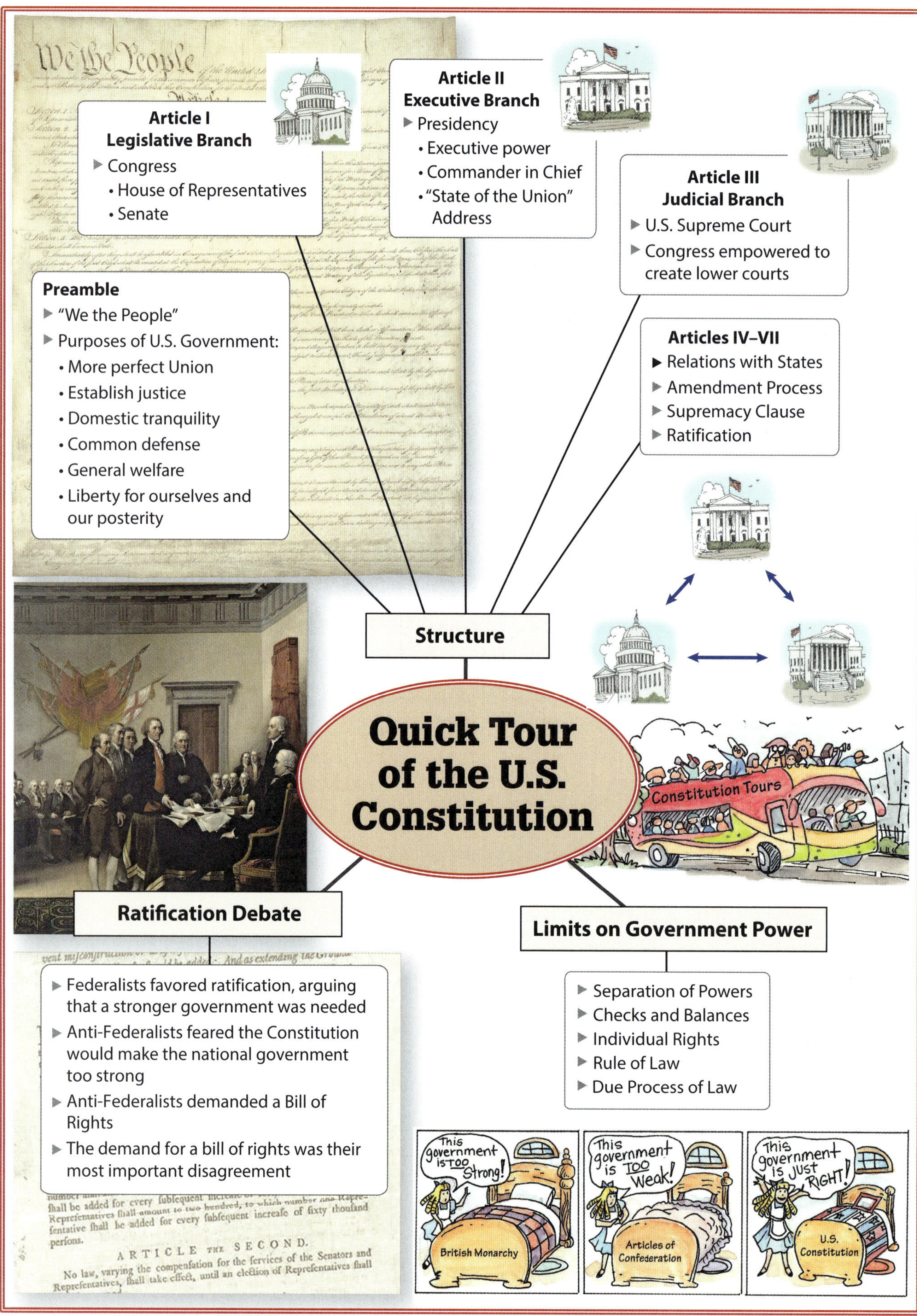
Quick Tour of the U.S. Constitution
Structure
Preamble
▶ "We the People"
▶ Purposes of U.S. Government:
• More perfect Union
• Establish justice
• Domestic tranquility
• Common defense
• General welfare
• Liberty for ourselves and our posterity
Article I
Legislative Branch
▶ Congress
• House of Representatives
• Senate
Article II
Executive Branch
▶ Presidency
• Executive power
• Commander in Chief
• "State of the Union" Address
Article III
Judicial Branch
▶ U.S. Supreme Court
▶ Congress empowered to create lower courts
Articles IV–VII
▶ Relations with States
▶ Amendment Process
▶ Supremacy Clause
▶ Ratification
Constitution Tours
Ratification Debate
▶ Federalists favored ratification, arguing that a stronger government was needed
▶ Anti-Federalists feared the Constitution would make the national government too strong
▶ Anti-Federalists demanded a Bill of Rights
▶ The demand for a bill of rights was their most important disagreement
Limits on Government Power
▶ Separation of Powers
▶ Checks and Balances
▶ Individual Rights
▶ Rule of Law
▶ Due Process of Law
This government is Too Strong!
British Monarchy
This government is Too Weak!
Articles of Confederation
This government is Just RIGHT!
U.S. Constitution
We the People
ARTICLE THE SECOND.
No law, varying the compensation for the services of the Senators and Representatives, shall take effect, until an election of Representatives shall

What Do You Know?

SS.7.CG.1.8

1. Why did the *Preamble* to the Constitution begin with the phrase, "We the People"?

   A. to indicate that the national government had limited powers

   B. to indicate that the states had been associated in a confederation

   C. to indicate that federal power was separated among three branches

   D. to indicate that the American people were the ultimate source of its authority

SS.7.CG.1.8

2. Which identifies one of the goals of government listed in the Preamble?

   A. to guarantee employment to all citizens

   B. to expand the nation's frontiers westward

   C. to establish independence from Great Britain

   D. to protect the rights and freedom of all citizens

SS.7.CG.1.9

3. The chart below shows the organization of the government of the United States, based on the Constitution.

The Legislative Branch: makes laws	The Executive Branch: enforces laws	The Judicial Branch: applies laws and settles disputes
Article I: Congress	Article II: Presidency	Article III: Supreme Court

   Which way in which the Constitution limited the power of government is illustrated by the chart?

   A. individual rights

   B. due process of law

   C. checks and balances

   D. separation of powers

SS.7.CG.1.9

4. When the President nominates an individual to serve as Secretary of State, the Senate must confirm the appointment. Which feature of the Constitution, limiting the power of government, does this illustrate?

   A. checks and balances

   B. separation of powers

   C. popular sovereignty

   D. due process of law

SS.7.CG.1.9

5. The list below provides three examples of actions by the U.S. government.

> - The President meets with the Prime Minister of the United Kingdom.
> - The Supreme Court applies an existing law to a new situation.
> - Congress passes a new environmental law.

Which feature of the Constitution do these examples illustrate?

A. limited government
B. due process of law
C. separation of powers
D. checks and balances

SS.7.CG.1.9

6. Which example illustrates the system of checks and balances?

A. The President vetoes legislation proposed by Congress.
B. The President confers with the members of the Cabinet.
C. The Supreme Court interprets the application of a law passed by Congress.
D. A state sets its own student learning standards while Congress regulates trade between states.

SS.7.CG.3.3

7. Which part of government in the U.S. Constitution was given the role of enforcing national laws?

A. Congress
B. the President
C. the Supreme Court
D. the House of Representatives

SS.7.CG.1.10

8. What was one of the Anti-Federalists' strongest arguments against the Constitution?

A. It did not create a national executive.
B. It did not include a list of protected rights for individuals.
C. The new central government would be too dependent on the states.
D. The new central government would be too weak to protect American interests abroad.

SS.7.CG.1.10

9. What was one outcome of the debate between Federalists and Anti-Federalists over the ratification of the Constitution?

A. the addition of the Bill of Rights
B. the state governments won the right to secede
C. the creation of a second house in Congress
D. the Federalists agreed to weaken the powers of the Presidency

CHAPTER 6

Congress: Our Legislative Branch

SS.7.CG.3.3 Describe the structure and function of the three branches of government established in the U.S. Constitution. (*This chapter describes the structure and function of Congress. For the other branches, see Chapters 7 and 8.*)

SS.7.CG.3.7 Explain the structure, functions and processes of the legislative branch of government. (*This chapter explains the legislative branch at the national level. For the local and state levels, see Chapter 12.*)

Content Focus Vocabulary in This Chapter

General powers described in Article I

Legislative branch

Congress

Structure of the legislative branch

House of Representatives

Senate

U.S. Congressmen/ U.S. Congresswomen

Functions of the legislative branch

Roles and responsibilities of the legislative branch

Enumerated powers

Delegated powers

Concurrent powers

Implied powers

"Necessary and proper"

Elastic Clause

Appointment confirmation

Processes of the legislative branch

Committees

Committee selection

How a bill becomes a law

Lawmaking process

Florida "Keys" to Learning

1. Article I established **Congress** as the **legislative branch**, or law-making part, of our national government.

2. **Structure of the legislative branch:** Congress has two chambers or "houses": the **House of Representatives** and the **Senate**. The House has 435 members. The number of representatives each state has in the House is proportional to the size of its population. Members of the House are known as Representatives, or **U.S. Congressmen** and **U.S. Congresswomen**. In the Senate, there are 100 members, known as **Senators.** Each state has 2 Senators.

3. **Functions of the legislative branch/Roles and responsibilities of the legislative branch:** The main role and responsibility of Congress is passing laws for the nation. Congress has the **general powers described in Article I**. These are known as the **enumerated powers** (*powers listed in the Constitution*). These enumerated powers are specifically listed in Article I, Section 8. They are also known as **delegated powers**, because these powers are delegated (*given*) to Congress. These powers include the power to tax and spend, to coin and print money, to declare war, to raise and support the armed forces (*army, navy, air force and marines*), to pass naturalization laws (*laws for how a foreign resident can become a U.S. citizen*), to pass laws for the regulation of immigration (*who can come to stay in the United States*), and to pass laws for the regulation of trade between states and with foreign countries.

4. **Concurrent powers** are those powers held by both the national government and the states, such as the power to tax.

5. Congress also has **implied powers**. These powers are not specifically listed in the Constitution. Instead, they are based on the "**Necessary and proper**" Clause. This clause gives Congress the power to make "all laws which shall be **necessary and proper** for carrying into execution" the enumerated powers. This clause permits Congress to do whatever it reasonably needs to do to perform its enumerated powers. It is also known as the **Elastic Clause** because it stretches the powers of Congress.

6. A second role of Congress is to check the other branches. For example, there is a system of **appointment confirmation.** Presidential appointments must be confirmed (*approved*) by the Senate. The Senate also must ratify (*approve*) all treaties (*official agreements between the United States and other countries*) before they go into effect, giving it a role in foreign relations (*relations with other countries*). Congress has the power of impeachment. This is the power to impeach (*accuse*) and remove the President and other officials from office.

7. Congress itself can be checked in several ways. The President can veto (*turn down; refuse*) legislation passed by Congress. Congress can only override the President's veto with a vote of two-thirds of each house. The Supreme Court can declare Congressional laws to be unconstitutional.

8. Constitutional qualifications are the requirements the Constitution states someone must meet to hold an office. To become a Representative, a person must be at least 25 years old, have been a U.S. citizen for at least seven years, and live in the state represented. To be a Senator, a person must be at least 30 years old, have been a U.S. citizen for at least nine years, and live in the state represented.

9. The key leaders of Congress are the Speaker of the House (*the leading member of the majority party in the House*), the Vice President of the United States (*who serves as President of the Senate*), and the President pro tempore of the Senate (*the leading member who presides over the Senate when the Vice President is absent*). Each house of Congress also has a majority leader, who directs the party members in that house with the most members. A minority leader leads members of the other major party in each house. (See Chapter 14 for political parties.)

10. **Processes of the legislative branch:** Congress does much of its work in **committees** (*small groups*

of people). Each committee usually consists of members of each party in the same proportion as they are in the whole house. House and Senate leaders decide on **committee selection** (*who is assigned to each committee*). Committee assignments are then approved by a vote of house members.

11. There are three types of Congressional committees. Standing committees are permanent committees that deal with all bills on particular subjects. Special committees, also known as select committees, are created for specific and temporary purposes. Conference committees are formed by members of both houses. The members of the conference committee work together to eliminate differences between the versions of a bill passed in each house. They amend the bill so that the exact same wording for the bill is passed by each house.

12. **How a bill becomes a law:** A bill is a proposed law. To become a law, a bill must pass through the **lawmaking process** (*steps to become a law*). First, it is introduced by a Representative or Senator in one of the two houses. Then it is sent to a standing committee, where it can either be set aside for consideraton later, disapproved or approved. If the bill is approved by the committee, it is reintroduced to the whole house. The whole house then debates and votes on the bill. If the bill is approved by a majority vote (*more than half*) in one house, it goes through the same stages in the other house. If approved by the second house, it goes to a conference committee to iron out differences between the two versions of the bill. Each house then votes to approve the same modified bill.

13. Lastly, the bill goes to the President for final approval. The President can sign, veto (*reject; refuse to accept*) or "pocket veto" (*not sign before the end of the session*) the bill. Congress can override the President's veto with a two-thirds majority in each house.

The delegates to the Constitutional Convention energetically debated which powers should be given to the new federal government. Following the suggestions of the Baron de Montesquieu, they separated the new government's powers among three branches. They hoped that each branch would watch over the others, making sure that no single branch becomes too powerful or oppressive (*abusive*). Congress was viewed at the time as the most powerful branch of government. Under the "Great Compromise," Congress was given two houses. The division of Congress into two houses was seen as another way to limit its power. For a bill (*a proposed law*) to become law, a majority (*more than half*) of both houses of Congress would be needed to approve it.

In this chapter, you will learn more about Congress, the legislative branch of our national government.

The Structure of Congress

> "All legislative powers . . . shall be vested in a Congress of the United States . . ."
>
> —U.S. Constitution, Article I, Section 1

Article I of the Constitution created **Congress** as the **legislative branch**. It makes all federal laws. The "structure" of something is how it is made up or put together. The **structure of the legislative branch**, consists of two separate houses or chambers: the **Senate** and the **House of Representatives**.

The Senate
100 members: Each state has two Senators

The House of Representatives
435 members: States are represented in proportion to the size of their population.

Be sure to know the enumerated and implied powers of Congress for the EOC test.

The Powers of Congress

The **functions of the legislative branch** (*its purpose; what it does*) are based on its roles and **responsibilities**. Its most important responsibility is passing laws for the nation. To meet these responsibilities, the Constitution gave Congress the **general powers described in Article I**.

The "Enumerated" Powers

The specific powers of Congress are listed in Article I, Section 8 of the Constitution. These are known as the "**enumerated**" (*listed*) **powers**. They are also known as the **delegated powers** because they are delegated, or handed over, to Congress:

1. The power to tax and to spend

Congress has the power to "lay (*raise*) and collect taxes, duties, imposts and excises, to pay the debts and provide for the common defense and general welfare of the United States." Congress thus has the power to raise money through taxes and to spend it for defense and the public welfare.

Originally, Congress' power to tax was limited to duties on imports (*foreign goods entering the U.S.*) and to taxes on the sale of some goods. The Sixteenth Amendment, passed in 1913, gave Congress the power to tax individual and corporate incomes. Since that time, income taxes have become the government's chief source of revenue (*income*). Since states also have the power to tax, this is known as a **concurrent power**—a power shared by the federal and the state governments. For more on concurrent powers, see Chapter 12.

2. The power to borrow money

Congress is able to borrow money. It does so by selling government bonds (*certificates*). These bonds entitle their owners to interest payments (*payments for the use of money*). This is also a concurrent power.

3. The power to regulate trade between states

Under the Articles of Confederation, economic rivalries between the states became intense. States restricted the flow of goods across state lines. The Constitution gave the new Congress the power "to regulate commerce with other nations, among the states, and with the Indian tribes." Commerce is the buying, selling and trading of goods and services. Commerce between parties in different states of the United States is known as "interstate commerce." Congress thus has power over the regulation of trade between states and with foreign countries. It can make rules for this trade. This is one of the most important powers of the federal government.

4. The power to regulate immigration and naturalization (*granting immigrants citizenship*)

The Constitution gave Congress the power to make laws regulating how immigrants (*those coming to the United States with the intention of staying*) can enter the United States. The regulation of immigration is by the federal government alone and is not shared with the states. Congress also is in charge of making naturalization laws (*setting rules for how immigrants living in the United States can become citizens*). See Chapter 13 for these rules.

5. The power to coin and print money, establish standard weights, and punish counterfeiters

Congress was given the power to coin and print money (*make coins and paper money*) and to "fix the standards of weights and measures." This provision allowed Congress to establish a common currency (*form of money*), ending the confusion that had existed when each state issued its own money. Congress was also given the power to punish counterfeiting (*making false money*), which became a federal crime.

6. The power to establish post offices

The Articles of Confederation had given the Confederation Congress "the sole and exclusive right and power of . . . establishing or regulating post offices from one State to another, throughout all the United States." The Constitution followed this example and gave Congress the power "to establish post offices and post roads," so that the mail might be delivered. Congress continues to regulate the U.S. Postal Service today.

7. The power to establish patents and copyrights

Copyrights provide authors with an exclusive right to their writings for a limited period of time. Patents give inventors similar exclusive rights to use, lease or sell their inventions for a limited period of time. These rights provide incentives to authors and inventors to develop new products and to share the fruits of their labors. Congress has the power to regulate both patents and copyrights.

8. The power to declare war

Only Congress can declare war. Although this power belongs solely to Congress, the President is able to send troops overseas for a short period of time in an emergency. This is part of the President's power as Commander in Chief. To prevent the President from sending troops overseas for longer periods of time without a declaration of war or the approval of Congress, Congress passed the War Powers Act in 1973. Based on this law, the President can send troops overseas in an emergency for 60 days, but must withdraw them if the approval of Congress is not obtained within that time period.

9. The power to establish a system of lower federal courts

The delegates to the Constitutional Convention could not agree on whether or not to create additional federal courts below the U.S. Supreme Court. As a compromise, it was left to the future Congress to decide. Congress was given the power to create lower federal courts but was not required to do so. When it met, the very first Congress decided to create "inferior" (*lower*) federal courts. You will learn more about these courts in Chapter 8.

10. The power to raise and support armies

The Confederation Congress had lacked the power to raise its own army. It was therefore dependent on the states. The new Constitution gave the power to raise and support armies to the federal government. Because of its powers to tax and spend money, Congress was given the power to decide on the budget (*spending allowance*) of the nation's armed forces (today, the U.S. Army, Navy, Marines, Air Force, Coast Guard, and Space Force).

11. The power to maintain a navy

Congress was given the power to build and maintain a navy, just as it is able to raise and support armies on land.

The Active Citizen

- Select one of the "delegated" or "enumerated" powers above. Then explain to another member of your class why that power is still important today. Consider the impact of the exercise of this power on the public, as well as its expense.
- Write a short letter to a friend explaining why you feel it was a good or bad idea to give the power you selected above to Congress.

The Implied Powers: The Elastic Clause

In addition to its enumerated powers, Congress also has **implied powers**. These are powers that are not directly stated in the Constitution, but that are implied (*strongly suggested*).

The basis for the implied powers is the Necessary and Proper Clause, found at the end of Article I, Section 8. (*A clause is a short section.*) This clause gave Congress the power "To make all Laws which shall be **necessary and proper** for carrying into

Execution the foregoing (*previous*) Powers, and all other Powers vested (*placed; put*) by this Constitution in the Government of the United States . . ."

The meaning of "necessary and proper" is not entirely clear. "Necessary" usually means needed, while "proper" means what is right or appropriate. Alexander Hamilton argued that the Necessary and Proper Clause gave Congress the power to create a national bank. He said that having a bank was necessary because it would help Congress to carry out its enumerated powers. Others felt that the creation of a national bank, while helpful, was not actually "necessary." They concluded that Congress had no power to create it.

In a famous case in 1819, the U.S. Supreme Court faced the same issue: did Congress have the power to establish a national bank? The creation of such a national bank was not one of the enumerated powers of Congress.

Those who interpreted the Constitution strictly made the following argument to the Court:

1. The power to create a national bank was not expressly granted to Congress by the Constitution. It was not one of the enumerated powers.
2. Congress did not absolutely need to create a national bank in order to exercise its enumerated powers. Congress could carry them out without the bank.
3. Therefore, Congress had no implied power to create a national bank.

The Supreme Court rejected this strict interpretation. Instead, it argued that it was "necessary and proper" for Congress to create a national bank in order to exercise many of its enumerated powers. The Constitution gave Congress specific powers to collect taxes and to borrow money. It also gave Congress the power to raise armies and to pay for them. Having a bank would give Congress a place to keep the money it collected from taxes. It would also create a place from which Congress could borrow money in an emergency. The Court concluded that having a bank would help Congress to carry out its enumerated powers. It was therefore "necessary and proper" for Congress to create a national bank.

> "*To its enumeration of powers* [the Constitution adds] *that of making 'all laws which shall be necessary and proper for carrying into execution the foregoing powers.'*
>
> *If the end be legitimate* (lawful and reasonable), *and within the scope* (range or limits) *of the Constitution, all the means* (ways) *which are appropriate* (proper or suitable; fitting), *which are plainly adapted to that end, and which are not prohibited, may constitutionally be employed to carry it into effect.*"
>
> —U.S. Supreme Court,
> *McCulloch v. Maryland*, 1819

The Court's interpretation gave Congress wide **implied powers.** Congress could do almost anything that was not prohibited (*forbidden*) by the Constitution, so long as it was undertaken in order to help it in the exercise of its enumerated powers.

Because the Necessary and Proper Clause stretched the powers of Congress, it has also come to be known as the **Elastic Clause**.

Other Roles and Powers of Congress

Another responsibility of Congress is checking the other branches of government. For these other roles, Congress has the following additional powers:

1. Impeachment

Congress has the "sole power of impeachment." This is the power to accuse members of the executive and judicial branches of abuses of power or unlawful activities, and to remove them from office.

In impeachment proceedings, the House of Representatives acts first. It has the power to "impeach" or accuse. Once a government official is successfully impeached in the House of Representatives, the Senate conducts an impeachment trial. Convicting the official requires a vote of two-thirds of the Senate. If the accused official is convicted, he or she is removed from office.

2. Choosing a President in Some Cases

Congress can sometimes play a role in the election of the President. The President is actually chosen by the electors of the Electoral College. The Constitution says that each state must choose a number of electors equal to the number of its Senators and Representatives combined. These electors vote for the President. If a candidate wins a majority of the electoral vote then he or she becomes the next President. However, if no candidate receives a majority, then the House of Representatives chooses the President. In this case, each state is given one vote.

3. Advice and Consent

Treaties. Congress plays a role in foreign relations (*U.S. relations with other countries*). The Constitution requires the President to obtain the "advice and consent" of the Senate for the ratification of a treaty—a solemn agreement between two or more countries. The Senate must approve (or "ratify") every treaty by a two-thirds vote.

Confirmation (*approval*) of Presidential Appointments. The President also nominates (*proposes*) and appoints ambassadors, Justices of the Supreme Court, other federal judges, and all other federal officers of the United States, including Cabinet members and military officers. The Senate must confirm (*approve*) such Presidential appointments by a simple majority vote.

For important nominations (such as a Supreme Court Justice or Cabinet member), a Senate committee usually conducts an investigation, holds hearings, and makes recommendations. Then the nomination is taken to the floor of the Senate, where it is debated and the entire Senate votes on the **appointment confirmation** (*approving the appointment*).

4. Propose Constitutional Amendments

Congress can propose amendments (*additions; changes*) to the Constitution. Amendments to the Constitution are usually proposed by a vote of two-thirds of each house of Congress. They then have to be ratified by three-fourths of the states. You will learn more about amendments in Chapter 9.

5. Investigative Powers.

Congress has powers of investigation. These are needed for Congress to perform its tasks. To write good laws, Congress needs to investigate social, economic, and political conditions. Congressional committees have the power to issue requests for documents and other evidence, and to require individuals to appear before them to answer questions and provide expert testimony.

The 435 members of the U.S. House of Representatives in full session

Structure and Powers of Congress

Structure

The Senate:
100 members. Each state has two Senators.

The House of Representatives:
435 members. Each state has a number of representatives (Congressmen and Congresswomen) in proportion to its population. Larger states thus have more representatives.

Powers

Enumerated Powers (also known as the "**Delegated Powers**"): These powers are specifically listed in Article I of the Constitution:

- The power to raise taxes and borrow money
- The power to coin and print money
- The power to raise and support the armed forces
- The power to declare war
- The power to regulate trade between states or with foreign countries
- The power to regulate immigration
- The power to regulate naturalization

Implied Powers: These powers are based on the Elastic Clause:

- The power to pass any law "necessary and proper" for carrying out the enumerated powers

Other Powers: Additional powers were given to Congress to check the other branches:

- The power to confirm Presidential appointments, including Supreme Court Justices
- The power to ratify (*approve/confirm*) treaties (*agreements with other nations*)
- The power to impeach and remove the President, federal judges and other federal officials for misconduct

Concurrent Powers: Shared with state governments

1. Which of the enumerated powers do you think are the most important? Why?

2. What limits are there to the "implied powers" of Congress?

Limits on Congressional Power

These are several important limits on the powers of Congress:

1. Some of these limits are based on the system of checks and balances. Congress can be "checked" by the other two branches (see Chapter 5). The President, for example, can veto proposed laws even though they have passed both houses of Congress.
2. The Supreme Court can rule that laws enacted by Congress are unconstitutional and therefore invalid (*not legal; not enforceable*).
3. Congress can only exercise those enumerated and implied powers granted to it by the Constitution.
4. The Constitution and the Bill of Rights prohibit Congress from passing laws denying certain individual rights. For example, Congress cannot pass a law that takes away freedom of religion. It also cannot pass a law that denies individuals the right to petition a court for a writ of habeas corpus. You will learn more about some of these specific prohibitions in Chapters 9 and 12.

Be sure to know the constitutional qualifications for serving in Congress for the EOC test. See Chapter 12 for state and local lawmakers.

Who Can Become a Member of Congress?

As you know, there are 435 Representatives in the House of Representatives. The number of seats in the House is fixed. The distribution of these seats is readjusted among the 50 states every ten years, based on their population size according to the U.S. Census.

There are constitutional qualifications (*requirements*) to hold a seat in Congress. To qualify to become a member of the House of Representatives (a **U.S. Congressman** or **Congresswoman**), an individual must:

1. Be a U.S. citizen for at least seven years;
2. Be at least 25 years old; and
3. Be a resident of the state in which he or she is elected.

Each member of the House is elected by the voters of a single Congressional district.

You also already know that there are 100 U.S. Senators in the Senate—two for each state. The constitutional qualifications for becoming a Senator are stricter than those for becoming a Representative.

To become a U.S. Senator, an individual must:

1. Be a U.S. citizen for at least nine years;
2. Be at least 30 years old; and
3. Be a resident of the state in which he or she is elected.

Senators are elected by the voters of an entire state.

There are no other constitutional requirements to serve in Congress. Most members of Congress today have backgrounds in business, law, or education.

The Active Citizen

- Why do you think the requirements for entering the Senate are stricter than for the House?
- Search on the Internet for information about the member in the House of Representatives from your Congressional district. What is his or her occupation? Why did he or she enter politics? Then write a letter asking your representative these same questions. Ask if your representative feels satisfied with what he or she has achieved by being a member of Congress. Finally, send your letter to the local office of your member of Congress and see what reply you receive.

Be sure to know the leaders of Congress and the types of committees.

Processes of the Legislative Branch: Congress at Work

Each branch of our government follows its own processes (*series of steps or actions*). Each Congressional term begins in January of an odd-numbered year, such as 2023, and lasts two years. Before the new term begins, the major political parties (the Democrats and Republicans) hold private meetings, known as "caucuses," to reach agreements on issues, and to choose leaders.

The House of Representatives on Opening Day. The term of a member of the House is two years. All members are elected to serve their two-year terms at the same time, so they all go through the process of re-election at the end of each term.

When Congress assembles for the new term, the members of the House elect the Speaker of the House, who presides over their proceedings. The Speaker is actually determined in advance by the majority party (*the party with the larger number of members*).

Next the House elects its other officers. Members are assigned to Congressional committees (*smaller working groups*) and committee chairs are appointed. Once these tasks are completed, the House sends a message to the Senate that it is ready for the President's "State of the Union" Address.

The Senate on Opening Day. The term of each Senator is six years. One third of all Senators face election every two years. Thus only one third of the Senators are serving new terms when the Senate opens. This method of electing its members provides continuity to the Senate.

The Vice President of the United States serves as the President of the Senate. The Senate also elects a "President pro tempore," who presides over the Senate when the Vice President is absent. The President pro tempore is the leading member of the majority party in the Senate. Senators are then assigned to fill vacancies on committees and other positions in the Senate.

In both the Senate and the House, the majority party chooses a majority leader—a member of their party who will manage their interests. The minority party in each house similarly chooses a minority leader. The Senate is then also ready to hear the President's "State of the Union" Address.

The President's "State of the Union" Address. The President is required by the Constitution to inform Congress of the "State of the Union." Since 1913, Presidents have personally appeared before Congress to give their "State of the Union" Address. Shortly after Congress tells the President that it is ready, the President delivers the address before Congress, other officials, and live television. The address covers both domestic and foreign affairs. It provides an agenda (or plan) for the coming term and recommends the legislation that the President believes is needed by the nation.

Congressional Committees

Imagine that your class is about to plan a party. It has to arrange music, food, decorations and invitations. It would be more efficient to divide students into several smaller groups, or "**committees**," to perform this work, rather than to have the whole class arrange all aspects of the party.

For greater efficiency, Congress is similarly organized into committees. Most of the work of Congress is actually performed in these committees. The three most important types of committees are:

Standing Committees. Each house currently has about 20 standing committees. These are by far the most important committees in Congress. Each standing committee is a permanent committee that deals with all bills on a particular subject. Standing committees continue from session to session of Congress. Each standing committee represents the entire House or Senate in miniature. The number of members each political party has on a committee reflects the strength of that party in the house as a whole. Thus, if there were 40 Democrats and 60 Republicans in the Senate,

Standing Committees: decide on bills on particular subjects

Special Committees: are temporary and formed for special purposes, such as to conduct an investigation

Conference Committees: make sure the same bill is passed by both houses

the Democrats would have 4 and Republicans would have 6 members on a standing committee of 10 there.

The chairperson of each standing committee and subcommittee belongs to the majority party. The chairperson holds important powers, such as the power to decide which of the many bills the committee will consider.

Special Committees. Each special committee (also known as a select committee) is created for a specific and temporary purpose. For example, a special committee might be formed to investigate the continuing effects of pollution in the Gulf of Mexico from the Deepwater Horizon oil spill in 2010.

Conference Committees. No bill can be sent to the White House to be signed into law unless it passes both houses in the exact same form. Members from both houses therefore act together in a conference committee to eliminate differences between the Senate and the House versions of the bill. You will learn more about the role of the conference committee in the lawmaking process in the next section of this chapter.

House and Senate leaders decide on **committee selection** (*who is assigned to each committee*). Each party makes its own selections. Committee assignments are then approved by a vote of all members of that house.

Examples of Standing Committees

House of Representatives

House Committee on Foreign Affairs

House Committee on Ways and Means

House Committee on Appropriations

Senate

Senate Committee on Foreign Relations

Senate Committee on the Judiciary

Senate Committee on Finance

The U.S. House of Representatives Finance Committee

The Active Citizen

- Research one of the standing committees from the Senate or House of Representatives on the Internet. You might also telephone or email the office of one of the members of this committee for additional information. Then give an oral presentation, PowerPoint or Prezi presentation to your class, or make a video, on the work of this committee.

How Congress is Organized

Constitutional Qualifications for Members

Senate: A Senator must be at least 30 years of age, be a U.S. citizen for 9 years and live in the state represented. Senators are elected to a 6-year term. Each Senator is elected by the voters of an entire state.

House of Representatives: A Representative must be at least 25 years of age, be a U.S. citizen for 7 years and live in the state represented. Representatives are elected to a 2-year term. Each Representative is elected by the voters of a single Congressional district.

Key Leaders

- **Speaker of the House:** Presides over House proceedings; elected by House members.
- **President pro tempore of the Senate:** Presides over Senate proceedings when the Vice President of the United States, who usually presides over the Senate, is absent.
- **Majority leader:** Manages the interests of the majority party (*the larger party*) in either the Senate or House of Representatives.
- **Minority leader:** Manages the interests of the minority party (*the smaller party*) in either the Senate or House of Representatives.

Committees

Committees are working groups of members from both parties, reflecting party strength in the house as a whole. Most of the work of Congress is done in committee.

- **Standing committees:** Permanent committees that deal with all bills on a particular topic, such as the House Committee on Foreign Affairs.
- **Special committees:** Special committees created for temporary purposes such as to conduct an investigation.
- **Conference committee:** A committee with members from both houses that eliminates differences between House and Senate versions of the same bill.

1. How do the terms for a Senator and member of the House of Representatives differ?
2. Why do the members of the House and Senate organize themselves into committees?
3. If there are 55 Republicans and 45 Democrats in the Senate, how many Republican members would there be in a standing committee of 20?

Be sure to know how a bill becomes a law for the EOC test.

The Lawmaking Process: How a Bill Becomes a Law

A bill is a proposed law. When a bill is proposed, it must go through a series of steps to become a law. This is known as the **lawmaking process**.

A Bill is Introduced

In the House of Representatives, a member of the House introduces the bill by placing it in the "hopper," a wooden box watched by the House clerk. In the Senate, a Senator introduces a bill by submitting the bill to the Senate clerk. Once the bill is introduced, it is numbered (preceded by H.R. for the House of Representatives or S. for Senate) and entered into the *House Journal* or *Senate Journal*, and the *Congressional Record*, which records all the proceedings (*activities*) of Congress.

The Committee Stage

Bills in the House are then sent to the Speaker of the House. The Speaker assigns them to the appropriate standing committee. The presiding officer of the Senate, usually the President pro tempore, decides which committee should receive bills in the Senate. The standing committee is the one that focuses on the subject of the bill.

Each committee usually receives many more bills than it has time to discuss. The chairperson of the committee has the power to decide which of the many submitted bills are actively considered by the committee. If the chairperson decides that the bill is not of great importance, the bill is pushed aside ("*pigeonholed*") and is not considered any further. Most bills, in fact, "die" in committee.

If the bill is not pushed aside, it is placed on the list of items for the committee to discuss when it meets. Using its investigative powers, the committee then conducts research on the bill. It may hold public hearings, and it may even visit locations affected by the bill. Special interest groups give their opinions. Experts and government officials may be required to appear before the committee to give testimony. The committee may make changes to the bill. Once it has approved the bill, it sends it back to the full house.

Action on the House and Senate Floors

Both houses of Congress require some discussion and debate before the final vote on any bill is taken. Members give speeches in favor of or against the bill.

Debate and Vote in the House. Due to the sheer number of Representatives in the House, strict rules limit its debate. The Speaker of the House can limit debate by selecting those members who are permitted to speak. The Speaker can also force those who are straying from the subject of the bill to stop speaking. Once a bill has been debated, the House is finally ready to vote. The bill must be approved by a majority vote (*more than half*). If the House approves the bill, the bill is sent to the Senate for consideration.

Debate and Vote in the Senate. With fewer members, rules for debate are looser in the Senate than in the House. Senators are permitted to speak freely and without any limit. They are not even required to stick to the subject of the bill. This freedom gives any Senator who opposes a bill and fears it is likely to pass the opportunity to speak endlessly for as long as he or she can remain standing. While the Senator speaks, the business of the Senate comes to a halt. This tactic of delay is called a filibuster. To end a filibuster, three-fifths of all Senators (60 Senators) must vote to limit further debate.

Once the debate is finished, the bill is put to a vote. If a majority of the Senate votes for the bill, it is sent to the House of Representatives for consideration, or if it came from there, the bill goes to a conference committee.

Conference Committee

A bill cannot become a law unless the House and Senate have both approved the bill in the ***same*** form. The exact same bill must pass each house. Yet by the time a bill has passed through each house of Congress, it has usually been amended, changing it in some way. To deal with the problems this creates, members of the House and Senate form a joint committee known as a "conference committee." This committee allows members of the two houses to confer (*talk to one another*). The conference committee reviews the different versions of the bill and then creates an acceptable compromise. This compromise bill is then sent back to both the House and Senate, where members can either vote for or against the bill. No further changes to the bill are permitted at this stage. If a majority in each house of Congress votes for the bill, then it is ready to go to the President for approval.

The President's Options

A bill that has successfully passed through both houses of Congress still requires the President's signature to become a law. This is part of our constitutional system of checks and balances.

After receiving a bill passed by Congress, the President has three options:

1. **Sign it:** The President can approve the bill by signing it. The bill then becomes a new law.
2. **Veto it :** The President can veto (*reject or disapprove*) the bill. The bill is then returned to Congress. If two-thirds of the members present in each house of Congress vote to "override" (*pass over*) the President's veto, then the bill becomes law. However, overriding a President's veto is usually difficult.
3. **Do nothing:** The President can refuse to either sign or veto a bill. Then what happens depends on whether Congress is still in session.
   - If Congress is in session at the end of the ten days (not counting Sundays), the bill becomes a law.
   - If Congress adjourns (*goes on a break*) within ten days of sending the bill to the President, the bill goes "into the President's pocket" and does *not* become a law. This method of killing a bill is known as a "pocket veto."

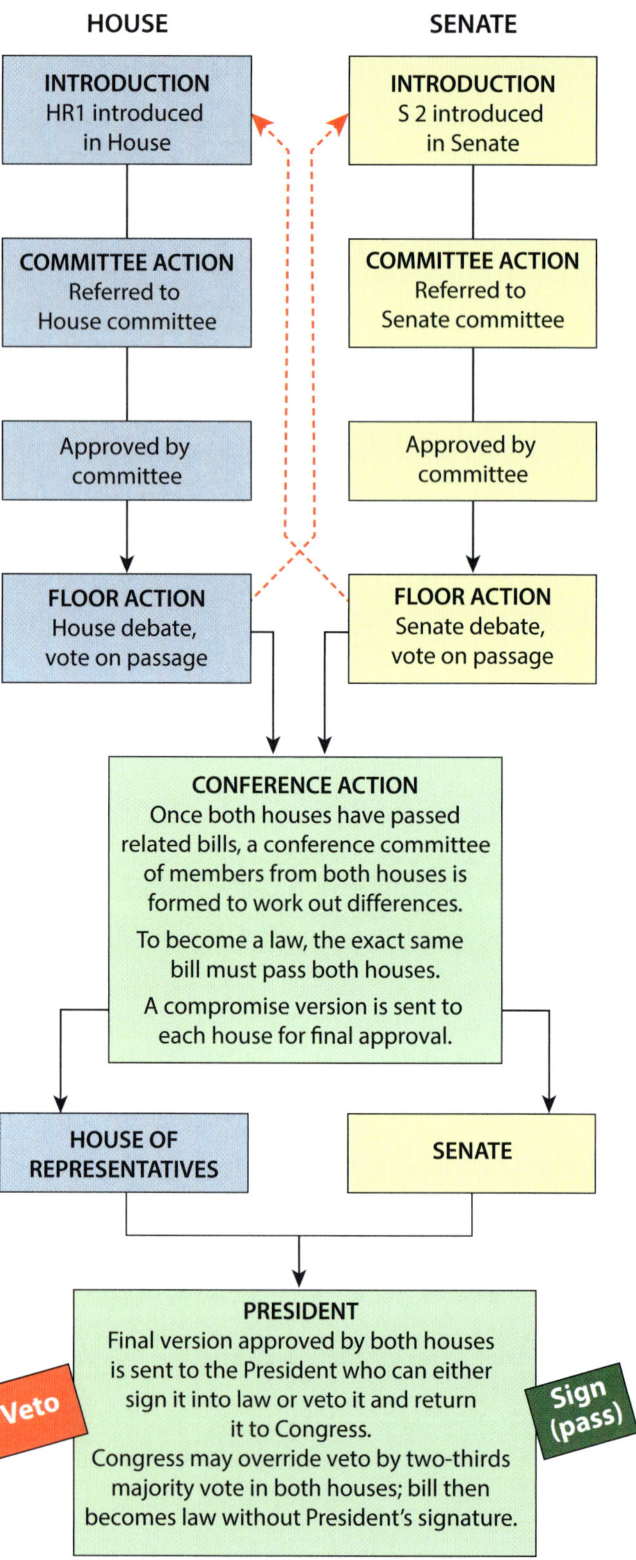

State and Local Law-making
The way in which a bill becomes a law in the State of Florida is very similar to the way in which a bill in Congress becomes a federal law. You will learn about how laws are passed at the state and local levels in Chapter 12.

The Active Citizen

▶ Why did the authors of the Constitution require the approval of the President, the head of the executive branch, before a bill could become a law?

▶ Why did the authors of the Constitution permit a two-thirds majority in each house to override the President's veto of proposed legislation?

▶ Imagine you are a member of the House of Representatives. Describe a typical day. (Hint: You might visit congress.gov for more details.)

A "Facebook" Page for Your Representative

Look up information on one of your U.S. Senators or your local member of Congress (House of Representatives). Then create a mock "Facebook" page for that Senator or House Member.

Name: ____

Position: (circle one) U.S. Senator Member of the U.S. House of Representatives for the ______________ District

About: ______________________________
____
____

Political Views: ______________________________
____
____

Worked at: ______________________________
____
____

Friends: ______________________________
____
____
____
____
____

Studied at: ______________________________
____
____

Details: ______________________________
____
____

Likes: ______________________________
____
____
____
____
____
____

Life Events: ______________________________
____
____

Photos:

Add Friend ··· | Add Friend ··· | Add Friend ··· | Add Friend ··· | Add Friend ···

Name ___________________________________

Review the following list of Congressional powers.*

Power to tax

Power to coin and print money

Power to regulate trade

Power to maintain a navy

Power to charter a national bank

Power to create a Space Force

Power to impeach federal officers

Power to approve Presidential appointments of federal officers (Senate)

Power to do whatever is "necessary and proper" to carry out the other powers

Power to investigate

Power to raise and support armies

Power to ratify treaties (Senate)

Now group these powers into the following two categories:

Enumerated/Delegated Powers*	Implied Powers

*Note: for reserved and concurrent powers, see Chapter 12

Answer these questions about the Elastic Clause:

The Elastic Clause	
What is the meaning of the Elastic Clause?	How was this clause interpreted by the U.S. Supreme Court in 1819?
What would be an example of an action taken by Congress that might be based on the Elastic Clause?	What would be an example of an action taken by Congress that could **not** be based on the Elastic Clause?

Name ___________________________________

Describe each step in the chart below, which shows how a bill becomes a law.

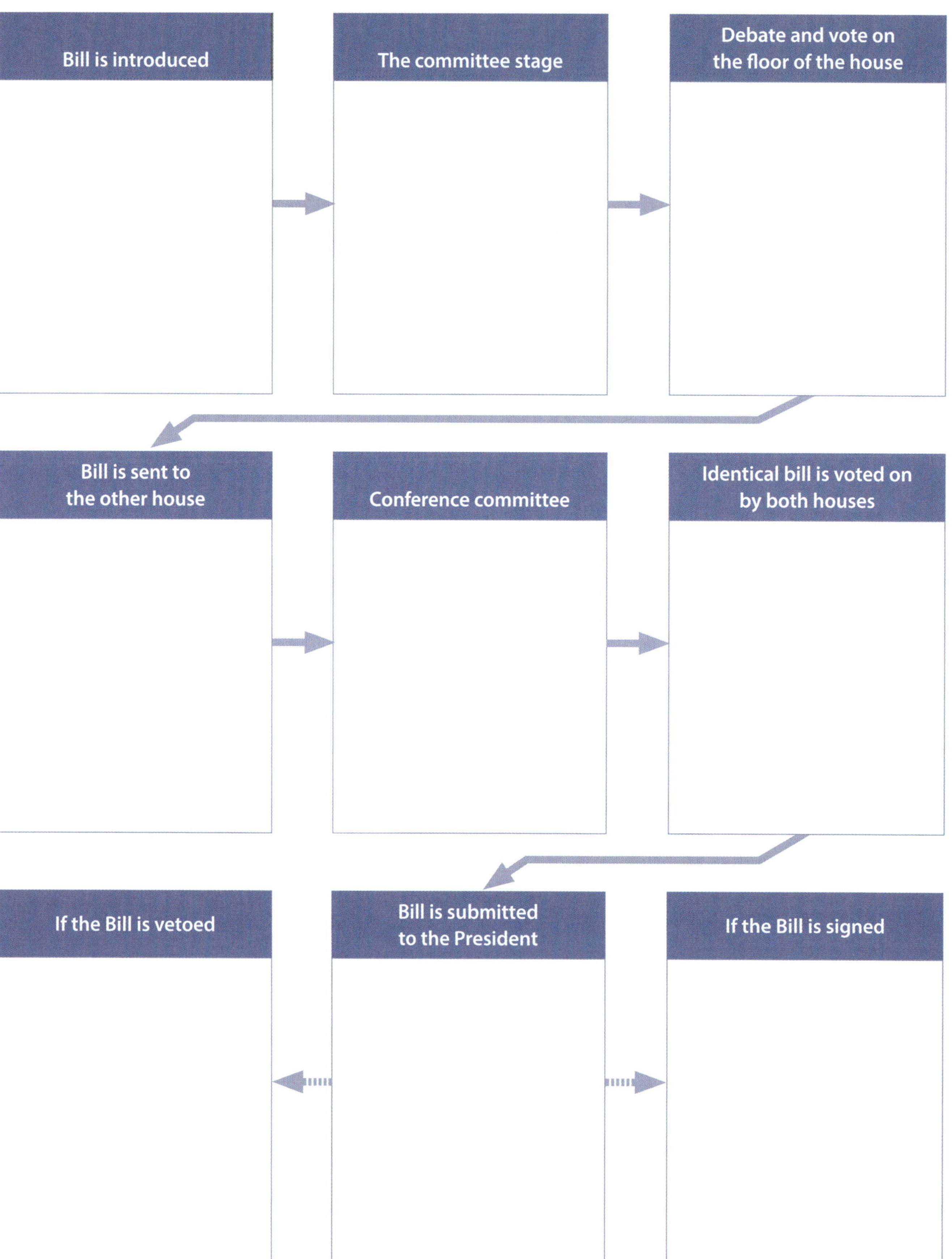

Constitutional Qualifications for Members
House: at least 25 years old; citizen for 7 years; reside in state
Senate at least 30 years old; citizen for 9 years; reside in state
Committees
Standing Committees
Special Committees
Conference Committees
House of Representatives: 435 members
Senate: 100 members
Both houses must agree to pass a law
President must sign bills
Judicial review can invalidate law
Structure
Checks on Congress
Tax
Borrow money
Coin and print money
Regulate interstate trade
Declare war
Establish patents & copyrights
Establish lower federal courts
Raise & support army and navy
Regulate immigration and naturalization
Confirm appointments
Ratify treaties
Impeach federal officials
United States Treasury
Enumerated/ Delegated Powers
Congress: Our Legislative Branch
Congressional Leaders
Speaker of the House
President Pro Tempore of the Senate
Majority and Minority Leaders
Implied Powers
Concurrent Powers
Shared with states
"Elastic" Clause: power to do what is "necessary and proper" to carry out enumerated powers
Example: create a national bank
Lawmaking Process: How a Bill Becomes a Law
Bill is introduced
Bill sent to committee
If reported favorably by committee, bill debated and voted on by house
Bill sent to other house where it goes through the same steps
Conference committee irons out differences in House and Senate versions
Bill given to President for approval or veto
Congress can override any veto with 2/3 vote in each house
UNITED STATES CONGRESS

Review Cards: Congress—Our Legislative Branch

The Structure of Congress

- Article I of the Constitution established **Congress** as the **legislative branch** (*law-making part*) of the national government.
- **The Structure of the Legislative Branch:** Congress has two houses: the **House of Representatives** and the **Senate.**
- The House has 435 members known as Representatives, or **U.S. Congressmen** and **U.S. Congresswomen**. Each state's number of Representatives is proportional to the size of its population. In the Senate, there are 100 members, known as Senators. Each state has two Senators.

The General Powers Described in Article I: The Enumerated Powers of Congress

Functions/Roles and Responsibilities of the Legislative Branch: The main role of Congress is to pass laws for the nation. The **"enumerated" powers** of Congress are those specifically listed in Article I, Section 8. They are also known as **"delegated" powers**. The first two of these (the taxing and borrowing powers) are also **concurrent powers**, shared with the states.

- Power to tax and spend
- Power to borrow money
- Power to coin and print money
- Power to declare war
- Power to raise and support armed forces
- Power to maintain a navy
- Power over the regulation of trade (between states and with foreign nations)
- Power to establish standard weights
- Power to punish counterfeiters
- Power to establish post offices
- Power to establish patent system
- Power to establish copyrights
- Power over the regulation of immigration
- Power to pass naturalization laws
- Power to establish lower federal courts

Other Powers of Congress

Additional Roles and Responsibilities of the Legislative Branch: The Constitution gives Congress several non-legislative powers (*powers other than law-making*). This is mainly because of the system of checks and balances. These non-legislative powers allow Congress to oversee and check the other branches.

- Power of impeachment—the ability to impeach the President, Vice President and other federal officers in the executive branch and to impeach Supreme Court Justices and other federal judges
- Power of **appointment confirmation**—the Senate confirms Presidential appointments by a majority vote
- Power to ratify treaties—the Senate ratifies treaties by a two-thirds vote giving it a role in U.S. foreign relations (*relations with other countries*)
- Power to propose constitutional amendments
- Power to choose the President if no candidate wins in the Electoral College—this is decided by the House of Representatives

The Implied Powers of Congress

- "Implied" means strongly suggested but not directly stated.
- The **implied powers** are not specifically listed in the Constitution but they are based on the **Elastic Clause**.
- This clause gives Congress the power "[t]o make all laws which shall be **necessary and proper** for carrying out the enumerated powers."
- Did this clause give Congress only those additional powers absolutely necessary to perform its "enumerated" powers? Or did this clause permit Congress to do anything that reasonably assisted it in performing its "enumerated" powers?
- In 1819, the U.S. Supreme Court ruled that the "Necessary and Proper" Clause gave Congress the power to do anything reasonably related to Congress's duties and not otherwise prohibited: "If the end be legitimate, and within the scope of the Constitution, all the means which are appropriate may constitutionally be employed to carry it into effect." On the basis of its **implied powers**, the Congress created a national bank. The power to create a bank was not one of the enumerated powers, but this step helped Congress to carry out its other powers. Another example of an implied power is the power of Congress to investigate an issue before passing a law.

Limits on Congressional Power

- As part of the system of checks and balances, there are important checks on Congress. The President can veto (*refuse; turn down*) legislation passed by Congress. However, Congress can override (*pass over*) the President's veto with a vote of two-thirds of each house. This turns the bill into a law despite the veto.
- Powers not given to Congress are reserved for the states and the people (see Chapter 10, for the 10th Amendment).
- Congress is prohibited from passing *ex post facto* laws, or suspending the right to request a writ of habeas corpus in peacetime (see Chapter 10).

Officers of Congress

- Speaker of the House: The leading member of the majority party, who is elected as Speaker by a vote in the House. The Speaker chairs the proceedings of the House and decides which committees bills are sent to.
- Vice President of the United States: Serves as President of the Senate and chairs proceedings of the Senate. The Vice President votes in the case of a tie in the Senate.
- President pro tempore of the Senate: The leading member of the majority party, who presides over the Senate when the U.S. Vice President is absent.
- Majority leader: Both the Senate and the House choose a majority leader—a member of the majority party who manages the interests of the party in that house of Congress.
- Minority leader: The minority party in each house similarly chooses a minority leader.

Processes of the Legislative Branch: Congressional Committees

The members of Congress organize themselves into **committees** (*small groups*) to get work done faster.

- **Standing committee:** One of several permanent committees in Congress that deals with all bills on a particular subject. Each standing committee represents the entire house (Senate or House of Representatives) in miniature. Each political party has a number of seats on the committee proportional to its representation in the house as a whole.
- **Special (or select) committee:** Committees created for a specific and temporary purpose such as to conduct an investigation.
- **Conference committee:** Members of both houses form a conference committee to eliminate differences between the versions of a bill passed in each house.

Processes of the Legislative Branch: How a Bill Becomes a Law

- **Introduction of the bill**: A bill is a proposed law. To become a law, it must go through the steps of the **lawmaking process**. Once the bill is introduced, it is numbered and submitted to the appropriate standing committee.
- **Committee stage**: The chairperson of the committee decides if the committee will consider the bill or if it should be left to die in committee. If it is considered, the committee will investigate the bill, hold public hearings, examine experts, and so on.
- **Debate and vote:** If the bill is approved by the committee, it will be sent back, often with changes, for discussion and a vote on the floor of the House or Senate. Often the bill will be amended (*changed*) in some way before it is passed. Bills need a simple majority vote (*more than half*) to pass.
- **Bill sent to other house:** Once the bill is passed in one house of Congress, it is sent to the other house, where it goes through the same stages.
- **Conference committee**: If a bill passes both houses of Congress, it is usually changed in some way in each house by amendments. To become a law, the bill must pass both houses of Congress in the same form. Members from each house join together in a conference committee, where they iron out the differences in the two versions of the bill. The same bill then goes back to both houses, which can either approve or deny the bill without amendment. If the exact same bill passes both houses, it is ready to be sent to the President for signature.
- **Submitted to the President**: The President can approve the bill, veto (*reject*) the bill with a message to Congress, or do nothing at all. If the bill is vetoed, a two-thirds (2/3) vote in each house can override the veto and pass the law. (See Chapter 12 for how state and local laws are made.)

Constitutional Qualifications: Who can be a Member of Congress?

	House of Representatives	Senate
Minimum Age	25 years old	30 years old
Minimum Length of U.S. Citizenship	7 years	9 years
Residence	Resident of state where elected	Resident of state where elected
Number of Members	435	100

What Do You Know?

SS.7.CG.2.7

1. The four individuals below are thinking of running for the office of U.S. Senator from Florida.

1.	2.	3.	4.
Joe Black was born in Canada and is 26 years old. He moved to Miami, Florida, when he was six and became a U.S. citizen in 2009.	Marisol Sanchez was born in Miami, Florida to two Cuban parents. She is now 35 years old and is a law student.	Roberto Mendez is a new arrival to Florida. He was born in New York City but has only lived in Florida two years. He is 29 years old.	Juan Fuentes was born in Cuba and has only lived in the United States for four years. He feels very strongly about immigration problems. He is 36 years old.

Which of these candidates is qualified to become a U.S. Senator?

A. Joe Black
B. Juan Fuentes
C. Roberto Mendez
D. Marisol Sanchez

SS.7.CG.3.3

2. Which is NOT an example of a delegated power?

A. regulation of trade
B. power to declare war
C. regulation of immigration
D. power to create a national bank

SS.7.CG.3.3

3. Which is an example of an "enumerated" power of Congress?

A. the power to tax exports
B. the power to declare war
C. the power to issue hunting licenses
D. the power to operate public school districts

SS.7.CG.3.3

4. The diagram on the right shows details about the U.S. government.

Which branch of government completes the diagram?

A. The Senate
B. The Cabinet
C. The Supreme Court
D. The House of Representatives

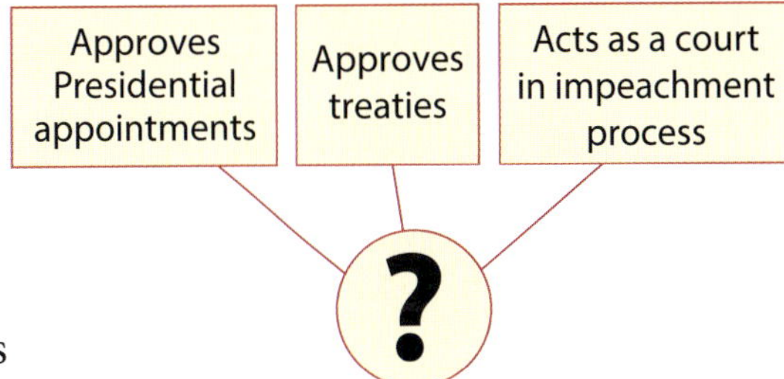

SS.7.CG.3.7

5. Why do most of the bills introduced in Congress never become law?
   A. They are defeated in floor votes.
   B. They never get out of committee.
   C. They are vetoed by the President.
   D. They are overruled by the U.S. Supreme Court.

SS.7.CG.3.7

6. In Congress, where does most of the work on bills take place?
   A. special committees
   B. standing committees
   C. conference committees
   D. floor of the House or Senate

SS.7.CG.3.7

7. What happens when the House and the Senate pass different versions of the same bill?
   A. The House bill is changed to conform to the Senate bill.
   B. The Senate bill is changed to conform to the House bill.
   C. A conference committee is appointed to resolve the differences.
   D. A standing committee from one house is chosen to resolve the differences.

SS.7.CG.3.3

8. What steps does the Constitution provide if there is persuasive evidence that the President of the United States has committed treason?
   A. The President can be arrested and forced to resign.
   B. The President can be impeached by the Supreme Court.
   C. The President cannot be removed until convicted in a court of law.
   D. The President can be impeached by the House and removed by the Senate.

SS.7.CG.3.3

9. Which action is an example of the exercise of an implied power?
   A. Congress votes to raise income taxes.
   B. Congress holds an investigation on women in the military.
   C. Congress declares war on a country for sponsoring terrorism.
   D. Congress decides to close post offices in rural areas on Saturdays.

SS.7.CG.3.7

10. A bill is passed by both the House and the Senate. The bill is then submitted to the President. Which is **not** an option for the President?

A. let the bill die in committee

B. sign the bill and it becomes law

C. veto the bill and inform Congress of the reasons for the veto

D. not sign the bill and after 10 days, if Congress is not in session, the bill dies

SS.7.CG.3.7

11. The diagram below shows some of the steps involved in passing a federal law.

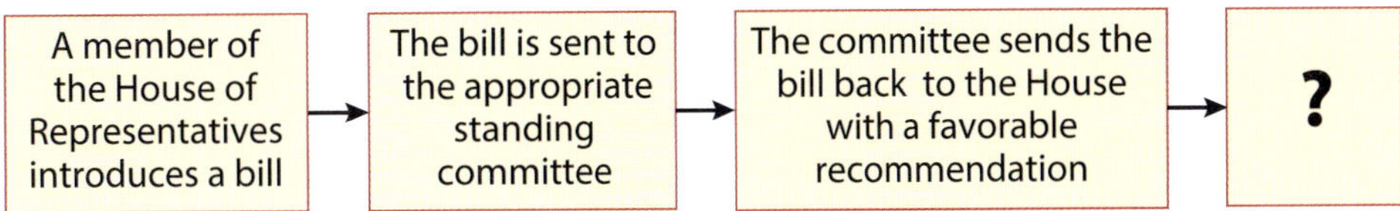

What is the next step in the lawmaking process?

A. The President signs the bill.

B. The bill is sent to the Senate.

C. The bill is sent to a conference committee.

D. The bill is debated on the floor of the House.

SS.7.CG.3.3

12. Which is an example of a check on congressional power?

A. the power of Congress to declare war

B. the power of the President to veto a bill

C. the power of the states to collect their own taxes

D. the power of the Supreme Court to try cases between states

SS.7.CG.3.7

13. Which official chairs the proceedings of the U.S. House of Representatives?

A. Sergeant-at-Arms

B. Speaker of the House

C. President pro tempore

D. Vice President of the United States

SS.7.CG.3.7

14. The President and Congress have different views on climate change. Congress sent the President a bill requiring all cars made in the United States to run on electricity. The President vetoed the bill. Which step is required to pass the bill over the President's veto?

A. approval of the bill by a majority of each house of Congress

B. approval of the bill by a majority of Supreme Court Justices

C. approval of the bill by two-thirds of each house of Congress

D. approval of the bill by three-quarters of the state legislatures

SS.7.CG.3.3

15. The Venn diagram below compares two types of powers under the U.S. Constitution.

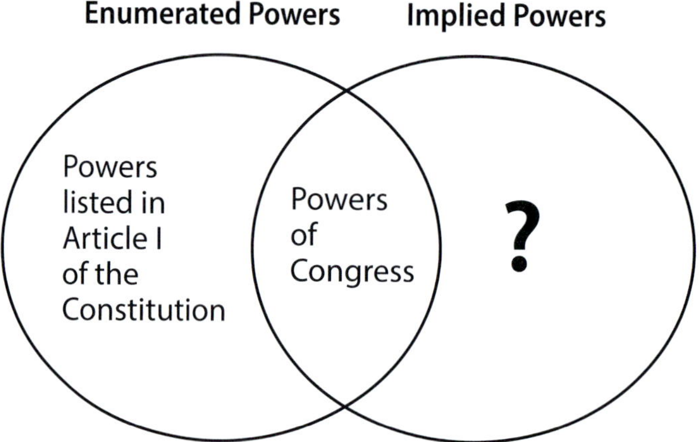

Which description completes the Venn diagram?

A. Powers required to interpret laws

B. Powers reserved for the Congress and the people

C. Powers needed to carry out the enumerated powers

D. Powers used to check the executive and legislative branches

SS.7.CG.3.7

16. What is the role of the President pro tempore of the Senate?

A. vote in the Senate in case of a tie vote

B. make sure fellow party members vote on important bills

C. preside over Senate proceedings if the Vice President is absent

D. become the next President of the United States if the President dies

CHAPTER 7

The Presidency: Our Executive Branch

SS.7.CG.3.3 Describe the structure and function of the three branches of government established in the U.S. Constitution. (*This chapter describes the executive branch; see Chapters 6 and 8 for the other branches of the national government.*)

SS.7.CG.3.8 Explain the structure, functions and processes of the executive branch of government. (*This chapter describes the executive branch at the national level. See Chapter 12 for the executive branch at the state and local levels.*)

SS.7.CG.3.14 Explain the purpose and function of the Electoral College in electing the President of the United States.

Content Focus Vocabulary in This Chapter

- General powers described in Article II
- Structure of the Executive branch
- President
- Functions/Roles and Responsibilities of the Executive Branch
- Processes of the Executive Branch
- Cabinet
- Executive order
- Veto
- Appointments
- Administrative agencies
- Advise
- Make regulations
- Enforce law and regulations
- Electoral College
- 12th Amendment

Florida "Keys" to Learning

1. **Structure of the Executive Branch: Article II** of the Constitution established the **executive branch**, the part of government that carries out the laws. It gave several important powers to the head of the executive branch, known as the **President**. The President is a single person, elected for a fixed term of office of four years. The President is limited to two elected terms.

2. **Functions/Roles and Responsibilities of the Exceutive Branch:** The main role of the President is to enforce our national laws. The President also has other responsibilities: to defend and represent the nation, to provide central leadership, and to check the other branches.

3. **General Powers under Article II:** The President has the "executive power" to enforce the laws. The President is also Commander in Chief, in charge of the armed forces. The President has the power to negotiate treaties. The President has the power to appoint ambassadors, chiefs of executive departments and Supreme Court Justices. The President delivers an annual (*yearly*) "State of the Union" Address to Congress. The President can veto bills passed by Congress and has the power to pardon (*excuse*) those accused or convicted for federal crimes.

4. The President also has other powers. These are implied, given by Congress, or based on the need to defend the nation. Such powers include consulting with the **Cabinet** (*the heads of the executive departments meeting together)*, exercising general control over U.S. foreign relations (*relations with other nations*), and assuming emergency powers in wartime.

5. **Processes of the Executive Branch:** To carry out these responsibilities, the President can make **appointments** (*place someone in a government position*), **veto** bills (*turn down; refuse to pass*) or issue an **executive order** (*a rule or order made by the President with the force of law*). As Commander in Chief, the President can send troops to foreign countries for a limited period without declaring war.

6. There are several checks on Presidential power. These are part of our Constitution's system of checks and balances. Congress can override a Presidential veto, choose not to fund the President's programs, refuse to approve Presidential appointments or treaties, or impeach the President. The Supreme Court can declare Presidential acts to be unconstitutional.

7. The President is assisted by **administrative agencies**. Each agency has responsibility over a particular field. Agencies **advise** the President. They also **make regulations** (*detailed rules to help carry out the law*). Finally, agencies **enforce the law and regulations**. They can fine those who violate their rules. An executive agency is usually led by a director appointed by the President. Independent regulatory agencies are usually managed by a board or commission of several members. Their members can often only be removed for misconduct.

8. The **constitutional qualifications** (*requirements*) for becoming President are that a person must be a U.S. citizen from birth, be at least 35 years old, and have been a U.S. resident for at least 14 years before taking office. A naturalized citizen (*a foreigner who becomes U.S. citizen*) cannot become President.

9. If the President is assassinated or unable to serve, the Vice President is next in line for the office.

10. The President and Vice President are chosen in a national election. Candidates for President first compete for their party's nomination. The nominees from each party then campaign against one another for election in November.

11. The President is actually chosen by the **Electoral College**. Electors from each state generally vote for the candidate who has won the most votes in their state in the November election. Sometimes a candidate wins a majority of the electoral votes without winning a majority of the popular votes.

12. The **12th Amendment** separated the election of the President and Vice President.

13. Congress can impeach and remove the President from office for treason or other high crimes. The impeachment process has two stages. First,

the House of Representatives impeaches the President (*here, "impeach" means to accuse or charge*). Then the Senate can remove the President by a two-thirds vote after a trial presided over by the Chief Justice of the Supreme Court.

The second branch of our national government is the **executive branch**, headed by the **President**. It executes (*carries out; enforces*) the laws. Many consider this to be the most dynamic of the three branches: the President today is vastly more powerful than the members of the Constitutional Convention could have ever imagined. In this chapter, you will study the Presidency.

You should know the powers of the President for the EOC test.

Structure and Powers of the Executive Branch

The Structure of the Executive Branch: From their knowledge of Roman history and their experiences under British rule, the delegates in Philadelphia in 1787 were afraid of a chief executive with too much power. Yet they also knew from their experience under the Articles of Confederation that without a chief executive, the national government could not manage the problems of a young democracy. They decided to create an executive branch headed by a single elected leader with a limited time in office. Each elected term would be four years. The main **functions/roles and responsibilities of the new executive branch** would be to enforce the law, defend and represent the nation, provide central leadership, and check the other branches.

General Powers of the Executive Branch under Article II: The President's "expressed" (or listed) powers are summarized below.

- First and foremost, the President was granted the "executive power":

> "The executive power shall be vested (*placed*) in a President of the United States of America."

The phrase "executive power" means the power to carry out or enforce the laws. The President is also to "take care that the laws be faithfully executed," and takes an oath to "faithfully execute" the office of President and to "preserve, protect and defend" the Constitution.

- The President is also the "Commander in Chief" of the armed forces of the United States:

> "The President shall be Commander in Chief of the Army and Navy of the United States, and of the militia of the several States, when called into the actual service of the United States."

The Constitution thus placed a civilian (*non-soldier*) at the head of the military.

- The President has the power to appoint members of the executive departments.

Particular departments are not specified in the Constitution, but from the beginning they have included the Secretary of State and the Secretary of the Treasury. Appointments must meet with the approval of a majority of the Senate. This is another example of the system of checks and balances in the Constitution.

> The President "shall nominate, and by and with the advice and consent of the Senate, shall appoint . . . all other officers of the United States."

The President can also request the advice of these officers in writing:

> The President "may require the opinion in writing of the principal officer in each of the executive departments, upon any subject relating to the duties of their respective offices."

- The President has the power to make treaties (*solemn agreements between foreign nations*), with approval of the Senate:

> The President "shall have Power, by and with the advice and consent of the Senate, to make Treaties."

While the President can negotiate treaties, approval by two-thirds of the Senate is required to "ratify" (*approve*) each treaty, putting it into force.

- The President has the power to appoint ambassadors—official representatives of the United States to other countries—and to receive the ambassadors and other diplomatic representatives of other nations:

> The President "shall nominate, and by and with the advice and consent of the Senate, shall appoint Ambassadors, other public Ministers and Consuls . . ."

> The President "shall receive Ambassadors and other public Ministers . . ."

- The President appoints the "Justices" (*judges*) of the U.S. Supreme Court. These must be approved by the Senate:

> The President "shall nominate, and by and with the advice and consent of the Senate, shall appoint . . . Justices of the Supreme Court . . ."

- The President has several specific powers with respect to Congress. The President delivers the "State of the Union" Address:

> The President "shall from time to time give to the Congress Information of the State of the Union, and recommend to their Consideration such Measures as he shall judge necessary and expedient . . ."

This responsibility gives the President the opportunity to share views with Congress and the American people and to make recommendations for the security and welfare of the country, which Congress can include in its annual budget.

- The President has the power to **veto** (*turn down*) bills submitted by Congress. The President's veto can be overridden by a two-thirds vote of the members present in each house of Congress (see Chapter 6). However, the President's veto power is so formidable that of the more than 2,500 Presidential vetoes, only about a hundred of them have been successfully overridden by Congress.
- The President has the power to call Congress into special session, or to adjourn the two houses of Congress if they cannot agree on the time of adjournment (*temporary recess or break*).
- Finally, the President has the power to grant pardons for federal crimes:

> The President "shall have the power to grant reprieves and pardons for offences against the United States, except in cases of impeachment."

A **pardon** forgives an individual for having committed a crime. It releases the person from prison, waives all penalties, and restores the person's civil rights. The power to grant pardons is often associated with executive power. Governors in every state can pardon those accused of state crimes.

Enrichment

In an article in *The New York Times*, President Bill Clinton justified the pardons that he granted on the last day of his Presidency: "A President may conclude a pardon or commutation is [justified] for several reasons: the desire to restore full citizenship rights, including voting, to people who have served their sentences and lived within the law since; a belief that a sentence was excessive or unjust; personal circumstances that [justify] compassion; or other unique circumstances . . . regardless of how unpopular a decision might be."

Bill Clinton

The President's Other Roles and Powers

Like Congress, the President also exercises "implied" and other powers, such as those delegated by Congress or necessary to defend our nation in an emergency.

Meeting with the Cabinet

The heads of fifteen departments in the executive branch meet together as the President's "**Cabinet**." The Cabinet is not mentioned in the Constitution. However, the Constitution gives the President the right to appoint heads of departments and to request their written opinions.

President George Washington began the first Cabinet in 1789 with four members: the Secretary of State (Thomas Jefferson), the Secretary of the Treasury (Alexander Hamilton), the Secretary of War, and the Attorney General. Today, there are fifteen heads of executive departments in the Cabinet, as well as the Vice President of the United States and seven other Cabinet officers.

The President not only appoints Cabinet members but also has the power to dismiss them. This is another implied power.

The Conduct of our Nation's Foreign Relations

President Washington was also the first to assert Presidential control of foreign relations (*our relations with other countries*). The basis of this power is to be found in the President's powers to make treaties, to receive and appoint ambassadors, and to act as Commander in Chief. You will learn more about American foreign policy in Chapter 18.

Emergency Powers in Wartime

Presidents typically exercise emergency powers in wartime, with or without the approval of Congress.

During the Civil War, Abraham Lincoln suspended several civil liberties guaranteed by the Constitution, including the right to a writ of habeas corpus. Lincoln also issued the Emancipation Proclamation, freeing the slaves in Southern states in rebellion, as an exercise of his emergency wartime powers. The Supreme Court later ruled that Lincoln did not have the authority to suspend habeas corpus.

During World War I, Congress gave President Wilson power to limit the exercise of free speech. During World War II, President Franklin D. Roosevelt ordered the internment of Japanese Americans on the West Coast on the basis of his emergency wartime powers. (See Chapter 10.)

Executive Orders

Since the time of George Washington, Presidents have issued **executive orders**. These orders have the force of laws, although they have not been passed by Congress. This practice is based on the responsibility of the President to execute laws passed by Congress. **Executive orders** are thus meant to implement (*put into effect*) the legislation of Congress. Past Presidents have issued executive orders to ration consumer goods, to control wages and prices, and to carry out laws affecting civil rights. One of the most famous of President Roosevelt's executive orders permitted the forced internment (*confinement; imprisonment*) of Japanese Americans during World

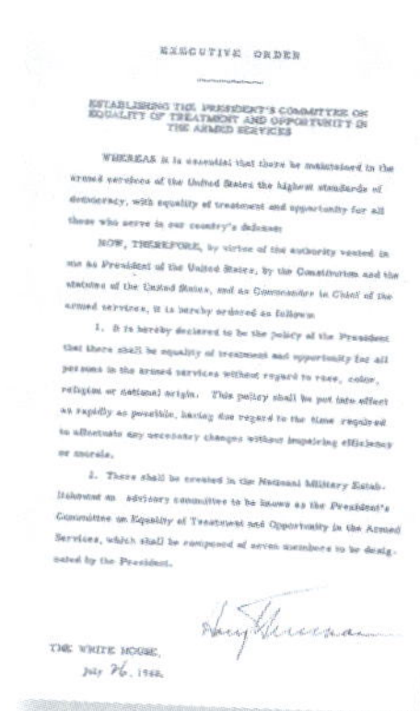

EXECUTIVE ORDER

ESTABLISHING THE PRESIDENT'S COMMITTEE ON EQUALITY OF TREATMENT AND OPPORTUNITY IN THE ARMED SERVICES

WHEREAS it is essential that there be maintained in the armed services of the United States the highest standards of democracy, with equality of treatment and opportunity for all those who serve in our country's defense:

NOW, THEREFORE, by virtue of the authority vested in me as President of the United States, by the Constitution and the statutes of the United States, and as Commander in Chief of the armed services, it is hereby ordered as follows:

1. It is hereby declared to be the policy of the President that there shall be equality of treatment and opportunity for all persons in the armed services without regard to race, color, religion or national origin. This policy shall be put into effect as rapidly as possible, having due regard to the time required to effectuate any necessary changes without impairing efficiency or morale.

2. There shall be created in the National Military Establishment an advisory committee to be known as the President's Committee on Equality of Treatment and Opportunity in the Armed Services, which shall be composed of seven members to be designated by the President.

THE WHITE HOUSE,
July 26, 1948.

War II. Another of his executive orders ended racial discrimination in the award of defense contracts. In 1948, President Truman issued an executive order ending racial discrimination in the armed services. On average, Presidents issue about a hundred executive orders a year. Over time, Presidents have issued more than 14,000 executive orders.

War-Making Powers/Military Interventions

According to our Constitution, only Congress can declare war. However, of the hundreds of armed conflicts in which the United States has engaged, only five have actually been declared wars. The most important armed conflicts of the past seventy years—the Korean War, the Vietnam War, and the two Gulf Wars—have been fought by American troops without any declaration of war at all.

When responding to an attack or planning an action against a foreign threat, it may not always be a good strategy to obtain a public declaration of war. Acting as Commander in Chief, the President is able to take immediate steps in defense of the nation.

Processes of the Executive Branch

As you can see, the President has these three main tools for carrying out the **roles and responsibilities** of the Presidency:

- **Appointments:** The President appoints the heads of Cabinet departments as well as the heads of government agencies. The President sits atop a vast federal bureaucracy. The President also appoints ambassadors and federal judges.
- **Executive Orders:** The President can issue executive orders, which have the force of law.
- **Veto:** The President can veto legislation proposed by Congress. It is difficult for Congress to override a Presidential veto.

Know these checks for the EOC test.

Checks on Presidential Power

As with the other branches, there are important checks on the President's powers. This is part of our Constitution's system of checks and balances:

- Congress can override a Presidential veto.
- All spending by the federal government is made by Congress. Without the support of Congress, the President is unable to fund (*pay for*) any government activities.
- The President must obtain Senate confirmation (*approval*) of appointments and treaties.
- The War Powers Act, passed by Congress in 1973, limits the President's ability to send troops overseas for longer than 60 days without the approval of Congress.
- The Supreme Court can declare acts of the President unconstitutional.
- Congress can impeach and remove the President for misconduct.

Administrative Agencies

For the EOC, be sure to know about administrative agencies.

Governing the United States is too difficult to be conducted by just a handful of officials. In addition to the Cabinet departments, the President is assisted by a large number of **administrative agencies**. An administrative agency is a group or organization in the government that has responsibility over a particular field or area. Examples of such agencies are the Food and Drug Administration (FDA), which regulates our food and drugs, and the Environmental Protection Agency (EPA), which protects the environment.

Agencies fulfill three goals:

(1) Agencies **advise** the President and other government officials.

(2) Agencies make detailed rules, known as **regulations**, about the area they oversee.

(3) Finally, agencies **enforce the law and regulations**.

Agencies develop special knowledge and expertise over the area they supervise. When Congress makes laws or the President issues orders, these are often not specific enough. It is left to the appropriate agency to spell out the details in their regulations. Agencies follow a special procedure for issuing regulations, known as "rule making." The agency must make every proposed regulation public and invite the public to make comments. The agency then holds a hearing to decide whether or not to adopt the proposed regulation.

Once the regulation is adopted, it is published and given the force of law. Citizens and companies must obey an agency's regulations or they can be required to pay a fine or other penalty. Agencies can order investigations, hold hearings, examine witnesses and documents, and issue fines. They can even hold their own trials of those accused of violating their rules. These trials may be decided by a special administrative law judge. Parties have the right to appeal agency decisions to a regular court.

There are two types of administrative agencies in our federal government:

- An executive agency is usually led by a single director appointed by the President and confirmed by the Senate. The President has the power to remove the director at any time. The Federal Bureau of Investigation (FBI) is an executive agency.

- Independent regulatory agencies are part of the executive branch but act independently. Often they are managed by a board or commission. The President appoints members but can only remove a director, a board member, or commissioner from an independent agency for misconduct. This preserves the agency's independence. Examples of this kind of agency are the Securities and Exchange Commission (SEC), which regulates the stock market, and the Federal Reserve Board, which controls monetary policy.

The Active Citizen

- A special law, the Administrative Procedure Act (APA), establishes the rules that all federal agencies must follow in their rule making and enforcement actions. For example, the APA requires all agencies to announce any new rules they are considering. The agency must then "give interested parties an opportunity to participate in the rule making through submission of written data, views

Continues ▸

or arguments with or without oral presentation." (APA, Section 553) Why is this opportunity for the public to submit comments so important?

____

____

____

You should know the requirements for becoming President for the EOC test.

Who Can Become President?

The constitutional qualifications (*requirements*) for becoming President of the United States, like those for becoming a member of the House of Representatives or the Senate, are few in number:

To be eligible to become President of the United States, an individual must:

1. Be a "natural born" citizen, born in the United States or having U.S. citizens as parents. "Naturalized" citizens (who became citizens after migrating here) cannot serve as President;
2. Be at least 35 years of age; and
3. Be a resident of the United States for at least 14 years before taking office.

There are no other constitutional requirements. Most recent Presidents have worked in law or business before entering politics.

Term in Office. The President is elected for a "term" of four years. President George Washington served for two terms in office before he stepped down. All later Presidents followed his example, until President Franklin D. Roosevelt ran for a third term while World War II was raging in Europe. Roosevelt was elected for a fourth term and died in office from a heart attack. The Twenty-second Amendment now limits the President to a maximum of two elected terms.

The Vice President. The Vice President must meet the same requirements and serves the same term as the President. If the President dies or leaves office for any reason, the Vice President becomes the next President.

How the President is Chosen

Have you ever dreamt of becoming President of the United States? You would get to live in the White House for free, and have your own cook, private movie theater and swimming pool. You could hold press conferences or go on television whenever you wanted, and telephone other world leaders.

So, you may be wondering, how does one actually go about becoming President? Meeting the minimal constitutional qualifications above is just the first step. Far more difficult, a candidate must win the nomination of a major political party, then campaign against the candidates of competing parties, and finally win votes in enough states to obtain a majority of electoral votes in the Electoral College. Let's look at each of these steps more closely.

The Nomination

The first step in running for President is usually winning the nomination of one of the two major political parties. A political party is an organization of citizens who share similar views and who work together to get some of their members elected to public office. Each of the two major national political parties—the Democrats and Republicans—will nominate only one candidate for President.

Usually, individuals announce their candidacy more than a year before the election itself. Powerful party leaders once selected their party's nominee in private. Today, party members vote on their party's candidates to determine which one should represent the party as its nominee in the coming election.

Each state follows its own rules and traditions. In most states, delegates to the party's national convention are chosen in special primary elections. A few states, however, use small gatherings known as "caucuses" to select their delegates. The candidates hold a lengthy competition as they debate one another and face each other in the various state primaries and caucuses, which are spread out in time. As the primaries continue, candidates start to calculate if they will have enough delegates to capture the nomination. Gradually, some of the candidates will drop out based on their performance in the primaries.

The nominees are finally chosen at each party's national convention, held in the summer before the election. The party determines, usually on the basis of committed delegates from the primary results, who the party's candidate will be. The candidate and other party members address the convention. Some of their speeches may appear on television. The nominee for President also selects and announces the nominee for Vice President. The two candidates run together on a single "ticket." Meanwhile delegates at the convention adopt a party platform with recommendations the party members view as important.

The Campaign for the General Election

Once the national conventions are over, the two nominees of the major parties have about three months to campaign against each other. The candidates conduct energetic campaigns—delivering speeches, attending meetings, and raising campaign funds—all to gain the support of voters. The candidates pay for political advertisements to be shown on television or printed in newspapers and journals. They are interviewed on radio talk shows and national television shows. The Presidential and Vice Presidential candidates also debate one another on national television.

Be sure to know about the Electoral College for the EOC test.

The Electoral College

The election for the President and Vice President occurs on the first Tuesday after November 1st. The final process of selecting the President and Vice President does not actually happen in the election itself, but in the Electoral College.

The authors of the Constitution did not trust the people enough to permit them to elect the President directly. Instead, they created the **Electoral College**—a group of individuals, called electors. Each elector has one electoral vote. Each state was given the same number of electoral votes as it had Senators and Representatives in Congress.

Originally, the electors could vote for anyone they wanted. Today, electors are required to vote for the candidate who won the most votes in their state in the general election. In all but two states, the winner of the popular vote receives all of that state's electoral votes. This rule also applies to the three electoral votes of the District of Columbia. In Maine and Nebraska, however, electoral votes are cast in proportion to the popular vote of that state.

There are 538 electoral votes in all in the Electoral College. To win the Presidential election, the candidate must receive more than half of these, or 270 electoral votes. It is possible under this system for a candidate to receive a majority of the popular votes in the general election and still lose the vote in the Electoral College. This occurs when a candidate wins several states by a large majority but loses others by a narrow margin. It happened three times in the nineteenth century. Most recently, it happened in the 2000 and 2016 elections. In 2000, Al Gore received more popular votes than George W. Bush, but Gore still lost the election. In 2016, Hillary Clinton received more popular votes than Donald Trump, but she also lost the election in the Electoral College.

The Twelfth Amendment

You will also have to know about the 12th Amendment for the EOC.

When the Constitution was first written, each elector in the Electoral College had two votes. The candidate receiving the most votes was to become President and the candidate with the second most votes was to become Vice President. This system often led to one candidate becoming President and his main opponent becoming Vice President. Once candidates began running in "tickets"—with one candidate for President and another from the same party for Vice President—a new problem arose. In the 1800 election, Thomas Jefferson ran against John Adams. Jefferson's running mate for Vice President was Aaron Burr. All the Democratic-Republicans who supported Jefferson gave one vote to Jefferson and their second vote to Burr. The result was that Jefferson and Burr each received the same number of votes. Burr refused to give way and the election went to the House of Representatives, which took 36 ballots (*separate votes*) to resolve the matter. Afterwards, Congress proposed and the states ratified the **12th Amendment**. This amendment separated the election for President from that of Vice President. The 12th Amendment also specified the way the Electoral College was to operate.

The Twelfth Amendment

"The electors shall meet in their respective states and vote by ballot for President and Vice-President . . . ; they shall name in their ballots the person voted for as President, and in distinct [*separate*] ballots the person voted for as Vice-President, and they shall make distinct lists of all persons voted for as President, and of all persons voted for as Vice-President, and of the number of votes for each, which lists they shall sign and certify, and transmit sealed to the seat of the government of the United States, directed to the President of the Senate. The President of the Senate shall, in the presence of the Senate and House of Representatives, open all the certificates and the votes shall then be counted . . . "

The Active Citizen

- Sometimes the winner of the most votes in the popular election does not win in the Electoral College. This happened in both 2000 and 2016. Should the Electoral College be eliminated? Hold a class debate on the following: "*Resolved: The Electoral College should be eliminated and the President should be elected by popular vote.*"

The Impeachment Process

The Constitution establishes procedures in case there is a need to remove the President from office for "treason, bribery, or other high crimes and misdemeanors." This process is known as *impeachment*. The impeachment of a government official does not impose any kind of penalties, fines or imprisonment at all. It simply removes the official from office. Once removed, the official may also face proceedings in a criminal or civil court.

The Constitution gives Congress the power to impeach the President. The impeachment process occurs in two stages. In the first, the President is impeached (*accused or charged*) in the House of Representatives. If a majority of the House votes to impeach the President, then the process moves into the second stage, where the President is tried in the Senate. The Chief Justice of the Supreme Court presides at the trial. A vote of two-thirds of the Senate is needed to convict and remove the President from office. If the President is removed, then the Vice President becomes the new President.

House of Representatives
Impeaches (*charges*) the President

Senate
Tries and removes the President

The Active Citizen

- How do the roles and responsibilities of the President differ from those of Congress? Make a chart or Venn diagram comparing these two branches.
- Suppose you were running for President. Make an action plan for your campaign. Consider what steps you would take to debate opponents, to raise money for advertisements, to win the nomination of a major party, and to win a majority of the electoral votes in the Electoral College.
- Many Americans believe that Abraham Lincoln was our best President. What actions did he take to exercise the powers of the Presidency so effectively? Conduct your own research on the Internet to answer this question.
- In a series of national crises over the past century, Presidents of the United States have taken on additional roles. For example, during the Great Depression, the President took on responsibility for the smooth running of the national economy. During the Korean War, Vietnam War, and two Gulf Wars, the President sent U.S. troops into foreign conflicts without any formal declaration of war by Congress. The President is now in charge of a large permanent military establishment and a vast federal bureaucracy. Has the modern Presidency become too strong, overshadowing the other two branches? Write three paragraphs giving your point of view on this question.

A Summary of the Presidency

Constitutional Qualifications to be President

- Must be a "natural born" citizen (***not*** a "naturalized" citizen)
- Must have lived in the United States for at least 14 years
- Must be at least 35 years old

Powers of the President

Expressed Powers (General Powers in Article II of the Constitution)

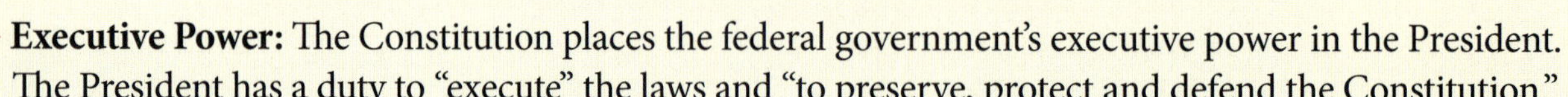

- **Executive Power:** The Constitution places the federal government's executive power in the President. The President has a duty to "execute" the laws and "to preserve, protect and defend the Constitution."
- **Commander in Chief:** The President is the Commander in Chief of the nation's armed forces.
- **Appointment Power:** With the advice and consent of the Senate, the President appoints (*chooses*) all U.S. ambassadors, all Justices of the U.S. Supreme Court, and all federal officers.
- **Treaty-Making Power:** With the consent of a two-thirds majority of the Senate, the President can make treaties with other countries.
- **Receive ambassadors:** The President receives ambassadors from foreign nations.
- **Veto Power:** The President can sign or veto a bill passed by Congress; Congress can override a Presidential veto with a two-thirds majority in each house.
- **Other Powers relating to Congress:** The President informs Congress of the "**State of the Union**"; recommends measures to Congress; and can convene (*call together*) and **adjourn** sessions of Congress.
- **Pardoning Power:** The President can **pardon** (*forgive; let free*) those accused of federal crimes.

Other Powers

- **Foreign Relations:** The President conducts our nation's **foreign relations**.
- **Cabinet:** The President often meets with the heads of **executive departments,** known as the **Cabinet**, which gives the President advice.
- **Executive orders:** The President issues **executive orders**.
- **Emergency Powers:** The President has an implied power to take immediate steps to defend our nation if it is attacked or if there is any kind of national emergency.
- **Administrative Agencies:** These (1) advise the President; (2) make regulations; and (3) enforce the law and regulations.

Choosing the President

The President is chosen by the **Electoral College**. Voters decide who their state's electors should support. All but two states give all their electors to one candidate.

The **12th Amendment** separated the election of the President and Vice President.

Impeachment

Congress has the power to **impeach** (*charge*) and remove the President. **Impeachment** is a two-step process:

- **Impeachment**: A majority of the House of Representatives must vote to impeach the President.
- **Removal:** Once impeached by the House, the President is tried in the Senate. The Chief Justice of the Supreme Court presides over the trial. To remove the President from office requires approval of two-thirds of the Senate.

Name ____

Fill in the chart below.

The Presidency
The President's general powers under Article II:
The President's other powers:
How Cabinet departments and administrative agencies assist the President:
How the President is chosen:
How the President may be removed:

The Presidency: Our Executive Branch
Constitutional Qualifications
Natural-born citizen
At least 35 years of age
U.S. resident at least 14 years
How to Become President
Announce candidacy
Run in primaries
Win nomination at party's national convention
Campaign for election
Presidential debates
Election Day voting
Win a majority of the Electoral College
Each state's electors = number of its Senators + Representatives
A candidate usually gets all or none of the state's electors
12th Amendment: separated the elections for President and Vice President
Cabinet
Vice President, 15 Executive Departments, other officers
Examples of Heads of Executive Departments: Secretary of State, Secretary of the Treasury
SEAL OF THE PRESIDENT OF THE UNITED STATES
Administrative Agencies
Advise the President
Make regulations
Enforce law and regulations
Other Powers
Foreign policy
Military interventions
Executive orders
Powers under Article II
Executive power: enforce the laws
Commander in Chief
Negotiate treaties
Appoint ambassadors
Appoint Supreme Court Justices
Appoint heads of departments
Inform Congress on "State of the Union"
Sign or veto bills from Congress
Receive ambassadors
Grant pardons
Responsibilities
Enforce the law
Defend the nation
Represent the nation
Provide central leadership
Check the other branches
Processes
Appointments
Executive orders
Veto power
Impeachment
Impeached/accused in House of Representatives
Trial in the Senate: 2/3 majority of Senate needed for removal
EXECUTIVE ORDER

Review Cards: The Executive Branch

Structure of the Executive Branch: The President

The delegates to the Constitutional Convention feared creating a national executive with too much power, similar to the English King. On the other hand, their experiences under the Articles of Confederation showed that a national executive was necessary to provide leadership. Article II of the Constitution established the **executive branch** (*part of governnent that enforces the law*) with an elected leader who serves for a fixed term in office, known as the **President**. Then main **roles and responsibilities** of the Presidency are to enforce the law, to defend and represent the nation, to provide central leadership, and to check the other branches.

Qualifications and Terms of the Presidency

- **Constitutional Qualifications:** The President must be a U.S. citizen from birth (a "natural born citizen"), be at least 35 years of age, and be a U.S. resident for at least 14 years before taking office.
- **Terms in Office:** Presidential terms are for four years. The Twenty-Second Amendment limits the President to two elected terms. If the President dies or leaves office for any reason, the Vice President becomes the next President.

How the President is Chosen

The contest to become President occurs in two stages: (1) the nominating process; and (2) the general election. To win in the general election, a candidate must receive a majority of the votes in the **Electoral College**.

The Nominating Process

Candidates are generally first nominated by one of the two major political parties (Democrats and Republicans). Candidates for the nomination compete in primary elections and state party caucuses. One nominee is finally chosen by each party at its national convention.

The General Election

The two nominees tour the country in an expensive campaign. They also engage in televised debates. Voters then cast their votes on Election Day—the first Tuesday after November 1.

The Electoral College

- The President is actually chosen by the **Electoral College**. The authors of the Constitution did not trust the people to elect the President directly. Instead, electors from each state make the final choice. Each state has the same number of electors as it has members in Congress (Senators and Representatives). These electors make up the "Electoral College."
- Today, electors are required to vote for the same candidate that their state's voters did in the general election. A candidate usually gets all or nothing of a state's electoral vote.
- A candidate can win the popular vote but lose in the Electoral College. This happens if they lose some states by a narrow margin. It happened in both 2000 and 2016.
- When the Constitution was first adopted, each elector had two votes. This created confusion between the election of President and Vice President. The **12th Amendment** separated the election of the President and Vice President into separate contests.

General Powers Described in Article II

The President has a number of **general powers under Article II** of the Constitution. These include the "executive power" (*the power to enforce the laws*), powers over military and foreign affairs, powers to make government appointments, and powers to check the actions of Congress:

- The President can consult with the **Cabinet** (see the card below).
- The President is Commander in Chief of the armed forces.
- The President has the power to negotiate treaties (with approval of two-thirds of the Senate), to appoint ambassadors, and to receive foreign ambassadors and other diplomats.
- The President has the power to appoint the heads of executive departments, as well as Supreme Court Justices. These appointments require confirmation by a majority of the Senate.
- The President delivers the "State of the Union" Address to Congress to share views and make recommendations. The President can **veto** (*refuse to approve*) legislation passed by Congress, and can summon Congress into a special session.
- The President has the power to pardon (*forgive; excuse*) those accused of federal crimes.

Processes of the Executive Branch

As you can see from the powers listed above, the President has several tools to carry out the responsibilities of the executive branch:

- The President has can make **appointments**. The President appoints heads of executive departments and administrative agencies. A large number of government workers assist the President.
- The President can issue **executive orders**—these have the force of law but do not require the approval of Congress.
- The President can **veto** legislation proposed by Congress.
- As Commander in Chief, the President commands our armed forces.

Executive Departments and the Cabinet

- The President is assisted by 15 executive departments.
- Each executive department is headed by a "Secretary" (except the Department of Justice, which is headed by the Attorney General). For example, the State Department—which handles foreign relations—is headed by the Secretary of State. The Treasury Department—which handles economic policies—is headed by the Secretary of the Treasury.
- The Vice President, the heads of the 15 executive departments, and a few other officers form the **Cabinet**. The Cabinet meets regularly and gives advice to the President. Although the Cabinet is not mentioned in the Constitution, every President has been advised by the Cabinet.

Administrative Agencies

- The executive branch includes a large number of administrative agencies.
- An **administrative agency** is an organization in the government that has responsibility over a particular field or area.
- An executive agency is usually led by a single director appointed by the President and confirmed by the Senate. The President has the power to remove the director of this type of agency at any time. Example: Federal Bureau of Investigation (FBI)
- Independent regulatory agencies are part of the executive branch but act independently of the executive. Many independent agencies are managed by a board or commission of several members. The President appoints each member of the agency. Unlike an executive agency, however, the President cannot remove a member from this type of agency except for misconduct. This protects the independence of the agency. Examples: Federal Reserve Board; Securities and Exchange Commission (SEC); Environmental Protection Agency (EPA).
- Administrative agencies fulfill three goals:

(1) They **advise** the President and other government officials.

(2) They make detailed rules, known as **regulations**, about the area they oversee. These detailed rules help to put existing laws into effect. The public is invited to comment on all proposed regulations.

(3) Finally, agencies **enforce the law and regulations**. They can hold trial-like hearings and fine offenders for violating their rules.

Checks on Presidential Power

- There are several checks on Presidential power: Congress can override a Presidential veto; can choose not to fund the President's suggested programs; can refuse to approve Presidential appointments or treaties; can apply the War Powers Act; and can impeach the President.
- The Supreme Court can declare Presidential acts, including executive orders, unconstitutional.

The Impeachment Process

- Congress has the power to impeach the President for treason or other high crimes. Impeachment can lead to removal from office but includes no other punishment. It has two stages:
  - First, a majority of the House of Representatives votes whether to impeach.
  - Second, if the House votes to impeach, then the President is tried in the Senate. The Chief Justice of the Supreme Court presides over the trial. Two-thirds of the Senate must vote to convict the President in order to remove the President from office.

The Impeachment Process

House of Representatives →

- Impeaches (*charges*) the President
- Majority vote needed to impeach the President

Senate

- Tries the President
- Chief Justice of the Supreme Court conducts the trial
- Two-thirds majority needed to remove the President

What Do You Know?

SS.7.CG.2.7

1. Which individual could qualify as a candidate for President of the United States?
   - **A.** Max is 67 years old; he has lived in Ontario, Canada for all of his life; he was born in Detroit.
   - **B.** Martha is 45 years old; she has lived in Chicago for the last 18 years; she was born in Tampa.
   - **C.** Samuel is 27 years old; he has lived in New York City for the past 3 years; he was born in Israel of American parents.
   - **D.** Karen is 42 years old; she has lived in Boston for the last 26 years; she was born in Ireland of Irish parents.

SS.7.CG.3.3

2. Which constitutional power provides the basis for the President's day-to-day control of U.S. foreign relations?
   - **A.** the power to appoint and receive ambassadors
   - **B.** the power to appoint Justices of the Supreme Court
   - **C.** the power to inform Congress of the "State of the Union"
   - **D.** the power to summon Congress in times of national emergency

SS.7.CG.1.9

3. The War Powers Act of 1973 restricted the powers of the President as Commander in Chief. Which principle of constitutional government did passage of this law illustrate?
   - **A.** federalism
   - **B.** limited government
   - **C.** checks and balances
   - **D.** separation of powers

SS.7.CG.3.3

4. Which power does the Constitution give to the President to check Congress?
   - **A.** the power to appoint heads of departments
   - **B.** the power to veto proposed federal legislation
   - **C.** the power to pardon offenders for federal crimes
   - **D.** the power to inform Congress of the "State of the Union"

SS.7.CG.3.8

5. Which of the following is an example of an administrative agency?
   - **A.** U.S. Army
   - **B.** U.S. Supreme Court
   - **C.** Federal Reserve Board
   - **D.** U.S. House of Representatives

SS.7.CG.3.3

6. During the 1976 Presidential campaign, Jimmy Carter promised to pardon draft evaders from the Vietnam War to help heal the wounds of the war. Shortly after he was elected, President Carter pardoned about 100,000 of them. How was he able to pardon so many at once?

   A. by exercising an implied power
   B. by exercising a customary power
   C. by exercising an emergency power
   D. by exercising a power found in the Constitution

SS.7.CG.3.14

7. Which argument is often raised against the Electoral College?

   A. Many electors do not honor the choice of most of their state's voters.
   B. The Electoral College encourages the growth of too many "third parties."
   C. A candidate can win the Presidency without a majority of the popular vote.
   D. Presidential elections are too often decided by the House of Representatives.

SS.7.CG.3.8

8. Which is an important task of an administrative agency?

   A. passing federal laws
   B. making detailed regulations
   C. running the United States armed forces
   D. resolving court cases between private parties

SS.7.CG.3.3

9. The headline shown on the left appeared in newspapers on December 20, 1998.

   Which step is next in the impeachment process?

   A. The President is tried in the Supreme Court.
   B. The President is tried by the United States Senate.
   C. The President can appeal to the U.S. Supreme Court.
   D. Three-fourths of the states must agree to the impeachment.

SS.7.CG.3.8

10. How does an executive order differ from a federal law?

   A. Executive orders are not subject to judicial review.
   B. Executive orders are not limited by the Constitution.
   C. Executive orders do not need to be approved by Congress.
   D. Executive orders are limited to military and foreign affairs.

SS.7.CG.3.14

11. The table below shows the popular vote in five states in the 2016 Presidential election.

	Popular Vote		
State	Hillary Clinton	Donald Trump	Number of Electoral Votes
North Dakota	93,758	216,794	3
South Dakota	117,458	227,721	3
North Carolina	2,189,316	2,362,631	15
South Carolina	855,373	1,155,389	9
Virginia	1,981,473	1,769,443	13

Based on the table, how many electoral votes did Donald Trump win in these five states?

A. none
B. 22
C. 30
D. 43

SS.7.CG.3.8

12. The following sections are found in the Administrative Procedure Act, a federal law governing administrative agencies:

> 5 U.S. Code Section 533(b) General notice of proposed rule making shall be published in the Federal Register . . .
>
> 5 U.S. Code Section 533 (c) After notice required by this section, the agency shall give interested persons an opportunity to participate in the rule making through submission of written data, views, or arguments with or without opportunity for oral presentation. . . .

Which statement best explains the reason for these sections?

A. Administrative agencies are required to advise the President.
B. Administrative agencies have the power to issue their own executive orders.
C. Administrative agencies must consider public views before issuing enforceable regulations.
D. Administrative agencies often enforce their own regulations in court-like settings.

SS.7.CG.3.3

13. Under the U.S. Constitution, which of the following tasks is assigned to the executive branch?

A. ratifying treaties with foreign countries
B. appointing Justices to the U.S. Supreme Court
C. determining whether a new law is constitutional
D. voting on funds to support U.S. armed forces stationed abroad

CHAPTER 8

The Federal Courts: Our Judicial Branch

SS.7.CG.3.3 Describe the structure and function of the three branches of government established in the U.S. Constitution. (*This chapter describes the structure and function of the judicial branch. For the other branches, see Chapters 6 and 7.*)

SS.7.CG.3.9 Explain the structure, functions and processes of the judicial branch of government. (*This chapter describes the federal courts; for summary judgment and Florida's state court system, see Chapter 9.*)

Content Focus Vocabulary in This Chapter

- Structure of the judicial branch
- General powers described in Article III
- Functions/roles and responsibilities of the Judicial branch
- U.S. Supreme Court
- Jurisdiction
- Trial process
- Appellate process
- Court order
- Writ of certiorari
- U.S. District Court
- U.S. Court of Appeals
- U.S. Circuit Court of Appeals
- Judicial review

Florida "Keys" to Learning

1. Article III of the U.S. Constitution established the **judicial branch** of our national government. **Roles and responsibilities of the judicial branch:** The role of the judicial branch is to administer justice (*help those who obey the law and punish offenders*), resolve disputes, interpret the law, and apply laws to specific cases.

2. **Structure of the judicial branch:** Article III created the **U.S. Supreme Court**. This court is superior to all other courts in the United States.

3. The Supreme Court is composed of the Chief Justice and eight Associate Justices. These Justices are not elected but are appointed by the President to serve for "good behavior"—that is, for life. The authors of the Constitution gave lifetime appointments to all federal judges to protect the independence of the judiciary. Judges are the public officials who preside over courts of law and who rule on cases. Supreme Court Justices are judges.

4. In the United States, there are different kinds of courts. The territory and type of cases over which each court exercises its authority is known as its **jurisdiction** (*the area over which it "says the law"*). A case can only be brought before a court that has jurisdiction over it. Federal courts derive (*obtain*) their authority from the U.S. Constitution. They have limited jurisdiction since the Constitution only gives the federal government limited powers.

5. **Processes of the judicial branch:** The U.S. Supreme Court has "original jurisdiction" in all cases affecting foreign ambassadors, foreign diplomats, or where states of the United States act as parties to the dispute. The Supreme Court acts as a trial court in these cases. It follows a **trial process** of hearing evidence and making a judgment. In all other cases, the U.S. Supreme Court exercises appellate jurisdiction. It acts as an appellate court and follows an **appellate process**. This means that it reviews decisions by lower courts to see if they have applied the law correctly.

6. The losing party must appeal the decision by the lower court. A party seeking review by the Supreme Court must file a petition for a **writ of certiorari** (*an order by the Supreme Court granting a request for review by that court*). This is a type of **court order** (*an instruction from the court with the force of law*). The Supreme Court is not required to hear all appeals. Only a small number of the petitions for a writ of certiorari are granted.

7. The Supreme Court generally makes its decisions after hearing "oral argument." Sometime after oral argument, the Justices discuss the case and take a vote to reach a decision. One Justice from the majority will be chosen to write an "opinion" on the decision. This opinion explains the Court's reasoning behind the decision. Other Justices are free to write their own dissenting opinions (*explanations of why they disagree with the majority opinion*).

8. Article III of the Constitution created the Supreme Court but no other federal courts. However, this article gave Congress the power to create "inferior" (*lower level*) federal courts if it chose to do so. The very first Congress decided to make lower federal courts. These federal courts now consist of 94 U.S. District Courts and 13 U.S. Courts of Appeals.

9. Each state has at least one **U.S. District Court**. Florida has three U.S. District Courts. These are trial courts that hear cases on federal issues or between citizens of different states. These courts follow a **trial process** and can have juries.

10. The 13 **U.S. Courts of Appeals** review cases on appeal. They are not trial courts. They are appellate courts. They follow an **appellate process**. They hear appeals from decisions by the U.S. District Courts in their "Circuit" (the region over which they have jurisdiction). They are sometimes known as Circuit Courts or as **U.S. Circuit Courts of Appeals**.

11. One of the most important powers of the U.S. Supreme Court and other federal courts is the power of **judicial review**. The U.S. Supreme Court and other federal courts can declare that a law is unconstitutional if they decide, after hearing a case, that the law violates the Constitution. When this happens, the law can no longer be enforced.

In the last two chapters, you learned about Congress and the Presidency. In this chapter, you will study the third branch of our federal government, the **judicial branch**. **Roles and responsibilities of the judicial branch:** The role of this branch is to administer justice (*help those who obey the law and punish offenders*), resolve disputes, interpret laws, and apply laws to specific cases.

The Supreme Court

The Articles of Confederation had lacked a national court system. The Constitution took care of this weakness by creating a national court. **Article III** of the Constitution established the **judicial branch** of our national government. This article created the **U.S. Supreme Court**. "Supreme" means the highest or most powerful—superior to all others. The Constitution also gave Congress the power to create "inferior" (*lower-level*) federal courts. The powers and authority of these courts are derived (*taken*) from the Constitution.

Composition of the Supreme Court

A **judge** is the public official who oversees a court of law. A judge on the U.S. Supreme Court is known as a "Justice." The Constitution did not establish the number of Supreme Court Justices. Instead, it left this decision up to Congress. As the new nation grew, Congress added new Justices to the Court. Since 1869, there have been nine Justices: one Chief Justice and eight Associate Justices.

The Chief Justice presides over the Court's proceedings. The Chief Justice also acts as the spokesperson for the Court, serves as the nation's highest judicial officer, gives the oath of office to the President of the United States, and presides over any impeachment trial of the President in the Senate.

Selection Process for U.S. Supreme Court Justices

Supreme Court Justices are not elected officials. Instead, they are nominated (*proposed; named*) by the President and confirmed by a majority vote in the U.S. Senate. The President nominates individuals with distinguished legal careers who often share the President's own general outlook. At one time, Senate confirmation was routine. However, in more recent years, the examination of nominees by the Senate Judiciary Committee has become more challenging. This is an important example of the Constitution's system of checks and balances.

Lifetime Appointments

Supreme Court Justices—and, in fact, all federal judges—hold their office for "good behavior." This means that they are appointed for life. The average length of time that Justices have served on the Supreme Court has been about 16 years.

Why do federal judges enjoy their appointments for life? The authors of the Constitution wanted to make sure that judges were truly independent and would base their decisions on an impartial interpretation of the law. They especially resented the pressure that King George III had placed on judges in the years leading to the American Revolution. By appointing judges for life, the authors of the Constitution made them less subject to popular and political pressures. Federal judges don't have to worry about being re-elected or re-appointed. Their lifetime positions support the independence of the judiciary. This maintains the separation of powers.

Federal judges remain in office unless they die, resign, or are impeached and removed by Congress for bribery, treason or other "high crimes."

Impeachment of federal judges has been rare. Samuel Chase is the only U.S. Supreme Court Justice ever to have been impeached. No Supreme Court Justice has ever been removed from office.

Justice Samuel Chase

The Active Citizen

- Should federal judges be appointed or elected? Write a short "letter to the editor" giving your view on this issue. State your position and write one paragraph giving your reasons.
- In small groups, discuss whether it is better for federal judges to be appointed for limited terms, such as six years, or to be appointed for life. Each group should report its conclusions to the whole class.

Jurisdiction

Be sure to know what jurisdiction is for the EOC test. You should know that the powers and jurisdiction of the federal courts are derived from the U.S. Constitution.

A court of law is a public place where decisions are taken affecting the enforcement of laws and the settling of disputes. As you know, a judge presides over the proceedings of the court. Court decisions have the force of law. Courts can issue court orders, make judgments, and publish opinions. (You will learn more about some of these in Chapter 9.) They can fine and even imprison those who come before it.

In the United States, there are many different kinds of courts—from traffic courts and municipal courts to federal courts. When a person is accused of a crime, when a person is injured by the carelessness of another, or when two businesses have a dispute, they go to court. But to which court should they look for help?

The territory and type of cases over which a court has legal authority is known as its **jurisdiction**. The word "jurisdiction" comes from *juris*, the Roman word for "law," and *dictio*, the word for "saying." A court's jurisdiction is the territory over which it "says the law."

One of the first jobs of a lawyer in taking any case is deciding *which* court has jurisdiction. Is this a case for state or federal court? And at which location should the case be filed?

The Active Citizen

- Imagine that you are a delegate at the Constitutional Convention in 1787. The Convention is discussing the possibility of a federal court system. Over which types of cases would you give jurisdiction to the new federal courts? Explain your answer.

Federal Jurisdiction

The **jurisdiction** of the federal courts is derived (*taken*) from the U.S. Constitution. Just as Congress has limited powers, federal courts have limited jurisdiction. They cannot decide all cases. Their jurisdiction is limited because federal power itself is limited.

Federal courts can only decide the following types of cases:

- Cases involving federal law, including the U.S. Constitution itself
- Cases involving the United States, individual states or foreign powers as parties
- Cases between citizens of different states—even if the dispute is under state law

The Active Citizen

How well can you interpret the actual language of the Constitution? Article III of the Constitution defines the jurisdiction of the federal courts. It states that the jurisdiction of federal courts includes:

1. "all Cases . . . arising under this Constitution, the Laws of the United States, and Treaties made, or which shall be made, under their Authority;"

   These are cases involving federal law, including the Constitution.

2. "all Cases affecting Ambassadors, other public Ministers and Consuls; . . . [all cases] to which the United States shall be a Party; [all cases] between two or more States; [or] between a State and Citizens of another State;"

   These are cases involving foreign diplomats, the United States, or one of the 50 states as a party.

3. [all Cases] "between Citizens of different States; . . . and between a State, or the Citizens thereof, and foreign States, Citizens or Subjects"

   These are cases between citizens from different states. Federal courts judge these cases because a state court might favor its own citizens.

- Why do federal courts have jurisdiction over only some kinds of cases? How does this demonstrate the constitutional principle of limited government?
- If you had been writing the Constitution, would you have given federal courts jurisdiction over any other types of cases? If so, which ones? Explain your answer.

The Processes of the Judicial Branch

Original Jurisdiction of the Supreme Court

The U.S. Supreme Court has "original jurisdiction" in all cases affecting foreign ambassadors and other diplomats, or where one of the states, such as Florida, is a party. "Original jurisdiction" means that the case begins—or originates—with this court. In other words, the U.S. Supreme Court is the first court to hear all cases involving these parties.

In these circumstances, the Supreme Court effectively acts as a "trial court." It follows the **trial process** of hearing evidence and making a judgment on the basis of the evidence. There have only been about thirty cases where the U.S. Supreme Court acted as a trial court. Most have involved disputes between states. For example, in *Florida v. Georgia* (1854), the U.S. Supreme Court resolved a border dispute between Florida and Georgia. In this case, the Court eventually ruled in favor of Florida, setting the boundary between the two states that still exists today.

The original jurisdiction of the U.S. Supreme Court was the subject of one of the most famous Supreme Court cases—*Marbury v. Madison*. You will learn more about this case later in this chapter and again in Chapter 10.

Appellate Jurisdiction of the Supreme Court

In all other cases, the U.S. Supreme Court exercises appellate jurisdiction. In these cases, the court acts as an appellate court. This means the Supreme Court cannot try these cases. It can only review decisions by lower courts sent to it on appeal. In these cases, the Court follows an **appellate process**. The party that has lost the case in the lower court asks the appellate court to look over the decision and determine if it was decided through the correct application of the law.The appellate court does not decide questions of fact—just interpretations of the law.

When the Constitution was first adopted, the Supreme Court was required to review all appeals sent to it. The number of such appeals soon became overwhelming. The U.S. Courts of Appeals were created in 1891. Since that time, parties in federal court must first appeal their cases to one of the U.S. Courts of Appeals. If a party loses its case in the U.S. Court of Appeals, it then has the right to appeal to the Supreme Court. Parties in state courts can also appeal to the U.S. Supreme Court if their case involves issues of federal law.

Be sure to know what a writ of certiorari is for the EOC test.

A party seeking review by the Supreme Court must file a petition for a **writ of certiorari**. About 10,000 such petitions are filed with the Supreme Court each year. The Supreme Court is not required to review all of these cases. If the Supreme Court decides to review a particular case, it issues a writ of certiorari. Courts are able to issue **court orders**—instructions that have the force of law. A writ of certiorari is an order by an appellate court granting a request for review of a lower court decision.

The Supreme Court carefully selects which cases to hear. It generally chooses those cases it believes to be of national importance. These cases typically involve the interpretation of an important federal law or the U.S. Constitution.

Fewer than one out of every 100 petitions to the Supreme Court are granted a writ of certiorari each year. The Court generally hears "oral argument" and issues written opinions on only 75 to 80 of these cases. It also usually resolves another 50 cases without oral argument.

A Day in the Life of the Supreme Court

Enrichment

The Court's term begins each year on the first Monday of October and usually lasts until the following July. When the Court is sitting, the Justices first meet privately in the morning to discuss cases. The Justices have already read "briefs"—written legal arguments—from both sides of the case. Law clerks or staff attorneys may have also written memoranda summarizing the key issues and the law. The Chief Justice may even ask for a preliminary vote by the Justices on a case.

Oral Argument

Public sessions begin promptly at 10:00 in the morning. The Justices enter the courtroom wearing their black robes. An attorney for each side of the case is given half an hour to make an oral presentation and to answer any questions that the Justices might ask. This is known as "oral argument." Usually the Court hears oral argument on two cases a day.

During oral argument, the Justices will usually interrupt the speaker with questions many times throughout the presentation.

Reaching a Decision

Sometime after oral argument, the Justices discuss the case among themselves in a private conference. After the case is fully discussed—which may take more than one meeting—a vote is taken.

Writing the Opinion

One of the Justices is assigned to write the decision for the majority. Justices who do not agree with part or all of the majority opinion may write their own dissenting opinions. A draft of the majority opinion is printed and given to all of the Justices. They reply with comments, which the author of the majority opinion often has to take into account. At this point, some of the Justices may have even changed their minds. In Chapter 11, you will read several excerpts from actual Supreme Court opinions. Here is how one Supreme Court Justice described the process:

Each Justice studies each case in sufficient detail to resolve the question for himself. In a very real sense, each decision is an individual decision of every Justice. The process can be a lonely, troubling experience. . . .

I would particularly emphasize that, unlike the case of a Congressional or White House decision, Americans demand of their Supreme Court judges that they produce a written opinion, the collective expression of the judges subscribing [agreeing] to it, setting forth the reason which led them to the decision.

These opinions are the exposition [explanation], not just to lawyers, legal scholars and other judges, but to our whole society, of the bases upon which a particular result rests . . .

—*Justice William J. Brennan, Jr., "How the Supreme Court Arrives at Decisions"*

The Active Citizen

- How did Justice Brennan see Supreme Court decisions as different from Presidential and Congressional decisions?
- Why did Justice Brennan believe that the practice of publishing Supreme Court opinions was so important?
- Is the practice of publishing dissenting opinions too divisive? Explain your answer.
- Imagine that you are a Justice of the U.S. Supreme Court. Write a letter to a friend in which you describe a typical day when the Court is in session.

Be sure to know the two types of lower federal courts for the EOC test.

The "Lower" Federal Courts

At the Constitutional Convention, the possibility of creating federal courts below the Supreme Court was hotly debated. The delegates could not agree. Many felt these courts were unnecessary. Others feared the Supreme Court would be flooded with petitions if lower federal courts were not created. As a skillful compromise, the members of the Constitutional Convention finally agreed to let the future Congress decide the issue. **Article III** created the **Supreme Court** but no other federal courts. However, the same article gave Congress the power to create "inferior" (*lower-level*) federal courts if it wished to do so. The very first Congress did so in the Judiciary Act of 1789.

U.S. District Courts

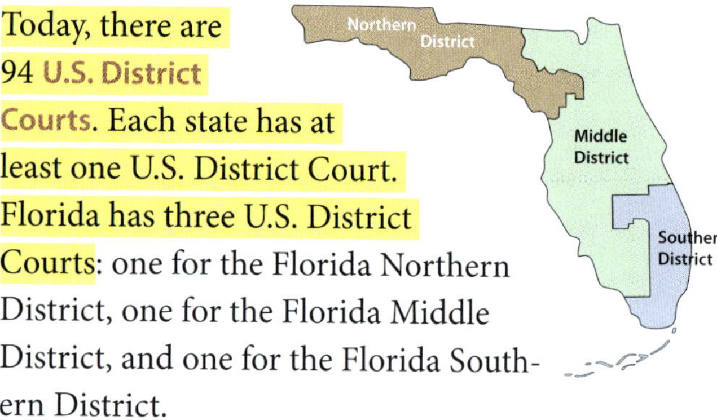

Today, there are 94 U.S. District Courts. Each state has at least one U.S. District Court. Florida has three U.S. District Courts: one for the Florida Northern District, one for the Florida Middle District, and one for the Florida Southern District.

Except for the U.S. Supreme Court in rare instances, the U.S. District Courts are the only federal trial courts. They follow a trial process. Because of this, the U.S. District Courts are also the only federal courts to have juries. A jury is a group of local citizens who hear the evidence at trial and decide the case. If a dispute involves federal law or if it involves citizens from different states, the parties have the right to have their case tried in U.S. District Court. There they will receive a trial, similar in many ways to one that might take place in a state court. In Chapter 9, you will learn more about how cases are tried in state courts.

U.S. Courts of Appeals

There are also now 13 U.S. Courts of Appeals. Twelve of these cover district courts from a specific region, forming a judicial "Circuit." A circuit is a circular route. The term comes from a time when judges traveled around their districts and held court sessions at various locations along their route. Sometimes a U.S. Court of Appeals may even be referred to as a "U.S. Circuit Court of Appeals." Florida, for example, belongs to the U.S. Court of Appeals for the Eleventh Circuit, which also includes Alabama and Georgia. The Eleventh Circuit covers nine U.S. District Courts.

The U.S. Courts of Appeals are not trial courts. Their judges do not try cases. They are appellate courts. They follow an appellate process. When a party loses in U.S. District Court, it has the right to appeal the decision to the U.S. Court of Appeals in its Circuit. The U.S. Court of Appeals then reviews the record of the trial to see whether the law was interpreted correctly and applied fairly. Three judges ordinarily review each case. If two of the three believe the trial court made an important error, they can send the case back to the trial court with instructions for a retrial. The party that loses on appeal has the right to look even farther to

Map showing U.S. Courts of Appeals

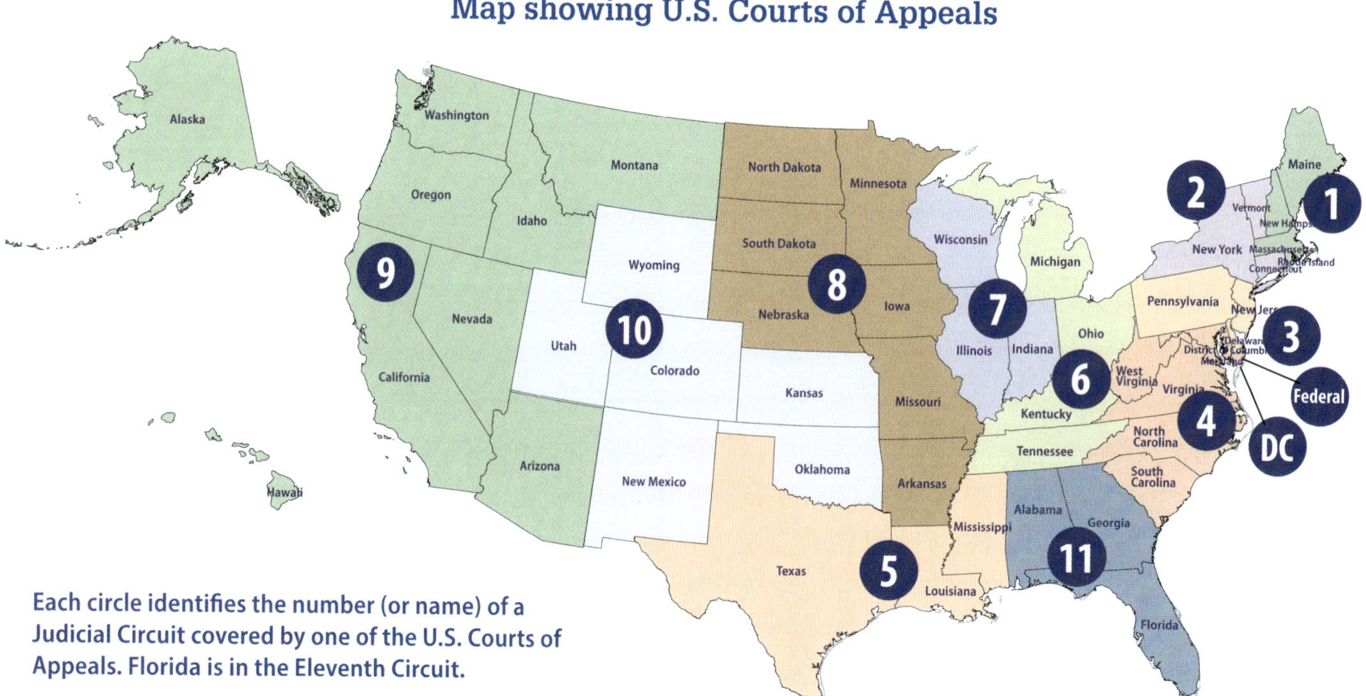

Each circle identifies the number (or name) of a Judicial Circuit covered by one of the U.S. Courts of Appeals. Florida is in the Eleventh Circuit.

obtain justice. If a party believes the law has been misinterpreted or misapplied by the U.S. Court of Appeals, it can petition for a **writ of certiorari** from the U.S. Supreme Court. There is no guarantee, however, that the Supreme Court will accept its petition and hear its case.

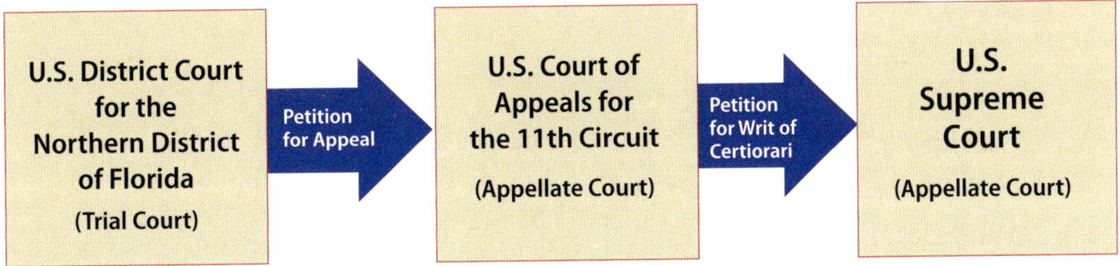

In the next chapter, you will learn more about the differences between trial and appellate courts.

Judicial Review

Chief Justice John Marshall

One of the most important powers of the Supreme Court and other federal courts is the power of **judicial review.** Federal courts can rule that either a law passed by Congress or an executive order issued by the President is unconstitutional. This means that the law or order is not permitted under the U.S. Constitution and cannot be enforced. Federal courts can also rule that a state law or action violates the U.S. Constitution. The power of judicial review is one of the most important checks on actions by Congress or the President. It also protects individual rights from actions by state and local governments.

The phrase "judicial review" is not to be found in the Constitution itself. Chief Justice John Marshall introduced the practice in the case of *Marbury v. Madison* in 1803. In this landmark decision, Marshall declared that part of the Judiciary Act of 1789 was, in fact, unconstitutional. Congress had exceeded its powers under the Constitution. This meant that this section of the Judiciary Act could not be enforced. Marshall argued that it was the Supreme Court's role to decide on the constitutionality of laws because it is the job of courts to interpret the law and to explain what the law is. You will study the case of *Marbury v. Madison* in more detail in Chapter 11.

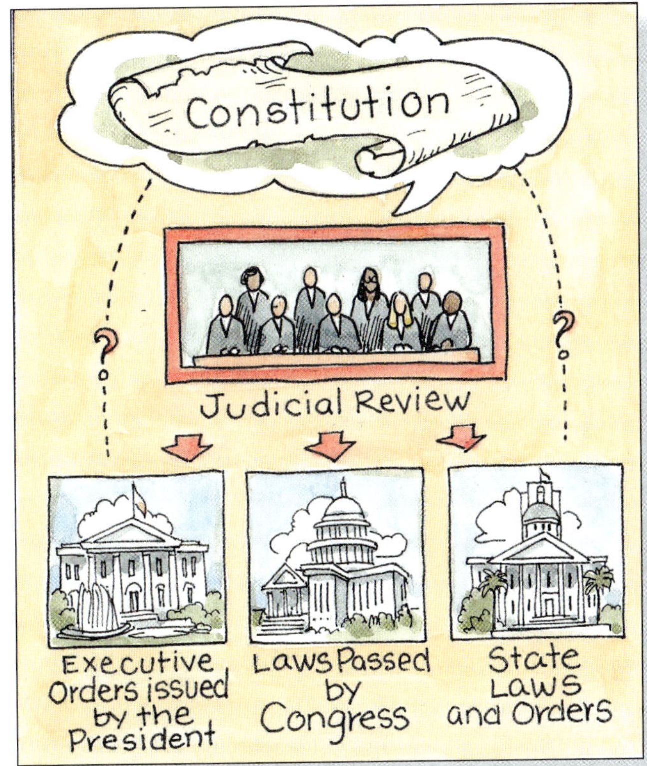

"Judicial review" is not a separate process in addition to the Court's other activities. Congress does not send bills or new laws over to the Court for advice on whether they are constitutional. The Supreme Court and other federal courts cannot issue "advisory opinions." They do not make recommendations to the legislature or the executive. They can only declare that a law is unconstitutional if that law comes before them as part of an actual dispute between two or more parties.

The Federal Judiciary

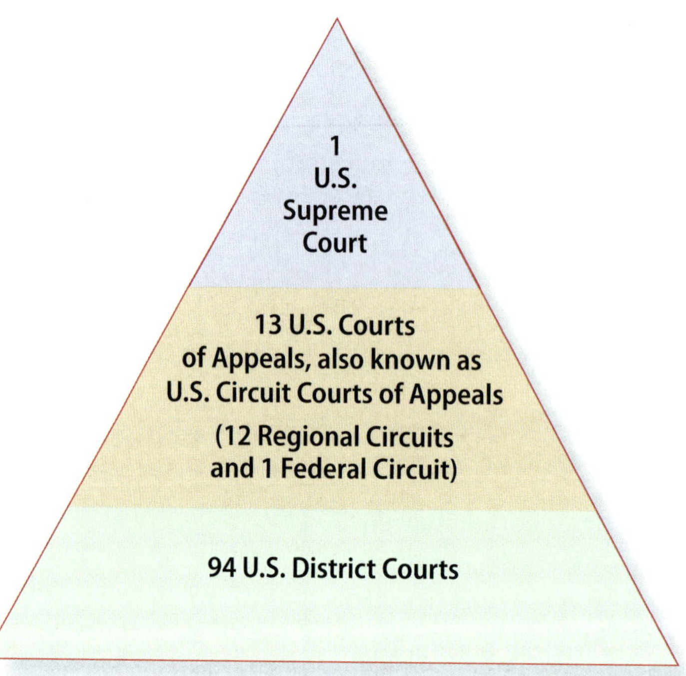

U.S. District Courts	▪ These are federal courts that try cases involving federal crimes, violations of federal law, or cases between parties from different states. ▪ U.S. District Courts are trial courts that hear witnesses, weigh evidence, and find facts. They can have juries.
U.S. Courts of Appeals	▪ These are appellate courts. ▪ They rule on appeals from decisions of the U.S. District Courts. They never have juries. ▪ These courts are organized into 12 geographic regions known as "Circuits." ▪ The U.S. Court of Appeals for the Federal Circuit reviews decisions concerning patents, claims against the U.S. government and other specialized matters.
U.S. Supreme Court	▪ The Supreme Court is the highest court in the land. ▪ It reviews decisions from the U.S. Courts of Appeals and can also review state supreme court decisions involving federal law. ▪ The Supreme Court also acts as a trial court in resolving disputes between different states of the United States, or in cases involving foreign ambassadors and other diplomats. ▪ The Supreme Court and other federal courts also have the power of judicial review: they can declare laws to be unconstitutional.

Name ____

Is there the basis for a successful appeal to an appellate court?

Scenario Number 1

Helen is accused of murdering Samuel. At her trial, a witness says he saw Helen shoot Samuel. Helen's lawyer said the witness was not trustworthy. Even so, the jury decided Helen was guilty. The trial was conducted fairly. The judge allowed all the evidence and testimony requested by Helen's lawyer. The jury instructions were clear, based on the law, and fair.

▸ Does Helen have any basis to appeal the decision? If so, on what basis?

Scenario Number 2

Albert is accused of robbing Margaret. Margaret's brother says he saw the robbery. Albert's lawyer had evidence that Margaret's brother was actually somewhere else at the time. The judge refused to admit this evidence, in violation of the rules of evidence. In the jury instructions, the judge told the jury that they should convict Albert if they thought he probably committed the crime, even if they had a reasonable doubt. This jury instruction was actually contrary to the law. The jury convicted Albert on the basis of the testimony they heard and the jury instructions they received.

▸ Does Albert have any basis for appealing this decision? If so, on what basis?

Define each of the following:

Jurisdiction ____

____

Writ of certiorari ____

____

Court order ____

____

Appellate court ____

____

Judicial review ____

____

Name ________________________________

Describe the role of each of these courts in the federal system:

U.S. Supreme Court

____

____

____

____

____

____

U.S. Court of Appeals

____

____

____

____

____

____

U.S. District Court

____

____

____

____

____

____

Name ______________________________

Comparing the Three Branches of our National Government

Branch	Legislative Branch	Executive Branch	Judicial Branch
Structure	Congress (Senate and House of Representatives): members elected for fixed terms	President (assisted by the Vice President, executive departments and administrative agencies): President elected for fixed term by the Electoral College	U.S. Supreme Court and "lower" Federal Courts (U.S. District Courts and U.S. Courts of Appeal): Justices and federal judges appointed by the President and confirmed by the Senate
Functions/ Roles and Responsibilities	▶ Passes laws for the nation ▶ Checks the other branches: confirm appointments; ratify treaties; impeach officials and judges ▶ Proposes amendments ▶ Chooses President if tie in the Electoral College	▶ Executes (enforce) our national laws ▶ Defends the nation: Commander in Chief of the armed forces ▶ Represents the nation ▶ Provides central leadership ▶ Checks the other branches: veto proposed legislation	▶ Administers justice (help those who obey the law and punish offenders) ▶ Resolves disputes ▶ Interprets the law ▶ Applies laws to specific cases ▶ Judicial Review: Determines the constitutionality of a law (checks the other branches)
Processes	Lawmaking process: introduce bill; committee stage; vote on floor of house; go to other house; conference committee; submit to President	Makes appointments (executive departments, agencies; Supreme Court Justices, ambassadors); issue executive orders; veto proposed legislation	Trial process; appellate process; court order; summary judgment; writ of certiorari; judicial review; case proceeds from U.S. District Court to U.S. Court of Appeals to U.S. Supreme Court

What similarities do you see between these three branches?

What differences do you see between these three branches?

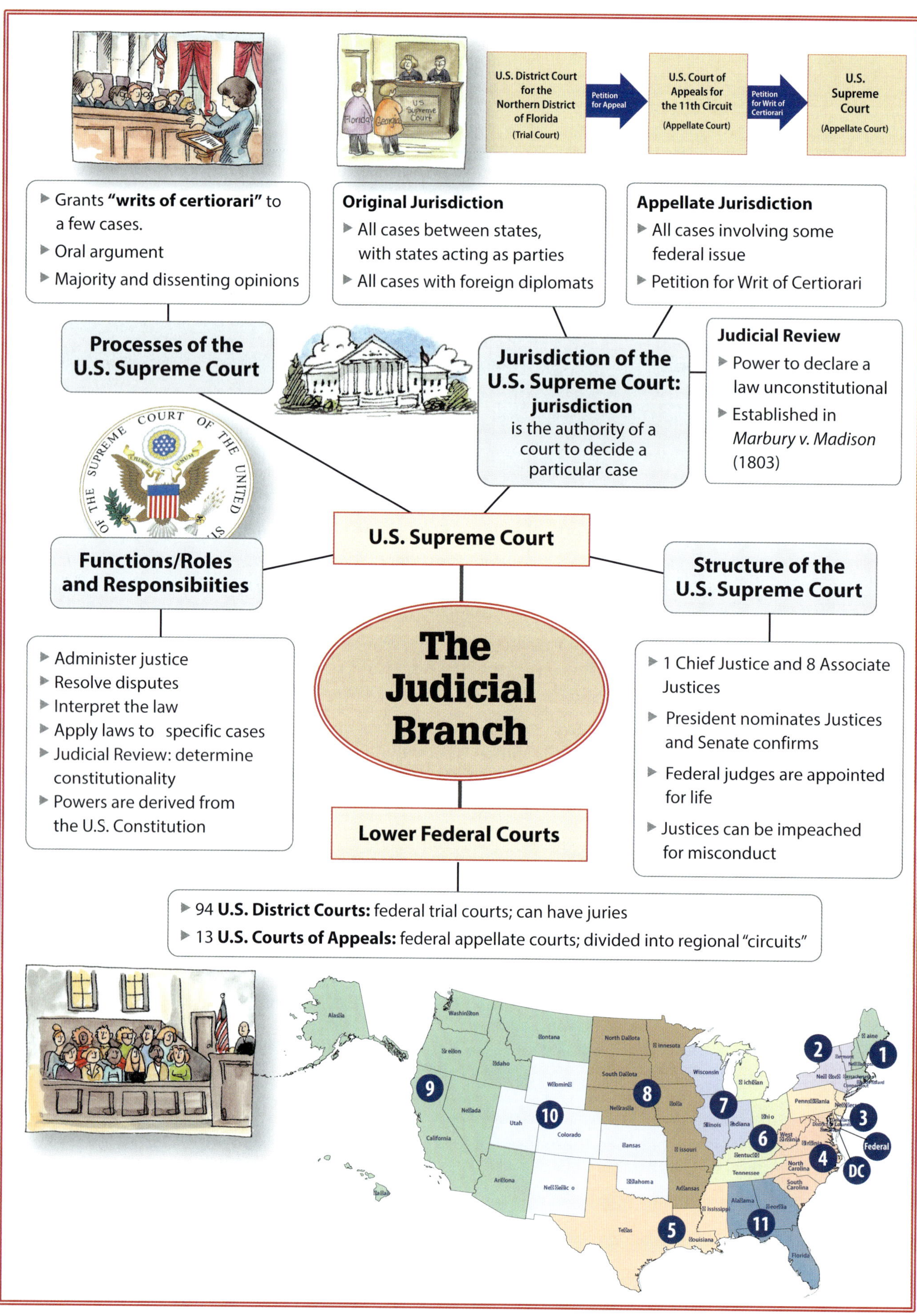

U.S. District Court for the Northern District of Florida (Trial Court)
Petition for Appeal
U.S. Court of Appeals for the 11th Circuit (Appellate Court)
Petition for Writ of Certiorari
U.S. Supreme Court (Appellate Court)
Grants "writs of certiorari" to a few cases.
Oral argument
Majority and dissenting opinions
Original Jurisdiction
All cases between states, with states acting as parties
All cases with foreign diplomats
Appellate Jurisdiction
All cases involving some federal issue
Petition for Writ of Certiorari
Processes of the U.S. Supreme Court
Jurisdiction of the U.S. Supreme Court: jurisdiction is the authority of a court to decide a particular case
Judicial Review
Power to declare a law unconstitutional
Established in Marbury v. Madison (1803)
U.S. Supreme Court
Functions/Roles and Responsibiities
Structure of the U.S. Supreme Court
The Judicial Branch
Administer justice
Resolve disputes
Interpret the law
Apply laws to specific cases
Judicial Review: determine constitutionality
Powers are derived from the U.S. Constitution
1 Chief Justice and 8 Associate Justices
President nominates Justices and Senate confirms
Federal judges are appointed for life
Justices can be impeached for misconduct
Lower Federal Courts
94 U.S. District Courts: federal trial courts; can have juries
13 U.S. Courts of Appeals: federal appellate courts; divided into regional "circuits"
1
2
3
4
5
6
7
8
9
10
11
Federal
DC

Review Cards: The Federal Courts

The Judicial Branch: The U.S. Supreme Court

- Article III of the Constitution established the **judicial branch**.
- **Functions/roles and responsibilities of the judicial branch:** The judicial branch of our federal government is in charge of administering justice (*helping those who obey the law and punishing those who break it*). It also resolves many disputes by interpreting and applying the law.
- **Structure of the Judicial Branch:** The Constitution created our country's first national court, the **U.S. Supreme Court**.
- The Constitution also gave Congress the power to create "inferior" (lower) federal courts.
- Public officials who preside over courts of law and sometimes decide cases are known as judges. Judges on the U.S. Supreme Court are known as Justices. The number of Justices on the Supreme Court has increased over time. There are now 8 Associate Justices and 1 Chief Justice. The Chief Justice presides over the Supreme Court and acts as its spokesperson. The Chief Justice also swears the President into office and presides over any Presidential impeachment trial.
- Supreme Court Justices are nominated by the President and confirmed by a majority vote in the Senate. This is an example of our system of checks and balances.
- All federal judges are appointed for life, so long as they maintain "good behavior" (do not commit "high crimes" or other misconduct, for which Congress can impeach them) or until they resign. This system of appointment for life helps federal judges to act independently of popular and political pressures. It helps to protect the independence of the judiciary and the separation of powers.
- Supreme Court Justices can be impeached by Congress, although no Supreme Court Justice has ever been removed from office.

Jurisdiction

- There are many different types of courts in the United States. The territory and type of cases over which a court exercises its authority is called its **jurisdiction**. The word *jurisdiction* comes from: "to say the law."
- Federal courts derive (*obtain*) their power from the Constitution. They have limited jurisdiction. They can only decide (1) cases involving federal law; (2) cases involving the United States, individual states or foreign powers as parties; or (3) cases involving citizens from different states.
- The **U.S. Supreme Court** has original jurisdiction in all cases involving foreign representatives (ambassadors, consuls, and other diplomats) or states (such as Florida) as parties. In these cases, the Supreme Court is the original, or first, court that the parties turn to. In these cases, it acts as a trial court. The Supreme Court considers the evidence in these cases and reaches its decision.
- In all other cases, the Supreme Court exercises appellate jurisdiction. In these cases, it acts as an appellate court. This means the Court follows an **appellate process**. It reviews appeals from the decisions of lower courts to see if they applied the law correctly, rather than trying the case itself.

The "Lower" Federal Courts

- The Constitution gave Congress the power to create "inferior"—or lower—federal courts. The Judiciary Act of 1789 created the first lower federal courts.
- Today, there are 94 **U.S. District Courts** and 13 **U.S. Courts of Appeals**.

U.S. District Courts

- Each state has at least one U.S. District Court. Florida has three. These are the only federal trial courts. They follow a **trial process**. This means they can have juries. These courts try those accused of federal crimes and resolve disputes involving federal law. They can also resolve disputes based on state law when these disputes are between citizens from different states.

U.S. Courts of Appeals

- The **U.S. Courts of Appeals** are appellate courts: they follow an **appellate process**. They review cases on appeal, but do not try them. They look for errors committed by the court below in interpreting and applying the law (such as admitting the wrong evidence or giving wrong jury instructions).
- Each U.S. Court of Appeals covers the U.S. District Courts in its "Circuit." For example, the U.S. Court of Appeals for the 11th Circuit covers the U.S. District Courts for Florida, Alabama and Georgia. The Court of Appeals for the 11th Circuit reviews appeals from all the U.S. District Courts in those three states. These are also known as **U.S. Circuit Courts of Appeals**.

Processes of the Judicial Branch: How a Case Proceeds through Federal Court

- First, the parties file the case in **U.S. District Court**. The District Court is a trial court.
- The losing party can appeal the decision to the **U.S. Court of Appeals** for that Circuit.
- The appellate court may agree with the lower court or it could reverse the lower court and send the case back with instructions for a retrial.
- The party losing the appeal can petition for a **writ of certiorari** from the U.S. Supreme Court. A **writ of certiorari** is a type of **court order**—an instruction from the court with the force of law.

Review by the Supreme Court

- Each year, the U.S. Supreme Court receives thousands of requests for review—called petitions for a **writ of certiorari**. Only about a hundred are usually granted. These are the cases heard by the Court.
- When a case reaches the Supreme Court, the Justices read papers known as "briefs" from both sides of the case. Then they hear oral arguments by the attorneys from both sides, during which the Justices ask questions. The Justices then discuss the case among themselves and reach their decision. One Justice writes a majority opinion, which is published. Justices who disagree with the majority opinion may write their own separate, dissenting opinions. These are also published.

Judicial Review

- In the case *Marbury v. Madison* in 1803, Chief Justice John Marshall established the power of **judicial review**. This is the power of the U.S. Supreme Court and other federal courts to declare that a law or executive order is unconstitutional if the court decides it violates the Constitution.
- Federal courts can only declare laws unconstitutional if they are brought before them in actual court cases.

What Do You Know?

SS.7.CG.3.9

1. Sam Morgan is convicted of committing mail fraud by the U.S. District Court for the Southern District of Florida. Sam believes the judge was unfairly biased against him. To which court should he send his appeal?

   A. U.S. Supreme Court
   B. Florida Circuit Court
   C. U.S. Court of Appeals
   D. Florida Supreme Court

SS.7.CG.3.3

2. Article III of the Constitution established the U.S. Supreme Court. Why does this article refer to this court as "supreme"?

   A. It hears more cases than any other court.
   B. It has authority over all other courts in the United States.
   C. Its officers are appointed by the President of the United States.
   D. It has authority over both the executive and legislative branches.

SS.7.CG.3.3

3. Why did the Constitution establish that federal judges be appointed for life?

   A. to ensure the system of checks and balances
   B. to strengthen their jurisdiction over state courts
   C. to limit the power of the legislative and executive branches
   D. to maintain the independence of the judiciary and separation of powers

SS.7.CG.3.9

4. An oil barge belonging to the State of Alabama has a massive oil leak in the Gulf of Mexico. The leaked oil damages the beautiful beaches of Destin, Panama City, and Ft. Walton. The oil also endangers the shrimp and crab industry of Florida. The State of Florida sues the State of Alabama. Which court has jurisdiction over the case?

   A. U.S. Supreme Court
   B. Florida Supreme Court
   C. U.S. Court of Appeals for the 11th Circuit
   D. U.S. District Court for the Northern District of Florida

SS.7.CG.3.9

5. How does an appellate court differ from a trial court?

   A. An appellate court usually has a jury.
   B. An appellate court decides issues of fact.
   C. An appellate court examines more witnesses.
   D. An appellate court reviews another court's decision.

SS.7.CG.3.9

6. The Rio Grande forms the international border between Texas and Mexico. Over the years, the Rio Grande has changed its course several times. This has led to a number of disputes between Texas, New Mexico, and Mexico. The Country Club dispute between Texas and New Mexico was decided by the U.S. Supreme Court in 1927.

Why did the Supreme Court follow a trial process in this case?

A. The case involved federal law.

B. The case was between several states as parties.

C. The case was between citizens of different states.

D. The case involved foreign ambassadors and other diplomats.

SS.7.CG.3.9

7. Which are the only federal courts to have juries?

A. U.S. District Courts

B. U.S. Supreme Court

C. U.S. Courts of Appeals

D. U.S. District Courts of Appeals

SS.7.CG.3.9

8. What kind of court order does the U.S. Supreme Court issue to indicate that it will review a case?

A. writ of certiorari

B. majority opinion

C. summary judgment

D. writ of habeas corpus

SS.7.CG.3.3

9. The headline on the left appeared in a newspaper.

Which statement would most likely follow this headline?

A. "Justice discovered to be ruling on cases solely to win votes."

B. "Justice found to be opposing the President's views on the case."

C. "Justice accused of accepting secret payments from a party in the case."

D. "Justice committed treason by ruling in favor of a foreign diplomat against the United States."

SS.7.CG.3.9

10. The diagram below provides details about the U.S. court system.

Which court completes the diagram?

A. Circuit Court

B. Supreme Court

C. Municipal Court

D. Court of Veterans Appeals

CHAPTER 9

The Rule of Law

SS.7.CG.1.11 Define the rule of law and recognize its influence on the development of legal, political, and governmental systems in the United States.

SS.7.CG.2.5 Describe the trial process and the role of juries in the administration of justice at the state and federal levels.

SS.7.CG.3.9 Explain the structure, functions, and processes of the judicial branch of government. (*For judicial review, writ of certiorari, and the federal court structure, see Chapter 8.*)

SS.7.CG.3.10 Identify sources and types (civil, criminal, constitutional, military) of law.

Content Focus Vocabulary in This Chapter

Legal system
Rule of law
Arbitrary and abusive use of government power
Governmental officials
Institutions
Accountability to the law
Consistent application and enforcement of the law
Decisions based on the law
Fair Procedures
Transparency of institutions
Due Process

Historical codes of law
Sources of law
Natural law
Statutory law
Common law
Case law
Constitutional law
Types of law
Civil law
Criminal law
Military law
Administration of justice

Trial process
Court order
Jury
Jury selection
Types of jury trial
Summary judgment
Appellate process
Florida County Court
Florida Circuit Court
Florida District Court of Appeal
Florida Supreme Court

Florida "Keys" to Learning

1. A law is a rule that is enforced by the government and includes some penalty (*punishment*) for breaking it. A community's set of laws is known as its **legal system**.

2. In many nations, the ruler's will (*desire*) is law. In contrast, Americans live under the **rule of law**. This means we live under a system of written laws that make it clear how people should behave with one another. All people are subject to the same laws, without exception. Our government leaders are subject to the same laws as everybody else.

3. The rule of law has an important impact on **governmental officials** (*those who serve in government*) and **institutions** (*parts of the government, such as agencies*). They must follow these principles: **accountability to the law** (*they are responsible for obeying the law*); **consistent application and enforcement of the law** (*they apply and enforce the law to everyone in the same way*); **decisions based on the law** (*decisions are based on existing laws, not on personal desires*); **fair procedures** (*the process of applying the law is fair and impartial*); and **transparency of institutions** (*procedures are conducted openly in public*).

4. **Due process** of law is an essential part of the rule of law and the American legal system. Before the government can take away our life, liberty or property, we are entitled to a fair process. This means a hearing of some kind, conducted in public before a neutral and impartial decision-maker or jury. We should be able to present our own evidence and see and hear all the evidence against us. Finally, the decision should be based solely on the law and the evidence presented at the hearing or trial.

5. Laws have evolved over time. **Historical codes of laws** (*collections of laws brought together*) have played an important role in the development of the law. They developed solutions to legal problems and made it possible to find a law by subject.

6. The United States has many **sources of law** (*places where the laws come from*). Laws passed by a legislature are known as **statutory law**. Medieval England established the **common law**—laws based on customs and the earlier decisions of judges in similar cases. **Case law** is law based on past court decisions. The U.S. Constitution and state constitutions are the sources of **constitutional law**.

7. There are many **types of laws**. These include **criminal laws**, which punish those who commit crimes, and **civil laws**, which resolve disputes between parties over accidents, property damage and other issues. **Constitutional law** concerns our rights under the Constitution; **military law** governs the members of our armed forces; and **juvenile law** applies to children who are not yet adults. Each type of law has its own rules.

8. Laws are enforced in courts by the decision of a judge or a judge and jury. A **jury** is a panel of citizens, chosen randomly from the community. Potential jurors receive a jury summons. During **jury selection**, lawyers interview potential jurors and eliminate those who show bias. There are different **types of jury trial**. A grand jury consists of 15 or more citizens. It meets in private and decides whether or not there is enough evidence to charge a person for a crime. A trial jury consists of six or 12 jurors. It meets in public, hears the evidence during a trial, and decides the case. Juries can decide both criminal and civil trials.

9. Juries protect the impartiality of the law. We don't always know what exactly occurred in an event, such as a crime. There are often many questions surrounding the facts. Juries are fact-finders: they hear the evidence and reach conclusions about the facts, based on what the evidence shows. The jury system protects citizens from **arbitrary and abusive uses of government power** (*government officals unfairly mistreating citizens*). Government officials cannot dictate the outcome of a jury trial. This makes it harder for them to arrest and punish opponents and critics.

10. A civil case concerns a dispute or injury between two or more parties. It begins when one party files a "complaint" against another. During pretrial

discovery, both sides must produce evidence. Lawyers investigate the facts and interview witnesses. A lawyer can file a motion for **summary judgment** to dismiss the case if overwhelming evidence favors one side. If a trial occurs, a jury is selected. Jurors who show bias (*prejudice*) are excused. During the trial, each side makes its case. The jury's role is to decide the facts based on the evidence. Their decision, including any monetary award, is known as the verdict.

11. If one side is not satisfied with the verdict, it can appeal to an appellate court. In the **appellate process**, the appellate court reviews the case for errors in law and decides whether to have a retrial.

12. A criminal case begins with the investigation of a crime. When a suspect is found, there is a hearing to decide if there is "probable cause" to arrest the suspect. A grand jury—a group of 15 or more citizens at the state level—may be used to determine probable cause. If probable cause exists, the suspect is "arraigned" and can plead guilty or not guilty. Then bail is set: if paid, the person is freed until trial. After a period of plea-bargaining, the case goes to trial. As in a civil trial, jurors are selected from local citizens. In a criminal case, the defendant is presumed not guilty unless the evidence shows guilt "beyond a reasonable doubt." If the defendant is found guilty by the jury, the judge imposes a sentence (*a punishment such as a fine or imprisonment*). The defendant can appeal both the verdict and the sentence.

13. Florida has four levels of courts. **Florida county courts** hear civil cases for $8,000 to $50,000 and cases of lesser crimes (misdemeanors). **Florida circuit courts** hear civil cases for more than $50,000 and more serious crimes (felonies). They also review appeals from the county courts. **Florida District Courts of Appeal** review cases from the circuit courts. Lastly, the **Florida Supreme Court** acts as the highest court in the state. It hears appeals from the lower state courts, including all death penalty cases, and can also issue some advisory opinions.

In the last chapter, you learned about the organization of the judicial branch of our federal government. In this chapter, you will look more closely at how laws are applied to specific situations by both state and federal courts.

Welcome to Law School!

You may only be in the middle grades, but in this chapter you are about to enter law school. You have probably already seen imaginary trials on television. What courts do is to interpret and apply the law. Therefore, you cannot truly understand what courts do until you first know what a law is.

So, what exactly is a law?

A law is a type of rule, such as having to stop at a stop sign. Unlike other rules, a law is enforced by the government. There is almost always some penalty (*punishment*) for breaking a law. If a driver doesn't stop at a stop sign, the driver may get a traffic ticket and have to pay a fine.

Laws help a community to organize and protect itself. They allow community leaders to take those steps needed to achieve cooperation for the common good. They also help the community to settle disputes without violence. Laws protect the safety of individuals and their property. Laws against crimes serve special purposes. They help the victims of a crime overcome their grief by punishing the criminal. They discourage potential criminals from committing future crimes. And finally, the experience of punishment can lead some individuals to reform and give up their criminal behavior.

Interpreting the Law

Although the wording of a law may seem clear at first, difficulties often arise in applying it to specific situations. Take, for example, the case of a town that decides to put up a sign in a local park. The sign says "No Vehicles Permitted in the Park." This seems clear enough. The town doesn't want cars, trucks, motorcycles or buses driving through the park.

But Ms. Smith wants to take her toddler in a stroller into the park. Is her stroller a "vehicle"? Would this action violate the rule? And her husband, Mr. Smith, is in a wheelchair. Is his wheelchair a "vehicle"? Can Mr. Smith take his wheelchair into the park?

Jack and Jill ride their bicycles to school. Can they take a shortcut through the park? Is a bicycle a "vehicle," as intended by the sign?

These are examples of the kinds of problems that can arise in interpreting the language of a particular law. It is the job of courts to interpret laws and to apply them to specific situations.

As one of the most famous U.S. Supreme Court Justices once explained:

> "*It is emphatically* (clearly; without a doubt) *the province and duty of the judicial department to say what the law is. Those who apply the rule to particular cases must of necessity [explain] and interpret that rule.*"
>
> —Chief Justice John Marshall, *Marbury v. Madison* (1803)

The Rule of Law

What is so special about having laws? As you can see, laws make it clear how we should conduct ourselves. Because of laws, we know how we should behave and how we can expect others to behave.

Laws are generally written and available in public so that everyone can know about them. We expect our laws to be fair and reasonable. Even if we disagree with a specific law, we are still willing to obey it.

In many societies throughout history, the ruler's will has been the law. Whatever the ruler desires at any moment suddenly becomes the law. In this kind of society, citizens cannot easily make future plans. From moment to moment, they do not know what they are permitted or not permitted to do. At any time, they may face harsh penalties. In this kind of society, everyone except the ruler is at risk.

Laws are therefore especially important in placing curbs on government. In a democratic society, the government itself is subject to the law. We say that we live under **the rule of law**. This means that we are ruled by laws rather than by our rulers' whims. Our laws protect us from the **arbitrary and abusive use of government power**. "Arbitrary" means dictatorial and unfair—doing whatever the ruler feels like doing, rather than doing what is fair and reasonable. Under the rule of law, government leaders can only do what the law permits them to do. The police, for example, must follow the law when questioning suspects. Judges must also follow the law when deciding whether to fine someone. Finally, our government leaders are themselves subject to the rule of law, just like everyone else.

The rule of law thus has an important impact on **government officials** (*those who serve in government*) and institutions (*parts of the government; official organizations*). It requires them to follow five key principles:

Accountability to the law

The government holds each of us "accountable" to the law. We must answer to it. Our conduct is subject to written laws that everyone knows and that everyone is subject to. We are legally responsible for our actions. No one is permitted to break the law without consequence. People who break the law must pay a penalty of some kind—either they pay a fine or go to prison. This even applies to our public officials.

Consistent application and enforcement of the law

"Consistent" means evenly, or always the same. The law should be applied and enforced for everyone in the same way, no matter how poor or rich they are or where they come from. Everyone should be treated the same under the law.

For this reason, the Supreme Court has held that even those who cannot afford to pay for a lawyer are entitled to the help of one if they are accused of a serious crime. If an accused person cannot afford a lawyer, then the court must provide one for free.

To make sure the law is applied and enforced consistently, our court decisions are recorded. Judges consider what was done in the past and try to apply the law to new cases in a similar way.

Decisions based on the law

When a government official or institution reaches a decision, such as to punish someone accused of a crime, this decision must be based on the law.

Fair procedures

Procedures are the steps the government takes to carry out its decisions. The procedures used to decide whether an accused person has violated the law, or to settle a dispute between people or groups, should be fair and impartial.

These fair procedures are sometimes known as our "due process" rights. We are "due" a fair process if we risk losing our freedom or our property in a court or government proceeding. These "due process" rights include the right to a public trial or hearing before our freedom or property can be taken away (see below). For example, a person accused of a crime has the right to see any evidence the police have collected and to question any witnesses. These "due process" rights make the law more fair and impartial for all of us.

Transparency of institutions

Something is transparent if we can see through it. In a society based on the rule of law, proceedings and decisions by government bodies affecting our rights are made openly and in public, not in secret. This is known as transparency of institutions. It means everyone can see what is going on. All our laws are public and all our government hearings and court proceedings, such as trials, are public and transparent. This way, everyone can see that the law is applied and enforced consistently, and that government decisions are fair and based on the law. Government officials cannot arbitrarily deny our rights in secret proceedings.

No one is above the law. The rule of law requires government officials and institutions to follow these five principles:

- Accountability to the law
- Consistent application and enforcement of the law
- Decisions based on law
- Fair procedures
- Transparency of institutions

The Importance of "Due Process" of Law

Due process is an essential part of the rule of law and the American legal system (*set of laws*). The Fifth and Fourteenth Amendments both guarantee our "due process of law." This means that before the government can take away our life, liberty or property, we are entitled to a fair and public "process" or hearing.

- We should receive advance notice about the possible future action and the reasons for it.
- We should be given enough time to prepare our response.
- We must be able to present our own evidence at the hearing or trial, as well as to see and hear all the evidence against us.
- We should be able to question witnesses who testify against us.
- We should have the right to receive the assistance of a skilled lawyer.
- The decision should be based solely on the law and the evidence presented at the hearing or trial. The ruling should be written and explain the reasons for the decision.
- The decision-maker who will decide the case—whether it be a judge, jury, or panel—should be neutral and impartial.
- Finally, there should be the right to appeal the decision.

Because of our "due process" rights, our lives, liberties, and property are protected from arbitrary actions by the government.

The Active Citizen

In the case of *Goldberg v. Kelly* (1970), New York State decided to end the financial assistance it was giving to several poor families with dependent children. The U.S. Supreme Court held that the way the state had ended the benefits for these families was unconstitutional because they had not been provided with due process of law. They were never given an opportunity to present evidence showing that their benefits should not be stopped: "The fundamental [requirement] of due process of law is the opportunity to be heard . . . The hearing must be 'at a meaningful time and in a meaningful manner' . . . In almost every setting where important decisions turn on questions of fact, due process requires an opportunity to confront and cross-examine adverse witnesses . . . Finally, the decisionmaker's conclusion . . . must rest solely on the legal rules and evidence [provided] at the hearing . . ."

—*Goldberg v. Kelly*, 397 U.S. 254, 270–271 (1970)

- How is each of the rights listed by the Court above important to the right of "due process"?

Where Do Laws Come From? How Laws Developed in Western Society

From the very earliest times, people have had laws. One of the earliest known written law codes was issued more than 3,700 years ago by Hammurabi, the ruler of Babylonia. With this written law code, people in ancient Babylon knew the rules to which they were accountable:

These excerpts from famous law codes are offered as examples. This one was written many thousands of years ago. You may find it difficult to read. **You will not have to know any specific law codes for the EOC test.**

The Code of Hammurabi

22. IF ANY ONE IS COMMITTING A ROBBERY AND IS CAUGHT, THEN HE SHALL BE PUT TO DEATH . . . .

196. IF A MAN DESTROYS THE EYE OF ANOTHER MAN, THEY SHALL DESTROY HIS EYE. IF ONE MAN BREAKS ANOTHER'S BONE, THEY SHALL BREAK HIS BONE. IF ONE MAN DESTROYS THE EYE OF A FREEMAN OR BREAKS THE BONE OF A FREEMAN, HE SHALL PAY ONE MINA OF SILVER. IF HE DESTROYS THE EYE OF A MAN'S SLAVE OR BREAKS THE BONE OF A MAN'S SLAVE, HE SHALL PAY ONE-HALF HIS PRICE . . . .

265. IF A HERDSMAN OR SHEPHERD, TO WHOSE CARE CATTLE OR SHEEP HAVE BEEN ENTRUSTED, BE GUILTY OF FRAUD . . . THEN HE SHALL BE CONVICTED AND PAY THE OWNER TEN TIMES THE LOSS . . . .

Word Helper

a code = a set of rules or laws

to commit = to do something

to destroy = here, to injure or damage

a freeman = a person who is not a slave

a mina of silver = an amount of money at that time; a coin

a herdsman = someone watching cattle

a shepherd = someone watching sheep

entrusted = to be trusted with something

fraud = cheating, lying or deceiving

The Active Citizen

Ancient law codes can be hard to read and understand. See if you can answer any of these questions.

- Were the penalties (*punishments*) for crimes in ancient Babylonia harsher than today? How would you explain the differences?
- Which of the laws above were made to deter (*discourage*) crime, and which ones were made to compensate (*reimburse; repay*) a victim for losses? Explain your answer.
- How were the penalties for hurting another person different, depending on his or her social status?
- Why were the penalties for fraud (*cheating; deceit*) in caring for animals so strict?
- What was the significance of written law codes like the Code of Hammurabi to the development of the rule of law?

The Roman Forum was a public square where the government made announcements.

Ancient Roman Law

In ancient Rome, the representatives of the common people insisted that their laws be written and displayed in a public place, so that the people would know what they could and could not do. These laws were written on **Twelve Tables** and placed on the main public square of Rome, known as the Forum, in 450 B.C.

Enrichment

Samples of Roman Laws from the Twelve Tables

Just like Hammurabi's Code, these ancient Roman laws may be difficult to understand. The rules here were used by Romans more than 2,000 years ago to resolve disputes and punish wrongdoers. You do not need to know any specific Roman laws for the EOC test.

Table VII

Law II.

If you cause any unlawful damage . . . accidentally and unintentionally, you must make good the loss, either by offering what has caused it, or by payment.

Law XIII.

If anyone knowingly and intentionally kills a freeman, he shall be guilty of a capital crime. If he kills him by accident, without malice or intention, let him substitute a ram to be sacrificed publicly to seek forgiveness . . .

Word Helper

intentionally = purposefully; deliberately
ram = male sheep
capital crime = crime punishable by death
malice = ill will; bad feeling
reparation = compensation; repayment

Table IX

Law III.

When a judge appointed to hear a case accepts money, or other gifts, for the purpose of influencing his decision, he shall suffer the penalty of death.

Table XII

Law III.

If a slave, with the knowledge of his master, commits a theft or causes damage to anyone, his master shall be given up to the other party by way of reparation for the theft, injury, or damage committed by the slave.

The Active Citizen

- Why did Roman commoners (*plebeians*) want to have these laws publicly displayed?
- Select two of these laws and explain them in a letter to a relative in a different part of the ancient world.
- What common principles can you find in these laws?

The Romans expanded their territories to create a far-flung empire that dominated the ancient world. With so many peoples and traditions under their rule, the Romans needed a well-organized set of laws that everyone could easily follow. Romans introduced many important legal concepts, such as the enforcement of contracts—solemn agreements made by private parties that can be publicly enforced in courts of law. In a contract, one party often promises to pay another party to do something. The Romans also improved procedures for investigating and prosecuting crimes and for resolving commercial disputes.

Between 529 and 534 A.D., the Emperor Justinian took all the known laws of the Roman Empire and brought them together into a single law code—the Code of Justinian. This made Roman laws easier to locate and refer to.

Law in the Middle Ages

During the Middle Ages in Europe (from 500 A.D. to about 1400 A.D.), laws came from many different sources. Some laws dated back to Roman times; others came from popular tradition.

A third group of laws came from the king. You already know, for example, that King John I of England signed *Magna Carta* in 1215. This royal charter gave certain rights to every freeborn Englishman. One of these rights was the right to a trial by jury.

Later in English history, laws were mainly passed by Parliament and approved by the king. Laws passed by Parliament or any other legislature such as Congress are known as statutes, or **statutory law**.

In the Middle Ages, England also established the **common law**. King John's father, Henry II, sent royal judges around the English countryside for part of each year in order to hear and decide cases. Henry told his judges to consider both local customs and past judgments in deciding cases. Later, these judges returned to London, where they discussed their cases and recorded their most important decisions. Henry's goal was to create a system of laws "common" to the entire kingdom. The **common law** thus took into account not only laws passed by the king and Parliament, but also customs and decisions reached by earlier judges on the same issue.

You should know the differences between statutory and common law for the EOC test.

People believed it was more just and fair when the law was applied consistently: all those in similar situations should receive the same treatment from the courts. The common law thus looked to precedents—previous decisions by courts. These served as models to guide later courts dealing with similar situations.

The common law came to be seen as a powerful force independent of the king's own authority. Chief Justice Sir Edward Coke (1552–1634) called the law "the perfection of reason." Coke considered the common law to be the "most general and ancient law of the realm."

Two Sources of Law

The Active Citizen

- What is meant by the "common law"?
- How does statutory law differ from the common law?

How Historical Codes of Law Have Influenced the United States

Historical codes of law are part of our heritage from ancient Greece, Rome, the Judeo-Christian tradition, and England. Above all, these codes established **the rule of law**—the basic principle that a stable society has a system of written laws that all its members agree to follow.

Over time, these earlier codes of law developed particular solutions to problems of everyday life that we still use today. For example, in primitive times if one person murdered another, the relatives of the murdered person attacked the relatives of the murderer in revenge. Fighting was common in these circumstances. Historical codes of law replaced this system of family revenge. They introduced a system in which the person accused of murder was tried, and a judge or jury decided on the proper punishment based on the evidence. This peaceful solution, first developed in earlier law codes, is what we still do today.

Historical codes of law also developed the first detailed rules for enforcing agreements, known as contracts, which make the conduct of modern business possible. They likewise developed solutions for what should happen when one person accidentally injures another. Earlier law codes further developed rules for the ownership of property and inheritance. All of these solutions from earlier codes of law are part of the laws of the United States today.

Finally, starting in the 1850s, American lawyers began to copy the example of the earlier law codes by bringing all their own laws together into state law codes and a single United States Code. This makes it possible to find a law by subject. The U.S. Code today contains all federal laws in a single source, organized by subject matter. Florida's laws are similarly organized into a single law code, with 48 "titles" (or subjects), ranging from the organization of Florida's state legislature (Title III), banks and banking (Title XXXVIII), and criminal laws (Title XLVI) to education (Title XLVIII). Each of these titles contains all of Florida's state laws on those subjects.

For the EOC test, be sure to know the different types of law—civil, criminal, constitutional, military and juvenile—as well as the different sources of law—natural law, statutory law, common law, case law, and constitutional law.

Sources and Types of American Law

Americans inherited several legal traditions—Judeo-Christian teachings, Roman law, English common law, and statutory law issued by the king and Parliament. In addition, colonial legislatures enacted many of their own laws. The Declaration of Independence appealed to the existence of **natural law**—rules based on human reason that apply to all societies, such as that each of us is entitled to our life, liberty and property, and that people have the right to choose their own government. Because of these different legal traditions, the United States has several **sources of law** (*places where its laws have come from*).

When the colonies became independent, each new state wrote its own constitution and established its own laws and court system. Each state continued to rely on both **statutory** and **common law**—that is, laws passed by state legislatures and laws based on the decisions of judges who had heard similar cases in the past. In the case of Florida, which became a state in 1845, its laws were also influenced by Spanish legal traditions.

Sources of Law

Natural Law	Basic laws that apply to all societies, such as that all individuals have inalienable rights to life, liberty and property.
Statutory Law	Statutory laws are all the laws passed by legislatures, also known as statutes.
Common Law	The common law is based on customs, traditions, and prior court decisions (*precedents*) on similar cases. Judges often have to fill gaps in the law in making their decisions. The common law is the sum of all these interpretations of laws.
Case Law	Case law is actually part of the common law. It is law based on prior court decisions (*precedents*).
Constitutional Law	These are laws based on the U.S. Constitution, including the Bill of Rights, and the state constitutions.

Federal, State and Local Laws

In the United States, there are different levels of laws. Federal courts can only decide some kinds of cases, such as those concerning federal law. State courts, in contrast, are more general. They can hear almost any type of case. Most legal matters today are, in fact, handled by state courts applying state law:

- If you are accused of committing a crime in Florida, you will be tried in a Florida state court for having broken a Florida law.
- If you have a contract dispute with a local business, you will seek to resolve your dispute in a Florida state court based on Florida law.
- If you suffered a personal injury in Florida because of someone else's carelessness, you seek compensation in a Florida state court.

In the United States, there are different levels of laws. As you know, government also creates its own laws. Whenever Congress passes a bill and the President signs it, it becomes a new federal law. Local governments also pass their own laws. We are thus surrounded by a web of laws. American citizens are subject to federal, state, and local laws.

Local, State, and Federal Laws

Local Laws	These laws are passed by local governments and only concern the local community. An example might be the speed limit on a local street. Local laws are often known as "ordinances."
State Laws	These laws are passed by state governments. They affect the citizens, residents and visitors in a single state. An example of a state law might be the speed limit on state highways or the requirements for graduating from a public high school in that state.
Federal Laws	These laws are passed by Congress, based on the powers granted to Congress by the U.S. Constitution. Federal laws concern the entire nation. An example of a federal law might be a law limiting air pollution from trucks used in interstate trade.

Types of American Law

Besides having different sources of law, we also have several **types of laws** today. Each type of law controls a different type of activity or relationship.

Civil Law—**Civil law** concerns everyday relations between citizens. Citizens can sue one another for personal injuries or for violations of contract in order to obtain compensation for their losses. Civil law also covers family matters, such as divorce, or the inheritance of property when someone dies.

Criminal Law—**Criminal law** concerns the prosecution and punishment of individuals for crimes. The government has an interest in the enforcement of justice to protect society from criminal behavior. If a person commits a crime, the state or national government puts the person on trial and punishes the person, if convicted, with a fine or imprisonment. Criminal laws thus punish those who have committed crimes and help to deter future crimes.

Constitutional Law—**Constitutional law** consists of the Constitution itself, including the Bill of Rights, and those federal laws that protect our rights under the Constitution. Laws based on state constitutions are also a form of constitutional law.

Military Law—**Military law** consists of the special laws and procedures that apply to the armed services. All members of the armed forces are subject to these special laws, found in the *Uniform Code of Military Justice*. These laws help to maintain discipline and security among our troops. For example, soldiers are tried by a special military tribunal, known as a court-martial, rather than by a jury. The rules of evidence, standards of proof, and punishments differ from those followed by civilian (*non-military*) courts.

Juvenile Law—Juvenile law consists of the special laws and procedures that apply to minors—those under the age of 18. Because of their younger age, minors are often not subject to the same penalties as adults. They are tried by judges in special juvenile courts.

The different types of laws can sometimes overlap. Suppose that Sandy steals Sarah's car. Sandy is arrested and prosecuted by the State of Florida for theft. This is a violation of the criminal laws of the State of Florida. But Sarah has also lost the use of her car for several days when it was stolen. Sandy may have also damaged Sarah's car. Sarah can therefore sue Sandy in state court in a civil suit, seeking money in compensation for her losses (known as monetary "damages"). All of these violations are matters of state law.

Examples Illustrating the Sources and Types of Laws*

Types of Laws	Sources of Laws: Common law/Case law	Statutory law	Constitutional law
Civil	A past decision by a state court about the conditions in which a driver is responsible for causing accidental injuries to another.	A law passed by Congress on how banks and other lenders must explain their finance charges to consumers.	A provision in the U.S. Bill of Rights stating that a person is entitled to just compensation when the government takes his or her property.
Criminal	A past decision by a state court about when to excuse someone for acting in self-defense.	A law passed by the Florida Legislature about the punishment for robbing a store.	A provision in the U.S. Bill of Rights stating that a person accused of a crime is entitled to the assistance of an attorney.
Military	A past decision by a court-martial about when a soldier may lawfully disobey an unreasonable order.	A law passed by Congress about the rights of soldiers on the battlefield.	A provision in the U.S. Constitution stating the President is the Commander in Chief.
Juvenile	A decision by the U.S. Supreme Court about the protections that minors (juveniles) should receive in juvenile courts.	A law passed by the Florida Legislature setting the maximum time that a minor can be kept in a juvenile detention center.	A section of the Florida Constitution stating when a child accused of breaking the law may be charged as a juvenile committing an act of delinquency.
Constitutional	A decision by the U.S. Supreme Court stating that the police must inform suspects of their right to speak to an attorney.	A law passed by Congress to enforce voting rights under the Fifteenth Amendment.	Each of the amendments in the U.S. Bill of Rights.

***Note:** Natural law has been omitted from this chart

The Active Citizen

How well can you identify the different sources and types of laws? Check all those that apply to each of the following excerpts from actual laws. Then explain why you made those selections.

Florida Statutes, § 812.014 Theft

(1) A person commits theft if he or she knowingly obtains or uses, or endeavors to obtain or to use, the property of another with intent to, either temporarily or permanently:

(a) Deprive the other person of a right to the property or a benefit from the property.

(b) Appropriate the property to his or her own use or to the use of any person not entitled to the use of the property. . . .

(2)(e) Except as provided in paragraph (d), if the property stolen is valued at $100 or more, but less than $300, the offender commits petit theft of the first degree, punishable as a misdemeanor of the first degree, as provided in §775.082 or §775.083.

Source: ☐ Common law/Case law ☐ Statutory law ☐ Constitutional law
Type: ☐ Criminal law ☐ Civil law ☐ Military law ☐ Juvenile law
Level: ☐ Federal law ☐ State law

Explain your selections. ____

10 U.S. Code, § 838. Article 38. Duties of Trial Counsel and Defense Counsel

(a) The trial counsel of a general or special court-martial shall prosecute in the name of the United States, and shall, under the direction of the court, prepare the record of the proceedings.

(b) (1) The accused has the right to be represented in his defense before a general or special court-martial or at an investigation under section 832 of this title (article 32) as provided in this subsection.

(2) The accused may be represented by civilian counsel if provided by him.

(3) The accused may be represented—(A) by military counsel detailed under section 827 . . . or (B) by military counsel of his own selection if that counsel is reasonably available.

Source: ☐ Common law/Case law ☐ Statutory law ☐ Constitutional law
Type: ☐ Criminal law ☐ Civil law ☐ Military law ☐ Juvenile law
Level: ☐ Federal law ☐ State law

Explain your selections. ____

Florida Statutes, § 768.81 Comparative fault. (c) "Negligence action" means, without limitation, a civil action for damages based upon a theory of negligence, strict liability, products liability, professional malpractice whether couched in terms of contract or tort, or breach of warranty and like theories. The substance of an action, not conclusory terms used by a party, determines whether an action is a negligence action. . . .

(2) Effect of Contributory Fault.—In a negligence action, contributory fault chargeable to the claimant diminishes proportionately the amount awarded as economic and noneconomic damages for an injury attributable to the claimant's contributory fault, but does not bar recovery.

Source: ☐ Common law/Case law ☐ Statutory law ☐ Constitutional law
Type: ☐ Criminal law ☐ Civil law ☐ Military law ☐ Juvenile law
Level: ☐ Federal law ☐ State law

Explain your selections. ____

How Our Laws Are Interpreted and Applied: the Job of Courts

Just as there are different sources of law, there are different places where these laws are applied:

- State laws are generally applied by state courts.
- Federal laws are generally applied by federal courts.
- Military laws are applied by military tribunals (courts-martial).

So, what happens when a case is tried in court?

You've seen plenty of courtroom dramas on television, but have you ever stopped to think about what a court really is? A court is a public place where disputes are resolved according to law. Every court has both a courtroom and a judge. In many cases, the judge alone makes the decision. In other cases, a jury decides the case. A **jury** is a panel of impartial, neutral citizens, chosen at random from the locality where the trial takes place. These citizens receive a jury summons to appear at the courthouse or to be on standby for possible jury service. The court then chooses the number of jurors it needs. Lawyers for each side have a chance to question jurors to remove any who appear to be biased (*prejudiced*). In cases submitted to a jury, the judge oversees the trial and instructs the jury to make sure the trial is reasonable and fair.

A court has special powers. It can issue court orders, which must be obeyed. These orders have the force of law. For example, a court can compel parties to produce documents and can compel witnesses to appear. It can order individuals to behave in the courtroom and can even fine or imprison those who disobey for "contempt of court." When a verdict is reached, the court issues a judgment that must be enforced.

You should know about the role of juries for the EOC

The Role of Juries in the Administration of Justice

As you can see, juries play an essential role in the **administration of justice** (*acting to protect citizens, punish wrongdoers and guarantee fairness*) in the United States. Juries act as basic fact-finders. When there is a dispute, or when a crime has been committed, people often disagree over basic facts. The role of the jury is to reach reasonable conclusions about such disputed facts, including deciding responsibilities.

For example, suppose a murder has taken place. When did it occur? How was the victim killed? Who was at the crime scene when the murder happened? Does the accused claim to have acted in self-defense? There may be disagreement about many of these facts.

We resolve such disagreements through the jury system. It is left to a panel of local citizens, who are neutral and impartial, to hear the evidence and decide these issues. Potential jurors are chosen at random from the community and summoned to the courthouse. During **jury selection**, lawyers eliminate those who appear to be biased and agree on the final jury.

The jury listens carefully to the testimony and evidence at the trial. The jury then goes into deliberation. Jurors discuss among themselves what they think the evidence shows. Their discussion occurs behind closed doors without any recording. Jurors are free to express their opinions and to change their minds.

As you know, the jurors do not decide what the law says. The judge determines the law. The law is explained to the jury by the judge in the jury instructions. The role of the jury is to decide the disputed facts and assign responsibilities. Based on the evidence presented at trial, which facts seem most likely? Who is responsible for any injury or wrong-doing?

There are different **types of jury trial**. The standard that the jury applies in making these decisions differs based on the type of jury trial:

- In a civil case, the jury decides what the evidence most likely shows. The jury decides which side has the most evidence in its favor.

- In a criminal case, the standard is different. The jury should only convict the accused if it believes the evidence shows the defendant committed the crime "beyond a reasonable doubt." That means the evidence is so compelling that a juror could not reasonably doubt that the accused person had committed the crime. Moreover, all the jurors have to agree that the defendant is guilty.

Our jury system guarantees that when we are involved in a dispute or accused of a crime, we receive a fair and impartial hearing. It also means that the government is unable to control the outcome. In colonial times, British judges, whom the King could recall at will, decided many disputes. Colonists did not feel they received a fair trial. In modern dictatorships, the dictator tells judges what they can do. Political opponents of the dictator often find themselves behind bars. In the United States the jury, not the government, decides the outcome.

The Active Citizen

1. Jack and Jill are having a dispute over their inheritance. Their parents have died and left each child with half of their belongings, which include the family's house. Jill has been living in the house and has already taken some furniture and other goods from the house before the inheritance is divided. Jack objects and sues his sister Jill in court. What should be the role of the jury in this case?
2. The Sixth Amendment guarantees our right to a trial by jury when we are accused of a crime. The Seventh Amendment guarantees our right to a trial by jury in civil cases above a certain value. Why did the Founders decide to guarantee the right to a jury trial in the Bill of Rights? (You will learn more about the Bill of Rights in the next chapter.) Explain the importance of the jury system.

- Fill in the chart below comparing trial and appellate processes. Place a checkmark in the column for each of the characteristics that apply to each type of process. A characteristic might apply to both processes.

Comparing Trial and Appellate Processes

Characteristic	Trial Process	Appellate Process
Holds a hearing with lawyers' opening and closing statements, the introduction of evidence, and testimony from witnesses		
Reviews the record of a prior court proceeding		
Hears new evidence		
Reviews evidence from the court records		
Has a jury		
Decides both questions of fact and questions of law		
Decides only questions of law		
Can order a lower court to retry the case		
Provides the losing party with an opportunity to appeal		

A government cannot, however, so easily control a panel of independent citizens acting as jurors. When a jury of our "peers" (*equals*) decides our court cases, we know we will not become the victims of **arbitrary and abusive use of government power** (*unfair and harsh mistreatment by government officials*). Finally, the jury system gives ordinary citizens an opportunity to participate in government and to learn more about our justice system.

One special type of jury is known as a grand jury. It is larger than a normal trial jury. A grand jury will have 15 to 21 members in state court and 16 to 23 members in federal court. It meets in private and hears evidence that a person may have committed a crime. If the jurors feel the evidence is sufficient, the suspect will be brought to trial. A grand jury can even conduct investigations on its own initiative and may hear evidence on more than one case. In Florida, a person must be charged by a grand jury before being tried for a capital crime (*a crime punishable by death*).

The Organization of Florida's State Courts

The organization of the judicial branch in most states is similar in many ways to that of the federal government. Florida's state courts were reorganized in 1972. The number of types of state courts was then reduced from ten to four:

> *"The judicial power shall be vested in a supreme court, district courts of appeal, circuit courts and county courts. No other courts may be established by the state, any political subdivision or any municipality"*
>
> —Florida State Constitution,
> Article V, Section 1 (as amended)

Florida's State Court System

- The **county courts** are at the bottom level of Florida's court system. The county courts handle lesser crimes (known as "misdemeanors"), small claims and civil cases involving from $8,000 to $50,000. A misdemeanor is any crime punishable by no more than one year in prison.
- At the next level, Florida is divided among 20 **circuit courts**. These courts handle more serious crimes (known as "felonies"), civil cases concerning more than $50,000, and family law matters. A felony is any crime punishable by more than one year in prison. These courts also review appeals from the county courts. Florida's circuit courts thus serve as both trial and appellate courts. Both county and circuit courts can have juries.
- Just above Florida's circuit courts are the state's five **District Courts of Appeal**. These are appellate courts. They review appeals from cases decided by the circuit courts. They do not try cases.
- Lastly, at the very top of Florida's court system is the **Florida Supreme Court**. It is the highest authority on Florida law: its decisions are binding on all other Florida courts (and on federal courts applying Florida laws). The Florida Supreme Court consists of seven Justices. The Justices are initially appointed by the Governor, based on the recommendations of a separate judicial qualifications commission. Justices can then remain in office after being elected for six-year terms. Each appellate district has at least one Justice.

  The Florida Supreme Court reviews cases from the District Courts of Appeal. In a few special situations, the Florida Supreme Court can also review a case directly from one of the state's circuit courts. Like the U.S. Supreme Court, it does not need to accept for review all the cases that are appealed to it. However, it must review all death penalty cases.

  The Florida Supreme Court is generally an appellate court but has original jurisdiction in a limited number of cases. Like the U.S. Supreme Court, it has the power of judicial review. Unlike the U.S. Supreme Court, the Florida Supreme Court can issue advisory opinions to the Governor or Attorney General. These are the opinions of the court on whether a law or proposed law is constitutional.

The Chief Justice of the Florida Supreme Court is chosen by a majority of the Florida Supreme Court Justices and oversees Florida's entire state court system.

As you can see, Florida state courts differ from the federal system in several important respects:

- The federal court system has three levels of courts, while Florida has four levels of courts.
- The Florida Supreme Court can give advisory opinions when asked by the Governor; the U.S. Supreme Court can never give advisory opinions.
- U.S. Supreme Court Justices and all federal judges are appointed for life; Florida judges may initially be appointed but then must be elected to retain their office.
- The Chief Justice of the U.S. Supreme Court is nominated by the President of the United States; the Chief Justice of the Florida Supreme Court is chosen by the Justices themselves.
- In the federal system, "circuit courts" (U.S. Courts of Appeals) are above "district courts" (U.S. District Courts); in Florida, the opposite is true: "district courts" (Florida District Courts of Appeal) are above "circuit courts" (Florida Circuit Courts).
- Florida's trial courts are courts of general jurisdiction: they can try all kinds of cases. Even at the bottom level of the federal court system, the U.S. District Courts are more limited: they can only try cases on issues of federal law or cases between parties from different states.

The Active Citizen

Complete the diagram below.

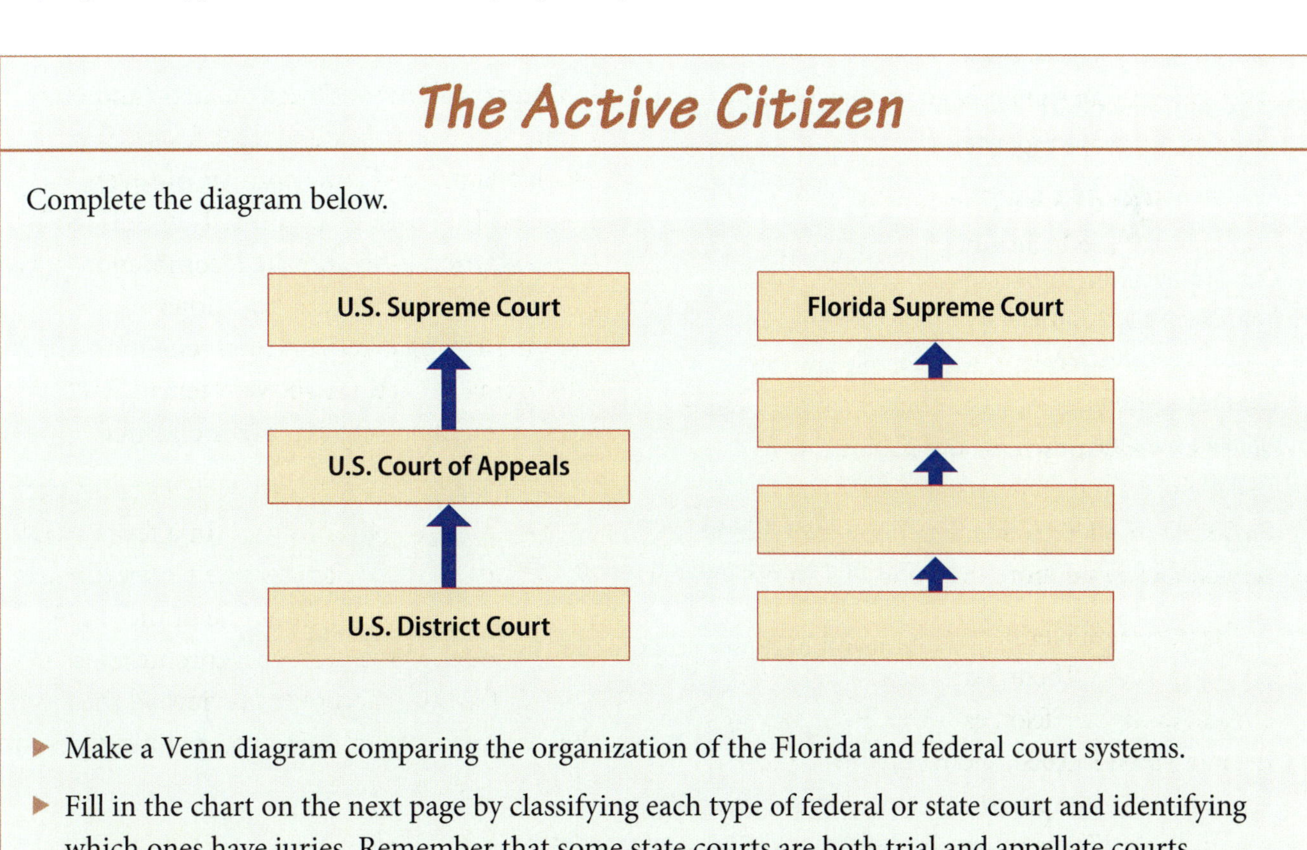

- Make a Venn diagram comparing the organization of the Florida and federal court systems.
- Fill in the chart on the next page by classifying each type of federal or state court and identifying which ones have juries. Remember that some state courts are both trial and appellate courts.

Continues ▶

Which Courts have Juries?

Name of Court	Federal Court	State Court	Trial Court	Appellate Court	Can Have a Jury	Never Has a Jury
U.S. Supreme Court						
U.S. Court of Appeals ("Circuit Court")						
U.S. District Court						
Florida Supreme Court						
Florida District Court of Appeal						
Florida Circuit Court						
Florida County Court						

Florida's State Court System

The Federal Judiciary

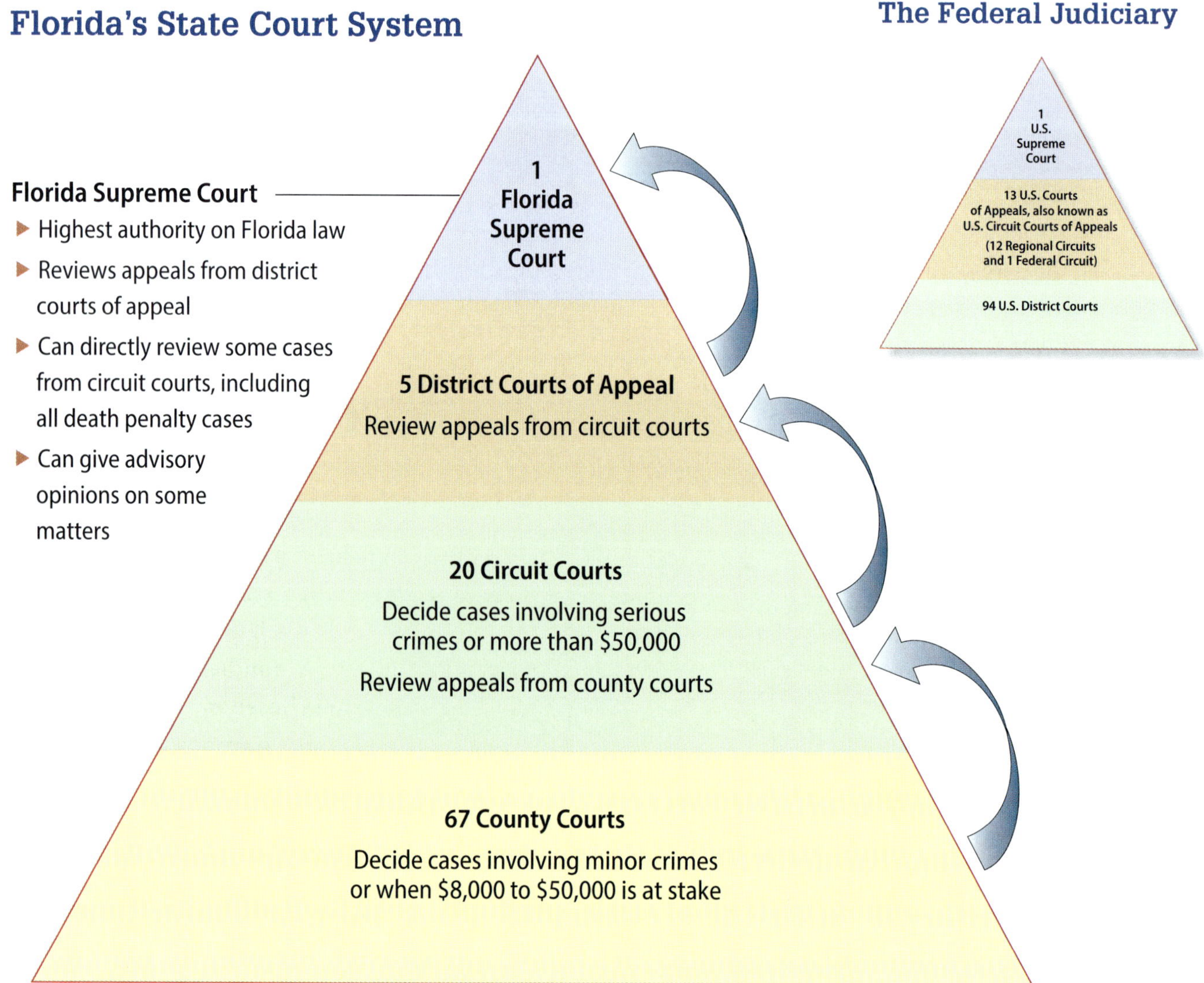

The Law in Action: Civil and Criminal Court Procedure

The **trial process** differs slightly for civil and criminal trials in both state and federal court. Let's look at how a typical civil case and criminal case would proceed in state court. You won't need to know all of these details for the EOC test, but you should be able to describe the trial process in general, especially the role of juries.

A Civil Case

The Pleadings: Complaint and Answer

A civil case begins when a person or business files a complaint. The person filing the complaint is known as the plaintiff (*complainer*). The person or business sued in a civil case is known as the defendant. The complaint gives background facts and states the plaintiff's grievances and request for relief. The defendant must file an answer with the court admitting or denying the claims made in the complaint.

Pretrial Discovery

Next comes a period of pretrial "discovery." Each side must turn over all relevant documents to the other side. Each side also has a chance to demand written responses to questions they ask.

Meanwhile, the attorneys conduct their own investigations. For example, they may look at police and hospital reports. They also interview witnesses.

Each party can also take depositions. This is a formal interview of a witness with a court reporter and all attorneys present. The court reporter types up the deposition. Evidence from depositions can be used later at the trial.

Be sure to know what a summary judgment is for the EOC test.

Pretrial Motions

A "motion" is a document requesting the court to do something. Before the trial, either party can file a "motion for **summary judgment**" if the evidence in its favor is so overwhelming that the other side cannot reasonably win. The motion for summary judgment could be on particular points, or on the whole case. The trial judge will grant the motion only if the evidence is so strong that any other outcome at trial would be unreasonable. Once a motion for summary judgment is granted, a trial on that point—or sometimes, on the whole case—becomes unnecessary. The court decides the issue without a trial because the evidence is so overwhelming.

The trial court will also encourage the parties to "settle" the case (*come to an agreement*) without the expense of a trial. Usually, the parties must have a settlement conference.

Be sure to know the role of the jury in the trial process for the EOC test.

Jury Selection

The Seventh Amendment guarantees our right to a jury trial in a civil case if a significant amount is at stake. Before the trial can begin, the court must therefore select a **jury**. A number of local citizens eligible for jury duty are chosen by the court at random. Each receives a jury summons. The citizens on this list must come to the courthouse or be on standby. The lawyers then have an opportunity to strike off any chosen jurors whom they think might be biased (*favor one side over the other*).

Continues ▶

The Trial

At the trial, each side presents its case. First, each lawyer will make an opening statement. The opening statement explains what the lawyer thinks the evidence will show.

Then the attorneys present their witnesses. Each side asks questions to its own witnesses (known as examination). It also asks questions to the opposing witnesses (known as cross-examination).

The attorneys also introduce documents and photographs, which must be identified by witnesses to show they are authentic. The lawyers may bring in qualified expert witnesses, such as doctors or professors, who give their opinions on what the evidence shows.

All of these proceedings must follow strict rules of evidence. A witness can say what he has personally seen, for example, but cannot tell the jury what he thinks his neighbor might have been thinking.

At the end of the trial, the attorneys present their closing statements.

Here is additional information about the role of the jury.

Jury Instructions and the Role of the Jury

After the lawyers have finished, the trial judge instructs the jury on what they must decide. This advice is known as jury instructions.

As you know, the main role of the jury is to act as a "fact-finder." They must decide if the claims made in the complaint are true, whether they were a violation of the law, if the plaintiff is entitled to any compensation, and if so, how much money should be awarded. In a civil case, the jury chooses the side it finds most persuasive.

Jury Deliberations and Verdict

The jury next goes into the jury room, where they discuss the case privately among themselves. Eventually, they reach a verdict (*decision or judgment in a court case*).

Be sure to know the difference between a trial court and an appellate court for the EOC test.

Appeal

In any lawsuit, the losing party can appeal the judgment to an appellate court. As you know from the last chapter, an appellate court reviews the decisions of trial courts. The appellate court does not retry the case on the basis of the facts. It does not take away the important job of the jury as "fact-finder." The only job of an appellate court is to **review how the law was applied to the facts of the case.** If the trial court made an error in its conduct of the trial or in its application of the law, the appellate court can send the case back with instructions for a retrial, or it can even reverse the decision.

How can a trial court make a mistake in its application of the law? It might, for example, have allowed the jury to hear evidence at the trial that should not have been admitted. This evidence might have unfairly prejudiced the jury. Or, the trial judge might have interpreted the law incorrectly in the court's instructions to the jurors. Such errors could lead an appellate court to order a retrial of the case.

The Active Citizen

- Have your class simulate a civil trial. One student should act as the judge, two students should act as attorneys, one student should act as the plaintiff, one student should act as the defendant, one student should act as the court bailiff, six students should act as jurors, and several other students should act as witnesses. Use the imaginary complaint below as the basis for your class's mock trial.
- Be sure to include all of the steps listed above for the trial: opening statements, submission of documents, examination and cross-examination of witnesses, closing statements, jury instructions from the judge, jury deliberations, and a final verdict.
- Make a chart or Venn diagram comparing the processes in a trial and appellate court.
- Interview a friend, relative or neighbor who has been involved in a civil case.

The Beginning of a Lawsuit in Civil Law

Smith and Smith
Attorneys at Law

NINTH CIRCUIT COURT FOR THE STATE OF FLORIDA

Leo Montague
Plaintiff,
vs.
Mary Capulet,
Defendant

) Case No.: 303
) Complaint for Personal Injury

NOW COMES LEO MONTAGUE, hereinafter Plaintiff, by and through his attorneys, John Smith and Joan Smith, and complaining of MARY CAPULET, hereinafter called Defendant, respectfully states as follows:

I

1. Plaintiff Leo Montague is an individual, and resident at 212 Sunshine Drive, Sarasota, Florida

2. Defendant Mary Capulet is an individual, and resident, who may be served at 3200 Orange Drive, Apartment 5B, Orlando, Florida.

II

1. That on April 8, 2018, at approximately 3:15 p.m., Defendant was driving southbound on Bullfrog Creek Road.

2. Plaintiff was a pedestrian who stepped into Bullfrog Creek Road at approximately 3:15 p.m. in order to cross to the other side of the road.

3. Defendant was talking on her cell phone prior to the accident.

4. Defendant continued driving and hit Plaintiff with her car.

5. Plaintiff could see that, immediately prior to the accident, Defendant was talking on her cell phone.

Complaint for Personal Injury - 1

III

6. The Defendant breached the duty of care owed to Plaintiff by failing to use reasonable care while driving her automobile, by talking on a cell phone while driving and by failing to pay attention to the road.

6. Immediately after the accident, Plaintiff was rushed to General Hospital.

7. As a result of Defendant's negligence, Plaintiff suffered personal injuries in the form of whiplash, cuts, scratches and bruises, and damage to his left leg.

8. Plaintiff was examined by Dr. William Jersey of General Hospital, who concluded that Defendant's left leg was badly damaged in the accident.

5. Despite physical therapy, Plaintiff has been unable to run again because of injuries sustained in his left leg, and will, in reasonable probability, incur a loss of earning capacity in future.

6. Defendant also experienced physical pain and suffering and mental anguish because of Defendant's negligence.

By reason of the foregoing, Plaintiff has been damaged by an amount of one million dollars ($1,000,000).

WHEREFORE, Plaintiff prays a Judgment be entered against Defendant for recovery of damages as set forth above.

Dated this 21 of July, 2018

John Smith

John and Joan Smith
Attorneys for Plaintiff

Complaint for Personal Injury - 2

A Criminal Case

Criminal cases follow somewhat different procedures from civil ones. In a criminal case, the state or the United States is actually a party to the proceeding. It acts in the interest of protecting society. In serious offenses, the defendant risks the loss of liberty through imprisonment.

Criminal Investigation

When a crime is first reported, the police conduct an investigation. They may obtain a search warrant from a judge to search places they have good reason to believe may provide important evidence. They will interview witnesses and possible suspects.

The Arrest

As a result of their investigation, the police may arrest a suspect if they have "probable cause" to believe this person committed the crime. The police cannot obtain a confession without first informing the suspect of his or her rights. Among these are the right to remain silent and the right to have an attorney present during questioning.

An informal hearing is held to decide whether there is "probable cause" to keep the suspect in custody. A person being charged with a capital crime (*punishable by death*) must be indicted (*officially charged*) by a grand jury—a group of 15 to 21 citizens in Florida state courts (and 16 to 23 citizens in federal courts).

Arraignment

If there are sufficient grounds to hold the suspect, the suspect is arraigned, or charged, in open court. The suspect is asked to plead "guilty" or "not guilty" to the charges. Then the court sets bail. This is an amount to be paid by the defendant to ensure that he or she will appear at trial. If bail is paid, the defendant is released until trial. If no bail is set or paid, the defendant must remain in jail until trial.

Plea-Bargaining

The defendant may enter into negotiations with the district attorney before trial. This process is known as plea-bargaining. The defendant may admit to a lesser crime if the charges against the defendant are dropped. If no plea bargain is made, the case goes to trial.

The Trial

In Florida, if a defendant could go to prison for six months or more, the defendant has the right to a jury trial. In criminal cases, the state (or the "People") is always against the defendant.

As in civil cases, both sides—the state and the defendant—have the right to strike off (*eliminate*) potential jurors during jury selection.

Once the case goes to trial, an attorney from the district attorney's office—the prosecutor—presents the state's case against the accused. Very special rules control the admission of evidence in a criminal trial. The district attorney's office is required to hand over to the defendant all the relevant evidence that the police have gathered. The police cannot use any evidence at trial that has been tampered with or obtained by them unlawfully.

The defendant has the right to face and question all witnesses. If the defendant cannot afford an attorney and has been accused of a serious crime, the court is required to appoint an attorney for the defendant, known as the "public defender."

After the evidence is presented and the attorneys make their closing statements, the judge will give instructions to the jury. The jury then deliberates in private to reach a verdict. The jury could decide to convict the defendant on all charges, it could find the defendant guilty of lesser crimes, or it could decide that the defendant is not guilty at all. In a criminal case, the "burden of proof" is on the prosecution. The standard is not the same as in a civil trial. If it cannot be shown beyond a reasonable doubt that the accused committed the crime, then the jury should find the defendant not guilty. To convict a defendant of a serious crime, all of the jurors must agree that the evidence shows beyond a reasonable doubt the defendant is guilty.

Sentencing

If the jury finds the defendant guilty, then the judge decides what the punishment should be. This process is known as sentencing. No cruel or unusual punishments are permitted. The amount of punishment should be in proportion to the severity of the crime. In sentencing, a judge must take into account many factors, including the severity of the crime, whether the defendant has previously been convicted of a crime, and whether the defendant shows any remorse (*sorrow for having committed the crime*). In Florida, when a person is unanimously convicted of a crime punishable by death, 8 of 12 jurors must agree before the judge can apply the death penalty.

Appeal

As with civil cases, the defendant has the right to appeal the verdict or sentence to an appellate court. The appellate court looks to see if the trial was handled correctly or if an error occurred in the application of the law.

Mary Smith was walking home when she saw a wallet on the street. She picked it up and continued on her way. In fact, Hector Garcia had slipped on the wet pavement and was lying on the ground around the corner. He saw Mary leave with his wallet and called the police with his cellphone to say it was stolen. Officer Sheila Swift read the message from the local police department and saw and arrested Mary. Mary said she was going to call the owner of the wallet once she reached home. Mary had a prior conviction for theft so the local district attorney decided to charge her.

Your class should simulate her questioning, arrest, arraignment and trial. Your teacher should select students to act as Mary, Mr. Garcia, Officer Swift, the judge, attorneys, witnesses and jurors.

The Active Citizen

- In your opinion, is the use of different procedures for civil and criminal cases justified? Explain your answer.
- Imagine you have been unfairly accused of a crime. Write a letter to a friend describing your ordeal.

Continues ▶

▶ Complete the following chart reviewing the steps of a civil and criminal case side-by-side. For each step, explain how the processes are similar or different.

Civil Case	Criminal Case	Explain how these are similar or different
Dispute	Crime and Police Investigation	
Complaint and Answer	Arrest and Arraignment	
Pretrial Discovery	Pretrial Discovery	
Settlement Conference	Plea Bargaining	
Pretrial Motions	Pretrial Motions	
Jury Selection	Jury Selection	
Trial: opening statements, examination and cross-examination of witnesses, closing statements	Trial: opening statements, examination and cross-examination of witnesses, closing statements	
Jury Instructions (each side's "burden of proof" is to show their case is more likely than not)	Jury Instructions (the prosecutor's "burden of proof" is to show guilt beyond a reasonable doubt)	
Jury Deliberations and Verdict (Decision)	Jury Deliberations and Verdict—verdict must be unanimous	
The jury determines the amount when compensation is awarded	Sentencing by the judge	
Appeal	Appeal	

Name ________________________________

Complete the chart below by describing the six principles that government officials and institutions follow to preserve the rule of law.

Principles the Government Follows Under the Rule of Law

Principle	Description
Accountability to the law 	
Consistent application and enforcement of the law for all parties 	
Decisions based on the law 	
Fair procedures 	
Transparency of Institutions 	

Name ______________________________

Complete the chart by identifying the different sources and types of law:

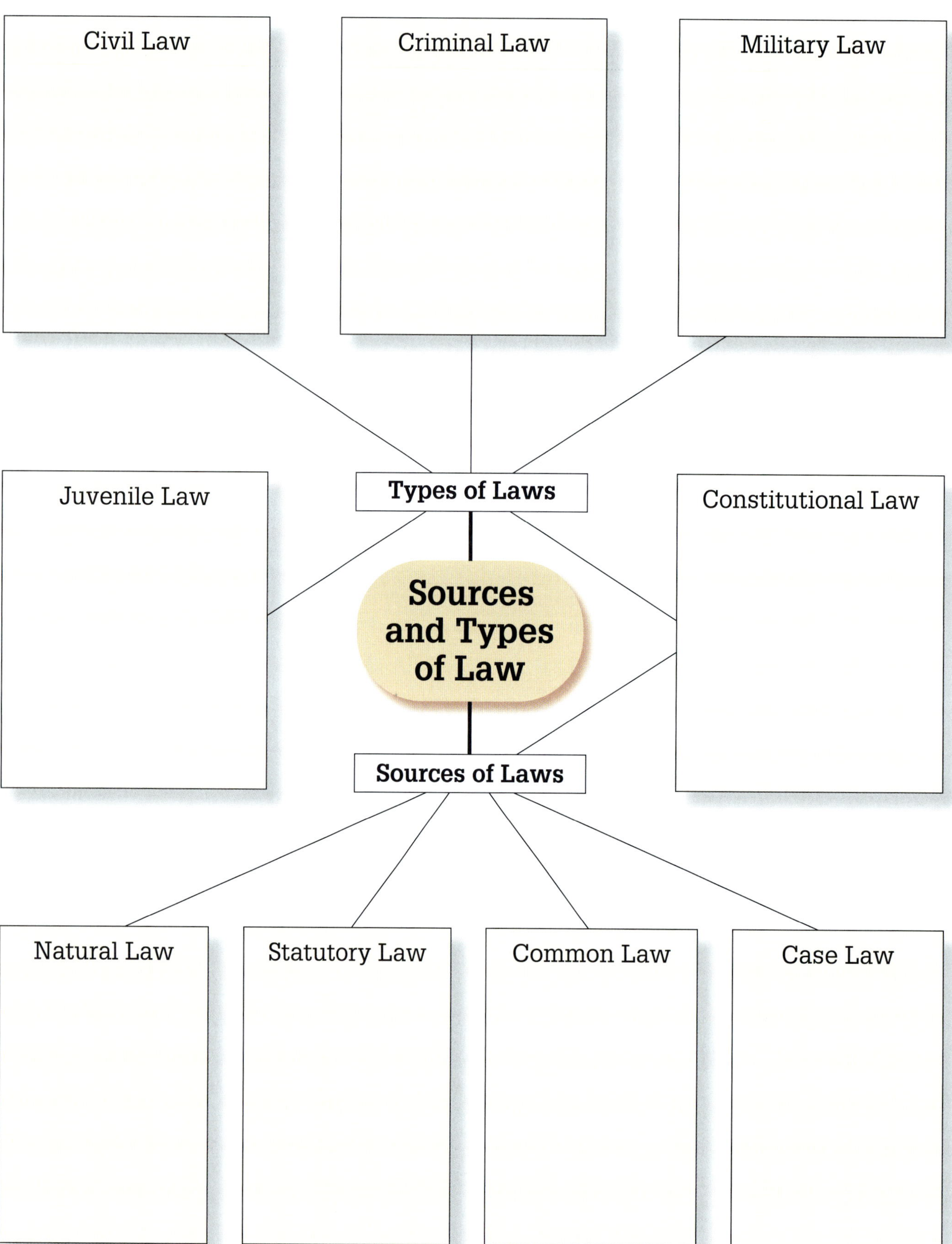

Name ______________________________

Make a question relating to each of the following clusters of terms and phrases:

Accountability to the law
Fair procedures
Decisions based on the law
Consistent application and enforcement of the law
Transparency

Natural law
Statutory law
Common law
Case law
Constitutional law

Civil law
Criminal law
Constitutional law
Military law

Florida Supreme Court
Florida District Courts of Appeal
Florida circuit courts
Florida county courts

Name ______________________________

Define each of the following:

Rule of law ______________________________

____

____

Jury ______________________________

____

____

Statutory law ______________________________

____

____

Common law ______________________________

____

____

Civil law ______________________________

____

____

Florida Supreme Court ______________________________

____

____

Florida District Courts of Appeal ______________________________

____

____

Florida Circuit Courts ______________________________

____

____

Florida County Courts ______________________________

____

____

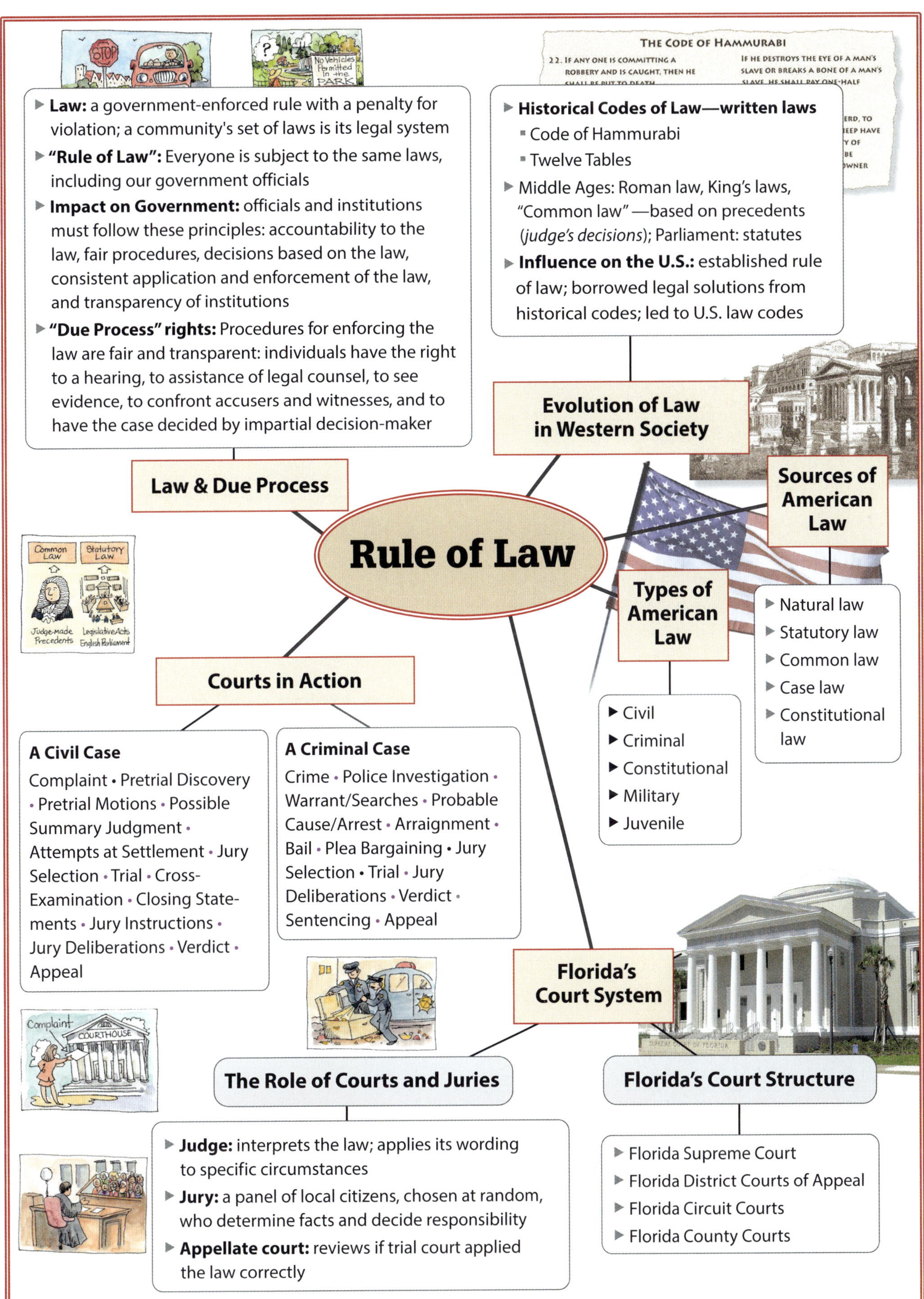
STOP
No Vehicles Permitted in the PARK
THE CODE OF HAMMURABI
22. IF ANY ONE IS COMMITTING A ROBBERY AND IS CAUGHT, THEN HE
IF HE DESTROYS THE EYE OF A MAN'S SLAVE OR BREAKS A BONE OF A MAN'S
▶ Law: a government-enforced rule with a penalty for violation; a community's set of laws is its legal system
▶ "Rule of Law": Everyone is subject to the same laws, including our government officials
▶ Impact on Government: officials and institutions must follow these principles: accountability to the law, fair procedures, decisions based on the law, consistent application and enforcement of the law, and transparency of institutions
▶ "Due Process" rights: Procedures for enforcing the law are fair and transparent: individuals have the right to a hearing, to assistance of legal counsel, to see evidence, to confront accusers and witnesses, and to have the case decided by impartial decision-maker
▶ Historical Codes of Law—written laws
▪ Code of Hammurabi
▪ Twelve Tables
▶ Middle Ages: Roman law, King's laws, "Common law"—based on precedents (judge's decisions); Parliament: statutes
▶ Influence on the U.S.: established rule of law; borrowed legal solutions from historical codes; led to U.S. law codes
Evolution of Law in Western Society
Law & Due Process
Sources of American Law
Rule of Law
Common Law
Statutory Law
Judge-made Precedents
Legislative Acts English Parliament
Types of American Law
▶ Natural law
▶ Statutory law
▶ Common law
▶ Case law
▶ Constitutional law
Courts in Action
▶ Civil
▶ Criminal
▶ Constitutional
▶ Military
▶ Juvenile
A Civil Case
Complaint • Pretrial Discovery • Pretrial Motions • Possible Summary Judgment • Attempts at Settlement • Jury Selection • Trial • Cross-Examination • Closing Statements • Jury Instructions • Jury Deliberations • Verdict • Appeal
A Criminal Case
Crime • Police Investigation • Warrant/Searches • Probable Cause/Arrest • Arraignment • Bail • Plea Bargaining • Jury Selection • Trial • Jury Deliberations • Verdict • Sentencing • Appeal
Florida's Court System
Complaint
COURTHOUSE
The Role of Courts and Juries
Florida's Court Structure
▶ Judge: interprets the law; applies its wording to specific circumstances
▶ Jury: a panel of local citizens, chosen at random, who determine facts and decide responsibility
▶ Appellate court: reviews if trial court applied the law correctly
▶ Florida Supreme Court
▶ Florida District Courts of Appeal
▶ Florida Circuit Courts
▶ Florida County Courts

Review Cards: The Rule of Law

What is Law?

- A law is a rule that is enforced by government and that has a penalty for breaking it.
- Laws help the members of a community organize and protect themselves, settle disputes and punish those who commit crimes. A community's set of laws is its **legal system**.
- Laws may seem clear but often need to be interpreted to see how they apply to specific situations.

The Rule of Law

- In some societies, the ruler's will is law. Ordinary subjects have little control over their lives. They are always subject to their ruler's desires.
- Americans live under the **rule of law**. This means we live under a system of written laws. These laws make it clear how we should behave and how we can expect others to behave.
- It also means that our government leaders cannot just do anything they please. They are subject to the rule of law like everyone else. No one is above the law.

The Impact of the Rule of Law on Government Officials and Institutions

Government officials and institutions must follow these principles, protecting citizens from the **arbitrary and abusive use of government power**:

- **Accountability to the law:** Their conduct is subject to written laws that everyone knows and that everyone is subject to.
- **Consistent application and enforcement of the law:** The law is applied to everyone in the same way. If two people commit the same crime, they should receive the same punishment.
- **Decisions based on the law:** When a court reaches a decision, such as to punish someone accused of a crime, the decision must be based on the law.
- **Fair procedures:** The procedures used to decide whether an accused person has violated the law, or to settle a dispute between two or more parties, must be fair and impartial. For example, an accused person has the right to see the evidence, hear witnesses and receive the help of an attorney. Fair procedures are known as our "due process" rights. "Due process" of law refers to our right to a public hearing or trial where we can present evidence, hear and refute evidence against us, and receive judgment from a neutral and impartial decision-maker.
- **Transparency of institutions:** Proceedings should be open and in public. This is known as transparency because it means everyone can see what is going on. It is important that our procedures, such as trials, are public and transparent so that we can see that decisions are based on a fair and consistent application of the law.

How Laws are Consistently Applied in the United States: the Work of Courts

- Laws are enforced in courts. Decisions of courts are recorded and serve as precedents for later cases.
- Sometimes court decisions are made by judges, and sometimes by a jury. A **jury** is a panel of impartial citizens, chosen at random from a pool of local citizens. These citizens receive a jury summons to appear at the courthouse or to be on standby for possible jury service. The court then chooses the number of jurors it needs. Lawyers for each side have a chance to question jurors to remove any who appear to be biased (*prejudiced*). The role of the jury is to hear the evidence, decide on the facts of the case, and assign responsibilities. The use of juries promotes the impartiality of the law and the independence of judicial proceedings.

Meaning and Importance of Due Process in the American Legal System

- The right of **due process** is an essential part of the American **legal system**.
- Before the government can take away our life, liberty or property, we are entitled to a fair process. This means a hearing of some kind, conducted in public before a neutral and impartial decision-maker or jury. We should be able to present our own evidence and see and hear all the evidence against us. Finally, the decision should be based solely on the law and the evidence presented at the hearing or trial.
- Because of our "due process" rights, our lives, liberties, and property are protected from the **arbitrary and abusive use** of government power.

Examples of Historical Law Codes: How Laws Developed in Western Society

- Many of the laws we have today developed slowly over time. Some of them were even recorded in **historical law codes**. Each law code brought all the laws of its society together.
- Hammurabi of Babylonia established one of the earliest known written law codes, more than 3,700 years ago. Having written laws that all could see was an important step in developing the rule of law. It meant that people knew what the laws permitted them to do and what they were prohibited from doing.
- Early Roman laws were displayed publicly on Twelve Tables, so everyone could see them. Roman law established rules that still influence modern law today, such as the enforcement of contracts.
- The Middle Ages had many sources of law. Laws came from old Roman codes, popular traditions, and kings. Laws passed by a legislature like Parliament were called statutes. Medieval England established the **common law**: laws based on customs and precedents (*earlier decisions*) found throughout the kingdom.
- The influence of **historical codes of law** on the United States: earlier law codes first established the rule of law; Americans took specific solutions to many legal problems from historical law codes; Americans then created their own law codes, making laws on particular subjects easier to find.

Sources of American Law

A **source of law** is where that law first came from. Because of the different legal traditions (above), Americans today have several sources for their laws:

- **Natural law:** Basic laws in nature that apply to all societies, such as that each person has an inalienable right to life, liberty and property; and that people have the right to govern themselves.
- **Constitutional law:** The source of these laws is the U.S. Constitution or state constitutions. They are the highest form of law.
- **Statutory law:** These are laws, known as statutes, passed by legislatures, such as by Congress or the Florida Legislature.
- **Common law:** These are laws based on customs and judicial precedents (the decisions of courts looking at similar cases).
- **Case law:** These are laws based on court decisions in prior cases.

Types of Laws

Americans have several different **types of law**, based on different kinds of activities and relationships:

- **Civil law:** concerns disputes between private parties. For example, two passengers may claim they were injured by another driver's carelessness, or one business may sue another for breaking a contract.
- **Criminal law:** concerns crimes. The government charges the accused of committing a crime.
- **Constitutional law:** concerns rights and responsibilities from the U.S. Constitution (including the Bill of Rights) or a state constitution.
- **Military law:** concerns the armed forces. Stricter rules apply in military courts. "Martial law" is enforced by a "court-martial."
- **Juvenile law:** concerns minors (those under 18 years of age). Juvenile courts take into account the younger age of minors accused of committing crimes.

How a Case Proceeds in Criminal Court

- Police respond to a crime report with an investigation, sometimes with a search warrant.
- If a suspect is detained, an informal hearing decides if there was probable cause of a crime.
- If there is probable cause, the suspect is arraigned (*charges are read*). For a capital crime (*punishable by death*), the accused must be indicted by a grand jury. This is larger than a trial jury. It meets in private and decides if there is enough evidence to bring the accused to trial.
- Bail is set: if paid, the person is released until trial. If not, he or she stays in jail awaiting trial.
- After a period of plea bargaining, when charges may be reduced for a plea of guilty, the case goes to trial. If a potential prison sentence is six months or more, a jury is assigned.
- During the trial, the police present their evidence. Lawyers for each side question witnesses. The "burden of proof" that the crime was committed is on the district attorney.
- The jury deliberates and reaches a verdict on the defendant's guilt. The jury must usually be unanimous to convict.
- If guilty, the judge imposes a sentence (*punishment*). A defendant can choose to appeal.

How a Case Proceeds in Civil Court

Pretrial:

- In a civil case, a complaint is first filed by one side against another.
- In the discovery period, both sides must produce evidence. They give each other documents and interview witnesses.
- A lawyer can file a motion for **summary judgment** if there is overwhelming evidence for one side leaving no real issues of fact. Then judgment is simply a matter of law. This may end the trial or take care of some of the disputed issues.
- The court will also encourage both sides to "settle" outside of court (*reach an agreement without going to trial*).

Jury Selection

- Members of the community are chosen at random and summoned (*called on to come*) to the courthouse. They are interviewed by lawyers and some are eliminated for possible bias (*prejudice*). The lawyers then agree on a set of jurors for the trial.

The Trial Process

- If a trial occurs, a **jury** is then chosen. A jury is a panel of local citizens chosen at random. Their role is to determine the facts of the case.
- During the trial, each side makes its case. Lawyers present evidence from witnesses, documents and photographs. Witnesses are questioned by both lawyers (*examined and cross-examined*). After all the evidence is presented, lawyers make closing statements.
- The judge then gives the jury their jury instructions on what they must decide. The judge tells the jury what law to apply to the case. The role of the jury is to decide on facts based on the evidence. The jury then issues a verdict, deciding how much the defendant is responsible for the damages that the lawsuit is about.

The Appeals Process

- If one side is not satisfied with the decision, it can appeal to an appellate court.
- The appellate court reviews the decision and decides if the trial court applied the law correctly or if there should be a retrial.

The Organization of Florida's Courts

- **Florida county courts:** Hear civil cases for $8,000 to $50,000, or lesser crimes (*misdemeanors*). A misdemeanor is any crime that is punishable by no more than one year in prison.
- **Florida circuit courts:** Hear civil cases when more than $50,000 is at stake, and for more serious crimes (felonies). A felony is any crime that is punishable by more than one year in prison. These courts also review cases from the county courts.
- **Florida District Courts of Appeal:** These are appellate courts that review cases from the circuit courts.
- **Florida Supreme Court:** The highest court in the state; hears appeals from the lower state courts, including all death penalty cases; can also issue some advisory opinions (advising the Governor or Attorney General if certain laws are constitutional).

What Do You Know?

SS.7.CG.3.10

1. Connie Hargrave's tree fell in the last storm and damaged the car of her neighbor, Andy Collin. Connie did not have insurance that covered this type of accident and has not paid Andy for the damage. Andy decides to sue Connie in court. Which type of lawsuit will this be?

   A. civil
   B. military
   C. criminal
   D. constitutional

SS.7.CG.1.11

2. Which actions identify an important impact of the rule of law?

   A. Decisions by the government are based on the law.
   B. Government leaders can change the law without notice.
   C. People accused of crimes against the state are tried in secret.
   D. Different social classes enjoy different legal rights and privileges.

SS.7.CG.3.10

3. Why were historical law codes like Hammurabi's Code and the Twelve Tables of Rome significant?

   A. They established official religions.
   B. They established new economic systems.
   C. They established democratic governments.
   D. They established written laws for the entire community.

SS.7.CG.2.5

4. Jack sues Jill in Florida Circuit Court for a personal injury. Jack claims Jill hit him while she was driving carelessly and texting on her cell phone. Jill denies his claim. On what grounds could the judge grant Jack's request for summary judgment on this claim?

   A. The judge doesn't think that Jill's witnesses are very believable.
   B. The jury has indicated that it prefers Jack's version of the accident.
   C. Many experts believe that texting while driving is likely to cause accidents.
   D. The evidence in Jack's favor is so overwhelming that it would be unreasonable to think otherwise.

SS.7.CG.3.9

5. Jack lives in Miami. He has a contract dispute with a hotel owner in Tampa for $40,000. In which court should Jack seek help?

   A. U.S. District Court
   B. Florida Circuit Court
   C. Florida County Court
   D. Florida District Court of Appeal

SS.7.CG.2.5

6. The table below lists several federal and state courts.

I.	U.S. Supreme Court
II.	U.S. Court of Appeals for the Eleventh Circuit
III.	U.S. District Court for the Middle District of Florida
IV.	Florida Supreme Court
V.	Fourth Judicial Circuit Courts of Florida
VI.	Brevard County Court

Which of the courts above have juries?

A. I, II and III
B. II, III and IV
C. III, V and VI
D. III, IV and V

SS.7.CG.3.10

7. The diagram below shows details about the law.

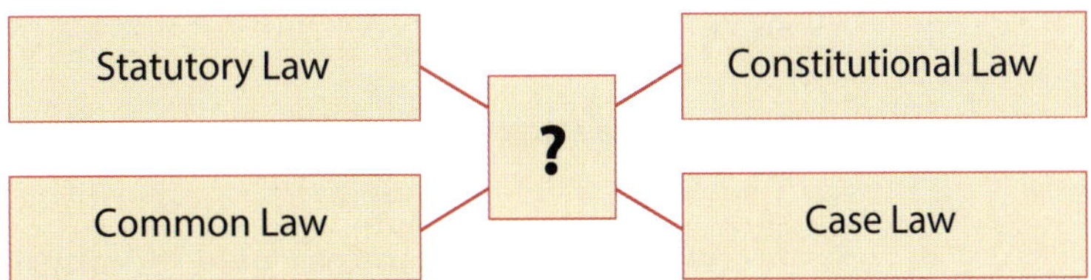

Which phrase completes the diagram?

A. Historical Law Codes
B. Sources of American Law
C. The Separation of Powers
D. The Enforcement of Contractual Agreements

SS.7.CG.3.9

8. The diagram below shows steps in a civil case in Florida.

Which statement completes the diagram?

A. Losing party appeals to U.S. District Court
B. Losing party appeals to Florida County Court
C. Losing party appeals to U.S. Circuit Court of Appeals
D. Losing party appeals to Florida District Court of Appeals

SS.7.CG.3.9

9. How does an appellate court differ from a trial court?

   A. An appellate court allows the defendant to cross-examine witnesses.

   B. Neither party to a lawsuit has any opportunity to address an appellate court.

   C. An appellate court reviews the record to see if errors were committed in applying the law.

   D. An appellate court uses a jury to reach conclusions from the evidence about disputed facts.

SS.7.CG.3.10

10. The four headlines below deal with incidents involving laws.

Which correctly identifies the type of law involved in each headline?

A.	1. civil law	2. civil law	3. military law	4. constitutional law
B.	1. civil law	2. criminal law	3. criminal law	4. military law
C.	1. criminal law	2. civil law	3. criminal law	4. common law
D.	1. juvenile law	2. criminal law	3. military law	4. constitutional law

SS.7.CG.2.5

11. Which statement describes a proper role for a jury in the administration of justice?

   A. The jurors authorize government officials to arrest their political opponents at a time of national crisis.

   B. After an accused person is convicted of a crime, the jurors decide on what should be the appropriate punishment for the accused.

   C. After hearing the evidence at trial, the jurors decide whether it is beyond a reasonable doubt that the accused committed the crime.

   D. After examining the record of an earlier trial, the jurors decide whether the law was applied correctly to the case or whether the case should be retried.

SS.7.CG.1.11

12. Which consequence is an important benefit of the rule of law?

   A. Bureaucratic government procedures are reduced.

   B. Government decisions are based on the will of the majority.

   C. Government officials can act on their own instincts in emergencies.

   D. Citizens are protected from the arbitrary and abusive use of government power.

public Confid...
nds of its Inſtitution—
ESOLVED, by the Senate and House of Representatives of
the United States of America in Congress assembled, two
ds of both Houſes concurring, That the following articles be propoſed
the Legiſlatures of the ſeveral States, as amendments to the Conſtitution
the United States, all or any of which articles, when ratified by three
rths of the ſaid Legiſlatures, to be valid to all intents and purpoſes, as
rt of the ſaid Conſtitution—Viz.
Articles in addition to, and amendment of, the Conſtitution of the United
ates of America, propoſed by Congreſs, and ratified by the Legiſlatures
the ſeveral States, purſuant to the fifth Article of the original Conſtitution.
ARTICLE THE FIRST.
After the firſt enumeration, required by the firſt article of the Conſtituti-
n, there ſhall be one Repreſentative for every thirty thouſand, until the
umber ſhall amount to one hundred; to which number one Repreſentative
hall be added for every ſubſequent increaſe of forty thouſand, until the
Repreſentatives ſhall amount to two hundred, to which number one Repreſentative ſhall be added for every ſubſequent increaſe of ſixty thouſand
perſons.
ARTICLE THE SECOND.
No law, varying the compenſation for the ſervices of the Senators and
Repreſentatives, ſhall take effect, until an election of Repreſentatives ſhall

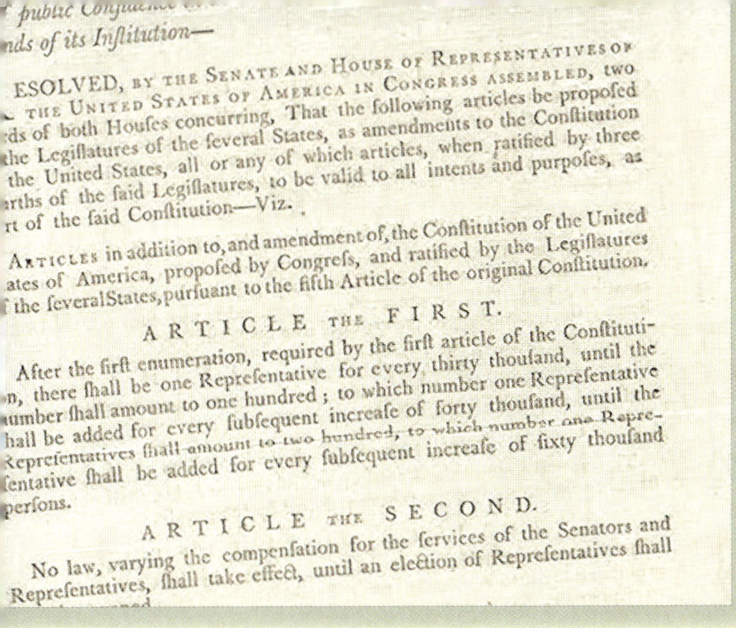

CHAPTER 10

The Bill of Rights and Later Amendments

SS.7.CG.2.3 Identify and apply the rights contained in the Bill of Rights and other amendments. (*See Chapter 11 for how the Supreme Court has interpreted some of these rights*)

SS.7.CG.2.4 Explain how the U.S. Constitution and the Bill of Rights safeguard individual rights.

SS.7.CG.3.5 Explain the amendment process outlined in Article V of the U.S. Constitution.

SS.7.CG.3.6 Analyze how the 13th, 14th, 15th, 19th, 24th and 26th Amendments broadened participation in the political process.

Content Focus Vocabulary in This Chapter

- U.S. Constitution
- Amendment
- Article V
- Formal amendment process
- Ratify
- Writ of Habeas Corpus
- *Ex post facto* law
- Bill of Rights
- Safeguard individual rights
- First Amendment
- Five freedoms
- Double jeopardy
- Due process
- Eminent domain
- Property rights
- Right to legal counsel
- Unenumerated rights
- Limits on rights
- Protected rights
- Government-imposed limitations
- Rationale
- Forced internment in wartime
- Limitations on speech
- Rationing during wartime
- Suspension of habeas corpus
- Equal protection under the law
- Suffrage
- Civil disobedience
- The 13th, 14th 15th, 19th, 24th, and 26th Amendments
- Participation in the political process
- Social interactions
- Civil Rights Act of 1964
- Voting Rights Act of 1965
- Civil Rights Act of 1968

Florida "Keys" to Learning

1. An addition or change to a law or other legal document is known as an **amendment. Article V** of the Constitution set up a **formal amendment process** that made it more difficult to amend the Constitution than it was to pass an ordinary law. Amending the Constitution is a two-step process. First, an amendment must be proposed. This has always been done by a vote of two-thirds of each house of Congress. Then, three-fourths of the state legislatures must **ratify** the proposed amendment. (An amendment can also be approved by special state ratifying conventions, but this has never been done.)

2. Two important individual rights were guaranteed in the original Constitution. These were the right to request a **writ of habeas corpus** (*a court order to bring before the court someone who is imprisoned*) and a prohibition of ***ex post facto* laws** (*laws punishing acts that occurred before they were made illegal*).

3. The first ten amendments to the Constitution are known as the "**Bill of Rights**." They were passed to meet the demands of Anti-Federalists during the debate over ratification of the Constitution. These amendments safeguard (*protect*) our **individual rights** (*the rights we enjoy as individuals*).

4. The **First Amendment** establishes **five freedoms**: freedom of religion, speech, the press, assembly and to petition. Congress cannot establish a state religion (*a government-supported church*), cannot prohibit (*forbid*) the free exercise of religion, cannot limit freedom of speech, cannot limit freedom of the press (*the right of newspapers and other sources to publish information*), cannot stop people from holding assemblies (*public gatherings*), and cannot prevent people from petitioning (*making formal requests to*) the government.

5. Other amendments guarantee individuals the right to bear arms, prohibit the sending of soldiers to live in people's homes without their consent, and protect citizens from search or seizure, including arrest, without good cause (usually indicated by a "warrant" signed by a judge). Several amendments safeguard (*protect*) the rights of those accused of a crime. They guarantee the right to a trial by jury, the **right to legal counsel**, and the right to due process, while they prohibit **double jeopardy** (*being tried for the same crime twice*) and cruel and unnatural punishments. They also protect our **property rights** by guaranteeing we will be paid fairly if our land is taken away for a pubic purpose by **eminent domain**. A summary of the Bill of Rights, listed by amendment, is found on the next page.

6. The Ninth Amendment states that the listing of specific rights in the Constitution does not mean that there are not also other **unenumerated rights**.

7. The Bill of Rights guarantees these **protected rights** (*rights protected by our laws and government*). However, there are also some **limits on rights**, including **government-imposed limitations**. The **rationale** (*justification; explanation*) is that our rights can be limited by the rights of others and by the needs of the community. In the past, such restrictions have included **limitations on speech** (*we cannot say things that could cause an immediate danger*), **rationing during wartime** (*limiting the amounts of some goods, such as food or gas, that people can buy*), **suspending habeas corpus** (*limiting the right to have a court challenge a person's imprisonment*)and even **forced internment** (*confinement in camps or prisons*) **during wartime.**

8. Several amendments to the Constitution have extended the rights of minorities and women, enabling their **participation in the political process** (*such as expressing their concerns, voting, and running for office*). Like the Bill of Rights, they influence both individual actions and **social interactions** (*how we act with others*).

9. The **13th Amendment** abolished slavery. The **14th Amendment** defined U.S. citizenship. It also required that states provide **due process** of law and **equal protection under the law** to all citizens. The **15th Amendment** prohibited federal and state governments from denying the right to vote on the basis of race.

10. The **19th Amendment** gave women **suffage** (*the right to vote*). The **24th Amendment** prohibited any requirement to pay poll taxes to vote in federal elections.The **26th Amendment** lowered the voting age to 18 years of age.

11. Acts of **civil disobedience** (*peacefully refusing to follow unjust laws*) helped promote the Civil Rights movement of the 1950s and 1960s. The **Civil Rights Acts of 1964 and 1968** and the **Voting Rights Act of 1965** protected the rights of minorities, including their right to equality under the law and their right to **participation in the political process.**

A SUMMARY OF THE BILL OF RIGHTS

First Amendment	The right to freedom of speech, freedom of the press, freedom of religion, freedom of assembly, and freedom to petition the government.
Second Amendment	The right to bear arms.
Third Amendment	The right not to have troops quartered without permission in one's home in peacetime.
Fourth Amendment	No search or seizure (*arrest*) without a warrant or a reasonable exception.
Fifth Amendment	No "double jeopardy" (*being tried twice for the same crime*); no "self-incrimination" (*being forced to testify against ourself*); no taking away of "life, liberty or property" without "due process of law"; and no taking of property by eminent domain (*for "public use"*) without just compensation.
Sixth Amendment	The right to a speedy and public trial by an impartial jury for a criminal offense; the right to be informed of all criminal charges; the right to face and question witnesses; and the right to have legal counsel (*a lawyer*).
Seventh Amendment	The right to a trial by jury in some civil matters.
Eighth Amendment	No excessive bail; no excessive fines; and no "cruel and unusual punishments."
Ninth Amendment	People may have other, "unenumerated rights," which are not mentioned in the Constitution or the Bill of Rights. Just because individuals are given several specific rights does not mean that they do not also have other unlisted rights.
Tenth Amendment	Rights not given to the federal government are "reserved" for the states and the people.

In this chapter, you will learn how the U.S. Constitution can be changed through the process of amendment, and how amendments have increased the protection of our individual rights and expanded our democracy.

For the EOC, be sure to know how the U.S. Constitution can be amended.

Amending the Constitution

The authors of the **U.S. Constitution** knew that they could not anticipate all future circumstances. Times and society change. If the Constitution were to succeed, it would have to be able to adapt to new realities and circumstances.

The authors therefore provided procedures for **formal amendment process**. To "amend" means to modify or change the Constitution. The process of amendment was deliberately made more difficult than passing an ordinary law. **Article V** established a two-step process for amendment. The first step was to introduce an amendment proposal. The second step was to **ratify** (*approve*) it.

Step 1. Proposing the Amendment

This can be accomplished in either of two ways:

1. By a two-thirds vote of both houses of Congress. All amendments of the Constitution so far have used this method.

   or

2. There is a second way of introducing a proposal. On the request of two-thirds of the state legislatures, Congress can call for a national convention to amend the Constitution.

Step 2. Ratifying the Amendment

There are also two ways to ratify a proposed amendment:

1. Ratification by three-fourths of the state legislatures.

   or

2. Ratification by special ratification conventions in three-fourths of the states.

For each proposed amendment, Congress will select one of these methods for ratification—so far, only the first has been used. The amendment process has been used successfully just 27 times since 1791.

Ways of Amending the Constitution

Proposes the Amendment

2/3 of each House of Congress proposes the amendment
or
2/3 of State Legislatures request a National Convention, which proposes amendments

Ratifies (*approves*) the Amendment

3/4 of the State Legislatures
or
3/4 of special State Conventions ratify the amendment

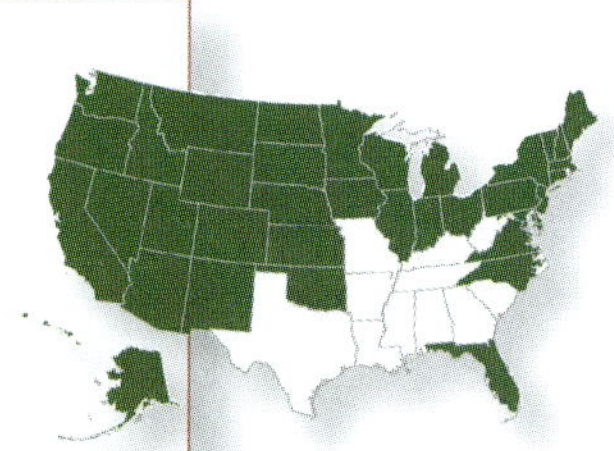

The Active Citizen

Did the authors of the U.S. Constitution make it too hard to amend? Hold the following debate in your classroom: "Resolved: That the process of amending the Constitution should be the same as the process for passing an ordinary law."

For the EOC, you should know the meaning of habeas corpus and an *ex post facto* law.

Two Rights Guaranteed in the Original Constitution

Before looking at the first ten amendments to the Constitution, it is worth identifying two rights that are guaranteed to individuals by the text of the original Constitution itself:

> "*The Privilege of the Writ of Habeas Corpus shall not be suspended, unless when in Cases of Rebellion or Invasion the public Safety may require it. No . . . ex post facto Law shall be passed.*"
>
> —U.S. Constitution, Article I, Section 9

Writ of Habeas Corpus

Article I, Section 9 prevents Congress from taking certain actions against citizens. These include suspending the right to a writ of habeas corpus. "Habeas corpus" means to "have the body." A "**writ of habeas corpus**" is a type of court order. It is a court order to an official to bring an imprisoned person before the court. The court will then decide whether there is enough evidence to justify the imprisonment. This right had existed under earlier English law.

A lawyer or relative can request a "writ of habeas corpus" to free someone who has been wrongfully imprisoned.

Federal courts can use the "writ of habeas corpus" to order the appearance of someone imprisoned by a state court, even if that person has been imprisoned on the basis of state law. This provides a pathway for citizens to use the federal courts to challenge the imprisonment of individuals they believe are unjustly imprisoned by state courts. Thousands of petitions are filed in federal courts each year for a writ of habeas corpus to free prisoners in state prisons. The Constitution states that the right to petition for a writ of habeas corpus cannot be suspended unless the nation is threatened by rebellion or invasion.

No *Ex Post Facto* Laws

Ex post facto is a Latin phrase meaning "after the fact." An ***ex post facto* law** is a law condemning an action that is passed ***after*** the action was taken. For example, suppose Congress passed a new federal law on June 30th, placing a penalty on all those who failed to wear helmets while riding on motorcycles on interstate highways. If the law placed the penalty on all those who had not worn a helmet since last January 1st, even though the law itself was only passed on June 30th, this would be an *ex post facto* law. How could a motorcyclist on an interstate highway have known, on January 1st, the requirements that Congress would introduce six months later? *Ex post facto* laws are obviously unfair. For this very reason, the Constitution forbids *ex post facto* laws.

The Active Citizen

Which of these illustrates a writ of habeas corpus and which is an *ex post facto* law?

A. "This U.S. District Court orders the state prison to bring prisoner Daniel Jones before it."

B. "All those who entered this building last month after 5:00 p.m. shall pay a $200 fine."

For the EOC, be sure to know the main rights in the Bill of Rights, especially each of the five freedoms in the First Amendment.

The Bill of Rights: Our First Ten Amendments

In the debate over ratification of the Constitution, Anti-Federalists loudly raised the criticism that the Constitution needed a bill of rights to protect the American people from a central government that might abuse its power. On June 8, 1789, James Madison, one of the leading Federalists, introduced 22 amendments in Congress. After some deletions and with many changes, these became the first ten amendments to the Constitution, known as the **Bill of Rights**.

The First Amendment

> *Congress shall make no law respecting an establishment of religion, or prohibiting the free exercise thereof; or abridging the freedom of speech, or of the press; or the right of the people peaceably to assemble, and to petition the government for a redress of grievances.*

The **First Amendment** set the tone for the Bill of Rights. It told the Congress what it could not do. This amendment placed a limit on the new federal government's exercise of power. The amendment actually establishes **five freedoms**:

1. **Freedom of Religion:** Congress cannot establish an official religion. At a time when England and other countries in Europe had established churches, this was interpreted to mean that there could be no law creating a national religion. Congress also cannot prohibit (*forbid*) the free exercise of religion by individual citizens. Americans are free to worship any faith or religion, or to have no religion at all.

2. **Freedom of Speech:** Congress cannot abridge (*cut short or limit*) freedom of speech. People

can express themselves in any way they choose: by speaking, making signs, or taking actions. Even "symbolic speech" actions are protected, such as wearing armbands or burning the American flag to protest American foreign policy. However, there are limits to free speech where public safety and the rights of others are involved. For example, one cannot "falsely shout fire in a crowded theatre." Speech is limited where it poses a clear and present danger.

3. **Freedom of the Press:** We have freedom of expression in print as well as in our spoken words. Congress cannot limit our freedom to write and publish our opinions or observations.

4. **Freedom of Assembly:** Congress also cannot prevent people from exercising their right to assemble peaceably. Without this right, the value of free speech is greatly weakened. It is especially with an audience that political speech has the greatest impact.

5. **Freedom to Petition:** A petition is a written request, usually signed by many people. Government cannot deny people the right to petition the government. If the government is to serve the people, people must be able to communicate their concerns to their government officials and leaders.

The Second Amendment

> **Word Helper**
> ***bear arms*** = carry guns
> ***infringed*** = limited; weakened

A well regulated militia, being necessary to the security of a free State, the right of the people to keep and bear arms, shall not be infringed.

The Second Amendment gives individuals the right to bear arms (*possess guns*). The U.S. Supreme Court has ruled that the Second Amendment guarantees the right to use arms for "traditional purposes," such as the defense of one's home.

The Third Amendment

No soldier shall, in time of peace be quartered in any house without the consent of the owner, nor in time of war, but in a manner to be prescribed by law.

> ***prescribed*** = laid down; stated

The Third Amendment was prompted by bitter memories of the British government's practice of quartering troops in the homes of American colonists without their consent before and during the Revolutionary War. This grievance was one of those listed in the Declaration of Independence. This amendment prohibits the quartering of soldiers in peacetime without the owner's permission.

The Fourth Amendment

The right of the people to be secure in their persons, houses, papers, and effects, against unreasonable searches and seizures, shall not be violated, and no warrants shall issue, but upon probable cause, supported by oath or affirmation, and particularly describing the place to be searched, and the persons or things to be seized.

This amendment protects our homes, the places where we work, our possessions, and our persons from unreasonable search and seizure. A "search" occurs when police enter a place to look for evidence. A "seizure" occurs when police either seize (*take*) something or arrest a person. If police officers want to make a search or seizure, they must first apply, under oath, to obtain a warrant. This is a document, signed by a judge, that permits police officers to conduct a search. In making their request for a warrant, the police must show "probable cause"—reasonable grounds for having suspicions and making the request.

In some cases, searches and seizures are permitted without a warrant. For example, if a police officer is in "hot pursuit," chasing a suspect who is fleeing the scene of a robbery in a car, it would be unreasonable to expect the officer to find a judge and obtain a warrant before continuing the chase. Searches without warrants are permitted in these cases.

Any evidence that the police obtain in violation of this amendment cannot be used in a court of law. The Fourth Amendment also protects our right to privacy—our ability to conduct our private lives without the interference of government.

The Fifth Amendment

No person shall be held to answer for a capital, or otherwise infamous crime, unless on an . . . indictment of a Grand Jury . . . nor shall any person be subject for the same offen[s]e to be twice put in jeopardy of life or limb; nor shall be compelled in any criminal case to be a witness against himself, nor be deprived of life, liberty, or property, without due process of law; nor shall private property be taken for public use, without just compensation.

indictment = formal accusation
jeopardy = danger
compelled = forced
compensation = payment

Like the First Amendment, the Fifth Amendment provides five separate rights. Four of these are rights of the accused:

1. A person cannot be charged for murder without an indictment by a grand jury. You already know that a jury is made up of a group of impartial local citizens. A federal grand jury is made up of 16 to 23 jurors (in Florida courts, 15 to 21). It provides a screening process to determine if there is enough evidence to make criminal charges and send a case to trial. The grand jury can call witnesses, examine evidence, and make an investigation to assist in its determination.
2. No person can be tried twice for the same crime. This is known as "**double jeopardy**" because the accused's liberty and life would be placed in danger twice.
3. No one accused of a crime can be forced to testify against himself or herself (*self-incrimination*). This is to prevent authorities from using pressure to frighten suspects into making false confessions or false testimony. Refusing to answer questions because the answers may be self-incriminating is sometimes called "pleading the Fifth."
4. No one can have life, liberty, or property taken away by government without "**due process of law.**" Due process means fairness. It means that one cannot lose life, liberty or property unless the procedures applied to the case are fair.
5. The last part of the Fifth Amendment focuses on **property rights** (*the right to be secure in the ownership of property*). It states that government can take private property for a valid public use (such as building a major highway), but the property owner must receive "just compensation." This means that the property owner must be paid what the property is truly worth. The power of government to take over private property for public purposes is known as the power of **eminent domain**.

The Sixth Amendment

In all criminal prosecutions, the accused shall enjoy the right to a speedy and public trial, by an impartial jury of the State and district wherein the crime shall have been committed ... and to be informed of the nature and cause of the accusation; to be confronted with the witnesses against him; to have compulsory process for obtaining witnesses in his favor, and to have the Assistance of Counsel for his defen[s]e.

confront = face
compulsory = involving compulsion; ability to compel
counsel = a lawyer

The Sixth Amendment also provides a person accused of a crime with several rights. In this amendment, these rights are focused on the trial itself:

1. The right to a speedy and public trial.

   The key words here are, "speedy and public." If one is accused of a crime and placed in jail, unless the case proceeds quickly to trial, the accused may have to wait in jail a long time before guilt or innocence is determined.

   The accused must not be tried in an isolated, secret court, but in a place where the public can see that the accused is fairly treated. Too often in dictatorships, innocent people are locked up while their cases are delayed for years without trial. Even if there is a trial, it is held in a hidden or secret place where no one can witness the unfair procedures that may result in sentencing the accused to long years of imprisonment or even death.

2. The right to a trial by jury.

   The accused is entitled to a trial by a group of "peers" or equals, known as jurors. They should be impartial and not be biased.

3. The right "to be informed of the nature and cause of the accusations."

   People have a right to hear the charges against them so that they can defend themselves. Charges must be stated at the time of any arrest or before any **forced internment** (*captivity or imprisonment*).

4. The right to "confront" witnesses.

   We have the right to face and question our accusers, in order to prove our innocence.

5. The right to require witnesses to appear in court for the accused.

6. The **right to legal counsel** (*an attorney*) for the defendant (*the person accused of committing the crime*).

In Chapter 11, you will learn how the U.S. Supreme Court interpreted this amendment in two cases: *Gideon v. Wainwright* and *Miranda v. Arizona*.

The Seventh Amendment

In suits at common law, where the value in controversy shall exceed twenty dollars, the right of trial by jury shall be preserved ...

This amendment guarantees the right to a jury trial in many civil (*non-criminal*) cases.

The Eighth Amendment

Excessive bail shall not be required, nor excessive fines imposed, nor cruel and unusual punishments inflicted.

There are three parts to this amendment:

1. The first part deals with the right of an individual accused of crime while awaiting trial. A defendant can usually remain outside of prison before trial by giving bail (*something of value, usually money, that the defendant gives the court to guarantee that he or she will come to the trial).* The Eighth Amendment requires that the bail not be "excessive" (*too high in proportion to the charges against the defendant*).
2. The amendment further provides that any fines on the defendant should also not be excessive.
3. Finally, the amendment guarantees that we should not have to suffer any "cruel and unusual punishment." (You may recall that this right was in the English Bill of Rights of 1689.)

Enrichment

The Active Citizen

Do you think that capital punishment (*execution*) should be prohibited as a "cruel and unusual punishment" in today's society? Write a persuasive essay with four paragraphs giving your point of view. In the first paragraph, write your introduction. In the second and third paragraphs, give your arguments with evidence to back them up. In the fourth paragraph, write your conclusion. Then exchange your persuasive essay with a partner from your class. After you read each other's papers, see if you influenced your partner's point of view. Which arguments did you both feel were most persuasive? Which arguments needed more support?

The Ninth Amendment

enumeration = listing
construed = interpreted
retained = kept

The enumeration in the Constitution, of certain rights, shall not be construed to deny or disparage others retained by the people.

When someone makes a list, others may think that whatever is not on the list is deliberately left off or excluded. The Ninth Amendment makes it clear that this is not the case for the individual rights listed in the Constitution and Bill of Rights. Other rights ***not*** listed in the Constitution may still exist and remain with the people. These are known as **unenumerated rights**.

The Tenth Amendment

The powers not delegated to the United States by the Constitution, nor prohibited by it to the States, are reserved to the States respectively, or to the people.

This amendment makes it clear that all rights and powers not granted to the national government by the Constitution are "reserved" to the states and to the American people. This amendment supports states' rights—the rights of states in our federal system. You will learn more about this amendment in Chapter 12 on federalism—the division of power between the national government and the states.

The Active Citizen

- Select your favorite amendment and draw your own political cartoon illustrating that amendment.
- Make a poster showing the rights of an accused person provided by the Bill of Rights.
- You may be surprised by how many of the rights in the Bill of Rights concern individuals accused of crimes. How are these rights about criminal procedure actually important safeguards of our political freedoms and our democratic system of government?

How the Constitution and Bill of Rights Safeguard Our Individual Rights

The Constitution tries to strike a balance that gives our government leaders enough power to govern effectively and yet protects our individual rights and liberties. This balance is found in our constitutional structure, which includes the separation of powers, the system of checks and balances, the division of power between the national government and the state governments, and the guarantees of individual rights found in the Constitution and the Bill of Rights. The Constitution, Bill of Rights, and several amendments guarantee individual rights that our government must respect. The result is a government that acts to **safeguard our individual rights** (*the rights we enjoy as individuals*). To "safeguard" is to protect.

Limits on Rights: At the same time, our individual rights must sometimes be limited to meet the demands of society. For example, as citizens of the United States we have certain obligations. We must obey the law, pay taxes, defend the nation, and serve on juries when summoned (see Chapter 13).

Furthermore, we cannot enjoy our own rights without respecting the rights of others. Courts have therefore placed certain common-sense limits on the exercise of some rights. Courts have held, for example, that:

- Free speech does not permit us to create an immediate danger to others or to publish harmful lies (known as libel) about others.

You won't have to know the numbers of amendments for the EOC test, but you should know these key groups of rights.

Summary: Individual Rights in the Bill of Rights

First Amendment Rights: The "Five Freedoms"

- **Freedom of religion:** People have the right to belong to any religion and to worship as they please; Congress cannot establish an official religion.
- **Freedom of speech:** People are free to say what they wish, including criticizing the government (but we cannot endanger the safety of others or violate their rights).
- **Freedom of the press:** People can write and publish what they wish, including criticism of the government (without violating the rights of others).
- **Freedom of assembly:** People have the right to meet publicly in groups.
- **Freedom to petition:** People have the right to write to their government officials to ask for change.

Rights of the Accused

- **No unreasonable search and seizure:** Police must have reasonable grounds for searching a place, taking goods, or arresting a person.
- **The right to due process:** The government must follow fair, public and transparent procedures before taking away someone's life, liberty or property.
- **The right to "plead the Fifth":** We cannot be forced to testify against ourselves.
- **The right to a trial by jury:** If accused of a crime, we have the right to be tried publicly by a group of impartial citizens.
- **The right to legal counsel:** A person accused of a crime has the right to the help of a lawyer.
- **No cruel and unusual punishment:** A person cannot be tortured or suffer a cruel and unusual punishment.
- **No double jeopardy:** A person cannot be tried twice for the same crime.

Other Rights in the Bill of Rights

- **The right to bear arms:** A person has the right to have a gun for self-defense.
- **The right to privacy:** We have a right to conduct our private lives without government interference.
- **The right to just compensation for property taken by eminent domain:** If the government takes our property for public use, it must pay us what it is worth.

- The right to bear arms does not mean we can carry dangerous guns in all public places.
- Permissible acts of civil disobedience (*refusing to obey laws we think are unjust*) do not include acts of violence.
- Protection against unreasonable searches and seizures does not mean the police need to get a court warrant if they are chasing a suspect they just saw commit a robbery.
- The freedom of religion does not allow us to interfere with others' freedom of belief.
- Property rights often are limited to protect the rights of others. We cannot, for example, burn down all the trees on our property because such a fire might endanger the homes and lives of our neighbors.

You will learn more about some of these interpretations of the Bill of Rights by the judicial branch in the next chapter. The limits that we place on ourselves and the powers that we grant our government to safeguard our rights are, in fact, closely related. We cannot have one without the other.

For the EOC, you should know these four examples of government-imposed limitations on individual rights.

Government-Imposed Limitations on Individual Rights

Sometimes the government places special limitations on individual rights for the sake of the community. This is especially true during wartime. Government officials become fearful that some individuals may act to harm the national war effort. To prevent this, government officials limit individual rights. It is often up to the judicial branch to decide whether the **rationales** (*explanations; reasons*) offered for these **government-imposed limitations** are justified.

Forced Internment during Wartime

Forced internment in wartime refers to relocating people to camps or prisons where they remain separated from the community and under guard. During World War II, many Americans feared that Japanese Americans living on the West Coast might be disloyal and commit acts of espionage or sabotage. The President issued an executive order allowing these Japanese Americans to be forced out of their homes and to be relocated to camps in desolate areas in the interior of the country. The Supreme Court upheld their forced internment as a wartime measure necessary for national security. Later, Congress apologized for the forced internment of loyal civilians during the war.

Japanese-American family awaiting internment in a camp shown on the right.

Limitations on Speech

During wartime, government officials also sometimes place **limitations on speech**. They fear that criticism of the war will weaken the war effort. During World War I, Congress passed the Espionage Act, which made it illegal to interfere with enforcement of the draft (*requiring citizens to serve in the armed forces*). The following year, Congress passed the Sedition Act, which prohibited any "disloyal" or "abusive language" about the government. Charles Schenck was arrested for violating the Espionage Act. Schenck had mailed leaflets advising men to resist the draft. He claimed his arrest violated his free speech rights. The Supreme Court, however, affirmed Schenck's arrest. It upheld government limitations on speech whenever "a clear and present danger" was evident.

Wartime Rationing

During World War II, eight million American men served in the armed forces. Gasoline, rubber, sugar, cooking oil, and canned foods were badly needed overseas by the American military and by America's allies. The government limited the freedom of Americans at home by **rationing during wartime**. People received a booklet of ration stamps for different types of goods. They had to give in a ration stamp whenever they bought one of the rationed goods. Once they used up their stamps for that type of item, they could not buy any more. Americans supported this limitation on their freedom to support the war effort.

Suspension of habeas corpus

A writ of habeas corpus requires the government to produce to the court someone who has been imprisoned. This is so the court can determine if the imprisonment is valid. This procedure helps prevent arbitrary arrest and wrongful imprisonment. The right to request a writ of habeas corpus is guaranteed by the

U.S. Constitution. The Constitution gives Congress the power to suspend this right in wartime. During the Civil War, Abraham Lincoln suspended habeas corpus and imprisoned opponents that he feared were sympathetic to the South. Congress supported his actions by passing the Habeas Corpus Suspension Act. The law authorized the President to suspend habeas corpus for the course of the war "whenever in his judgment the public safety may require it."

The Role of the Judicial Branch

The judicial branch has the job of protecting individual rights and freedoms. Courts balance our rights as individuals against the rights of other individuals and the rights of the community as a whole. In each of the cases above, courts had to decide whether the **government-imposed limitations** of rights was justified or whether it unnecessarily violated individual rights.

A cartoon critical of Lincoln for suspending the right to habeas corpus and other civil liberties

You will learn more about the role of the U.S. Supreme Court in interpreting the Constitution and the Bill of Rights in the next chapter.

The Impact of Later Amendments in Broadening Participation in the Political Process

Be sure to know the impact of these later amendments for the EOC.

One key to the success of American democracy has been the involvement of citizens through **participation in the political process** (*how our government leaders are chosen and government policies are made*). At first, however, many groups were left out of American political life: African Americans, women, those who could not pay poll taxes, and those under 21 years of age all could not vote. In order to participate fully in the political process, these groups needed to gain the rights and responsibilities of citizenship, including the right to vote.

The ability of our Constitution to change through the power of amendment opened the door to the granting of equal political rights to all these groups. The amendments described below made it possible for these groups to enter into the political process. These amendments influenced the way many individuals acted as well as their **social interactions** (*how they acted with others*).

As different groups achieved their right to vote, their views were considered more fully by others. Women and minorities were able to achieve other rights, such as equal opportunities in education and equal pay for equal work.

The 13th, 14th, and 15th Amendments

These three amendments were passed during and just after the Civil War, the great conflict between North and South that ended the practice of slavery.

The Thirteenth Amendment

Neither slavery nor involuntary servitude, except as a punishment for crime whereof the party shall have been duly convicted, shall exist within the United States, or any place subject to their jurisdiction.

servitude = state of being a servant or slave

Impact: The Thirteenth Amendment abolished slavery and involuntary servitude. Involuntary servitude is any form of forced labor.

Despite the abolition of slavery, some minorities were still treated as second class citizens. In Florida, many African Americans were forced to labor in camps under harsh conditions where they made turpentine, a major commercial product of the state. This form of involuntary servitude survived in Florida until the 1940s, despite the Thirteenth Amendment.

The Fourteenth Amendment

Section 1. All persons born or naturalized in the United States, and subject to the jurisdiction thereof, are citizens of the United States and of the State wherein they reside. No State shall make or enforce any law which shall abridge the privileges or immunities of citizens of the United States; nor shall any State deprive any person of life, liberty, or property, without due process of law; nor deny to any person within its jurisdiction the equal protection of the laws.

Impact: The Fourteenth Amendment guaranteed equality to African-American freedmen (*freed slaves*). It was ratified in 1868, just after the end of the Civil War. It further guaranteed all U.S. citizens certain rights against the actions of state governments.

Citizenship. The first section of this amendment stated that all persons born or naturalized in the United States were citizens of the United States and of the state in which they lived. Its purpose was to make it clear that the freed slaves were U.S. citizens with all the rights of citizenship.

Privileges and Immunities. The amendment also stated that no state could pass laws that limited the benefits of citizenship. These benefits are referred to as the "privileges and immunities" of citizenship.

"Due Process" Rights. The amendment further guaranteed citizens their "due process" rights in actions by state governments. The Fourteenth Amendment forbids any state government from taking "life, liberty, or property without due process of law. Both the procedures used and the laws applied must be fair, reasonable, and just. Based on the Fourteenth Amendment, the Bill of Rights applies to the states as well as to the federal government.

Equal Protection Clause. Lastly, the Fourteenth Amendment stated that all citizens are entitled to the equal protection under the law. This means that states must treat all people equally. It reflected the concerns of Congress over the treatment of African-American freedmen in Southern states. The Equal Protection Clause said that states could not legally discriminate against any citizen. It became a pillar in the struggle for civil rights in America.

The Fifteenth Amendment

The right of citizens of the United States to vote shall not be denied or abridged by the United States or by any State on account of race, color, or previous condition of servitude.

Impact: Despite the Fourteenth Amendment, many African Americans were still denied the right to vote, including in Northern states. The Fifteenth Amendment addressed this problem directly. The Amendment forbade the national and state governments from denying any citizen the right to vote on the basis of race, color, or having once been enslaved.

The Expansion of Democracy: the 19th, 24th, and 26th Amendments

The Nineteenth Amendment

The right of citizens of the United States to vote shall not be denied or abridged by the United States or by any State on account of sex.

Impact: Throughout the nineteenth century, American women were denied the right to vote, known as suffrage, in most states. Women reformers sought an amendment that would give women the right to vote across America. They used many tactics on behalf of women's suffrage, including, in some cases, **civil disobedience** (*refusing to obey laws considered unjust*). After many campaigns and struggles, women finally secured the right to vote in all states with the ratification of the **Nineteenth Amendment** in 1920.

While women secured suffrage with the Nineteenth Amendment, women reformers in the 1960s and 1970s wanted greater equality of opportunity. They failed, however, to achieve adoption of the Equal Rights Amendment. This amendment was proposed by Congress in 1972, but was never ratified by enough states. It stated that "Equality of rights should not be denied . . . on account of sex." Women themselves became divided over whether to support the amendment, and many claimed it was unnecessary. They felt women's rights were already protected by other amendments.

The Twenty-fourth Amendment

> *The right of citizens of the United States to vote in any primary or other election for President or Vice President, for electors for President or Vice President, or for Senator or Representative in Congress, shall not be denied or abridged by the United States or any State by reason of failure to pay any poll tax or other tax.*

Impact: Tactics such as poll taxes (*a special tax paid in order to vote*) were once used, even as late as the 1960s, by Southern states to discourage African-American voters. The **Twenty-fourth Amendment** prohibited any state from requiring the payment of a poll tax by citizens to vote in federal elections.

The Twenty-fourth Amendment was ratified at the height of the Civil Rights Movement of the 1960s. African-American leaders like Dr. Martin Luther King, Jr., held rallies and demonstrations, conducted boycotts, went on marches, and committed acts of **civil disobedience**. Their actions led to several laws that helped end racial discrimination and promoted greater social justice. These included:

abridged = limited

- **The Civil Rights Act of 1964.** Many restaurants and hotels in the South would not serve African Americans. This law prohibited such discrimination in restaurants, hotels and many forms of employment on the basis of race, sex (*gender*), religion or ethnic origin.
- **The Voting Rights Act of 1965.** This law echoed the Fifteenth and Twenty-fourth Amendments. It prohibited poll taxes and racial discrimination in voting, and permitted special federal officials to register voters.
- **The Civil Rights Act of 1968.** This law prohibited racial discrimination in the sale or rental of housing.

The Twenty-sixth Amendment

> *The right of citizens of the United States, who are eighteen years of age or older, to vote shall not be denied or abridged by the United States or by any State on account of age.*

Impact: During the War in Vietnam, young men were being drafted (*conscripted for compulsory military service*) at the age of 18 years, but they were often not permitted to vote until they reached 21 years of age. Critics argued that if an 18-year-old man was old enough to be required to fight and die for his country, then surely he was old enough to vote. The amendment process again made it possible to expand voting rights. The **Twenty-sixth Amendment** lowered the minimum voting age from 21 years to 18.

◆ ◆ ◆

The general impact of these amendments has been to make women, young adults and minorities equal partners with other voters in the American system of democracy. We now see representatives of every race, ethnic background, gender and age at every level of our government. This was not always the case. There was a bitter struggle to provide the rights of citizenship to all, thus permitting Americans to live up to their original creed (*belief*), that all people are created equal. The ability of Americans to amend the Constitution helped to make this transformation possible.

Name ____________________________________

Our individual rights are precious. We cannot protect our rights, however, if we cannot recognize when those rights are violated. Complete the chart below by identifying which rights in the Bill of Rights have been violated in each scenario.

Events	Which rights have been violated and how
Sarah robs a bank. The police arrest her and interrogate her. No lawyer is present and the police do not tell her about her rights. Sarah confesses to the crime.	
Jasmine writes an article in the newspaper about corruption in her local government. The mayor orders the police to arrest her for publishing her article. Jasmine is arrested and sent to jail without a trial.	
Edgar wants the United States to withdraw its troops from a Middle Eastern country. He writes to his member of Congress. He also meets with other people to demonstrate in the street against the government's actions. The police arrest Edgar for participating in a demonstration against government policy.	
Jim lives in a state that decides to tax its citizens to provide funding for religious schools. All different types of religious schools can request funding from this new tax, so state officials feel the tax is fair. Jim, however, refuses to pay the tax.	
Sandra is accused of shoplifting. She is placed on trial and the jury finds her "not guilty." Shortly after the trial, the store finds a videotape showing Sandra committing the crime. The District Attorney decides to charge her again for shoplifting. Sandra is put on trial a second time for the same crime.	
Leroy is arrested for causing a public nuisance when he repeatedly refuses to stop playing loud music after 10:00 pm at night. The judge refuses to set any bail before his trial. After Leroy is found guilty, the judge sentences him to three years in prison.	

Name ______________________________

Complete the Internet chat below by filling in the text messages on some of the limits placed on the rights guaranteed by the Bill of Rights.

What the amendment says	Limits placed on that right in order to protect the rights of others or the demands of society
The First Amendment guarantees free speech.	Yes, but ______________________________
The First Amendment also guarantees a free press.	Yes, but ______________________________
The Second Amendment says that we have the right to bear arms.	Yes, but ______________________________
The Fourth Amendment says that the police need to obtain a warrant before searching a place or seizing a suspect.	Yes, but ______________________________

Name ____

Complete the chart below by describing each right and evaluating how it influences people's actions.

First Amendment: "Five Freedoms"	Description/Influence
Freedom of religion 	
Freedom of speech 	
Freedom of the press 	
Freedom of assembly 	
Freedom to petition 	

Name ______________________________

Complete the chart below by describing each right and evaluating how it influences people's actions.

Rights of the Accused	Description/Influence
No unreasonable search and seizure 	
Right to "due process" 	
Right to "Plead the Fifth" 	
Right to a trial by jury 	
Right to the assistance of legal counsel 	

Name ______________________________

Complete the chart below by describing each right and evaluating how it influences people's actions.

Rights of the Accused	Description/Influence
No "double jeopardy" 	
No "cruel and unusual" punishment 	

Other Rights in the Bill of Rights	Description/Influence
Right to bear arms 	
Right to privacy 	
Right to just compensation for property taken by eminent domain 	

The Principles Underlying America's Founding Ideas

In Chapters 1 and 2, you learned about the origins of the basic principles that influenced the founders of the American constitutional republic. These principles are reflected in America's founding documents—the Declaration of Indpendence, the Articles of Confederation, the Constitution and the Bill of Rights. Now that you have studied those documents, you can identify where these important principles can be found. For each principle, identify at least one place in the founding documents where that principle is located.

Principle	Explanation	Example(s) of this Principle in the Founding Documents
Rule of Law	We are all subject to the same rules. Even government officials and wealthy citizens must obey these laws. Because we live under the rule of law, we are safe from arbitrary actions by our government officials. No one is above the law	
Natural Rights	There are certain basic rights, based on human reason, that apply to all people in societies. These rights cannot be taken away. They include the right to life, liberty and property.	
Limited Government	We give our government certain powers over us, but the powers of our government are not unlimited. There are limits on what government officials can do. These limits prevent our government from becoming too strong and threatening our individual rights.	
Due Process	We are entitled to a fair and public trial or some other public hearing before our lives, liberty or property can be taken away. Our due process rights protect us from arbitrary actions by government officials.	
Equality of Mankind	We are all equal as human beings. Each of us is entitled to the same natural rights.	
Protection of Religious Liberty	There is no official religion in the United States, and everyone has the freedom to practice their own religious beliefs or no religion at all. Because of this protection of religious liberty, Americans have avoided religious wars.	

Name ___________________________________

Complete the chart below on the later amendments and laws expanding American democracy.

Amendment	What it says	Impact on the participation of minorities, women or young people in the political process
Nineteenth Amendment		
Twenty-fourth Amendment		
Twenty-sixth Amendment		
Civil Rights Act of 1964		
Voting Rights Act of 1965		
Civil Rights Act of 1968		

Based on the table, what was the impact of Civil Rights legislation in broadening political participation?

African Americans in Government		
Year	Members of Congress	Total Elected Officials
1965	6	[not available]
1970	10	1,469
1975	18	3,503
1980	17	4,912
1985	20	6,056
1990	26	6,131

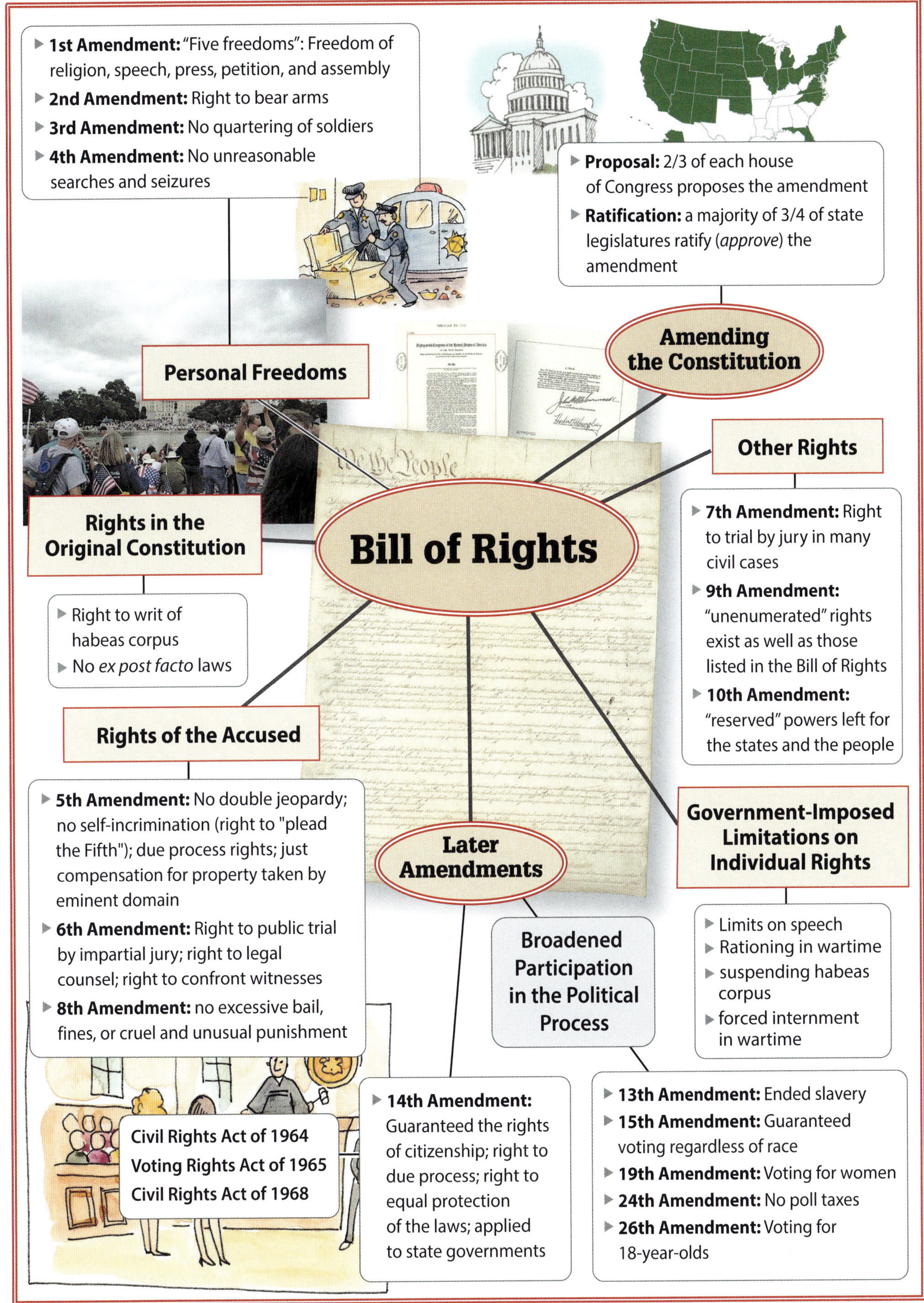

1st Amendment: "Five freedoms": Freedom of religion, speech, press, petition, and assembly
2nd Amendment: Right to bear arms
3rd Amendment: No quartering of soldiers
4th Amendment: No unreasonable searches and seizures
Proposal: 2/3 of each house of Congress proposes the amendment
Ratification: a majority of 3/4 of state legislatures ratify (approve) the amendment
Personal Freedoms
Amending the Constitution
Other Rights
Bill of Rights
Rights in the Original Constitution
Right to writ of habeas corpus
No ex post facto laws
7th Amendment: Right to trial by jury in many civil cases
9th Amendment: "unenumerated" rights exist as well as those listed in the Bill of Rights
10th Amendment: "reserved" powers left for the states and the people
Rights of the Accused
5th Amendment: No double jeopardy; no self-incrimination (right to "plead the Fifth"); due process rights; just compensation for property taken by eminent domain
6th Amendment: Right to public trial by impartial jury; right to legal counsel; right to confront witnesses
8th Amendment: no excessive bail, fines, or cruel and unusual punishment
Later Amendments
Government-Imposed Limitations on Individual Rights
Limits on speech
Rationing in wartime
suspending habeas corpus
forced internment in wartime
Broadened Participation in the Political Process
Civil Rights Act of 1964
Voting Rights Act of 1965
Civil Rights Act of 1968
14th Amendment: Guaranteed the rights of citizenship; right to due process; right to equal protection of the laws; applied to state governments
13th Amendment: Ended slavery
15th Amendment: Guaranteed voting regardless of race
19th Amendment: Voting for women
24th Amendment: No poll taxes
26th Amendment: Voting for 18-year-olds

Review Cards: The Bill of Rights and Later Amendments

Amending the Constitution

The **U.S. Constitution** allows for changing times through a **formal amendment process**. However, to amend the Constitution is more difficult than passing an ordinary law. **Article V** of the Constitution established a two-step process for amendments:

Step 1. Proposing the Amendment

First, it must be proposed. An amendment can be proposed in either of two ways:

1. By a two-thirds vote of both Houses of Congress. All amendments of the Constitution so far have used this method.
   or
2. On the request of two-thirds of the state legislatures, Congress can call for a national convention to amend the Constitution.

Step 2. Ratifying the Amendment

Then it must be ratified. There are two ways to **ratify** (*approve*) an amendment. Congress selects which one to apply:

1. Ratification by three-fourths of the state legislatures. So far, only this method has been used.
   or
2. Ratification by special ratification conventions in three-fourths of the states.

Two Rights in the Original Constitution

- Everyone is guaranteed the right to apply for a **writ of habeas corpus**, a court order to bring a prisoner before the court to determine if the imprisonment is lawful.
- Everyone is protected against *ex post facto* laws. An ***ex post facto* law** punishes people for doing something that only became illegal after they did it.

The Bill of Rights: The First Ten Amendments

The **Bill of Rights** consists of the first ten amendments to the Constitution. They were proposed by the first Congress to meet the demands of the Anti-Federalists, who had demanded a bill of rights during the debate over ratification of the Constitution. The Bill of Rights originally just protected individuals from actions by the federal government. Only later did the Fourteenth Amendment apply these rights to actions by state governments.

First Amendment

Establishes **five freedoms**. Congress *cannot*:

1. limit freedom of religion or establish a state religion (*a government-supported church or religion*)
2. limit freedom of speech
3. limit freedom of the press (*the right of newspapers and other media sources to publish information*)
4. prevent people from holding assemblies (*public gatherings*)
5. prevent people from petitioning (*making formal requests to*) the government

Continues ▶

The Bill of Rights: The First Ten Amendments (*continued*)

Second Amendment

Protects citizens' right to bear arms (*possess guns*).

Third Amendment

Prohibits (*forbids*) government from quartering (*sheltering*) soldiers in citizens' homes in peacetime without the owners' consent.

Fourth Amendment

Protects citizens from unreasonable search and seizure of their persons, houses, papers and other belongings. To "search" is to look through and to "seize" is to take something or arrest someone.

Fifth Amendment

Provides several rights, most of which protect those accused of a crime:

1. **"Double Jeopardy":** No person can be tried twice for the same crime.
2. Freedom from Self-Incrimination: No person can be compelled to testify against himself or herself ("Pleading the Fifth"—refusing to answer questions where the answers might be self-incriminating).
3. **"Due Process"** rights: No person can be deprived of life, liberty, or property without **due process**—a process that is fair and that respects the person's rights.
4. **Eminent Domain:** Private property may be taken over by government for public use, but the owner must be fairly compensated (*paid*). This provision helped protect **property rights** (*private ownership of property*).

Sixth Amendment

Guarantees rights of the accused in criminal proceedings. These rights are:

1. The right to a speedy and public trial
2. The right to a trial by jury
3. The accused must be informed of the charges
4. The right to face witnesses against the accused
5. The right to require witnesses to come to the court, who can testify in the accused's favor
6. The **right to legal counsel** (*an attorney*)

Seventh Amendment

Provides the right to a jury trial in many civil cases.

Eighth Amendment

1. Prohibits excessive bail (*money given by the accused to guarantee appearance at trial*).
2. Prohibits excessive fines.
3. Prohibits cruel and unusual punishment.

Ninth Amendment

The enumeration (*listing*) of some rights in the Constitution does not mean that other rights may not also exist. These other rights are known as **unenumerated rights**.

Tenth Amendment

Any rights not given to the federal government or prohibited to the states are reserved for the states or for the people. These powers are known as the "reserved" powers. (See Chapter 12.)

Later Amendments Contributed to the Expansion of Democracy

Later amendments have played an important role in the expansion of democracy by bringing previously excluded groups into the American political process. The impact of these amendments has been to expand American democracy. These amendments have also shaped our **social interactions** (*how we relate to one another*).

- The **13th Amendment** abolished slavery and involuntary servitude in the United States.
- The **14th Amendment** protected the rights of freedmen and other citizens:
  1. It made all persons born or naturalized in the United States into citizens of the United States.
  2. **Due Process** Clause prohibits any state from taking "life, liberty, or property without due process of law." Courts have interpreted this to mean the Bill of Rights applies to the state governments.
  3. **"Equal protection of the laws"** requires states to treat people equally under the law. The Equal Protection Clause became an important weapon in the struggle for civil rights in America.
- The **15th Amendment** prohibited the national and state governments from denying the right to vote to any citizen on the basis of race, color, or having been a slave.
- The **19th Amendment** gave women the right to vote (known as *suffrage*).
- The **24th Amendment** abolished poll taxes as a requirement to vote in federal elections. Poll taxes had been used to deny African-American citizens their right to vote.

  The 24th Amendment was passed at the time of the Civil Rights Movement when Civil Rights leaders were using **civil disobedience** (*peaceful refusal to obey laws considered unjust*) demonstrations, and other efforts to end racial segregation and achieve equality. This amendment was accompanied by the **Civil Rights Act of 1964** (*banning discrimination in restaurants, hotels, and most employment*), **Voting Rights Act of 1965** (*enforcing the 15th and 24th Amendments*), and **Civil Rights Act of 1968** (*banning discrimination in housing*). An Equal Rights Amendment, guaranteeing equality to women, was never ratified.
- The **26th Amendment** lowered the voting age to 18 years old.

How the Constitution and Bill of Rights Safeguard Individual Rights

- The Constitution seeks to find a balance between limiting government power to protect **individual rights** and allowing government sufficient power to govern effectively.
- The balance is found in a constitutional structure that has a separation of powers, checks and balances, the division of power between the national and state governments, and guarantees of individual rights. The Bill of Rights and later amendments identify which particular individual rights are **protected rights** (*rights protected by the Constitution and federal law*).

Limitations on Individual Rights

- Courts have upheld individual rights but have also placed common-sense restrictions on our exercise of them to protect the rights of our fellow citizens and meet the needs of the community: for example, free speech does not permit us to create an immediate danger to others or to tell lies about others; freedom of religion does not allow us to interfere with others' rights; the right to bear arms does not mean we can carry any kind of gun into every public place; protection against unreasonable searches does not mean the police have to get a court warrant if they are engaged in a chase; acts of **civil disobedience** do not include the right to use violence.
- **Government-imposed limitations on individual rights:** Sometimes, especially in wartime, the government limits our individual rights. The **rationale** (*reason; explanation*) for these limits is to protect the community. Examples of such limits are: **limitations on speech** (*we cannot say things that could cause an immediate danger*), **rationing during wartime** (*limiting the amounts of some goods, such as food or gas, that people can buy*), **suspending habeas corpus** (*limiting the right to have a court challenge a person's imprisonment*) and even **forced internment during wartime** (*confinement of people in camps or prisons*).

What Do You Know?

SS.7.CG.2.3

1. What is one of the five freedoms protected by the First Amendment?

   A. freedom of speech
   B. freedom from self-incrimination
   C. freedom from unreasonable search and seizure
   D. freedom from cruel and unusual punishments

SS.7.CG.3.5

2. What is usually the first step in amending the U.S. Constitution?

   A. Three-fourths of the state legislatures propose the amendment.
   B. Two-thirds of each house of Congress propose the amendment.
   C. Conventions in three-fourths of the states propose the amendment.
   D. The President, after consulting with the U.S. Supreme Court, proposes the amendment.

SS.7.CG.2.3

3. Juanita owns unused property in her town. Her city council decides to use part of her property to build a new bus terminal. The council votes to give Juanita $20,000 for this part of her property. She claims her land is worth much more. The city clerk sends her a check for $20,000, and the city starts building the terminal. Which two rights of Juanita have been violated?

   A. right to assistance of counsel and trial by jury
   B. right to privacy and protection from unreasonable seizure
   C. equal protection of the law and prohibition of double jeopardy
   D. right to due process and just compensation in case of eminent domain

SS.7.CG.3.5

4. The diagram below shows the most common method of amending the U.S. Constitution.

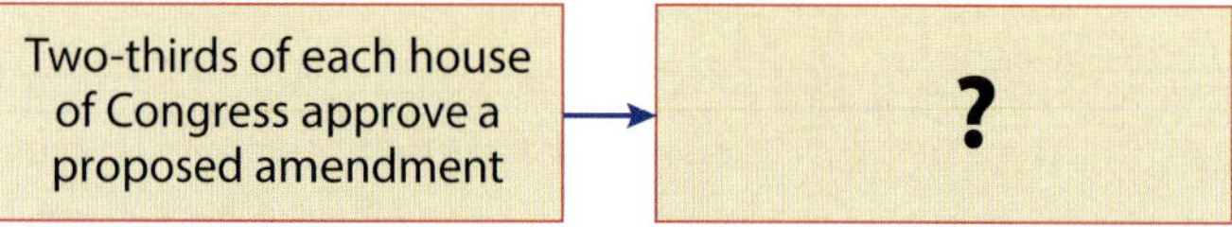

Which completes the diagram?

A. Two-thirds of the states hold a constitutional convention

B. Three-fourths of the state legislatures ratify the amendment

C. The President of the United States approves the amendment

D. Three-fourths of both houses of Congress ratify the amendment

SS.7.CG.2.3

5. Which of these rights from the Bill of Rights helps people accused of crimes?

A. the right to bear arms for self-defense

B. the right to have the assistance of counsel

C. the right not to have troops quartered in one's home

D. the right to petition government for a redress of grievances

SS.7.CG.2.3

6. While Alex was at school, police officers broke into his home and took his computer. They did not have a warrant and there was no reason to believe that Alex had broken any laws. Alex was not avoiding the police or planning to move away from his home. Which right did the police officers violate?

A. the right to due process of law in the Fourteenth Amendment

B. the right to assistance of legal counsel in the Sixth Amendment

C. the right to the equal protection of the laws in the Fourteenth Amendment

D. the right against unreasonable searches and seizures in the Fourth Amendment

SS.7.CG.2.4

7. Which example illustrates a government-imposed limitation on individual rights that is permitted by the Constitution?

A. Government officials arrest a newspaper editor for criticizing their policies.

B. A defendant pleads the Fifth Amendment rather than testifying at her trial.

C. Congress suspends the right to petition for a writ of habeas corpus during wartime.

D. The police conduct the search of a private home without a warrant or "probable cause."

SS.7.CG.2.4

8. What did the rationing of goods during World War II illustrate?
   A. the operation of the due process of law
   B. a government-imposed limitation on individual rights
   C. one of the checks and balances in the U.S. Constitution
   D. the broadening of the political process through amendment

SS.7.CG.2.4

9. Joe Smith was tried in state court a second time for the same crime, found guilty and sent to prison. Joe's lawyer believes Joe has been wrongly imprisoned. What could the lawyer do?
   A. protest against an unfair *ex post facto* law
   B. petition for a writ of habeas corpus
   C. demand Joe's "due process" rights
   D. petition for a writ of certiorari

SS.7.CG.3.6

10. Which statement describes an impact of the Due Process and Equal Protection Clauses of the Fourteenth Amendment?
   A. Women were guaranteed the right to vote in all states.
   B. African-American freedmen were guaranteed the right to vote.
   C. Americans were protected against abuses by state governments.
   D. Opponents of the government no longer feared forced internment.

SS.7.CG.3.6

Times-Union
26th Amendment Ratified by North Carolina, the 38th State
Those Fighting for Their Country Now Have a Voice in its Government

11. The newspaper headline on the left announces an amendment to the U.S. Constitution.
   What was the impact of the passage of this amendment on the American political process?
   A. Women were allowed to vote in elections in all states.
   B. Citizens from 18 to 20 years of age were allowed to vote in elections.
   C. Those who could not afford to pay poll taxes could still vote in federal elections.
   D. Restaurants and hotels could not practice discrimination against Vietnam veterans.

SS.7.CG.2.4

12. The statement below about free speech is from the Supreme Court decision of *Schenck v. United States* (1919).

   > *The most stringent protection of free speech would not protect a man in falsely shouting fire in a theater and causing a panic.*

   Which conclusion can be drawn from this reasoning?
   A. Our constitutional rights are limited by the rights of others.
   B. Not all Supreme Court decisions uphold the U.S. Constitution.
   C. Since 1917, Americans no longer enjoy the freedom of speech.
   D. The U.S. Supreme Court generally favors the powers of the federal government over the rights of individuals.

SS.7.CG.2.4

13. What protects a citizen from being punished for an act that only became a crime after the act was committed?

A. the right to petition for a writ of habeas corpus
B. the Constitution's prohibition of *ex post facto* laws
C. the unenumerated rights of the Ninth Amendment
D. the powers reserved to citizens by the Tenth Amendment

SS.7.CG.2.4

14. The statement from the U.S. Supreme Court below gives the rationale for a government-imposed limitation on individual rights.

> Korematsu was excluded because we are at war with the Japanese Empire, because the properly constituted military authorities feared an invasion of our West Coast and felt constrained to take proper security measures, [and] because they decided that the military urgency of the situation demanded that all citizens of Japanese ancestry be [removed] from the West Coast temporarily . . .
>
> —*Korematsu v. United States* (1944)

Which action did this rationale attempt to justify?

A. limitations on speech
B. a suspension of habeas corpus
C. forcible internment in wartime
D. an exercise of the power of eminent domain

S.7.CG.2.3

15. John Wilkinson's property was needed to complete a section of the new state highway. The State of Florida took his property and paid John $100,000. Based on the prices of nearby homes, John thought he should have received twice that amount. He demanded a hearing and the return of his property. What are John's rights in these circumstances?

A. John is entitled to receive an additional $100,000 from the State of Florida.
B. John is entitled to the return of his property because he was denied due process of law.
C. John is entitled to a public hearing to determine whether he received just compensation for his property.
D. Because of its power of eminent domain, the State of Florida is entitled to keep John's property without any further payment.

CHAPTER 11

"May It Please the Court": The Supreme Court in Action

SS.7.CG.3.11 Analyze the effects of landmark Supreme Court decisions on law, liberty and the interpretation of the U.S. Constitution.

Content Focus Vocabulary in This Chapter

Constitutional principles

Individual rights

Impact on society

Law, liberty, and the U.S. Constitution

Marbury v. Madison

Dred Scott v. Sandford

Hazelwood v. Kuhlmeier

Gideon v. Wainwright

Miranda v. Arizona

In re Gault

Plessy v. Ferguson

Brown v. Board of Education

United States v. Nixon

Florida "Keys" to Learning

1. The U.S. Supreme Court interprets the **individual rights** promised by the Constitution. Its power of judicial review often helps it to protect those rights. The Court's decisions affect our understanding of the **law, liberty and the U.S. Constitution**: what the law means, what freedoms we should enjoy, and how the U.S. Constitution is to be interpreted. The Court's decisions are often based on **constitutional principles** and can have a major **impact on society**, affecting people's everyday lives.

2. In ***Marbury v. Madison*** (1803), the Supreme Court firmly established the power of judicial review: the principle that the Supreme Court has the power to rule that laws passed by Congress or state governments are unconstitutional and that the Court can invalidate (*cancel; overturn*) them.

3. In ***Dred Scott v. Sandford*** (1857), the Supreme Court held that African Americans, whether enslaved or free, could not sue in federal courts because they were never intended to be U.S. citizens. The Court also held that the Missouri Compromise, which prohibited slavery in northern territories, was unconstitutional because it took away slave owners' "property" (*enslaved persons*) without providing the slave owners with "due process" (*a hearing or other procedure*). This decision caused a storm of controversy and helped lead to the Civil War. The 14th Amendment later overturned the Court's ruling on citizenship.

4. In ***Hazelwood School District v. Kuhlmeier*** (1988), the Supreme Court placed limits on students' free-speech rights. It stated that school officials could censor (*examine and edit*) school-sponsored student publications so long as such restrictions served a proper educational purpose.

5. Several of the rights in the Bill of Rights protect the rights of the accused. In ***Gideon v. Wainwright*** (1963), the Supreme Court ruled that the Sixth Amendment guarantees the right to legal counsel (*a lawyer*) to a defendant charged with a felony (*a serious crime*) who is too poor to afford one. Ever since this case, courts are required to provide the service of a "public defender" to persons accused of serious crimes who cannot afford to hire a lawyer.

6. In ***Miranda v. Arizona*** (1966), the Supreme Court ruled that suspects must be informed of their Fifth and Sixth Amendment rights before being questioned by police. Suspects have the right to remain silent and to have a lawyer.

7. In ***In re Gault*** (1967), a juvenile (*minor; someone under 18 years old*) was imprisoned after an unfair process under juvenile law. He was denied "due process" rights and was given an unjustly harsh penalty for supposedly making an obscene phone call he said he did not make. The Supreme Court ruled that most "due process" rights apply to minors as well as to adults.

8. Segregation means separation and often refers to the separation of people by race. In the 1880s and 1890s, many Southern states passed segregation laws. In ***Plessy v. Ferguson*** (1896), the U.S. Supreme Court affirmed the constitutionality of state segregation laws, so long as the facilities offered to each race were of "equal standards" (known as "separate-but-equal").

9. In ***Brown v. Board of Education*** (1954), the Court ruled that racial segregation in public schools violated the Equal Protection Clause of the Fourteenth Amendment. This was because segregated public schools were "inherently unequal"—unequal by their very nature. The Court overruled *Plessy v. Ferguson*. The *Brown* decision was the first step toward ending racial segregation in the South.

10. In ***United States v. Nixon*** (1974), the Supreme Court weighed President Nixon's claim of "executive privilege" against the needs of prosecutors to collect evidence of wrongdoing. His claim was overruled by the Court, which ordered the President to hand over tapes of White House conversations to investigators. The Court's decision proved that even the President of the United States is not above the "rule of law."

Imagine a close relative promised you a special present: a favorite book or computer game, or a trip to an amusement park. Such a promise would surely be wonderful, but if you never actually received the present, you would soon become disappointed. The Bill of Rights was a splendid promise made to the American people. But without a means of enforcement, the Bill of Rights would have become an empty promise and nothing more. What made the Bill of Rights and later constitutional rights so very effective was the fact that these promises were combined with the active protection of the federal courts, and especially by the U.S. Supreme Court.

In this chapter, you will witness the Supreme Court in action. You will see how the Court has interpreted the **individual rights** promised by the Constitution, especially those rights found in the Bill of Rights and the Fourteenth Amendment. Its decisions affect our understanding of the **law, liberty and the interpretation of the U.S. Constitution**—what the law means, what freedoms we should enjoy (and their limits), and how the U.S. Constitution is to be interpreted. The Court determines how **constitutional principles** are to be applied to specific situations.

Be sure to know the facts, outcome and significance of *Marbury v. Madison* and the other eight cases in this chapter.

The Power of Judicial Review

Marbury v. Madison (1803)

This decision, perhaps the single most important one in the history of the Supreme Court, took place against a background of political rivalry. *Marbury v. Madison* was not about individual rights, but about the powers of the Court itself. It laid the foundation for many later decisions by the Court.

The Political Background

John Adams was the second President of the United States. Adams was defeated by Thomas Jefferson in the Presidential election of 1800. In December 1800, Adams' supporters in Congress passed laws creating new judicial posts. Their aim was to fill the judiciary with sympathetic judges before Jefferson took power.

President Adams nominated new judges from his own political party to fill all of these posts. The Senate only completed confirmation of his new appointments on March 3, 1801—Adams' last day in office. The new appointments were quickly signed by Adams and sealed by his Secretary of State, John Marshall. Most of the new commissions *(official signed documents of the appointment)* were delivered (*handed over*), but in the last-minute rush, a few were not.

Meanwhile, the Chief Justice of the Supreme Court had resigned in January. Adams appointed John Marshall to take his place. In February 1801, Marshall assumed office as Chief Justice of the Supreme Court. Marshall also remained as Secretary of State during Adams' final month in office.

On March 4, 1801, Thomas Jefferson took the oath of office as the third President of the United States. He appointed James Madison as his Secretary of State. Jefferson and Madison refused to deliver any remaining last-minute commissions made by Adams. One of these undelivered commissions was to William Marbury.

Marbury's Lawsuit

After writing to Madison, Marbury applied to the Supreme Court for the delivery of his commission.

The Judiciary Act of 1789 had given the U.S. Supreme Court the power to issue a court order to a government official to perform his duties (*writ of mandamus*). Marbury filed his suit in the Supreme Court, seeking such an order to Madison, requiring him to deliver the commission.

The lawsuit placed Chief Justice Marshall in a delicate situation. As former Secretary of State, Marshall had set the seal of the United States on the very commission he was now asked to enforce. Could his decision be impartial in these circumstances?

The Legal Issues

The case brought two issues before the Court:

1. Should the Supreme Court issue a court order to Madison, as Secretary of State, requiring him to deliver the commission to William Marbury?
2. Can the Supreme Court rule on the constitutionality of a law passed by Congress?

The Decision/Outcome

Marshall found an ingenious solution to his situation in this case.

First, Marshall made it clear that Marbury was fully entitled to his appointment, which had already been signed and sealed.

Then Marshall turned to the question of enforcement. Did the Supreme Court actually have the power to order the Secretary of State to deliver Marbury's commission?

Marshall explained that the Constitution had given the U.S. Supreme Court "original jurisdiction" in only a small number of cases. Congress did not have the right, under the Constitution, to enlarge this original jurisdiction. Only a constitutional amendment could do this. Therefore, the section of the Judiciary Act of 1789 that gave the Supreme Court the power to issue court orders to officials to perform their duties was an "unconstitutional" expansion of the Court's original jurisdiction.

Since this section of the Judiciary Act was unconstitutional, Marshall concluded that it could not be enforced. Therefore, the Supreme Court lacked the power to order Madison to deliver Marbury's commission.

This raised a second issue, which was actually far more important than the first: **Which branch of government had authority to determine the constitutionality of laws?** Marshall explained that it was the U.S. Supreme Court that held the final power in determining whether or not a law, or parts of it, were constitutional.

Here was his argument:

1. The Constitution was the fundamental (*basic*) law of the United States.
2. When the Constitution and an ordinary law were in conflict, the Constitution had to be upheld.
3. It was the job of the U.S. Supreme Court to interpret and apply the law.
4. It was therefore the job of the Supreme Court to interpret both the Constitution and individual laws passed by Congress.
5. The Supreme Court could declare laws unconstitutional if it found them to be in conflict with the Constitution.
6. Finally, unconstitutional laws were invalid (*not valid; not lawful*) and could not be enforced.

Ironically, Marshall had limited the Supreme Court's authority by denying it the power to issue certain types of court orders (*writ of mandamus*). At the same time, Marshall had greatly expanded the Court's authority by establishing the principle of judicial review.

Justice John Marshall

Analysis of Effects: The Interpretation of the Constitution

The decision in *Marbury v. Madison* firmly established the principle of judicial review: the principle that the Supreme Court has the power to rule that laws passed by Congress are unconstitutional and to invalidate (*cancel; overturn*) them.

With this decision, the Supreme Court took on the role of "guardian" of our Constitution. It became the final authority for the interpretation of the U.S. Constitution. The Court uses its power of judicial review to protect our individual rights. But remember: the U.S. Supreme Court only determines the constitutionality of a law if it comes before the Court in a real case.

Case Summary

Summarize this case and the Supreme Court's decision in your own words.

What **constitutional principle** did this case establish? What impact has this case had on American society and government?

The Active Citizen

"It is emphatically the province and duty of the Judicial Department to say what the law is. Those who apply the rule to particular cases must, of necessity, expound and interpret that rule. If two laws conflict with each other, the Courts must decide on the operation of each. So, if a law be in opposition to the Constitution: if both the law and the Constitution apply to a particular case, so that the Court must either decide that case conformably to the law, disregarding the Constitution; or conformably to the Constitution, disregarding the law: the Court must determine which of these conflicting rules governs the case. This is of the very essence of judicial duty . . ."

—*Marbury v. Madison*, 1803

Word Helper

emphatically = unmistakably; without a doubt

province = area of responsibility

expound = explain

in opposition to = in disagreement with

conformably = in agreement with

disregarding = ignoring; paying no attention to

essence = the very core; the most basic part

- Do you agree with John Marshall that the Supreme Court is the branch of government best suited to determine the constitutionality of laws? Write an editorial for a newspaper in 1803, in which you either support or attack his reasoning in *Marbury v. Madison*. An **editorial** is a type of newspaper article presenting an opinion on an issue.
- How did Marshall's reasoning in *Marbury v. Madison* make it difficult for his opponents in Congress to attack his decision?
- Why was this decision so important for later ones?

Main Events behind *Marbury v. Madison*

Enrichment

1787: Article III of the Constitution defines the "original jurisdiction" of the U.S. Supreme Court. These are situations in which the Court has immediate authority to take action.

1789: The first Congress passes the Judiciary Act of 1789, creating lower federal courts. The same act expands the "original jurisdiction" of the U.S. Supreme Court. It gives the Court the power to issue orders to federal officials.

1796: John Adams is elected second President of the United States.

June 6, 1800: John Marshall takes office as President Adams' Secretary of State.

October-December 1800: John Adams loses the Presidential election to Thomas Jefferson. Adams and Jefferson lead opposing political parties.

February 4, 1801: John Marshall becomes Chief Justice of the Supreme Court, while also remaining Secretary of State in the final month of Adams' Presidency.

March 2, 1801: Two days before he leaves office, President John Adams nominates William Marbury as a judge.

March 3, 1801: On Adams' last day in office, the Senate confirms Marbury's appointment. President Adams signs and Secretary of State John Marshall puts the seal of the United States on Marbury's commission (*a signed official document with the appointment*) along with 41 others. Marshall's brother James Marshall is unable to take all of the commissions for delivery. He fails to deliver the commission to Marbury and two other appointees.

March 4, 1801: Thomas Jefferson becomes President. He finds Marbury's undelivered commission on the table in the office of the Department of State.

March 5, 1801: Jefferson appoints James Madison as his Secretary of State. Jefferson and Madison refuse to deliver Marbury's commission.

December 16, 1801: Marbury writes to Madison that he will seek an order from the U.S. Supreme Court forcing Madison to deliver Marbury's commission.

December 17, 1801: Marbury applies to the Supreme Court for an order requiring Madison to deliver his commission. His application is based on the Court's power to issue such orders under the Judiciary Act of 1789.

February 24, 1803: Fourteen months later, Chief Justice Marshall issues his decision. Marshall rules that part of the Judiciary Act of 1789 is **unconstitutional**. Congress cannot expand the "original jurisdiction" of the Court, which is stated in the Constitution. This can only be changed by a constitutional amendment. Therefore, the Supreme Court has no power to issue orders to federal officials to perform their duties. This means the Court cannot order Madison to deliver the commission. In this decision, Marshall further explains that the Supreme Court must have the power to overturn any laws that it believes are in conflict with the Constitution. This is the power of **judicial review**.

- Based on his earlier involvement in Marbury's appointment, should Chief Justice Marshall have excused himself from ruling on the case?
- How did Marshall's decision expand the power of the Supreme Court?

A List of Landmark Supreme Court Cases

Judicial Review

- ***Marbury v. Madison*** (1803): In this case, the U.S. Supreme Court established its power of judicial review—the right to overturn laws it finds unconstitutional.

Slavery and Citizenship

- ***Dred Scott v. Sandford*** (1857): The Supreme Court ruled that African Americans, whether enslaved or free, cannot sue in court because they were never intended to be U.S. citizens or to enjoy the rights of citizenship. In addition, the Missouri Compromise was unconstitutional because it deprived slave owners of their "property" (enslaved persons) without "due process." (Later overturned by the 14th Amendment.)

First Amendment – Free Speech

- ***Hazelwood School District v. Kuhlmeier*** (1988): School authorities can edit/censor school-supported student newspapers, consistent with their educational mission.

Rights of the Accused

- ***Gideon v. Wainwright*** (1963): Poor defendants charged with committing serious crimes have a right to be provided with free legal counsel.

- ***Miranda v. Arizona*** (1966): Police must inform suspects of their rights before questioning them. These rights include the right to remain silent and the right to have the assistance of an attorney.

- ***In re Gault*** (1967): Juveniles (those under 18) in juvenile law proceedings are entitled, just like adults, to reasonable "due process" rights when facing possible detention (*imprisonment*).

Racial Segregation

- ***Plessy v. Ferguson*** (1896): State segregation laws do not violate the Equal Protection Clause of the Fourteenth Amendment if the state offers "separate but equal" facilities to members of each race. (Later overturned by *Brown.*)

- ***Brown v. Board of Education*** (1954): Since separate schools are by their very nature unequal, segregation has "no place" in public education. This decision ended racially segregated schools.

The Presidency and the Rule of Law

- ***United States v. Nixon*** (1974): The Supreme Court denied President Nixon's claim of "executive privilege" and ordered Nixon to hand over White House tapes to investigators. The decision showed that the President of the United States is not above the rule of law. It led to President Nixon's resignation rather than face impeachment.

Slavery and Citizenship

You should know that before the Civil War, the Supreme Court denied African Americans the rights of citizenship in the Dred Scott decision.

*Dred Scott v. Sandford** (1857)

The Facts

In the United States, slavery was legal in Southern states until the Emancipation Proclamation (1863) and Thirteenth Amendment (1865). In 1820, Congress passed the Missouri Compromise, which prohibited slavery in federal territories north of the "Missouri Compromise line."

Dred Scott was an enslaved person. Scott's "owner" was Dr. Emerson, a doctor in the U.S. Army who moved from post to post. Emerson brought Scott with him to Illinois, a free state. He then took Scott to Wisconsin, a federal territory where slavery was prohibited by the Missouri Compromise. Emerson later returned to Missouri, a slave state. After Emerson died, Dred Scott and his wife sued for their freedom. The Scotts pointed out that they had been brought to a free state and a free territory. Once there, they claimed, their enslavement had ended. The State of Missouri, the Scotts argued, was required to respect this change. So when they returned to Missouri, they were no longer slaves.

The trial court in Missouri where the Scotts sued for their freedom agreed with them. It ordered the Scotts to be freed. Emerson's widow, their "owner," appealed. The Supreme Court of Missouri reversed the trial court's decision. It sided with Ms. Emerson. The state's supreme court said that Missouri was not required to respect the laws of other states on slavery. Because Dred Scott and his wife had returned to Missouri, a slave state, they should remain as slaves.

Ms. Emerson gave the Scotts to her brother, John Sanford, a citizen of New York.* Under federal law, a citizen has the right to sue a citizen from a different state in federal court. Dred Scott next sued John Sanford for his freedom in the U.S. Circuit Court for Missouri, a federal court. Scott again argued that since he had lived in a free state and a free territory, he had been emancipated at that time and was no longer a slave when he returned to Missouri.

Sanford's lawyer argued that Scott was not a citizen; therefore, he had no right to sue someone in federal court. Sanford's lawyer also said that Congress had no right to take away a slave owner's "property" by prohibiting slavery. The U.S. Circuit Court sided with Sanford. Scott immediately appealed to the U.S. Supreme Court to obtain his freedom.

The Legal Issues

1. Was Dred Scott, an enslaved African American, a citizen with the right to sue in federal court?
2. After being taken to both a free state and a free federal territory (where slavery was prohibited), had Dred Scott become a free man?

The Decision/Outcome

In 1857, four of the nine Justices on the Supreme Court were Southern slave owners. Three of the Northern Justices on the Court were also known supporters of slavery. Chief Justice Taney, who wrote the Court's majority opinion, was a Southerner who had served on the Court since 1836.

In his opinion, Taney first addressed the question of jurisdiction–whether Court had the authority (*jurisdiction*) to hear the case. Taney held that Scott, as an African American, was not a citizen and in fact had no rights at all. Therefore, Scott did not have the right to sue in federal court and the Court had no jurisdiction to decide the case.

> *The question is simply this: Can [an African American], whose ancestors were imported into this country, and sold as slaves, become a member of the political community formed and brought into existence by the Constitution of the United States, and as such become entitled to all the rights . . . guarant[e]ed by that instrument to the citizen? One of which rights is the privilege of suing in a court of the United States . . .*

*The Supreme Court mistakenly used "Sandford" when it reported the case

We think... that [African Americans] are not included, and were not intended to be included, under the word "citizens" in the Constitution, and can therefore claim none of the rights . . . and privileges which that instrument provides . . . On the contrary, they were at that time [of America's founding] considered as a subordinate and inferior class of beings who had been subjugated by the dominant race, and, whether emancipated or not, yet remained subject to their authority, and had no rights or privileges but such as those who held the power and the Government might choose to grant them . . .

[African Americans] had no rights which the white man was bound to respect; and [an African American] might justly and lawfully be reduced to slavery for his benefit. He was bought and sold and treated as an ordinary article of merchandise, whenever profit could be made by it . . .

Word Helper

ancestor = one of the people from whom one is descended

instrument = a legal document

privilege = a special right or benefit

subordinate = someone who is lower in position or importance

subjugate = to make someone subordinate; to place someone under control

dominant = controlling; ruling; powerful

emancipated = freed from slavery

prevailed = was common; existed

bound to respect = required to respect

merchandise = goods; products that are bought and sold

According to Taney, the Founding Fathers, many of whom were slaveholders, never meant to include enslaved Africans and their descendants in the Declaration of Independence, Constitution or Bill of Rights.

Although Taney said the Court had no authority to decide the case, he went on to do so anyway. He noted that in previous cases the Court had ruled that an enslaved person was not freed by entering a free state. No court, however, had ever ruled on whether a slave was freed by entering a federal territory where slavery was prohibited.

Taney thought of an enslaved person as no more than a piece of property. He said that a person—the owner—could not have his or her property taken away without "due process." Therefore, the owner should not lose his or her property just by entering a free territory:

[A]n act of Congress which deprives a citizen of the United States of his liberty or property merely because he . . . brought his property into a particular territory of the United States, and who had committed no offense against the laws, could hardly be dignified with the name of due process of law.

For this reason, Taney concluded that Congress could not really prohibit slavery on federal lands. The Missouri Compromise, he concluded was, therefore, unconstitutional. This was the first time the Supreme Court had overruled a federal law since the decision in *Marbury v. Madison* more than 50 years earlier. Based on this reasoning, Scott was not a freed man.

Analysis of Effects: Impact on Society

The *Dred Scott* decision had an important **social impact**. It was shocking to many Northerners. It permitted slavery in the northern part of the Louisiana Purchase, where it had previously been prohibited. This caused a strong reaction, especially in the North.

Frederick Douglass, an escaped slave and famous abolitionist, treated the decision with disgust. He believed the Court's ruling would actually contribute to the eventual end of slavery: "To decide against this right in the person of Dred Scott . . . is to decide against God . . . [W]e, the abolitionists and colored people, should meet this decision . . . in a cheerful spirit. This very attempt to blot out forever the hopes of an enslaved people may be one necessary link in the chain of events preparatory to the downfall and complete overthrow of the whole slave system." Abraham Lincoln, a candidate for U.S. Senator in Illinois, also thought the decision could not survive because it left the United States half-slave and half-free. Debates over the *Dred Scott* decision brought Lincoln to national attention and contributed to his later election as President. This led to the Civil War and the end to slavery.

The *Dred Scott* decision also affected citizenship. The Supreme Court had ruled that Dred Scott was not a citizen even though he was born in the United States. This was changed by the Fourteenth Amendment, which stated that all people born in the United States are U.S. citizens:

"All persons born . . . in the United States . . . are citizens of the United States and of the state wherein they reside." This first section of the amendment was a direct attempt to overturn the *Dred Scott* decision.

First Amendment Rights

You should know that the Supreme Court has ruled that public school officials can censor student publications without violating the First Amendment

As you learned in the last chapter, the First Amendment guarantees American citizens the right to free speech: "Congress shall make no law . . . abridging (*limiting*) the freedom of speech." But does this right extend to students?

Hazelwood School District v. Kuhlmeier (1988)

Background

In 1969, the Supreme Court held that students had First Amendment rights, even when they were in school. A group of students had worn armbands into their public school to protest against the Vietnam War. The Supreme Court stated that school officials did not have a right to stop the exercise of free speech, unless that speech interfered with school work or safety.

In the aftermath of this decision, there was a flourishing (*thriving*) of student expression. Several lower courts ruled against censorship of school-sponsored student publications. Censorship refers to the revising of a publication (such as a magazine or book) by authorities before it is made public, or even a refusal to permit its publication at all. In *Kuhlmeier,* the U.S. Supreme Court looked at student newspapers and defined some of the limits on students' free-speech rights.

The Facts

Students in a journalism class in Hazelwood East High School in Missouri published their own student newspaper. The school district paid for the printing as well as their academic adviser's salary. In 1983, the academic adviser showed the next issue to the school principal for approval. The principal objected to a story on teenage pregnancy in which student reporters had interviewed three pregnant students. The principal also objected to a story about divorce. The paper was printed without the two stories.

Cathy Kuhlmeier, the student editor of the newspaper, and the two student reporters sued the school district for violating their free speech rights. Their claims were upheld by the U.S. Court of Appeals for the Eighth Circuit.

The Legal Issue

Does the First Amendment protect school-sponsored publications from censorship by school authorities?

The Decision/Outcome

The Supreme Court reversed the ruling of the U.S. Court of Appeals.

According to the Supreme Court, the right to publish in a school-sponsored newspaper was not the same as the right to wear armbands. In the case of school-sponsored activities like student newspapers, school officials have the right to exercise control "so long as their actions are reasonably related to legitimate pedagogical concerns."

Word Helper

legitimate pedagogical concerns = valid educational concerns; concerns about teaching

The situation was seen as different from the student armband case because in this case the school was actually promoting the publication through its sponsorship: "A school need not tolerate student speech that is inconsistent with its basic educational mission, even though the government could not censor similar speech outside the school."

> **Word Helper**
>
> ***tolerate*** = permit; put up with
>
> ***mission*** = purpose; goal
>
> ***inconsistent with*** = in conflict with; in disagreement with
>
> ***censor*** = when officials examine and edit a writing, taking out any unacceptable parts, before it is published
>
> ***contempt*** = dislike; hatred

The Supreme Court concluded that school-sponsored student publications were ***not*** protected by the First Amendment. The school principal's refusal to publish the three articles thus did not violate the students' rights. Three of the Justices dissented from the majority opinion, arguing that it showed an "unthinking contempt for individual rights."

Analysis of Effects: Individual Rights

Kuhlmeier concerned **individual rights**. It qualified some of the free speech rights previously given to students. It stated that school officials could censor school-sponsored student publications so long as such restrictions served a valid educational purpose. In decisions since *Kuhlmeier*, the Supreme Court has further explained that "the constitutional rights of students in public school are not [the same as] the rights of adults in other settings." While students do not lose their rights when they enter school, "the nature of those rights is what is appropriate (*proper*) for children in school."

Case Summary

Summarize the facts of this case and the Supreme Court's decision in your own words.

> You should know that several landmark decisions have helped define the rights of the accused and juvenile rights.

Rights of the Accused

Several of the rights in the Bill of Rights protect the **individual rights** of the accused (*those who have been accused of a crime*). These safeguards serve two purposes:

1. They protect innocent persons who may be wrongfully accused; and
2. They protect us all from arbitrary (*dictatorial; unfair*) actions by the government.

Although the rights of the accused were established by the Bill of Rights, several Supreme Court decisions were needed to determine how these constitutional rights applied to specific situations.

Gideon v. Wainwright (1963)

The Facts

Clarence Gideon was arrested in Florida. He was accused of robbing the jukebox in a pool hall. A witness had seen Gideon walking from it with a bottle of wine and change in his pockets. Gideon faced a prison sentence but was too poor to afford a lawyer. He requested a lawyer but was told that, under the

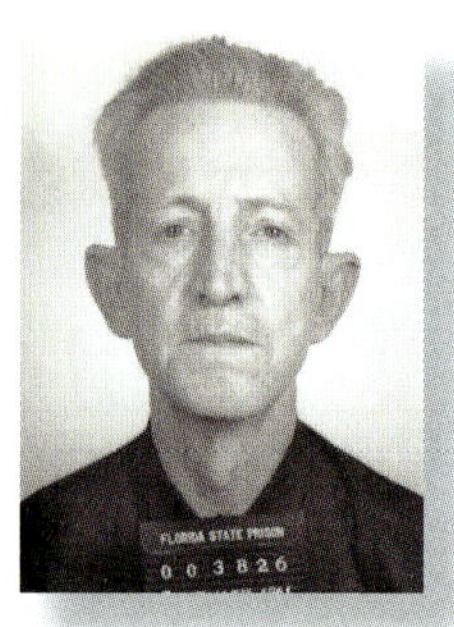

laws of Florida, the court would only pay for a lawyer if he faced the death penalty. Gideon defended himself and was sentenced to five years imprisonment. From prison, Gideon appealed his case in a hand-written letter to the U.S. Supreme Court.

The Legal Issue

Does the Sixth Amendment require a court to provide legal counsel (*a lawyer*) to an indigent (*poor*) defendant accused of a felony (*a crime punishable with imprisonment of more than one year*)?

The Decision/Outcome

The U.S. Supreme Court heard Gideon's case. It then held that the government must provide a lawyer to anyone accused of a felony who is too poor to afford one. The right to a lawyer was a fundamental right, essential to a fair trial. The Sixth Amendment guaranteed this right, while the Fourteenth Amendment placed this requirement on state as well as federal courts. When he was tried again with the help of a lawyer, Gideon was acquitted (*found to be innocent*) and released.

Analysis of Effects: Impact on Society

Based on the decision in *Gideon*, states must now provide free lawyers to defendants charged with felonies who cannot pay for their own attorney. Public defenders, special court-appointed lawyers who are paid by the government, generally fill this role.

Case Summary

Summarize the facts of this case and the Court's decision in your own words. ....

What is your opinion? Should the rest of society have to pay for a lawyer to defend a poor person who may have actually committed a crime? ....

Miranda v. Arizona (1966)

The Fifth Amendment protects us from self-incrimination (*making a statement that incriminates ourselves*), and the Sixth Amendment guarantees a person accused of a serious crime the right to an attorney.

The Facts

In 1963, Ernesto Miranda was arrested in Arizona for kidnapping and rape. After two hours of police questioning, Miranda signed a confession (*a statement admitting he had committed the crime*).

However, Miranda was never told that he had the right to remain silent or to have a lawyer present during the questioning. Miranda was convicted and sentenced to 20 to 30 years imprisonment. Miranda appealed on the grounds that he had not been informed of his rights to remain silent or to see an attorney before he gave his confession.

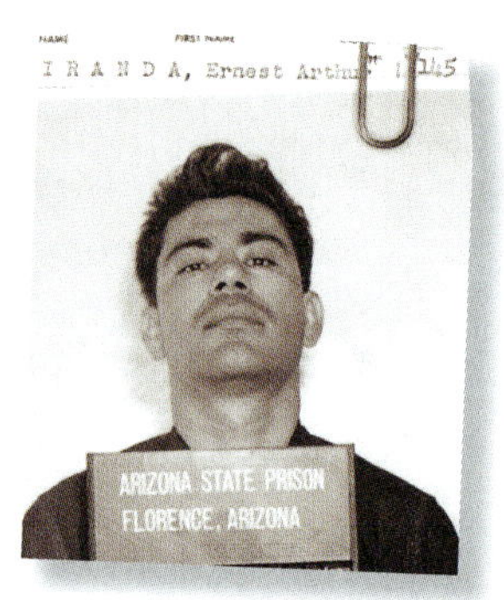

The Legal Issue

Can the police interrogate (*question*) a suspect without informing him of his rights to remain silent and to have a lawyer present?

The Decision/Outcome

The U.S. Supreme Court overturned Miranda's conviction on the grounds that Miranda had not been properly informed of his rights:

> *"The person in custody must, prior to interrogation, be clearly informed that he has the right to remain silent, and that anything he says will be used against him in court; he must be clearly informed that he has the right to consult with a lawyer and to have the lawyer with him during interrogation, and that, if he is indigent, a lawyer will be appointed to represent him. . . .*
>
> —*Miranda v. Arizona*, 1966

Word Helper

custody = under police control
interrogation = questioning
to be informed = to be told
to consult = to discuss with; to get advice from
indigent = poor

Analysis of Effects: Individual Rights

The rights established by the Supreme Court in this case are now referred to as "Miranda" rights. Police must state these rights before questioning a suspect; otherwise, any self-incriminating statements or confession cannot be used in court. These requirements reduce the risk that police treat suspects unfairly.

Miranda himself was retried and convicted a second time without the use of his confession. Miranda was released in 1972, but he was killed in a fight four years later.

> "You have the right to remain silent. Anything you say can and may be used against you in a court of law. You have the right to talk to a lawyer before we ask you questions. You also have the right to have a lawyer present during questioning. If you cannot afford a lawyer, you have the right to have one appointed at public expense."
>
> —Miranda rights

Case Summary

Summarize the facts of this case and the Supreme Court's decision in your own words. ______

In *Miranda*, the Court ruled that before the police question someone, the person must "be clearly informed that he has the right to remain silent, and that anything he says will be used against him in court." Explain, in your own words, what the Court meant. ______

Did the Court in *Miranda* make it too difficult for police to convict criminals? ______

In re Gault (1967)

States have different procedures and penalties for criminal offenses committed by minors (those under 18 years old) and by adults. *In re,* "in the matter of," is used in juvenile proceedings to indicate that there are no opposing parties as there are in adult criminal cases. **"Juvenile"** means having to do with minors—generally, those under 18 years old.

In the 1960s, juvenile courts had no attorneys or juries. Decisions were made by juvenile court judges. The reasons for these differences were generally to protect children, to keep them from being branded as criminals, and to discourage them from becoming criminals. The existence of a separate juvenile justice system permitted some states, however, to act without fully respecting the rights of minors.

The Facts

Gerald Gault was 15 years old when he was accused of making an obscene telephone call to a neighbor. Gault was arrested and taken to a children's detention home. Gault's parents were away at work when he was arrested, and no notice was left for them.

A hearing was scheduled for the next day without notice and without sufficient time to prepare. The hearing was informal: Gault was questioned by a judge from the superior court acting as a juvenile judge. Gault denied making the obscene remarks. No witnesses were present at the hearing.

A second hearing was held the following week. The neighbor again did not appear for the hearing, and no transcript was made of either hearing. Gault never had the benefit of an attorney. Gault was convicted of making the obscene call and sentenced to a juvenile detention home until he was 21 years old—a period of six years. The maximum penalty for an adult making an obscene phone call at that time was only $50 and two months' imprisonment. Moreover, under Arizona law, a juvenile court order could not be appealed.

To release their son, the parents petitioned for a *writ of habeas corpus* (a special court procedure for the release of someone unjustly imprisoned). Their petition was denied by the Arizona Supreme Court on the grounds that the procedures applied to Gault's case had met "due process" requirements.

Legal Issue

What "due process" rights are owed to a juvenile (*a minor; someone under the age of 18*) facing a possible loss of liberty?

The Decision/Outcome

The U.S. Supreme Court overturned the decision by an 8 to 1 vote. While there are good reasons for treating juveniles and adults differently, the Court held that juveniles were still entitled to all reasonable "due process" rights when facing possible detention (*imprisonment*).

These "due process" rights include: (1) timely notice of criminal charges; (2) the right to face and question witnesses; (3) the right against self-incrimination; (4) the right to counsel (*an attorney*); (5) the right to a transcript (*typed record*) of the proceedings; and (6) the right to appellate review. Gerald Gault had been denied all of these rights.

> *"Due process of law is the primary and indispensable foundation of individual freedom. It is the basic and essential term in the social compact which defines the rights of the individual . . . .*

Word Helper

due process of law = the right to a fair, public and just procedure

primary = main; most important

indispensable = something we cannot do without

social compact = social contract; agreement to form a community

The Supreme Court considered how Gault would have been treated if he had been tried as an adult instead of as a juvenile. It began with the fact that his maximum punishment would have been far less:

The essential difference between Gerald's case and a normal criminal case is that safeguards available to adults were discarded in Gerald's case. The summary procedure as well as the long commitment was possible because Gerald was 15 years of age instead of over 18. If Gerald had been over 18, he would not have been subject to Juvenile Court proceedings. For the particular offense immediately involved, the maximum punishment would have been a fine of $5 to $50, or imprisonment in jail for not more than two months. Instead, he was committed to custody for a maximum of six years.

discarded = thrown out
summary procedure = shortened procedure
long commitment = long imprisonment
maximum = the greatest amount
committed to custody = imprisoned; put under the control of authorities

The Court continued by listing the many "due process" rights that Gault would have enjoyed as an adult:

If he had been over 18 and had committed an offense to which such a sentence might apply, he would have been entitled to [important] rights under the Constitution of the United States as well as under Arizona's laws and constitution. The United States Constitution would guarantee him rights and protections with respect to arrest, search and seizure, and pretrial [questioning]. It would [give him] specific notice of the charges and adequate time to . . . prepare his defense. He would be entitled to clear advice that he could be represented by counsel, and, at least if a felony were involved, the State would be required to provide counsel if his parents were unable to afford it. . . . If the case went to trial, confrontation and opportunity for cross-examination would be guaranteed.

offense = crime
sentence = punishment given by a court
specific notice of the charges = provide specific information about what one is accused of
adequate time = enough time
be entitled to = have a right to
felony = a crime punishable by imprisonment for more than one year
confrontation = facing accusers
cross-examination = questioning of opposing witnesses

All of these "due process" rights had been denied to Gault. Instead, special procedures that were supposed to protect juveniles from the harshness of adult courts had in fact been abused.

Although Arizona claimed its juvenile law system was designed to protect minors accused of a crime, the U.S. Supreme Court found the very opposite to be true:

So wide a gulf between the State's treatment of the adult and of the child requires a bridge sturdier than mere verbiage, and reasons more persuasive than cliché can provide."

—*In re Gault*, 1967

gulf = divide; space between
sturdier = stronger; more sturdy
mere verbiage = words and nothing else
cliché = an overused phrase or saying

Analysis of Effects: Individual Rights

As a result of Gault's case, state juvenile justice systems must now provide minors with the "due process" rights guaranteed by the Constitution and listed in the Court's decision. These rights are known as juvenile rights.

Case Summary

Summarize the facts of this case and the Supreme Court's decision in your own words. ______________________

What was the impact of this decision on American society?

You should know that the Supreme Court once allowed state segregation laws but later prohibited segregation in public schools.

Racial Segregation and "Equal Protection"

One of the most important issues ever to face American courts has been that of racial segregation—the separation of people by race. Following the Civil War and period of Reconstruction, Southern states passed "Jim Crow" laws imposing racial segregation on public places, such as trains, buses, parks and schools. These laws required African Americans to use different facilities than whites did.

Yet the Fourteenth Amendment had promised all American citizens the "equal protection of the laws." White Southerners argued that so long as the facilities offered to African Americans were "separate but equal," the requirements of the Fourteenth Amendment were satisfied.

In the following two cases, you will see how the Supreme Court's views on the meaning of "equal protection" under the Fourteenth Amendment have shifted over time. These two court cases were among the most influential in all of American history.

Plessy v. Ferguson (1896)

The Facts

In 1890, Louisiana passed a "Jim Crow" law requiring railroad companies to "provide equal but separate" passenger cars to members of different races. Opponents of segregation persuaded Homer Plessy, who was one-eighth African American and appeared to be white, to challenge this law. Plessy sat in a railroad passenger car reserved for whites. He told the conductor of his mixed ancestry and was arrested. He fought this case all the way up to the U.S. Supreme Court.

The Legal Issue

Can a state impose racial segregation by offering "separate-but-equal" facilities, without violating the Equal Protection Clause of the Fourteenth Amendment?

The Decision/Outcome

The U.S. Supreme Court saw nothing in the Louisiana law itself that stated that some races were inferior (*below; not as good as*) to others. Therefore, the separation of races it required did not violate the Equal Protection Clause of the Fourteenth Amendment. If African Americans or others chose to see themselves as inferior, the Court said, this had nothing to do with the law itself. The law merely separated these races without indicating that either one of them was superior or inferior.

"We cannot say that a law which requires the separation of two races is unreasonable. We consider the [error] of [Plessy's] argument to consist in the assumption that the enforced separation of the two races stamps the colored race with a badge of inferiority. If this be so, it is not by reason of anything found in the act, but solely because the colored race chooses to put that construction upon it. . . .

When the government . . . has secured to each of its citizens equal rights before the law, and equal opportunities for improvement and progress, it has accomplished the end for which it was organized, and performed all of the functions respecting social advantages with which it is endowed . . . .

If the civil and political rights of both races be equal, one cannot be inferior to the other civilly or politically. If one race be inferior to the other socially, the Constitution of the United States cannot put them upon the same plane."

—*Plessy v. Ferguson*, 1896

Word Helper

assumption = belief
inferior = of lesser quality
badge of inferiority = sign or mark of lesser quality
construction = interpretation
secured = obtained
end = purpose; goal
functions = tasks; responsibilities
respecting = having to do with
endowed = given
same plane = same level

Analysis of Effects : Impact on Society

In *Plessy v. Ferguson*, the U.S. Supreme Court upheld the constitutionality of state segregation laws, so long as the facilities offered to each race were of "equal standards." This became known as the "separate-but-equal" doctrine. In *Plessy*, the Court held that such segregation did not violate the Equal Protection Clause of the Fourteenth Amendment. As a result of this decision, states across the South strengthened their segregation laws.

Case Summary

Summarize the facts of this case and the Supreme Court's decision in your own words. ______________________

____

____

____

____

What was the impact of this decision on American society between 1896 and 1954? ______________________

____

____

____

Brown v. Board of Education (1954)

For the next 50 years after *Plessy v. Ferguson*, white and African-American children continued to attend separate public schools across the South.

Starting in the 1930s, African-American lawyers at the National Association for the Advancement of Colored People, or "NAACP," began challenging the "separate-but-equal" doctrine in public education. They launched an ambitious strategy by filing a series of lawsuits challenging state laws.

The Facts

Linda Brown was a schoolgirl in Topeka, Kansas. Her father sued the local school board because Linda was forced to attend an all-black school when an all-white school was closer to their home. Brown lost the case in state court. In 1953, the NAACP appealed Linda Brown's case along with a number of others to the U.S. Supreme Court.

The Legal Issue

Did racial segregation in public schools violate the Equal Protection Clause of the Fourteenth Amendment?

The NAACP's Legal Argument

Thurgood Marshall, the NAACP lawyer handling the case, did not argue that the facilities given to African-American children were inferior (although this was generally the case). Instead, he argued that the system of segregated education was, by its very nature, unequal because it sent a psychological message to African-American children that they were not "good enough" to be taught with whites.

Marshall supported his argument with the findings of an African-American psychologist, Dr. Kenneth Clark. Clark showed white and black dolls to young African-American children and found that these children preferred the white dolls to black ones. Clark concluded that the system of racial segregation had led to this painful sense of inferiority. It denied these children "equal protection."

The Decision/Outcome

Earl Warren, a former Governor, had only just been appointed as Chief Justice of the Supreme Court. Warren wanted to avoid a divided decision. With great effort, he obtained the support of all nine Justices. They were persuaded in part by Thurgood Marshall's reasoning. Warren wrote the Court's unanimous opinion, which declared racial segregation in public schools to be a violation of the Fourteenth Amendment:

> *"Does segregation of children in public schools solely on the basis of race, even though the physical facilities and other 'tangible' factors may be equal, deprive the children of the minority group of equal educational opportunities? We believe that it does.*
>
> *. . . Segregation of white and colored children in public schools has a detrimental effect upon the colored children. The impact is greater when it has the sanction of the law, for the policy of separating the races is usually interpreted as denoting the inferiority of the [African-American] group. A sense of inferiority affects the motivation of a child to learn. . . .*
>
> *We conclude that, in the field of public education, the doctrine of 'separate but equal' has no place. Separate educational facilities are inherently unequal."*
>
> —*Brown v. Board of Education,* 1954

Word Helper

solely = only
tangible = things you can touch; physical
deprive = deny; keep from having
detrimental = harmful
sanction = blessing; approval
denoting = meaning
affects = influences
motivation = desire; willingness
doctrine = principle; belief
inherently = see *The Active Citizen below*

The Active Citizen

- Look up the word "inherent" in the dictionary. Why did Chief Justice Earl Warren conclude that segregated schools were "inherently" unequal? Why did this mean that "in the field of public education, the doctrine of 'separate but equal' has no place"? How was this conclusion important to the Supreme Court's judgment?

Analysis of Effects: Impact on Society

The *Brown* decision had an enormous impact on society. It required the entire system of public education in the South to change. Southern Senators in Congress immediately signed a public protest against the *Brown* decision. Local officials across the South swore they would never enforce it. Violence in the South increased.

Southern resistance required the U.S. Supreme Court to make a separate ruling on how the *Brown* decision was to be carried out a year later. Enforcement of the *Brown* decision was handed over to the lower federal courts, which were to see that local school districts carried out the desegregation order "with all deliberate speed."

The *Brown* decision would take many years to carry out. As a result of the *Brown* decision, the first steps were taken towards ending racial segregation in the South and creating the more equal, multicultural society we enjoy today.

Case Summary

Summarize the facts of this case and the Supreme Court's decision in your own words.

What was the impact of the *Brown* decision on American society?

The Active Citizen

- Complete the Venn diagram below comparing the two decisions, *Plessy* and *Brown*. How would you account for the differences in outcome?

Plessy v. Ferguson (1896) | *Brown v. Board of Education* (1954)

Ruled on the constitutionality of racial segregration

- Imagine you are presenting oral argument to the Supreme Court in the case of *Brown v. Board of Education*. Which points would you emphasize?
- Prepare an oral presentation, PowerPoint or Prezi presentation, or video on the impact of either of these two decisions on American society.

In *U.S. v. Nixon*, the Supreme Court held that not even the President is above the rule of law.

The Presidency

The Supreme Court has only occasionally ruled on questions of Presidential power. In the case below, the Court ruled on whether "executive privilege" allowed a President to avoid handing over documents in a criminal investigation.

United States v. Nixon (1974)

The Facts

During the Presidential election campaign of 1972, a group of former government agents broke into Democratic Party headquarters in the Watergate Hotel and office complex in downtown Washington, D.C. President Nixon, a Republican, tried to protect these agents from investigation by claiming that they were acting for national security. At Congressional hearings, it was revealed that Nixon had taped all his conversations in the White House. Nixon refused to hand over the tapes to investigators, claiming that as President of the United States, he was entitled to "executive privilege."

The Legal Issue

Does "executive privilege"—the need of the President of the United States for privacy and confidentiality in making high-level decisions of national importance—excuse the President from turning over documents needed as evidence in a criminal proceeding?

The Decision/Outcome

President Nixon's claim of "executive privilege" was overruled by the U.S. Supreme Court, which ordered the President to hand over the tapes.

> *"A President and those who assist him must be free to explore alternatives in the process of shaping policies and making decisions, and to do so in a way many would be unwilling to express except privately. These are the considerations justifying a presumptive privilege for Presidential communications. . . . But this presumptive privilege must be considered in light of our historic commitment to the rule of law . . . To ensure that justice is done, it is imperative to the function of courts that compulsory process be available for the production of evidence needed either by the prosecution or by the defense."*
>
> —*United States v. Nixon*, 1974

Word Helper

alternatives = options; other choices
compulsory process = ability of the courts to give orders
production of evidence = handing over of documents; appearance of witnesses
presumptive privilege = a privilege one can presume exists; all things being equal, one can assume the President has this privilege

Analysis of Effects: The Law

The tapes revealed that President Nixon was indeed behind the Watergate "cover-up." President Nixon resigned rather than face impeachment. The decision proved that even the President of the United States is not above the "rule of law."

Case Summary

Summarize this case by completing the paragraph frame on the next page.

In 1972, Richard Nixon faced re-election as President. A special unit in the White House was created to conduct secret investigations and prevent government "leaks" to the press. Members of this unit broke into the headquarters of the __________ Party at the Watergate Hotel to spy on their campaign activities.

When they were caught and arrested by police, President Nixon tried to cover up their ties to the ________________. White House officials told the FBI not to investigate the break-in. The White House secretly tried to pay the arrested men to lie about their connections.

A special independent prosecutor was appointed to investigate the break-in. Congress also conducted its own investigation. A former member of Nixon's staff told a Congressional committee that the President had ____.

President Nixon denied this.

The same staff member next revealed that Nixon had taped all his White House conversations. Congress and the special prosecutor demanded to listen to these tapes. Nixon refused to hand over the tapes, claiming "executive privilege." By this he meant the right of the President to _______________ ________________________________.

The demand for the tapes reached the U.S. Supreme Court. The Court weighed the President's need for freedom in making decisions of national importance with the needs of investigators for evidence in a criminal proceeding. In the end, the Court ordered President Nixon to hand over the tapes. These tapes proved that he was lying all along. Nixon resigned the Presidency rather than face impeachment.

The great significance of the decision was that it showed that even the President is not above the __________. This is an essential part of our legal system, in which all citizens alike live under the rule of _________.

The Active Citizen

▸ In *United States v. Nixon*, did the U.S. Supreme Court strike the right balance between the needs of the executive and judicial branches? Or did their decision upset the traditional separation of powers? Write a short essay of two to three paragraphs giving your views on whether the Supreme Court was right in ordering President Nixon to turn over his tapes.

President Richard Nixon with transcripts from the White House Tapes, April 22, 1974

Other Supreme Court Cases

In addition to the issues above, the U.S. Supreme Court has ruled on many other matters. These include:

- The Rights of Students
- Political Campaign Contributions
- Privacy Rights
- Individual Rights in Wartime
- The Powers of the Federal Government
- Freedom of Speech
- Legislative Representation
- Freedom of Religion

The Active Citizen

- Your teacher should divide your class into groups. Each group should select one of these topics and research two cases in that area. For each case, they should investigate the background facts, the legal issues, the reasoning of the Supreme Court, the Court's decision, and the significance of the case. Then each group should make an oral presentation, a PowerPoint or Prezi presentation, or a video to share what they have learned with the rest of the class.
- Turn your classroom into the U.S. Supreme Court! Select one of the cases discussed in this chapter. Your teacher should appoint nine students to act as the Justices of the U.S. Supreme Court, and should appoint a group of students to represent the team of attorneys on each side of the case. Attorneys from each team should take turns in representing their case before the Justices, while the Justices should ask penetrating questions during oral argument. Then the Justices should confer among themselves to see if they reach the same decision that the Supreme Court did in the actual case, and briefly present their "majority opinion" to the class. Finally, the rest of the class should complete a questionnaire evaluating how well each of the participants performed his or her part.

How well can you recognize these excerpts from several of the most famous decisions of the U.S. Supreme Court?

> *"But it is too clear for dispute that the enslaved African race were not intended to be included and formed no part of the people who framed and adopted this declaration; for if the language, as understood in that day, would embrace them, the conduct of the distinguished men who framed the Declaration of Independence would have been utterly . . . inconsistent with the principles they asserted.*

- From which decision is this excerpt taken?____________________________
- Based on the excerpt, what was the signficance of this case?____________________________

____

____

"So wide a gulf between the State's treatment of the adult and of the child requires a bridge sturdier than mere verbiage, and reasons more persuasive than cliché can provide."

- From which decision is this excerpt taken?____________________________________
- Based on the excerpt, what was the signficance of this case?____________________________________

"The person in custody must, prior to interrogation, be clearly informed that he has the right to remain silent, and that anything he says will be used against him in court; he must be clearly informed that he has the right to consult with a lawyer and to have the lawyer with him during interrogation, and that, if he is indigent, a lawyer will be appointed to represent him."

- From which decision is this excerpt taken?____________________________________
- Based on the excerpt, what was the signficance of this case?____________________________________

"We cannot say that a law which requires the separation of two races is unreasonable. . . . If the civil and political rights of both races be equal, one cannot be inferior to the other civilly or politically."

- From which decision is this excerpt taken?____________________________________
- Based on the excerpt, what was the signficance of this case?____________________________________

"We conclude that, in the field of public education, the doctrine of 'separate but equal' has no place. Separate educational facilities are inherently unequal."

- From which decision is this excerpt taken?____________________________________
- Based on the excerpt, what was the signficance of this case?____________________________________

"These are the considerations justifying a presumptive privilege for Presidential communications . . . But this presumptive privilege must be considered in light of our historic commitment to the rule of law . . . To ensure that justice is done, it is imperative to the function of courts that compulsory process be available for the production of evidence."

- From which decision is this excerpt taken?____________________________________
- Based on the excerpt, what was the signficance of this case?____________________________________

Name ______________________________

Complete the chart below and on the following pages. For "Effects," consider the social impact of the decision and how the decision affected Americans' understanding of the law, individual rights, and the interpretation of the U.S. Constitution.

Case	Background Facts	Legal Issue(s)	Decision/Outcome	Analysis of Effects
Marbury v. Madison (1803)				
Dred Scott v. Sandford (1857)				
Hazelwood v. Kuhlmeier (1988)				

Name ______________________________

Case	Background Facts	Legal Issue(s)	Decision/Outcome	Analysis of Effects
Gideon v. Wainwright (1963)				
Miranda v. Arizona (1966)				
In re Gault (1967)				

Name ______________________________

Case	Background Facts	Legal Issue(s)	Decision/Outcome	Analysis of Effects
Plessy v. Ferguson (1896)				
Brown v. Board of Education (1954)				
United States v. Nixon (1974)				

Name ____

Imagine you are making an argument before the U.S. Supreme Court for one of the cases that you read about in this chapter.

Name of case: ____

Mr. Chief Justice and may it please the Court.

I come today representing ____.

We believe that ____

____

____

____

____

____

____

____

____

In conclusion, we firmly believe that the Court should rule that ______________________________

____

____

____

because ____

____

____

____

Thank you for this opportunity to appear before the Court.

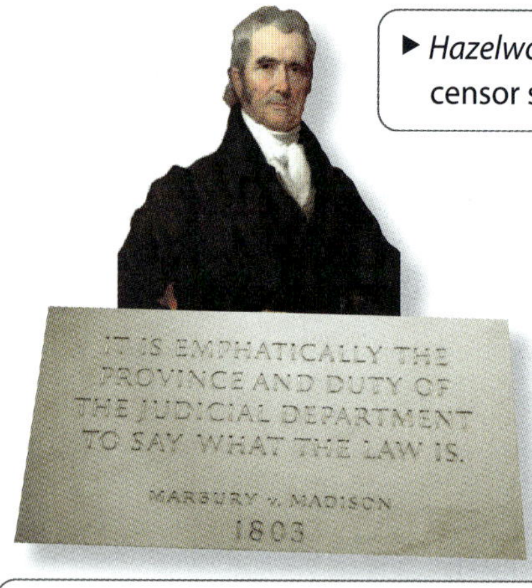

U.S. Supreme Court Key Decisions:

- Decisions affect our understanding of the law, liberty, and interpretation of the U.S. Constitution
- Decisions safeguard individual rights
- Decisions often have a social impact

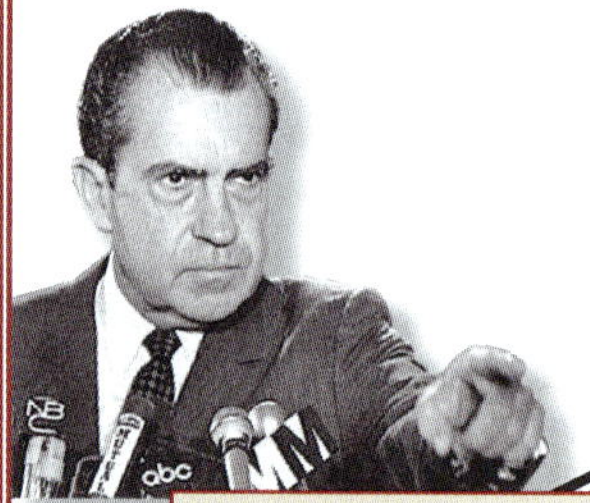

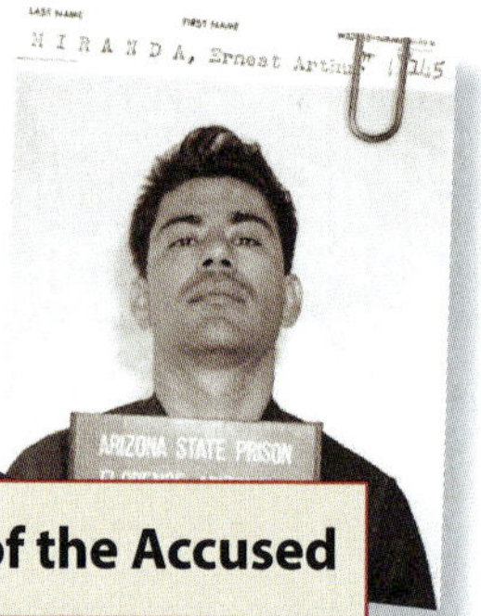

First Amendment Rights

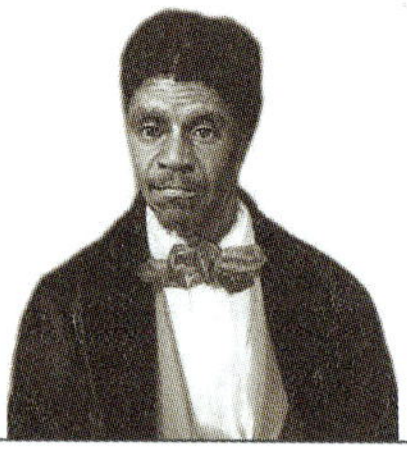

- *Hazelwood School District v. Kuhlmeier* (1988): schools can censor school-sponsored student newspapers

Judicial Review

IT IS EMPHATICALLY THE PROVINCE AND DUTY OF THE JUDICIAL DEPARTMENT TO SAY WHAT THE LAW IS.
MARBURY v. MADISON
1803

- *Marbury v. Madison* (1803): established power of judicial review

Slavery and Citizenship

- *Dred Scott v. Sandford* (1857): African Americans, whether enslaved or free, are not citizens and have no rights; Congress has no right to limit slavery in federal territories; was later overturned by the 13th and 14th Amendments, which ended slavery and gave citizenship to all those born in the United States.

Presidential Power

The New York Times
NIXON RESIGNS

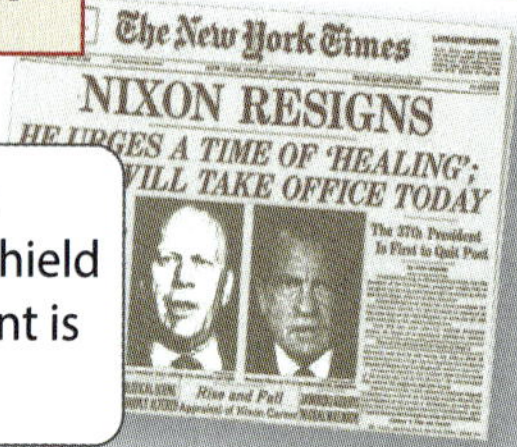

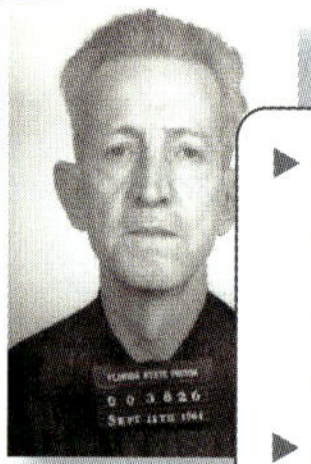

- *United States v. Nixon* (1974): executive privilege did not shield President Nixon: the President is not above the law

Rights of the Accused

- *Gideon v. Wainwright* (1963): poor criminal defendant accused of a felony (*a serious crime*) entitled to court-appointed attorney
- *Miranda v. Arizona* (1966): Suspect must be told of rights prior to interrogation
- *In re Gault* (1967): minors have many of the "due process" rights of adults

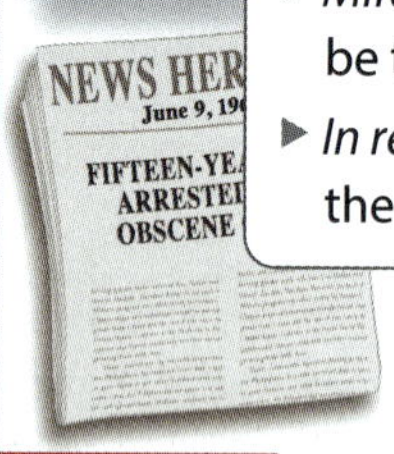

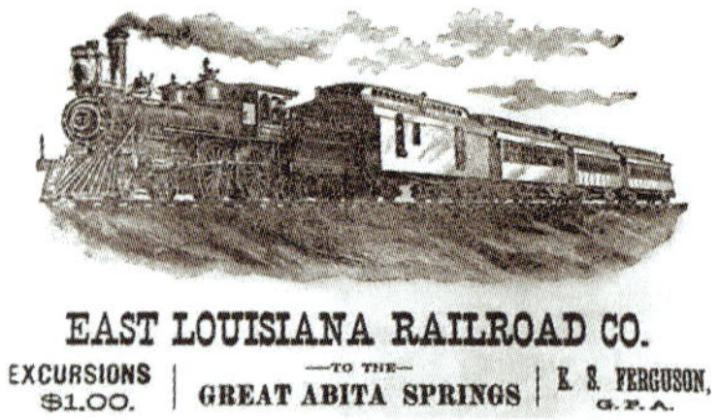

Racial Segregation

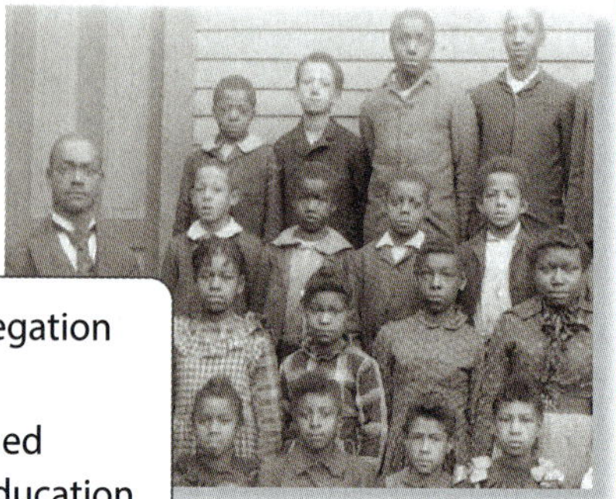

EAST LOUISIANA RAILROAD CO.
EXCURSIONS $1.00. —TO THE— GREAT ABITA SPRINGS | E. S. FERGUSON, G. P. A.

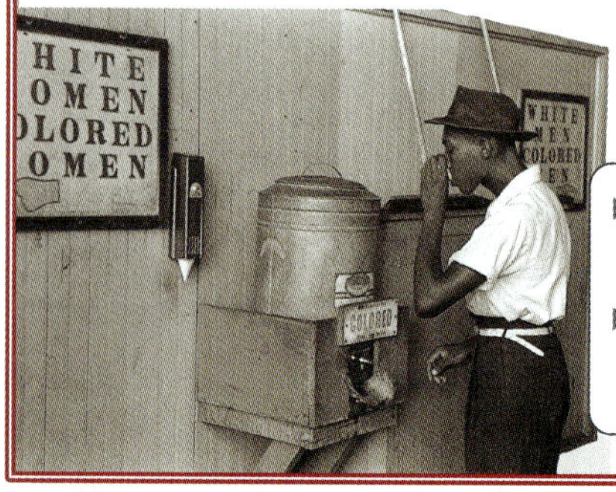

- *Plessy v. Ferguson* (1896): upheld racial segregation if "separate but equal"
- *Brown v. Board of Education* (1954): overturned *Plessy*; segregation has no place in public education

Review Cards: The Supreme Court in Action

Judicial Review

The Supreme Court is the final authority in interpreting the Constitution. It interprets and protects constitutional rights, especially the **individual rights** in the Bill of Rights and the Fourteenth Amendment. The Court's decisions affect our understanding of the **law, liberty and the interpretation of the U.S. Constitution**: what the law means, what freedoms we should enjoy, and how the U.S. Constitution is to be interpreted. The Court's decisions often are based on **constitutional principles** and have a major **impact on society**, affecting people's everyday lives.

Marbury v. Madison (1803)

- **Facts:** William Marbury sued the Secretary of State, James Madison, for failing to deliver his commission.
- Marbury filed his suit directly with the Supreme Court so that it would order Madison to send the commission. In the Judiciary Act of 1789, Congress had given the Supreme Court the power to issue such orders (***writs of mandamus***).
- **Issues:** (1) Should the Supreme Court issue a court order to Madison, as Secretary of State, requiring him to deliver the commission to William Marbury? (2) Can the Supreme Court rule on the constitutionality of a law passed by Congress?
- **Decision/Outcome:** Chief Justice John Marshall believed that Marbury was entitled to his commission. However, the Supreme Court did not have the power to order its delivery. The Constitution had defined the "original jurisdiction" of the Supreme Court, and Congress had no power to enlarge it. The section of the Judiciary Act giving the Court the power to issue *writs of mandamus* thus conflicted with the Constitution. This section was unconstitutional.
- The Court had the duty of interpreting the law, and where it saw that a law was in conflict with the Constitution, the law was invalid. The Court's power to overturn laws it views as unconstitutional is known as **judicial review**.
- **Effects:** The case established the Court's power of judicial review and made the Court the final authority in the **interpretation of the U.S. Constitution.**

Slavery and Citizenship

The following decision threatened to expand the system of slavery and denied citizenship rights to all African Americans. It is generally considered the worst decision in the Court's history.

Dred Scott v. Sandford (1857)

Facts: Dred Scott was a slave who was brought by his owner to a free state and a free territory. Later, Dred Scott went back with his owner to Missouri, a slave state. When his owner died, Scott sued his widow for his freedom. Scott won the case at the trial court but lost on appeal. He later sued in federal court. His new owner, John Sanford, claimed that Scott was not a citizen of the United States and had no right to sue in federal court.

Issues: (1) Was Scott, an enslaved African American, a citizen with the right to sue in federal court?

(2) After living in a free state and a free federal territory, was Scott a free man?

Slavery and Citizenship (*Continued*)

Dred Scott v. Sandford (1857)

Issues: (1) Was Scott, an enslaved African American, a citizen with the right to sue in federal court?

(2) After living in a free state and a free federal territory, was Scott a free man?

Decision/Outcome: Chief Justice Roger Taney, who wrote the Court's opinion, was a Southerner. Taney held that African Americans had been brought to America by force and had always been treated as mere property, not as people. It had never been thought that they should have rights under the Constitution. Taney said that even if freed, African Americans could not become citizens. Scott therefore had no right to file a claim in federal court. Taney further stated that Congress had no right to take away a slaveholder's "property" without due process. A man could not lose his property instantly just by crossing a state line. The prohibition of slavery in some territories by the Missouri Compromise was therefore unconstitutional.

Effects: The **impact on society** of this decision was explosive. The Missouri Compromise, which had divided the Louisiana Purchase into free and slave territories, was no longer lawful. Even settlers probably could not bar slavery. This increased tensions and helped lead to the Civil War. In 1868, the 14th Amendment guaranteed that anyone born in the United States, regardless of race, was a U.S. citizen. This amendment overturned *Dred Scott.*

First Amendment Rights (Free Speech)

Hazelwood School District v. Kuhlmeier (1988)

- **Facts:** A previous Supreme Court case had established that students have free speech rights, even while they are in school. Two articles in a school-sponsored student newspaper were censored by the school principal. The students claimed this violated their First Amendment rights.
- **Issue:** Does the First Amendment protect school-sponsored publications from censorship by school authorities?
- **Decision/Outcome:** The Supreme Court ruled that schools have the right to censor speech in activities they sponsor (*pay for*), if the restrictions are for valid educational purposes.
- **Effects:** *Kuhlmeier* restricted an earlier free speech ruling by allowing censorship in this case. It gave school officials the right to limit student speech in some circumstances. In this case, the Court identified a limit on **individual rights.**

Cathy Kuhlmeier holding a copy of her school newspaper.

Fifth and Sixth Amendment Rights (Rights of the Accused)

Several amendments in the Bill of Rights protect the rights of accused. This is to protect innocent people who have been wrongfully accused of a crime, and to guard against government abuse.

Gideon v. Wainwright (1963)

- **Facts:** Clarence Gideon, a poor defendant, was accused of robbery. He asked the court to provide him with a free lawyer, but was refused. At the time, Florida only provided a free lawyer in capital (*death penalty*) cases.
- **Issue:** Does the Sixth Amendment require a court to provide counsel (*a lawyer*) to a poor defendant accused of a **felony** (*a crime punishable with imprisonment of one year or more*)?
- **Decision/Outcome:** The Supreme Court ruled that the Sixth Amendment guarantees the **right to legal counsel**. Governments are therefore required to provide one to defendants too poor to afford one if they are charged with a felony.
- **Effects:** States now offer poor defendants the services of a public defender.

Miranda v. Arizona (1966)

- **Facts:** Ernesto Miranda was convicted for kidnapping and rape after he confessed during police interrogation. He appealed the case because he had not been informed of his Fifth and Sixth Amendment rights to remain silent and to have a lawyer present before his confession.
- **Issue:** Can the police **interrogate** (*question*) a suspect without informing him of his rights to remain silent or to have a lawyer present?
- **Decision/Outcome:** The Supreme Court ruled that suspects must always be informed of their Fifth and Sixth Amendment rights before interrogation; otherwise their confession cannot be used in court.
- **Effects:** Police now must read suspects their "Miranda" rights.

In re Gault (1967)

- **Facts:** Juvenile courts were established to shield minors (those under 18 years old) from the harshness of adult courts. However, in some states, juvenile courts adopted summary procedures and failed to protect minors. Gerald Gault's parents appealed a case where a juvenile court had denied Gault's "due process" rights and given him an unjustly harsh penalty. He was accused of making a single obscene call to a neighbor, which he denied. He was sent away to a juvenile home with no right of appeal. Gault was given no advance notice of his hearing, faced no witnesses, had no lawyer, had no transcript of the hearing, and had no right of appeal. The maximum penalty for an adult was 2 months, yet Gault was sent away for 6 years.
- **Issue:** What "due process" rights are owed to a juvenile (*a minor*) facing a possible loss of liberty?
- **Decision/Outcome:** The Supreme Court ruled that although juvenile courts should have different procedures than adult courts, normal "due process" rights still applied to minors. The Court listed some of the basic "due process" rights that minors shared with adults--such as receiving adequate notice, having time to prepare, being able to cross-examine witnesses, having the help of an attorney, and being able to appeal the decision. These rights of minors are now known as juvenile rights.
- **Effects:** Because of *In re Gault*, states reformed their juvenile justice procedures.

Fourteenth Amendment Rights (Racial Segregation and "Equal Protection")

Segregation refers to the practice of separating people by race. Southern states introduced segregation laws in the late 19th century. These two cases, for and against segregation, are among the most influential in U.S. history.

Plessy v. Ferguson (1896)

- **Facts:** An African-American man, Homer Plessy, appealed his arrest for ignoring Louisiana's "Jim Crow" segregation laws by sitting in the "whites only" passenger car of a train. Plessy himself was seven-eighths white.
- **Issue:** Can a state impose racial segregation by offering "separate-but-equal" facilities, without violating the Equal Protection Clause of the Fourteenth Amendment?
- **Decision/Outcome:** The Supreme Court ruled against Plessy: it held that racial segregation did ***not*** violate the **Fourteenth Amendment's** right to "equal protection," so long as the facilities provided to each race were "**separate but equal**." The Louisiana law itself, said the Court, did not say that one race was either superior or inferior to the other.
- **Effects:** As a result, segregation laws were further strengthened across the South.

Brown v. Board of Education (1954)

- **Facts:** The **NAACP** (National Association for the Advancement of Colored People) appealed a case in which an African-American girl, Linda Brown, was forced to attend a segregated, African-American public school when a white school was closer to her home.
- **Issue:** Does racial segregation in public schools violate the Equal Protection Clause of the Fourteenth Amendment?
- **NAACP's Legal Argument:** **Thurgood Marshall**, the NAACP lawyer, argued that segregated education sent young African-American children the message that they were inferior to whites. Psychologist Dr. Clark supported this claim with a study in which African-American children preferred white dolls. Therefore racial segregation in public schools was "inherently unequal."
- **Decision/Outcome:** Chief Justice Earl Warren wrote the unanimous Court decision: racially segregated public schools violated the Fourteenth Amendment because they made African-American children feel inferior, not equal. Segregation, the Court said, had no place in public education.
- **Effects:** The Supreme Court ruled that the lower federal courts should enforce the decision "with all deliberate speed." Though it took many years, the *Brown* decision was the first step toward ending racial segregation in the South. It led to a transformation of American society.

Before *Brown v. Board of Education*

After *Brown v. Board of Education*

Presidential Power

Despite the separation of powers, the Supreme Court has occasionally ruled on issues concerning Presidential power.

United States v. Nixon (1974)

- **Facts:** In 1973, a group was caught breaking into Democratic headquarters in the Watergate Hotel and office complex. Journalists and Congressional hearings gradually learned that the White House might be involved. They also discovered that President Nixon had taped all his White House conversations. Nixon claimed he had "executive privilege" and refused to hand over tapes of White House conversations to investigators.
- **Issue:** Does "executive privilege"—the need of the President of the United States for privacy and confidentiality in making high-level, national decisions—excuse the President from turning over documents needed as evidence in a criminal proceeding?
- **Decision/Outcome:** The Supreme Court ruled that "executive privilege" did not justify withholding the tapes in these circumstances. The President was ordered to hand over the tapes.
- **Effects:** The tapes were handed over and President Nixon was implicated in the Watergate scandal. Nixon resigned rather than be impeached. The decision emphasized that even the President is not above the rule of law.

What Do You Know?

SS.7.CG.3.11

1. What was the significance of the U.S. Supreme Court decision in *Marbury v. Madison* (1803)?
   - **A.** It gave the Court the power to mediate disputes between different states.
   - **B.** It gave the Court original jurisdiction in disputes involving foreign governments.
   - **C.** It established the power of the Court to declare an act of Congress unconstitutional.
   - **D.** It established the right of the Court to advise Congress in advance on the validity of proposed laws.

SS.7.CG.3.11

2. Which statement describes the significance of the U.S. Supreme Court's decision in *Miranda v. Arizona* (1966)?
   - **A.** Southern states could no longer maintain racially segregated public schools.
   - **B.** States could no longer have racial quotas as part of their affirmative action programs.
   - **C.** Individuals accused of serious crimes unable to pay for an attorney were entitled to a state-sponsored one.
   - **D.** Suspects had to be told of their right to have an attorney present or to remain silent during police interrogations.

SS.7.CG.3.11

3. The passage below is from the U.S. Supreme Court decision in *Dred Scott v. Sandford* (1857).

> *We think . . . that [African Americans] are not included, and were not intended to be included, under the word "citizens" in the Constitution, and can therefore claim none of the rights . . . and privileges which that instrument provides . . .*

Based on this reasoning, what did the Supreme Court conclude?

A. African Americans should seek justice in the state courts rather than in the federal courts.

B. The practice of slavery clearly violates the U.S. Constitution, but African Americans still have no rights in court.

C. The Court has no jurisdiction over the case because an African American has no right to sue in federal court.

D. African Americans have a right to file lawsuits in Northern states, where slavery is prohibited, but not in Southern states, where slavery is permitted.

SS.7.CG.3.11

4. Which statement identifies the social impact of the U.S. Supreme Court decision in *Brown v. Board of Education* (1954)?

A. It overturned racial segregation in public schools.

B. It overturned the earlier decision of *Gideon v. Wainwright*.

C. It upheld state laws requiring the payment of poll taxes to vote.

D. It upheld state laws requiring racial segregation on railroad cars.

SS.7.CG.3.11

5. In which U.S. Supreme Court decision did Chief Justice John Marshall establish the power of the Court to invalidate a "law repugnant to [*in conflict with*] the Constitution"?

A. *U.S. v. Nixon*

B. *Miranda v. Arizona*

C. *Marbury v. Madison*

D. *Brown v. Board of Education*

SS.7.CG.3.11

6. What lesson did state courts learn from the 1963 U.S. Supreme Court case *Gideon v. Wainwright*?

A. Minors are entitled to many of the same "due process" rights as adults.

B. Evidence cannot be presented in a court trial if obtained by police in an unlawful search.

C. Suspects must be informed of their 5th and 6th Amendment rights prior to police interrogation.

D. A person accused of a felony who cannot afford an attorney is entitled to have one appointed by the court.

SS.7.CG.3.11

7. The passage below is from the U.S. Supreme Court decision *In re Gault* (1967).

> *From the inception of the juvenile court system, wide differences have been tolerated . . . between the procedural rights accorded to adults and those of juveniles. In practically all jurisdictions, there are rights granted to adults, which are withheld from juveniles. . . .*
>
> *[H]istory has again demonstrated that unbridled discretion, however benevolently motivated, is frequently a poor substitute for principle and procedure. . . .*

Which conclusion did the Court draw from this reasoning?

A. Evidence cannot be presented in a court of law if obtained by police in an unlawful search.

B. States must provide minors accused of crimes with most of the same "due process" rights given to adults.

C. Suspects must be informed of their Fifth and Sixth Amendment rights prior to being questioned by the police.

D. A person accused of a felony who is unable to afford an attorney is entitled to have one provided by the court.

SS.7.CG.3.11

8. The passage below is from the U.S. Supreme Court decision in *Plessy v. Ferguson* (1896).

> *We consider the underlying fallacy of the plaintiff's argument to consist in the assumption that the enforced separation of the two races stamps the colored race with a badge of inferiority. If this be so, it is not by reason of anything found in the act, but solely because the colored race chooses to put that construction upon it. . . .*
>
> *If the civil and political rights of both races be equal, one cannot be inferior to the other civilly or politically. If one race be inferior to the other socially, the constitution of the United States cannot put them upon the same plane.*

What was the impact on society of the reasoning above?

A. Racial segregation remained in place in the South for another half century.

B. Southern state governments were forced to end their practice of racial segregation.

C. State governments had to ensure the economic and social equality of their residents.

D. State governments no longer had to provide equal facilities to members of different races.

SS.7.CG.3.11

9. The timeline below shows several Supreme Court cases and constitutional amendments.

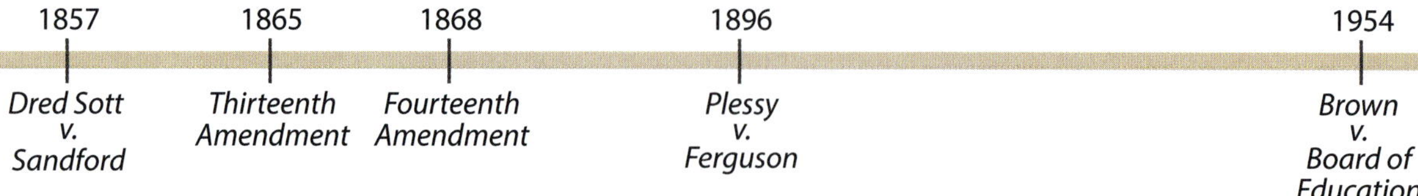

Which conclusion can be drawn from the events shown on the timeline?

A. The Supreme Court has never reversed its earlier decisions.

B. State courts are not required to follow the decisions of the Supreme Court.

C. The Supreme Court's interpretation of the Constitution may be changed by later decisions or amendments.

D. The institution of slavery and racial segregation were both ended by the decisions of the Supreme Court.

SS.7.CG.3.11

10. The passage below is from the U.S. Supreme Court decision in *Brown v. Board of Education* (1954).

> *Segregation of white and colored children in public schools has a detrimental effect upon the colored children. The impact is greater when it has the sanction of the law, for the policy of separating the races is usually interpreted as denoting the inferiority of the [African-American] group. . . . We conclude that, in the field of public education, the doctrine of 'separate but equal' has no place.*

What was the impact of this reasoning by the U.S. Supreme Court?

A. Southern states were forced to end all racial segregation in public schools.

B. Southern states were required to ensure the economic and social equality of all races.

C. Racial segregation was discontinued in public elementary schools but continued in higher grades.

D. Southern states could maintain separate schools for African-American and white children if they were of equal quality.

SS.7.CG.3.11

11. Which Supreme Court decision was overturned by the ratification of the 13th and 14th Amendments?

A. *Marbury v. Madison*

B. *Dred Scott v. Sandford*

C. *Plessy v. Ferguson*

D. *Brown v. Board of Education*

Florida Governor Ron DeSantis

CHAPTER 12

Federalism: National, State and Local Governments Acting Together

In this chapter you will learn about the types of constitutional powers; federalism; the Florida Constitution; and state and local government. You will also compare different levels of government and government services.

SS. 7.CG.3.4 Explain the relationship between state and national governments as written in Article IV of the U.S. Constitution and the 10th Amendment.

SS.7.CG.3.7 Explain the structure, functions and processes of the legislative branch of government. (*This chapter explains the legislative branch at the state and local levels; see Chapter 6 for the national level.*)

SS.7.CG.3.8 Explain the structure, functions and processes of thwwwwe executive branch of government. (*This chapter explains the executive branch at the state and local levels; see Chapter 7 for the national level.*)

SS.7.CG.3.12 Compare the U.S. and Florida constitutions.

SS.7.CG.3.13 Explain government obligations to its citizens and the services provided at the local, state and national levels.

Content Focus Vocabulary in This Chapter

Federalism
Article IV
10th Amendment
Enumerated powers
Delegated powers
Concurrent powers
Reserved powers
Supremacy Clause
"Supreme law of the land"
Level of government
Constitution
Framework for government
Florida Constitution
Preamble
Articles
Amendments
Florida Declaration of Rights
State legislators
State Senators
State Representatives
Amendment process
Statute
Act
Governor
Executive authority
Lawmaking process
Local government
Ordinance
City/County Commissioners
Council members
Mayor
Lawmakers
Government obligations
Government services

Florida "Keys" to Learning

1. A **constitution** is a written plan of government. It serves several purposes: it (1) provides a **framework for government** (*its basic structure or system of organization*); (2) defines and limits the powers of government; and (3) protects the rights of individuals.

2. The U.S. Constitution spelled out which powers were given to the new national government and which powers were left to the states. Those powers given to the national government became known as the **enumerated powers**. These powers are also called the **delegated powers**. The **10th Amendment** states that all powers not delegated to the national government are "reserved" for the states and the people. Powers given to the state governments are therefore known as **reserved powers**. Examples of reserved powers are the control of elections and public education within a state. Finally, powers given to both the national government and the states, such as the power to tax, are known as **concurrent powers**. This system of dividing power between the national and state governments is known as **federalism**.

3. **Article IV** of the Constitution spells out relations between the national government and the states, as well as between the states themselves. State governments must respect the legal acts of other states, including court judgments. The national government promises to preserve the "republican form of government" (*government by elected representatives*) in each state and to protect each state from invasion.

4. Article VI of the Constitution contains the **Supremacy Clause**. This clause declares the supremacy (*superiority*) of federal law (*laws passed by the national government*) over state law. Federal law is the "**supreme law of the land**" (*the highest form of law*) in all those areas where the Constitution gives the national government the power to act. It means that whenever federal and state laws conflict, federal law wins.

5. Each state has its own state constitution. The first **Florida Constitution** was written in 1838 and has been rewritten several times. The current Florida Constitution was ratified (*adopted*) in November 1968.

6. There are many similarities between the U.S. Constitution and the Florida Constitution. Both have a **preamble** (*an introduction*), a series of **articles** (*major sections*), and **amendments** (*later additions or changes*). Both constitutions identify "We the people" as the final source of all governmental power. The Florida Constitution includes the **Florida Declaration of Rights**, which echoes the U.S. Bill of Rights.

7. Both constitutions established governments with similar structures. The U.S. Constitution created a national legislature known as Congress, with a Senate and House of Representatives. Florida has its own state legislature, with the Florida Senate and Florida House of Representatives. **State legislators** are known as **State Senators** and **State Representatives**. Both constitutions created executive branches led by a chief executive (the President at the national level and the **Governor** of Florida at the state level), and established their own court systems.

8. There are some important differences between these two constitutions. The U.S. Constitution gave the national government powers to deal with the concerns of the nation as a whole, such as defense and foreign affairs. The Florida Constitution gave the state government powers over matters specific to Florida, such as statewide elections, state finances, local government, and public education.

9. The Florida Constitution also has several unique provisions, such as its taxpayer's bill of rights. The Florida Constitution establishes English as the official language and prohibits state income taxes on individuals.

10. The Florida Constitution also has an easier **amendment process** than the U.S. Constitution provides. An amendment to the Florida Constitution can be proposed in five different ways and requires only 60% of the voters to ratify it. In contrast, an amendment to the U.S. Constitution needs to be ratified by three-fourths (75%) of the states. The Florida Constitution has been amended hundreds of times; the U.S. Constitution fewer than 30 times.

11. Florida's **Governor** enforces the law, meets with the Cabinet, represents the state, oversees state agencies, proposes laws, and can veto bills and issue pardons.

12. The **lawmaking process** of the Florida State Legislature is similar to that of Congress: bills first go to committees, must be approved by each house, and are signed or vetoed by the executive.

13. There are two main forms of **local government** in Florida: counties and municipalities. County governments are run by elected **county commissioners** and make laws for an entire county. Counties provide health services, maintain county courts and jails, supervise local elections, and maintain county records. They may also handle waste disposal, maintain local roads, and have police and fire departments. Each county is also a public school district.

14. A municipality is a city, town or village with its own government. A municipality often has an elected executive known as the mayor. **Council members** (elected members of the city council) or **city commissioners** (elected members of the city commission) act as a legislative body, passing municipal laws. Municipal governments serve many of the same functions as county governments.

15. Comparing the **lawmaking process**: Processes at the national and state level are similar. In contrast, lawmakers in local government usually make up just one body. Proposed laws go through fewer steps. Laws passed by Congress or by the Florida state legislature are called **acts** or **statutes**. Laws passed by local governments are known as **ordinances**.

16. Comparing **lawmakers**: Legislators at the national level (U.S. Senators and Representatives, or Congressmen and Congresswomen), state level (State legislators), and local level (commissioners and council members) are all elected officials who serve a fixed term in office. Term lengths and constitutional and legal requirements differ.

17. Comparing **executive authority**: At each level of government, the executive enforces the law. The President has executive authority for the entire nation and the Governor for the state. A sheriff, mayor or city manager acts as the executive at the local level: local executives have authority over their local areas.

18. Different levels of government have different **government obligations**—services the government must provide to citizens. Our national governmnent meets the needs of the nation as a whole, such as for national defense. State government meets the needs of state residents, such as setting requirements for high school graduation or for practicing medicine in the state. **Local governments** in Florida provide **government services** that address local needs.

The authors of the U.S. Constitution not only separated government powers among three branches; they also created a system in which the new federal government and state governments shared power. This division of power is known as **federalism**. In this chapter, you will study federalism and the role of state and local governments in our federal system.

You should know the different types of powers for the EOC

The Division of Power in the Federal System

The Enumerated and Reserved Powers

From the beginning, our national government has had only limited powers. These are the **enumerated powers** listed in the Constitution. These listed powers are also known as the **delegated powers.** (You can look back at Chapter 6 to see examples of these powers.)

All other powers are "reserved" (*saved for*) for the states or the people. The **10th Amendment**, the last amendment in the Bill of Rights, makes this clear:

> *"The powers not delegated to the United States by the Constitution, nor prohibited by it to the States, are* ***reserved*** *to the States...or to the people."*

Because of the words used in the Tenth Amendment, the powers left to state governments are frequently called the "reserved powers."

The Supremacy of Federal Law

In all areas where the national government lawfully exercises power, federal law is supreme (*the highest authority*). It is treated as superior to state law.

This principle was established by the **Supremacy Clause** of the Constitution:

> *"This Constitution, and the Laws of the United States . . . and all treaties made. . . under the authority of the United States, shall be the supreme law of the land; and the judges in every state shall be bound thereby . . ."*
>
> —U.S. Constitution, Article VI, Clause 2

If a state law and federal law are seen to be in conflict, judges are required by the Supremacy Clause to rule in favor of the federal law. Federal law is thus considered to be the "supreme law of the land."

For example, some states had once allowed poll taxes (*special taxes paid in order to vote*). The Twenty-fourth Amendment to the U.S. Constitution outlawed poll taxes in 1964. Because of the supremacy of federal law, this amendment made all state poll taxes invalid.

The Concurrent Powers

Under our federal system, many of the enumerated powers (like the power to declare war) are exclusive: they are held only by the national government. Other government powers are reserved just for the states. There is a third group of powers that are actually shared by state governments and the national government. These shared powers are known as the **concurrent powers**. Several of the enumerated powers, like the power to tax, are also concurrent powers. Both the national government and the state governments have the power to tax their citizens.

Several examples of enumerated, concurrent and reserved powers are shown on the chart below:

Exclusive Enumerated Powers	Concurrent Powers (Both)	Reserved Powers (States Only)
Coin and print money	Tax	Regulate elections
Regulate interstate commerce	Borrow money	Regulate a state's internal commerce
Declare war	Provide for the general welfare	Establish local governments
Manage relations with foreign nations	Legislate and enforce laws	Establish and maintain state militia
Punish counterfeiters of U.S. securities and money	Create and maintain court systems	Provide for the health, safety, and education of state residents
Raise, maintain, and command the military forces of the United States		Ratify amendments to the U.S. Constitution
Establish systems of patents and copyrights		Regulate the practice of law and medicine
Establish standard weights and measures		Keep all powers not granted to the federal government (10th Amendment)
Make naturalization rules for immigrants to become U.S. citizens		
Establish post offices		

The Active Citizen

▶ Classify the power to conduct each of the following government activities by type:

	Exclusively National	Concurrent	Reserved
Set the requirements for the practice of medicine in Florida	☐	☐	☐
Explain your choice: ______________________________			
Set the speed limits on a state highway	☐	☐	☐
Explain your choice: ______________________________			
Set requirements for the safety of meat products sold in several states	☐	☐	☐
Explain your choice: ______________________________			
Collect taxes to pay for government services	☐	☐	☐
Explain your choice: ______________________________			
Sell bonds to finance government programs	☐	☐	☐
Explain your choice: ______________________________			
Sign a nuclear arms treaty with Russia	☐	☐	☐
Explain your choice: ______________________________			
Set standards for high school graduation	☐	☐	☐
Explain your choice: ______________________________			
Negotiate a treaty of commerce with Singapore	☐	☐	☐
Explain your choice: ______________________________			
Require all U.S. citizens to have health insurance	☐	☐	☐
Explain your choice: ______________________________			
Require bicycle riders in the state to wear helmets	☐	☐	☐
Explain your choice: ______________________________			

Continues ▶

▶ "You've Got the Power!" Complete the table below by defining the various types of government powers in our federal system. Then provide one example of each.

Type of Power	Definition	Example
Enumerated Powers (also known as Delegated Powers)		
Implied Powers (see Chapter 5)		
Concurrent Powers		
Reserved Powers		

For the EOC, you should know that Article IV concerns the states.

Article IV of the U.S. Constitution

Article IV describes relations between the states and the national government, as well as between the states themselves.

	What it says	What it means
Section 1	"Full faith and credit shall be given in each state to the public acts, records, and judicial proceedings of every other state . . ."	Court judgments, marriages, wills, and other public records from one state will be valid (*legally binding; enforceable*) in all other states.
Section 2	"The citizens of each state shall be entitled to all privileges and immunities of citizens in the several states."	A state cannot give special privileges to its own citizens and deny those privileges to citizens from other states—all U.S. citizens enjoy the same rights in all states.
	"A person charged in any state with treason, felony, or other crime, who shall flee from justice, and be found in another state, shall on demand of the . . . state from which he fled, be delivered up . . ."	A state can demand that an accused person who flees to another state be returned to stand trial.

	What it says	What it means
Section 3	"New states may be admitted by the Congress into this Union . . ."	Congress can admit new states.
Section 4	"The United States shall guarantee to every state in this Union a republican form of government, and [the United States] shall protect each of them against invasion, and on application of the legislature, or of the executive (when the legislature cannot be convened) against domestic violence."	The national government guarantees the representative form of government in each state. It also promises to protect each state from foreign invasion. In the event of domestic (*internal*) unrest, the national government will assist a state if requested.

Article IV requires each state to recognize legal documents and court judgments from other states. It thus guarantees U.S. citizens some degree of uniformity across the United States. For example:

- If a couple is married in one state, their marriage license will be valid in all other states.
- If a customer owes money to a business owner, the customer cannot move to another state to avoid paying the business owner.
- If a driver accidentally injures someone and a court orders the driver to pay the injured person's medical bills, the driver cannot move to another state to avoid paying.
- If a family moves to a different state, they will be treated by the state government as equal to those already living in that state.

Article IV also makes the national government responsible for preserving the "republican form of government" in every state, and for protecting states from foreign invasion. Finally, it requires the national government to assist any state applying for help in putting down violent domestic unrest.

The Active Citizen

- Why was it important to include Article IV in the Constitution?
- What would it be like if one state did not recognize legal documents or court judgments from another state?

Different Levels of Government Acting Together

In the rest of this chapter, you will learn how these different **levels of government**—national and state—work together. You will also learn about a third level of government: local government. Finally, you will see that citizens have two responsibilities in common at each of these levels of government: to obey the law and pay taxes.

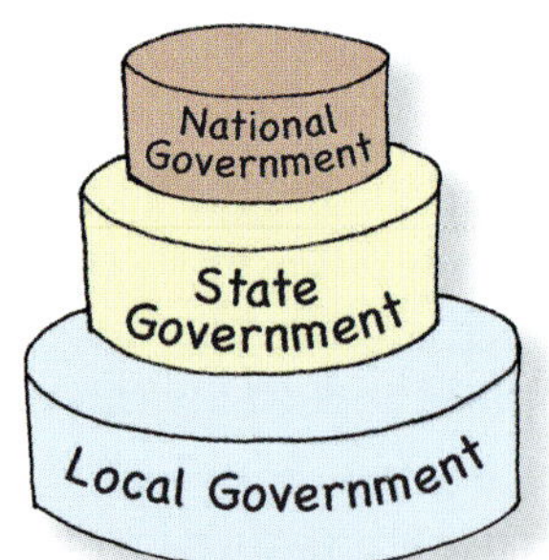

Under our system of federalism, each "layer" of our government has its own powers and responsibilities.

For the EOC, know the purposes of a written constitution and the similarities and differences between the Florida and U.S. Constitutions.

A Comparison of the Florida Constitution and the U.S. Constitution

A written constitution actually serves several purposes: (1) it provides a **framework** (*basic structure*) **for government**; (2) it defines and limits the power of government; and (3) it protects individual rights.

Like our national government, the state government of Florida is based on a written constitution: the Constitution of the State of Florida, known as the **Florida Constitution**. This document is the source of authority for Florida's state government.

The current state constitution was adopted in 1968. This constitution is similar to the U.S. Constitution in many ways. Both documents begin with a **preamble** (*an introduction*) followed by a series of **articles** (*main sections, with each section describing a different part or feature of the government*). Finally, both include **amendments** (*later additions or changes*). The U.S. Constitution ends with a series of amendments. In the Florida Constitution, amendments lead to changes in the text of the Constitution itself rather than to a separate list of amendments at the end.

The Florida Constitution begins with this Preamble:

> *We, the People of the State of Florida, being grateful to Almighty God for our constitutional liberty, in order to secure its benefits, perfect our government, insure domestic tranquility, maintain public order, and guarantee equal civil and political rights to all, do ordain and establish this constitution.*

This is, in fact, very similar to the Preamble to the U.S. Constitution, which you have studied in Chapter 5. Both Constitutions begin with "*We the People*"—a recognition that the powers of government in a democratic society are based on the consent of the people. It is the people who, in the spirit of John Locke's social contract, form the government.

The Florida Constitution further provides these basic definitions:

> "*Section 1.* ***Political power***—*All political power is inherent in the people.*"

> "*Section 2.* ***Basic rights***—*All natural persons, female and male alike, are equal before the law and have inalienable rights, among which are the right to enjoy and defend life and liberty, to pursue happiness, to be rewarded for industry, and to acquire, possess and protect property . . .*"

Much of this language is borrowed directly from the U.S. Declaration of Independence.

Both constitutions follow this opening statement with a list of their purposes. The Florida Constitution borrows many of its purposes directly from the U.S. Constitution. To these, it adds the goals of maintaining public order and guaranteeing equal civil and political rights to all.

A Comparison of the U.S. Constitution and Florida Constitution

U.S. Constitution	Florida Constitution
Preamble Begins: "We the People" Describes purposes of government	**Preamble** Begins: "We, the people of the State of Florida . . ." Describes purposes of government
Articles (7 Articles) (**Bill of Rights**: see Amendments I-X below) **Article I Legislature** ◆ Congress ▪ Senate ▪ House of Representatives **Article II Executive** ◆ President and Vice President **Article III Judiciary** ◆ U.S. Supreme Court **Article IV States** * * * * **Article V Amending Process** ◆ Proposing the amendment: 2/3 vote of both houses of Congress ◆ Ratifying the amendment: 3/4 of state legislatures (or special state conventions) * * * * **Article VI Supremacy Clause** ◆ Federal law is "supreme law of the land" **Article VII Ratification of Constitution**	**Articles (12 Articles)** **Article I Declaration of Rights** **Article II General Provisions** ◆ Section 1 State boundaries ◆ Section 9 English is official language **Article III Legislature** ◆ Florida State Legislature: ▪ Senate ▪ House of Representatives **Article IV Executive** ◆ Governor, Lieutenant Governor and Cabinet **Article V Judiciary** ◆ State courts, judges, attorneys and public defenders **Article VI Suffrage and Elections** ◆ Regulations; term limits for state offices; campaign spending **Article VII Finance and Taxation** ◆ Taxes, bonds ◆ Section 5: no personal income tax **Article VIII Local Government** ◆ Counties, municipalities **Article IX Education** **Article X Miscellaneous** * * * * **Article XI Amending Process** ◆ Proposing amendments (five methods): ▪ 3/5 of each house of legislature proposes ▪ Constitutional convention ▪ Voter initiative ▪ Constitution Revision Commission ▪ Taxation and Budget Reform Commission ◆ Approving amendments: 60% of voters must approve most amendments in referendum * * * * **Article XII Schedule** (transition from older constitution to new one of 1968)
Amendments ◆ Only 27 Amendments ▪ **Bill of Rights** (1791): First Ten Amendments ▪ 13th Amendment ended slavery ▪ 14th Amendment defined the rights of U.S. citizens ▪ 15th, 19th, 24th and 26th Amendments—expanded the right to vote	**Amendments** ◆ The Florida Constitution has been amended more than 100 times since 1968. ◆ Once approved, amendments are placed as changes in the text of the Florida Constitution itself.

The Florida Declaration of Rights

The first article of the Florida Constitution is the **Florida Declaration of Rights**. This Declaration is very similar to the U.S. Bill of Rights. It guarantees the following rights and freedoms to the citizens of Florida:

- Freedom of religion
- Freedom of speech and the press
- Freedom of assembly
- The right to bear arms
- The right to due process
- The right to be secure against unreasonable searches and seizures
- No *ex post facto* laws*
- No laws reducing contract obligations
- A guarantee of the right to a writ of habeas corpus, except in times of invasion or rebellion*
- Protection against double jeopardy
- One cannot be forced to testify against oneself (no self-incrimination)
- No cruel or unusual punishment
- The right to bail
- The right to an attorney if accused of a crime
- The right to a speedy and public trial by an impartial jury

*For the meaning of these rights, see Chapter 10.

Ties between the Florida and U.S. Constitutions are so close that in several places the Florida Constitution adopts standards from the U.S. Constitution by reference. For example, it provides that Florida's rules against unreasonable searches and seizures should "be construed *(interpreted)* in conformity with the 4th Amendment to the United States Constitution, as interpreted by the United States Supreme Court" (Florida Constitution, Article I, Section 12).

How Florida's State Government Is Organized

In Articles II–IV, the Florida Constitution establishes the organization of its state government. There are many similarities between Florida's state government and the national government. Like the federal government, Florida's government has three branches: legislative, executive, and judicial. Also like the national government, the three branches of Florida's state government serve to check one another to prevent abuses of government power.

The Legislative Branch: The Florida State Legislature

> **Composition.** *The legislative power of the state shall be vested in a legislature of the State of Florida, consisting of a senate composed of one senator elected from each senatorial district and a house of representatives composed of one member elected from each representative district.*
>
> —*Florida Constitution, Article III, Section 1*

The Florida State Legislature, like Congress, has two houses. It consists of:

1. the Florida House of Representatives, with up to 120 members; and
2. the Florida Senate, with up to 40 members.

These **state legislators** are known as **State Representatives** and **State Senators**. A Florida State Representative is elected for a term of two years and a Florida State Senator is elected for a term of four years.

	National Government	Florida State Government
Legislative Branch	Congress: U.S. Senate U.S. House of Representatives	Florida State Legislature: Florida Senate Florida House of Representatives
Executive Branch	President Vice President Appointed Cabinet Members	Governor Lieutenant Governor Elected Cabinet Members (Attorney General, etc.)
Judicial Branch	U.S. Supreme Court U.S. Circuit Court of Appeals U.S. District Court	Florida Supreme Court Florida District Courts of Appeal Florida Circuit Courts Florida County Courts

For the EOC, be sure to know the constitutional qualifications for serving in state government.

To be a legislator in either house, a candidate must:

- be 21 years old;
- be a resident of Florida for at least two years; and
- be a resident of the district he or she will represent.

Florida's legislative branch has the power to make laws, just as Congress does at the federal level. Laws made either by Congress or by a state legislature are known as **acts** or **statutes**.

Like Congress, the Florida Legislature also has investigative powers. It can order the appearance of witnesses and documents to assist state legislators in deciding which state laws to pass.

And like Congress, the Florida Legislature can override a veto by the executive with a two-thirds majority vote in each house. It also has the power to impeach officials in the other two branches of government for wrongdoing, corruption, or crime.

The Executive Branch: The Governor, Lieutenant Governor and Cabinet

Both Florida and our national government have one individual in charge of the executive branch. Instead of a President, Florida has a **Governor**; and instead of a Vice President, Florida has a Lieutenant Governor.

"The supreme executive power shall be vested in a governor, who shall be commander-in-chief of all military forces of the state not in active service of the United States. The governor shall take care that the laws be faithfully executed, commission all officers of the state and counties, and transact all necessary business with the officers of government. The governor may require information in writing from all executive or administrative state, county or municipal officers upon any subject relating to the duties of their respective offices. The governor shall be the chief administrative officer of the state responsible for the planning and budgeting for the state."

—Florida Constitution, Article IV, Section 1

The Governor of Florida has many powers and responsibilities similar to those of the President of the United States. The Governor serves as chief executive of the state government, can veto proposed legislation, commands the state militia, and can pardon those convicted of state crimes. The Governor oversees a large number of departments and administrative agencies, including the Florida Citrus Commission, the Florida Department of Health, the Florida Department of Elder Affairs, the

Florida State Board of Education, and the Florida Fish and Wildlife Conservation Commission.

Just as the President represents the United States, the Governor represents the State of Florida.

One additional power that the Governor has, which the President lacks, is the power to request advisory opinions from the Florida Supreme Court.

To serve as Governor or Lieutenant Governor, an individual must:

- be at least 30 years old
- have lived in Florida for the past 7 years before the election.

While the Cabinet is not even mentioned in the U.S. Constitution, it is described in the Florida Constitution, where its three members are listed:

> *"There shall be a cabinet composed of an attorney general, a chief financial officer, and a commissioner of agriculture."*
>
> —*Florida Constitution, Article IV, Section 4*

Unlike the national government, these three members of the Cabinet in Florida are elected officials. Each must meet the same minimum qualifications for office as the Governor, except that the Attorney General needs only to have lived in Florida for the five years before the election. The Governor, Lieutenant Governor and Cabinet members are all elected to 4-year terms in office.

The Judicial Branch

Florida's court system likewise has several similiarities to the federal one, although Florida has four—not three—levels of courts.

> **Courts** *"The judicial power shall be vested in a supreme court, district courts of appeal, circuit courts and county courts. No other courts may be established by the state, any political subdivision or any municipality."*
>
> —*Florida Constitution, Article IV, Section 4*

At the very top of Florida's court system sits the Florida Supreme Court; just below that are Florida's five District Courts of Appeal; below these are two levels of trial courts—20 circuit courts for more important cases and 67 county courts for less important ones. You can review Florida's court structure in Chapter 9.

Other Differences between the U.S. and Florida Constitutions

There are many other differences between the Florida Constitution and the U.S. Constitution. The most important is that the U.S. Constitution addresses the concerns of our nation as a whole, while the Florida Constitution addresses matters specific to the State of Florida. Some of these more specific concerns are found in the Florida Constitution's provisions for:

- elections and voting (Article VI)
- state finances and taxation (Article VII)
- local government (Article VIII)
- public education (Article IX)

In general, the Florida Constitution is more detailed than the U.S. Constitution. The U.S. Constitution lays out broad principles and concepts. The Florida Constitution includes broad principles but frequently enters into specific details. This is typical of most state constitutions.

Enrichment

Many of the similarities between the Florida Constitution and the U.S. Constitution can be traced to the history of the state constitution. In 1838, Florida was still a territory. To become a state, Florida had to submit a written constitution to Congress for approval. Using the constitutions of several Southern states as models, Floridians developed a constitution that included many concepts already found in the U.S. Constitution.

There have actually been six Florida constitutions. The first was the one drafted in 1838 and approved by Congress when Florida became a state in 1845. It was repealed in 1861 when Florida became one of the first states to secede from the Union just before the Civil War.

After the Civil War, Florida sought to rejoin the Union. In 1868, Congress required a new constitution from Florida. The new state constitution had to conform to the U.S. Constitution, especially the 13th and 14th Amendments, which ended slavery. John Pope, commander of the Union occupation force in Florida, ordered the election of delegates to attend a state constitutional convention. This assembly drafted the Florida Constitution of 1868. Reconstruction (the period just after the Civil War) ended shortly afterwards and Florida was readmitted to the Union.

The state constitution was revised again in 1885. Florida's present-day constitution was adopted in 1968. While later constitutions introduced several changes, most of the basic principles of the current constitution can be traced back to the Constitution of 1838.

Florida's first Constitution (1838).

The Florida Constitution thus has many provisions without similar ones in the U.S. Constitution:

- It specifically names English as the "official language of the State of Florida" (Article II, Section 9).
- It prohibits the collection of any state personal income taxes or inheritance taxes (Article VII, Section 5). Florida is one of only a handful of states that do not collect personal income taxes. However, Florida does collect corporate income tax.
- It requires the state legislature to draft and adopt a Taxpayer's Bill of Rights.
- It gives the state legislature the power to create the Department of Veterans Affairs and the Department of Elder Affairs.
- It permits the Governor of Florida to reduce expenditures whenever there is less state revenue (*income*) than expected.
- It creates a trust fund to conserve and protect the Florida Everglades.
- It provides for the licensing of professionals, such as attorneys and doctors.
- It places limits on marine net fishing in Florida waters.
- It provides for education about tobacco and the prevention of smoking.
- It places restrictions on smoking in indoor workplaces.

The Active Citizen

▶ Complete the Venn diagram below comparing the organization of the national government and the state government of Florida. One common element is that each government has three branches.

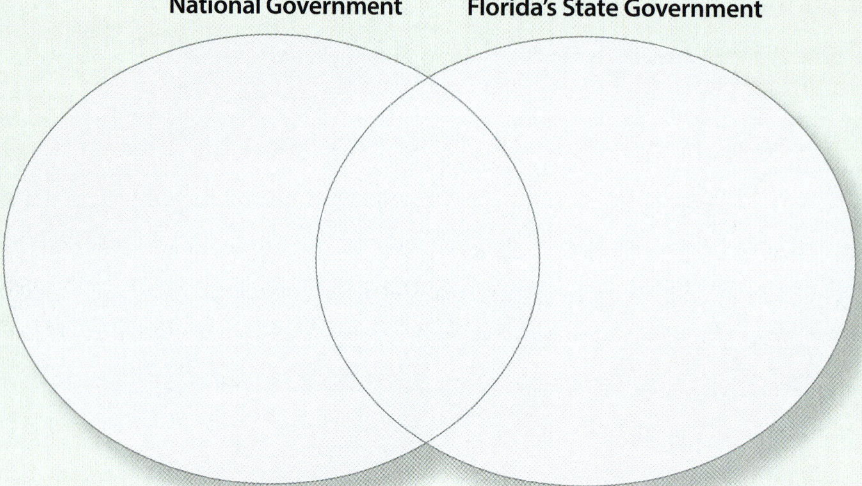

▶ Why do you think the Florida Constitution and the constitutions of most states are more specific than the U.S. Constitution?

For the EOC, be sure to know the differences in the amendment process

The Amendment Process: Florida *vs.* United States

One area in which the U.S. Constitution and the Florida Constitution are especially different is the **amending process**. You will recall that "to amend" is to revise, add to, or change. Both the U.S. Constitution and the Florida Constitution permit amendments so that these constitutions can change along with society's changing needs. However, amending each constitution was deliberately made more difficult than passing an ordinary law.

As you learned in Chapter 10, the U.S. Constitution can be amended through a two-step process. First, proposals for amendments are made either by a vote of two-thirds of each house of Congress, or by a national convention that can be called for by two-thirds of the state legislatures. Then the proposed amendment must be ratified by three-fourths of the state legislatures or by special conventions in three-fourths of the states.

The Florida Constitution can also be amended through a two-step process. In the first step, an amendment is proposed; in the second step, the proposed amendment is approved by voters and adopted.

In Florida, there are more ways for proposing amendments than in the federal system. In Florida, final adoption of an amendment is also not as difficult as at the federal level. As a result, there have been many more amendments to the Florida Constitution than to the U.S. Constitution.

Thousands of amendments to the U.S. Constitution have been suggested. However, only 17 amendments have actually been added to the U.S. Constitution since the ratification of the Bill of Rights in 1791.

In contrast, there have already been more than 100 amendments to the Florida Constitution since 1968. With five methods for proposing amendments and the requirement that only 60% of the voters need to approve most amendments, the Florida Constitution is just much easier to amend.

For example, Florida voters amended the Florida Constitution in 2000 to require high-speed rail throughout the state. Then in 2004, another amendment successfully repealed that provision. Even an amendment to care more humanely for pigs has become part of Florida's State Constitution (Article X, Section 21). There is no similar provision in the U.S. Constitution and none is likely.

Amending the Florida Constitution

Step 1. Proposal

There are five ways in which a constitutional amendment may be proposed:

1. By a three-fifths (3/5) vote of both houses of the Florida legislature.
2. By a Constitutional Revision Commission, which meets every 20 years. Its members are the Florida Attorney General and 36 members selected by the Speaker of the Florida House of Representatives, the President of the Florida Senate, the Chief Justice of the Florida Supreme Court, and the Governor.
3. By the Taxation and Budget Reform Commission, which also meets every 20 years. It has members appointed by the Governor, the Speaker of the House, and the President of the Senate.
4. By voters directly proposing an amendment. (At least 8% of voters in the last election must sign petitions proposing the amendment.)
5. By a majority of voters calling for a constitutional convention to revise the constitution.

Step 2. Adoption

1. To adopt a proposed amendment, sixty percent (60 %) of the voters must approve the amendment in a referendum (*a vote on an issue*), held in the next general election after it is proposed.
2. If the proposed amendment concerns taxes, then the approval of two-thirds (66.7%) of the voters is required for the amendment to be adopted.

The Active Citizen

Make a chart or Venn diagram comparing how an amendment is proposed and adopted at the national level and in Florida.

For the EOC, be sure to know Florida's lawmaking process

The Lawmaking Process at the State Level

The Florida Legislature meets for regular session, starting in March, for 60 days each year. The Governor can also summon special sessions.

The lawmaking process in Florida is quite similar to the process at the federal level (see Chapter 6). A bill can be introduced in either house when the legislature is in session. As in Congress, committees are a part of the legislative process. After a bill is introduced, it is referred to a committee, where the bill is discussed and may be changed. The committee can report the bill favorably, amend the bill, or report the bill unfavorably. If the bill is killed in committee, it is dead for the rest of the legislative session.

If the bill is reported favorably by the committee, it is then placed on the calendar for a discussion on the floor of the house. This is followed by a vote. Passage of the bill requires a simple majority vote in support of the bill.

Once a bill has passed in one house, it is sent to the other house. If it passes in the other house without amendment, the bill can be immediately sent to the Governor. However, if the bill is amended in the second house, it is then sent to a conference committee, just as bills are in Congress. The members of the conference committee iron out the differences in the two versions of the bill and the new bill is sent to both houses. They must approve or reject the revised bill in its entirety.

Once the bill has passed in both the Florida Senate and the Florida House of Representatives, it is submitted to the Governor for approval. The Governor can sign the bill, making it into a law. The Governor can also veto the bill. If the Governor vetoes the bill, the legislature can override the veto by a two-thirds vote in each house. The Governor must sign or veto the bill within 7 days if the legislature is in session. If the legislature has adjourned, the Governor must sign or veto the bill within 15 days. Otherwise, it becomes law.

How a Bill in the State Legislature becomes a Law

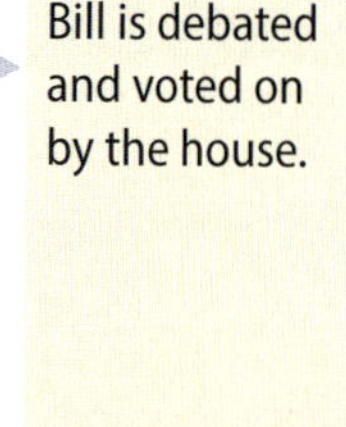

The Active Citizen

- Imagine that you are a Florida State Senator. Write to a friend or colleague describing a bill you have sponsored and its progress in becoming a law.
- You can check on current bills being considered by the Florida Legislature by going to flsenate.gov or myfloridahouse.gov.

Be sure to know what ordinances, city and county commissioners, and school boards are for the EOC test. You do **not** need to know the differences between county and municipal governments.

Local Government in Florida

Local government is the level of government that is closest to us. It affects our daily lives. There are two main types of local governments in Florida: counties and municipalities. These local governments handle such matters as local roads and bridges, public schools, public parks, libraries, garbage collection and recycling, building permits, and providing police and fire protection.

County Governments

The largest unit of local government in Florida is the county. Florida is divided into 67 counties. The citizens of each county elect a sheriff, tax collector, county clerk, property appraiser, and other county officials. They also elect five to seven **county commissioners**. These form a board of commissioners, which makes laws for the county. The commission-

Florida's Ten Largest Municipalities

Municipality	Type of Government
Jacksonville	Mayor-council
Miami	Mayor-commission
Tampa	Mayor-council
St. Petersburg	Mayor-council
Orlando	Mayor-commission
Hialeah	Mayor-council
Tallahassee	Commission-manager
Fort Lauderdale	Commission-manager
Port St. Lucie	Council-manager
Pembroke Pines	Commission-manager

ers deal with matters affecting residents of the county. Laws passed by county commissioners are known as **ordinances**. The county also collects property tax and sales tax to pay for county services.

County governments provide health care, offer assistance to the homeless, maintain county courts and jails, supervise elections, and keep records for the county, including births, deaths, marriages and divorces. They also provide garbage collection, recycling and utilities in some areas.

School Boards

Each county in Florida also forms its own public school district. Voters in the county elect five or more members to a school board for the district. The school board operates and supervises all public schools in the district. The school board also sets the rates of local school district taxes to support its schools.

Municipal Governments

A municipality is any city, town or village that establishes its own government. Municipalities are formed within counties, but they are considered to be separate. There are hundreds of incorporated municipalities in Florida. The government of a municipality is known as a municipal government.

There are several different forms of municipal government. The most common has a **mayor** and a city council or commission. The mayor is elected by all of the voters of the town or city. He or she acts as the chief executive—appointing other city officials, preparing a budget, enforcing city laws, and proposing new laws. The city council or commission acts as a legislature. Its members, known as **council members** or **city commissioners**, are also elected. The city council or commission passes local laws. Like county laws, these are also known as **ordinances**.

Jacksonville, for example, has an elected mayor. The city has 19 elected members on its city council. Miami has an elected mayor and five elected commissioners. Tampa has an elected mayor and a city council with seven council members.

Some cities in Florida have a special city manager. In these cities, voters elect city commissioners. The commissioners in turn appoint the city manager and other officials to run the administration of the city. Both Tallahassee and Fort Lauderdale have city managers. In these cities, the elected commissioners set policies but the city manager heads the city administration. Both cities also have an elected mayor, who sits on the commission. The mayor represents voters from throughout the city, but does not act as a chief executive.

The Active Citizen

What form of local government do you live under? Research your local government on the Internet and write a brief description for a friend in another part of Florida.

Comparing Lawmaking Processes at the Local, State, and National Levels

Similarities between all three levels: At the national, state, and local levels of government, laws are made by officials who are elected for a fixed term in office. The laws they create apply to the area over which their level of government has control.

Differences: At the county level, the board of county commissioners acts as a local legislature. In municipalities, a city council or board of city commissioners serves as a local legislature. Unlike the state legislature or Congress, county boards of commissioners and city councils consist of a single body. A proposed law does not have to go into another house or chamber. In some cases, once the proposal is approved by a majority vote, it becomes law without having to be approved by the executive. In other cases, the mayor's approval is needed for the proposal to become law.

In contrast, both the state legislature and Congress consist of two houses—the Senate and House of Representatives. At both the state and national levels, bills are first introduced into one house and then referred to a committee. If the committee approves the bill, it is discussed and voted on by the whole house. If it is approved by a majority of the house, it is then presented to the other house. Once it passes the second house, a conference committee removes any differences between the two bills. If this new version of the bill is passed by both houses, the bill is then presented to the chief executive (the President or Governor). The executive can sign the bill into law or veto it. At both the state and national levels, the legislature has the power to override a veto with the approval of two-thirds of the members of each house. These steps are identical at both the state and national level, but do not exist for lawmaking at the local level.

Comparing Local, State, and National Lawmakers

At all three levels of government—local, state and national—lawmakers are elected for a fixed term of office. They also must be living in the area that they represent. The qualifications for serving and the length of their terms in office may differ. Florida has term limits (how many terms an official can serve) on its state legislators. They can serve no more than 8 continuous years in either house. There are no term limits on U.S. Representatives or U.S. Senators.

Within local government, there are further variations. Counties and municipalities may have either commissioners or council members. The qualifications for holding office are usually set by local charter and can vary. Typically there is a residence requirement but no age requirement. There are also term limits on many local lawmakers.

National	State	Local
U.S. Congressmen and Congresswomen (U.S. Senators and U.S. Representatives)	State Legislators (State Representatives and State Senators)	City Commissioners, County Commissioners, or Council Members
U.S. Senators are at least 30 years old and are elected to a term of 6 years; U.S Representatives are at least 25 years old and elected to a term of 2 years	Florida Senators are at least 21 years old and are elected to a term of 4 years; Florida Representatives are at least 21 years old and elected to a term of 2 years	According to the State Constitution, County Commissioners are elected to 4-year terms unless changed by charter; most City Commissioners and Council Members are also elected for 4-year terms

Comparing Executive Authority at the Local, State, and National Levels

At the national level, the head of the executive branch is the President. At the state level, it is the Governor. At the local level, the executive might be the county sheriff, mayor or city manager.

Similarities between the state and national executives: You have already read about some of the similarities and differences between the President and Governor. Both are elected by voters for fixed terms of office (in the case of the President, through the Electoral College); both enforce the law; both serve as the commanders of armed forces; both can veto proposed legislation; both have pardoning powers; both are in charge of a large number of administrative agencies; and both are advised by a Cabinet.

Differences between the state and national executives: At the national level, the President selects all Cabinet members; in Florida, Cabinet members are elected officials. In Florida, the Governor can ask the Florida Supreme Court for advisory opinions on some matters. The greatest difference is that the President has **executive authority** over national matters, such as national defense, while the Governor has authority over matters of concern to the state, such as state highways, state employment opportunities, and public education.

Similarities and differences with local government: In county governments, an elected sheriff acts as an executive, in charge of law enforcement and preserving the peace. Some city governments have an elected mayor or appointed city manager who acts as executive. Like the President and Governor, the mayor enforces the law, carries out policies, proposes a budget for the government, makes appointments, and acts as the ceremonial head of government. Their **executive authority**, however, only extends over local matters. They may appoint a police chief, but they do not command a militia or military force.

For the EOC, you should know the types of services each level of government provides.

Government Obligations and Services at Three Levels

Our three levels of government—local, state and national—work together to provide services to their citizens. Each level of government has a **government obligation** (*requirement*) to provide particular services. Local governments provide **government services** to local residents, while state governments meet statewide needs. The national government promotes the general welfare of our nation as a whole. Sometimes the services offered by these different levels of government overlap.

National Government. Our national government provides services at the national level. These include maintaining the armed forces, controlling immigration into the United States, conducting relations with foreign countries, and regulating trade between the states. Our national government checks the quality of food and drugs sold in the United States to protect consumer safety. It also regulates banks and the stock market. The national government operates U.S. Post Offices, prints money, issues passports, and operates U.S. embassies in other countries. It collects taxes and pays social security benefits, Medicare and Medicaid. In cases of natural disaster such as hurricanes, the national government provides emergency relief. Its courts enforce federal laws and protect the constitutional rights of U.S. citizens. Its prisons hold criminals who have broken federal laws.

State Government. The state government of Florida protects the lives and property of Florida citizens. It provides necessary statewide services, works to improve the state's economy, and promotes the general welfare of the people of Florida.

Florida's state government regulates business, industry, and insurance in the state. It establishes licensing requirements for professions (doctors, lawyers, nurses, and teachers). It maintains state highways and enforces statewide rules for safe driving. The state government issues driving licenses, marriage licenses, hunting licenses and fishing licenses. It regulates utilities in the state such as electricity and natural gas; establishes statewide building codes; sets statewide education requirements; and supervises public education across the state. The state government establishes standards for hospitals and public health; looks after the special needs of veterans, disabled workers, and the elderly in Florida; operates state parks; and performs other vital services that affect all Floridians.

Local Government. Florida's county and municipal governments provide services to their residents. They run the public schools. They provide police and fire protection. They provide garbage collection and recycling. They make local zoning decisions (*how property can be used in an area*), enforce state building codes, and issue building permits to allow new construction. Local governments build and maintain local roads and bridges. In some places, local governments provide forms of public transportation, such as buses or trolleys. They provide local health care; issue business licenses; license and inspect local restaurants; operate local parks and beaches; and record births, marriages, divorces and deaths. What all these services have in common is that they concern citizens in a smaller area than services provided by the state or national government.

Overlapping Services. When the powers of the national government and state governments are concurrent, their services can sometimes overlap.

- National, state and local governments each offer their own court systems for the administration of justice.
- National, state and local governments provide their own forms of law enforcement. The national government has the FBI, Florida has its own Department of Law Enforcement, and many counties and municipalities have their own police departments.
- National, state and local governments maintain their own parks and recreation areas. The national government has the National Park Service, Florida has its own state parks, and many counties and municipalities have their own local parks and recreation areas.

Services Typically Provided by Local Governments

- Building and maintaining local roads and bridges
- Law enforcement
- Fire protection
- Regulating local business and industry/ issuing business licenses
- Zoning and building permits
- Regulating utilities (electricity, gas, water)
- Garbage collection/sanitation
- Collecting property and sales taxes
- Supervising elections
- Operating public schools
- Maintaining public libraries
- Managing local parks and recreation areas
- Keeping public records: births, marriages, divorces, deaths

The Active Citizen

Which level of government would be primarily responsible for providing this service?

	Local	State	National
Defending American ships attacked overseas in neutral waters	☐	☐	☐
Providing summer school programs for middle school students in your town	☐	☐	☐
Negotiating changes to trade agreements with Mexico	☐	☐	☐
Setting health and safety standards for amusement parks throughout Florida	☐	☐	☐
Building a new town hall	☐	☐	☐
Repairing a state highway that crosses several counties	☐	☐	☐
Building a new firehouse for a major city	☐	☐	☐
Introducing a new recycling program to accompany local garbage collection	☐	☐	☐
Establishing new civics requirements for all Florida middle school students	☐	☐	☐
Introducing a zoning ordinance that creates a new shopping district in your town	☐	☐	☐
Making rules for banks with branches in several states	☐	☐	☐
Setting rules for visitors to Everglades National Park	☐	☐	☐
Issuing driving licenses to residents of Florida	☐	☐	☐

Compare and contrast executive authority at the national, state and local levels by describing the executive branch at each level on the chart and answering the questions below. (Use details from this chapter and Chapter 7.)

National	State	Local
President of the United States	Governor of Florida	County Sheriff/ Mayor/ City Manager/

What similarities do you see? ______________________________

____

What differences to you see? ______________________________

____

Name ______________________________

In this chapter you learned about the system of federalism: how our local, state and national governments have both different and overlapping powers and responsibilities. Complete the chart below by showing the obligations of each level of government and some of the services it provides.

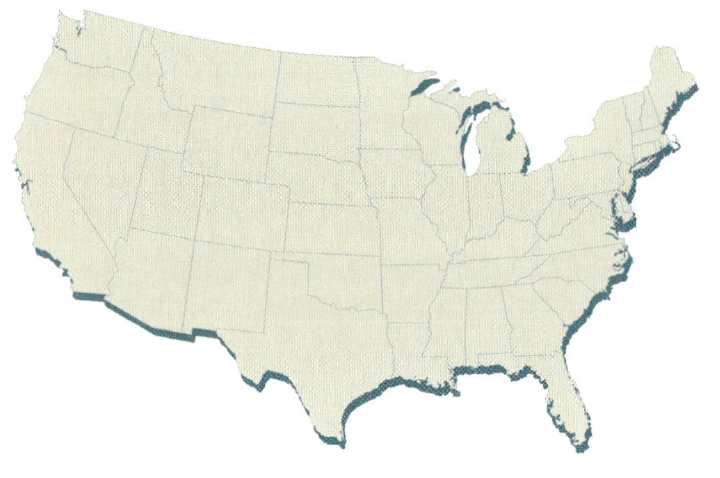

Obligations and services of the national government

____

____

____

____

____

____

____

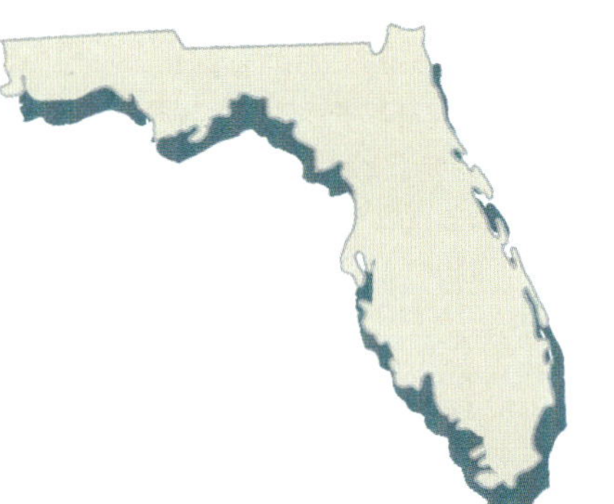

Obligations and services of Florida's state government

____

____

____

____

____

____

Obligations and services of your local government

____

____

____

____

____

____

Federalism: National, State, and Local Governments

Federalism

- Division of power between national and state governments
- Types of powers
  - **Enumerated** or **delegated powers** held by national government
  - **Reserved powers** (left to the states)—**10th Amendment**
  - **Concurrent powers** (shared by federal and state)
- **Supremacy Clause**—federal laws are superior to state laws
- **Article IV** defines relations with states—states must recognize court judgments and legal acts of other states; guarantees republican government in states.

Obligations and Services of Governments

- National government meets national needs, such as defense and foreign policy
- State governments meet statewide needs, such as setting state educational requirements
- Local governments meet local concerns, such as running a local school district

Comparing Levels of Government

- Lawmaking processes
- Executive authority
- Lawmakers' qualifications and terms

The U.S. Constitution vs. Florida Constitution

Both have a preamble, articles and amendments

U.S. Constitution

- Preamble: "We the People"; purposes of government
- Government of 3 branches:
  - Congress
  - President and Vice President
    Appointed Cabinet (not in Constitution)
  - Federal Courts: 3 levels

Florida Constitution

- Preamble: "We the People of Florida"; purposes of government
- Florida Declaration of Rights (like Bill of Rights)
- State Government of 3 branches:
  - Governor and Lt. Governor (at least 30 years old and lived in Florida past 7 yrs)
  - Elected Cabinet
  - Florida State Legislature (members must be 21 years old and lived in Florida for 2 years)
    Florida House of Representatives: up to 120 members
    Florida Senate: up to 40 members
  - Florida Courts: 4 levels

Local Governments in Florida

- **County Governments**
  Largest unit of local government; counties together cover the entire state; governed by a board of commissioners
- **Municipal Governments**
  Governed by mayor and a council or commission; sometimes has city manager

- Local legislative bodies have only one "house"; laws are discussed and passed by a majority of the board or council
- A sheriff, mayor or city manager often acts as a local executive, who enforces the laws.

Differences between Florida and U.S. Constitutions

- Elected Cabinet in Florida
- No state income tax in Florida
- English is the official language in Florida
- Florida Constitution is easier to amend
  - 5 ways to propose amendment
  - 60% of voters must approve for adoption
- Florida Constitution is more detailed than the U.S. Constitution

Review Cards: Federalism—Federal, State and Local Governments Acting Together

Division of Power between the National and State Governments

Federalism = Division of power between the national government and the state governments.

Enumerated powers = The powers granted to the national government and listed in Article I, Section 8 of the Constitution. Also known as the **delegated powers**.

Examples: power to declare war; power to regulate interstate commerce; power to coin money

Reserved powers = The powers held back from the national government and reserved for the state governments. The **10th Amendment** specifically states that these powers are "reserved" for the states and the people.

Examples: power to establish local government; power to provide statewide public education

Concurrent powers = The powers shared by the national and state governments. Both can exercise these powers.

Examples: power to tax; power to borrow money

Supremacy Clause (Article VI of the Constitution) = states that whenever there is a conflict between federal and state law, the federal law is supreme (*the highest authority*): federal law is the **"supreme law of the land"**.

Article IV of the Constitution deals with the states. States must honor the court judgements and legal acts of other states ("Full Faith and Credit" Clause). The national government guarantees the "republican form of government" and pledges to protect the states from invasion.

A Comparison of the Florida Constitution and the U.S. Constitution

Similarities

1. Both constitutions have a **preamble** (*introduction*), **articles** (*main sections dealing with different parts or features of the government*) and **amendments** (*later changes*). Both constitutions recognize the people as the source of all government power. This is stated in their preambles and in Article I of the Florida Constitution: "All political power is inherent in the people." Both Preambles also identify the purposes of the government they establish.
2. Both constitutions state that all people are equal before the law and have inalienable rights.
3. The **Florida Declaration of Rights**, found in the first article of the Florida Constitution, echoes the U.S. Bill of Rights.
4. Ties between the two constitutions are so close that the Florida Constitution adopts several standards from the U.S. Constitution by reference.
5. Both Constitutions establish similar government structures with three branches.
6. Both the Florida Legislature and the U.S. Congress have two houses: the Senate and House of Representatives.
7. Both the U.S. President and the Florida **Governor** are chief executives, who serve as Commanders in Chief of their armed forces, are assisted by a Cabinet, hold veto power, and have the right to pardon. Each executive oversees a great number of departments.
8. Both the federal and state judicial branches have several levels. Both have a supreme court, appellate courts, and trial courts.

A Comparison of the Florida Constitution and the U.S. Constitution

Differences

1. The U.S. Constitution and the federal government it created address national concerns, such as foreign affairs, while the Florida Constitution and state government focus on matters specific to Florida, such as elections and voting, state finances and taxation, local government and public education. Like most state constitutions, the Florida Constitution is more detailed than the U.S. Constitution.
2. The Florida Constitution has some provisions that are not found in the U.S. Constitution, such as identifying English as the official language, prohibiting state income taxes, having elected Cabinet officials, and providing a taxpayer's bill of rights.
3. The **Amendment Process**: Amending the Florida Constitution is easier than amending the U.S. Constitution. There are five ways to introduce an amendment to the Florida Constitution and only a 60% majority of voters is needed for ratification. At the national level, three-fourths of the states must approve for ratification. The U.S. Constitution has been amended fewer than 30 times; the Florida Constitution has been amended hundreds of times.

State Government in Florida

Legislative branch: **Florida State Legislature** with House of Representatives and Senate.

Qualifications to be a **State legislator:** (1) be at least 21 years old; (2) have been in Florida for two years; and (3) live in the district represented.

Lawmaking process: The steps for a bill to pass through the Florida State Legislature are similar to a bill passing through Congress: the bill goes into committee; if approved it is debated and put to a vote on the floor of the house; goes to the other house and a conference committee; the bill goes to the Governor who signs or vetoes it; the legislature can override a veto with 2/3 of each house.

Executive branch: The **Governor** serves as Florida's executive. The Governor enforces the laws, meets with the Cabinet, represents the state in ceremonies, commands the state militia, and can veto bills and issue pardons.

Qualifications to be Governor: (1) be at least 30 years old; (2) have lived in Florida for the 7 years before the election.

Local Governments in Florida

Local governments make decisions that affect local residents, such as operating schools, parks, libraries, and fire and police departments. There are two main kinds of local governments in Florida:

1. **County Governments**

   Florida has 67 counties. Citizens in each county elect a sheriff, tax collector, and other officials. They also elect **county commissioners** to serve as members of the county board of commissioners, which make laws—known as **ordinances**—for the county. Unlike lawmaking at the state and national levels, these lawmaking bodies usually have just one "house."

2. **Municipal Governments**

   These are cities, towns, and villages that set up their own local government. Voters in a town or city may elect a chief executive, known as the **mayor**, who is assisted by a city council or city commission. **Council members** and **city commissioners** are elected officials. In some municipalities, the city council or city commission appoints a city manager to head the city administration. The city council or commission acts as a local legislature and passes local laws, known as ordinances.

   Comparing Executive Authority: The mayor or city manager acts as an executive, enforcing local laws similar to the executives at the national and state levels. However mayors, city managers and sheriffs do not command an army, conduct foreign relations, or appoint judges like the President or Governor.

   Comparing Lawmakers: Local, state and national lawmakers are elected to fixed terms in office. Term lengths and qualifications for office differ. U.S. Senators must be at least 30 years old and are elected for 6-year terms; U.S. Representatives must be at least 25 years old and are elected for 2-year terms; Florida State Legislators must be at least 21 years old and are elected for 2- or 4-year terms. Terms of local officials vary and are set by local charters or laws.

Government Obligations and Services

Each level of our government has a **government obligation** (*responsibility*) to provide particular **government services**:

National Government

Our national government handles national issues, such as national defense, foreign policy, and regulation of the the American economy. Federal courts protect the rights of citizens guaranteed by the Constitution and the Bill of Rights, and interpret federal law.

State Government

Florida's state government regulates state businesses and insurance, licenses professionals (such as teachers, lawyers and doctors), builds and maintains state highways, issues and enforces rules for traffic safety, licenses drivers, regulates state utilities, and creates building construction codes. It also sets the rules for the state's public education system and regulates conservation, pollution, and public health throughout the state.

Local Government

Florida's local governments address the daily local needs of their people, such as operating their public school districts, managing local police and fire departments, and overseeing local sewage and garbage disposal.

What Do You Know?

SS.7.CG.3.4

1. Which is an example of a reserved power?

   A. the power to collect taxes
   B. the power to establish post offices
   C. the power to educate young citizens
   D. the power to declare war on foreign enemies

SS.7.CG.3.12

2. How does the process for amending the Constitution of Florida compare to that of amending the U.S. Constitution?

   A. It is more difficult to amend the Florida Constitution than to amend the U.S. Constitution.
   B. It is more difficult to amend the U.S. Constitution than to amend the Florida Constitution.
   C. The Florida Constitution and the U.S. Constitution follow the exact same procedures for amendment.
   D. The U.S. Constitution requires two steps for amendment, while the Florida Constitution can be amended in just a single step.

SS.7.CG.3.7

3. What is a law passed by a Florida county or municipality called?

   A. an act
   B. a statute
   C. a precedent
   D. an ordinance

SS.7.CG.3.13

4. Which is an obligation owed by local governments to their citizens?

   A. the operation of public school districts
   B. the establishment of statewide curricular requirements
   C. the provision of professional certification requirements for teachers
   D. the setting of national economic policies to promote full employment

SS.7.CG.3.13

5. The table below identifies services provided by different levels of government.

Level of Government	National	State	Local
Service Provided	Provides for the country's defense	?	Operates public school districts

Which completes the diagram?

A. Enforces local building codes
B. Operates police and fire departments
C. Conducts diplomacy with foreign leaders
D. Establishes high school graduation requirements

SS.7.CG.3.12

6. Which statement identifies a basic similarity between the U.S. and Florida Constitutions?

   A. Both have a preamble, articles and amendments.
   B. Both prohibit the collection of personal income taxes.
   C. Both provide details on the qualifications for voting in elections.
   D. Both have detailed provisions on public education and local government.

SS.7.CG.3.8

7. What is one way that the government of the State of Florida differs from the national government?

   A. Florida judges hold their positions with lifetime appointments.
   B. Members of the Cabinet in Florida also sit in the state legislature.
   C. Several Cabinet members in Florida are elected rather than appointed.
   D. Unlike the Vice President of the United States, the Lieutenant Governor of Florida is appointed.

SS.7.CG.3.4

8. What is guaranteed by the "Supremacy Clause" of the U.S. Constitution?

   A. the supremacy of federal over state law
   B. the supremacy of individual rights over government power
   C. the supremacy of Congress over the President
   D. the supremacy of the people over their government

SS.7.CG.3.8

9. The diagram below shows several steps in how a bill becomes a law in Florida.

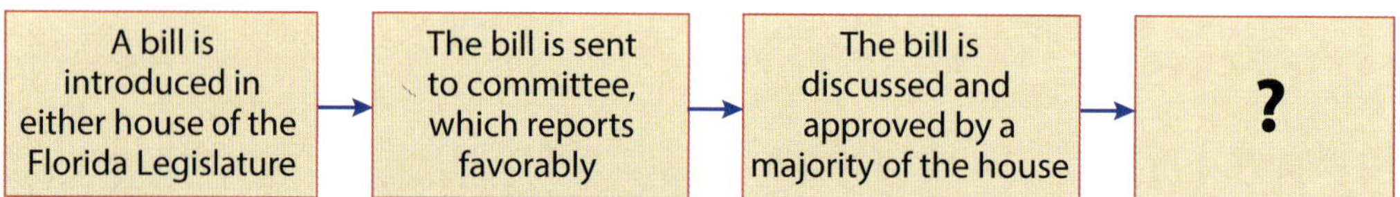

   What is the next step in this process?

   A. The bill is sent to a conference committee.
   B. The bill is sent to the Governor for approval.
   C. Two thirds of both houses need to support the bill.
   D. The bill is sent to the other house of the legislature.

SS.7.CG.3.4

10. Based on the 10th Amendment to the U.S. Constitution, which powers are reserved for state governments or individual citizens?

   A. all powers needed to conduct U.S. foreign policy
   B. all powers needed by Congress to carry out its enumerated powers
   C. all powers not delegated to the national government by the Constitution
   D. all powers needed to prevent corruption and abuse by the national government

SS.7.CG.3.4

11. How does the system of federalism limit the power of the national government?

    A. by guaranteeing citizens their individual rights

    B. by making federal law the "supreme law of the land"

    C. by reserving some of the powers of government to the states

    D. by separating the powers of government between three branches

SS.7.CG.3.7

12. Which identifies an important similarity between local mayors in Florida, Florida state legislators, and U.S. Congressmen and Congresswomen from Florida?

    A. They have term limits for how long they can serve.

    B. They must reside in the area they are representing.

    C. They must meet special age qualifications for the offices they hold.

    D. They must meet qualifications established by the Florida or U.S. Constitution.

SS.7.CG.3.12

13. Which goal identifies one of the main purposes of a constitution?

    A. to limit government authority

    B. to raise money for government officials

    C. to make it more difficult to pass new laws

    D. to prevent citizens from interfering with the government

SS.7.CG.3.13

14. Use the chart below to answer Questions 14 and 15.

Levels of Government		
I U.S Government	II Government of the State of Florida	III County and Municipal Governments

Which governments provide garbage collection services to homes and businesses?

A. I only

B. I and II

C. III only

D. I, II, and III

SS.7.CG.3.13

15. Which levels of government establish and implement educational requirements for minors?

    A. I only

    B. I and II

    C. II and III

    D. I, II, and III

SS.7.CG.3.4

16. What do enumerated and concurrent powers have in common?

A. They are both types of powers that the national government can exercise.

B. They are both types of powers that are reserved for the state governments.

C. They are both powers that are implied from the "Necessary and Proper" Clause.

D. They are both powers that were added to the Constitution by later amendments.

SS.7.CG.3.8

17. How are a local mayor, a state governor and the President of the United States similar?

A. Each decides the constitutionality of laws.

B. Each makes the laws for an entire community.

C. Each leads an executive branch of government.

D. Each acts as commander in chief of the armed forces.

SS.7.CG.3.7

18. How are the lawmaking processes of the Florida State Legislature and the U.S. Congress similar?

A. Bills are usually approved on the floor of the house without going to a committee.

B. Bills have to be approved by both houses of the legislature before they can become law.

C. Members of the public can introduce bills directly in the House of Representatives but not in the Senate.

D. The head of the executive branch can ask the Supreme Court for an advisory opinion on the constitutionality of a proposed law.

SS.7.CG.3.12

19. Which provision is found in the Florida Constitution but not the United States Constitution?

A. English is the official language.

B. The people are the source of government authority.

C. The executive branch can veto bills passed by the legislature.

D. The powers of government are separated into three branches.

CHAPTER 13

The Obligations, Responsibilities, and Rights of Citizens

SS.7.CG.2.1 Define the term "citizen," and explain the constitutional means of becoming a U.S. citizen.

SS.7.CG.2.2 Differentiate between obligations and responsibilities of U.S. citizenship, and evaluate their impact on society.

Content Focus Vocabulary in This Chapter

- Citizen
- Citizenship
- U.S. citizen
- 14th Amendment
- Constitutional means
- Naturalized citizen
- Naturalization process
- Impact of the naturalization process
- Immigrant
- Law of Blood
- Law of Soil
- Permanent residency
- Obligations (*duties*) of U.S. citizenship
- Obey the law
- Pay taxes
- Jury service
- Selective Service
- Responsibilities of U.S. citizenship
- Active participation
- Attending civic meetings
- Voting
- Running for office
- Petitioning government
- Political process
- Common good

Florida "Keys" to Learning

1. A **citizen** is a legally recognized member of a country. **Citizenship** (*membership as a citizen*) brings both rights and responsibilities.

2. A **U.S. citizen** is a legally recognized member of the United States. The **14th Amendment** defines who is a citizen. U.S. citizenship is obtained through two **constitutional means** (*ways according to the Constitution*): by birth or by becoming a citizen through the **naturalization process** (*process of becoming a citizen*).

3. U.S. citizenship is obtained at birth either by the "**Law of Soil**" or the "**Law of Blood**." The "Law of Soil" is that any child born on American soil automatically becomes an American citizen. The "Law of Blood" is that if a child is born in another country and both his or her parents are American citizens, the child is also an American citizen.

4. **Impact of the naturalization process**: This process is the way in which someone who does not have U.S. citizenship at birth can become a U.S. citizen. To become a **naturalized citizen**, a person must be lawfully admitted to the United States, become a permanent resident, reside in the United States for five years, take a citizenship test, be of good character, and swear an oath of allegiance to the United States.

5. The **naturalization process** affects American society, government and the **political process** (*how people participate in government*). **Immigrants** to the United States (*those who come here to live*) see the possibility of becoming full citizens in future. This encourages people to come and share their knowledge and skills. They later contribute as citizens by voting and by serving in government.

6. A person does not need to become a citizen to live and work lawfully in the United States. Many people from other countries living in the United States are lawful **permanent residents**. Their permanent residence permit is sometimes known as a "green card."

7. American citizens have obligations and responsibilities as well as rights. The **obligations (*duties*) of U.S. citizenship** are the things that citizens *must* do. These obligations are to **obey the law, pay taxes, serve on a jury** if summoned, and register with the **Selective Service** (if male and aged 18–25) in order to defend the nation if called on. Our society and government depend on citizens performing these obligations.

8. American citizens also have responsibilities. These are things they *should* do to make our democratic system effective. Citizens fulfill these responsibilities to promote the **common good** (*the good or benefit of the community*). Examples of the **responsibilities of U.S. citizenship** include **attending civic meetings** (*meetings of citizens held for a public purpose*), **voting, petitioning government** (*writing to government officials, agencies or legislators asking for changes to be made*), and **running for office** (*seek election to a government office*). These are all forms of **active participation** (*participating in government or the political process*).

9. Citizens have rights as well as obligations and responsibilities. All people in the United States have rights guaranteed in the Constitution. These include the individual rights guaranteed by the Bill of Rights. (See Chapter 10 for these rights.)

10. Having U.S. citizenship provides some additional rights. The most important rights held exclusively by U.S. citizens are the right to vote and the right to run for political office. These are rights as well as responsibilities. Other benefits of U.S. citizenship include the right to carry a U.S. passport, the ability to serve on a jury, a preference in bringing relatives into the United States, and the ability to hold many government jobs.

In the introduction to this book, you learned what a "citizen" is: a legally recognized member of a nation like the United States. Such citizenship (*membership as a citizen*) brings with it obligations, responsibilities and rights.

After the Civil War, leaders in Congress wanted to make it clear that all Americans—including the freed slaves—were U.S. citizens with the same rights as other citizens. This principle was established by the 14th Amendment:

> *"All persons born or naturalized in the United States, and subject to the jurisdiction thereof, are citizens of the United States and of the State wherein they reside."*

This Amendment made it clear that there were actually two constitutional means of becoming a U.S citizen: (1) by birth; or (2) by becoming a citizen through the naturalization process.

You should know that people can have U.S. citizenship at birth or through naturalization.

American Citizenship

Citizenship at Birth

In fact, there are two ways to become an American citizen at birth. They are based on where you are born and who your parents are.

- The "Law of Soil": Any person born on American soil is automatically an American citizen.

This amendment also overturned the earlier ruling of the Supreme Court in *Dred Scott v. Sandford.* Dred Scott was born in the United States and therefore was a citizen.

- The "Law of Blood": A baby born in another country is an American citizen at birth if (1) both parents are American citizens and one parent lived at some time in the United States, or (2) one parent is an American citizen who has lived at least one year continuously in the United States. If the father but not the mother is an American citizen and the parents are ***not*** married, special rules will apply. For the child to qualify for U.S. citizenship, the father has to provide convincing evidence of fatherhood.

Enrichment

The Active Citizen

Here is a part of the current law, passed by Congress, on citizenship at birth:

"The following shall be nationals and citizens of the United States at birth:

(a) a person born in the United States, and subject to the jurisdiction thereof;

(b) a person born in the United States to a member of an Indian, Eskimo, Aleutian, or other aboriginal tribe . . .

Continues ▶

(c) a person born outside of the United States . . . of parents both of whom are citizens of the United States and one of whom has had a residence in the United States . . . , prior to the birth of such person;

(d) a person born outside of the United States . . . of parents, one of whom is a citizen of the United States who has been physically present in the United States . . . for a continuous period of one year prior to the birth of such person, and the other of whom is a national, but not a citizen of the United States . . ."

—8 U.S. Code §1401

- Sandra's father works for a large company with offices all around the world. Sandra was born while her parents were living in Costa Rica for more than a year. Her father is a U.S. citizen, but her mother is from Costa Rica and is not a U.S. citizen. Her father grew up overseas and has never actually lived one year continuously in the United States. However, her American grandmother came to Costa Rica when Sandra was born. Sandra's parents are married. Based on these facts and the law above, was Sandra a U.S. citizen at birth? Explain your answer.
- James was born overseas while his parents were visiting his father's parents in Morocco. Both of James' parents were born overseas, but became naturalized American citizens before James was born. Was James an American citizen at birth? Explain your answer.
- Maria lives in Mexico. Both her parents are Mexican. Maria is a Mexican citizen. She was born in an American hospital while her parents were on a short vacation in San Diego, California. Was Maria an American citizen at birth? Explain your answer.

Be sure to know the steps of the naturalization process.

The Naturalization Process

The **Fourteenth Amendment** provides a second **constitutional means** of becoming a U.S, citizen: the **naturalization process**. This is the process by which an immigrant (*a person who comes to the United States with an intent to stay*) becomes a U.S. citizen. Those who acquire citizenship through this process are known as "**naturalized citizens**."

The Constitution gives Congress the power to regulate the naturalization process. To apply for naturalization, a resident alien (a foreign-born person) must be at least 18 years old, be a lawful permanent resident, have lived in the United States for five years, be of "good character," and know basic English. The candidate must complete an N-400 application form and submit the form with accompanying documents (such as a "green card" and two photographs). If the application is approved, the candidate is interviewed by the U.S. Citizenship and Immigration Services. At the interview, the candidate is given a brief oral test on American history and government. If the applicant knows enough English and passes the test, he or she can attend a naturalization ceremony to swear an oath of allegiance to the United States and become a U.S. citizen. (Older permanent residents who have been in the United States a long time may be exempt from the test.)

A person does not need to become a citizen to lawfully live and work in the United States. Many foreign nationals—known as "aliens"—are lawful permanent residents. This means they have been legally admitted into the United States and have **permanent residency**—permission to stay and work here. Their lawful permanent residence card is sometimes known as a "green card" because of its green color. Lawful permanent residents have many rights. They have the right to live and work in the United States. They have the right to become certified in professions like teaching and law. They generally have the right to leave and re-enter the United States. Having **permanent residency** is an important step in the path towards citizenship. It demonstrates that the applicant is responsible and reliable.

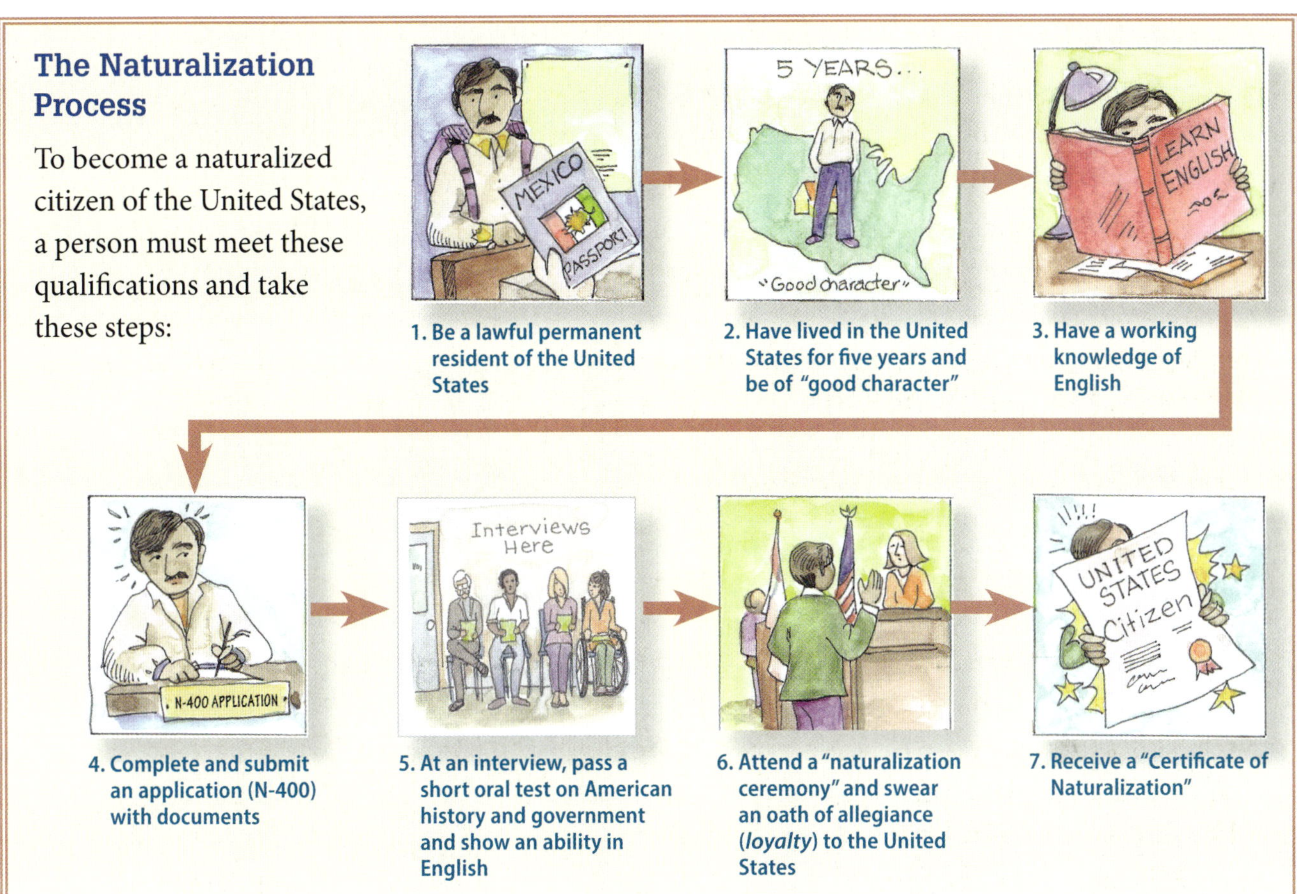

1. Be a lawful permanent resident of the United States

2. Have lived in the United States for five years and be of "good character"

3. Have a working knowledge of English

4. Complete and submit an application (N-400) with documents

5. At an interview, pass a short oral test on American history and government and show an ability in English

6. Attend a "naturalization ceremony" and swear an oath of allegiance (*loyalty*) to the United States

7. Receive a "Certificate of Naturalization"

The Impact of the Naturalization Process

The **naturalization process** has had an important impact on American society, government and the political process. It has meant that people arriving in the United States have the possibility of becoming citizens—full and equal partners in American society. They are not forced into becoming a separate group without the same rights as other members of society. It has meant that immigrants have a chance to contribute their talents and skills to selecting leaders as voters, to running for office and providing to government service, and to enhancing American society as a whole. The fact that immigrants can become fully integrated into American society makes the United States very attractive to newcomers, who bring knowledge and skills. Finally, the arrival of so many people from foreign lands—with their own foods, languages, customs, and ideas—has greatly enriched American culture.

For the EOC, you should know the difference between the obligations and responsibilities of citizenship.

The Obligations (*duties*) of U.S. Citizenship

American citizens have **obligations** (*duties*) as well as rights. These obligations are things that all citizens ***must*** do. Citizens can be fined or even imprisoned if they fail to meet the obligations of citizenship.

The Obligations of Citizenship: the "Musts" of Citizenship

- Obey the law.
- Pay taxes.
- Register with the Selective Service and defend the nation if called upon.
- Serve on a jury if summoned.

Obey the Law

Not only citizens but visitors to the United States and permanent residents must all **obey the law**.

Pay Taxes

Citizens must **pay taxes** to support government services. Visitors and residents also pay taxes if they buy goods or earn income here.

Defend the Nation

In times of war, all citizens are required to help defend the nation. Even in peacetime, all males living in the United States must register with the **Selective Service** system once they reach the age of 18 years old. This applies to both residents and citizens.

The purpose of the Selective Service System is to help defend the United States. The Selective Service keeps the names and addresses of registrants on file in case the United States ever needs to re-establish conscription (*compulsory military service*)—also known as the "draft." During the Civil War, World War I, World War II, the Korean War and the War in Vietnam, young men were required to serve in the military.

If you are a man age 18 through 25 and living in the U.S., then you must register with Selective Service. It's the law. According to law, a man must register with Selective Service within 30 days of his 18th birthday. Selective Service will accept late registrations but not after a man has reached age 26. You may be denied benefits or a job if you have not registered. You can register at any U.S. Post Office and do not need a social security number.

Not all draft-age men were needed in every year of every war. The task of Selective Service was to select those men who would be required to serve. Typically, the Selective Service drew the days of the year at random and assigned each day a number. Those numbers determined the order in which eligible men were called up each year for military service.

The first lottery drawing for the War in Vietnam was in December 1969.

The last "draft" ended in January 1973. Since that time, the United States has had an all-volunteer military force. Citizens volunteer to serve in the armed forces out of patriotism (*love of country*) and to obtain the many benefits of military service—good pay, physical and vocational training, work experience, funding for future education, health benefits, and opportunities for travel. Of course, there is also hard work associated with a tour of military duty and the risk of injury or even loss of life in combat.

Although the draft has ended, all draft-age males living in America must still register with the Selective Service System in case the United States ever needs to draft its young men to help defend the nation again.

Serve on Juries

Only citizens are asked to **serve on juries**. For jury service, a court will usually choose names by lot (*at random*) from a list of licensed drivers and those with Florida identification cards who live in the

area. Courts have the power to summon individuals to appear before them. Potential jurors are sent a jury summons. A "summons" is an order to appear in court. The summons tells the potential juror where and when (both day and time) to appear. The citizen receiving the summons can ask for a postponement or to be excused from jury duty, but must provide a valid reason to the court.

When potential jurors arrive at the courthouse, they become part of a juror pool. Only some of them will ever serve on a jury. The actual jurors for each case are chosen at random from members of the juror pool. Lawyers have the right to question these citizens before they are placed on a specific jury. The lawyers may "strike" (*eliminate*) a number of potential jurors without giving any reason. They can also eliminate jurors on the grounds of possible juror prejudice.

If selected to serve on a jury, citizens attend a trial. They hear and see witnesses and evidence. Then they discuss the evidence with other jurors to reach a verdict. Good citizens pay attention at trial and try to reach fair conclusions without bias or prejudice.

By serving on juries, citizens help protect our constitutional right to be tried by our peers (*equals*). In this case, it is easy to see how our rights and obligations are closely related. The Sixth Amendment guarantees us the benefit of a trial by jury, but our help is needed to serve as jurors for others if this right is to be effective.

For the EOC, be sure to know these responsibilities of citizenship.

The Responsibilities of U.S. Citizenship

In addition to the legal obligations (or duties) of citizenship, citizens have **responsibilities** that are not enforced by penalties. These are things citizens ***should*** do. All of these are forms of **active participation** (*participating in government and the political process*). They are ways of being an active citizen.

If ordinary citizens do not devote some of their time to public affairs, democracy simply cannot work. Passive citizenship cannot ensure the success of our democratic system of government. Our system depends on the willingness of its citizens to perform their responsibilities as well as their legal obligations.

Be Informed. To influence public policy and to make wise decisions when voting, citizens need to be informed. They should read or listen to reliable sources of information—such as books, newspapers and news magazines, radio, television, and the Internet.

Voting. Democracy depends on citizens carefully choosing their own representatives. Good citizens therefore exercise their right to vote both by being informed and by **voting** in every election. When they cannot be at home on the day of an election, they send in an absentee ballot in advance. These are special ballots, usually sent by a voter by mail, when he or she cannot go in person to the polling place (*the place where voting takes place*) to vote on "Election Day" (*the day of the election*). You will learn more about elections in the next chapter.

Runing for Office. Good citizens join political parties and may even run for public office themselves. **Running for office** gives citizens a chance to share their views with a wider audience. You will learn more about elections and political parties in the next chapter.

Attending Civic Meetings. Another responsibility of citizenship is **attending civic meetings**—both to remain informed and to provide their views to government leaders who must make decisions. A civic meeting is a group of citizens meeting for a public purpose, such as informing the public or giving citizens a chance to express their views to public officials. These could be public meetings of the local school board, deciding which programs to fund; or public meetings of the town planning commission, deciding where to build a new road; or "town hall meetings" called by a member of the state legislature or Congress, who is trying to sound out local opinion on future legislation.

Petition the government. Citizens have the right to **petition government**. A petition is a formal written request to government officials to make some change. Usually a petition addresses a single issue. Most petitions are addressed to legislators—such as the members of the Congress. Petitions often include the signatures of other citizens who agree with the request. It takes time and effort to write a petition and obtain signatures. Good citizens are willing to make this effort to let their representatives know how they would like their government to act on important issues.

Volunteer. Finally, good citizens will volunteer from time to time on local projects for the good of the community—such as cleaning up local roads on a special "pick-up litter" day, working in a local school library, reading to elderly citizens at a local community center, or serving on a student or parent committee that is making recommendations to the local school board.

The aim of all of these forms of **civic participation** is to promote the "**common good**"—simply, what is good for the community as a whole.

The Impact on Government and Society

By meeting our citizenship obligations and responsibilities, we make it possible for our government and society to work. Just imagine the consequences if we failed to fulfill these:

- Our government could not provide safety and order if people refused to obey the law.
- Our government could not provide services if people refused to pay taxes.
- We could have no jury trials if citizens refused to serve on juries.
- Our nation could not be defended if citizens refused to serve in the armed forces when required.
- Our leaders could not know the opinions of the public if all citizens refused to attend civic meetings or petition government.
- Our government could not have elected leaders if all citizens refused to vote or run for office.

The Active Citizen

How important would you rate each of these obligations and responsibilities of citizenship?

	Not important	Important	Very important
Obeying the law	☐	☐	☐
Justify your evaluation ______			
Paying taxes	☐	☐	☐
Justify your evaluation ______			
Defending the nation	☐	☐	☐
Justify your evaluation ______			
Serving on a jury	☐	☐	☐
Justify your evaluation ______			
Voting in elections	☐	☐	☐
Justify your evaluation ______			
Attending civic meetings	☐	☐	☐
Justify your evaluation ______			
Petitioning the government	☐	☐	☐
Justify your evaluation ______			
Running for office	☐	☐	☐
Justify your evaluation ______			

The Active Citizen

Enrichment

Select one local issue or one thing you would like to change in your community. Then write a letter expressing your views. Send your letter to a local newspaper, to your representatives in the Florida State Legislature, or to your member of Congress:

- First, think about the issue you would like to address. You might want to conduct some research to get details about the problem or situation you would like to change.
- Then think about the changes you would like to introduce. What evidence do you have that these changes would work? Can you explain why your ideas might help to solve the problem? Has your approach been used successfully elsewhere? Do you have the names of any experts who support your ideas? In writing your letter, be sure to introduce who you are, to describe the problem, to explain your solution, to provide evidence to support your ideas, and to conclude by showing how your solution will solve the problem. Then thank your reader.
- Next search the Internet to see what local newspapers might be interested in printing your letter. Search the Internet to find the names of local newspapers, or ask your school librarian.
- Then find the name of your representatives in the Florida House of Representatives, the Florida Senate, and Congress. Send each of them your letter.

The Rights of Citizenship

Citizenship brings rights as well as obligations and responsibilities. Some of these rights are shared with visitors and lawful permanent residents. Other rights, such as voting, belong exclusively (*only*) to citizens of the United States.

As you know, some of our individual rights, such as the right to petition for a writ of habeas corpus and not to be punished by an *ex post facto* law, were guaranteed in the text of the Constitution when it was first ratified. Other individual rights were added to the Constitution by the Bill of Rights in 1791. You have already studied these rights in Chapter 10. A summary of those important individual rights appears on the next page.

These rights belong not only to American citizens but to all individuals present in the United States—visitors, lawful permanent residents, and citizens.

There are other rights and privileges, however, enjoyed only by American citizens.

For Citizens Only: The Benefits of U.S. Citizenship

The most important rights held exclusively (*only*) by U.S. citizens are: (1) the right to vote; and (2) the right to hold political office. As you know, exercising these important rights is part of the responsibilities of citizenship.

In addition to these rights, only U.S. citizens have the right to carry a U.S. passport, to re-enter the United States after living abroad, and to serve on juries. Their children, even if born abroad, become U.S. citizens.

Most federal jobs and several other occupations also require U.S. citizenship. Only U.S. citizens, for example, can work in the U.S. Post Office. Lawful permanent residents are permitted to enlist in the armed services, but some positions in the U.S. military are only open to U.S. citizens.

A SUMMARY OF THE BILL OF RIGHTS

First Amendment	The right to freedom of speech, freedom of the press, freedom of religion, freedom of assembly, and freedom to petition the government.
Second Amendment	The right to bear arms.
Third Amendment	The right not to have troops quartered without permission in one's home in peacetime.
Fourth Amendment	No search or seizure (*arrest*) without a warrant or a reasonable exception.
Fifth Amendment	No "double jeopardy" (*being tried twice for the same crime*); no "self-incrimination" (*being forced to testify against ourself*); no taking away of "life, liberty or property" without "due process of law"; and no taking of property by eminent domain (*for "public use"*) without just compensation.
Sixth Amendment	The right to a speedy and public trial by an impartial jury for a criminal offense; the right to be informed of all criminal charges; the right to face and question witnesses; and the right to have legal counsel (*a lawyer*).
Seventh Amendment	The right to a trial by jury in some civil matters.
Eighth Amendment	No excessive bail; no excessive fines; and no "cruel and unusual punishments."
Ninth Amendment	People may have other, "unenumerated rights," which are not mentioned in the Constitution or the Bill of Rights. Just because individuals are given several specific rights does not mean that they do not also have other unlisted rights.
Tenth Amendment	Rights not given to the federal government are "reserved" for the states and the people.

The Exclusive Benefits of U.S. Citizenship

- Only U.S. citizens can vote in U.S elections or serve on juries.
- Only U.S. citizens can carry a U.S. passport.
- A U.S. citizen can never lose his or her right to reside in the United States.
- U.S. citizens have a priority over permanent residents when applying to bring family members to the United States.
- Only U.S. citizens can run for elective office in the federal government and most state and local government offices.
- Many federal government jobs and some state government jobs require U.S. citizenship.
- Many college financial aid programs are limited to U.S. citizens.
- Other government benefits may be open only to U.S. citizens.

The Active Citizen

Rights

Freedom to express yourself.

Freedom to worship as you wish.

Right to a prompt, fair trial by jury.

Right to vote in elections for public officials.

Right to apply for federal employment requiring U.S. citizenship.

Right to run for elected office.

Freedom to pursue "life, liberty, and the pursuit of happiness."

Obligations and Responsibilities

Support and defend the Constitution.

Stay informed of the issues affecting your community.

Participate in the democratic process (including voting and running for office).

Respect and obey federal, state, and local laws.

Respect the rights, beliefs, and opinions of others.

Participate in your local community.

Pay income and other taxes honestly, and on time, to federal, state, and local authorities.

Serve on a jury when called upon.

Defend the country if the need should arise.

The chart above was taken from the website of the U.S. Citizenship and Immigration Service. It has been changed slightly. It lists the rights, obligations and responsibilities of U.S. citizenship.

- Select one right and one obligation/responsibility that apply to both U.S. citizens and to lawful permanent residents. Explain each one.
- Select one right and one obligation/responsibility from the chart above that apply to U.S. citizens but ***not*** to lawful permanent residents. Explain each one.
- Imagine that you have a friend whose parents are lawful permanent residents. They have already lived in the United States for 12 years. Write a letter explaining the benefits of U.S. citizenship to them and outlining what they must do to become naturalized citizens.

Name ____

Look at each of the scenarios below. Then explain the obligations and responsibilities of a good citizen in each situation.

Scenario	What a Good Citizen Would Do
The United States is under attack. The President of the United States has asked Congress for a declaration of war. Congress has declared war and has authorized the Selective Service System to call up all men between the ages of 18 and 25 for military service.	
A resident of Alcoma in Polk County has received a jury summons from the County Circuit Court. However, this resident has an operation scheduled for eye surgery the same day that cannot be easily changed.	
Andrew and Rachel Jackson have received a notice from the Internal Revenue Service that they have made an error in last year's income taxes. The notice states that they owe an additional $3,345 to the federal government, as well as a $600 penalty.	
A young hospital worker has registered to vote but has not had time to study the issues closely. The Presidential election is this coming Tuesday.	
The town is holding a civic meeting to decide whether to allow property developers to build a new entertainment complex and residential development of single-family homes.	
The local middle school is looking for parent chaperones so that fifth graders can take their annual trip to watch state government in action in Tallahassee.	
Stan is on a jury that has already been deliberating for two days. He believes that the accused is innocent, but he is tired of the jury deliberations. If he changes his vote to convict the accused, he can leave for home in a few hours. Stan believes the accused will only have to serve six months in prison at most, if convicted.	
Nancy is driving home after a long day at work. She is at a red light that always seems to take a long time to change. She notices there is no traffic and there are no police cars or police officers in sight.	
There is a leaky fire hydrant in Mr. Smith's neighborhood. It seems to be wasting water, but nothing has been done to fix it for more than three weeks.	
Ms. Jamie disagrees strongly with recent cuts in school funding, which have caused her local high school to eliminate its art program. Ms. Jamie is a professional artist. She believes that students should have the opportunity to study art in high school. She argues that art is important, not only for art appreciation and the enjoyment of life, but also to develop vital skills in spatial reasoning needed for engineering, artificial intelligence, computer programming, physics, anatomy, medicine, graphic design, architecture, interior design, and fashion.	

Name ______________________________

Explaining the Naturalization Process

Can you explain the basic steps for becoming a naturalized citizen of the United States? Complete the chart below. First list the qualifications you need to be eligible for U.S. citizenship. Then identify and explain the steps you would have to take to become a naturalized citizen.

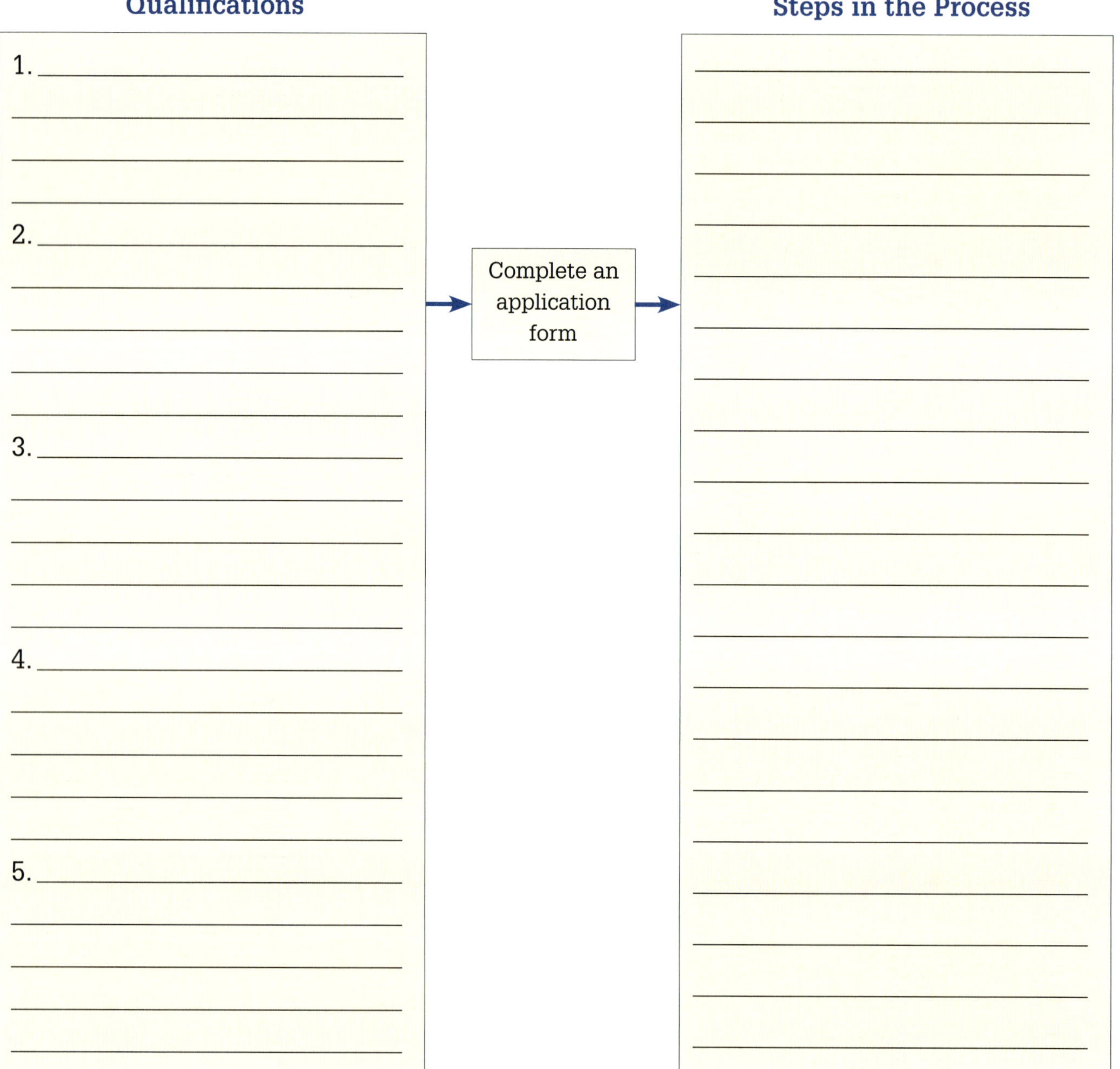

Name ____________________

Identify the terms and phrases in the concept circles below and explain how they fit together.

Five years residence

Permanent residency

History and Government Test

Oath of allegiance

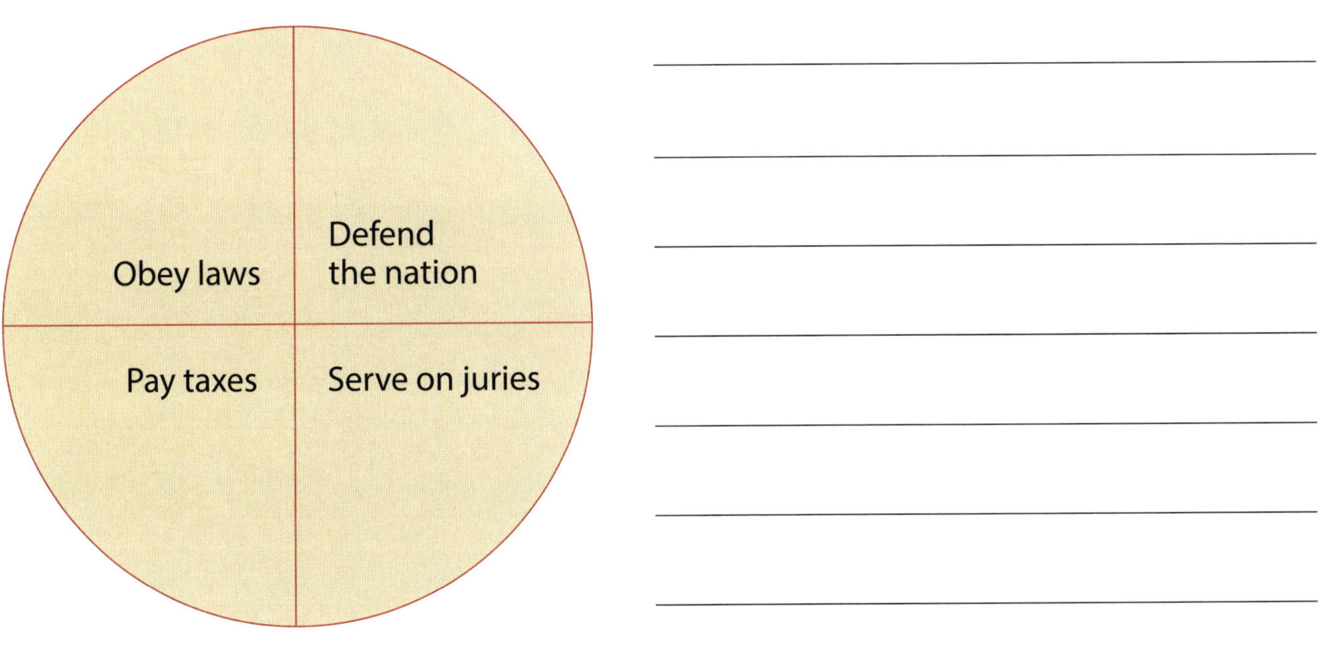

Name ______________________________

Identify the terms and phrases in the concept circles below and explain how they fit together.

Vote	Petition government
Run for public office	Attend civic meetings

Becoming a U.S. citizen	Obligations of U.S. citizenship
Responsibilities of U.S. citizens	Rights of U.S. citizens

Name ____

Imagine that you are making your own comic strip to explain the obligations, responsibilities and rights of U.S. citizenship to elementary school children. You can include captions, characters and speech bubbles in your comic strip.

In these panels, make your comic strip explaining the obligations of U.S. citizenship:

In these panels, make your comic strip explaining the responsibilities of U.S. citizenship:

In these panels, make your comic strip explaining the rights of U.S. citizenship:

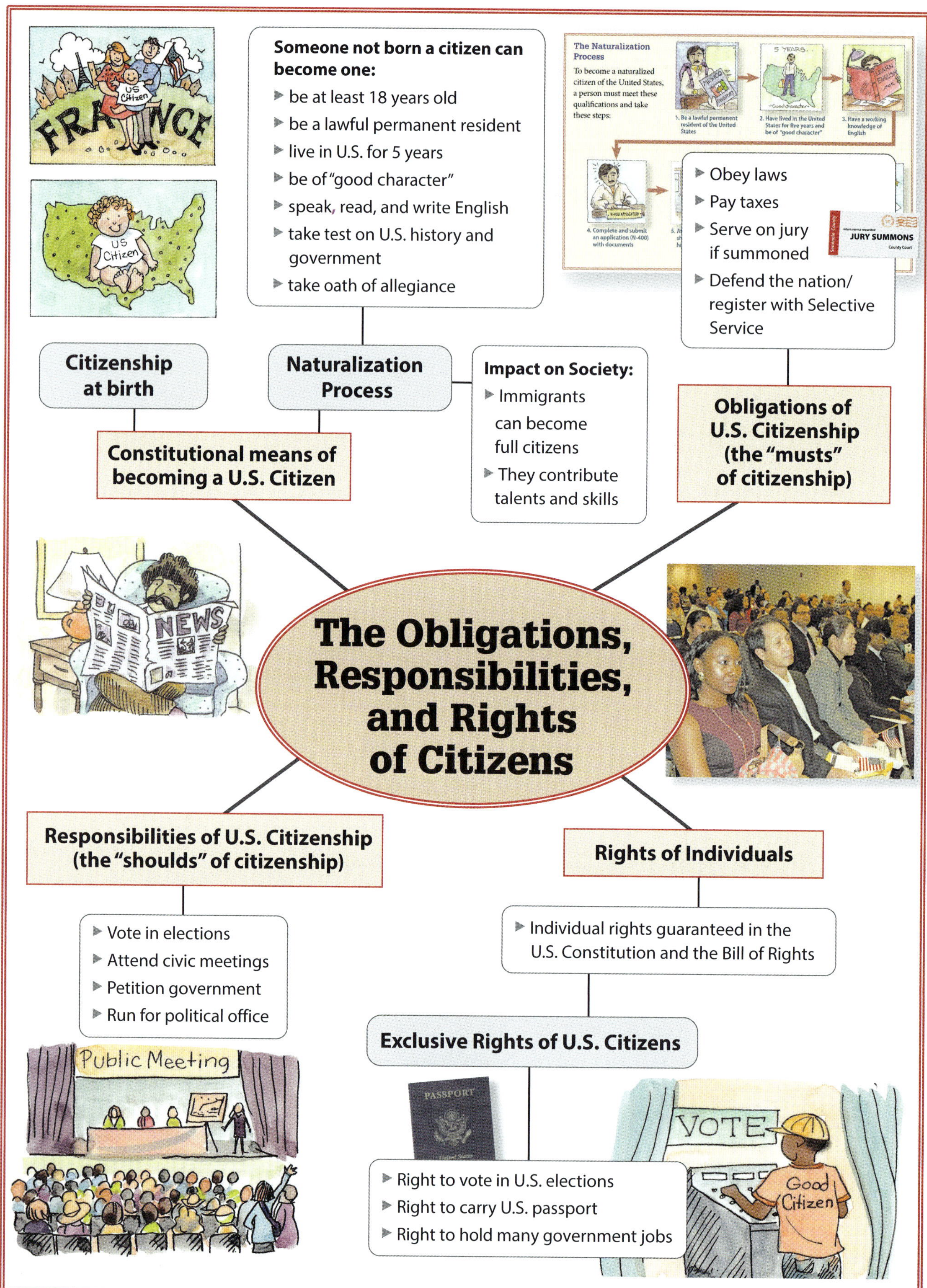
FRANCE
US Citizen
US Citizen
Someone not born a citizen can become one:
▶ be at least 18 years old
▶ be a lawful permanent resident
▶ live in U.S. for 5 years
▶ be of "good character"
▶ speak, read, and write English
▶ take test on U.S. history and government
▶ take oath of allegiance
The Naturalization Process
To become a naturalized citizen of the United States, a person must meet these qualifications and take these steps:
1. Be a lawful permanent resident of the United States
2. Have lived in the United States for five years and be of "good character"
3. Have a working knowledge of English
4. Complete and submit an application (N-400) with documents
▶ Obey laws
▶ Pay taxes
▶ Serve on jury if summoned
▶ Defend the nation/ register with Selective Service
JURY SUMMONS
Citizenship at birth
Naturalization Process
Impact on Society:
▶ Immigrants can become full citizens
▶ They contribute talents and skills
Obligations of U.S. Citizenship (the "musts" of citizenship)
Constitutional means of becoming a U.S. Citizen
NEWS
The Obligations, Responsibilities, and Rights of Citizens
Responsibilities of U.S. Citizenship (the "shoulds" of citizenship)
Rights of Individuals
▶ Vote in elections
▶ Attend civic meetings
▶ Petition government
▶ Run for political office
▶ Individual rights guaranteed in the U.S. Constitution and the Bill of Rights
Exclusive Rights of U.S. Citizens
Public Meeting
PASSPORT
VOTE
▶ Right to vote in U.S. elections
▶ Right to carry U.S. passport
▶ Right to hold many government jobs
Good Citizen

Review Cards: The Obligations, Responsibilities, and Rights of Citizens

Obtaining United States Citizenship

- A **citizen** is a legally recognized member of a nation.
- In the United States, the Fourteenth Amendment specifies two **constitutional means to citizenship**: at birth and through naturalization.
- A person receives citizenship at birth by the "**Law of Soil**," if they are born in the United States, or by the "**Law of Blood**," if born outside but both parents are American citizens and one has lived at some time in the United States. If only one parent is an American citizen, the "Law of Blood" still applies if that parent has lived at least one year continuously in America.
- **Immigrants** to the United States (*those who come from other countries with an intent to live here*) can become citizens through the **naturalization process**. To become a "naturalized" U.S. citizen, a person must know English, be of good character, be at least 18 years old, and have been a lawful permanent resident for at least 5 years. Then he or she must complete an application, show an ability to communicate in English, pass a test on American history and government, and swear an oath of allegiance.
- A person who is not a citizen but who lawfully lives and works in the United States has lawful **permanent residency**. Lawful permanent residents hold "green cards."
- Permanent residents have the right to live and work in the U.S., to receive professional certification, to leave and re-enter the United States, and to be protected under the Bill of Rights. They cannot vote.
- **Impact of the Naturalization Process:** The naturalization process has made America more attractive to immigrants, who enrich America with their own talents, cultures and traditions. Immigrants can become full members of American society, rather than remaining as a separate group. They provide their talent, work, and knowledge to their adopted country. Once they become citizens, they help to elect the best leaders and may even serve in government themselves.

The Obligations of Citizenship: What Citizens Must Do

- The **obligations (*duties*) of U.S. citizenship** are things that U.S. citizens must do. These are to **obey the law**, to **pay taxes**, to defend the nation, and to **serve on a jury** if summoned. Visitors and permanent residents must also obey the law and pay taxes, such as local sales taxes, or income taxes if they work. Citizens, residents, and visitors can be punished for failing to meet those obligations.
- Citizens have an obligation to help defend the nation. All draft-age males, whether citizens or residents, must register with the **Selective Service**. They also have an obligation to serve in the military if conscripted; however, conscription has not happened since 1973.
- Citizens have an obligation to **serve on a jury** when called on. Citizens are called to jury duty with a jury summons.

The Responsibilities of Citizenship: What Citizens Should Do

- The **responsibilities of U.S. citizenship** are things that U.S. citizens should do. They are not enforced by law, but they are encouraged. These include participation in and having knowledge of local, state, and national affairs and events.
- Citizens fulfill their citizenship responsibilities by **voting, running for office, attending civic meetings** (*meetings of citizens held for a public purpose*), and **petitioning the government** (*writing to government officials requesting a change*). They can also volunteer for local service projects to promote the **common good** (*what is good for the community*).
- By fulfilling our citizenship obligations and responsibilities, we make it possible for our government and society to work. If citizens did not obey the law, there would be no order or safety. If they did not pay taxes, government could not provide services. If citizens refused to serve on juries, we could not have jury trials. If citizens did not vote or run for office, we could not have elected officials.

The Rights of Citizenship

- U.S. citizens have rights as well as obligations and responsibilities.
- The U.S. Constitution guarantees certain rights to all people in America, both citizens and non-citizens. State constitutions, like the Florida State Constitution, also protect citizens' rights.
  - Everyone is guaranteed the right to apply for a writ of habeas corpus..
  - Everyone is protected against *ex post facto* laws..
- The Bill of Rights applies to everyone in the United States—citizens and non-citizens alike (see Chapter 10).
- Some rights are only enjoyed by U.S. citizens. Only U.S. citizens can vote and hold political office in the United States.
- Other benefits of U.S. citizenship include the right to live permanently in the United States, the right to have a U.S. passport, the right to hold certain jobs and military offices that require citizenship, the right to have priority in applying to bring family members from other countries to the United States, and the right to enjoy certain other government and private benefits, such as some college scholarships.

Permanent residents about to become citizens of the United States at a naturalization ceremony. What new rights, obligations and responsibilities will they have as U.S. citizens?

What Do You Know?

SS.7.CG.2.2

1. The list below identifies several activities.

- Attending a school board meeting
- Voting in a primary election
- Sending a petition to local officials
- Putting a candidate's sign in your yard
- Registering voters at a community college

What do these activities illustrate?

A. ways that citizens can meet their citizenship obligations
B. opportunities for citizens to participate in national elections
C. ways in which citizens can meet their citizenship responsibilities
D. opportunities for citizens to influence political action committees

SS.7.CG.2.1

2. The diagram below shows the requirements for becoming a naturalized citizen.

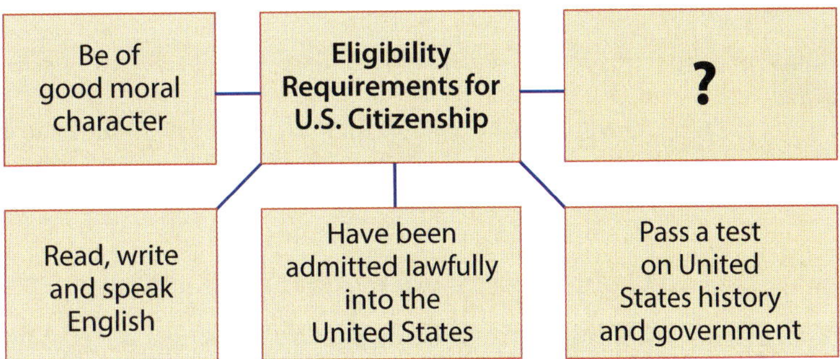

Which statement completes the diagram?

A. Pay federal income tax
B. Have an annual income of $20,000 or more
C. Have resided in the United States for five years
D. Have a parent, spouse or child who is a U.S. citizen

SS.7.CG.2.2

3. Which practice is part of the obligation of a U.S. citizen to help defend the nation?

A. serve on a jury
B. register for Selective Service
C. vote in all national elections
D. keep informed about national issues

SS.7.CG.2.2

4. The document below was part of a summons to perform an important civic duty.

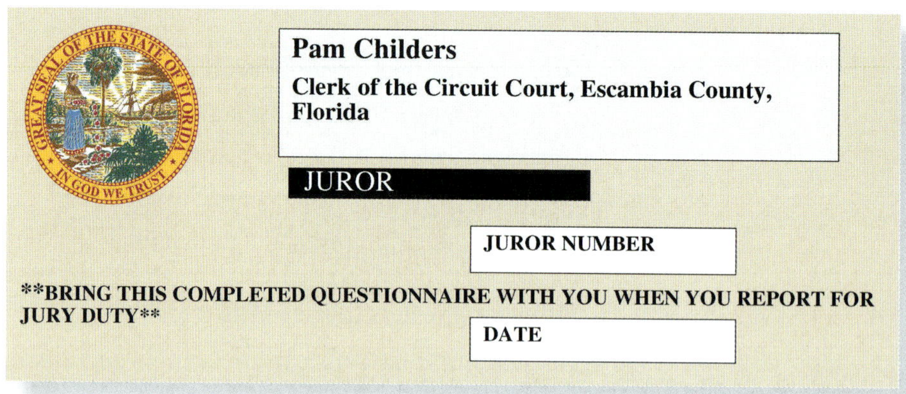

Pam Childers

Clerk of the Circuit Court, Escambia County, Florida

JUROR

JUROR NUMBER

BRING THIS COMPLETED QUESTIONNAIRE WITH YOU WHEN YOU REPORT FOR JURY DUTY

DATE

Why is it important for citizens to meet the obligation indicated in this document?

A. to guarantee our right to confront witnesses
B. to preserve constitutional limits on governmental power
C. to guarantee our right to be judged by a jury of our peers
D. to protect our right to petition for a writ of habeas corpus

SS.7.CG.2.1

5. Which is a constitutional means of obtaining U.S citizenship??

A. paying U.S. income taxes
B. being born in the United States
C. buying real estate in the United States
D. agreeing to obey the laws of the United States

SS.7.CG.2.1

Ester Tua Caballa becomes a citizen in the U.S. District Court in Pensacola, Florida in June 2014.

6. The photograph on the left shows an accomplishment of Ms. Ester Tua Caballa.

What are three of the requirements she had to fulfill for this accomplishment?

A. reside in the United States for five years; be of "good character"; pass a U.S. history test
B. be of "good character"; pass a test of general knowledge; have a high school diploma
C. be of "good character"; enter the United States lawfully; earn more than $20,000 annually
D. reside in the United States for five years; enter the United States lawfully; serve in the armed forces

SS.7.CG.2.2

7. The notice below was posted by Florida Americorps.

May 8, 2014: Governor Announces a Disaster Fund for Floridians Affected by Flooding

The company, Florida Americorps, will coordinate the volunteers and donations in the disaster. They urge all Floridians to serve their local community. They raise funds to aid the Commission in accomplishing its goals of meeting human needs in Florida. They are guided by a voluntary Board of Directors.

What statement best describes the notice shown above?

A. Florida Americorps is asking Floridians to fulfill their citizenship obligations.

B. Florida Americorps is encouraging Floridians to take action to promote the common good.

C. Florida Americorps is urging Floridians to demand the rights of citizenship.

D. Florida Americorps is advising Floridians to apply to local government agencies to provide assistance.

SS.7.CG.2.2

8. The sign below was placed in public view by members of United Way.

GET CONNECTED!

Powered by Orange County, Florida United Way Volunteers

Commit to Help by:

- ☑ Bagging & Distributing food
- ☑ Stocking shelves
- ☑ Tutoring a homeless child
- ☑ Mentoring, playing with children, ages 4–12, facing homelessness
- ☑ Helping sand and stain bunk beds inside the Thomas House Family Shelter

Why would citizens volunteer to perform some of the activities listed above?

A. to earn more money

B. to promote the common good

C. to earn additional citizenship rights

D. to fulfill their obligations under the law

SS.7.CG.2.2

9. Which act is considered a citizenship responsibility rather than an obligation?

A. paying taxes
B. obeying the law
C. attending civic meetings
D. registering for Selective Service

SS.7.CG.2.1

10. The Venn diagram below compares two means of becoming a U.S. citizen.

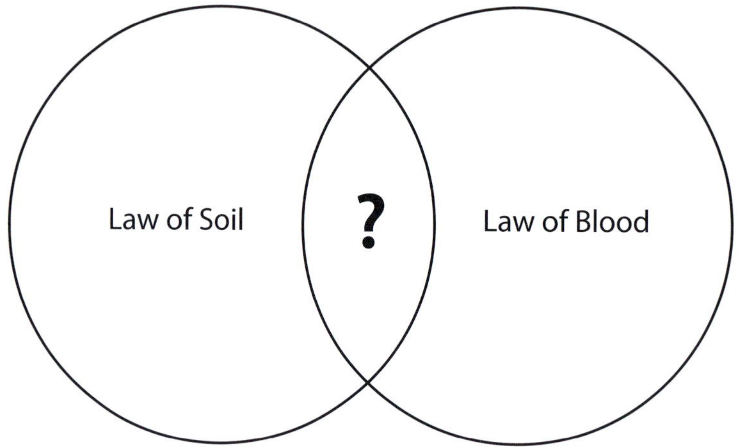

Which characteristic completes the Venn diagram?

A. Obtained at birth
B. Does not include voting rights
C. Obtained through naturalization
D. Requires residence in the United States

SS.7.CG.2.2

11. What would be the most likely consequence to society if citizens began refusing to fulfill their citizenship responsibilities?

A. People would face the threat of losing their individual rights and freedoms.
B. People would have more free time because they would have fewer social obligations.
C. People would benefit from the direction of strong leaders who would guard their freedoms.
D. People would find that society was able to look after itself without the help of civic participation.

SS.7.CG.2.1

12. What is an important impact of the naturalization process?

A. More foreign residents in the United States obtain "green cards."

B. Permanent residents in the United States are required to pay taxes.

C. An increased number of illegal immigrants come to the United States.

D. Immigrants to the United States see the possibility of becoming citizens.

S.7.CG.2.4

13. The diagram below shows some of the rights of U.S. citizens and of lawful permanent residents.

Rights of U.S. Citizens Alone	Rights of Both U.S. Citizens and Lawful Permanent Residents
• **?** • Right to hold U.S. passport • Priority in bringing relatives to the United States • Right to work at jobs in the federal government	• Right to petition for habeas corpus • No ex post facto laws • Rights in the Bill of Rights • Right to work and reside in the United States

Which completes the diagram?

A. Right to vote

B. Right to refuse to pay taxes

C. Right to freedom of speech

D. Right to freedom of religion

S.7.CG.2.2

14. Which of these is a legal obligation of U.S. citizenship?

A. to reside in the United States

B. to save money for retirement

C. to vote in Presidential elections

D. to serve on a jury when summoned

SS.7.CG.2.1

15. Which of these is one of the legal requirements for becoming a citizen?

A. registering to vote

B. paying income taxes

C. having relatives in the United States

D. living in the United States at least five years

SS.7.CG.2.2

16. The list below identifies several responsibilities of U.S. citizens.

- ?
- Attending civic meetings
- Petitioning the government
- Running for public office

Which phrase completes the list?

A. Voting in elections
B. Paying federal income tax
C. Answering a jury summons
D. Registering with Selective Service

S.7.CG.2.2

17. What is the impact on society when citizens fail to perform their citizenship obligations?

A. Citizens are still able to maintain their protected rights.
B. Most citizens benefit from not having to pay taxes or obey laws.
C. Government leaders seize control because of the lack of civic participation.
D. Governments can no longer perform services, maintain order or defend citizens.

S.7.CG. 2.1

18. Which statement identifies a positive impact of the naturalization process on American society?

A. It increases American power and influence overseas.
B. It leads to greater divisiveness on domestic political issues.
C. It attracts talented immigrants who contribute knowledge and skills.
D. It costs taxpayers money to enforce immigration and naturalization laws.

SS.7.CG.2.1

19. The diagram below shows the naturalization process.

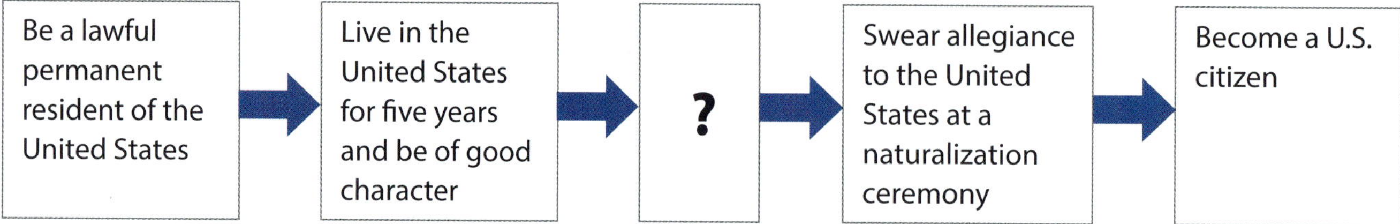

Which statement completes the diagram?

A. Pay income tax for five years
B. Serve in the U.S. armed services
C. Be sponsored by an American employer
D. Pass a test on American history and government

CHAPTER 14

Elections and Voting

SS.7.CG.2.6 Examine the election and voting process at the local, state and national levels.

SS.7.CG.2.7 Identify the constitutional qualifications required to hold state and national office.

For SS.7.CG.3.14 on the Electoral College, see Chapter 7 on the Presidency

Content Focus Vocabulary in This Chapter

Election and voting processes
Elections
Voting
Impact of elections
Political party
Role of parties
Republican Party
Democratic Party
Public policy
Constitutional qualifications
State office
National office
Local office
Free and fair elections
Democratic institutions
Preserve the republic

Florida "Keys" to Learning

1. **Election and voting processes**: American citizens exercise their control over government by **voting** in **elections**. In order to vote, a citizen must be a registered voter. State governments handle election procedures. In Florida, voters must register before the election takes place. To register in Florida, a person must be a U.S. citizen, a resident of Florida, and 18 years or older. The person cannot have committed a felony (unless voting rights have been restored) or be mentally incapable. Finally, the applicant must provide a current and valid identification card, such as a driver's license.

2. Citizens vote at a polling place. They mark their choices on a paper or electronic ballot. The election of national, state, and local officials usually takes place at the same time. The ballot presents choices in election contests based on the districts in which the voter lives.

3. **Impact of elections:** Elections impact citizens at the local, state and national levels. At each level of government, citizens are able to influence their officials through the election process. Leaders know that if their policies are unpopular, they will not be re-elected. Their policies, in turn, influence citizens at the local, state, and national levels. For example, government officials at the national level may decide to raise or lower taxes. This will affect how much of their income citizens have to save or spend. Voters elect state officials who, in turn, will establish policies that affect access to educational programs. These policies affect citizens at the state level. The same holds true at the local level. Citizens elect local officials who will make decisions on school spending or new construction in the community.

4. When voters register, they can identify themselves as members of a political party. A **political party** is a group of people who share political beliefs. They organize to promote their shared beliefs by electing party members to government offices.

5. **The role of parties:** The United States has a two-party system. Most elected officials belong to either the Democratic Party or Republican Party. The **Democratic Party** was formed in 1828 to represent the "common man"—the newly enfranchised working man. The **Republican Party** was formed in 1854 by those who opposed the extension of slavery into western territories. Abraham Lincoln became the first Republican President in 1860.

6. Both parties have evolved over time. In the 1930s and 1960s, the Democratic Party introduced new government programs to address social and economic problems. Republicans favor less government interference and lower taxes. Whichever party is in power can have a major impact on **public policy** (*actions of government to meet public needs*).

7. Often, individuals from the same party compete in a primary election to win their party's nomination. The nominees from the opposing parties then run against each other. During the campaign, candidates debate, give speeches and use political advertisements to win support.

8. The U.S. Constitution establishes the **constitutional qualifications** for **national offices**: to be a Representative in Congress, one must be at least 25 years old, be a citizen for 7 years, and live in the represented state. To be a U.S. Senator, one must be at least 30 years old, be a citizen for 9 years, and live in the represented state. To be President of the United States, one must be at least 35 years old, be a "natural born" citizen, and be a U.S. resident at least 14 years. The President is chosen by the **Electoral College**.

9. The Florida Constitution sets the **constitutional qualifications** for state offices: the Governor of Florida and other elected Cabinet

members must be at least 30 years old and have lived in Florida at least 7 years. Florida Senators and Representatives must be at least 21 years old, have lived in Florida at least two years, and live in the districts they represent. The qualifications for local offices, such as mayor or county commissioner, are set by charters and local laws. They vary across Florida.

10. The United States has **free and fair elections**. People do not have to pay any fees to vote. Free speech allows candidates to criticize government policies and campaign for public support. Citizens mark their ballots in private, and impartial officials oversee the vote count.

11. Because the United States has free and fair elections, its citizens can place their trust in the country's **democratic institutions** (*organizations of government based on the rule of the people*). Their trust helps **preserve the republic**. Not all countries have free and fair elections. Some have no elections at all. In others, opponents are jailed, voters have no real choice among the candidates, and the government in power cheats in reporting the election results.

In our American constitutional republic, ordinary citizens hold the final power over their government officials and institutions. But how do they exercise this power? Like the citizens of ancient Rome, Americans today exercise their control over government by electing public officials to limited terms in office. If citizens do not like what an official is doing, they can vote the person out of office when the time comes for re-election. In this chapter, you will learn more about **election and voting processes**.

The Voting Process

In an **election**, qualified citizens exercise their power over government by **voting**.

How Voting Takes Place

Citizens with the right to vote go to a special place, known as a "poll." Polling places are usually a school, library or other public building located close to where the voter lives. When voters arrive at the poll, they proceed to a "check-in" table where poll workers check their names against an official list of registered voters in that area. State governments determine election rules and procedures. In Florida, voters must show a current identification card with a picture and signature, such as a driver's license, U.S. passport, or Florida identification card.

After checking in, qualified citizens are able to vote. They are given a paper ballot to fill out in private, or they enter into a voting booth and pull the levers of a voting machine. The ballot (*the piece of paper used to record the vote*) presents a series of choices with the names of candidates running for public office. Voters usually elect candidates for local, state and national offices at the same election. The ballot may also include several issues for voters to decide directly.

Voters make their selections by filling in ovals on the paper ballot, punching holes, or by pulling levers in the voting booth. The votes are only counted after the election is closed. If the vote is close, there is a recount to check the accuracy of the count.

A sample ballot from the Presidential election of November 2020 appears on the next page. This ballot appeared in Miami Dade County. A voter was supposed to fill in one oval on the left for each group of names, next to the name of the candidate the voter wished to select. For example, for President and Vice President, the instructions say "Vote for 1."

As you can see, the name of each candidate is followed by the name of his or her political party. "REP" stands for Republican Party, and "DEM" stands for Democratic Party. You will learn more about political parties later in this chapter.

In addition to presenting the candidates for U.S. President, this ballot had a number of other candidates who were running for local, state and national offices. These included candidates for Congress, for the Florida State Legislature, and for state judgeships. You can see that on this "Election Day," local, state and national elections were all held at the same time. Everyone in Florida had the same seven choices on their ballot for President and Vice President, but voters living in different districts had different choices on their ballots for other public offices. (Because this is a sample ballot, it shows several districts for each contest; an actual ballot in this election had only one district for each contest.)

There is an instruction above each office to be filled, stating how many candidates the voter should choose. In addition to selecting candidates for these government offices, voters were also asked to decide several issues directly, including whether or not to support various proposed amendments to the Florida State Constitution.

Sometimes citizens cannot go to the polling place, where they usually vote. In this case, they have an opportunity to complete a mail-in ballot.

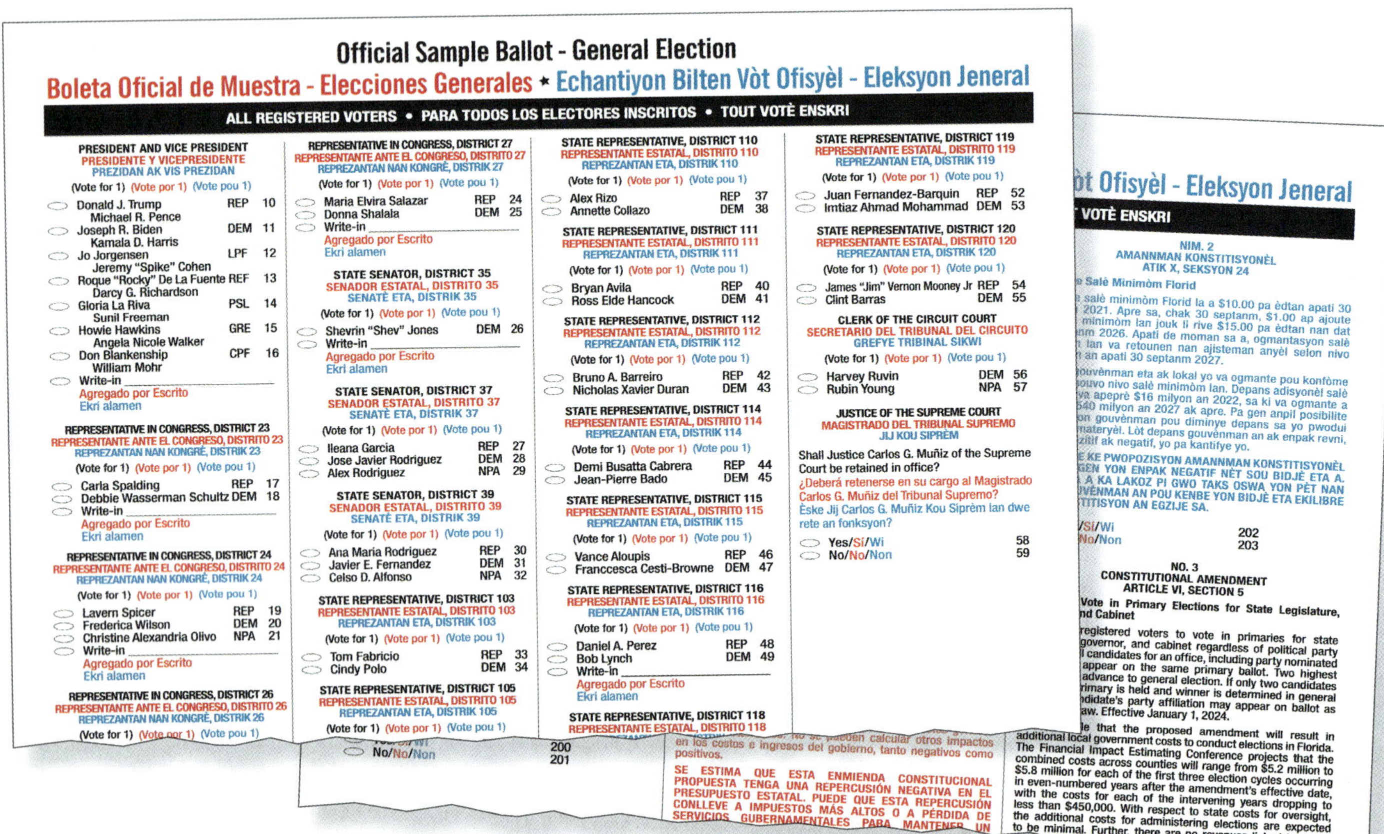

Official Sample Ballot - General Election

Boleta Oficial de Muestra - Elecciones Generales ★ Echantiyon Bilten Vòt Ofisyèl - Eleksyon Jeneral

ALL REGISTERED VOTERS • PARA TODOS LOS ELECTORES INSCRITOS • TOUT VOTÈ ENSKRI

PRESIDENT AND VICE PRESIDENT
PRESIDENTE Y VICEPRESIDENTE
PREZIDAN AK VIS PREZIDAN
(Vote for 1) (Vote por 1) (Vote pou 1)
Donald J. Trump / Michael R. Pence REP 10
Joseph R. Biden / Kamala D. Harris DEM 11
Jo Jorgensen / Jeremy "Spike" Cohen LPF 12
Roque "Rocky" De La Fuente / Darcy G. Richardson REF 13
Gloria La Riva / Sunil Freeman PSL 14
Howie Hawkins / Angela Nicole Walker GRE 15
Don Blankenship / William Mohr CPF 16
Write-in / Agregado por Escrito / Ekri alamen

REPRESENTATIVE IN CONGRESS, DISTRICT 23
REPRESENTANTE ANTE EL CONGRESO, DISTRITO 23
REPREZANTAN NAN KONGRÈ, DISTRIK 23
(Vote for 1) (Vote por 1) (Vote pou 1)
Carla Spalding REP 17
Debbie Wasserman Schultz DEM 18
Write-in / Agregado por Escrito / Ekri alamen

REPRESENTATIVE IN CONGRESS, DISTRICT 24
REPRESENTANTE ANTE EL CONGRESO, DISTRITO 24
REPREZANTAN NAN KONGRÈ, DISTRIK 24
(Vote for 1) (Vote por 1) (Vote pou 1)
Lavern Spicer REP 19
Frederica Wilson DEM 20
Christine Alexandria Olivo NPA 21
Write-in / Agregado por Escrito / Ekri alamen

REPRESENTATIVE IN CONGRESS, DISTRICT 26
REPRESENTANTE ANTE EL CONGRESO, DISTRITO 26
REPREZANTAN NAN KONGRÈ, DISTRIK 26
(Vote for 1) (Vote por 1) (Vote pou 1)

REPRESENTATIVE IN CONGRESS, DISTRICT 27
REPRESENTANTE ANTE EL CONGRESO, DISTRITO 27
REPREZANTAN NAN KONGRÈ, DISTRIK 27
(Vote for 1) (Vote por 1) (Vote pou 1)
Maria Elvira Salazar REP 24
Donna Shalala DEM 25
Write-in / Agregado por Escrito / Ekri alamen

STATE SENATOR, DISTRICT 35
SENADOR ESTATAL, DISTRITO 35
SENATÈ ETA, DISTRIK 35
(Vote for 1) (Vote por 1) (Vote pou 1)
Shevrin "Shev" Jones DEM 26
Write-in / Agregado por Escrito / Ekri alamen

STATE SENATOR, DISTRICT 37
SENADOR ESTATAL, DISTRITO 37
SENATÈ ETA, DISTRIK 37
(Vote for 1) (Vote por 1) (Vote pou 1)
Ileana Garcia REP 27
Jose Javier Rodriguez DEM 28
Alex Rodriguez NPA 29

STATE SENATOR, DISTRICT 39
SENADOR ESTATAL, DISTRITO 39
SENATÈ ETA, DISTRIK 39
(Vote for 1) (Vote por 1) (Vote pou 1)
Ana Maria Rodriguez REP 30
Javier E. Fernandez DEM 31
Celso D. Alfonso NPA 32

STATE REPRESENTATIVE, DISTRICT 103
REPRESENTANTE ESTATAL, DISTRITO 103
REPREZANTAN ETA, DISTRIK 103
(Vote for 1) (Vote por 1) (Vote pou 1)
Tom Fabricio REP 33
Cindy Polo DEM 34

STATE REPRESENTATIVE, DISTRICT 105
REPRESENTANTE ESTATAL, DISTRITO 105
REPREZANTAN ETA, DISTRIK 105
(Vote for 1) (Vote por 1) (Vote pou 1)

STATE REPRESENTATIVE, DISTRICT 110
REPRESENTANTE ESTATAL, DISTRITO 110
REPREZANTAN ETA, DISTRIK 110
(Vote for 1) (Vote por 1) (Vote pou 1)
Alex Rizo REP 37
Annette Collazo DEM 38

STATE REPRESENTATIVE, DISTRICT 111
REPRESENTANTE ESTATAL, DISTRITO 111
REPREZANTAN ETA, DISTRIK 111
(Vote for 1) (Vote por 1) (Vote pou 1)
Bryan Avila REP 40
Ross Elde Hancock DEM 41

STATE REPRESENTATIVE, DISTRICT 112
REPRESENTANTE ESTATAL, DISTRITO 112
REPREZANTAN ETA, DISTRIK 112
(Vote for 1) (Vote por 1) (Vote pou 1)
Bruno A. Barreiro REP 42
Nicholas Xavier Duran DEM 43

STATE REPRESENTATIVE, DISTRICT 114
REPRESENTANTE ESTATAL, DISTRITO 114
REPREZANTAN ETA, DISTRIK 114
(Vote for 1) (Vote por 1) (Vote pou 1)
Demi Busatta Cabrera REP 44
Jean-Pierre Bado DEM 45

STATE REPRESENTATIVE, DISTRICT 115
REPRESENTANTE ESTATAL, DISTRITO 115
REPREZANTAN ETA, DISTRIK 115
(Vote for 1) (Vote por 1) (Vote pou 1)
Vance Aloupis REP 46
Franccesca Cesti-Browne DEM 47

STATE REPRESENTATIVE, DISTRICT 116
REPRESENTANTE ESTATAL, DISTRITO 116
REPREZANTAN ETA, DISTRIK 116
(Vote for 1) (Vote por 1) (Vote pou 1)
Daniel A. Perez REP 48
Bob Lynch DEM 49
Write-in / Agregado por Escrito / Ekri alamen

STATE REPRESENTATIVE, DISTRICT 118
REPRESENTANTE ESTATAL, DISTRITO 118

STATE REPRESENTATIVE, DISTRICT 119
REPRESENTANTE ESTATAL, DISTRITO 119
REPREZANTAN ETA, DISTRIK 119
(Vote for 1) (Vote por 1) (Vote pou 1)
Juan Fernandez-Barquin REP 52
Imtiaz Ahmad Mohammad DEM 53

STATE REPRESENTATIVE, DISTRICT 120
REPRESENTANTE ESTATAL, DISTRITO 120
REPREZANTAN ETA, DISTRIK 120
(Vote for 1) (Vote por 1) (Vote pou 1)
James "Jim" Vernon Mooney Jr REP 54
Clint Barras DEM 55

CLERK OF THE CIRCUIT COURT
SECRETARIO DEL TRIBUNAL DEL CIRCUITO
GREFYE TRIBINAL SIKWI
(Vote for 1) (Vote por 1) (Vote pou 1)
Harvey Ruvin DEM 56
Rubin Young NPA 57

JUSTICE OF THE SUPREME COURT
MAGISTRADO DEL TRIBUNAL SUPREMO
JIJ KOU SIPRÈM
Shall Justice Carlos G. Muñiz of the Supreme Court be retained in office?
¿Deberá retenerse en su cargo al Magistrado Carlos G. Muñiz del Tribunal Supremo?
Èske Jij Carlos G. Muñiz Kou Siprèm lan dwe rete an fonksyon?
Yes/Sí/Wi 58
No/No/Non 59

NO. 3
CONSTITUTIONAL AMENDMENT
ARTICLE VI, SECTION 5
Vote in Primary Elections for State Legislature, ... and Cabinet

Who Can Vote?

Only qualified citizens can lawfully vote. In order to vote in an election, a citizen must be "registered." To register is to enter information into an official record. Through this process, the government prevents fraud (*cheating*) in elections.

Each state government determines its own voter registration rules. In Florida, voters must be registered 29 days before any election in which they wish to vote.

The National Voter Registration Act of 1993, also known as the "Motor Voter" law, requires state governments to offer voter registration at the same time that residents apply for or renew their drivers' licenses. This information is forwarded by the Department of Motor Vehicles to the state's election officials. Most Americans now register to vote while applying for their driver's license.

The same law requires states to register voters at state offices offering services to Americans with dis-

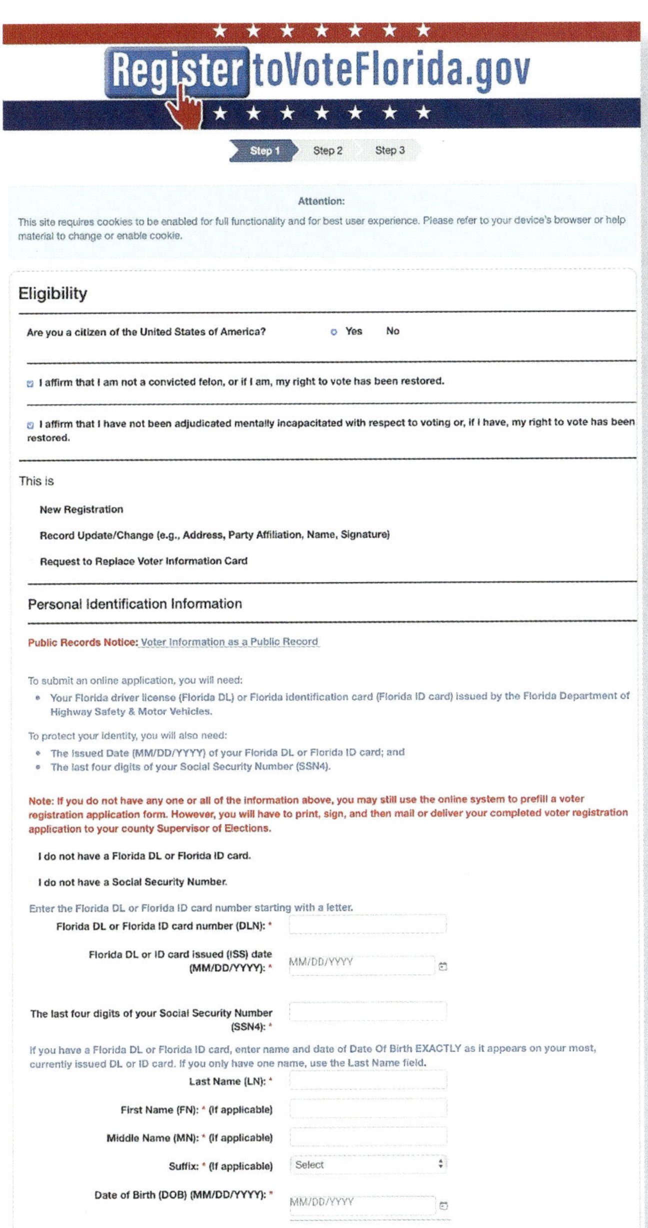

RegistertoVoteFlorida.gov

Step 1 Step 2 Step 3

Attention:

This site requires cookies to be enabled for full functionality and for best user experience. Please refer to your device's browser or help material to change or enable cookie.

Eligibility

Are you a citizen of the United States of America? Yes No

I affirm that I am not a convicted felon, or if I am, my right to vote has been restored.

I affirm that I have not been adjudicated mentally incapacitated with respect to voting or, if I have, my right to vote has been restored.

This is

New Registration

Record Update/Change (e.g., Address, Party Affiliation, Name, Signature)

Request to Replace Voter Information Card

Personal Identification Information

Public Records Notice: Voter Information as a Public Record

To submit an online application, you will need:

- Your Florida driver license (Florida DL) or Florida identification card (Florida ID card) issued by the Florida Department of Highway Safety & Motor Vehicles.

To protect your identity, you will also need:

- The Issued Date (MM/DD/YYYY) of your Florida DL or Florida ID card; and
- The last four digits of your Social Security Number (SSN4).

Note: If you do not have any one or all of the information above, you may still use the online system to prefill a voter registration application form. However, you will have to print, sign, and then mail or deliver your completed voter registration application to your county Supervisor of Elections.

I do not have a Florida DL or Florida ID card.

I do not have a Social Security Number.

Enter the Florida DL or Florida ID card number starting with a letter.

Florida DL or Florida ID card number (DLN): *

Florida DL or ID card issued (ISS) date (MM/DD/YYYY): * MM/DD/YYYY

The last four digits of your Social Security Number (SSN4): *

If you have a Florida DL or Florida ID card, enter name and date of Date Of Birth EXACTLY as it appears on your most, currently issued DL or ID card. If you only have one name, use the Last Name field.

Last Name (LN): *

First Name (FN): * (If applicable)

Middle Name (MN): * (If applicable)

Suffix: * (If applicable) Select

Date of Birth (DOB) (MM/DD/YYYY): * MM/DD/YYYY

abilities or offering public assistance (such as food stamps). State election offices, public libraries and armed services recruitment offices also offer in-person voter registration.

To register to vote in Florida, a person must meet these six requirements:

- Be a citizen of the United States
- Be a Florida resident
- Be at least 18 years old (you may preregister if you are 16 years old)
- Not have been judged as "mentally incapacitated" (*incapable*) with respect to voting in Florida or any other state, without having had your voting rights restored (*given back*)
- Not have been convicted of a felony (serious crime) in Florida, or any other state, without having had your voting rights restored
- Provide a current Florida driver's license number or Florida identification card number.

Most states allow voters to register online. Florida residents can register online at: RegisterToVoteFlorida.gov. To register online, a voter needs his or her driver's license or Florida identification card and the last four digits of his or her Social Security number.

There is also a National Voter Registration Card, which can be filled out and sent to election officials in every state.

The Impact of Elections and Voting on Citizens at Different Levels of Government

Although national, state and local elections often take place at the same time and follow similar procedures, they impact citizens at the three levels of government in different ways. Each level of government has different responsibilities. Voters are able to influence each level through its own election contests. The officials that voters elect at each level make decisions that influence citizens' lives. At the same time, officials know that if their policies are unpopular, they will not be re-elected.

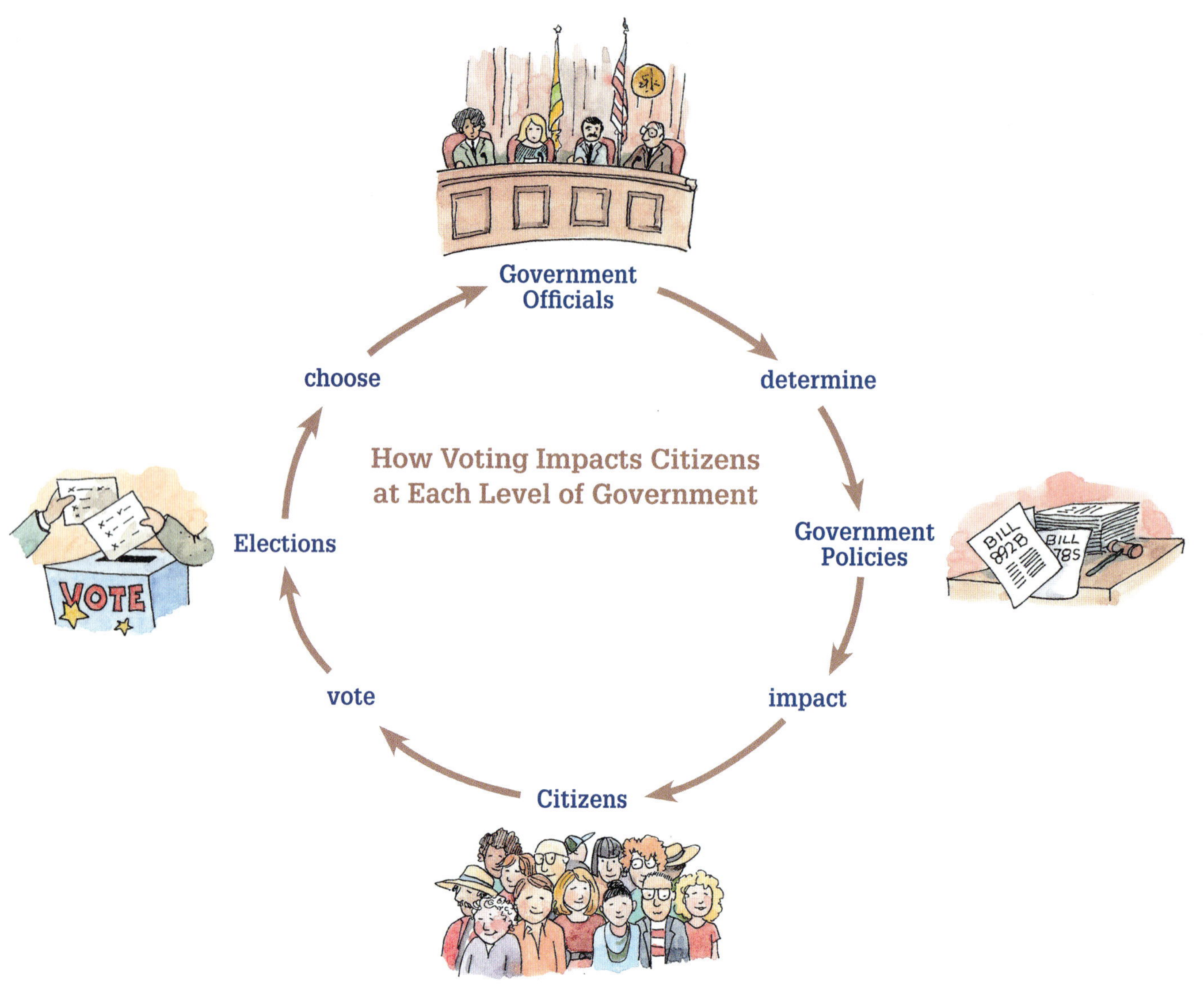

National elections	All registered voters in Florida can vote for President and for U.S. Senator; only the registered voters living in a particular Congressional district can vote for the U.S. Representative for that district. By voting for President and members of Congress, voters are able to choose which leaders hold power. These leaders in turn make decisions that affect citizens across the nation: such as whether the United States goes to war; or whether personal income taxes are increased or decreased.
State elections	All registered voters in Florida can vote for the Governor of Florida and for elected Cabinet members; only the registered voters living in a particular district can vote for that district's State Senator or State Representative. By voting for state officials, voters are able to choose which leaders hold power at the state level. These leaders in turn make decisions that impact citizens across the state, such as whether to build new state roads or whether to change how many days students in the state attend school. Voters also sometimes vote directly on some state issues, like amendments to the state constitution.
Local elections	Only local voters can vote in local elections. Voters elect their own leaders at the local level. They also vote directly on some issues, such as local school finance or property taxes. In this way, community members are able to determine which policies their community will follow. These policies in turn impact citizens.

The Role of Political Parties

You should know the origins of the two major parties for the EOC

When registering to vote, a citizen can declare being a member of a political party. A **political party** is a group of people who share political beliefs. Party members hold similar ideas about the role of government in society. Political parties promote their beliefs and work to get their party members elected into positions in government.

When the United States became independent, many American leaders, including George Washington, hoped that Americans would not form political parties. These leaders feared that competition between parties would threaten American unity. Their wish to avoid parties was not realized. The very first American political parties formed as early as Washington's first term as President. In fact, the **role of parties** has been essential to the success of our system of government. Parties unite voters and officials with similar beliefs, introduce new ideas, pay for election campaigns, and help to manage legislative bodies.

Americans have usually had a two-party system. For the past 160 years, the two main political parties in the United States have been the Democrats and the Republicans.

Origins of the Democratic Party

At the time when Americans declared their independence, only adult white males who owned a certain amount of property could vote. Ordinary working men could not vote at all. The property qualifications for voting were gradually ended state by state. By the 1820s, all adult white men, even if they were poor, had the right to vote.

In 1828—during this period of expanding voting rights—Andrew Jackson founded the **Democratic Party**. The Democratic Party was the first modern political party with a broad membership. It introduced new campaigning methods for the age of mass politics. A self-made man who was raised in poverty, Jackson saw himself as the champion of the "common man." In the Presidential election of 1832, the Democratic Party held one of the first national party conventions. These conventions opened up the nominating process, which had once been controlled by a handful of party leaders, to ordinary party members. The Democratic Party thus began as the party representing the average citizen.

To show that the new Democratic Party represented the "common man," President Andrew Jackson invited the public to celebrate his inauguration at the White House

Origins of the Republican Party

The **Republican Party** was formed less than thirty years later. In the 1850s, Americans were sharply divided over the issue of slavery. Slavery had been previously banned in federal territories in the North, but the Kansas-Nebraska Act of 1854 had reopened the possibility of introducing slavery there. Those who opposed the extension of slavery formed the Republican Party that same year.

Because he opposed the spread of slavery to western territories, Abraham Lincoln joined the Republican Party in 1856.

Lincoln was elected as the first Republican President in November 1860. During the Civil War, the Republican Party came to stand for loyalty to the Union and for greater rights for African Americans.

Democrats and Republicans Today

Over time, our nation's two major political parties evolved. In the 1930s and 1960s, Democratic Presidents Franklin D. Roosevelt and Lyndon B. Johnson introduced new social programs and civil rights legislation. Democrats favored using the power of the national government to solve social and economic problems and to improve peoples' lives.

During this same period, Republicans became the party of less government, more private enterprise, lower taxes, less public debt, and a strong foreign policy. They believe that private initiatives—from education to energy and the environment—often do a better job at solving problems than government programs do. Republicans favor less government control and greater personal freedom. They believe this approach promotes stronger economic growth and better job creation.

The cartoonist Thomas Nast introduced the donkey as a symbol of the Democratic Party in 1870. He also introduced the elephant to represent the Republican Party—known as the "GOP," or Grand Old Party.

The Role of the Two Major Parties in Shaping Public Policy

The two major parties have had a major impact in shaping **public policy** (*the policies followed by the government*). Because Democrats and Republicans disagree on many issues, when members of either party are elected to office they often make changes in public policy with lasting effects. Here are two examples:

- President Woodrow Wilson was a Democrat. He wanted to establish a new international organization known as the League of Nations. However, Republicans in the U.S. Senate refused to ratify the treaty that would have made the United States a member of this new organization. Wilson tried to win more popular support for the Democrats but failed. Democrats lost both the Presidential election and congressional elections in 1920. As a result, the United States never joined the League of Nations.
- In the 1960s and 1970s, Presidents from the Democratic Party introduced many new social programs. These expanded social services but also increased tax rates. In 1980, Ronald Reagan was the Republican candidate for President. Reagan told voters that the government was not the solution to the nation's problems but the source of its difficulties. Reagan wanted to see less government with greater personal freedom and private intiative. Reagan was elected and scaled back many federal programs.

As these examples show, each of the two major political parties—the Democrats and Republicans—has had a major role in shaping public policy. Whichever party is in power tries to achieve its goals. At the same time, the separation of powers and system of checks and balances often prevents the party in power from changing public policy as much as it might like to do.

The Active Citizen

Was George Washington right in warning his fellow Americans against forming political parties? Are political parties good or bad for a democracy? Here are some of the benefits that modern political parties provide:

- **Education:** Political parties educate voters by informing them about the issues.
- **Debate:** Political parties offer alternatives and encourage debate.
- **Legislation:** Political parties help local, state and national lawmakers organize into groups on behalf of a legislative program.
- **Critics:** Political parties closely monitor and criticize what opposing parties are doing.

With a partner, think of two disadvantages of political parties. Then discuss whether the advantages of political parties above outweigh those two disadvantages. Finally, share your conclusions with the rest of the class.

For the EOC, be sure to know these constitutional qualifications for office

Who Can Run? Meeting the Constitutional Qualifications for Office

In elections, voters select candidates to fill elected offices. Before an individual can run for state or national office, however, he or she must meet certain **constitutional qualifications**. The qualifications for holding a **national office** (*an elected position in the national government*) are found in the U.S. Constitution.

The requirements for holding a **state office** (*an elected position in the state government*) in Florida are found in the Florida Constitution.

You have already learned about some of these constitutional requirements in earlier chapters:

Office	Requirements
United States (Federal)	
President	Be a "natural born citizen"; be at least 35 years of age; and have lived in the United States for 14 years.
U.S. Senator	Be at least 30 years of age; have been a U.S. citizen for nine years; and live in the state he or she will represent.
U.S. Representative	Be at least 25 years of age; have been a U.S. citizen for seven years; and live in the state from which he or she is chosen.
Florida (State)	
Governor, Lieutenant Governor and Cabinet Members	Be at least 30 years old and have been a resident of Florida for seven years.
Florida Senator	Be at least 21 years old; have been a resident of Florida for two years; and live in the district he or she will represent; cannot serve in the Senate continuously more than 8 years.
Florida Representative	Be at least 21 years old; have been a resident of Florida for two years; and live in the district he or she will represent; cannot serve in the House continuously more than 8 years.

The Active Citizen

The excerpts below show the constitutional qualifications for national and state offices.

United States Constitution

Article I, Section 2:

"No Person shall be a Representative who shall not have attained to the Age of twenty five Years, and been seven Years a Citizen of the United States, and who shall not, when elected, be an Inhabitant of that State in which he shall be chosen."

Article I, Section 3:

"No Person shall be a Senator who shall not have attained to the Age of thirty Years, and been nine Years a Citizen of the United States, and who shall not, when elected, be an Inhabitant of that State for which he shall be chosen."

Article II, Section 1:

"No person except a natural born citizen, or a citizen of the United States, at the time of the adoption of this Constitution, shall be eligible to the office of President; neither shall any person be eligible to that office who shall not have attained to the age of thirty five years, and been fourteen Years a resident within the United States."

Florida Constitution

Article III. Legislature

Section 15. Terms and qualifications of legislators.

"(a) Senators shall be elected for terms of four years . . .

(b) Members of the house of representatives shall be elected for terms of two years . . .

(c) Each legislator shall be at least twenty-one years of age, an elector and resident of the district from which elected and shall have resided in the state for a period of two years prior to election."

Article IV. Executive

Section 5. Election of governor, lieutenant governor and cabinet members; qualifications; terms."

"(b) When elected, the governor, lieutenant governor and each cabinet member must be an elector not less than thirty years of age who has resided in the state for the preceding seven years. The attorney general must have been a member of the bar of Florida for the preceding five years. No person who has, or but for resignation would have, served as governor or acting governor for more than six years in two consecutive terms shall be elected governor for the succeeding term."

Why were these requirements for holding national and state offices made into constitutional provisions instead of just being ordinary laws?

The Qualifications for Holding Local Office

The qualifications for holding elected local offices (mayor, county commissioner, etc.) are not defined in the U.S. or Florida Constitutions. They are based on local laws or the charter (*a grant of powers by the state legislature*) of a municipality. Qualifications to hold local office differ from place to place. There are almost always residence requirements (*how long someone has lived in a place*) but usually no special age requirements. Many local governments have term limits: an official can serve only a limited number of continuous terms in the same elected position.

The Active Citizen

Azem Hadzic was born in Bosnia in 1985. His family came to the United States as political refugees in 1993. He became a naturalized citizen in 2005. Azem has lived in Pensacola, Florida, since 2010. For which national and state offices would Azem be qualified to serve? Check all that apply:

☐ U.S. President	☐ U.S. Representative	☐ Florida Senator
☐ U.S. Senator	☐ Governor of Florida	☐ Florida Representative

Abebe Lee was born in Jacksonville, Florida. She moved to Orlando when she was 25 years old. She just celebrated her 30th birthday last week. For which national and state offices would Abebe be qualified to serve? Check all that apply:

☐ U.S. President	☐ U.S. Representative	☐ Florida Senator
☐ U.S. Senator	☐ Governor of Florida	☐ Florida Representative

Lucy Smith was born in New York City. She is 40 years old. Lucy moved to Fort Lauderdale, Florida, five years ago. For which national and state offices would Lucy be qualified to serve? Check all that apply:

☐ U.S. President	☐ U.S. Representative	☐ Florida Senator
☐ U.S. Senator	☐ Governor of Florida	☐ Florida Representative

The Election Process

Meeting the legal requirements for serving in office is only just the first step. Candidates next have to be elected. For most government offices, the **election process** has two stages:

- First, a candidate must be nominated by his or her political party
- Second, he or she must be elected by voters in the general election.

Winning the Party Nomination

One of the most important roles played by political parties is finding good people to run for office. Each major party usually nominates (*names*) one candidate for each office to be filled in the election. Smaller parties may also offer candidates.

Very often, several members of the same party want to run for the same political office (such as the Presidency or a seat in Congress). They compete against each other to win their party's nomination.

Primary Elections

Candidates from the same party generally compete by participating in primary elections. A primary is a special election that indicates the preference of party members for the party's nominees. Florida has a "closed primary." Only registered party members can vote in each party's primary elections. Independent voters and voters from opposing parties do not participate.

Party Conventions

The Democratic and Republican Parties both hold state and national party conventions. A convention is a large meeting. National conventions are held every four years to nominate candidates for President and Vice President. Most of the delegates who attend these conventions are already pledged to a candidate, based on earlier primary results.

Besides choosing their party's nominees, the delegates at a political convention also adopt a party platform—a detailed statement of the party's policies on key issues. A state or national party convention helps to ignite party enthusiasm behind the party's candidates for their campaign against the candidates of the opposing party. The convention also provides opportunities to display party unity and strength, especially in the media (*television, radio, newspapers and the Internet*).

Conducting the Election Campaign

After being nominated by their party, candidates campaign against the nominees of other parties in the final months before the election. The methods that candidates use to win the nomination and the general election are similar:

▶ Political Advertisements

Candidates purchase time on television and radio, or space in magazines, newspapers and the Internet in order to present their message to voters.

▶ Direct Mail and Telephone Campaigns

Candidates send out flyers or have volunteers call voters by telephone. Sometimes candidates will send recorded messages to large numbers of voters.

▶ The Internet and Social Media

Candidates often post detailed policy statements on key issues on their websites.

▶ Rallies and Demonstrations

Candidates hold rallies in auditoriums, stadiums, or even in the street, where they give speeches to their supporters.

▶ Volunteers

Unpaid volunteers host meetings, contact voters, spread the messages of their candidates, make contributions, and help raise additional funds.

▶ Debates

In most elections, candidates hold public debates. A debate is a form of public speaking in which two sides face each other and take turns presenting their views. Voters get to see candidates face-to-face and judge for themselves how capable they are.

▶ Campaign Finance

Political campaigns are paid for by private contributions. There are limits on individual campaign contributions, but individuals are allowed to form political committees. There are no limits on the amount that can be contributed to some types of committees. Corporations and labor unions cannot make direct contributions to candidates, but they can make contributions to separate "political action committees," known as PACs.

Winning the General Election

For most elections, candidates must win the popular vote in a district or state. For Presidential elections, a candidate must win a majority of the electoral votes in the Electoral College (see Chapter 7). Sometimes the winner of the popular vote does not win the Electoral College. This can happen if the candidate loses several states narrowly.

How Free and Fair Elections Develop Trust in Democratic Institutions

For the EOC, be sure to know how having free and fair elections in the United States helps develop trust in our democratic institutions and preserve our constitutional republic.

Voting is a form of civic participation and an important citizenship responsibility. By voting, we signal that we are proud to be part of a democracy in which ordinary citizens are the final source of all political power and authority. We express our choices and agree to follow the will of the majority of our fellow citizens. Government leaders learn what the majority of citizens really want. This helps inform and shape public policy.

To **preserve our constitutional republic**, elections are **free and fair**. Every qualified citizen has the right to vote without paying any poll tax or other fee. Public officials oversee that elections are conducted honestly and fairly. Voting takes place in private in a public place, so the process is transparent. Citizens can demand a recount if the election results are very close. Candidates have the right to criticize government policies without fearing imprisonment.

Having free and fair elections is one of the pillars of the American system of government. Because we believe our elections are fair, we believe that our government officials represent the will of the majority of the American people. Even if we do not agree with all of our leaders' policies, we can accept their actions as the will of the majority. We also know that we have the opportunity—through our freedoms of speech, press, and assembly—to persuade our fellow citizens to change their views and to elect different officials in the next election. Finally, our individual rights and the rule of law protect us from arbitrary actions by the political party in power.

In contrast, many nations do not have free and fair elections. Citizens may not enjoy the right to vote at all. These citizens are subject to the whims of a dictator or a military government, and have no voice of their own in the direction of the government or public policy.

In other countries, citizens may have to pay some fees to vote, limiting who is able to participate in the election process.

In still other countries, citizens appear to have the right to vote, but in fact there is no real choice between the candidates. Political opponents of the government are arrested and imprisoned, limiting the choices for voters. There is no free speech, so people cannot campaign against government policies. When the voting does take place, the party in power cheats in reporting the results. Under this kind of government, people have no faith in the election process. Citizens realize that they are living in a dictatorship without individual rights and that their elections are fake.

In the United States, we believe that our elections are **free and fair**, that our elected officials represent the will of the majority, that we have an opportunity to change their policies in the future, and that our basic individual rights are safeguarded. Therefore, we can place our trust in our nation's **democratic institutions**—our organizations of government that follow democratic principles, such as the rule of the majority and the protection of individual rights. Our confidence in the integrity (*honesty; truthfulness*) of our democratic institutions protects and preserves our constitutional republic.

The belief that our elected officials represent the will of the majority and that they will respect the rule of law and individual rights discourages any thoughts of overthrowing our government institutions and therefore helps to protect our republican system of government.

Name ________________________________

Complete the exercise below.

ELECTION PROJECT

Evaluating Candidates for Public Office

INTRODUCTION:

In this project, you and your classmates will evaluate candidates running for office in the next election. Then you will create a candidate profile that appeals to young voters.

TASK:

1. Create a new notebook in OneNote for this project.
2. Select a public office, such as Governor of Florida or U.S. Senator, that is being decided in the next election.
3. Conduct Research:
   - Identify the candidates from the two major parties (Democratic and Republican) who are running for that office.
   - In your OneNote notebook, create two tabs (one for each candidate).
   - Gather background information on each candidate and place findings in appropriate tabs.
   - Evaluate how qualified each candidate is based on education, experience, and views on the issues.

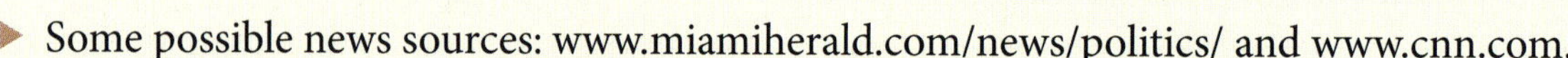

   - Some possible news sources: www.miamiherald.com/news/politics/ and www.cnn.com.

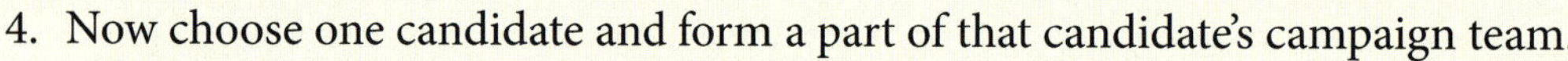

4. Now choose one candidate and form a part of that candidate's campaign team.
   - Work in small groups. Your group should create a Facebook profile of your candidate that will appeal to young voters, ages 18–25. Your Facebook profile should include a photograph of the candidate and sections on the candidate's background and education, experience, views on key issues, and why that individual is the most qualified candidate for the office. Your Facebook profile should be aimed at young voters.
5. Finally, your group will make a presentation to the rest of the class on behalf of your candidate.
   - Your group should base its presentation on its Facebook profile.
   - Provide feedback to other groups in the form of written comments on how accurate you thought their presentation was, how polished and professional they appeared, and how compelling you think their case would have been to young voters.

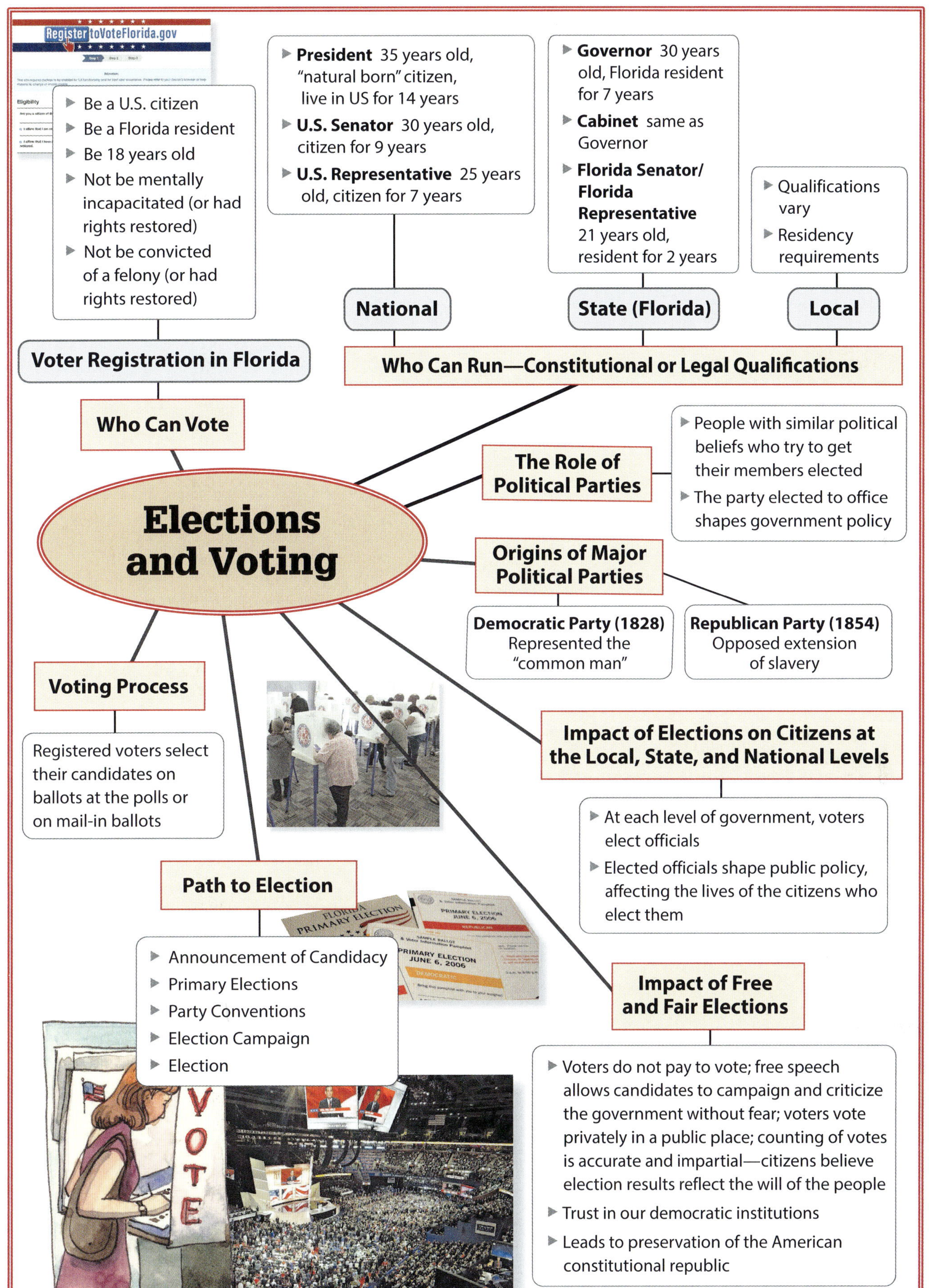
RegistertoVoteFlorida.gov
Be a U.S. citizen
Be a Florida resident
Be 18 years old
Not be mentally incapacitated (or had rights restored)
Not be convicted of a felony (or had rights restored)
Voter Registration in Florida
Who Can Vote
President 35 years old, "natural born" citizen, live in US for 14 years
U.S. Senator 30 years old, citizen for 9 years
U.S. Representative 25 years old, citizen for 7 years
Governor 30 years old, Florida resident for 7 years
Cabinet same as Governor
Florida Senator/ Florida Representative 21 years old, resident for 2 years
Qualifications vary
Residency requirements
National
State (Florida)
Local
Who Can Run—Constitutional or Legal Qualifications
Elections and Voting
The Role of Political Parties
People with similar political beliefs who try to get their members elected
The party elected to office shapes government policy
Origins of Major Political Parties
Democratic Party (1828) Represented the "common man"
Republican Party (1854) Opposed extension of slavery
Voting Process
Registered voters select their candidates on ballots at the polls or on mail-in ballots
Impact of Elections on Citizens at the Local, State, and National Levels
At each level of government, voters elect officials
Elected officials shape public policy, affecting the lives of the citizens who elect them
Path to Election
Announcement of Candidacy
Primary Elections
Party Conventions
Election Campaign
Election
FLORIDA PRIMARY ELECTION
PRIMARY ELECTION JUNE 6, 2006
VOTE
Impact of Free and Fair Elections
Voters do not pay to vote; free speech allows candidates to campaign and criticize the government without fear; voters vote privately in a public place; counting of votes is accurate and impartial—citizens believe election results reflect the will of the people
Trust in our democratic institutions
Leads to preservation of the American constitutional republic

Review Cards: Voting and Elections

Voting and Voter Registration

- American citizens exercise their control over government by **voting** in **elections**.
- In order to vote, a citizen must be a registered voter. In Florida, voters must register 29 days or more before the election takes place. Most Americans register when they renew their driver's licenses.
- To register in Florida, a person must be a U.S. citizen, be a resident of Florida, and be 18 years of age or older. The person cannot have committed a felony or be mentally incapable (and not have had his or her rights restored). Finally, the applicant must provide a current and valid identification card, such as a driver's license.

The Voting Process: How Qualified Citizens Vote

- Citizens vote at a polling place. They mark their choices on a paper or electronic ballot.
- The election of national, state, and local officials usually takes place at the same time. The ballot presents choices to each voter for that voter's election contests, based on the districts in which the voter lives.
- Voting has an important impact on voters. It gives them pride in their government and an understanding that they have the ability to influence public policy.

Political Parties

- When citizens register to vote, they can identify themselves as members of a **political party**. A political party is a group of people who share political beliefs. They organize to promote their shared beliefs by electing party members to government offices.
- The United States has a two-party system. Most elected officials belong to either the Democratic Party or Republican Party. The **Democratic Party** was formed in 1828 to represent the "common man"—the newly enfranchised working man. The **Republican Party** was formed in 1854 by those who opposed the extension of slavery into western territories. Abraham Lincoln became the first Republican President in 1860.
- Both political parties have evolved over time. In the 1930s and 1960s, the Democratic Party introduced new government programs to address social and economic problems. Republicans favor less government interference and lower taxes. Whichever party is in power can have a major impact on **public policy** (*the actions taken by government to meet public needs*).

The Path to Office: Nomination and Election

- Political parties find suitable people to run for political office. Each party nominates (*names*) one candidate for each government office that is up for election.
- Primary elections: When several individuals from the same party seek the same political office, they usually compete in a primary election to obtain their party's nomination.
- Party Conventions: Political parties hold state and national party conventions. National party conventions are usually held every four years to nominate candidates for President and Vice President.
- Party nominees then compete in a general election campaign. They hold rallies, make political advertisements, and have debates with other candidates.

The U.S. Constitution: Qualifications for National Office

The U.S. Constitution sets the **constitutional qualifications** for serving in national offices:

- Every U.S. Representative must be at least 25 years old, must have been a U.S. citizen for seven years, and must be a current resident of the state he or she represents.
- Every U.S. Senator must be at least 30 years old, must have been a U.S. citizen for nine years, and must be a current resident of the state he or she represents.
- The President of the United States must be at least 35 years old, must be a "natural born" citizen (not "naturalized"), and must have lived in the United States for at least 14 years.

The Florida Constitution: Qualifications for State Office

The Florida Constitution sets the **constitutional qualifications** for serving in state offices:

- The Governor of Florida, Lieutenant Governor, and other elected Cabinet members must be at least 30 years old, and must have been residents of Florida for at least seven years.
- Each Florida Senator or Florida Representative must be at least 21 years old, must have been a resident of Florida for at least two years, and must be current resident of the district he or she represents.

Local Government in Florida: Qualifications for Local Office

The qualifications for elected local offices (mayor, county commissioner, etc.) are defined by local laws or charters (*grants of powers by the state legislature*) of a municipality rather than by the Florida or U.S. Constitution. Qualifications to hold local office differ from place to place. There are almost always residence requirements (*how long someone has lived in a place*) but usually no restrictions based on age. Many local governments have term limits.

How Free and Fair Elections Build Trust in Democratic Institutions

- Because we have free and fair elections, we believe that our government officials represent the will of the majority of the American people.
- We also know that we have the opportunity—through our freedoms of speech, press, and assembly—to persuade our fellow citizens to change their views and to elect different officials in the next election. Meanwhile, our individual rights protect us from arbitrary actions by those in power.
- Our **free and fair elections** help build **trust in our democratic institutions** (*government bodies that follow democratic principles, such as having elected officials, and protecting individual rights*). Our confidence in our democratic institutions helps **preserve our constitutional republic**.
- In contrast, many nations do not have free and fair elections. People may not enjoy the right to vote at all. These citizens are subject to the whims of a dictator or a military government. In some countries, citizens appear to have the right to vote, but in fact there is no real choice between the candidates. Political opponents of the government have been arrested and imprisoned. There is no free speech, so people cannot campaign against government policies. When the voting takes place, the party in power cheats in reporting election results. Under this kind of government, people have no faith in the election process.

The Impact of Voting and Elections on Citizens at the Local, State and National Levels

- At each level of government, citizens influence their state officials through the election process. Leaders know that if their policies are unpopular, they will not be re-elected. Their policies, in turn, influence citizens at the local, state and national level.
- In national elections, voters elect the President and members of Congress. These officials set our national policies. For example, they may decide to raise or lower taxes. This will impact how much of their income citizens have to save or spend.
- Voters elect state officials who will establish policies that affect citizens at the state level—such as access to state educational programs.
- At the local level, citizens elect local officials (such as a mayor, county commissioners or school board members, These locial officeholders will make decisions affecting the community, such as on school spending or new housing in the community.

What Do You Know

SS.7.CG.2.7

1. Which candidate meets the constitutional requirements for becoming Governor of Florida?

   A. Eileen was born in Ireland, is 32 years old, is a naturalized citizen, and has lived in Florida for 20 years.

   B. James was born in Florida, is 27 years old, and has lived in Florida his whole life.

   C. Amy was born in New York, is 45 years old, and has lived in Florida for five years.

   D. Steven was born in Massachusetts, is 28 years old, and has lived in Florida for six years.

SS.7.CG.2.6

2. What was the reason for the formation of the Democratic Party?

   A. to oppose the extension of slavery

   B. to urge granting the right to vote to women

   C. to represent recently enfranchised working men

   D. to promote a safety net to ordinary citizens during the Depression

SS.7.CG.2.6

3. Why is having free and fair elections important to a democratic society?

   A. Citizens have greater trust in their institutions.

   B. The rights of minority groups may not be respected.

   C. Government leaders can act without restraint in a crisis.

   D. Citizens fear to criticize their leaders after they are elected.

SS.7.CG.2.6

4. The chart below lists different elections.

I.	Election of the President of the United States
II.	Election of the Governor of Florida
III.	Election of U.S. Senator from Florida
IV.	Election of Attorney General of Florida
V.	Election of Representative to Florida Legislature
VI.	Election of Representative to the U.S. House of Represenatives

Which of the elections above are conducted at the state level?

A. I, III, VI

B. II, IV, V

C. II, III, V

D. I, IV, VI

SS.7.CG.2.7

5. The chart below lists the constitutional requirements for serving as a member of the Florida House of Representatives

- Be 21 years old
- ____ **?** ________
- Live in the district of Florida represented

Which constitutional requirement completes the chart?

A. Be a natural born citizen

B. Have lived in the United States for 14 years

C. Have been a resident of Florida for two years

D. Have previously served in local government

SS.7.CG.2.6

6. The diagram below shows a series of events in a city in Florida.

Registered voters elected new city commissioners

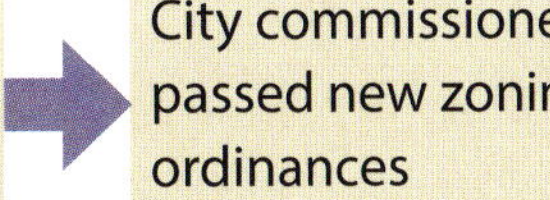

City commissioners passed new zoning ordinances

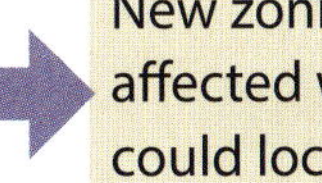

New zoning ordinances affected where residents could locate businesses

What would be the best title for this diagram?

A. The impact of voting laws on election contests

B. The impact of elections on citizens at the local level

C. The impact of elections on citizens at the state level

D. The impact of elections on citizens at the national level

SS.7.CG.2.6

7. Which American political party was established to oppose the extension of slavery into western territories?

A. Federalist Party
B. Democratic Party
C. Republican Party
D. Abolitionist Party

SS.7.CG.2.6

8. The following chart shows the requirements to register to vote in Florida.

- Be a U.S. citizen
- ____?________
- Be 18 years old or older
- Not be judged as mentally incapacitated
- Not be convicted of a felony (or have rights restored)

Which requirement completes the chart?

A. be a Florida resident
B. live in Florida for two years
C. have a high school diploma
D. be able to read and write in English

SS.7.CG.2.6

9. In November 1932, Democratic candidate Franklin D. Roosevelt was elected as President of the United States. He replaced Herbert Hoover, a Republican. Roosevelt changed Hoover's policies by providing direct relief to unemployed workers through programs such as the Civilian Conservation Corps.

What conclusion can be drawn from this example?

A. Political parties have done more harm to society than good.
B. Disagreements between the two main parties caused the Great Depression.
C. Both of the major political parties have had an important role in shaping public policy.
D. The existence of political parties distracts leaders from promoting the common good.

SS.7.CG.2.7

10. Azra is 29 years old. She was born in Istanbul, Turkey. Fifteen years ago, Azra moved to the United States with her family. She became a U.S. citizen eight years ago. Just last year, Azra moved to Florida. She has decided to run for public office. For which office is she qualified to run?

A. Governor of Florida
B. Florida State Senator
C. U.S. Senator from Florida
D. Member of U.S. House of Representatives

CHAPTER 15

The Impact of Individuals, Interest Groups, and the Media

SS.7.CG.2.8 Examine the impact of media, individuals, and interest groups on monitoring and influencing government.

SS.7.CG.2.9 Analyze media and political communications and identify examples of bias, symbolism and propaganda.

Content Focus Vocabulary in This Chapter

Methods used by individuals
Monitor government
Influence government
Hold government officials accountable
Attend civic meetings
Peacefully protest
Petition government
Vote
Run for office
Impact
Interest group
Methods used by interest groups
Lobbying
Media
Methods used by media
Watchdog
Freedom of the press
1st Amendment
Political communications
Bias
Symbolism
Propaganda
Public opinion

Florida "Keys" to Learning

1. **The methods used by individuals** to **monitor** (*watch over; keep track of*), **hold accountable** (*make responsible for*), and **influence government** are **attending civic meetings** (*meetings held for public purposes*), **peacefully protesting, petitioning government** (*writing to government officials requesting a change*), **voting**, and **running for office** (*seeking election to a government position*). The **impact** (*effect*) of these actions is often to change the course of public policy (*the steps taken by government*).

2. An **interest group** is a group of individuals with common interests who seek to influence public policy. While political parties try to elect candidates and have positions on a wide number of issues, interest groups try to influence legislators and government officials directly, and only have positions on a narrow range of issues based on their specific interests.

3. **Methods used by interest groups:** Interest groups often "**monitor**" (*watch over; keep track of*) developments in legislatures and government agencies, and report to their members or to the public.

4. Interest groups hire lobbyists, who speak to state legislators, members of Congress, or other government officials. The goal of **lobbying** is to **influence government**, especially new legislation or regulations.

5. Interest groups also try to influence elections and election activities. Each interest group is allowed to form its own political action committee, or PAC, in order to help politicians get elected or re-elected.

6. Interest groups sometimes promote their causes by filing lawsuits (*suing in court*), known as litigation.

7. Interest groups usually try to sway public opinion—the views of the general public—through advertising, press releases, publishing articles, and television and radio appearances. The **impact** of the methods used by interest groups is to shape legislation and public policy.

8. The **media** consist of newspapers, television, radio and the Internet. These are all ways of communicating with the public.

9. The **methods used by media** to **monitor government**: Newspapers, television networks, and news agencies send reporters to follow government activities. The media act as "**watchdogs**" over our government—questioning government leaders about their actions and exposing government wrongdoing.

10. **Impact**: People learn about their government from the media. Government leaders are careful in their actions because they know they will be reported by the media.

11. Because of its important function in our democracy, the media are protected by the **1st Amendment**, which guarantees "**freedom of the press**." This means government officials cannot censor (*edit in advance*) what is published, and reporters and media cannot be prosecuted for criticizing the government.

12. **Political communications** are messages that attempt to influence voters, public opinion and government actions. They appeal to both reason and emotion to persuade readers and viewers. They often use **symbolism** and **bias**. A symbol is something that represents something else, such as a flag, which represents a country. Being biased means being one-sided or prejudiced without considering all sides of an issue fairly.

13. Political communications that are extremely biased and that appeal to fears and emotions in order to persuade public opinion are known as **propaganda**. Propaganda makes use of exaggerations, half-truths, name calling, glittering generalities, and over-simplification. The aim of propaganda and other forms of political communication is to influence **public opinion** (*the views of the general public*).

Political parties are not the only groups not found in the Constitution that influence government policies. Newspaper and television reporters and special interest groups are not mentioned there either. Yet they can have a tremendous impact on government decision-making. In fact, the press and other media are so influential they have even been called the "Fourth Branch" of government.

In this chapter, you will learn how individuals, interest groups, and the "media" monitor and influence government. You will also learn how they sometimes use bias, symbolism and propaganda to shape public opinion.

> To **monitor the government** means to closely observe what its different officials, agencies or branches are doing; for example, following a bill that is passing through Congress.
>
> To **influence the government** means to persuade members of the government to adopt policies or programs you prefer.

How Individuals Can Monitor, Hold Accountable, and Influence Government

Be sure to know how individuals monitor, hold accountable, and influence government for the EOC.

In the United States, any individual can **monitor the government** (*watch over or keep track of government actions*), **hold government officials accountable,** and **influence government policy**. We hold our government officials "accountable" by seeing them as responsible for what they accomplish in office. We especially compare their conduct in office with the campaign promises they made to get elected.

There are several **methods used by individuals** to monitor, hold accountable and influence government. These include:

Attending Civic Meetings

Individuals can **attend civic meetings**. These meetings may be held by community leaders to discuss local issues, or by a national political party to choose candidates. At these meetings, individuals learn information and express their views.

Peacefully Protesting

Sometimes attending a meeting on a public issue does not seem to be enough. Individuals may feel very strongly about a particular cause. It could be civil rights, an overseas war, taxes, protecting the environment, or some other important issue. Individuals can **peacefully protest** by marching, demonstrating in front of government buildings, or holding a rally. The purpose of such peaceful protests is to attract publicity and persuade lawmakers to act.

Petitioning Government

Another way that individuals can influence government is by petitioning. A petition is a formal document, signed by citizens, requesting the government to do something. The petition might be sent to state legislators or members of Congress. Our right to **petition government** is guaranteed by the **1st Amendment**.

Voting

One of the most basic ways that individuals **influence government** and **hold government officials accountable** is by **voting**. Voters will often refuse to re-elect government officials who have not kept their campaign promises, or who have not done a good job in office. By either re-electing government officials or voting them out of office, citizens hold them accountable for their actions.

> **Some Methods Used by Individuals to Monitor and Influence Government**
>
> - Attending civic meetings
> - Peacefully protesting
> - Petitioning government
> - Voting
> - Running for office

Running for Office

Finally, individuals are able to **run for office** (*seek a government position*). During the campaign they can make their views known. Even if they lose the election, their views will be considered and have some influence on government. Those individuals who are elected to public office have the opportunity to move government policy in a new direction. The impact of all these methods used by individuals is to influence government decisions and shape public policy (*steps taken by the government*).

Interest Groups

We all have interests—some of us like sports while others enjoy music or being outdoors. An **interest group** is a group of individuals with common interests who seek to influence public policy. There are now thousands of such interest groups in the United States.

Many of these interest groups are based on common economic interests. For example, American manufacturers have formed an interest group known as the "National Association of Manufacturers." Other groups, such as the American Medical Association, the National Association of Home Builders, and the American Bankers Association, are focused on a single industry. The AFL-CIO (American Federation of Labor and Congress of Industrial Organizations) represents the interests of more than ten million workers. The National Education Association and the Service Employees International Union represent specific groups of workers.

Environmental interest groups, such as the Sierra Club, protect wildlife and attempt to reduce pollution. Other interest groups, like the NAACP (National Association for the Advancement of Colored People) and NOW (National Organization of Women) promote the interests of groups that were disadvantaged in the past.

Some interest groups form over specific issues, such as the National Right to Life Committee and the American Israel Public Affairs Committee. The National Rifle Association is now largely concerned with protecting the right to own guns.

A public interest group attempts to promote the common good—the interests of Americans as a whole rather than of any specific group. A non-profit public interest group does not pay federal income tax.

An interest group differs from a political party. A political party focuses on electing its candidates to office. A political party usually has a platform addressing a large number of issues. An interest group attempts to influence public policies directly, rather than by electing its members as government officials. It generally focuses on a specific issue or area, rather than on all the problems facing our government leaders.

The Active Citizen

- Make a chart or Venn diagram comparing political parties and interest groups.
- Research one of the interest groups mentioned above. Give an oral presentation or PowerPoint presentation to your class describing how this group was formed, where it is located today, how many members it has, what its goals are, and what it has accomplished.

How Interest Groups Monitor and Influence Government

There are several methods used by interest groups to influence the government and further their goals.

Monitoring

As you know, to monitor something is to watch over it and check what is happening. Interest groups often "monitor" developments. This means they keep track of everything legislatures and government agencies are doing that might affect their area of focus. Interest-group officers or agents attend legislative sessions and committee hearings. They develop friendly relations with legislators and their staff to get copies of bills. Then the interest group sends newsletters to its members informing them of key developments. This keeps members informed and allows them to take steps to influence new laws or to react to new requirements. Some interest groups even rate legislators, based on how well they support the interest group's goals.

Lobbying

A lobby is a long hall or corridor. In the past, the hired representatives of interest groups often tried to corner legislators in the lobbies of their hotels or of legislative buildings to speak to them. Today, the paid agent of an interest group who speaks to state legislators, members of Congress, or government officials in order to influence new legislation or regulations is known as a lobbyist. Their activities are known as lobbying.

Lobbying is an activity protected by the right to free speech. Lobbyists must register with Congress, or with their state legislature. They also have to file reports showing how much each of their clients has paid for their lobbying services. All of this information is made available to the public.

At present, there are thousands of lobbyists working in Washington, D.C., and state capitals around the country. Some of these lobbyists are former legislators themselves. The main goal of these lobbyists is to influence members of Congress or state legislators. Very often lobbyists have special subject-area expertise and can provide very useful information to legislators. They may even help friendly legislators plan a strategy for passing or blocking proposed legislation.

Campaigning

Interest groups and their lobbyists also help politicians to get elected or re-elected. Campaign finance reform has limited the amount of money that individuals can contribute to candidates. However, the law permits any interest group, including corporations and labor organizations, to form its own political action committee, or PAC. Each PAC must register with the Federal Election Commission. PACs can contribute larger sums of money to support candidates than individuals are permitted to do.

In addition to providing funds through PACs, interest groups provide endorsements to candidates and supply volunteers to work in election campaigns.

Litigation

Litigation refers to filing and defending against lawsuits in court. One important way in which interest groups—particularly public interest groups and those supporting minority rights—promote their causes is by filing lawsuits. Civil Rights groups used litigation to overturn racial segregation in the South. Consumer groups and environmental groups also sometimes use lawsuits. Even when they lose, lawsuits bring public attention to issues raised by interest groups.

Publicity

Interest groups also take other steps to win public support for their causes and to influence public opinion (*the views of the general public*). This is sometimes called "grass roots" lobbying. Interest groups may advertise in newspapers, magazines, radio or television. They may publish articles promoting their point of view. They may send out advertisements or persuasive literature by mail. They may even phone members of the public directly in a telephone campaign or use social media. This puts pressure on lawmakers and other decision makers.

The Impact of Interest Groups

The activities of interest groups affect public opinion, legislators and other government officials. Because of their subject matter expertise, campaign contributions and lobbying efforts, interest groups have a special **impact** (*effect*) on the laws and regulations passed by government.

Methods Used by Interest Groups to Monitor and Influence Government

- There are many different types of interest groups, from those representing particular industries to public interest groups protecting the environment.
- Interest groups offer different points of view.
- Interest groups can be one-sided and biased.
- Interest groups encourage public participation in government.
- Interest groups help to provide specific details for proposed legislation.
- Interest groups bring subject-area expertise to legislators, government officials and the public.
- Interest groups monitor events in government for their members, for legislators and for the public.
- Interest groups influence public opinion ("grass roots" lobbying).
- Interest groups can influence the legislative process by lobbying legislators.

The Active Citizen

- Imagine that you are a paid lobbyist. Write a newsletter to your clients (those who pay for your lobbying services).
- Are interest groups too powerful? Interview two adults (relatives, neighbors or friends) and ask them this question. Then share your results with your classmates.
- Identify the type of activity—monitoring, lobbying, litigation, or publicity—used by interest groups in each of the examples in the chart below.

Scenario	Type of Interest Group Activity
The National Association of Armadillo Watchers, a public interest group, files a lawsuit to protect nine-banded armadillos in Florida from real estate developers.	
A hired representative of the Acme interest group contacts members of Congress, urging them to vote "yes" on a new bill.	
The staff of the Unicycle Association of America, an interest group, prepares its monthly newsletter telling its members about new legislation on unicycle lanes.	
The National Society of French Bakers of America starts a newspaper, radio and television campaign to increase public awareness of new government regulations on French breakfast pastries.	

What is the Media?

You do not need to know the history of the media for the EOC test, but you do need to know how the media monitor the government and hold government officials accountable.

The term **"media"** refers to "mass media"—methods of communicating to large numbers of people. The media include newspapers, magazines, radio and television programs, Internet websites and "blogs," and "social media" like Facebook and Instagram.

Like political parties and interest groups, the media are not mentioned in the Constitution. And yet they have played just as important a role in American politics and government from the very beginnings of our nation.

Enrichment

At one time, most Americans learned about current events and politics from newspapers. In the early nineteenth century, newspapers were often filled with the debates of Congress and state legislatures. By the 1930s, Americans started learning about public events from the radio. President Franklin D. Roosevelt appealed directly to Americans in his weekly "Fireside Chats," broadcast over

the radio. Most Americans listened by radio to President Roosevelt's speech on December 8, 1941, the day after the attack on Pearl Harbor, when he asked Congress for a declaration of war on Japan. Americans also saw occasional current events on newsreels when they went to the movies.

After World War II, a majority of Americans started watching news at home on television. Each of the three major networks—ABC, CBS, and NBC—had its own nightly news program. These network news programs were hosted by one or two highly visible news anchors—such as Walter Cronkite for CBS. President John F. Kennedy began the practice of giving televised press conferences and live addresses to the nation on television.

Even as recently as 1981, when President Reagan addressed Congress for the very first time, almost two-thirds of the public watched his address that evening on one of the three major networks. Half of the public read about Reagan's speech the next day in the newspaper.

This situation has greatly changed in recent years with the rise of cable television and the Internet. There are now more television stations reporting the news than ever before. Many people also learn about current events from social media and other sources on the Internet, which are being constantly updated, instead of watching news programs on television or reading articles in a printed newspaper.

News Articles and Editorials

The media have two main kinds of articles or programs for their readers. Most articles are intended to inform readers. They tell readers the "who," "what", "when," "where," "how," and "why" of an event or news story. These articles usually attempt to give a balanced picture, often reporting more than one point of view.

Newspapers, magazines, Internet sources, and television networks also present a second kind of article (or television program): "opinion" pieces. These tell the opinions of the writer or producer. The purpose of an opinion piece is not to give balanced, informative reporting but to persuade readers to adopt a particular point of view.

Sometimes articles, especially on the Internet, will present opinion pieces as informational and may even report facts that are untrue. It is now the reader's responsibility to check information, especially if the source is unknown.

How the Media Monitor and Hold Government Accountable

Investigative Journalism: The Media Acting as "Watchdog"

Like interest groups, the media monitor government and hold government officials accountable. The media thus act as "**watchdogs**" of our government. They question government officials and research government activities to identify issues and to expose possible wrongdoing by government officials.

This has always been one of the roles of the media. The "muckrakers" of the Progressive Era (1890–1920), for example, exposed the abuses of rapid industrialization. Upton Sinclair reported that meat packers put dead rats and other impurities into their sausages. Outrage over his reports led Congress to pass the Meat Inspection Act in 1906.

Upton Sinclair

The role of the media as "watchdog" became especially significant when public mistrust of government grew during the Vietnam War in the 1960s and early 1970s. Investigative journalists then played an important role in the Watergate scandal. Reporters from the *Washington Post* investigated and publicized a break-in into Democratic Party national headquarters in the Watergate Hotel and office complex in 1972. Their newspaper articles led to Congressional hearings. These hearings eventually exposed the White House cover-up of the break-in. President Nixon resigned from office rather than face impeachment.

As you can see, journalists are considered "**watchdogs**" because they watch over public officials and report what they see to the public. Without their oversight, the public would have far less information about the workings of our government. Politicians and government leaders would then be able to act without the same accountability to the public.

For this reason, "**freedom of the press**" is a protected right. The **1st Amendment** states that: "Congress shall make no law . . . abridging (*limiting*) the freedom . . . of the press." Government officials do not censor (*read in advance and edit*) newspaper or other media reports before they are published. They also cannot prosecute journalists for reporting the truth. This is not always the case in other countries.

The Impact of the Media

The media thus **monitor government, hold government officials accountable**, and **influence government**. They do this in many ways:

- Newspapers, television stations and news agencies assign reporters to monitor the Presidency, Congress and key agencies as well as state and local governments. They follow their activities and report them to the American people.
- Reporters need information and interviews for their news stories. Legislators need to communicate their views and activities to the public. By giving an interview, a politician or legislator can often reach millions of voters. The media therefore make it easier for government leaders to communicate with the public.
- Government officials, legislators, and politicians are less likely to be dishonest because they know that they are being constantly monitored by journalists.
- When reporters suspect wrongdoing by government officials, they investigate the situation further.
- While the media help keep government officials accountable, there may be some drawbacks. Surrounded by the media, politicians tend to focus on getting re-elected. They may be afraid to take necessary steps that are unpopular. The constant pressure of the media may also discourage some talented individuals from entering government service.

The Active Citizen

- Write one or two paragraphs describing what American politics would be like if there were no journalists, newspapers, radio, television, or the Internet.
- In the past, reporters focused on public issues but overlooked officials' private lives. This is no longer true. Should journalists be able to report on the private lives of public leaders? Write a short essay giving your views on this topic. First identify your point of view. Then give your reasons with supporting facts.

Evaluating the Impact of Bias, Symbolism and Propaganda on Public Opinion

Political communications are statements from political parties, interest groups and others. They provide information but are mainly designed to persuade readers and listeners. Editorials in newspapers and other media have the same purpose.

These types of communications use special persuasive techniques to influence public opinion. Three of the most important of these techniques are **bias**, **symbolism**, and **propaganda**.

- **Bias** is a prejudice in favor of or against something. People are biased when they favor one side over another without really looking at an issue or situation carefully. They may have a personal or economic interest at stake in the issue.

  Political communications and media are similarly biased when they give only one point of view on an issue or situation. They focus on information that favors their position while they ignore opposing information. They also show bias when they repeat popular prejudices and stereotypes (*general beliefs about different groups of people based on emotion*).

- **Symbolism** is the use of symbols in speech, writing or art. A symbol is something that actually stands for something else. It is often a simple image that represents a group, place, or set of ideas. For example, an eagle in a political cartoon could represent the United States, a donkey in a political poster could represent the Democratic Party, and an elephant could represent the Republican Party.

  How many of these symbols can you identify?

People trying to persuade others often associate themselves with a popular symbol. They try to link themselves to the positive feelings that the audience has about that symbol. For example, when American politicians appear on television, they often show the American flag in the background. They hope their viewers will associate them with the flag as a symbol of patriotism.

- **Propaganda** is a form of public communication that provides biased and one-sided information. The purpose of propaganda is to influence and persuade "**public opinion**"—the views of average citizens.

  Propaganda is always one-sided. It gives evidence in support of its point of view but not evidence for other points of view. Usually it is exaggerated and misleading.

  Propaganda appeals to people's emotions rather than to their reason. It may, for example, encourage people's fears. Propaganda relies on emotionally charged "loaded language," rather than presenting logical reasoning and actual facts.

Fact or Opinion?

A **fact** is a statement that can be verified by checking with other sources. It is either true or false. An **opinion** is an expression of belief. There are different kinds of opinions. Some opinions are mere expressions of taste: "I like the taste of a fresh, crisp apple." No one can dispute that the speaker likes apples. Other opinions are statements of belief about the future, or about factual matters where the facts remain unknown: "I think people will watch less television in the future" or "I believe Florida had more visitors last year than any other state."

You will not need to identify specific propaganda techniques on the EOC but you will need to recognize propaganda, symbolism and bias.

Some of the ways that propaganda attempts to influence public opinion are the following:

- **Opinions disguised as facts:** The propaganda presents opinions as though they were facts.

  "People on food stamps are clearly too lazy to work."

- **Endorsements:** The propaganda emphasizes the support of famous people, suggesting that this makes something reasonable or right.

  "Jennifer Lawrence, Lady Gaga and Taylor Swift support Amendment 10 as the best choice. Shouldn't you support it, too?"

- **"Bandwagon" technique:** The propaganda points out that a large number of people are doing something, so the listener or reader should do the same.

  "Most Floridians support Amendment 10. Shouldn't you support it, too?"

- **"Labeling" or "name calling":** The propaganda puts down opponents or ideas by calling them names and making fun of them. It uses "loaded language" (*terms with emotional meanings*).

  "Those against sending more U.S. troops to Syria are cowards afraid of their own shadows."

- **"Glittering generalities":** The propaganda makes vague, general statements that sound good but that are not specific enough to be checked.

  "This is the best product ever invented. Everyone loves using it."

- **Oversimplification:** The propaganda makes a complex situation or problem seem simpler than it really is. The propaganda may propose a simple solution to a group of complex problems.

  "Drug companies are responsible for our current health care crisis."

- **Half-Truths and Exaggerations:** The propaganda makes statements that give part of the truth but that are not really accurate. Exaggerations (*saying something is more of something—stronger, larger, smarter—than it actually is*) are a form of half-truth. Images in visual propaganda often contain exaggerated features, based on common biases and stereotypes (*a popular but oversimplified image of a person or thing*).

  "Our candidate risked his life in the military in the last war." (This is a half-truth if the candidate was in the military but was never actually sent into combat.)

The Active Citizen

Examine the following two American posters from World War II. During this war (1941–1945), American soldiers fought against soldiers from Imperial Japan and Nazi Germany. Look for examples of bias, symbolism, and propaganda in these posters.

Continues ▶

1. How does the first poster show bias? Consider the images and expressions of the two soldiers, and the use of loaded language like "Murdering Jap."
2. How does the second poster use symbolism? Consider the helmet and the statue the figure is holding.
3. Which common propaganda devices do these two posters use?
4. What impact do you think posters like these had on public opinion in wartime?

Identify whether each of the following statements illustrates bias, symbolism or propaganda. The same example could illustrate more than one of these. Then explain how this example would be likely to affect a reader,

Statement	Bias, Symbolism or Propaganda?	Probable Impact on a Reader
"Our community has done more to help the homeless than any other community in recorded history."		
"As we approached the house, we could tell that there was something wrong inside even before we got there."		
"The American taxpayer has suffered for far too long. It is time for us to object to all these unnecessary taxes that just encourage government waste. Stand up for yourself by joining our new political party!"		
"As the smoke cleared on the battlefield, we could see the American flag still waving proudly."		
"We need to send more of our troops to this foreign country. We have never been defeated in war before and we don't want to start here. Sending a few thousand more troops should do the job."		
"People in other countries don't share the same concerns that we do. A quick glance at history is all that is needed to see that."		
"Most of our problems are caused by lazy people who come from other countries. If we could stop them from coming here, prosperity would return to our nation."		
"There is a reason why the tasty orange is our state fruit. Florida is clearly the best state. All the nicest and smartest people live here."		

Name ______________________________

Fill in the boxes in the concept ladder below by adding your own definitions and explanations.

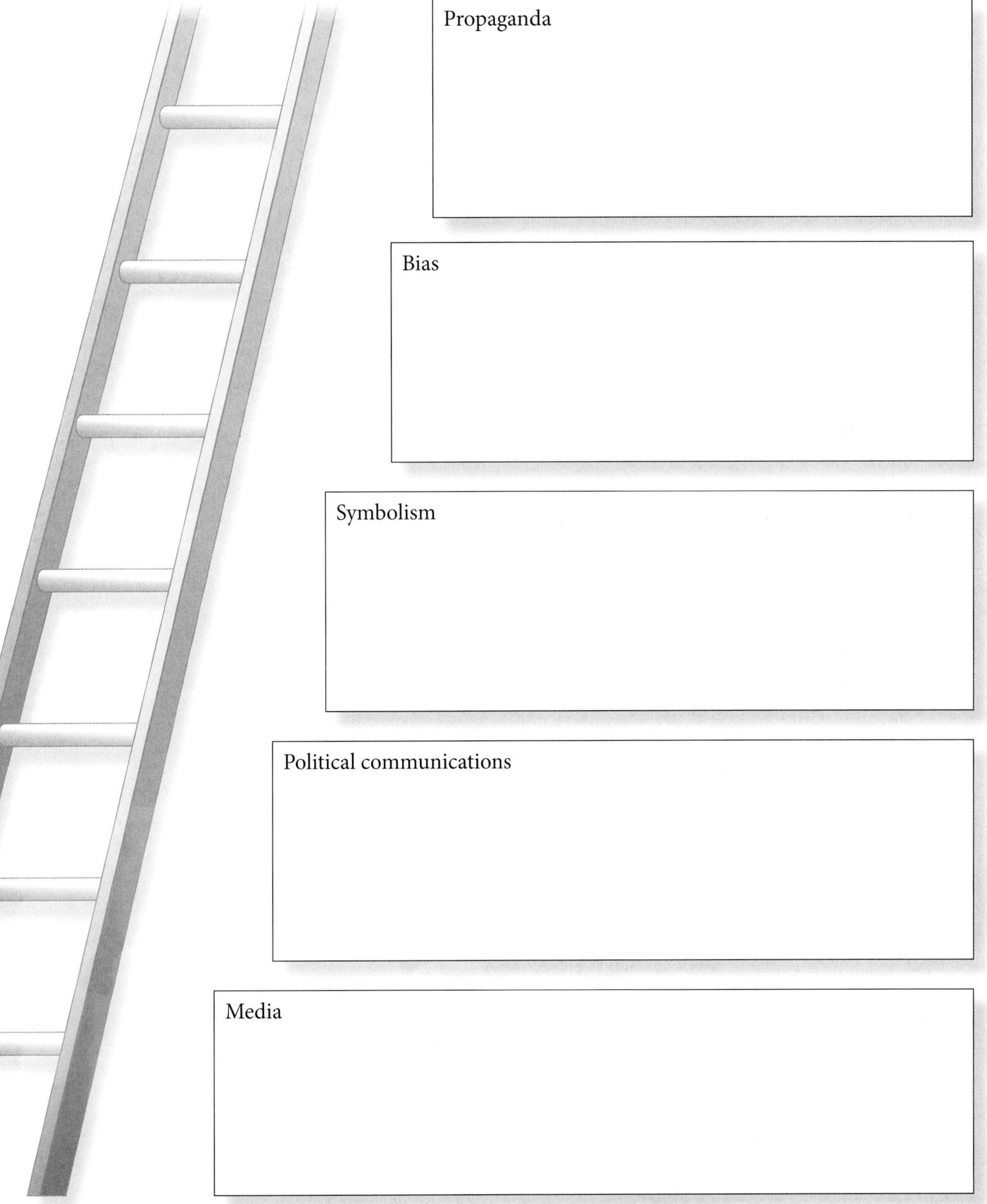

The Dangers of Distortion: Nazi Propaganda and the Holocaust

Today, **propaganda** is seen as something largely negative, but this wasn't always the case. In Nazi Germany (1933–1945), there was an official "Ministry of Public Enlightenment and Propaganda." Propaganda played an essential role in the Holocaust—the systematic persecution and destruction of the Jewish people of Europe by Nazi Germany.

In ancient times, the Jewish people had lived in Israel where they were the first people known to believe in one God. The Romans forced the Jewish people to leave Israel and to move to other parts of the Middle East and Europe. In Europe, Jews were a small minority. They had different beliefs and customs than the majority of Europeans, who were Christian. During the Middle Ages, Jews were often the targets of groups unhappy with their own conditions. Jews were unfairly blamed for the spread of disease, wars, and other disasters. Hatred of Jews is known as antisemitism.

In more modern times, Jews were blamed for economic depressions. New political parties arose that asserted that Jews had formed a giant conspiracy to take over the world. Adolf Hitler, a soldier who had fought in World War I, joined the new Nazi Party after the war. This party blamed the Jews for Germany's defeat in World War I, even though they had nothing to do with it. The Nazis attacked Jews for being communists, but also attacked them for being bankers and owning large businesses (the very opposite of communism).

In the 1930s, the "Great Depression" spread to Germany. In desperation, many Germans turned to the Nazi Party for solutions. Hitler was appointed as leader of the German government at the beginning of 1933. Hitler acted quickly to put all power in the hands of the Nazi Party. He also appointed a Minister of Propaganda to promote Nazi ideas. The Nazi Minister of Propaganda gave speeches, made radio broadcasts, wrote newspaper articles, published books, printed posters and produced newsreels—all of which distorted the truth by making fun of Jews and blaming them for all of Germany's problems. Nazi propaganda films, for example, showed Jewish people living in filth, and compared them to rats. The aim of this propaganda was to demonize and dehumanize the Jewish people. The Nazi government prohibited free speech. So there was no one to challenge these ideas.

Many German people were persuaded by this powerful propaganda. They pledged complete loyalty to the Nazi government and accepted its antisemitic ideas. When the German government openly attacked Jewish people in the streets, few protested. In 1941, with World War II raging, Hitler and the Nazis took an unthinkable step. They decided to murder all of the millions of Jews of Europe—every Jewish man, woman, and child. Nazi propaganda made this tragedy possible by distorting the truth, and making unchecked lies and exaggerations. The Holocaust demonstrated the dangers of modern propaganda.

Even today, antisemitism still exists. Private groups and even some governments create propaganda—often using negative symbols and stereotypes to attack Jewish people and the country of Israel, the Jewish state in the Middle East created in the aftermath of the Holocaust.

Jewish people about to be murdered in the Holocaust—a direct effect of the Nazi propaganda campaign

Analyzing Media and Political Communications

As an active citizen, you may have to interpret communications from the media, interest groups, and political parties. Some of these communications may be speeches or written texts; others might be visual images, such as posters, signs or cartoons; still others could be moving images, such as political advertisements on television.

Remember that a political communication is not impartial. It is created by a specific political party or interest group, whose general aim is to persuade you to adopt their point of view. The goal of political communications—including propaganda—is to influence public opinion. You therefore must be able to identify any bias, symbolism or propaganda found in such communications.

1. The first step in analyzing any media or political communication is to see who created the message. Was it an individual, a reporter, a political party, or an interest group?
2. The second step is to determine the purpose of the article or communication. What were the authors of this communication trying to do? Remember that there are different types of communications, depending upon their purpose. Some articles, images or other communications are informational—their purpose is to give the reader impartial information. Other communications are persuasive—their purpose is to persuade the reader to adopt a particular point of view.

   How does this purpose influence what is said in the communication? In particular, does the communication show any bias? Does it make use of symbolism in order to persuade the reader? Is it actually a piece of propaganda—relying more on its appeal to emotions than on reasoning and facts?
3. Now read or listen to the text of the communication very carefully. What is the main idea it expresses? What arguments does the author use?
4. Next identify any facts or opinions in the communication. You should decide whether each of these facts is accurate. If the communication includes opinions, you should decide if those opinions are reasonable and justified by the evidence.
5. The final step is to evaluate (*determine the value of*) the reasoning in the communication. Is it logical? Or does it contain logical errors?
   - Does it include any of the propaganda devices that you just read about? Is it one-sided? Does it contain "glittering generalities," half-truths, or exaggerations? Does it rely on endorsements or the bandwagon effect?
   - How does it relate to other information you know about the topic?

The Impact on Public Opinion

The aim of propaganda and other forms of political communication is to influence **public opinion**. Yet no one can ever know for sure what the "public" is thinking. In fact, there really is no single public at all—only various groups of people within the public. To measure public opinion, experts take opinion polls. By selecting a sample that accurately represents a cross section of voters, an opinion poll can often predict voting results and measure popular attitudes. In this way, experts also try to determine how bias, symbolism, and propaganda have actually influenced the public.

Enrichment

The Active Citizen

Professor Joseph F. Truman includes several speeches in the appendix to his book, *Political Communication in American Campaigns*. Two of the speeches he includes are by President Ronald Reagan and Reverend Al Sharpton. The first excerpt below is from President Reagan's First Inaugural Address, given in January 1981. This was at a time when the country faced economic difficulties.

The second excerpt is from Reverend Sharpton's speech in favor of John Kerry at the Democratic National Convention in 2004. Kerry ran for President but lost to George W. Bush, who was seeking a second term. John Edwards was Kerry's running mate. He ran for the Vice Presidency.

In this activity, you are asked to compare the two speeches and the methods they use to persuade listeners. Both of these are examples of political communication.

President Reagan's First Inaugural Address

"*The economic ills* (problems) *we suffer have come upon us over several decades. They will not go away in days, weeks, or months, but they will go away. They will go away because we as Americans have the capacity* (ability) *now, as we've had in the past, to do whatever needs to be done to preserve this last and greatest bastion* (stronghold) *of freedom.*

In this present crisis, government is not the solution to our problem; government is the problem. . . .

We hear much of special interest groups. Well, our concern must be for a special interest group that has been too long neglected (ignored). *It knows no sectional boundaries or ethnic and racial divisions, and it crosses political party lines. It is made up of men and women who raise our food, patrol our streets, man our mines and factories, teach our children, keep our homes, and heal us when we're sick— professionals, industrialists, shopkeepers, clerks, cabbies, and truck drivers. They are, in short, 'We the people,' this breed (type of people) called Americans.*

—President Ronald Reagan, First Inaugural Address (1981)

Summarize each paragraph in your own words:

Summarize each paragraph in your own words:

With the idealism and fair play which are the core of our system and our strength, we can have a strong and prosperous America, at peace with itself and the world."

Reverend Al Sharpton's Speech to the Democratic National Convention

Summarize each paragraph in your own words:

"I have come here tonight to say, that the only choice we have to preserve (keep) *our freedoms at this point in history is to elect John Kerry the President of the United States.*

I stood with both John Kerry and John Edwards on over 30 occasions during the primary season. I looked into their eyes. I am convinced that they are men who say what they mean and mean what they say.

I'm also convinced that at a time when a vicious (mean; cruel) *spirit in . . . this country attempts to undermine America's freedoms—our civil rights, and civil liberties—we must . . . organize this nation for victory for our party and John Kerry and John Edwards in November . . .*

Look at the current view of our nation worldwide as a result of our unilateral (single-handed) *foreign policy. We went from unprecedented* (more than ever before) *international support and solidarity* (unity; agreement) *on September 12, 2001, to hostility and hatred as we stand here tonight. We can't survive in the world by ourselves.*

—Reverend Al Sharpton, Speech to the Democratic National Convention (2004)

Continues ▶

▸ Which of the following statements are opinions, and which are facts? Explain your answers.

President Ronald Reagan:

"The economic ills (illnesses; problems) *we suffer have come upon us over several decades."*

Opinion ☐ Fact ☐

Explanation: ____

____

"In this present crisis, government is not the solution to our problem; government is the problem."

Opinion ☐ Fact ☐

Explanation: ____

____

"With the idealism and fair play which are the core of our system and our strength, we can have a strong and prosperous America, at peace with itself and the world."

Opinion ☐ Fact ☐

Explanation: ____

____

Reverend Al Sharpton:

"I stood with both John Kerry and John Edwards on over 30 occasions during the primary season."

Opinion ☐ Fact ☐

Explanation: ____

____

"We went from unprecedented (more than ever before) *international support and solidarity* (unity; agreement) *on September 12, 2001, to hostility and hatred as we stand here tonight.*

Opinion ☐ Fact ☐

Explanation: ____

____

"We can't survive in the world by ourselves."

Opinion ☐ Fact ☐

Explanation: ____

____

- What was the purpose of each speech?

- What exaggerated statements, if any, were made in either speech?

- Did either of these speeches show **bias**? Explain your answer.

- How did President Reagan use the phrase "We the People" and Reverend Sharpton use the expression "America's freedoms" for **symbolism**? Explain your answer.

- Should either of these political communications be considered as **propaganda**? Explain your answer.

Name ____

Complete the chart below on how individuals, interest groups, and the media monitor and influence government.

The Impact of Individuals, Interest Groups and the Media

	How they monitor the government	How they influence the government	How they hold government officials accountable
Individuals			
Interest groups			
Media			

Name ______________________________________

Complete the chart below by describing the different activities of interest groups and their impact in influencing government.

Activity	Description/Impact
Monitoring 	
Lobbying 	
Campaigning (helping candidates get elected) 	
Litigation (filing lawsuits) 	
Publicity (winning public opinion) 	

Name ______________________________

You are the chairperson of a nonprofit organization such as Habitat for Humanity, the American Red Cross, the American Cancer Society, the Make-A-Wish Foundation, the Girl Scouts of the USA, the Boy Scouts of America, or the American Society for the Prevention of Cruelty to Animals. Design a campaign to help you win support for your nonprofit organization—both in Congress and with the general public. Fill in the "action list" below.

Name of Nonprofit Organization: ______________________________

Action List

1. Steps to take to lobby support in Congress:

____

____

____

____

____

____

2. Steps to take to win support from the public:

____

____

____

____

____

____

3. Ways to use the media in support of your cause:

____

____

____

____

____

____

How Individuals Monitor, Hold Accountable, and Influence Government:

- Attend civic meetings
- Peacefully protest
- Petition government officials
- Vote
- Run for office
- Impact: individuals can affect policies

- These are groups that organize to promote their interests with legislators and public opinion
- Different types of interest groups: based on economic interests, unions, environmental protection, political action committees (PACs), etc.
- Activities of interest groups: monitoring, lobbying, litigation, campaigning, publicity
- Impact: Lobbyists often bring expert subject-matter knowledge to legislators; lobbyists can influence legislation; interest groups can sway public opinion

Individuals

Interest Groups

How Individuals, Interest Groups, and the Media Monitor and Influence Government

The Media

- Television, newspapers, magazines, radio, the Internet
- News reporters monitor government activities
- The media act as "watchdogs" exposing corruption, wrong-doing or error, and holding government officials accountable
- Media are protected by freedom of the press in the 1st Amendment
- Impact: The media inform the public; government officials are more careful

Analyzing Political Communication/Advertising: Aim at influencing public opinion

- **Bias** = one-sided; not based on evidence; prejudiced
- **Symbolism** = represents something
- **Propaganda** = appeals to emotions: Look for bias, exaggeration, being one-sided, half-truths, glittering generalities

Review Cards: Interest Groups and the Media

How Individuals Can Monitor, Hold Accountable, and Influence Government

Individuals can **monitor government** (*watch over; keep track of*), **hold government officials accountable** (*make them responsible for their actions*), and **influence government** by:

- **Attending civic meetings** (*meetings held for a public purpose*)
- **Protesting peacefully**
- **Petitioning government** (*writing to government officials requesting a change*)
- **Voting**
- **Running for office**

Impact: Individuals can affect public policy (*government actions*)

Interest Groups

- An **interest group** is a group of individuals with common interests who seek to influence public policy. Interest groups attempt to influence public policies directly, rather than by electing their members as government officials. Unlike a political party, an interest group tends to focus on a specific issue or area, rather than on all the problems facing government leaders.
- There are many different types of interest groups: environmental interest groups (which protect wildlife and reduce pollution), economic interest groups like the American Bankers Association and American Medical Association (which often focus on their single industry), civil rights interest groups, and interest groups that are formed over particular issues.

Methods Used by Interest Groups to Monitor and Influence Government

- Monitoring: Interest groups often "**monitor**" developments. This means they keep track of everything legislatures and government agencies are doing that might affect their area of focus.
- **Lobbying**: Interest groups hire lobbyists, who speak to state legislators, members of Congress, and other government officials in order to influence new legislation or government regulations.

  Lobbyists usually specialize in a particular subject. They therefore bring subject-area expertise to legislators, government officials and the public. Interest groups often help to provide specific details for proposed legislation.
- Campaigning: Interest groups and their lobbyists also help politicians to get elected or re-elected. In 1974, a law was passed that allowed each interest group to form its own political action committee, or PAC. PACs can provide larger sums of money to political candidates than individuals are permitted to contribute.
- Litigation (lawsuits): Interest groups—particularly public interest groups and those supporting minority rights—sometimes promote their causes by filing lawsuits.
- Publicity: Interest groups usually try to influence public opinion—the views of the general public—through advertising, press releases, publishing articles, and television and radio appearances.

Methods Used by the Media to Monitor Government and Hold Officials Accountable

The word "media" is the plural of "medium." A medium is something that transfers or carries something, including messages, from one place to another. Here, "**media**" refers to "mass media"—methods of communication to large numbers of people through television programs, newspapers, magazines, radio, Internet websites, Internet blogs, and social media.

- The media **monitor** and **influence government**. Media play an important role in our democratic system of government because they inform citizens what is happening in government. The **1st Amendment** protects "**freedom of the press**." A free press is important to a democratic society because it is how citizens become informed.
- The media act as a **watchdog** over our government, questioning government leaders about their actions and exposing government wrongdoing. "Investigative journalists" investigate issues or suspected wrongdoing through research and by interviewing witnesses and participants.

Political Communications: Bias, Symbolism, and Propaganda

- Individuals, interest groups and political parties create **political communications** in order to persuade readers. Sometimes these communications show bias, make use of symbolism, or become a form of propaganda.
- Some communications show **bias**—they provide only a partial perspective and may be prejudiced for or against something. They may take advantage of popular beliefs and stereotypes.
- **Symbolism** refers to the use of symbols in a communication, like a donkey on a poster to represent the Democratic Party. The authors may try to associate themselves with popular symbols like the U.S. flag.
- Political communications that are very biased and that mainly appeal to fears and emotions are known as **propaganda**. Propaganda often relies on unsupported opinions, exaggerations, half-truths, name calling, stereotypes, oversimplifications, and "glittering generalities" (*claims that cannot be checked*).

Analyzing Media and Political Communications

To analyze a political communication, media message or political advertisement, take the following steps:

1. Determine who created the message.
2. Determine the purpose of the article or communication. Is it meant to be informational or persuasive?
3. Read or listen to the text carefully.
   - What is the main idea?
   - What arguments does the author use?
4. Identify facts and opinions in the communication.
   - Determine if its facts are accurate.
   - Decide if its opinions are reasonable, based on the evidence.
5. Does it show any obvious **bias**? Consider the use of any **symbols** in the article or communication. Is it a form of **propaganda**?

What Do You Know?

SS.7.CG.2.8

1. What is an important difference between interest groups and political parties?

   A. Interest groups have more members than political parties.
   B. Interest groups have platforms addressing all issues of public concern.
   C. Interest groups are organized to elect their candidates to political office.
   D. Interest groups attempt to influence government directly on particular issues.

SS.7.CG.2.8

2. Which of the following is NOT one of the ways in which the media influence government?

   A. by providing information to the public
   B. by contributing to election campaign funds
   C. by focusing public attention on particular issues
   D. by making public officials accountable for their actions

SS.7.CG.2.8

3. The diagram below gives details about the American political system.

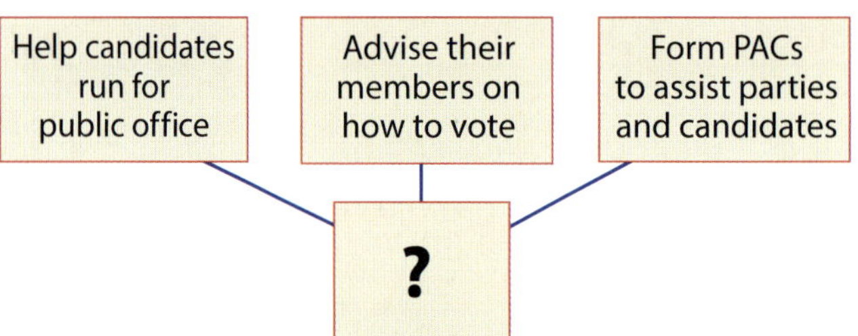

   Which title completes the diagram?

   A. How interest groups influence elections
   B. How interest groups use publicity to win support
   C. How interest groups monitor government activities
   D. How interest groups lobby state and federal legislators

SS.7.CG.2.8

4. Sarah felt very strongly about an issue in the news. She wrote to her representative in Congress and expressed her feelings on the issue. Then started a petition on the same issue, collected signatures from her neighbors, and sent it off. Which statement describes Sarah's activities?

   A. She was acting as a lobbyist.
   B. She was forming her own political party.
   C. She was starting her own special interest group.
   D. She was influencing government as an individual.

SS.7.CG.2.8

5. The graph below shows where Americans obtain their news.

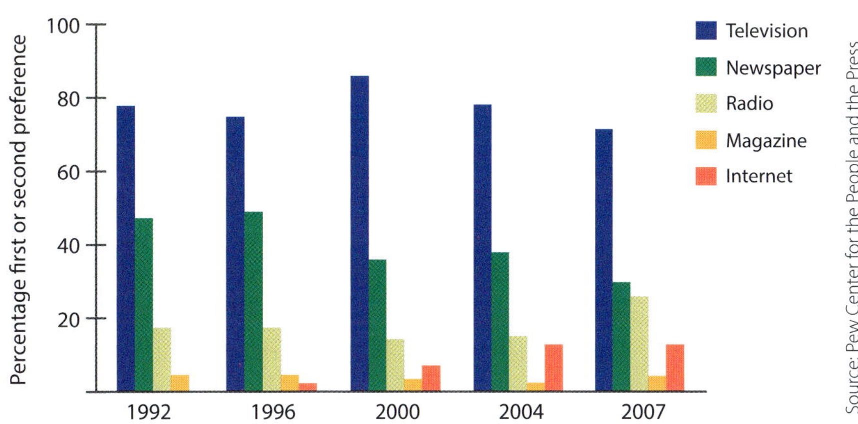

Based upon the information in the graph, where should a candidate in 2007 have spent the most campaign funds for advertising?

A. newspaper
B. television
C. Internet
D. radio

SS.7.CG.2.9

6. "Italians make the best chefs in the world." What does this statement show?

A. a form of media
B. being a watchdog
C. an example of bias
D. an example of symbolism

SS.7.CG.2.8

7. The table below describes four interest groups.

Interest Group 1	Supporters of the interests of workers
Interest Group 2	Activists who protect wildlife and struggle to reduce pollution
Interest Group 3	Defenders of the Second Amendment who protect the right to own guns
Interest Group 4	Advocates of greater equality for women through education and advocacy

Which of these interest groups would be mostly likely to support a ban on deepwater drilling in the Gulf of Mexico?

A. Interest Group 1
B. Interest Group 2
C. Interest Group 3
D. Interest Group 4

SS.7.CG.2.8

8. How does the media hold government officials accountable?

A. by voting them out of office
B. by informing government officials on public issues
C. by acting as a watchdog, reporting officials' actions to the public
D. by raising campaign funds to help re-elect officials they prefer

SS.7.CG.2.8

9. What is one method that interest groups use to influence government?
   - **A.** bribing legislators to support their proposals
   - **B.** impeaching their opponents in the legislature
   - **C.** sponsoring news programs on major television networks
   - **D.** giving legislators the benefit of their subject-area expertise

SS.7.CG.2.9

10. A U.S. government poster from World War I is shown at the right.

    Which evidence supports the view that this poster is an example of wartime propaganda?
   - **A.** the use of symbolism
   - **B.** the use of bandwagon claims
   - **C.** the mention of Liberty Bonds
   - **D.** the exaggerated characteristics of the soldier

SS.7.CG.2.9

11. The sign shown at the right was posted all over the town of Mayberry.

    Which method does this political communication have in common with propaganda?
   - **A.** using symbolism
   - **B.** name-calling of opponents
   - **C.** presenting an opinion as a fact
   - **D.** appealing to readers' greatest fears

Vote for Joe Everyman
for City Commissioner.
He is the only candidate
who truly cares about
your future!

SS.7.CG.2.9

12. The statement below was made by President George W. Bush at the start of the 2004 Presidential election campaign against Democratic candidate Senator John Kerry.

    > *It's a choice between keeping the tax relief that is moving the economy forward, or putting the burden of higher taxes back on the American people . . . It's a choice between an America that leads the world with strength and confidence, or an America that is uncertain in the face of danger.*

    How was this political communication intended to win public support for President Bush?
   - **A.** by using political symbolism
   - **B.** by giving the reasons for his policies
   - **C.** by labeling his opponent as uncertain
   - **D.** by presenting a one-sided claim as a fact

CHAPTER 16

Public Policy

SS.7.CG.2.10 Explain the process for citizens to address a state or local problem by researching public policy alternatives, identifying appropriate government agencies to address the issue, and determining a course of action.

Content Focus Vocabulary in This Chapter

Process to address a problem
State or local problem
Public policy
Research
Level of government
Government agency
Public policy alternatives
Course of action

Florida "Keys" to Learning

1. Actions taken by governments to solve problems and to achieve goals are known as **public policy.** In our system of democratic government, citizens can have a direct voice in shaping public policy.

2. There is a **process to address a problem**. A process is a series of steps that are followed to do something. Citizens who want to address a **state or local problem** (*a problem that either affects the whole state or affects a local area*) should follow this process: (1) identify a problem; (2) conduct **research** about the problem; (3) develop and evaluate various **public policy alternatives** (*possible ways of solving the problem*); (4) identify the appropriate (*proper*) **level of government** (*local, state, or national*) and the right **government agency** to address the problem; and (5) determine a recommended **course of action**. These steps may vary depending on the problem faced.

3. Local government is usually involved if the problem only concerns a local area; the state government becomes involved if the problem is statewide; the national government becomes involved if the situation is part of a larger national problem.

What is Public Policy?

Governments make laws, issue executive orders and regulations, and make other decisions that affect the public. Actions taken by governments to solve problems and achieve goals are known as **public policy**. This is because our government acts on behalf of the public. In this chapter, you will study public policy.

Public policy decisions can lead to new laws or actions by the government. Many of the examples in this book concern public policy decisions by our national government. Congress may pass a new law. For example, the President may issue an executive order affecting the national parks. The Environmental Protection Agency (EPA) may announce a new regulation changing air pollution standards.

State and local governments also make many public policy decisions. A state conservation commission may issue regulations banning (*prohibiting*) construction in an area in order to protect an endangered bird species. The Florida Department of Education may issue new academic requirements for student graduation from high school. A local town planning commission may approve a request to build a group of commercial buildings near the town center. A city council may raise local sales taxes to cover rising costs.

Citizens Influence Public Policy

In our system of democratic government, citizens can have a direct voice in public policy. Almost every important decision by government agencies allows some opportunity for public comment. Before a local committee or state or federal agency makes an order or regulation, it usually holds hearings. It may ask specific experts to testify and generally invites all interested citizens to submit oral or written comments.

In addition to these formal steps, citizens have the right to address their public officials and legislators by writing letters or sending petitions (*formal requests to government officials, signed by citizens who agree with the demand*). Citizens can also attend civic meetings, hold peaceful protests, vote, and run for office to influence public policy. You have already learned how individuals can influence the government in the previous chapter.

Steps in the Public Policy Process: Developing a Plan to Resolve a State or Local Problem

The following steps are often used to address a public policy problem:

> In answering questions about public policy on the EOC test, remember that you should first research the problem, identify the level of government and agency to address, then think of alternative solutions, and finally evaluate these alternatives before determining a course of action.

1. Identify a **state or local problem**.
2. Conduct **research** about the problem. This research may focus on determining what has caused the problem.
3. Develop and evaluate various **public policy alternatives** (or "options"). Consider the pros and cons of each alternative.
4. Identify the appropriate (*proper*) **level of government** and **government agency** to address the problem.
5. Determine your **course of action**. Consider possible private solutions along with public policy solutions.

Now that you have learned the main steps of the process for addressing a local or state problem, let's see how those steps might actually work in addressing a specific problem.

Your teacher should divide your class into groups. Each group will identify a local or state problem and develop a solution to that problem. Then you will send your proposal (*suggested plan*) to the appropriate government agency.

1. Identify a Problem

First of all, your group should identify a local or state problem. Some examples of potential problems are listed below, but feel free to think of a different problem on your own. Be sure to select a problem that really concerns you.

The Environment

- How can local air, water and land pollution be reduced in your community?
- How can local residents be encouraged to recycle waste?

Public Education

- How can students in your school be better motivated?
- How can your school district help prevent bullying?
- How can class sizes in the state be reduced?
- Should your school district offer after-school programs for children with working parents?

Safety and Crime

- How can local crime be reduced?
- How can local homes and businesses be made safer?
- How can Florida prevent identify theft and Internet crime?

Bicycle Lanes, Roads, and Highways

- How can the roads in your community be made safer for bicycle riders?
- How can traffic accidents in the community be reduced?
- How can local rush-hour traffic be reduced?

The Regulation of Retail Stores

- How can local shopping hours be made more convenient?
- How can your town attract more shoppers?

Parks and Recreation

- How can local parks be made more attractive?
- Which recreational facilities would local residents most enjoy?
- Should your town build a new sports center or outdoor stadium?

Insurance

- How can Florida reduce insurance rates for residents and businesses?

Taxation

- How can Florida improve its social services without raising sales taxes?

Real Estate Development and Construction

- How can your town or neighborhood promote development without damaging the environment?

Health and Food

- How can Florida let consumers know which foods are healthy choices?
- How can Florida help fight child obesity?
- How can Florida encourage children to be vaccinated?
- How can Florida help its residents obtain better health care?
- How can Florida help fight Alzheimer's disease?
- How can Florida reduce costs while maintaining quality health care?

Which local or state problem has your group identified?______________________________________

____

____

2. Conduct Research

The next step is to conduct **research** (*finding information about something*). Be an aggressive researcher! Think of yourself as a reporter or a detective trying to solve a problem.

Your research might begin by defining the problem more precisely. Your group may wish to research the causes of the problem. Knowing what has caused a problem often helps in developing a solution to it. Then you should research different ideas for solving your problem. See whether any of these ideas have actually been tried.

There are many ways to find information about a problem and possible solutions. Members of your group may want to start by searching the Internet for information. You might also visit your school or local library for books, magazines and newspapers with information about the problem. Your school or local librarian should be able to help you locate good sources of information.

If your problem is a local one, you might look at local newspapers and community records at your local library or town hall. For example, there may have been a town meeting about the issue in the past. It could be helpful to see what solutions were discussed, what was tried, and what was rejected.

In addition to looking at the Internet and printed sources, you may want to interview experts or public officials about the problem your group has chosen. You might, for example, look at the website of a government agency that is related to the problem. Then you might look for "Contact Us" or "Staff" on that website. Once you click this link, you will often find the names and email addresses of one or more experts or government officials who have information about your problem. You can then email these experts. Be sure to introduce yourself and to ask specific, focused questions. Also be sure to send a thank you letter if one of these experts responds to your questions.

If your problem is a local one, you may also want to interview local community leaders in person or by telephone. You can ask them what they know about the problem and if there had been any efforts to solve the problem in the past. You can also ask these leaders for their ideas on what is causing the problem and what they think would be the best solution to the problem.

It may help for members of your group to put the information they find on index cards so that your group can bring all the results of its research together. Each index card should deal with a particular aspect of the problem—such as defining the problem, possible causes of the problem, previous attempts by officials to deal with the problem, and proposals to resolve the problem in the future. Be sure to record information about your sources on each card. Once your group has completed its research, it can organize all the index cards from group members by topic—such as details about the problem, causes of the problem, and alternative solutions to the problem. Write three sources that your group has consulted (or plans to consult) below. These sources could be books, magazine articles, websites, or people that your group has interviewed.

____

____

____

Complete one or two sample index cards from your own research:

Topic: ________________________

____

____

Source: ________________________

____

Topic: ________________________

____

____

Source: ________________________

____

3. Develop and evaluate various public policy alternatives (or "options")

Now comes the fun part! You should "brainstorm" with the other members of your group to think of possible solutions to your problem. When you brainstorm, you simply think of every idea you possibly can that might help to solve the problem. No reasonable idea is rejected. Sometimes hearing the ideas of classmates can even inspire you to think of new ideas.

- ☑ Think about what caused the problem. What solutions might eliminate the causes of the problem?
- ☑ Think about what has been proposed to solve the problem in the past, and why it wasn't tried or didn't work.
- ☑ Think about what has been proposed or tried successfully elsewhere, and how that might be adapted to your situation.
- ☑ Think about the resources you have and how they might be best used to solve the problem.

Try to be as creative as possible!

Because each proposal is an alternative solution to the problem, proposed solutions are sometimes called "**public policy alternatives**" or "options."

List two of the public policy alternatives that your group has developed in its brainstorming session on the top lines of the two cards on the next page.

Now you are ready to look at each public policy alternative more closely to evaluate it. You should consider the "pros" (*advantages*) and "cons" (*disadvantages*) of each alternative. "Pros" and "cons" may also be referred to as the "benefits" and "costs" of a proposed solution.

In thinking of pros and cons—or costs and benefits—begin by thinking how effective the proposed solution will be in solving the problem. Will it solve the problem completely? If not, will it help reduce the problem? Is the proposed solution something that government agencies will be able to accomplish? Will the solution bring additional benefits besides solving the problem?

Then look at the disadvantages for each proposed policy alternative. What will each alternative cost? What resources would each require? What additional disadvantages might each bring?

Write down the pros and cons for two of the public policy alternatives you are evaluating:

Public Policy Alternative #1

Proposed Solution: ______________________

____

____

____

____

Pros:	Cons:
__________	__________
__________	__________
__________	__________
__________	__________

Public Policy Alternative #2

Proposed Solution: ______________________

____

____

____

____

Pros:	Cons:
__________	__________
__________	__________
__________	__________
__________	__________

Look again at all of the policy alternatives your group came up with during its brainstorming. Compare your evaluations with those of other members of your group and rank all the alternatives from best to worst.

- The *best alternative* is the one that brings the most benefits at the least cost.
- The *worst alternative* is the one that brings the least benefits for the most cost.

In the space below, write down your choice for the three best public policy alternatives from those proposed by your group. Put the one you consider the very best at the top of your list.

1. ______________________________________

____

2. ______________________________________

____

3. ______________________________________

____

Explain why you feel the one at the top of your list is better than the other two.

____

____

____

____

Now give each of your top three alternatives a score:

Alternative 1	3 points
Alternative 2	2 points
Alternative 3	1 points

Compare your choices with those of your classmates. To calculate the score for each alternative, add together all the points it has received from all of the members of your group. The public policy alternative with the most points is the one your group has selected as the best course of action in response to the problem.

4. Identify the appropriate level of government and agency to address the problem

Now that your group has researched the problem and chosen its proposed solution, it is ready to identify which **level of government** and which particular **government agency** is best able to address the problem. In general, problems across the state are best handled by state agencies, while local problems are best handled by local agencies. If the situation is part of a larger national problem, then it might be dealt with by the national (or federal) government.

- Which level of government would best be able to deal with the problem your group has identified?

  - ☐ State of Florida
  - ☐ Local Government
  - ☐ Agency of the National Government

Once you determine the level of government for your problem, you should look on the Internet for the particular agency or department that would deal with this problem. You already learned about federal government agencies in Chapter 7. State and local governments also have their own agencies.

Government agencies generally deal with a specific subject matter. For example, a problem in a state forest area would be handled by the Florida Forest Service, while a problem with state educational requirements would be handled by the Florida Department of Education.

You can find a listing of major state agencies on the Internet by using the search term: "Florida state agencies."

You can usually find the names of local agencies by looking on your local government website.

- Which government agency would best be able to deal with this problem? Include contact information below.

Department, Agency or Office:

____

____

____

Email and/or Address:

____

____

____

Why is this the appropriate (*proper; suitable*) level of government and government agency? Explain your answer.

____

____

____

5. Determine a course of action

Now that you and the other members of your group have chosen the right agency, you can really go into action. You have to determine a **course of action** (*steps the government or private citizens should take to solve the problem*), based on your selection of the best public policy alternative. In other words, this is when you implement your plan.

To "implement" means to put it into effect.

To implement a public policy solution, you usually have to win the support of the government agency in charge of that aspect of public policy.

There are many ways in which your group can directly influence such policy-makers. Members of your group can petition or write directly to the policy-makers in the government agency or department you have identified. You can offer to meet with these policy-makers to give them your opinions. You can even visit the offices of your state legislators.

Your group can also try to build public support by writing letters to the editor of the local newspaper. You can create a campaign using social media like Facebook and Twitter, or create your own website or blog devoted to the problem. You can hold a public meeting or conference on the problem.

Enrichment

Not every problem requires a public policy solution. Some problems are better solved through the voluntary efforts of private individuals than they are by government. Many problems can be solved through private community service solutions—unpaid, voluntary efforts by private individuals.

For example, your community may have a food pantry or food bank. Food banks collect unsold food donated by grocery stores and restaurants. Food banks store and distribute this food to people in need. These food banks are private charities, usually run by unpaid volunteers.

All such public service projects aim to promote the "common good" (or "public good")—what is good for all the members of the community.

List three steps that you might take with your group to implement (*put into effect*) your decision through a course of action.

1. ______________________________

2. ______________________________

3. ______________________________

Once you have implemented your plan, it is helpful to keep track of how well it works. This will help you become a better policy-maker in the future.

To evaluate the effectiveness of your plan, consider how well it works at solving the problem, what it costs (in time, money and other resources), and what additional advantages or disadvantages it brings.

How do you plan to keep track of the implementation of your plan?

____

____

How well has it solved the problem?

____

____

What have been its costs?

____

____

What other advantages/disadvantages has it had?

____

____

The Active Citizen

Enrichment

You can discover some of the actual problems facing Florida today by looking at the websites of the Florida Senate (www.flsenate.gov) or the House of Representatives (www.myfloridahouse.gov). Click on "bills" on each website to find proposals currently before the state legislature. Many of these bills are attempts by legislators to resolve important state problems.

1. Choose one of the bills on an important problem that interests you.
2. Study the problem and how the bill proposes to resolve it. Then write a letter to the editor of a local or regional newspaper giving your views.
3. Contact your state legislator for his or her views on the problem and how the bill intends to solve it.
4. Invite your legislator or a staff member to your class to explain his or her views on the issue and to answer questions.

Name ___________________________________

Now that you have experienced the process of addressing a local or state problem, how would you explain this process to others? Review the steps in the chapter and explain each step in the chart below.

Step	Explanation
Identify a problem 	
Conduct research 	
Develop and evaluate policy alternatives  OPTION 1 OPTION 2	
Identify level of government and agency  Florida Department of Environmental Protection	
Determine a course of action  Petition We the undersigned ask Congress to pass a law stating... Signed,	

Florida Department of Environmental Protection
ENOUGH
Respect MY VOTE!
Petition
We the undersigned ask Congress to pass a law stating...
Signed,
Actions taken by governments to solve problems and achieve goals
Send petitions
Attend civic meetings
Hold peaceful protests
Vote
Run for office
What is Public Policy?
How Citizens Influence Public Policy (See Chapter 15)
Public Policy
OPTION 1
OPTION 2
REZONING NOTICE PUBLIC HEARING
CASE NO.: Z-13-18724
PHONE #:
FROM: R-75 (S-F RESIDENTIAL)
PURPOSE: MIXED COMM. & RESIDENTIAL DEVELOPMENT
PLACE: DEKALB COUNTY AUDITORIUM
1300 COMMERCE DRIVE, DECATUR, GEORGIA
PLANNING COMMISSION
The Process for Addressing a State or Local Problem
Identify a state or local problem
Conduct research
Develop and evaluate public policy alternatives
Identify the appropriate level of government and government agency to address it
Determine a course of action
Public Policy Alternative #1
Proposed Solution:
Pros:
Cons
Public Policy Alternative #1
osed Solution:
Cons

Review Cards: Public Policy

Public Policy

- **Public policy** concerns actions taken by governments to solve problems and to achieve goals for the common good (*the good of the community*).
- Individual citizens can influence public policy by proposing programs or policy alternatives, by speaking at a public hearing, by petitioning government officials, or by working through an interest group or political party. (See Chapter 15 for how individuals can influence government.)

Addressing a State or Local Problem

A "process" is a series of steps taken to do something. Citizens should follow this **process to address a problem**:

1. Identify a **state or local problem**.
2. Conduct **research** about the problem.
3. Develop and evaluate various **public policy alternatives** (or "options"). Consider the "pros" and "cons" of each alternative.
4. Identify the **level of government** (*local, state, or national*) and appropriate **government agency** to address the problem.The local level of government usually addresses problems that only affect a local area. The state level of government addresses problems affecting the entire state. The national government only gets involved when the local situation is part of a larger national problem or becomes a national emergency.
5. Determine a **course of action** (*adopting the public policy alternative that should be taken to solve the problem*).

What Do You Know?

SS.7.CG.2.10

1. Juan and Maria have noticed that all the frogs in their local pond have been very quiet recently. When they went to the pond, they could no longer hear any of them. Then they saw a few of them were dead. To which government agency should they report this problem?
   A. Florida Department of Education
   B. Florida Department of Elder Affairs
   C. Florida Department of Veterans Affairs
   D. Florida Department of Environmental Protection

SS.7.CG.2.10

2. The local library has reduced its opening hours in order to save the community money. Many students and parents are upset at this change. Many students liked to go to the library after school. How should concerned citizens address this local issue?
   A. replace the community library with an online digital library
   B. develop a list of alternative solutions and send this list to local officials
   C. send a letter to the Governor of Florida in support of community libraries
   D. file a lawsuit in federal court challenging the reduction of library opening hours

SS.7.CG.2.10

3. John Smith lives in the downtown area. He is upset that local motorcycle riders sometimes come through his town in the early evening and make loud noises with their motorcycles. Which of the following should be John's first step in addressing this local problem?
   A. conduct research on how nearby communities deal with the same problem
   B. write a letter to the local newspaper demanding a town ordinance against motorcycles
   C. propose a local ordinance against motorcycle use at the next town council meeting
   D. ask local police officers to arrest any motorcyclists who appear in the town

SS.7.CG.2.10

4. John and Maria have become concerned about the large number of stray pets that are often lost in their community. To which level of government should they address their concerns?
   A. the local level of government
   B. the state level of government
   C. the national level of government
   D. the scientific level of government

CHAPTER 17

Types of Government and Economic System

SS.7.CG.3.1 Analyze the advantages of the United States' constitutional republic over other forms of government in safeguarding liberty, freedom and a representative government.

SS.7.CG.3.2 Explain the advantages of a federal system of government over other systems in balancing local sovereignty with national unity and protecting against authoritarianism.

SS.7.CG.3.15 Analyze the advantages of capitalism and the free market in the United States over government-controlled economic systems (e.g., socialism and communism) in regard to economic freedom and raising the standard of living for citizens.

Content Focus Vocabulary in This Chapter

Organizational structure
Political philosophy
Form of government
Republic
Monarchy
Oligarchy
Theocracy
Autocracy
Safeguard liberty
Checks and balances
Consent of the governed
Democracy
Due process of law
Federalism
Individual rights
Limited government
Representative government
Republicanism
Rule of law
Separation of powers
Constitutional republic
Authoritarianism
Authoritarian nation
Totalitarian nation
System of government
National unity
Local sovereignty
Federal system
Confederal system
Unitary system
Economic system
Capitalism
Free market economy
Government-controlled economy
Communism
Socialism
Standard of living
Economic freedom
Opportunity
Economic prosperity

Florida "Keys" to Learning

1. Governments help people cooperate, enforce rules, provide public services, and protect the community. Governments have different **organizational structures** (*ways of being organized*), based on their **political philosophy** (*beliefs about government*). One way to classify the organizational structures of governments is by their **form of government**: who holds power.

2. A **monarchy** has a government ruled by one person, whose claim to rule is hereditary (*inherited; passed from one family member to another*).

3. In a **democracy**, the people rule. In some democracies, citizens debate and decide public issues for themselves; in a representative democracy, also known as a **republic**, citizens elect representatives to act on their behalf. The people rule through their representatives and place limits on what the government can do.

4. The United States is a **constitutional republic** (*a representative government based on a written constitution*). Its principles **safeguard liberty** (*protect freedom*) and prevent our representative government from ever becoming an **authoritarian nation** (*a country governed by an all-powerful ruler with absolute authority*) or a **totalitarian nation** (*a country where the government controls all aspects of life*). These principles include: **democracy** (*government based on rule by the people*), **representative government** (*rule by elected representatives*), **consent of the governed** (*citizens agree to follow their representatives' decisions*), **republicanism** (*support for representative government*), **rule of law** (*everyone is subject to the same rules*), **due process of law** (*everyone is entitled to a fair hearing*), **individual rights** (*personal rights are guaranteed by the Bill of Rights*), **limited government** (*the government has only those powers specified in the Constitution*), **federalism** (*division of power between the national and state governments*), **separation of powers** (*division of power between the branches of government*), and **checks and balances** (*different branches of government check each other*).

5. In an **autocracy**, one ruler holds all political power. The autocrat might be an absolute monarch or a modern dictator.

6. In an **oligarchy**, the members of a small group, such as nobles (*wealthy, hereditary landowners*) or army officers, hold power.

7. A **theocracy** is a government controlled by religious leaders.

8. The organizational structures of governments can also be classified based on their **system of government**—the relationship between their central and local governments. (The "central government" is the organizational structure at the center of national power.) Governments have to balance the need for **national unity** with the demands for **local sovereignty** (*local control*).

9. In a **unitary system** of government, the central government holds all the power. It creates local governments and delegates (*assigns; hands over*) certain powers to them. It can abolish them at any time.

10. In a **federal system** of government, the central and local governments exercise independent powers and cannot abolish each other. This system allows local authorities to control local affairs but also has a strong central government to meet national needs. The United States has a federal system of government. This system has important advantages in preventing **authoritarianism** (*government by an all-powerful absolute ruler*). Strong local authorities would resist any attempt at seizing absolute power.

11. In a **confederal system** of government, a group of independent states or nations form an association to cooperate. Most power remains with the separate states (acting as local governments), which are free to leave at any time. The United States under the Articles of Confederation had a confederal system of government.

12. All societies have to answer three basic economic questions: what to produce; how to produce it; and who gets what is produced. The way a society answers these questions is known as its **economic system**. Under **capitalism**, or the

free market system, people make their own economic choices. They can decide what to produce and what to consume (*buy and use*). This system provides the most **opportunity** and **economic freedom**. The "laws of supply and demand" (*the interactions of consumers' demands and producers' supplies*) act as an "invisible hand," determining what gets produced.

13. Communism and socialism are **government-controlled economic systems**. Under **communism**, the government owns all natural resources, farms and industries. Central planners in the government make five-year plans, which establish which goods and services the nation will produce. There is little private initiative.

14. Under **socialism**, the government owns some basic industries, including transportation and communications. It also provides extensive public services, including health care and college education. At the same time, private ownership of businesses is also allowed.

15. **Capitalism** has been successful as an economic system. People enjoy **economic freedom**, while the market eliminates inefficient producers. The profit incentive encourages producers to improve, raising **standards of living** (*levels of income and comfort*), providing **opportunity**, and promoting **economic prosperity** (*success; wealth*). Communism turned out to be inefficient as an economic system. Central planners could not predict all of a society's needs. Workers had little incentive to work harder or improve. **Standards of living** remained at a standstill. Socialism has been successful in small countries rich in natural resources, but less successful in larger countries.

In previous chapters, you learned about the American **constitutional republic**. This is the type of government you have probably known all of your life. But in fact, there are other types of government. In this chapter, you will explore how some of these forms and systems of government are organized.

Enrichment

How Did Governments Develop?

Wherever you go in the world today, you will find some sort of government. But where did all these governments come from?

During the Enlightenment, people asked this very same question. Some writers came up with the idea that, once upon a time, there had been no governments at all. People had lived as separate individuals in a "state of nature." But people soon realized they could not protect themselves. They also could not do many of the things that they would be able to do in cooperation with others. So they banded together in small groups.

This was the thinking behind John Locke's social contract theory, which you learned about in Chapter 2. According to this theory, societies were formed by agreement. People also agreed to create an organization to make rules for their community, to organize work and land ownership, to settle disputes, and to provide for the community's defense. As you know, this organization is known as **government**. Because people had formed their own government, Locke believed they also had the right to change it if it did not protect their rights and meet their needs.

Today, social scientists no longer believe there was once a time when people lived as isolated individuals without governments. They realize that people have lived together in groups for as long as they have existed on Earth. The first human groups may have been small bands of hunters and gatherers, but each group had its own leaders and rules. With the introduction of agriculture, humans were able to settle in one place. Their communities grew larger, and their forms of government became more complex.

The governments that ruled over the world's first civilizations were created by force and violence as much as by agreement. A ruler and his warriors forced others to obey. Then they conquered neighboring peoples to create vast empires. In some places, religious beliefs encouraged the rise of governments. Egyptian pharaohs, for example, combined both military and religious power.

Whatever their origin, all governments fulfill several essential roles. They help the people of a community to cooperate and defend themselves; they enable communities to develop rules that everyone should follow; and they enforce those rules.

Be sure to know the different forms of government and advantages of our constitutional republic

Forms of Government: Who Holds the Power? Monarchy, Democracy, Autocracy, Oligarchy, and Theocracy

As you look around the world today, you will quickly see that governments have different **organizational structures** (*ways they are organized*), based on their **political philosophy** (*their beliefs about government*). There are also several ways in which these governments can be classified. One of the most useful ways to compare governments is by looking at who holds power. This is known as the **form of government**.

Monarchy

In the earliest civilizations, one leader often arose as the most powerful member of society. This ruler then passed power on to one of his or her children, or to another member of the family. This **form of government** is known as a **monarchy**. A monarch inherits political power. The monarch might be known as a king, queen, emperor, or empress. A monarch rules by hereditary right.

In a monarchy, a king or queen inherits power.

In the Middle Ages, European monarchs were not all-powerful. They were limited by tradition, law, and the Catholic Church. Monarchs also had to respect the rights of their nobles. Even a monarch's sources of revenue (*income*) could be limited. If a monarch wanted additional income, he or she usually had to ask an assembly of nobles for help.

In the 1600s, a new type of monarchy emerged in Europe. It was known as an absolute monarchy. These rulers claimed *absolute*, or total, power. Each asserted control over their nobles and over religious life. They established large standing armies and sharply increased tax collection. Absolute rulers claimed to hold their power by "divine right." This meant they were chosen by God. Their will was law.

In a constitutional monarchy, the monarch is often a ceremonial figurehead. Real power is held by the people, who elect Parliament or other legislature.

King Louis XIV of France

"I am the state," proclaimed King Louis XIV of France.

English kings tried to imitate the example of France and Spain by establishing their own absolute monarchy. They attempted to rule and collect taxes without Parliament. This effort failed when Parliament and its supporters rose up in rebellion. The British Parliament established its supremacy over the King in the English Bill of Rights of 1689. Great Britain became a constitutional monarchy. Real power was held by Parliament, and the monarch only acted as a symbol of national unity.

Today, there are very few absolute monarchies. Saudi Arabia, Oman, Brunei and Eswatini (former Swaziland) are examples of absolute monarchies. There are many more constitutional monarchies, including the United Kingdom, Japan, Sweden, Denmark, Thailand, Cambodia, Belgium, and the Netherlands.

Enrichment

The Active Citizen

- Conduct research on one of the following absolute monarchs: Philip II of Spain, Louis XIV of France, Peter the Great of Russia, or Catherine the Great of Russia. How "absolute" was their power?
- Imagine you are a monarch. Write a short letter or speech explaining the advantages of your form of government.

Democracy

Another form of government is **democracy**. As you know, this system first arose in ancient Greece. Democracy means "people power" in ancient Greek.

In the Athenian form of democracy, all the adult male citizens had the right to participate in the assembly, which served as both a legislature and a court. Citizens directly debated and decided important issues facing the *polis* (*city state*).

Most experts believe this form of democracy, in which all citizens decide issues in a common assembly, works best for small communities.

In larger communities, there is no single place for all citizens to assemble. It becomes impossible for so many people to discuss proposals and to make decisions together effectively. In these larger communities, citizens elect representatives. These

In all forms of democracy, the people hold the final power.

Direct Democracy

Representative Democracy

© FTE ▪ Unlawful to photocopy without permission

elected representatives debate proposals and make decisions for the rest of the community. All the members of the community are bound by these decisions. This form of government, first developed in ancient Rome, is known as a **representative government** or a **republic**.

In a republic, the people remain the final source of the government's power but act through their elected representatives. Republics are also able to place limits on the powers of the government, especially to protect individual rights.

The United States is a **constitutional republic**. It has a written constitution and a **representative government**. Its citizens elect representatives to the House of Representatives and the Senate. Citizens also elect the members of the Electoral College, who choose the President. These elected officials in turn make important decisions on the public issues facing the nation. They act on the people's behalf. In a **republic**, government leaders are responsible to the public—not to a king or queen. If citizens disagree with the decisions of their representatives, they vote them out of office in the next election.

Theocracy

A **theocracy** is a government run by religious leaders. In a theocracy, leaders claim to be acting on behalf of God. There is no separation of church and state. Citizens who do not belong to the official religion may face discrimination and persecution because of their religious beliefs. Iran is an example of a theocracy. The Iranian Constitution emphasizes the importance of the Quran (*the holy book of Islam*) and Sharia (*Islamic law*). Its preamble states that, "The Constitution of the Islamic Republic of Iran sets forth the cultural, social, political and economic institutions of the people of Iran, based on Islamic principles and rules, and reflecting the fundamental desires of the Islamic people."

Iranian citizens elect a President and representatives to a national assembly, but these elected leaders remain under the authority of Iran's Supreme Leader—a religious leader who is appointed for life. The assembly can enact laws but not any that would violate Islamic law. Other countries with theocratic governments are Afghanistan, Yemen, Mauritania, and Vatican City.

The Supreme Leader of Iran meeting with authorities.

Autocracy and Oligarchy

Autocracy and oligarchy refer to the number of people in control of a government.

An **autocracy** is a form of government in which one person enjoys absolute power. An absolute monarchy is one type of autocracy. So is a modern dictatorship—a system in which one political leader, like Hitler or Stalin, has total power.

Oligarchy means rule by a few. In this form of government, a small group rules over a country. There are many types of oligarchies. In a plutocracy, a group of rich people rule over society. In other oligarchies, an aristocracy (nobles who inherit their wealth and status) controls the government. In still another type of oligarchy, power is held by leading members of the military or of a political party.

The Advantages of the American Constitutional Republic over other Forms of Government in Safeguarding Liberty, Freedom, and Representative Government

The American system of government is designed to protect individual liberty while also ensuring **national unity**. To achieve this goal, it applies basic principles that distinguish it from the governments of authoritarian and totalitarian nations.

- In an **authoritarian nation**, an all-powerful individual or small group holds complete authority and can order other members of society at will.
- In a **totalitarian nation**, an authoritarian government controls all aspects of its people's lives. Its control over society is total.

Two examples of nations that were authoritarian and totalitarian are Nazi Germany (1933–1945) and the Soviet Union under the rule of Stalin (1922–1953). In these countries, citizens had no **individual rights**. The government controlled all social and political organizations. Military forces pledged absolute obedience to the leader. Opposition political parties were strictly prohibited. Opponents of the regime were placed in prison or murdered.

The American **constitutional republic** has important safeguards (*protections*) aimed at preventing the rise of such a system:

Safeguards of the American Constitutional Republic

Democratic Principles

- **Democracy:** A democracy is a government ruled by the people. The United States follows democratic principles, which make it difficult for an authoritarian leader to take charge.
- **Representative government:** The United States has the type of democracy known as representative government. In this form of government, citizens elect their representatives and public officials. Because our officials are elected for limited periods in office, they cannot seize power easily. If they act in ways against the public, they will be voted out of office.
- **Consent of the governed:** Through our elections, our government leaders are selected with the consent of the governed. Officials act with the support of a majority of citizens. This makes it difficult for an authoritarian leader to seize control.
- **Republicanism:** Republicanism refers to support for the republican system of government, also known as representative government. Again, by having elected representatives, Americans are protected from a dictator or other form of authoritarian government that might abuse their rights.

The Rule of Law and Individual Rights

- **Rule of law:** The rule of law is one of the strongest protections of the American constitutional republic. It means that our government officials must follow established law. We are not subject to the whims of our governing officials.
- **Due process of law:** Due process of law guarantees that citizens cannot have their lives, liberties or properties taken away by the government without a hearing and a fair process before a neutral and impartial decision-maker. This means an authoritarian leader cannot just seize our property or put us in prison if we criticize the government.

Continues ▶

- **Individual rights:** Americans enjoy individual rights, specified in the Constitution and the Bill of Rights. Because we have individual rights that cannot be taken away, governments cannot act against us arbitrarily. This prevents the rise of authoritarian leaders who wish to have life-and-death power over other citizens.

Checks on Government Power

- **Limited government:** The powers of our government are defined in the Constitution. The national government only has those powers given to it by the Constitution. The Constitution and Bill of Rights further establish individual rights that the government cannot take away. Because the power of the government is limited, the United States cannot become a totalitarian society in which national leaders exercise control over all aspects of life without limit.
- **Federalism:** Federalism divides power between the central government and the state governments. The state governments provide a check on any central government that might grow too strong.
- **Separation of Powers:** Power is divided among several branches, so that no single part of the government can become too strong. This makes it more difficult for a single person or small group to seize control and establish an authoritarian state.
- **Checks and balances:** Different parts of the government can check each other, so no one part of the government becomes too strong or authoritarian.

Because of these features, the American form of government has many advantages in **safeguarding liberty**, freedom and representative government compared to other forms of government. It has the advantage that government policies are based on the will of the people, as expressed in periodic elections. At the same time, this form of government guarantees the **rule of law**, **individual rights**, and the **due process of law**. Our government thus acts for the majority while also protecting minority rights.

- Because our leaders are elected, the American constitutional republic has advantages over a **monarchy**. Our leaders are chosen on the basis of their talent and skill, not because they have inherited power.
- Because the people elect their leaders, the American constitutional republic has advantages over an **oligarchy**. The views of the general public are considered, and voters act for the common good. In an oligarchy, a small group runs the government, usually for its own benefit. The group running the government tends to enrich itself at the expense of the general public. In our constitutional republic, citizens are able to hold their officials accountable.
- The American constitutional republic also has advantages over an **autocracy**. In an autocracy, one man or woman rules an entire society. The autocrat may listen to advisers and may even achieve some remarkable accomplishments. Over time, however, autocrats tend to lose touch with ordinary citizens and the needs of their nation. They often become all-consumed with the need to perpetuate their own power. Criticism of public policies is not allowed, so mistakes are made. Ordinary citizens suffer because they have no rights.
- In a **theocracy**, religious leaders run the government. In this kind of government, there is generally no freedom of religion and often no freedom of thought. People expressing different religious beliefs may face persecution and punishment. Religious matters take up

a large proportion of government concerns. Religious leaders consult sacred texts or one another, with less concern for the views of the public. Because they believe they are acting with divine authority, theocratic leaders tend to be authoritarian and totalitarian. They tell the rest of society how to behave. This is in sharp contrast to the American constitutional republic, where government officials have only limited power and ordinary citizens are protected by the due process of law and individual rights, including freedom of religion.

A Summary of the Advantages and Disadvantages of Three Major Forms of Government

Type of Government	Major Advantages	Major Disadvantages
Constitutional republic *(American system of government based on a written constitution, the rule of law, and elected representatives)*	Ordinary citizens are represented in government; the government operates by the rule of law; people enjoy individual rights and the due process of law.	Disagreements between citizens may slow down government processes.
Monarchy *(rule by an individual who inherits power)*	It is usually clear who the ruler is. The government is often stable and may be able to act rapidly in a crisis.	If the monarch lacks talent, the government will become corrupt and the nation will stagnate. Sometimes when a ruler dies, there is fighting to determine the new ruler.
Autocracy *(rule by one person)*	The autocrat can respond quickly to a crisis. A powerful autocrat can also focus all national energies on particular goals.	In an autocracy, ordinary citizens often live in fear. There are no guarantees of individual rights and laws are based on the whims of the autocrat. The autocrat often makes mistakes.

For the EOC, be sure to know the different systems of government and the advantages of our federal system

Systems of Government: Unitary, Federal and Confederal

All countries must cover some geographic area. Most governments cover an area large enough to need separate local authorities to govern all of their territory effectively. Another way to classify governments is by their **system of government**—the relationship between the national government and these local authorities. Governments must balance the need for **national unity** with the demands of citizens for **local sovereignty**—letting local authorities have the final say over local matters. They have different organizational structures (*ways of being organized*) to deal with this relationship.

Unitary Systems of Government

In a **unitary system**, the central government is all-powerful. Local areas (which may be called states, provinces, departments, or counties) may have their own governments, but these local governments exercise only those powers given to them by the central government. The central government has the power to abolish (*eliminate*) these local units at any time.

This system of government is known as **unitary** because the whole government of the nation exists as a single unit. Local governments are mere extensions of the central government. The central government delegates (*assigns*) various tasks and responsibilities to the local governments to carry out.

You won't need to know the names of specific countries with particular systems of government for the EOC test. But you will need to be able to identify a system of government from its characteristics and know the advantages of our federal system.

Most states in the world today have unitary systems of government. For example, the United Kingdom (Great Britain and Northern Ireland), France and Sweden all have unitary governments.

In the United Kingdom, Parliament rules over the entire nation. The United Kingdom actually consists of four historic kingdoms—England, Wales, Scotland and Northern Ireland. Each of these areas has its own local institutions, but these are all subject to Parliament. England, for example, is divided into "regions," which in turn are divided into county councils, borough councils, and unitary authority councils. But Parliament has the power to change or even to abolish these local authorities at any time.

Similarly, France is a unitary state. Its local government units—called "regions" and "departments"—were created by the national government and remain under its control. Sweden is also a unitary state. It has 21 counties, managed by administrators appointed by the central government. Other examples of unitary states include Algeria, China, Colombia, Cuba, Ghana, Egypt, Ireland, Israel, Italy, Japan, Poland, Saudi Arabia, South Korea, Thailand and Turkey.

Unitary government: local governments are extensions of the central government.

Memory Hint: To remember unitary government, remember that this system of government is based on a single unit.

Federal Systems of Government

In some countries, the central government and local governments each have their own powers. Local areas—often known as states or provinces—have an independent basis of authority. The central government has no right to abolish them. This is known as the **federal** system of government (or a federation). This system arises when several sovereign states join together to make a separate "federal" government with its own independent power.

In a federation, individual states do not have the right to leave the federation without the agreement of the other member states. At the same time, the central government does not have the right to take away the powers of the state governments. These powers are sometimes known as states' rights.

As you learned in earlier chapters, the United States has a **federal system**. Power is shared between the national government and the states. Each state has

Central government

Regional (state) governments

Federal government: a division of power between the central government and regional (state) governments. Each level has its own powers and responsibilities.

its own government with an elected state legislature and an elected governor. The Supremacy Clause guarantees the supremacy of the national government over the state governments, but the powers of the national government are limited. The 10th Amendment protects states' rights. Local authorities control local affairs but rely on the national government to meet national needs.

Advantages of the federal system. This system gives people control over their local affairs and makes it difficult for one person or party to seize dictatorial power. Local authorities would resist attempts at authoritarianism (*government by an all-powerful ruler with absolute authority*). At the same time, this system provides **national unity.** Other examples of modern federal governments include Germany, Mexico, Brazil, Nigeria, and India.

Enrichment

The Active Citizen

By its very name and based on its constitution, the Russian Federation is a federation with 22 republics and several provinces and territories. However, since 2004, the President of Russia appoints all the governors and presidents of Russia's local regions. Is Russia still a federation, or has it become a unitary state? Members of your class should conduct a debate on the following resolution:

"Resolved: That Russia, despite its name, is no longer a federation but has become a unitary state."

Confederal Systems of Government

A number of independent states or countries may decide to form an association in order to act together. Often, such countries wish to cooperate over trade or foreign policy. At the same time, the independent states or countries joining the association do not wish to give up their sovereign (*supreme*) power. Such associations usually have very little power of their own. They depend on the cooperation of their members. Each member of the association is free to leave at any time.

This kind of association is known as a **confederal system** (or a confederation). The central government of a confederation is far weaker than the local governments. Most power remains with the member states that joined together to create the confederation.

As you learned in earlier chapters, the thirteen new American states joined together to form a confederation in 1781. However, the type of government established by the Articles of Confederation proved to be too weak. By adopting the Constitution, Americans moved from a confederal system to a federal system.

Some political scientists consider the European Union an example of a confederal system. The European Union consists of member states that continue to have their own governments. These member states cooperate in a number of common European institutions, such as the European Parliament. They have created a large free trade area across Europe where goods, services, money, and people can move freely. All members also agree to follow certain European regulations. But many decisions remain

In a confederal government, several member states agree to cooperate in a central association with limited powers.

with the members' national governments. Member countries can also leave, as the United Kingdom did in 2020. German courts define the European Union as "an association of sovereign national states."

Most centralized ⟷ Least centralized

Unitary	Federal	Confederal
The central government is all-powerful. The entire government exists as a single unit. (*Disadvantage*: This system would allow a dictator to establish absolute control quickly after seizing power.)	The central government shares power with regional governments. (In the United States, these regional governments are the states.) Regions control local affairs while the central government meets national needs.	Several independent regions create an association, known as a confederation, for limited cooperation and common action.
Regional (local) governments are simply extensions of the central government. The central government may delegate some tasks and responsibilities to regional governments.	A constitution usually defines which powers and tasks are given to the central government and which powers are given to the regional governments.	Primary power remains with the members of the confederation. However, they may assign some tasks, such as managing trade and foreign policy, to the confederal government.
Regional governments owe their very existence to the central government. They can be abolished (eliminated) by the central government at any time.	Regional governments exist independently of the central government. The central government does not have the right or the power to abolish these regional governments.	The members of the confederation have the right to withdraw at almost any time. (*Disadvantage*: This system might be too weak to resist a dictator.)

The Active Citizen

- Some experts consider the European Union to be a federation rather than a confederation. Conduct your own research on the organization of the European Union. Then state your opinion on whether the EU is a confederation or federation in a brief written paper or oral presentation.
- Imagine you are a member of a constitutional convention for a new country. Prepare a speech on whether this new country should adopt a unitary, federal or confederal system of government.

Economic Systems

For the EOC, you should know the three major economic systems and how much freedom and prosperity each provides.

Economics is the study of how people meet their needs. Our needs and wants are unlimited. They are greater than the limited resources each society has to satisfy them. Societies therefore have to decide how to use their scarce resources to satisfy the unlimited desires of their members. All societies must answer these three basic economic questions:

- What should be produced?
- How should it be produced?
- Who should receive what is produced?

How a society answers these three basic economic questions is known as its **economic system**. An economic system is how a society produces goods (*things people make*) and services (*actions people do for others*), and how it distributes those goods and services to its members.

There are three main types of economic systems you should know:

Capitalism

Under **capitalism**, also known as the **free market system**, individuals are able to own their own private property. They are free to use this property without government interference. They can invest their time and property in creating businesses that provide services and goods to others. They can sell these services and goods to other citizens in the hopes of making a profit (*the difference between the price of the product and the cost of making it*). "Capital" refers to the resources (including money) that people and businesses save and invest.

- Under capitalism, the three basic economic questions are answered by individuals and private businesses pursuing their own interests. Individuals and companies decide which goods and services to produce. They also decide what price to charge for these products. Consumers (*those who buy products*) decide for themselves whether or not they want to purchase those products. The government does not tell the producers or consumers what to do.
- Producers will become successful if there is a demand for their products. If people are willing to pay for their goods and services, they can even make more of them and raise their prices. If people don't want to buy their products, they will lower their prices and produce less.
- If consumers need more of a good or service, they will pay more for it and the price goes up. As the demand for the product increases, it becomes profitable for producers to make more of it. On the other hand, if the supply of the product is greater than the demand, the price that purchasers are willing to pay for it will fall. Producers will compete with one another to sell off their supplies by reducing their prices.
- What economists call the "laws of supply and demand" thus determine what gets produced and how much. The same "laws" determine the prices at which those goods and services are sold. The "laws of supply and demand" act as an "invisible hand," guiding society in what to produce. In this way, the free market, without government interference, answers the three basic economic questions—deciding what goods and services are made, what their prices will be, and who receives what is produced.

Prosperity and Opportunity under Capitalism

Economic Freedom

Capitalism provides **opportunity** and the maximum **economic freedom**. Producers and consumers make their own economic choices with limited government interference.

Living Standards

Living standards (*levels of income and comfort*) in capitalist economies tend to be high. The free market eliminates inefficient producers. The profit incentive spurs producers to develop new technologies and better ways of providing goods and services—so that living standards are constantly improving. On the other hand, the social "safety net" under capitalism is often not as complete as in government-controlled economies, so some groups may feel left out.

Communism

During the Industrial Revolution, workers were badly treated. They had to work long hours for low wages under poor and unhealthy conditions. Reformers tried to reduce the suffering of factory workers, miners and other laborers. Their concerns gave birth to two new systems—**socialism** and **communism**. Unlike capitalism, these are both **government-controlled economic systems**.

Karl Marx

Communists believed that the rich would never give up their wealth and privileges peacefully. A violent revolution would therefore be necessary to improve conditions for workers. After workers rose up, they could defeat the factory owners and other business owners who had amassed riches by taking unfair advantage of them. The workers would then abolish private property altogether. Everything would be owned in common, and all citizens would work for the good of the community.

Communists seized power in Russia in November 1917. Russia—renamed as the Soviet Union—became the world's first communist state. After World War II, communism spread to the countries of Eastern Europe, North Korea, China, North Vietnam, and Cuba.

Under **communism**, the government has complete control over what is produced and how it is distributed:

- In the communist economic system, the central government controls all natural and human resources. Industries are owned and managed by the government.
- Farms are taken away from private farmers and given to state-owned collective farms.
- Production is based on five-year plans set by government officials known as central planners. Central planners establish production quotas for farms and factories. They decide how resources will be used.

Prosperity and Opportunity under Communists

Economic Freedom

In practice, communist leaders set up brutal dictatorships. Political opponents were arrested and sent to labor camps or murdered. Under communism, the government answered the basic economic questions. There was little **economic freedom**—the freedom to make one's own economic choices. Government authorities determined what to produce in their five-year plans. People were not able to own businesses of their own.

Joseph Stalin

Living Standards

The **standard of living** is a measure of how well the people of a society are doing. Communist economies did not make progress at the same pace as free market economies. There were not enough incentives for their citizens to work hard or take risks. Communist economies eventually stagnated (*stayed still; did not grow*). The Soviet Union and the countries of Eastern Europe abandoned communism in the 1990s.

China kept the communist political system but allowed private ownership and free enterprise in its economy. These developments raised living standards and turned China into one of the world's fastest growing economies.

Socialism

Unlike communists, socialists did not think a violent revolution was necessary for workers to improve their conditions. They believed that workers could improve their conditions if they acted together and elected government leaders sympathetic to their needs. The government could then take over some industries, impose stricter regulations on employers, and provide more social services.

Under socialism, the government greatly influences what is produced, but there is also private property and free enterprise:

- The government owns basic industries (steel and energy), transportation facilities (bus and subway systems, railroads, airlines), and communications (radio and television). Government-owned companies in socialist economies are known as "state-owned" industries. Other businesses remain under private ownership.
- The government provides a large range of social services to the public at no cost. Citizens enjoy free health care and free education, including free college and professional training. The government also provides free museums, sports facilities, and entertainment. Local authorities may even own houses and apartments, which they rent to citizens at low cost.
- People have the right to own private property and are free to use it as they wish. They can also form their own businesses.
- To pay for the large range of government services, taxes in socialist economies are generally high.

Prosperity and Opportunity under Socialism

Socialist political parties achieved power in several countries in Europe after World War II (1939–1945). Socialist leaders then created "welfare states" in Britain, Sweden, Norway and other countries. These governments increased taxes in order to provide free medical care, higher education and other services to all their citizens. Socialist governments also took over businesses providing essential services, such as transportation, communication, and electric power. Socialist governments then provided cheap or free transportation, electricity and other services to their citizens.

In a few countries, such as Norway, socialist policies are still followed today. In other countries, socialism was only a partial success. High taxes and lack of opportunity limited growth. Productivity fell. New businesses found it hard to succeed. In Britain, conservative political parties defeated socialists in elections. Once in power, these conservatives sold off state-owned industries to private investors. They lowered taxes and raised tuition for attending university, but kept free health care.

Economic Freedom

Economic freedom under socialism is greater than it is under communism but not as great as under capitalism.

Living Standards

Socialism has been successful in small countries with additional resources, such as Norway. Norway has North Sea oil, which helps pay for public services. In other countries, like Great Britain, socialism was less successful. By the 1980s, the British economy was not advancing. British leaders sold off the country's state-owned industries. Businesses became more competitive and living standards improved.

Comparing the Economic Prosperity and Opportunity of Nations Today

The type of economic system affects the degree of economic opportunity. In capitalist and socialist societies, there are more opportunities for individual initiative than in communist economies.

The type of economic system also affects a nation's economic prosperity—how well an economy is performing. But because other factors, such as resources, can also impact national prosperity, it is often difficult to determine the exact effect that the type of economic system has.

To judge national prosperity, economists (*people who study economics*) look at various indicators (*something that measures the level of something*).

One important economic indicator is Gross National Income. That is the amount of goods and services produced in a country in one year. Gross National Income per capita (per person) is GNI divided by a country's population. It is the amount produced in a year by an average person in that country.

The World Bank has classified countries based on their GNI per capita. According to the World Bank website (date.worldbank.org), there are currently about 80 "high income" countries with GNI per capita of more than $12,696. These "high income" countries include many with capitalist economies, such as the United States ($64,210), Singapore ($86,480), Switzerland ($69,170), Germany ($56,370), Australia ($52,230), France ($47,730), South Korea ($45,570), and Japan ($43,130). "High income" countries also include some nations with socialist economies, including Norway ($65,500) and Sweden ($56,740).

In contrast, many countries with government-controlled communist economies or that previously had communist economies are not performing as well—for example, Russia ($29,110), Belarus ($19,400), China ($17,090), Venezuela ($17,090), Vietnam ($8,150), Laos ($7,800), and Cuba (estimated at $9,000).

The Active Citizen

1. Choose one country with a capitalist economy, one country with a socialist economy, and one country with a communist economy. Select countries that are about the same in the size of their population.

Type of Economic System	Country	Population
Capitalist		
Communist		
Socialist		

2. Next, research how well each of these three countries has provided economic prosperity and determine the country's level of economic prosperity. You can record your findings below.

3. Finally, compare your findings with the rest of the class. See if you can draw any conclusions about the relationship between a country's economic system and its economic prosperity and opportunity.

The Comparative Government Game

Now you are ready to play a game based on what you have just learned about the different types of governments and economic systems.

Rules of the Game

1. Your teacher should divide your class into small groups of 3–5 students.
2. Each group should research the governments and economic systems of four countries on the Internet.
3. The group should write a short description of the governments of each of these countries on a separate index card. Be sure to include characteristics that indicate (1) whether that government is a monarchy, democracy, autocracy, oligarchy, or theocracy; (2) whether it has a unitary, federal or confederal system; and (3) whether it has a capitalist, communist or socialist economic system.
4. On the bottom of the same card, include all those classifications that your group believes apply to that country. For example, the United States is a democracy, has a federal system, and has a capitalist economy.
5. After all the groups are done, your teacher should collect the cards.
6. After mixing up the cards, your teacher should read aloud the description on each card. After hearing each description, you should write down on a separate sheet of paper all the classifications you have studied that fit that country's description (such as being a monarchy with a unitary system).
7. For every classification that you identify correctly, you will receive one point. After the cards are all read, the student with the most points wins the game!

Here are four descriptions to help start the Comparative Government Game: What kind of government and economic system does each country have?

The government of Saudi Arabia is headed by a hereditary king with total power. The King is assisted by the Crown Prince and a Council of Ministers, or Cabinet. The King is also assisted by a legislative council, the Majlis Al-Shura, which recommends new laws. Its 150 members are appointed by the King. The country's judicial system is based on Islamic law. The King appoints the governors of 13 regional governments. There are many state-owned industries, and the government provides many public services.

What kind of government and economic system does Saudi Arabia have? ______________________

Continues ▶

The Constitution of the People's Republic of China guarantees the position of the Communist Party. The all-powerful Politburo, consisting of about ten individuals, makes the most important decisions. The Communist Party and the People's Liberation Army follow the orders of the Politburo. The Paramount (*supreme*) Leader is chosen by the Politburo. China's Paramount Leader acts as General Secretary of the Communist Party and as President of the People's Republic of China. China also has a State Council and National People's Congress with nearly 3,000 elected members. The central government appoints officials to run China's provinces and regions. People have some freedom to start and operate their own businesses.

What kind of government and economic system does China have? ____________________

Norway adopted a written constitution in 1814. A hereditary king or queen acts as its head of state. The king or queen holds symbolic power and represents Norway in state ceremonies. Voters elect members of the legislature, known as the Storting. The leader of the parliamentary bloc holding a majority is appointed as Norway's Prime Minister. The Prime Minister appoints other ministers to form a government. There are private businesses but the government has an ownership share in oil, aluminum, telecommunications and other industries. Taxes are high but the government provides many social services to citizens, including retirement benefits, health care and higher education. Norway's county governments have some powers but are under the complete control of the national government.

What kind of government and economic system does Norway have?

____

Brazil has a national government with a President, National Congress, Supreme Court, and other national courts. The President and members of Congress are elected. Brazil has 26 states and a federal district where the capital is located. Each state has its own powers. Voting in Brazil is compulsory for those over 18 years old who can read and write. The economy allows free enterprise, while the government provides some social services.

What kind of government and economic system does Brazil have? ____________________

Name ______________________________

Complete the following imaginary dialogue between Thomas Jefferson and King George III on the advantages and disadvantages of democracy and monarchy.

Thomas Jefferson: Governments are created to protect the rights of individual citizens. A democracy is the best form of government because it places power directly in the hands of its citizens.

King George III: There are many different groups in every society. Each of these groups tries to use the powers of government for its own benefit. A hereditary king or queen is the only person who stands above all these groups and represents society as a whole. A hereditary monarch is a neutral judge who will do what is best for all citizens.

Thomas Jefferson

____

King George III

____

Thomas Jefferson

____

King George III

____

A Summary of the Forms of Government And Economic Systems

Who Holds the Power: One, Few or Many?

Monarchy: Government by a king, queen, emperor or empress who inherits power.

Autocracy: Rule by one person who claims total power. An absolute monarchy is one form of autocracy. Rule by a dictator is another example of an autocracy.

Oligarchy: Rule by a small group of people, such as a few very rich people, or the leaders of a political party.

Democracy: A form of government in which ordinary people hold the final power.

Theocracy: Religious leaders hold power.

Representative Government: A form of democratic government in which citizens elect representatives to make decisions for them. If citizens are unhappy with the decisions that their representatives make, they can vote them out of office in the next election.

Republic: Another name for a representative government. The government belongs to the "public." The United States is a constitutional republic with additional safeguards to protect individual rights and its form of government.

Economic Systems

Socialism: In socialist economies, the government owns some industries and provides many public services, such as health care and education, at no charge. Private enterprise exists alongside "state-owned" industries. Taxes are generally high to pay for public services.

Capitalism (Free Market): People own private property and make their own economic choices. They are free to buy what they want and to invest in producing goods and services they can sell to others. The "laws of supply and demand" determine what is produced and the prices at which it is sold. Standards of living are high because the free market eliminates inefficient producers.

Communism: Communism is a government-controlled economic system. The government controls all farming and industry. Central planners decide people's needs, and they tell farms and factories what to produce to meet those needs. In practice, communist governments became brutal dictatorships. Standards of living fell because the system was inefficient.

A Summary of the Systems of Government

Relationship between the Central Government and Local Authorities

Governments can by classified by system--how the national government relates to the local governments. Governments must balance the need for **national unity** with the desire of local authorities for **local sovereignty**.

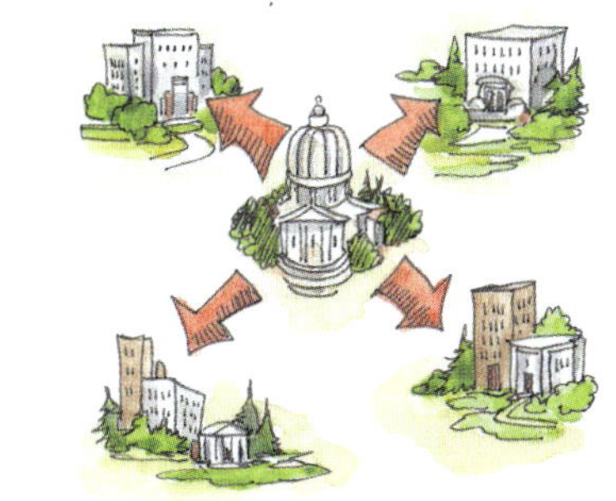

Unitary System: In this system, the central government holds all power. The central government can create or abolish local governments, and it tells those local governments what to do.

Federal System: In the federal system, the central government and local governments share power. States do not have the power to leave the federal government on their own authority, and the central government cannot abolish the states or take away their power. This system gives local authorities power over their own affairs, yet also creates a strong central government for national needs. The United States has a federal system.

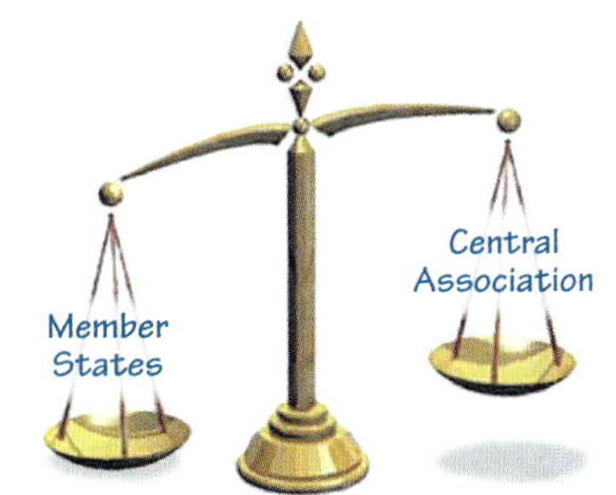

Confederal System: This system of government is an association of independent states. The central government is weak and can only do what the states agree to let it do. Member states can leave the confederal government at any time. The United States had a confederal government under the Articles of Confederation.

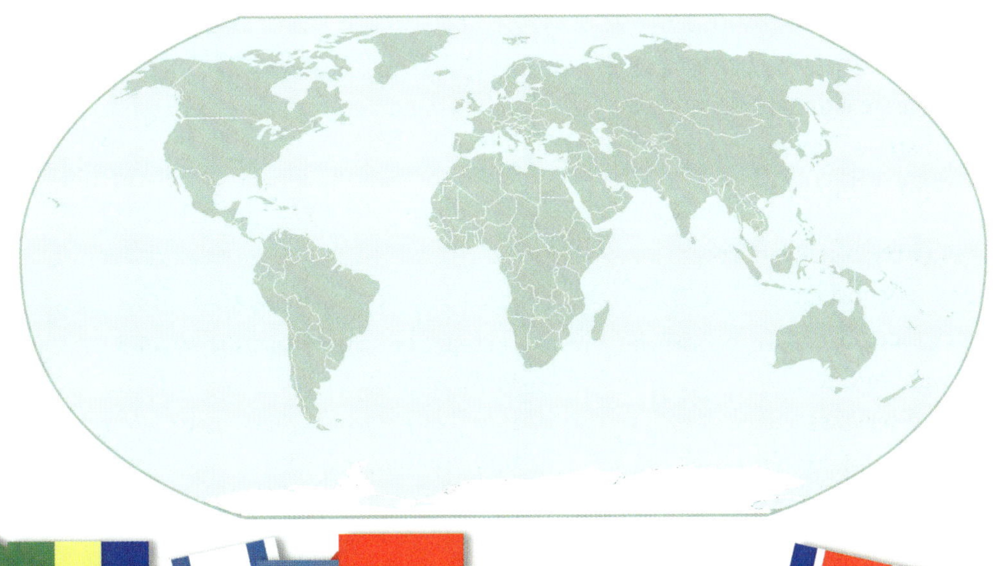

Name ____

Fill in the charts below.

Capitalism (Free Market)	
Define this economic system:	How much freedom does this economic system allow?
An example of a country with this economic system:	How does this economic system affect standards of living?

Communism	
Define this economic system:	How much economic freedom does this system allow?
An example of a country with this economic system:	How does this economic system affect standards of living?

Socialism	
Define this economic system:	How much economic freedom does this system allow?
An example of a country with this economic system:	How does this economic system affect standards of living?

Name ______________________________

Fill in the chart below on the characteristics of the different forms of government.

Forms of Governments

Form	Description of its Organizational Structure	Example
Monarchy		
Democracy		
Republic		
Autocracy		
Oligarchy		
Theocracy		

Name ______________________________

Fill in the chart below on the characteristics of the different systems of government.

Systems of Governments

System	Description of its Organizational Structure	How well does this system protect against authoritarianism?
Unitary		
Federal		
Confederal		

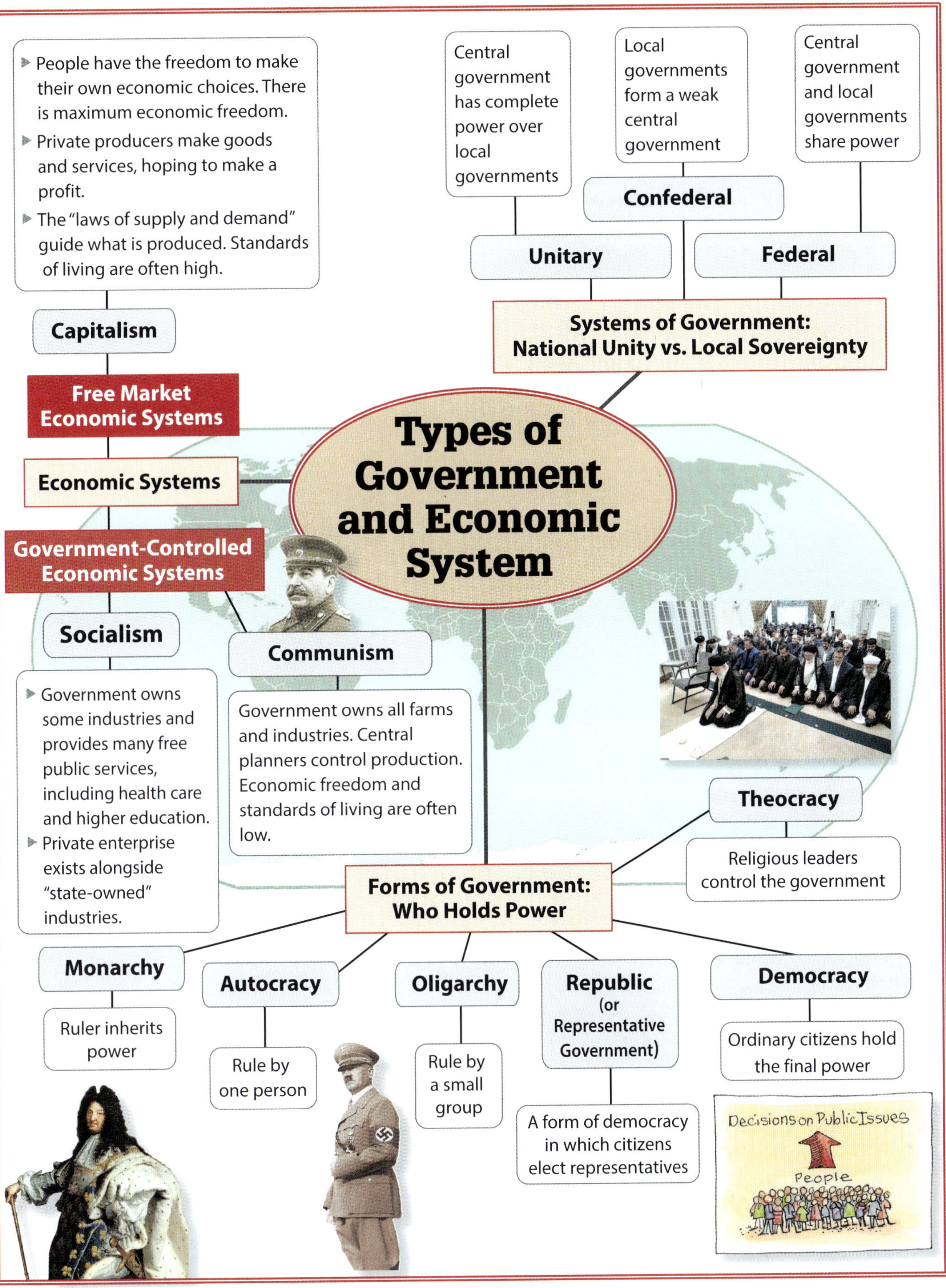

Types of Government and Economic System
Economic Systems
Free Market Economic Systems
Capitalism
People have the freedom to make their own economic choices. There is maximum economic freedom.
Private producers make goods and services, hoping to make a profit.
The "laws of supply and demand" guide what is produced. Standards of living are often high.
Government-Controlled Economic Systems
Socialism
Government owns some industries and provides many free public services, including health care and higher education.
Private enterprise exists alongside "state-owned" industries.
Communism
Government owns all farms and industries. Central planners control production. Economic freedom and standards of living are often low.
Systems of Government: National Unity vs. Local Sovereignty
Unitary
Central government has complete power over local governments
Confederal
Local governments form a weak central government
Federal
Central government and local governments share power
Forms of Government: Who Holds Power
Theocracy
Religious leaders control the government
Monarchy
Ruler inherits power
Autocracy
Rule by one person
Oligarchy
Rule by a small group
Republic (or Representative Government)
A form of democracy in which citizens elect representatives
Democracy
Ordinary citizens hold the final power
Decisions on Public Issues
People

Theories of Government

Government is the organization that makes up rules for the community, settles disputes, protects the community and provides public services. It has power to enforce its rules, defend the community and take other actions.

Today, there are many different types of governments around the world. Governments have different **organizational structures** (*ways of being organized*) based on their **political philosophy** (*beliefs about government*).

Forms of Government: Monarchy, Democracy, Autocracy, Oligarchy, and Theocracy

To classify items is to arrange them into groups of related items (known as "classes"). One way to classify the **organizational structures** of governments is by identifying who holds power in that **form of government**.

Monarchy

- A **monarchy** is a government ruled by one person, who holds hereditary power. Power passes down from one family member to the next—usually the monarch's oldest son or daughter.

Democracy

- **Democracy** ("people power") is a government in which the people rule. They are the final source of government authority and power.
- The first democracy arose in Athens, Greece. All male citizens could participate in government. Citizens directly debated and decided public issues in a public assembly.

Republic (or Representative Government)

- A **republic** is a form of democracy in which the people rule through elected representatives, who make decisions on their behalf. It is suitable for larger communities where it would not be possible for all citizens to assemble together to make decisions. The United States is a **constitutional republic** with a representative government based on a written constitution.

Autocracy and Oligarchy

- In an **autocracy** (such as an absolute monarchy or a dictatorship, one ruler holds all political power.
- In an **oligarchy**, a small group, such as a group of noblemen or the military, holds power.

Theocracy

- In a **theocracy**, religious leaders hold supreme political power.

Advantages of the American Constitutional Republic in Safeguarding Liberty and Representative Government

The American **constitutional republic** has many safeguards to protect our freedom and prevent our country from becoming either an **authoritarian nation** (*a country under the control of an all-powerful, absolute ruler*) or a **totalitarian nation** (*a country where the government closely controls all aspects of life*).

These safeguards include:

- **Democracy** (*government is based on the will of the people*): opposes authoritarianism
- **Representative government** (*rule by elected representatives*): opposes rule by an individual or a small group
- **Consent of the governed** (*government based on citizens' approval*): leaders cannot act against the will of the majority of the people
- **Republicanism** (*support for representative government*): opposes rule by an individual or a small group
- **Rule of law** (*everyone is subject to the same rules*): leaders cannot do what they please or seize power in violation of the law
- **Due process of law** (*everyone is entitled to a fair hearing*): allows people to criticize the government without fear of punishment
- **Individual rights** (*personal rights are guaranteed by the Bill of Rights*): people are permitted to criticize the government
- **Limited government** (*the government has only those powers specified in the Constitution*): a leader cannot seize unlimited power
- **Federalism** (*division of power between the national and state governments*): local authorities would resist an authoritarian leader
- **Separation of powers** (*division of power between the branches of government*): prevents one branch from becoming too strong
- **Checks and balances** (*different branches of government check each other*): other branches would check any attempt to establish authoritarian rule

National Government and Local Authorities: Unitary, Federal and Confederal Systems of Government

Governments can also be classified based on the relationship between their central and local governments. There are three **systems of government** based on this relationship: unitary, federal, and confederal. Governments must balance the need for **national unity** with the demands of citizens for **local sovereignty** (*local control*).

Unitary System

- In a **unitary system**, the central government holds complete power.
- The central government creates local governments and gives them some powers, but it can take back these powers at any time. It can change or even abolish these local governments if it likes.
- Most nations in the world today have unitary systems.

Continues ▶

National Government and Local Authorities: Unitary, Federal and Confederal Systems of Government (*continued*)

Federal System

- In a **federal system**, the central and local governments exercise independent powers and cannot abolish each other.
- States can join together to form a federal government, but a state cannot leave a federal government without the agreement of the other states.
- In the United States, the national (central) and state governments share power. The federal government has limited powers and other powers are reserved for the states. Wherever the federal government can lawfully exercise power, its power is supreme.
- Advantages of the federal system: This system gives people control over their own local affairs. By dividing power, it makes it harder for a potential dictator to seize power. Local authorities would resist any attempt to establish **authoritarianism** (*a system of government by an all-powerful ruler with complete authority*). At the same time, this system promotes **national unity**.

Confederal System

- In a **confederal system**, a group of independent states or nations form an association to cooperate.
- The majority of power remains with the separate states, which are free to leave at any time.
- The Articles of Confederation created this type of government in the United States in 1781. The U.S. Constitution then changed the United States from a confederal to a federal system. Another example of a confederation is today's European Union, which consists of various sovereign European governments cooperating with one another. Each has a right to leave the European Union.

Economic Systems

Economics is the study of how people use their resources to produce goods and services to meet their needs and wants. Our resources are limited but our needs and wants are unlimited. All societies must therefore answer three basic economic questions:

- What to produce?
- How to produce it?
- Who gets what is produced?

The way in which a society answers these three questions is known as its **economic system**.

Three different types of economic system are capitalism (or free market system), communism and socialism.

Capitalism

- Under **capitalism**, also known as the **free market system**, the three basic economic questions are answered by individuals and private businesses pursuing their own interests freely.
- People can invest their own time and property in creating businesses that provide services and goods to others. They sell these services and goods in the hopes of making a profit. Consumers (*those who buy products*) decide for themselves if they want to purchase what is made. Producers are successful if there is a demand for their products.
- The "laws of supply and demand" determine what gets produced and the prices at which those products are sold. These laws act as an "invisible hand" guiding society in what to produce.
- Capitalism provides the most **economic freedom** and **opportunity** of any system. Producers and consumers make their own economic choices. **Standards of living** (*levels of income and comfort*) in capitalist economies tend to be high. The free market eliminates inefficient producers, while the profit incentive spurs producers to improve.

Government-Controlled Economic Systems: Socialism and Communism

Socialism and **communism** arose in reaction to the harsh treatment of workers during the Industrial Revolution. Both systems rely on government controls instead of the free market. In socialism, the government exercises some control; in communism, the government exercises total control.

Socialism

- Socialists believe that it is the government's job to improve conditions for citizens. Socialist governments establish "welfare states" in which the government takes over some industries and increases taxes in order to provide more public services, like free health care, free higher education, and inexpensive public transportation.
- In a few countries with small populations and plentiful resources, such as Norway, socialism has been successful. In larger countries, the high taxation, large number of government industries, and lack of **opportunity** discouraged workers and kept standards of living from rising. Eventually, most of these countries gave up socialism, sold off their state-owned industries, and returned to the **capitalist** or **free market system**.

Communism

- Communists believe that a violent social revolution is necessary in which workers overthrow the rich and abolish private property. Everything will then be owned in common and the government will eventually disappear.
- In practice, actual communist revolutions, like the Russian Revolution in 1917, resulted in brutal dictatorships. In these countries, the Communist Party took over everything and suppressed opposition. A party leader, like Joseph Stalin in Russia and Mao Zedong in China, became an all-powerful dictator. These dictators imprisoned or murdered their opponents, silencing all criticism. The central government took control of all human and natural resources and owned all property.

Continues ▸

Government-Controlled Economic Systems: Socialism and Communism (*continued*)

▶ In the communist economic system, the government controls all farming and industry. Central planners decide people's needs, and they tell farms and factories what to produce to meet those needs. Communism was inefficient in practice: people had little **economic freedom**, planners could not predict social needs, and there was little incentive to improve. **Standards of living** fell. By the 1980s, the Soviet Union and Eastern Europe, with their **communist** economies, had fallen behind Western nations with **free market systems**. In the 1990s, these countries gave up communism and adopted capitalist economies.

What Do You Know?

SS.7.CG.3.1

1. What do an autocracy and oligarchy have in common?
   - **A.** The head of state is chosen by Parliament.
   - **B.** Their citizens decide public issues for themselves.
   - **C.** The majority of citizens have little or no control over government.
   - **D.** Political power is exercised by representatives elected by the people.

SS.7.CG.3.1

2. What is one advantage of the American constitutional republic over autocratic nations in safeguarding individual liberties?
   - **A.** Its national government has unlimited power over its citizens.
   - **B.** The conduct of its government officials is limited by the rule of law.
   - **C.** It places power in a single person without any checks and balances.
   - **D.** It gives local authorities final authority over the national government.

SS.7.CG.3.15

3. Which type of economic system provides the most economic freedom and has historically provided high standards of living?
   - **A.** socialism
   - **B.** capitalism
   - **C.** totalitarian
   - **D.** communism

SS.7.CG.3.15

4. How do communist economies determine what goods and services to provide to their citizens?
   - **A.** Central planners set quotas for state-owned farms and factories.
   - **B.** Private businesses decide what to produce based on consumer demand.
   - **C.** Private citizens determine their own needs and produce for themselves.
   - **D.** State-owned industries determine some production while private businesses produce goods based on consumer demand.

SS.7.CG.3.2

5. The Venn diagram below compares two forms of government.

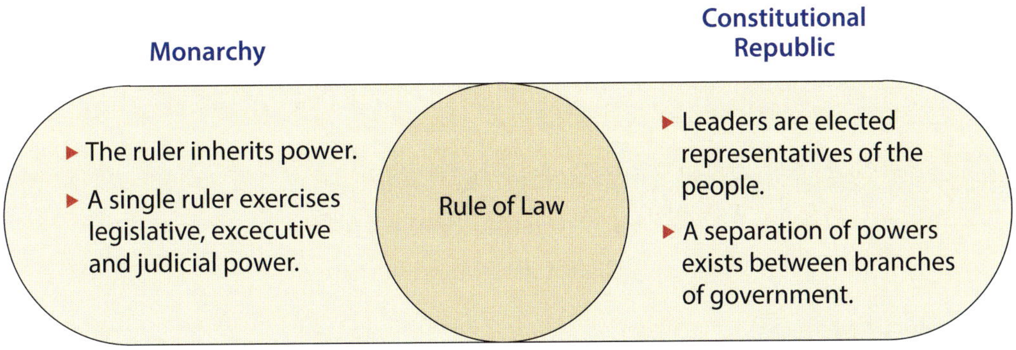

What would be considered an advantage of the government on the right?

A. There are fewer disagreements over public policy.

B. It is able to act more quickly in a crisis or emergency.

C. It provides better safeguards for protecting individual liberties.

D. Members of the government are able to meet with foreign officials.

SS.7.CG.3.2

6. Which statement is true of a federal but not of a unitary system of government?

A. Its local governments are extensions of the central government.

B. Its local governments cannot be abolished by the central government.

C. Its central government usually appoints the leaders of local governments.

D. Its central government delegates responsibilities to local governments to carry out.

SS.7.CG.3.1

7. The excerpt below is from "The Form of Islamic Government" by Ayatollah Khomeini, Supreme Leader of Iran.

> *The fundamental difference between Islamic government, on the one hand, and constitutional monarchy and republics, on the other, is this: whereas the representatives of the people or the monarch in such regimes engage in legislation, in Islam the legislative power and competence to establish laws belong exclusively to God Almighty.*

Based on this excerpt, which form of government would Ayatollah Khomeini have preferred?

A. oligarchy

B. autocracy

C. theocracy

D. democracy

SS.7.CG.3.1

8. John lives in the country of Devonia. Devonia has an absolute leader in charge of its government. This leader holds unlimited power. She can imprison or even execute citizens at will. She has opened special internment camps, where she sends critics of her government. The government controls all aspects of people's daily lives—education, work, social organizations, and media. No rival organizations are permitted. Under which form of government does John live?

   A. a monarchy
   B. an oligarchy
   C. a constitutional republic
   D. a totalitarian government

SS.7.CG.3.2

9. What is an advantage of the federal system of government in balancing local sovereignty with national unity?

   A. In this system, local governments can leave the nation at any time because they are sovereign.
   B. In this system, national unity is secure because the national government exercises complete control over local governments.
   C. In this system, freedom is protected because local governments have sovereignty over the national government in all matters.
   D. In this system, the national government is strong enough to protect the nation but local governments prevent it from becoming authoritarian.

SS.7.CG.3.2

10. Why did the authors of the Constitution create a federal system of government rather than a unitary system?

   A. They did not trust the state governments.
   B. They feared a central government that was too powerful.
   C. They wanted to limit the role of the people in government.
   D. They had seen how inefficient a weak central government was under the Articles of Confederation.

SS.7.CG.3.15

11. Which statement identifies an advantage of capitalism over government-controlled economic systems in raising standards of living?

   A. Central planners identify where economic needs are greatest.
   B. The profit incentive spurs producers to develop new technologies.
   C. Government leaders punish critics who challenge economic policies.
   D. Workers have no reason to work hard since their jobs are guaranteed.

SS.7.CG.3.2

12. The diagram below represents three systems of government.

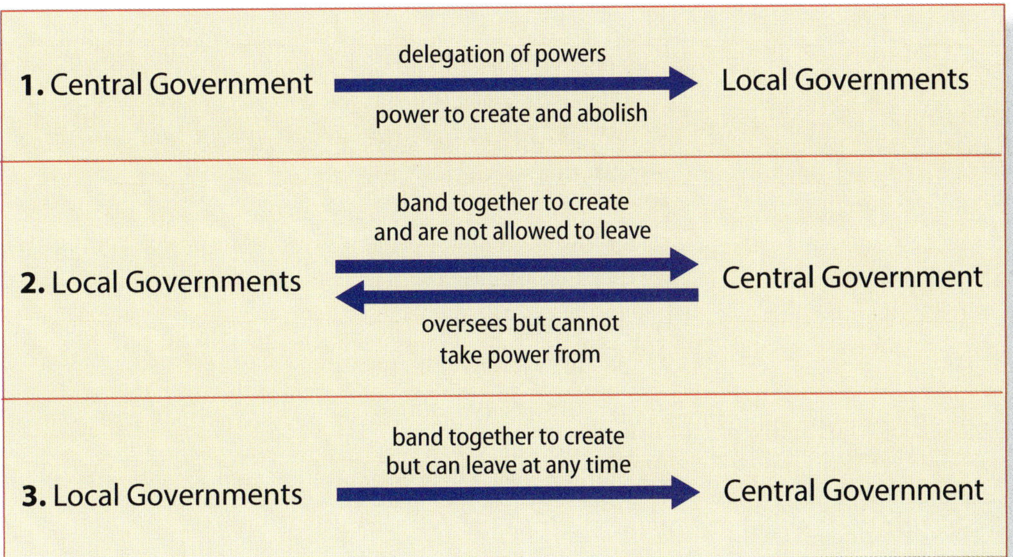

Which list correctly identifies the three types of governments in the diagram?

A. 1. Unitary; 2. Federal; 3. Confederal
B. 1. Federal; 2. Confederal; 3. Unitary
C. 1. Monarchical; 2. Autocratic; 3. Theocratic
D. 1. Confederal; 2. Democratic; 3. Monarchical

SS.7.CG.3.15

13. What do socialist and communist economic systems have in common?

A. They often resulted in brutal dictatorships and economic stagnation.
B. They believed that the ideal society was one in which the government abolished all forms of private property.
C. They both promoted a violent social revolution in which workers would take control of the government.
D. They believed that government should provide services to the community to raise the average standard of living.

SS.7.CG.3.1

14. Which form of government gives the most power to ordinary citizens?

A. autocracy
B. oligarchy
C. theocracy
D. democracy

SS.7.CG.3.15

15. Which statement best describes a socialist economy?

A. Private businesses provide all goods and services.
B. Taxes are low, but government services are extremely limited.
C. The government owns several basic industries and provides many services at no cost.
D. Private property is abolished and all goods and services are provided to citizens by the government.

SS.7.CG.3.1

16. The excerpt below comes from the writings of Jacques Bénigne Bossuet, a French bishop in the early 1700s.

> *Rulers act as the ministers of God and as his lieutenants on earth. It is through them that God exercises his empire. . . . It appears from all this that the person of the king is sacred, and that to attack him in any way is sacrilege. . . .*

Based on this excerpt, which form of government would Bishop Bossuet most likely favor?

A. oligarchy
B. democracy
C. monarchy
D. confederation

SS.7.CG.3.15

17. The list below describes the characteristics of an economic system.

- People can own private property.
- Producers can make whatever they want.
- Consumers can buy whatever they want.
- Producers act to make a profit.

What is an important consequence of this type of economic system?

A. Many people enjoy economic freedom and high standards of living.
B. Living standards drop when the country falls behind in its use of technology.
C. People are helped by the government, which provides many free public services.
D. Government leaders take over all farms and industries to provide greater equality.

SS.7.CG.3.2

18. Which statement identifies an advantage of the federal system of government in resisting authoritarianism?

A. Local authorities possess greater power than the central government.
B. Local authorities have the right to secede from the nation at any time.
C. Local authorities have enough independent power to resist the rise of an overpowering central government.
D. The central government cannot become too strong because it is a weak association of stronger local governments.

CHAPTER 18

American Foreign Policy

SS.7.CG.4.1 Explain the relationship between U.S. foreign and domestic policy.

SS.7.CG.4.2 Describe the United States' and citizen participation in international organizations.

SS.7.CG.4.3 Describe examples of the United States' actions and reactions in international conflicts.

Content Focus Vocabulary in This Chapter

- Domestic policy
- Foreign policy
- Secretary of State
- Ambassador
- National interest
- Means available to the national government
- Methods used to deal with international conflicts
- Diplomacy
- Espionage
- Humanitarian efforts
- Peacekeeping operations
- Sanctions
- War
- International incidents
- International conflicts
- U.S. actions and reactions
- Reasons for U.S. Involvement
- World War I
- World War II
- Korean War
- Bay of Pigs
- Cuban Missile Crisis
- Vietnam War
- First and Second Gulf Wars
- Iran Hostage Crisis
- International organization
- United States participation
- Citizen participation
- United Nations
- North Atlantic Treaty Organization
- International Court of Justice
- World Trade Organization

Florida "Keys" to Learning

1. **Domestic policy** is any government policy that concerns affairs at home. **Foreign policy** is any government policy that deals with foreign affairs.

2.The Constitution gives both the President and Congress some control over U.S. foreign policy.

3. The **Secretary of State** is the member of the Cabinet entrusted with the day-to-day running of U.S. foreign policy. The Secretary of State heads the State Department. **Ambassadors** are diplomats who act as representatives between nations.

4. U.S. foreign policy pursues our **national interest** (*what is in the best interest of the United States*). The national interest includes these goals: the security of the United States; the protection of U.S. citizens and their property and investments abroad; the promotion of trade with the United States; the encouragement of democracy and free enterprise; protecting the environment; the humanitarian goals of world peace and improving global living standards; and the prevention of armed conflicts and genocide (*murder of an entire people*).

5. There are several **means available to the national government** to pursue the national interest. These are also the **methods used to deal with international conflicts**: **diplomacy** (*dealings and negotiations*), **espionage** (*spying*), **humanitarian efforts** (*aid to help people*), **peacekeeping operations** (*sending troops to keep peace*), **sanctions** (*bans and boycotts*), and **war**.

6. Americans have reacted to several **international incidents** (*events*) and entered a number of **international conflicts**. There have been various **reasons for U.S. involvement**. In 1917, the United States entered **World War I** to protect freedom of the seas and helped lead Allied forces to victory.

7. In December 1941, Japan attacked the U.S. fleet at Pearl Harbor. Americans joined **World War II**, helped defeat Germany and Japan, and developed the first atomic bomb.

8.The Cold War began when the Soviet Union turned the nations of Eastern Europe into communist satellites. Americans feared the spread of communism.

9.When communist North Korea invaded South Korea in 1950, Americans became involved in the **Korean War**. The war ended in 1953 with an armistice (*truce*) that left Korea divided as it had been before.

10.When Castro established a communist dictatorship in Cuba, America cut off trade and diplomatic relations. In 1961, Cuban exiles landed at the **Bay of Pigs** but were defeated. In 1962, American spy planes discovered Cuban bases for Soviet nuclear missiles, triggering the **Cuban Missile Crisis**.

11. Americans sent troops to fight communism in South Vietnam but proved unable to win the **Vietnam War**.

12. In 1978, a revolution turned Iran into an Islamic Republic. In 1979, U.S. embassy staff were seized, creating the **Iran hostage crisis**.

13. In the 1980s, Soviet leaders introduced reforms into Soviet society. The Berlin Wall fell in 1989 and the Soviet Union itself dissolved at the end of 1991.

14. In 1990, Iraqi dictator Saddam Hussein invaded Kuwait. U.S. and coalition forces drove Iraqi forces out of Kuwait in the **First Gulf War**.

15. On September 11, 2001, the terrorist group al-Qaeda attacked the World Trade Center. President Bush declared a global "War on Terror" and sent U.S. forces to Afghanistan.

16. President Bush feared Saddam Hussein might be hiding weapons of mass destruction. In 2003, U.S. forces invaded Iraq in the **Second Gulf War**.

17. **United States participation in international organizations** (*organizations of several nations*): The U.S. participates in the **United Nations**, the **North Atlantic Treaty Organization (NATO)**, the **International Court of Justice**, and the **World Trade Organization (WTO)**. There are advantages and disadvantages to membership depending

on the type of organization. Membership can be expensive but may help to promote peace, security, justice and trade. **Citizenship participation** in some international organizations is also possible, such as the International Red Cross/Red Crescent.

In this chapter, you will learn how the United States conducts its relations with other countries.

What is Foreign Policy?

There are two types of government policies: domestic and foreign.

Domestic policy is any government policy that concerns affairs "at home"—such as setting tax rates, regulating safety in factories, or determining the academic requirements for students in middle school. Domestic affairs refers to things happening in the United States.

Foreign policy is any government policy that concerns foreign countries and events taking place outside the United States: for example, making an alliance with a foreign country, fighting a war overseas, or entering into a trade agreement with another country. Foreign affairs refers to things happening in other countries, outside the United States.

Foreign policy and domestic policy are closely related. They often affect each other. When domestic policy leads to economic prosperity, American leaders can provide more assistance to other countries. When the United States is involved in an overseas conflict, this can reduce the resources available at home. Some historians believe, for example, that U.S. involvement in the Vietnam War led to a decrease in spending on domestic programs.

The Active Citizen

▸ Which of these are examples of domestic policy and which are examples of foreign policy?

Activity	Domestic Policy	Foreign Policy	Your Explanation:
Adopting health care reform	☐	☐	
Reducing carbon emissions in the United States	☐	☐	
Signing a treaty with the country of Jordan in the Middle East	☐	☐	
Attending a conference with leaders of the European Union	☐	☐	
Participating in negotiations between Israelis and Palestinians	☐	☐	
Increasing funding to public schools to reduce class sizes	☐	☐	
Negotiating with Russian leaders to reduce the number of nuclear warheads	☐	☐	

What's So Special about International Relations?

Foreign policy deals with "international relations." This phrase refers to relations between independent countries all around the world.

International relations is special because international law is not as powerful as the rule of law within a single country. To some extent, independent, sovereign nations still live in a "Wild West" atmosphere. They could be attacked, invaded or destroyed at any time. They might be able to defend themselves or to find allies, but they could just as easily be conquered and wiped off the map. Therefore, nation-states are constantly worried about their own security.

Who Makes Foreign Policy?

The U.S. Constitution gives authority over foreign relations to the federal government rather than to the states. Control over foreign policy is actually exercised by two branches of our federal government: the Presidency and Congress. This sharing of power illustrates both the separation of powers and the system of checks and balances.

Powers of the President

- The President appoints and receives ambassadors.
- The President acts as Commander in Chief of the armed forces.
- The President negotiates treaties.
- The President appoints the heads of executive departments, including the Secretary of State and the Secretary of Defense.

Powers of Congress

- The Senate confirms the President's appointments.
- The Senate ratifies U.S. treaties by a two-thirds vote.
- Congress has the power to declare war.
- Congress approves funding for all federal programs, including defense, foreign aid and the State Department budget.

The Secretary of State and the State Department

The **Secretary of State** is the member of the Cabinet entrusted with the day-to-day running of our nation's foreign policy.

The Secretary of State is the head of the State Department. This department manages our nation's foreign policy.

The State Department keeps in contact with our ambassadors and other diplomats sent to foreign countries. An **ambassador** is the official representative of one country sent to reside in another.

Ambassadors are diplomats—officials who act as representatives between nations. They learn and practice **diplomacy**—the skill of handling relations between states.

The ambassador and other staff at the U.S. Embassy officially represent the United States. The ambassador will occasionally meet with the political leaders of the host country to exchange views. At the same time, the ambassador and embassy staff gather information and send it back to the U.S. State Department in Washington, D.C.

Although the Secretary of State manages the day-to-day foreign relations of the United States, the President frequently becomes involved. The President can give instructions to the Secretary of State at any time, and can even dismiss the Secretary of State in the event of disagreement.

The President also meets with foreign leaders, and is regularly advised by U.S. military leaders, the National Security Advisor, and the Central Intelligence Agency (CIA), as well as by the Secretary of State.

Congress also takes an active interest in foreign affairs. Both the House and the Senate have important committees that focus on foreign affairs. The President and Congress are both equally concerned about public opinion on foreign-policy issues. If they ignore public views on these issues, they may easily lose the next election.

The Aim of U.S. Foreign Policy: Pursuit of the National Interest

The President, Congress, and the State Department generally agree that the basic aim of U.S. foreign policy is the pursuit of the **national interest** of the United States.

The "national interest" refers to what is good for our nation and its people. This includes the security and prosperity of the United States. To promote the national interest, those in charge of American foreign policy promote the following goals:

The U.S. National Interest: The Goals of American Foreign Policy

- Protect the security of the United States.
- Protect American citizens, their property, and investments abroad.
- Encourage other countries to trade with the United States.
- Spread the American system of democracy and free enterprise.
- Promote U.S. economic success and prosperity.
- Promote international peace and stability.
- Provide economic assistance to developing countries.
- Make humanitarian efforts to improve health, education, and living conditions around the world.

The EOC test may ask you what steps to take in an international crisis. Remember that the use of armed force is usually the last step, not the first.

Methods for Pursuing the National Interest and Dealing with International Conflicts

There are several **means available to the national government** to pursue the national interest. These means are also the **methods used to deal with international conflicts**. You can think of these means or methods as the various tools used by American leaders in conducting foreign policy.

Diplomacy

Diplomacy refers to direct dealings between countries, usually handled by the representatives of each country. Whenever there is an international dispute or conflict, the first step towards a settlement is usually for the countries involved to enter into talks, also known as negotiations. These talks may occur at special conferences between top leaders, in secret negotiations in a neutral country, or on a simple day-to-day basis between ambassadors and government leaders in each country.

The aim of negotiation is always to find some compromise, or middle ground, that all the parties to the dispute can somehow accept. Usually, each side has to be willing to give up something for the negotiations to be successful.

Diplomats (*people who practice diplomacy*) are trained negotiators. They recognize that it is almost always better to compromise than it is to go to war. However, they will not want to appear too "weak" in negotiations and give up too much to obtain a compromise solution. Sometimes giving in to the demands of aggressors to avoid a conflict can be a mistake.

In conducting diplomacy, American leaders have the following additional tools:

- **Alliances.** An alliance is an agreement between two or more countries to act together. During the Cold War, the United States formed an alliance with the countries of Western Europe, known as the North Atlantic Treaty Organization, or NATO. The United States has pledged to defend these countries, with nuclear weapons if necessary, from any attack.
- **Membership in International Organizations.** Another "tool" of American diplomacy is membership in international organizations, such as the United Nations. These international organizations provide a place for member nations to discuss issues and establish rules. By joining such organizations, the United States shows its support for cooperation among nations and a peaceful world order. American diplomats use these international organizations as places where they can explain American foreign policy actions to the rest of the world.
- **Diplomatic Recognition.** The President of the United States has the power to receive the representatives of other nations. Sometimes the President uses this power to refuse to recognize new leaders or new states. In other cases, the United States has been among the first to extend diplomatic recognition to new states to further its foreign policy goals.
- **Cultural Exchanges.** Another way that the United States conducts its diplomacy is through cultural exchanges. These might be visits of ballet companies, art exhibits, or joint sporting events. The goal of such exchanges is to develop good will.
- **Public Opinion and the Media.** American diplomacy attempts to create favorable public opinion towards the United States throughout the world. Favorable public opinion places pressure on foreign governments to support U.S. foreign-policy goals.
- **Treaties.** The United States enters into treaties with other countries. A treaty is a solemn agreement concluded between two or more countries, which is enforceable under international law.

Espionage

Espionage means spying. Like other countries, the United States relies on gathering secret information (known as "intelligence") about foreign countries, their military capabilities, and their leaders' plans. This information is gathered and analyzed by the Central Intelligence Agency, or "CIA."

Americans use satellites and surveillance aircraft with long-distance cameras as well as human agents ("spies") to obtain this information. For example, surveillance aircraft flying over Cuba in 1962 discovered that the Soviet Union was about to install medium-range nuclear missiles in Cuba. President Kennedy took immediate steps to oppose this action. He protested in the U.N. Security Council and placed a blockade around Cuba. Oleg Penkovsky, a Russian spy working for the United States, gave Americans secret information about Soviet weaknesses that made President Kennedy more confident during the Cuban Missile Crisis (see later in this chapter).

American espionage today includes spying on companies and cyber-espionage (spying on computer networks). For example, the United States cooperated with Israel to use cyber-espionage to disrupt Iran's nuclear program. Sometimes the United States has even used cyber-espionage to gain advantages in trade negotiations.

Sanctions

Sanctions are measures that a country takes to try to persuade another country to change its policies. These sanctions are generally economic in nature. They often include bans (*prohibitions*) and boycotts (*refusals to buy goods or have commerce*). The United States may ban travel and trade with any country that is violating international rules, committing acts of aggression, or developing nuclear weapons in violation of international treaties.

American leaders have used sanctions against Cuba, Sudan, Iran, North Korea, and Russia. For example, to stop Iran's nuclear program, American leaders "froze" Iranian bank accounts in the United States. The government and citizens of Iran had no access to their money in American banks. It also became illegal for Americans to trade with Iran. The invasion of Ukraine by Russia led to U.S. sanctions against Russia. The United States froze Russian bank accounts and shut Russia out of the international system for the changing of money between currencies. American companies withdrew from Russia. The export of high-technology goods to Russia was prohibited. Imports of Russian oil and other goods were also banned. These sanctions will only be "lifted" (*ended*) when Russia ends its war against Ukraine.

Humanitarian Efforts

Americans also engage in **humanitarian efforts.** These are attempts to improve living conditions around the world. The United States provides economic assistance to many countries around the world to help them develop their economies and improve their standards of living. Americans offer to help countries facing destruction from war or hurricanes, drought, famine, disease, and other disasters.

One of the most famous American humanitarian efforts occurred after World War II. Under the Marshall Plan, Americans gave economic assistance to the war-torn countries of Western Europe. This humanitarian assistance helped Western Europeans rebuild their economies, encouraged them to trade with the United States, and enabled them to resist Communism. Another example of U.S. humanitarian efforts occurred in Sudan. Although the United States had imposed sanctions against Sudan, it nevertheless provided humanitarian aid to the Sudanese people

Today, American humanitarian efforts are spearheaded by the U .S. Agency for International Development (or "USAID"). USAID reaches more than 40 million people each year with food assistance. This agency has provided essential relief in Burma, Venezuela, and Haiti. In 2022, USAID established a "Special Disaster Assistance Response" team to provide humanitarian aid to civilians in Ukraine, which was attacked by Russia. Over six million Ukrainian refugees have left the country. In March and April 2022, USAID provided 87,000 blankets and 18,000 kitchen sets to Ukrainians; by May 2022, USAID had provided four million Ukrainians with food.

Peacekeeping Operations

Sometimes the United States sends military forces to a troubled "hot spot" as part of a **peacekeeping operation.** Peacekeepers monitor and observe an area after a conflict has ended. They make sure each side keeps to the agreement and try to prevent new outbreaks of violence. Peacekeepers are given clear instructions based on what is achievable. For example, the United States sent peacekeepers to Sudan to help enforce an end to the Darfur conflict between local rebel groups and the Sudanese government (then under the control of a military dictator).

U.N. peacekeeping forces with American participation have been sent to Liberia, Kosovo, the Democratic Republic of the Congo, and other places. The United States is currently the largest contributor to the U.N.'s peacekeeping budget and pays for almost one fourth of all U.N. peacekeeping missions.

War

War is armed conflict between nations. It is the most extreme way of dealing with international disagreements and should always be the last resort in resolving a dispute.

The United States spends more money on its armed forces than any other nation, and it has the most advanced military technologies in the world. The President can use American air power, naval power, and/or troops to intervene overseas. Usually the United States will only go to war if its national security is at stake. The United States will also try to cooperate with its allies to obtain their assistance before employing military force. It will generally seek the help or at least the approval of the other members of the UN Security Council. Using air strikes generally has lower costs for the United States than sending in ground troops and may be tried first.

The U.S. armed forces can win most wars, but Americans have sometimes had difficulties achieving their long-term objectives after defeating the enemy on the battlefield. Moreover, the United States cannot use its powerful military directly against either Russia or China without great risk because of those countries' nuclear weapons.

Even without going to war, American leaders have used American military power as a tool of diplomacy. They can threaten the use of military power to prevent action by a potential enemy. For example, the United States deterred Russia from attacking members of the NATO alliance in 2022 by promising swift retaliation if it did.

Enrichment

The Active Citizen

Crisis Management

You have just been appointed as a special adviser to the President during a dangerous international crisis. A group of more than 100 terrorists have surrounded the U.S. Embassy in Nairobi, Kenya in Africa. The terrorists may belong to al-Qaeda. The U.S. Ambassador and his staff are all trapped inside the embassy building. The embassy is guarded by five U.S. Marines. It is not clear if the government of Kenya is going to take any action or will ignore the crisis.

The President of the United States has called an emergency meeting with the Vice President, the U.S. Secretary of State, the National Security Advisor, the Director of National Intelligence, the Chairman of the Joint Chiefs of Staff, and several other close advisers. You have been invited to the meeting. The purpose of this special meeting is to review all the options available for responding to the crisis at the embassy. Some of the alternatives being considered are the following:

- The U.S. could demand a special meeting of the UN Security Council.
- The U.S. could airlift a force of paratroopers to the embassy in Nairobi.
- The U.S. could denounce the actions of the terrorists on Alhurra, the Voice of America, and its other radio and television stations.
- The U.S. could offer to assist the Kenyan military in defeating the terrorists.
- The U.S. could impose economic sanctions on any country shown to have links to the terrorists.
- The U.S. could enter into negotiations with the terrorists to find out what they want.
- The U.S. could threaten to invade Kenya if Kenyan authorities fail to take action against the terrorists.
- The U.S. could wait patiently to see how the government of Kenya reacts.

Form a small group with some of the President's other "special advisers" (your classmates). Then decide which of these options you should recommend to the President. Next, decide in what order these options should be used. Finally, are there any other alternatives your group would recommend besides those listed above? Either have a member of your group present your recommendations to the class during a "debriefing" session, or write down your recommendations in the form of a memorandum to the President.

China now has a very strong economic relationship with the United States. It exports a large number of goods to America, and it frequently purchases U.S. Treasury Notes. Imagine that the U.S. Ambassador to China has just informed the Secretary of State that a series of human rights violations have been reported in Tibet, once an independent country, which China annexed by force in the 1950s. Which tools of U.S. foreign policy would you recommend that the United States adopt? Which step should be taken first, which steps should follow, and what would be an appropriate last resort? Some possibilities to consider are: diplomatic talks, public protests, economic sanctions, condemnation by international organizations, and military intervention. Prepare a PowerPoint or Prezi presentation, or a written memorandum to the Secretary of State, presenting your ideas.

U.S. Actions and Reactions in International Conflicts

In this section, you will examine the actual record of American foreign policy—with a focus on **United States actions and reactions** to **international conflicts**.

In the early years of our history, American leaders tried to separate our nation from wars in Europe and to focus our energies on opportunities in the Western Hemisphere. A major goal of U.S. foreign policy in these years was to avoid conflicts involving Europe.

A second major goal of early American foreign policy was westward expansion. After defeating Mexico in the Mexican-American War (1846–1848), the United States obtained California and the Southwest, stretching the nation's boundaries to the Pacific Ocean. Fifty years later, the United States defeated Spain in the Spanish-American War (1898), and gained overseas colonies in the Pacific and Caribbean. It also increased its trade with Europe, Asia, and Latin America.

By the beginning of the twentieth century, the United States—with its growing population, powerful economy, and strong navy—had emerged as one of the world's "great powers." These were leading nations with greater military and economic resources than other countries. As a "great power" with global interests, the United States began responding to **international incidents** (*events occurring in world affairs*). Americans became involved in several international conflicts, described in the following pages.

World War I

Who fought: United States, Great Britain, France, Italy, Russia (Allies) vs. Germany, Austria-Hungary, Ottoman Turkey (Central Powers)

When: 1914–1918

U.S. Entry: April 1917

Reason for U.S. involvement: German submarine warfare; German telegram offer to Mexico

World War I broke out in Europe in the summer of 1914. A group of terrorists assassinated (*killed for political purposes*) Archduke Franz Ferdinand, heir to the Austro-Hungarian Empire, while he was visiting the small country of Serbia. Serbian officials were secretly involved in the murder.

Austria-Hungary, encouraged by Germany, attacked Serbia in revenge. Serbia's ally, Russia, rushed to its defense. Russia also called on its own allies, France and Great Britain, for support. By August 1914, all the "great powers" of Europe had become involved in the conflict.

Because of advances in warfare—such as the invention of the machine gun—the armies on both sides became tied down in trenches (*long, fortified ditches*), which spread the length of eastern France. Soldiers could not advance without being mowed down by machine gun fire or choked by poison gas.

The British set up a naval blockade of Germany and Austria-Hungary. The Germans, with a smaller navy, established a submarine blockade of Britain. A submarine is a ship that can travel underwater for long periods. Submarines carry explosive torpedoes that they fire at ships.

For the first three years of the war, Americans remained neutral. However, German submarine attacks on allied ships with American passengers, such as the *Lusitania*, turned American public opinion against Germany. Early in 1917, Germany announced unrestricted submarine warfare and began sinking American ships. A secret German note to the Mexican government was also discovered by the British and published. The note promised Mexico the return of its former lands if it would ally with Germany against the United States. This telegram further inflamed American public opinion.

In April 1917, President Woodrow Wilson finally asked Congress for a declaration of war against Germany:

> *"The present German submarine warfare against commerce is a warfare against mankind. It is a war against all nations. American ships have been sunk, American lives taken . . . The challenge is to all mankind."*

Woodrow Wilson

U.S. entry into the war broke the deadlock in Europe. In just over a year, the United States sent an expeditionary force of a million men to France, forcing the Germans to surrender.

President Wilson sailed to Paris, where he helped to negotiate the Treaty of Versailles—the peace treaty between the Allies and Germany. Wilson promised to re-organize Europe along national lines, to promote democracy, and to establish a new international peacekeeping organization known as the League of Nations. The final treaty was harsh towards Germany and greatly resented by the German people. It did, however, include creation of the League of Nations just as Wilson had promised.

In the United States, there was a strong reaction against the bloodshed of World War I. The U.S. Senate rejected membership in the League of Nations and refused to sign the peace treaty. Americans retreated into a policy of isolationism, in which they generally ignored the rest of the world and focused more on their own domestic affairs.

World War II

Who fought: United States, Great Britain, Soviet Union (three main Allies) vs. Germany, Italy, Japan (Axis Powers)

When: 1939–1945

U.S. Entry: December 1941

Reason for U.S. involvement: Japanese attack on Pearl Harbor

In Germany, the Nazi Party, led by Adolf Hitler, obtained power in 1933. Hitler blamed Germany's troubles on the Treaty of Versailles, Germany's democratic government, and the Jewish people of Europe. He believed that different races were competing for world domination, and that Germans were a superior race. Hitler had ambitious plans for the German conquest of Europe. In September 1939, Hitler attacked the neighboring country of Poland. Meanwhile, the Soviet Union attacked Poland from the east. Britain and France were allied to Poland and declared war on Germany. **World War II** began in Europe.

Adolf Hitler

This time, Germany had developed a new form of warfare, based on the use of airplanes, tanks, and troop carriers (*modified trucks*). Airplanes bombed positions from overhead; then tanks and motorized vehicles with troops advanced. German armies quickly overran Poland; next they conquered Belgium, Denmark and France.

Italy's dictator had already concluded an alliance with Hitler before the outbreak of the war. The ambitious military leaders of Imperial Japan also decided to ally with Nazi Germany. Together, Germany, Italy and Japan became known as the Axis powers.

Most Americans were determined to stay out of the war. President Franklin D. Roosevelt grew alarmed, however, at the successes of the anti-democratic powers. In 1940, Great Britain stood almost alone against Germany, Italy and Japan. In June 1941, Hitler suddenly launched an invasion of the Soviet Union, bringing the Soviets into the war.

Five months later, on December 7, 1941, Japan launched a surprise attack on the U.S. Pacific fleet at Pearl Harbor in Hawaii. President Roosevelt told Congress:

> *"Yesterday, December 7, 1941—a date which will live in infamy—the United States of America was suddenly and deliberately attacked by naval and air forces of the Empire of Japan."*

Germany and Italy also declared war on the United States. These events brought the United States into the war on the side of Britain and the Soviet Union.

The U.S. Navy ended Japanese supremacy in the Pacific Ocean at the Battle of Midway, only six

Spanish-American War
1898

1914–1918: World War I
1914

1939: World War II begins in Europe
1939

1941: U.S. enters World War II

1945: Germany and Japan surrender; World War II ends
1945

1945: United Nations formed

Beginning of "Cold War"

1950–1953: Korean Conflict
1950

months after the attack on Pearl Harbor. But American and British troops were not strong enough to fight the German army in France. The two Western Allies sent their troops instead to North Africa, Sicily and Italy. Meanwhile, enormous Soviet and German armies fought each other inside the Soviet Union. Germans also organized the mass murder of Jews and other groups. Finally in June 1944, American and British forces landed on the beaches of Normandy, France, on "D-Day." They quickly moved westward, freeing Paris from Nazi rule by August 1944.

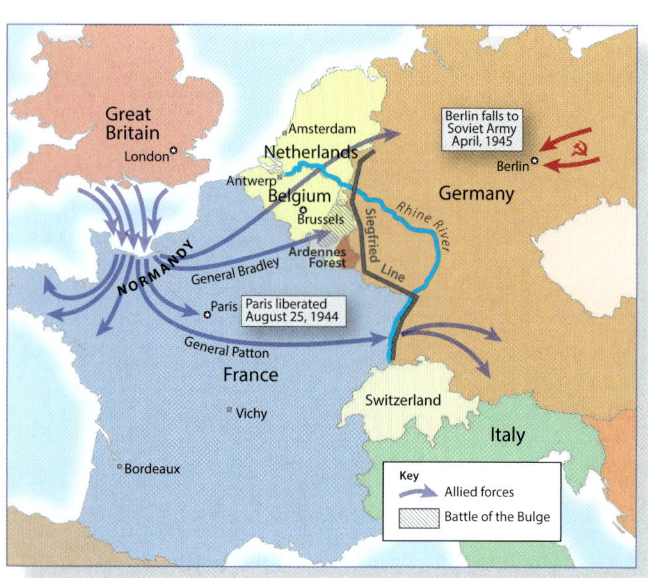

The American advance was temporarily halted in the cold winter of 1944–1945. Once German resistance collapsed, American troops resumed their advance. They entered Germany from the west, while Soviet troops came from the east. Hitler committed suicide at the end of April 1945, and Germany surrendered in May 1945.

In the Pacific, American troops fought a series of bloody battles against Japanese forces on a string of islands. After the surrender of Germany, U.S. forces planned a massive invasion of Japan, which would have cost more than a million lives. Instead, the United States dropped two atomic bombs on Japan, forcing its surrender in August 1945. World War II, the bloodiest conflict in human history, was finally over. More than 50 million people lost their lives in the war.

Unlike 1919, this time Americans welcomed the creation of a new peacekeeping organization, known as the **United Nations** (or UN). The UN replaced the unsuccessful League of Nations.

1961: Bay of Pigs Invasion

1962: Cuban Missle Crisis

1964–1973: War in Vietnam

1979: Iran Hostage Crisis

1989: Berlin Wall removed

End of "Cold War"

1990: First Gulf War

2001: Terrorists strike World Trade Center and Pentagon

2001: U.S.-led coalition forces deployed to Afghanistan

2003–2011: Second Gulf War

1960 | 1980 | 1990 | 2000 | 2010

Enrichment

Outbreak of the Cold War

Who was involved: United States and Western allies vs. the Soviet Union and communist nations

When began: 1945–1948

Reason for U.S. involvement: To prevent the spread of communism

Almost as soon as World War II ended, Americans found themselves in the middle of a new contest, known as the "Cold War."

Relations between the democratic United States and the communist Soviet Union had always been uneasy, even during World War II. The Soviet Union was under the control of Joseph Stalin, a brutal communist dictator. The United States was a representative democracy with a free market economy. Both countries looked at the other with suspicion.

After the heavy Soviet losses of World War II, Stalin demanded Soviet control of Poland and the rest of Eastern Europe. U.S. President Harry Truman believed, on the other hand, that Eastern Europeans wanted to establish democracies. Truman could do little because the Soviet army was still occupying the area. It established communist governments across Eastern Europe. An "Iron Curtain" fell on Eastern Europe, cutting off all contacts between it and the West.

When it seemed that communism might next spread to Greece and Turkey, President Truman offered to give these countries military and economic aid. He announced a new foreign policy **doctrine**—the "Truman Doctrine." Truman promised to give U.S. support to all free peoples resisting communism. American foreign policy now aimed at the "containment" of communism—preventing it from spreading any further.

The Korean War

Who fought: United States, South Korea, and other Allies (UN forces) vs. North Korea, China

When: 1950–1953

Reason for U.S. involvement: To contain communism in Asia and to stop an aggressor

President Truman's "containment" policy succeeded in stopping the spread of communism in Europe, but in 1949, communists seized power in China, the world's most populous nation.

Meanwhile, after World War II, the country of Korea was divided into North and South Korea. North Korea, with Soviet support, established a communist government. A Western-style government was established in the South. In 1950, North Korea invaded South Korea in an attempt to re-unite the country under communist rule.

When President Truman received news of the invasion, he immediately decided to send U.S. troops to South Korea to resist the North Koreans. "The attack upon Korea," Truman announced, "makes it plain beyond all doubt that Communism has passed beyond the use of subversion (*undermining*) to conquer independent nations and will now use armed invasion and war." Truman was able to get the support of the UN Security Council since the Soviet Union was boycotting it (*refusing to participate*) at the time. Congress, however, never officially declared war on North Korea.

UN forces, mainly consisting of U.S. troops, went to South Korea under the command of General Douglas MacArthur, former U.S. commander in the Pacific during World War II. MacArthur quickly defeated the North Koreans and advanced UN troops through North Korea. He took U.S. troops so close to the Chinese border with Korea that he actually brought Communist China into the war. The **Korean War** lasted two more years and only ended in an armistice (*truce*) in 1953. Korea remained divided just as it had been before the war.

The Bay of Pigs Invasion

Who fought: Cuban exiles aided by the United States (CIA) vs. Cuba

When: April 1961

Reason for U.S. involvement: The CIA hoped to overturn Castro in Cuba

The Cold War was far from over. By 1949, the Soviet Union had developed its own atomic weapons. By the early 1950s, both the United States and the Soviet Union had developed much more powerful and destructive hydrogen bombs.

In 1959, Fidel Castro and his force of guerilla fighters overthrew the dictator ruling in Cuba. Castro had raised money from supporters in the United States and had promised to establish a democracy in Cuba. Once in power, however, Castro imprisoned opponents and set up a communist dictatorship.

Castro next took over property belonging to American companies. U.S. President Dwight Eisenhower reacted by cutting off American trade and diplomatic relations with Cuba. Eisenhower also gave his approval to a secret plan to train an army of Cuban exiles (*people who leave their native country*). The exiles planned to invade Cuba and overthrow Castro. They were armed and given special training by the CIA (Central Intelligence Agency) in Guatemala and Florida.

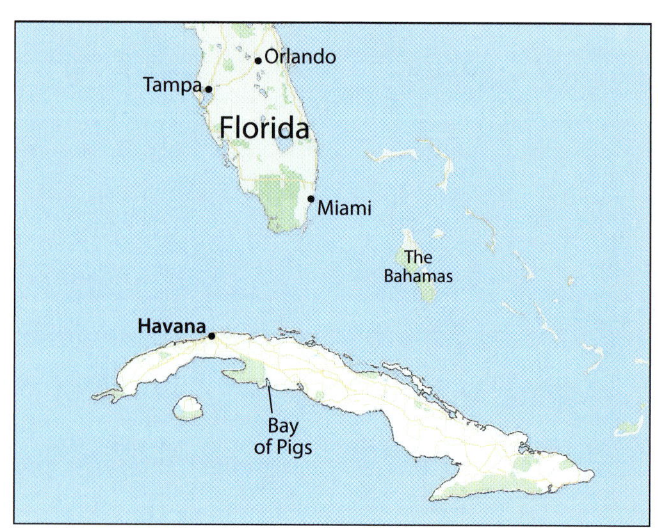

In 1960, Democratic candidate John F. Kennedy was elected President. Kennedy was told of the secret plan to help the Cuban exiles invade Cuba. He decided to go ahead with the plan. In April 1961, only four months after Kennedy took office, 1,400 Cuban exiles landed at the **Bay of Pigs**. The night before the attack, CIA planes bombed Cuban airfields. Kennedy refused, however, to give air support to the exiles on the day of the invasion, and the exiles were defeated.

The Cuban Missile Crisis

Who was involved: United States vs. Cuba and the Soviet Union

When: October 1962

Reason for U.S. involvement: To stop placement of nuclear missiles on Cuba

After the Bay of Pigs invasion, Castro strengthened his ties with the communist Soviet Union. Soviet leader Nikita Khrushchev sent nuclear warheads to Cuba. These warheads were to be placed on missiles that could be fired at the United States.

In October 1962, American spy planes discovered that Cubans were secretly building bases for these nuclear missiles, only 90 miles from Florida. This discovery triggered the **Cuban Missile Crisis**—the closest the world has ever come so far to a nuclear war.

> *"This urgent transformation of Cuba into an important strategic base by the presence of these large, long range, and clearly offensive weapons of sudden mass destruction,"* President Kennedy said in a televised address, posed a clear *"threat to the peace and security of all the Americas . . ."*

Kennedy brought the matter before the UN Security Council. After consulting with his advisers, he also established a naval blockade of Cuba. The blockade prevented the Soviet Union from sending ships to Cuba. Next, Kennedy threatened to invade the island if the missiles were not immediately withdrawn. Khrushchev agreed to remove the missiles, and Kennedy promised that the United States would not invade Cuba. He also agreed to withdraw U.S. missiles from Turkey that had been aimed at the Soviet Union. After the crisis, the two leaders set up a special "hot line"—a direct telephone connection between their offices in Washington, D.C., and Moscow.

The War in Vietnam

Who fought: United States, South Vietnam and allies vs. Viet Cong and North Vietnam

When: 1955–1975

U.S. Involvement: 1964–1973

Reason for U.S. involvement: To stop the spread of communism in Southeast Asia ("Domino Theory") and to help an ally

The Cold War also spread to Southeast Asia. Vietnam is a country in Indochina, a large peninsula on the southeastern edge of Asia. At one time, Vietnam was a French colony. After World War II, Vietnamese nationalists fought to drive the French out of their country. Vietnam was then divided, just as Korea had been, into two halves.

North Vietnam was placed under the control of a communist government. South Vietnam came under the rule of a dictator with ties to the West. The South Vietnamese government refused to hold elections to reunite the country. South Vietnamese communists—known as "Viet Cong"—reacted by launching a rebellion. The Viet Cong were helped by North Vietnam. President Kennedy sent advisers to help the South Vietnamese government. American leaders felt that they were aiding a friendly democracy. They also believed in the "Domino Theory"—that if communists took over South Vietnam, the other countries of Southeast Asia would quickly fall to communism like a row of dominoes.

In 1964, President Lyndon B. Johnson announced that North Vietnam had attacked U.S. ships in international waters. Congress passed a resolution giving the President authority to send U.S. ground troops to Vietnam. The **Vietnam War** was never officially declared, but by the end of 1965, almost 200,000 U.S. troops were in Vietnam; by 1968, there were half a million U.S. troops there. President Johnson also authorized bombing missions over North Vietnam. Americans used poisonous chemicals to bomb the Viet Cong and destroy their jungle cover.

Over the next eight years, American troops proved unable to win the war in Vietnam even though they had jet planes, helicopters, and superior weapons. American leaders had underestimated the determination of the leaders of North Vietnam to reunite Vietnam under their rule. The North Vietnamese continued to send supplies and troops to the South. The Viet Cong and North Vietnamese set booby traps and used guerrilla warfare (*a form of warfare in which they made attacks and then disappeared*) against American forces. Meanwhile, American soldiers were unfamiliar with the language, history and geography of South Vietnam. The South Vietnamese government became increasingly corrupt and unpopular. The war grew divisive in the United States.

American leaders began trying to find a way out of Vietnam. Richard Nixon won the Presidential election of 1968 by promising "peace with honor." Nixon started replacing U.S. troops with South Vietnamese soldiers. The United States conducted negotiations with the North Vietnamese in Paris while also increasing its bombing missions over North Vietnam. In 1973, the United States finally signed a treaty agreeing to withdraw its forces from South Vietnam. Two years later, North Vietnamese forces defeated the South Vietnamese and took over the country.

The Iran Hostage Crisis

Who was involved: United States vs. Islamic Republic of Iran

When: 1979–1981

Reason for U.S. involvement: Iranian protestors had seized staff of U.S. Embassy in Tehran

In 1979, popular demonstrations overthrew the Shah of Iran, one of America's strongest supporters in the Middle East. Religious leader Ayatollah Khomeini returned to Iran from exile, and Iranians created a new Islamic Republic. Laws were based on the *Quran*, the Islamic holy book.

The Shah first fled to Egypt, and then went to the United States to seek medical treatment. When the Shah was admitted into the United States, the Iranian government let an angry mob seize the staff of the U.S. Embassy in their capital city of Tehran.

For more than a year, U.S. Embassy staff were held as hostages during the **Iran hostage crisis**. President Jimmy Carter tried to negotiate their release without success. He even attempted a secret military operation to free them, which also failed. The hostages were not finally freed until January 1981, on the same day that Ronald Reagan took office as President.

The End of the Cold War

Enrichment

A strong anti-communist, President Reagan wanted to go beyond containment to "roll back" communism in countries where it already existed. He gave aid to anti-communist fighters in Afghanistan. Reagan built up the military resources of the United States and threatened to create a new anti-ballistic system against Soviet missiles.

The Soviet Union, in contrast, was facing severe economic difficulties. Soviet leader Mikhail Gorbachev withdrew Soviet forces from Afghanistan and introduced greater "openness" in Soviet society. His efforts unleashed nationalist feelings in Eastern Europe and the Soviet Union. People demanded an end to Soviet rule. Rather than use force to put down popular demonstrations, Gorbachev permitted Eastern Europeans to enjoy greater freedom. In November 1989, the Berlin Wall, a hated symbol of the Cold War, came tumbling down. The Soviet Union itself dissolved at the end of 1991, and was replaced by the Commonwealth of Independent States, a loose confederation. The long and icy Cold War was finally over.

The First Gulf War

Who was involved: United States, Great Britain, Saudi Arabia, Egypt and allied coalition vs. Iraq

When: 1990–1991

Reason for U.S. involvement: Saddam Hussein, dictator in Iraq, had invaded neighboring Kuwait; the United States and its allies forced Iraqi forces out of Kuwait

At the end of the Cold War, the United States was the world's only "superpower." When Saddam Hussein, a dictator in Iraq, invaded neighboring Kuwait, President George H.W. Bush decided to act. He built up an impressive coalition of international forces to oppose Hussein's bold act of aggression (*unjustified attack*). Bush acted both for humanitarian reasons and to save Kuwait's oil. U.S. and coalition forces were first sent to Saudi Arabia to protect the Saudi kingdom from possible Iraqi attack. Then, when Hussein refused to withdraw from Kuwait, U.S. and coalition forces entered Kuwait in the **First Gulf War**. Iraqi forces were quickly defeated and retreated back to Iraq. As the Iraqis withdrew, they set Kuwaiti oil wells on fire. President George H.W. Bush refused, however, to topple Hussein from power in Iraq.

The Attacks of September 11, 2001 and the "War on Terror"

Who was involved: United States vs. al-Qaeda and Taliban

When: September 11, 2001

Reason for U.S. involvement: Al-Qaeda terrorists took control of commercial jet planes and crashed them into the World Trade Center and Pentagon; the United States invaded Afghanistan when the Taliban refused to hand over al-Qaeda leaders

On September 11, 2001, Americans were shocked when commercial airplanes flew into the World Trade Center in New York City and the Pentagon building in Washington, D.C. Al-Qaeda, an Islamic Fundamentalist terrorist group, was responsible. Members of al-Qaeda had boarded several planes, taken their passengers as hostages, entered the cockpits, and flown each of the planes into their targets on a suicide mission. The two towers of the World Trade Center in New York City collapsed, leading to the deaths of almost three thousand people.

In response to the attacks, President George W. Bush (the son of President George H.W. Bush) declared a global "War on Terror."

> *"These acts of mass murder were intended to frighten our nation into chaos and retreat,"* President Bush told the nation. *"But they have failed. Our*

country is strong. . . . Terrorist attacks can shake the foundations of our biggest buildings, but they cannot touch the foundation of America."

When the Taliban, the Islamic Fundamentalist government of Afghanistan, refused to turn over Osama bin Laden, the mastermind behind the attacks, President Bush sent U.S. forces to Afghanistan, where they overthrew the Taliban government.

The "War on Terror" also led to changes inside the United States. Americans introduced tighter security at U.S. airports, and Congress passed the USA PATRIOT Act, expanding the federal government's powers of surveillance (*ability to observe and spy on potential terrorists*).

The Second Gulf War

Who was involved: United States, Great Britain, Poland, Australia, Spain, and others vs. Iraq

When: 2003 (forces stayed until 2011)

Reason for U.S. involvement: To overthrow Iraqi dictator Saddam Hussein, who was suspected of having "weapons of mass destruction"

In Iraq, Saddam Hussein remained in power as a brutal dictator. President George W. Bush feared that Hussein might be hiding biological or chemical "weapons of mass destruction," which could be turned over to al-Qaeda terrorists. After presenting the U.S. position to the UN Security Council, President Bush warned Saddam Hussein to step down from power or face an attack from the United States. Bush then ordered the invasion of Iraq in March 2003.

During this **Second Gulf War**, the Iraqi army was quickly defeated. Saddam Hussein fled but was later captured, tried and executed by the new Iraqi government.

Although the American victory over Hussein was swift, a rebellion led by Hussein's former supporters and Fundamentalist Muslims broke out against moderate Iraqi leaders and the U.S. occupation force. This rebellion was much harder to defeat and resulted in American forces remaining in Iraq for eight more years.

President Barack Obama finally withdrew the last U.S. forces from Iraq at the end of 2011. Just a few months earlier, President Obama also sent special forces into Pakistan, where they captured and killed Osama bin Laden, the terrorist leader responsible for the attacks of September 11, 2001.

The Active Citizen

Complete the chart below.

How the United States Has Dealt with International Conflicts

Conflict	Reasons for U.S. Involvement	Impact of U.S. Involvement
World War I		
World War II		
Korean War		
Bay of Pigs Invasion		
Cuban Missile Crisis		
War in Vietnam		
Iranian Hostage Crisis		
First Gulf War		
Second Gulf War		

- Select any one of the conflicts on the chart above and write a speech defending American policy. Be sure to mention one or more of the methods of dealing with international conflicts that either were used or that might have been used to resolve the conflict.
- Make an illustrated timeline showing the history of American foreign policy from 1917 to the present with an emphasis on U.S. involvement in international conflicts.

Name ____________________________________

United States Actions and Reactions in International Conflicts

Primary Source Document, No. 1

"[I]t is absolutely necessary to increase our measures against England as soon as possible . . . to obtain a swift victory. . . . [M]y conclusion is that a campaign of unrestricted submarine warfare, launched in time to produce a peace [with England], . . . has to accept the risk of American [entry into the war], because we have no other option. In spite of the diplomatic break with America, the unrestricted submarine warfare is . . . the right means to conclude this war victoriously. It is also the only means to this end."

—Admiral Henning von Holtzendorff, Imperial German Navy's Chief of the Admiral Staff, December 22, 1916, Secret Memorandum

Based on this secret memorandum, why did the German military resume unrestricted submarine warfare in 1917?

Primary Source Document, No. 2

"I have called the Congress into extraordinary session because there are serious, very serious, choices of policy to be made, and made immediately, which it was neither right nor constitutionally permissible that I should assume the responsibility of making. On the third of February last, I officially laid before you the extraordinary announcement of the Imperial German Government that on and after the first day of February it was its purpose to put aside all restraints of law or of humanity and use its submarines to sink every vessel that sought to approach either the ports of Great Britain and Ireland or the western coasts of Europe or any of the ports controlled by the enemies of Germany within the Mediterranean. . . ."

—President Woodrow Wilson, Joint Address to Congress, April 2, 1917

Based on the events described in this address, what course of action should the United States take?

Primary Source Document, No. 3

"From the standpoint of Imperial General Headquarters, based on the assumption that a peaceful solution has not been found and war is inevitable, the Empire's oil supply, as well as the stockpiles of many other important war materials, is decreasing day by day with the result that the national defense power is gradually diminishing. If this deplorable situation is left unchecked, I believe that, after a lapse of some time, the nation's vitality will deteriorate and ultimately fall into dire straits."

—Admiral Osami Nagano at the Imperial Conference of September 6, 1941 in Tokyo, Japan

Based on the information in this document, why did Japanese leaders decide to attack Pearl Harbor in 1941?

Primary Source Document, No. 4

"Yesterday, December 7, 1941—a date which will live in infamy—the United States of America was suddenly and deliberately attacked by naval and air forces of the Empire of Japan. The United States was at peace with that nation, and . . . was still in conversation with its government and its Emperor, looking toward the maintenance of peace in the Pacific. . . . [T]he distance of Hawaii from Japan makes it obvious that the attack was deliberately planned many days or even weeks ago . . . The facts of yesterday and today speak for themselves . . ."

—President Franklin D. Roosevelt before a Joint Session of Congress, December 8, 1941

Based on the facts described in this speech, what course of action should the United States take?

Primary Source Document, No. 5

"[T]his secret, swift, and extraordinary buildup of Communist missiles—in an area well known to have a special and historical relationship to the United States and the nations of the Western Hemisphere, in violation of Soviet assurances, and in defiance of American and hemispheric policy—this sudden, clandestine decision to station strategic weapons for the first time outside of Soviet soil—is a deliberately provocative and unjustified change in the status quo which cannot be accepted by this country, if our courage and our commitments are ever to be trusted again by either friend or foe. . . ."

—President John F. Kennedy, Radio and Television Address, October 22, 1962

Based on the information in this speech, what course of action should the United States take?

Primary Source Document, No. 6

"Whereas naval units of the Communist regime in Vietnam, in violation of the principles of the Charter of the United Nations and of international law, have deliberately and repeatedly attacked United Stated naval vessels lawfully present in international waters, and have thereby created a serious threat to international peace; and

Whereas these attackers are part of deliberate and systematic campaign of aggression that the Communist regime in North Vietnam has been waging against its neighbors . . .

Now, therefore be it *Resolved by the Senate and House of Representatives of the United States of America in Congress assembled*, That the Congress approves and supports the determination of the President, as Commander in Chief, to take all necessary measures to repel any armed attack against the forces of the United States and to prevent further aggression."

—Joint Resolution of Congress, August 7, 1964

Based on the events described in this resolution, what course of action should the United States take?

Primary Source Document, No. 7

> "Today, our fellow citizens, our way of life, our very freedom came under attack in a series of deliberate and deadly terrorist acts. The victims were in airplanes or in their offices: secretaries, businessmen and women, military and federal workers, moms and dads, friends and neighbors. Thousands of lives were suddenly ended by evil, despicable acts of terror. . . .These acts of mass murder were intended to frighten our nation into chaos and retreat. But they have failed. . . . The search is underway for those who were behind these evil acts. I have directed the full resources of our intelligence and law enforcement communities to find those responsible and to bring them to justice. We will make no distinction between the terrorists who committed these acts and those who harbor them . . ."
>
> —President George W. Bush, Television Address, September 11, 2001

Based on this television address, what course of action should the United States take?

Based on these primary source documents, what conclusions can you reach about why the United States sometimes becomes involved in international conflicts?

U.S. Participation in International Organizations

Earlier in this chapter, you learned that one of the most important tools that American diplomats have to promote American foreign policy is **participation** in international organizations. An **international organization** is a group of nations that join together in a formal body for some purpose. Some of the international organizations that the United States has joined are alliances with other representative democracies for mutual defense; others are trade organizations; still others are peacekeeping or humanitarian organizations.

Many of these organizations have their headquarters (*central offices*) in New York City or some other city in the United States. Others have their headquarters in places such as Geneva, Switzerland.

In addition to official U.S. membership in these intergovernmental organizations, some individual American citizens participate directly in international non-governmental organizations (INGO) like the Red Cross, by giving money or volunteering service.

The United Nations (UN)

After the destruction of World War II, the United States and other nations created the **United Nations**. According to the United Nations Charter, the major aim of this organization is to maintain the peace of the world, while promoting friendship and cooperation among nations. The United Nations also seeks to eliminate hunger, disease, and ignorance in the world. The United Nations has its own peacekeeping forces, contributed by member nations.

All member nations belong to the UN General Assembly. This body provides a world forum for the discussion of important affairs.

Five nations serve as permanent members of the UN Security Council. These permanent members—the United States, Great Britain, Russia, China and France—enjoy special powers, including veto power over all UN peacekeeping operations. There are also

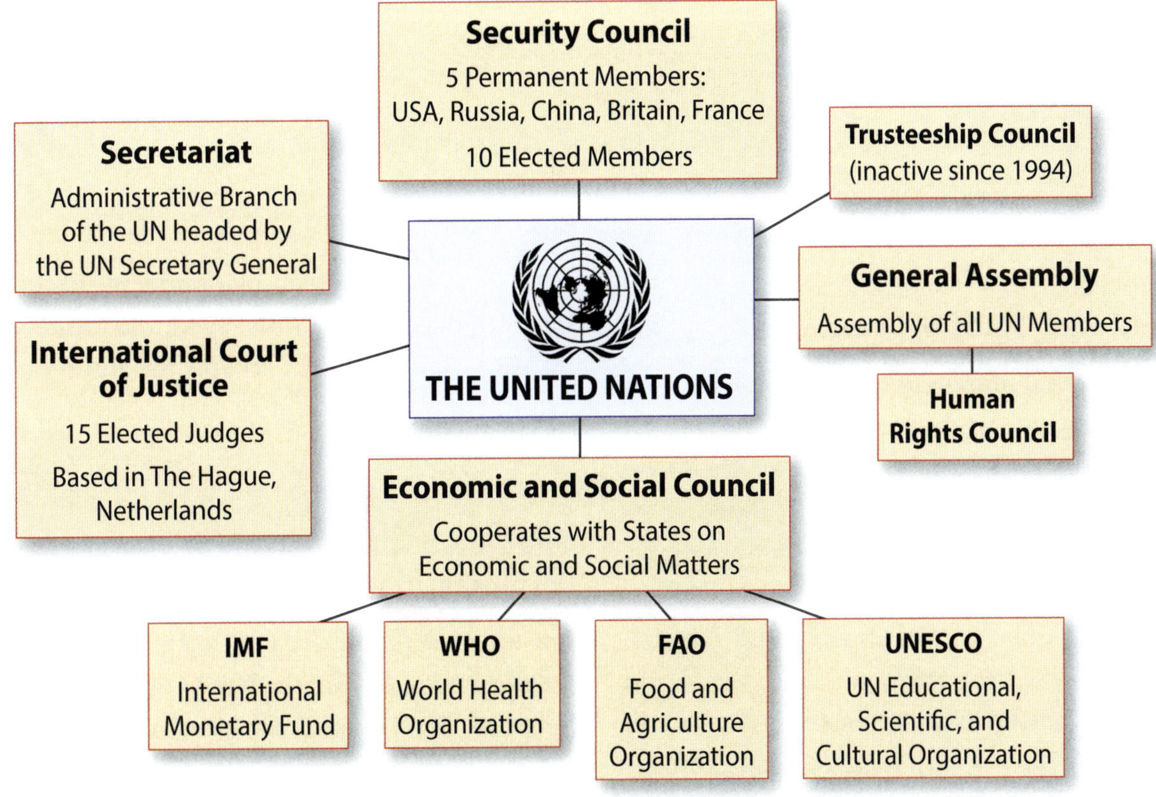

ten elected non-permanent members on the Security Council.

Other important bodies in the United Nations are the International Court of Justice and the Economic and Social Council. Other institutions of the United Nations, such as UNESCO, support programs encouraging economic development and social reform. The UN Secretariat manages this complex organization. Its head, the UN Secretary-General, acts as spokesperson for the entire United Nations.

The UN Secretariat, Security Council and General Assembly are all located in New York City.

Enrichment

The Active Citizen

Article 1 The Purposes of the United Nations are:

"1. To maintain international peace and security, and to that end: to take effective collective measures for the prevention and removal of threats to the peace, and for the suppression (*ending*) of acts of aggression or other breaches (*breaks*) of the peace, and to bring about by peaceful means, and in conformity (*agreement*) with the principles of justice and international law, adjustment or settlement of international disputes or situations which might lead to a breach of the peace;

2. To develop friendly relations among nations based on respect for the principle of equal rights and self-determination of peoples, and to take other appropriate measures to strengthen universal peace;

3. To achieve international co-operation in solving international problems of an economic, social, cultural, or humanitarian character, and in promoting and encouraging respect for human rights and for fundamental freedoms for all without distinction as to race, sex, language, or religion; and

4. To be a center for harmonizing the actions of nations in the attainment of these common ends."

—*Charter of the United Nations* (1945)

- Which of these purposes do you think was most important to American leaders in 1945? Explain your answer.
- Which of these purposes is most important today? Explain your answer.

The "World Court" (International Court of Justice)

This is the judicial branch of the United Nations. It meets in The Hague in the Netherlands. The Court settles legal disputes between countries. The **International Court of Justice** does not hear cases between individuals or organizations—only nations. The Court consists of fifteen international judges elected by the UN Security Council and General Assembly for nine-year terms. In 1986, the World Court ruled against the United States in the case of *Nicaragua v. United States*. The American government was accused of aiding opponents of the Nicaraguan government. Since 1986, the United States no longer automatically accepts the authority of the World Court, which it now accepts only on a case-by-case basis.

The North Atlantic Treaty Organization (NATO)

The **North Atlantic Treaty Organization,** or **NATO** was formed in 1949 at the height of the Cold War. Its purpose was to defend Western Europe against possible Soviet attack. It reassured Western Europeans

NATO Headquarters in Brussels, Belgium

that the United States would come to their defense, with nuclear weapons if necessary. NATO headquarters are in Brussels, Belgium.

Since the end of the Cold War, NATO has expanded its functions and membership. Its focus remains on the defense of its member states, but it also acts to discourage militarism and to encourage a peaceful transition to democracy. Several Eastern European nations have joined NATO, including Poland, the Czech Republic, Hungary, Slovakia, Slovenia, Latvia, Estonia, Lithuania, Bulgaria, Albania, and Croatia.

Membership in NATO remains open to any European state that supports its principles and that can contribute to the security of the North Atlantic area.

The World Trade Organization (WTO)

The United States had signed the General Agreement on Tariffs and Trade, or GATT, in 1947. Its aim was to encourage international trade by eliminating tariffs. In 1995, GATT was replaced by the **World Trade Organization**, or **WTO**. Members of the WTO have agreed to a set of rules for world trade, including rules for settling disputes. WTO members have further agreed to take steps to reduce tariffs and to eliminate other obstacles to world trade. The WTO now has more than 150 member countries, covering 95% of world trade. The WTO has a general council and several specific councils, such as the Council for Trade in Goods, the Council for Trade in Services, and the Trade Negotiations Committee. Its headquarters are in Geneva, Switzerland.

The Advantages and Disadvantages of U.S. Membership in International Organizations

Because there are different kinds of international organizations, the advantages and disadvantages of U.S. membership will depend on the type of international organization.

- International trade associations, like the World Trade Organization, open up opportunities for increased trade. They increase the foreign market for many U.S. goods and make it possible for Americans to buy many less expensive foreign goods. At the same time, they increase globalization and may lead to the loss of some U.S. jobs.
- Defensive alliances, such as NATO, help to increase U.S. security. Alliance partners helped the United States in the fight against terrorism and in putting up a united front against acts of aggression by countries such as Russia. At the same time, such alliances are expensive to maintain and risk drawing the United States into military conflicts to defend other alliance members.
- International organizations, like the United Nations and the World Court, promote international cooperation. The United Nations provides an important forum for discussion. At the United Nations, the United States can point out international problems, discuss potential solutions, and directly challenge world aggressors. The United Nations also provides essential economic and social assistance to many developing countries, which the United States supports. The chief disadvantages to UN membership are that (1) maintaining the United Nations can be

expensive, (2) U.S. policies are sometimes challenged at its meetings, (3) participating in international organizations limits American freedom of action, and (4) the UN has been ineffective in stopping many cases of aggression because China and Russia have veto powers over UN actions.

The Active Citizen

- Review the advantages and disadvantages of U.S. membership for each type of international organization above.
- Discuss with a partner in which of the following international organizations the United States should continue to remain as a member:

International Organization	Remain	Leave
World Trade Organization (WTO)	☐	☐
North Atlantic Treaty Organization (NATO)	☐	☐
World Court	☐	☐
United Nations	☐	☐

How Citizens and Governments Participate in International Organizations

There are different ways that both individual citizens and governments can participate in international organizations.

The four organizations you just learned about only permit countries to become members:

- United Nations (UN)
- World Court
- North Atlantic Treaty Organization (NATO)
- World Trade Organization (WTO)

Governments join these international intergovernmental organizations ("IGOs") by signing a treaty or a charter. Member governments agree to follow the rules of the organization. Usually they also agree to pay dues to the organization to finance its operations.

Individual citizens cannot join these organizations but they can sometimes support them by joining separate, private associations that promote their work. For example, the Friends of the United Nations is a private group that makes people aware of the activities of the United Nations.

Both individual citizens and companies can also join international non-governmental organizations (INGOs). These are private associations. Individuals can contribute money, volunteer their time, or enroll as members in these organizations, such as the International Red Cross/Red Crescent, which helps with relief efforts around the world.

Describe the relationships between the terms and phrases in the concept circles below and explain their significance.

Name ______________________________

Foreign affairs | Domestic affairs
Foreign policy | Domestic policy

Preserve U.S. security | Protect citizens abroad
Encourage foreign trade | Promote democracy and free enterprise

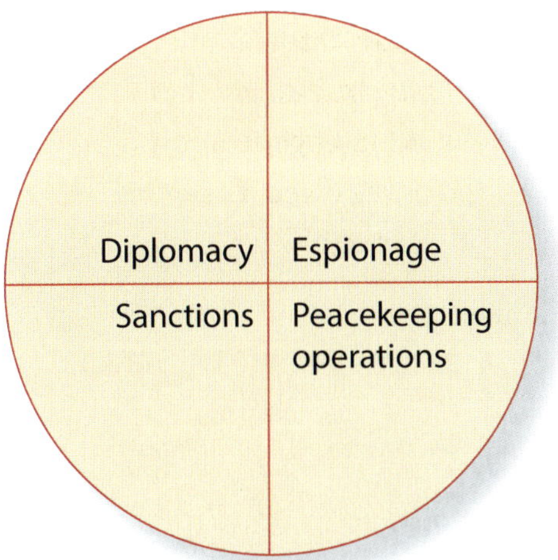

Name ___________________________________

What were each of these important international conflicts about? Fill in the chart below.

Conflict	Description and Reason for U.S. Involvement
World War I (1917–1918) 	
World War II (1941–1945) 	
Korean War (1950–1953) 	
Bay of Pigs Landing (1961) 	
Cuban Missile Crisis (1962) 	

Name ___________________________________

What were each of these important international conflicts about? Fill in the chart below.

Conflict	Description and Reason for U.S. Involvement
War in Vietnam (1964–1973) 	
Iran Hostage Crisis (1979) 	
First Gulf War (1990–1991) 	
September 11, 2001 Terrorist Attack on World Trade Center and Pentagon 	
Second Gulf War (2003–2011) 	

Name ______________________________

Do you agree with past U.S. policies abroad? Identify one of the conflicts you studied in this chapter. Then research that conflict in your school library or on the Internet. Decide if you agree with U.S. policy in that instance. Then complete an official "White Paper" (an official government report on a complex issue) presenting your findings and conclusions.

Office of the Historian, U.S. Department of State

Official White Paper on ______________________________
(name of conflict)

Sources of information about the conflict:

____

____

How did this conflict arise?

____

____

Why did the United States become involved in this conflict?

____

____

What was the impact of U.S. involvement?

____

____

What was the final outcome of the conflict?

____

____

Would you have agreed with U.S. policy? Yes [ ] No [ ]

Explain your point of view.

____

____

Name ______________________________________

Fill in the chart below.

U.S. Participation in International Organizations

International Organization	What It Does
United Nations	
World Court	
NATO	
WTO	

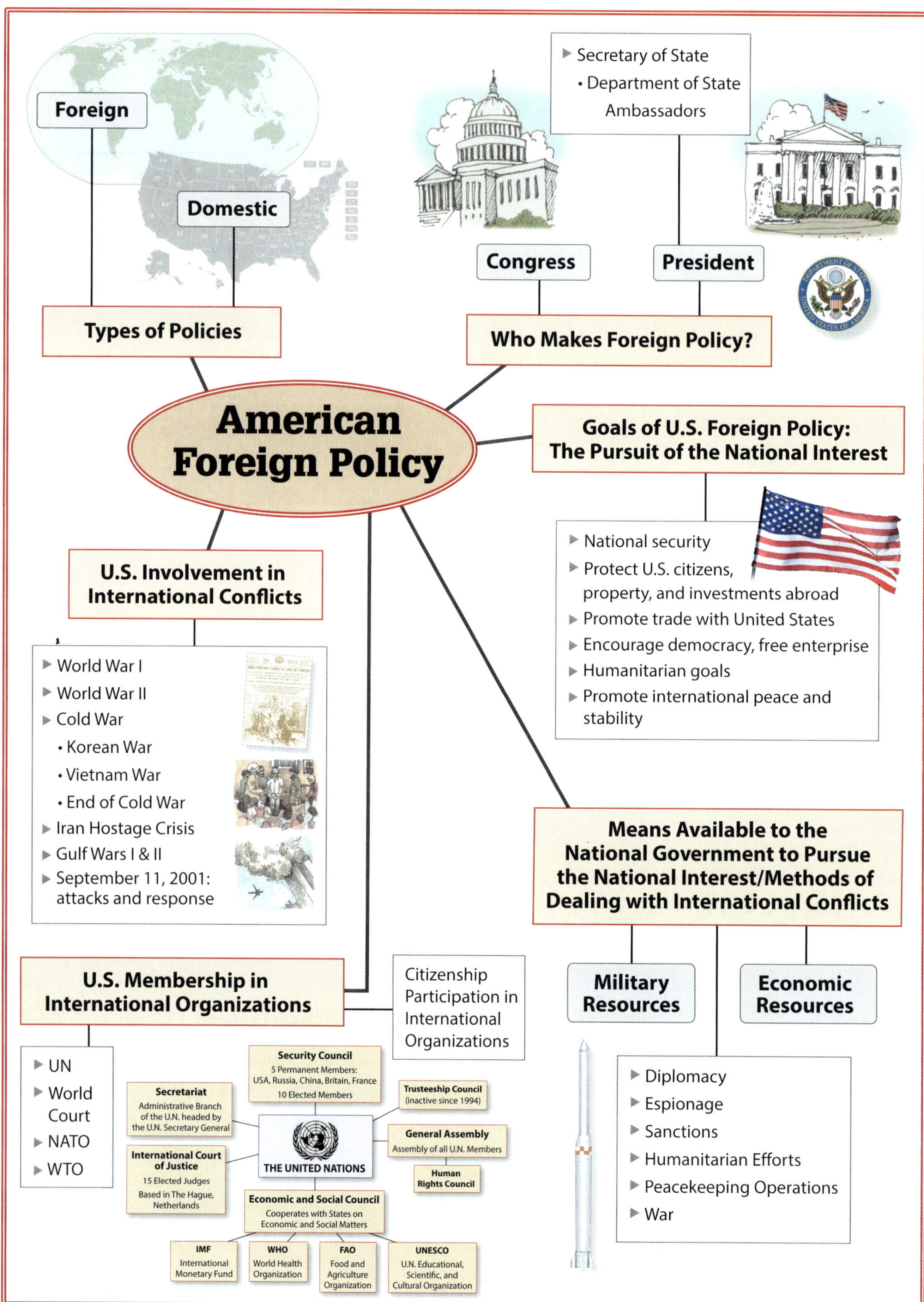

American Foreign Policy
Types of Policies
Foreign
Domestic
Who Makes Foreign Policy?
Congress
President
Secretary of State
• Department of State
Ambassadors
Goals of U.S. Foreign Policy: The Pursuit of the National Interest
National security
Protect U.S. citizens, property, and investments abroad
Promote trade with United States
Encourage democracy, free enterprise
Humanitarian goals
Promote international peace and stability
U.S. Involvement in International Conflicts
World War I
World War II
Cold War
• Korean War
• Vietnam War
• End of Cold War
Iran Hostage Crisis
Gulf Wars I & II
September 11, 2001: attacks and response
Means Available to the National Government to Pursue the National Interest/Methods of Dealing with International Conflicts
Military Resources
Economic Resources
Diplomacy
Espionage
Sanctions
Humanitarian Efforts
Peacekeeping Operations
War
U.S. Membership in International Organizations
Citizenship Participation in International Organizations
UN
World Court
NATO
WTO
THE UNITED NATIONS
Security Council
5 Permanent Members: USA, Russia, China, Britain, France
10 Elected Members
Secretariat
Administrative Branch of the U.N. headed by the U.N. Secretary General
Trusteeship Council (inactive since 1994)
General Assembly
Assembly of all U.N. Members
International Court of Justice
15 Elected Judges
Based in The Hague, Netherlands
Human Rights Council
Economic and Social Council
Cooperates with States on Economic and Social Matters
IMF
International Monetary Fund
WHO
World Health Organization
FAO
Food and Agriculture Organization
UNESCO
U.N. Educational, Scientific, and Cultural Organization

Review Cards: American Foreign Policy

American Foreign Policy

- **Domestic policy** is any government policy that concerns affairs "at home"—such as setting tax rates or regulating safety in factories.
- **Foreign policy** is any government policy that concerns foreign countries and events taking place outside the United States: for example, making an alliance with a foreign country, fighting a war overseas, or entering into a trade agreement with another country.
- Foreign policy thus deals with "**foreign affairs**," or "**international relations**." These terms refer to relations between independent countries all around the world.
- **International relations** are special because international law is not as powerful as the rule of law within a single country. Therefore nations are always concerned about their own security.

Who Makes Foreign Policy?

Control over foreign policy is actually exercised by two branches of our federal government: the Presidency and Congress.

Powers of the President

- The President appoints and receives ambassadors.
- The President negotiates treaties.
- The President acts as Commander in Chief of the armed forces.
- The President appoints the heads of executive departments, including the Secretary of State and the Secretary of Defense.

Powers of Congress

- The Senate confirms the President's appointments.
- The Senate ratifies U.S. treaties by a two-thirds vote.
- Congress has the power to declare war.
- Congress approves funding for all federal programs, including defense, foreign aid and the State Department.

The Secretary of State and the State Department

- The **Secretary of State** is the member of the Cabinet entrusted with the day-to-day running of our nation's foreign policy and heads the **State Department**.
- **Diplomats** are officials who practice **diplomacy**—the skill of handling relations between states. An **ambassador** is the official representative of one country sent to reside in another.

The Objectives of U.S. Foreign Policy

The President, Congress, and the State Department generally agree on the fundamental objective of U.S. foreign policy: to pursue the **national interest** of the United States:

- Protect the security of the United States.
- Protect American citizens, their property and investments abroad.
- Encourage other countries to trade with the United States.
- Spread the American system of democracy and free enterprise.
- Promote U.S. economic success and prosperity.
- Promote international peace and stability.
- Provide economic assistance to developing countries.
- Make humanitarian efforts to improve health, education and living conditions around the world.

Means Available to Pursue the National Interest

There are several **means available to the national government** to pursue the **national interest**. These are also often the **methods used for dealing with international conflicts**, and include:

- **Diplomacy:** This refers to direct dealings between countries through their representatives. Diplomats negotiate to resolve problems and disagreements. Often they compromise (each side gives up something). American diplomats also rely on alliances, international organizations, use of diplomatic recognition, cultural exchanges, public opinion and treaties to achieve their goals.
- **Espionage:** This refers to spying, to obtain information about other countries. The United States and other countries now also engage in industrial and cyber espionage. They use satellites and aircraft with cameras as well as human spies.
- **Sanctions:** Taking steps against a country like freezing its bank accounts and prohibiting trade.
- **Humanitarian Efforts:** Giving food, money and other assistance, especially in times of disaster.
- **Peacekeeping Operations:** Sending soldiers to enforce the peace after a conflict ends.
- **War:** Armed conflict between nations. War should always be the last resort.

World War I (1914–1918: U.S. entry in 1917)

World War I broke out in Europe in the summer of 1914 between the Central Powers (Germany, Austria-Hungary, Ottoman Empire) and the Allies (Russia, France, Great Britain). At first, Americans tried to stay out of the war. Publication of a secret German offer to return U.S. lands to Mexico outraged American public opinion. When Germany announced unrestricted submarine warfare (sinking vessels without warning) and began sinking American ships in 1917, President Woodrow Wilson asked Congress for a declaration of war. The United States sent a million-man army to France. This broke the deadlock in Europe and forced Germany to surrender, bringing victory to the Allies.

World War II (1939–1945: U.S. entry in 1941)

In the 1930s, the Nazi (National Socialist) Party, led by Adolf Hitler, gained control in Germany. Hitler believed Germans were a superior race and planned to conquer the rest of Europe. Nazi Germany attacked Poland in 1939, beginning **World War II.** Americans were at first determined to stay out of the war, but in December 1941, Japan attacked the United States at Pearl Harbor in Hawaii. Germany and Italy also declared war on the United States. Americans became involved in the most bloody and destructive war in human history. The Axis Powers (Germany, Italy and Japan) were opposed by the Allied Powers (United States, Great Britain, and Soviet Union). Eventually, the Germans were defeated, Hitler committed suicide, and Germany surrendered in May 1945. In August 1945, Americans dropped atomic bombs on two Japanese cities. Japan then surrendered, ending World War II. More than 50 million people were killed in the war.

Korean War (1950–1953)

America wanted to contain communism, so that it would not spread to countries across Europe and beyond. Korea had been divided into North and South Korea after World War II. North Korea established a communist government and invaded South Korea in 1950. President Harry Truman sent U.S. troops to South Korea to prevent further communist expansion. The U.S. army quickly defeated the North Koreans in South Korea and advanced into North Korea. U.S. troops went so close to the Chinese border that communist China entered the war. The **Korean War** ended in 1953 and Korea remained divided the same way it had been before the war.

Bay of Pigs (1961)

In 1959, Fidel Castro and his force of guerilla (*rebel*) fighters overthrew the dictator Batista and took control of Cuba. Once in power, Castro imprisoned those speaking out against him and established a communist dictatorship. When Castro's government took control of property belonging to American companies, the United States cut off trade and diplomatic relations. President Eisenhower gave his approval to a secret plan to train Cuban exiles (*refugees*), who planned to invade Cuba and remove Castro. The exiles were armed and given special training by the CIA (Central Intelligence Agency). Newly elected President John F. Kennedy decided to continue with Eisenhower's plan. In April 1961, The Cuban exiles landed at the **Bay of Pigs**. When Kennedy refused to give air support on the day of the invasion, the exiles were defeated.

Cuban Missile Crisis (1962)

After the Bay of Pigs invasion in 1961, Castro increased his ties with the communist Soviet Union. In October 1962, American spy planes discovered that Cubans were secretly building bases for Soviet nuclear missiles, only 90 miles from Florida. During the **Cuban Missile Crisis**, President Kennedy established a naval blockade of Cuba, preventing any ships from passing through the area. Then President Kennedy threatened to attack the island of Cuba if the missiles were not immediately removed. Soviet leader Khrushchev agreed to remove the missiles, and Kennedy promised not to invade Cuba and to remove U.S. missiles from Turkey that were aimed at the Soviet Union. The world had come close to, but had avoided, a nuclear war.

Vietnam War (1964–1973)

After winning independence from France in 1954, Vietnam was divided. North Vietnam established a communist government. South Vietnam came under the control of a dictator with Western ties, who refused to hold elections to reunite the country. South Vietnamese communists (known as Viet Cong), with the help of the North, began a rebellion against the government of South Vietnam. American leaders believed that if communists took over South Vietnam, the rest of Southeast Asia would fall to communism like a row of dominoes ("Domino Theory"). In 1964, Congress authorized the President to send ground troops to Vietnam. Over the next eight years, American troops and bombing missions proved unable to win the **Vietnam War**. The war became unpopular in the United States and President Nixon began removing U.S. troops while secretly negotiating with the North Vietnamese in Paris. In 1973, the United States signed the Paris Peace Accords, agreeing to leave Vietnam. Two years later, South Vietnam fell to the North Vietnamese army and the country was reunited under communist rule.

Iran Hostage Crisis (1979–1981)

In 1979, popular demonstrations overthrew the Shah (*ruler*) of Iran and installed an Islamic Republic. Iran began following Islamic law and was governed by religious leaders. The Shah first fled to Egypt, and then went to the United States to seek medical attention. The new Iranian government objected when U.S. leaders let the Shah enter the United States. They responded by allowing an angry mob to seize (*take*) the staff of the U.S. Embassy in the capital city of Tehran as hostages. For more than a year, U.S. Embassy staff were held as hostages during the **Iran hostage crisis**, until they were finally released in January 1981. President Jimmy Carter finally negotiated to their release, although they were not freed until his Presidency ended in January 1981.

The First Gulf War (1990–1991)

Saddam Hussein was a dictator who ruled over Iraq from 1979 to 2003. When Hussein invaded and occupied oil-rich Kuwait in 1990, President George H.W. Bush decided to act. He put together an alliance of countries to oppose Hussein's actions. At first, the U.S. and allied forces were sent to protect Saudi Arabia from attack. When Hussein refused to leave Kuwait they advanced into Kuwait. Iraqi forces were defeated and retreated (*went back*) to Iraq in the **First Gulf War**. However, President Bush refused to send U.S. forces into Iraq to overthrow Hussein.

Attacks of September 11, 2001 and the "War on Terror"

On September 11, 2001, commercial airplanes flew into the World Trade Center in New York City and the Pentagon in Washington, DC. Al-Qaeda, a terrorist group, was responsible for the attack. Members of al-Qaeda had boarded several planes, taken the passengers aboard as hostages, entered the cockpits, and flown each of the planes into their targets on a suicide mission. Almost 3,000 people died when the twin towers of the World Trade Center in New York City collapsed. Following the attacks, President George W. Bush declared a global "War on Terror." When the Taliban, the government of Afghanistan, refused to turn over Osama bin Laden, the mastermind behind the "9/11" attacks, President Bush sent U.S. forces to Afghanistan, where they overthrew Taliban rule.

Second Gulf War (2003)

Saddam Hussein remained in power as the dictator of Iraq. After the terrorist attack by al-Qaeda on September 11, 2001, President George W. Bush feared that Hussein might be hiding nuclear, biological, or chemical "weapons of mass destruction," which could be turned over to al-Qaeda terrorists. Because of this, in March 2003, President Bush demanded that Hussein resign from office. When Hussein refused, Bush ordered the invasion of Iraq. In the **Second Gulf War**, the Iraqi army was quickly defeated by American forces. Hussein fled but was later captured and executed by the new Iraqi government. Despite their swift victory, American troops soon found they could not leave Iraq. They became involved fighting Hussein's supporters, Islamic Fundamentalists and other groups challenging the new Iraqi government. President Barack Obama finally withdrew the last U.S. forces from Iraq at the end of 2011.

U.S. Participation in International Organizations

- The **United Nations (UN)**. According to the United Nations Charter, the major aim of this organization is to maintain world peace, while trying to promote friendship and cooperation among nations. All member nations belong to the UN General Assembly. This organ provides a world forum for the discussion of important affairs. The United States and four other nations serve as permanent members on the UN Security Council. These permanent members enjoy special powers, including veto power over all UN peacekeeping operations.
- The **"World Court" (International Court of Justice)**. This is the judicial branch of the United Nations. It meets in The Hague in the Netherlands, where it settles legal disputes between countries.
- **The North Atlantic Treaty Organization (NATO)**. NATO was formed in 1949 to defend Western Europe against possible Soviet attack. It reassured Western Europeans that the United States would come to their defense, with nuclear weapons if necessary. Since the end of the Cold War, NATO has expanded its functions and membership. Its focus remains on the defense of its member states.
- The **World Trade Organization (WTO)**. Members of the WTO have agreed to a set of rules for world trade, including rules for settling disputes. WTO members have further agreed to take steps to reduce tariffs and to eliminate other obstacles to world trade. The WTO now has more than 150 member countries.

The Advantages and Disadvantages of U.S. Membership in International Organizations

The advantages and disadvantages of U.S. membership will depend on the type of international organization:

- **International trade associations, such as the World Trade Organization**

  Pro (*advantages*): these associations open up opportunities for increased trade.

  Con (*disadvantages*): they increase globalization and lead to the loss of some U.S. jobs.

- **International defensive alliances, such as NATO**

  Pro: helps to increase U.S. security.

  Con: (1) such alliances are expensive to maintain; (2) they risk drawing the United States into a military conflict to defend other alliance members.

- **International peacekeeping organizations, such as the United Nations**

  Pro: (1) they promote international cooperation; (2) they provide places where the United States can point out international problems, discuss potential solutions, and directly challenge world aggressors; (3) they provide essential economic and social assistance to many developing countries.

  Con: (1) maintaining the United Nations is expensive; (2) U.S. policies can be challenged at its meetings; (3) participation may limit American freedom of action; (4) the UN and other international organizations have often been ineffective in stopping aggression.

What Do You Know?

SS.7.CG.4.2

1. What is the purpose of the International Court of Justice?

A. to settle legal disputes between countries
B. to provide economic aid to struggling nations
C. to try war criminals for crimes against humanity
D. to provide a place where citizens can sue governments

SS.7.CG.4.1

2. The diagram below shows details about the federal government.

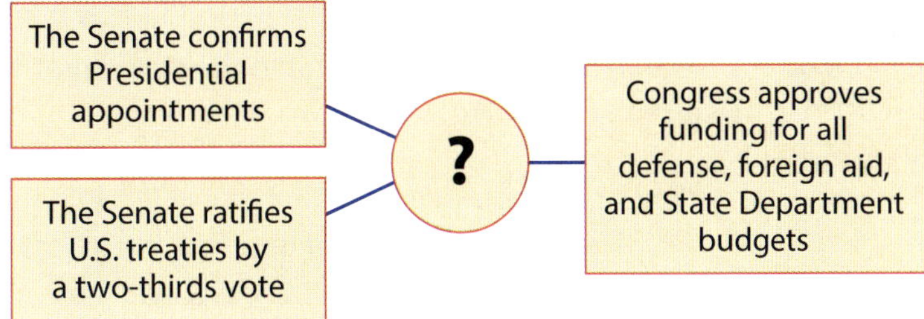

Which phrase completes the diagram?

A. How Congress influences U.S. domestic policy
B. How Congress influences U.S. foreign policy
C. How the State Department manages U.S. domestic affairs.
D. How the House Committee on Foreign Affairs investigates issues

SS.7.CG.4.1

3. The speech below was delivered to Congress by President Harry Truman in 1947.

I believe that it must be the policy of the United States to support free peoples who are resisting attempted subjugation by armed minorities or by outside pressures. . . If we falter in our leadership, we may endanger the peace of the world and we shall surely endanger the welfare of our own nation.

Which goal of U.S. foreign policy did President Truman have in this speech?

A. to prevent genocide around the world
B. to protect the security of the United States
C. to encourage foreign trade with the United States
D. to achieve world peace through international organizations

SS.7.CG.4.3

4. What was the primary reason for U.S. involvement in Korea and Vietnam?

A. an imperialist longing to annex new colonies
B. a fear of the international spread of communism
C. the hope of expanding American frontiers westward
D. a humanitarian desire to help these peoples improve their economies

SS.7.CG.4.1

5. Which action would be an example of a foreign-policy decision?

   A. Congress changes the naturalization rules for immigrants wishing to become citizens.

   B. The President signs an executive order modifying emissions standards for power plants burning coal.

   C. Congress passes a law providing tax benefits to companies manufacturing cars using electrical power.

   D. The President accepts an invitation to mediate between China and Japan over ownership of the Senkaku Islands.

SS.7.CG.4.3

6. President George W. Bush gave the statement below in a televised address on September 11, 2001.

   > *"Today, our fellow citizens, our way of life, our very freedom came under attack in a series of deliberate and deadly terrorist acts. . . . The search is underway for those who were behind these evil acts. I have directed the full resources of our intelligence and law enforcement communities to find those responsible and to bring them to justice. We will make no distinction between the terrorists who committed these acts and those who harbor them . . .*

   Which action was taken by the United States in reaction to the situation described in this address?

   A. boycotting Russia for its role in the crisis

   B. joining the European Union to obtain more allies

   C. invading Afghanistan when the Taliban refused to hand over the terrorists

   D. leaving the United Nations when the Security Council failed to punish the terrorists

SS.7.CG.4.3

7. President George Washington gave the advice below in his Farewell Address of 1796.

   > *The great rule of conduct for us in regard to foreign nations is in extending our commercial relations, to have with them as little political connection as possible. So far as we have already formed engagements, let them be fulfilled with perfect good faith. Here let us stop.*

   Which later event most closely followed President Washington's advice?

   A. The United States annexed the Philippines in 1898.

   B. Congress supplied ships to Britain for cash in 1940.

   C. Americans attempted to remain neutral at first during both World Wars I and II.

   D. Americans sent troops to Korea and Vietnam in order to prevent the spread of communism in Asia.

SS.7.CG.4.2

8. Which international organization protects the United States and Western Europe through collective security?

A. NATO

B. the United Nations

C. the World Trade Organization

D. the International Court of Justice

SS.7.CG.4.1

9. The two paragraphs below describe events during the Presidency of Bill Clinton.

"In response to the nuclear tests, people in New Delhi took to the streets lighting firecrackers, thanking Hindu gods and crying out 'Bharat Mata Jai!' (Victory to Mother India)."

"President Bill Clinton decided tonight to impose . . . sanctions on India's government for detonating three underground nuclear explosions."

Which would be an example of the sanctions that President Clinton might have imposed?

A. sending U.S. troops to India

B. prohibiting U.S. trade with India

C. ordering aerial surveillance of New Delhi

D. banning news from Indian television stations

SS.7.CG.4.1

10. A country that has a military alliance with the United States faces a civil war from ethnic conflict. What would be an appropriate first response by the United States in dealing with the conflict?

A. threaten the parties in the civil war

B. impose economic sanctions against the country

C. send U.S. troops to that country to restore order

D. encourage peaceful negotiations between the parties

SS.7.CG.4.2

11. The list below identifies three organizations in which the United States is a member.

- World Trade Organization (WTO)
- United Nations (UN)
- North Atlantic Treaty Organization (NATO)

What purpose is common to all three of these organizations?

A. military isolation

B. collective security

C. defensive alliances

D. international cooperation

SS.7.CG.4.2

12. Which argument is used by opponents of U.S. membership in the United Nations?

A. The United Nations is expensive and has failed to prevent international aggression.

B. The United Nations provides a forum where the United States can present its views.

C. The United Nations maintains peacekeeping forces in many parts of the world today.

D. The United Nations plays an essential role in providing economic and social assistance.

SS.7.CG.4.3

13. The newspaper headline on the left describes an event that took place in the Middle East.

Which course of action did the United States take in reaction to this international incident?

A. It refused to give Iraq any additional humanitarian aid.

B. It launched an invasion of Iraq to topple dictator Saddam Hussein.

C. It organized a military alliance that forced the Iraqis out of Kuwait.

D. It seized the staff of the Iraqi Embassy in Washington, D.C., as hostages.

SS.7.CG.4.3

14. Why did President Roosevelt consider December 7, 1941, a "date which will live in infamy"?

A. Japan attacked Pearl Harbor.

B. Nazi Germany invaded Poland.

C. North Korea attacked South Korea.

D. Terrorists attacked the World Trade Center.

SS.7.CG.4.3

15. The Joint Resolution below was passed by Congress on April 6, 1917.

Therefore be it resolved by the Senate and the House of Representatives of the United States of America in Congress assembled, that the state of war between the United States and the Imperial German Government which has thus been thrust upon the United States is hereby formally declared; and that the President be, and he is hereby, authorized and directed to employ the entire naval and military forces of the United States and the resources of the Government to carry on war against the Imperial German Government.

Which action led to this Joint Resolution?

A. the German invasion of Poland

B. a surprise attack on Pearl Harbor

C. submarine attacks on American ships

D. a terrorist attack on the World Trade Center and Pentagon

Chapter 19 A Practice End-of-Course Assessment in Civics and Government

SS.7.CG.1.5

1. How did the British government respond to the colonial concerns expressed during the Boston Tea Party?
   A. It passed the Intolerable Acts, closing Boston Harbor.
   B. It recognized colonial grievances and agreed not to pass any more taxes.
   C. It ordered troops to fire on colonial demonstrators in a public square of Boston.
   D. It declared the colonists to be in a state of open rebellion and outside the King's protection.

SS.7.CG.1.9

2. How does the rule of law limit the powers of government?
   A. Citizens expect to be punished if they commit unlawful acts.
   B. Citizens know which rules to follow in their relations with others.
   C. Government officials are accountable to the law for their actions.
   D. Government officials must provide a hearing before punishing critics.

SS.7.CG.1.6

3. The photograph below shows Dr. Martin Luther King after giving his "I Have a Dream" speech during the Civil Rights Movement.

Which part of the Declaration of Independence influenced the events shown in this photograph?
   A. its list of colonial grievances
   B. its outrage at the British use of force
   C. its theory of government based on natural rights
   D. its claim of the right to overthrow a tyrannical government

SS.7.CG.1.7

4. Which was an important weakness of the Articles of Confederation?
   A. It was based on the principle of limited government.
   B. There was no national executive to supply leadership.
   C. It gave the central government too much power over the states.
   D. It maintained a form of association between the former colonies.

SS.7.CG.1.8

5. The passage below is from the Preamble to the U.S. Constitution.

We the People of the United States, in order to form a more perfect Union, establish justice, insure domestic tranquility, provide for the common defense, promote the general welfare, and secure the blessings of liberty, to ourselves and our posterity, do ordain and establish this Constitution for the United States of America.

In 1957, President Eisenhower sent the National Guard into Little Rock, Arkansas, in order to prevent violence. Which goal of government, listed in the Preamble, did this action illustrate?

A. to ensure domestic tranquility
B. to form a more perfect Union
C. to secure the blessings of liberty
D. to provide for the common defense

SS.7.CG.1.9

6. Suppose the following sequence of events occurs in our federal government:

- ▶ Congress passes a bill and sends it to the President.
- ▶ The President vetoes the bill and returns it to Congress.
- ▶ Both houses of Congress override the veto.
- ▶ The bill becomes a law.

Which two constitutional principles do these events illustrate?

A. federalism and limited government
B. federalism and checks and balances
C. individual rights and popular sovereignty
D. separation of powers and checks and balances

SS.7.CG.1.10

7. Below are views for and against ratification of the Constitution.

1	2
The Constitution will create a national government more tyrannical than the British government ever was. Our individual liberties will be under a constant threat. We need better safeguards than the assurances of the Constitution's supporters.	We must have a stronger national government to protect our interests against foreign powers and domestic unrest. The separation of powers and federalism will sufficiently curb the ambitions of the new national government.

Which conclusion can be drawn from these views?

A. The proposed Constitution lacked a bill of rights.
B. The proposed Constitution guaranteed free speech.
C. The proposed Constitution had no national executive.
D. The proposed Constitution strengthened state governments.

SS.7.CG.1.10

8. During the ratification debates, Anti-Federalists demanded that the rights below be added to the Constitution in order for them to support it.

- Guarantee of a speedy trial
- Freedom from illegal searches and seizures
- Right not to have troops quartered in one's home

Which document guaranteed these rights?

A. The Bill of Rights
B. The *Federalist Papers*
C. The Articles of Confederation
D. The Declaration of Independence

SS.7.CG.3.3

9. The final clause of Article I, Section 8 of the Constitution gives Congress the power to make all laws that are "necessary and proper" to fulfill its other responsibilities. What name is sometimes given to this clause?

A. Elastic Clause
B. *Ex Post Facto* Clause
C. Bill of Attainder Clause
D. Writ of habeas corpus Clause

SS.7.CG.3.7

10. The diagram below shows some of the steps involved in passing a federal law.

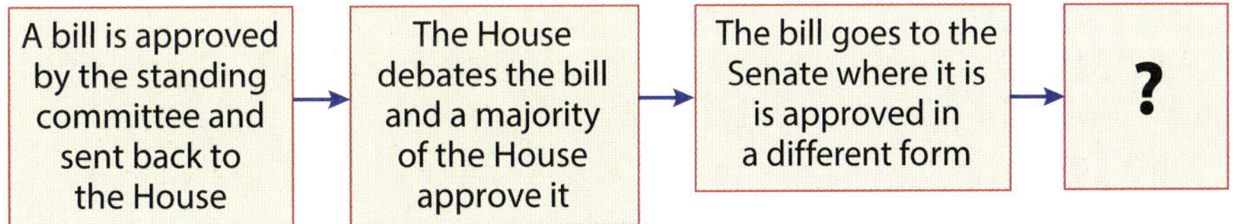

Which step completes the diagram?

A. The bill is sent to a conference committee.
B. The bill is sent back to the House to be amended.
C. The bill is pigeonholed until the next session of Congress.
D. Both bills are sent to the President to choose which to sign.

SS.7.CG.1.9

11. Which of the following is an example of the system of checks and balances?

A. Government powers are divided among three branches
B. The President can veto laws proposed by Congress.
C. Government officials are elected for fixed terms in office.
D. Government powers are divided between the national and state governments.

SS.7.CG.3.9

12. Why does the U.S. Supreme Court have only limited jurisdiction?
    - **A.** People prefer to go to their local courts because they are closer.
    - **B.** Supreme Court Justices have only limited time at their disposal.
    - **C.** Congress has decided to limit the jurisdiction of the Supreme Court.
    - **D.** The U.S. Constitution grants federal courts authority over only some matters.

SS.7.CG.1.11

13. The chart below describes some of the characteristics of the "due process" of law.

Due Process of Law

- The right to a hearing
- The right to present evidence
- The right to question witnesses
- The right to an impartial decision maker
- **?**

Which phrase completes the chart?
- **A.** The right to elect government officials
- **B.** The right to petition representatives in government
- **C.** The right to a decision based on the law and the evidence
- **D.** The right to criticize government leaders for their policies

SS.7.CG.3.4

14. How does a reserved power differ from a concurrent power?
    - **A.** It is implied from the Constitution.
    - **B.** It is denied to the national government.
    - **C.** It is delegated to the national government.
    - **D.** It is exercised by both the state and national governments.

SS.7.CG.3.3

15. Which branch of government is responsible for interpreting laws and applying them to specific situations?
    - **A.** judicial branch
    - **B.** executive branch
    - **C.** legislative branch
    - **D.** administrative branch

SS.7.CG.3.5

16. In 1971, two-thirds majority of the House of Representatives approved a proposed Equal Rights Amendment to the U.S. Constitution. In 1972, a two-thirds majority of the Senate approved the same amendment. What was the next step for amending the Constitution?

A. A majority of the state governments had to approve the amendment
B. A popular election would determine whether to adopt the amendment
C. A majority in three-fourths of the states had to approve the amendment
D. The amendment had to be signed by the President of the United States to be adopted.

SS.7.CG.3.14

17. The statement below was published in support of the Constitution.

"Measures are too often decided, not according to the rules of justice and the rights of the minor party, but by the superior force of an interested and overbearing majority of ordinary citizens."

—James Madison, *The Federalist, No. 10*

Which feature of the Constitution was introduced to reduce the possible influence of an "overbearing majority"?

A. the creation of an Electoral College to select the President
B. the decision to place the executive branch in the hands of one person
C. the requirement that the Senate confirm nominations by the President
D. the establishment of a House of Representatives to represent the people

SS.7.CG.3.12

18. Which provision of the Florida Constitution has no equivalent in the United States Constitution?

A. Preamble with "We the People"
B. the election of Cabinet officials
C. the "Necessary and Proper" Clause
D. the ability of the legislature to override an executive veto

SS.7.CG.4.2

19. What is the purpose of the World Trade Organization (WTO)?

A. to protect global peace and stability
B. to create and maintain rules for international trade
C. to prosecute those responsible for crimes against humanity
D. to provide collective security for North America and Europe

SS.7.CG.3.9

20. The diagram below provides details about the U.S. court system.

Which court completes the diagram?

A. Court-martial
B. U.S. County Court
C. U.S. District Court
D. Florida Supreme Court

SS.7.CG.2.7

21. What is one of the constitutional qualifications to become the Governor of Florida?

A. be a natural born citizen
B. be at least 35 years old
C. have paid federal income taxes for five years
D. have lived in Florida for the past seven years

SS.7.CG.3.10

22. Naval Commander John Hart is accused of stealing $10,000 from the payroll purser during his tour of duty in the Arabian Sea near the Persian Gulf. Which type of law will he be subject to?

A. civil
B. criminal
C. military
D. constitutional

SS.7.CG.1.11

23. The list below includes some of the rights of American citizens in legal proceedings.

- Right to have an attorney
- Right to be heard if accused
- Right not to have cruel or unusual punishment
- Right not to have double jeopardy

Which term is used to describe these rights?

A. Equal protection of the laws
B. Arraignment rights
C. Due process of law
D. Eminent domain

SS.7.CG.2.5

24. Which statement identifies an important difference between civil and criminal trials?

A. Juries only hear criminal cases.

B. Only a criminal proceeding can be appealed.

C. Lawyers only cross-examine witnesses in criminal trials.

D. Proof must be beyond a reasonable doubt to convict in criminal trials.

SS.7.CG.3.9

25.

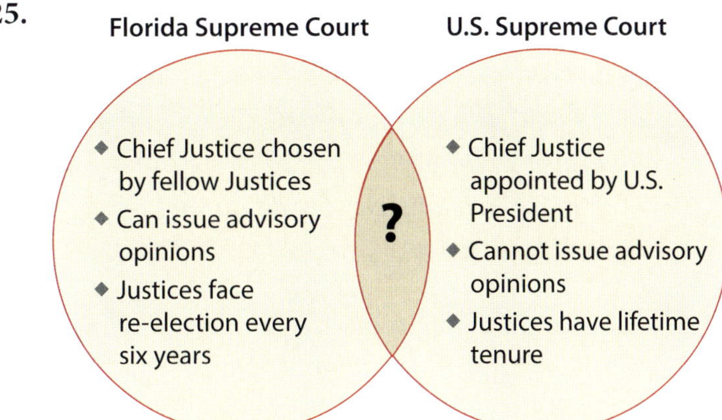

Which statement completes the Venn diagram?

A. Consists of 9 Justices

B. Exercises powers of judicial review

C. Is the highest authority on federal law

D. Is required to review all death penalty cases

SS.7.CG.3.7

26. The diagram below shows some of the steps involved in passing a Florida state law.

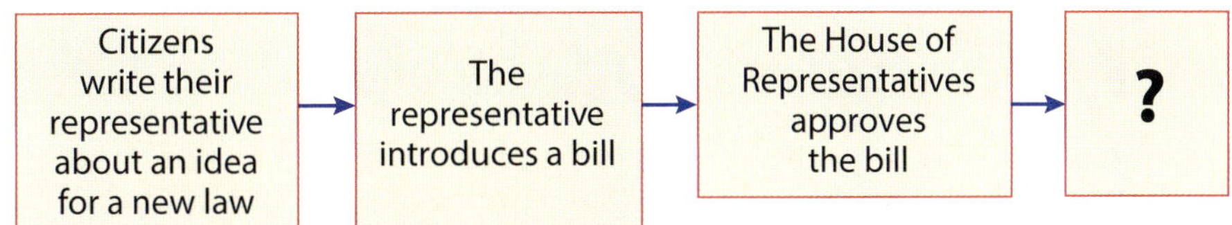

Which step comes next in the diagram?

A. The Governor signs the bill into law.

B. The bill goes to the Senate for action.

C. The people vote on the bill in an election.

D. The bill goes to the Supreme Court for a hearing.

SS.7.CG.3.10

27. Which type of law protects our fundamental rights as individuals?

A. civil law

B. military law

C. criminal law

D. constitutional law

SS.7.CG.2.6

28. What is an important consequence of free and fair elections?

A. People lose confidence in the ability of their leaders.

B. People develop greater trust in their democratic institutions.

C. People regret the lack of continuity in their government's policies.

D. People fear interference by other countries in their electoral processes.

SS.7.CG.2.3

29. The passage below is from the Sixth Amendment to the U.S. Constitution.

In all criminal prosecutions, the accused shall enjoy the right to a speedy and public trial, by an impartial jury . . . and to be informed of the nature and cause of the accusation; to be confronted with the witnesses against him; to have compulsory process for obtaining witnesses in his favor, and to have the assistance of counsel for his defen[s]e.

How do the rights provided in this amendment help to protect democracy?

A. They make it difficult for police officials to search citizens without just cause.

B. They make it difficult for government officials to imprison political opponents.

C. They protect the rights of citizens to publish remarks criticizing the government.

D. They prevent government officials from taking private property without fair compensation.

SS.7.CG.3.11

30. Which statement summarizes the outcome of the 1954 U.S. Supreme Court case *Brown v. Board of Education*?

A. Students had the right to protest government policies by wearing armbands in school.

B. Amish parents could not be forced to send their children to public high schools.

C. Mexican-American children were entitled to protection from discrimination.

D. States could not maintain segregated schools since racial segregation in public education is "inherently unequal."

SS.7.CG.1.2

31. What has been a long-term effect of the First Amendment's guarantee of religious liberty?

A. Americans have avoided divisive religious wars.

B. Americans are less religious than people in most countries.

C. Americans have established different official churches in each state.

D. Americans with strong religious beliefs have generally left the United States.

SS.7.CG.3.11

32. Chief Justice Roger Taney made the statement below in an 1857 Supreme Court decision.

We think . . . that [African Americans] are not included, and were not intended to be included, under the word "citizens" in the Constitution, and can therefore claim none of the rights . . . and privileges which that instrument provides . . .

What was an immediate consequence of this decision?

A. The fugitive slave law was overturned.
B. Southern states seceded from the Union.
C. Divisions over slavery across the country intensified.
D. Congress added two new Justices to the Supreme Court.

SS.7.CG.4.3

33. Which conflict did the United States enter after a surprise attack on the U.S. naval fleet in Pearl Harbor, Hawaii?

A. World War II
B. Vietnam War
C. First Gulf War
D. Spanish-American War

SS.7.CG.1.3

34. Which important idea was found in the English Bill of Rights (1689)?

A. The members of humankind are all equal.
B. Government institutions should be transparent.
C. The government should not impose excessive punishments
D. Government officials have a right to demand that citizens lend their money.

SS.7.CG.1.1

35. Which statement identifies an important influence that ancient Greece had on the American constitutional republic?

A. Americans believed in the equality of humankind.
B. Americans believed that religious liberty was a protected right.
C. Americans believed that ordinary citizens should participate in government.
D. Americans believed that a separation of powers would protect individual rights.

SS.7.CG.3.13

36. Which is a service provided by local governments to their citizens?

A. national defense
B. issuing drivers' licenses
C. police and fire protection
D. establishing rules for banks

SS.7.CG.3.8

37. What is an important function of an administrative agency?

    A. writing detailed regulations to implement existing laws
    B. passing new laws without the approval of Congress
    C. deciding on the constitutionality of law through judicial review
    D. helping the government exercise powers otherwise reserved to the states

SS.7.CG.2.9

38. A U.S. government poster from World War II is shown at the left.

    Which media technique is used in this poster to encourage women to leave their homes and go to work?

    A. negative propaganda
    B. bias against foreigners
    C. demonizing opponents
    D. appeals to patriotic emotion

SS.7.CG.3.2

39. The passage below describes the government of Saudi Arabia.

    The Kingdom of Saudi Arabia is divided politically into thirteen provinces. Each is headed by an emir who is appointed by the King and who answers to the Ministry of the Interior. These 13 provinces are further divided into 118 governorates headed by local mayors. The provinces are created by the King's authority and can be eliminated at any time.

    Based on this passage, which system of government does the Kingdom of Saudi Arabia have?

    A. unitary
    B. federal
    C. oligarchy
    D. confederal

SS.7.CG.3.1

40. Which statement applies to all types of monarchies?

    A. The monarch inherits his or her power.
    B. They combine the executive and legislative branches.
    C. Their ruler holds absolute power, unlimited by Parliaments or constitutions.
    D. The monarch's power, whether total or limited, is established in a written constitution.

SS.7.CG.3.2

41. In Country X, the leader of the national government appoints deputies who are placed in charge of local governments. The deputies can be recalled by the leader at any time. The leader can also alter the powers of the local governments. What type of system of government does Country X have?

  A. federal system
  B. unitary system
  C. confederal system
  D. republican system

SS.7.CG.4.3

42. How did President John F. Kennedy respond to the threat of nuclear missiles in Cuba?

  A. He sent an army of exiles to invade Cuba at the Bay of Pigs.
  B. He launched air strikes on Cuba to destroy the missile sites.
  C. He placed economic sanctions on both Cuba and the Soviet Union.
  D. He established a blockade around Cuba and threatened a U.S. invasion.

SS.7.CG.2.2

43. Which action is a legal obligation of U.S. citizenship?

  A. voting in all Presidential elections
  B. serving on a jury when summoned
  C. supporting one's parents in their old age
  D. keeping informed about major public issues

SS.7.CG.2.1

44. The diagram below shows some of the requirements for becoming a naturalized citizen.

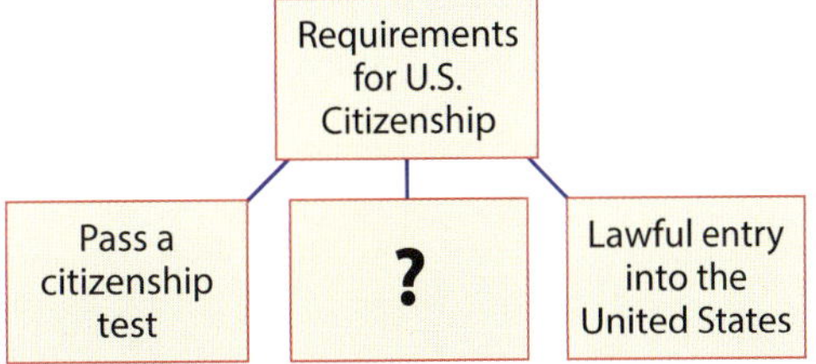

Which statement completes the diagram?

  A. Be at least 21 years of age
  B. Have served in the U.S. armed forces
  C. Have a close relative who is a U.S. citizen
  D. Have resided in the United States for five years

SS.7.CG.2.1

45. The passage below is from the Fourteenth Amendment.

"All persons born or naturalized in the United States, and subject to the jurisdiction thereof, are citizens of the United States and of the State wherein they reside."

What is an additional constitutional means for a person to have U.S. citizenship?

A. by treaty agreements
B. by purchasing citizenship
C. by having valuable work skills
D. by having U.S. citizens as parents

SS.7.CG.3.1

46. What is an advantage of the United States' constitutional republic over a theocracy?

A. Citizens can vote in elections.
B. Citizens have freedom of religion.
C. Citizens generally pay less in taxation.
D. Citizens receive public services from the government.

SS.7.CG.3.11

47. What was the outcome of the 1974 Supreme Court decision *United States v. Nixon*?

A. Government surveillance of antiwar demonstrators during the Vietnam War was halted.
B. President Nixon was unable to block the publication of *The Pentagon Papers* in *The New York Times.*
C. A manual recount of votes in Florida was halted because of insufficient guidelines and inconsistent practices.
D. Executive privilege did not excuse President Nixon from handing over tapes of his conversations to investigators.

SS.7.CG.1.4

48. The diagram shows an impact of Enlightenment ideas on the founding of the United States.

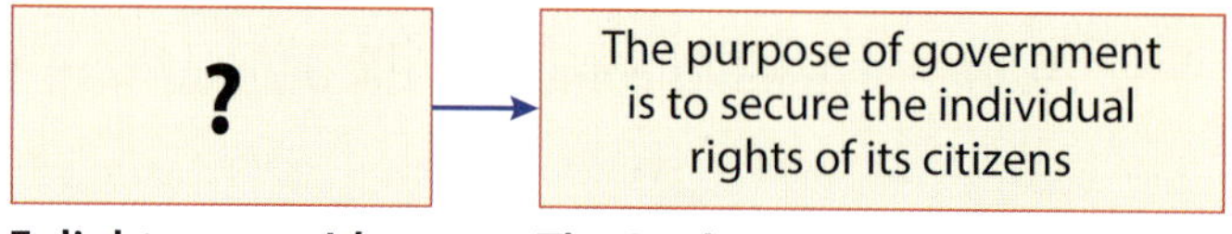

Which phrase completes the diagram?

A. Spread of scientific inquiry
B. John Locke's social contract
C. Growth of religious tolerance
D. Montesquieu's separation of powers

SS.7.CG.2.3

49. Police entered Mr. Anderson's home without a warrant and without "probable cause." Which constitutional right of Mr. Anderson was violated?
    - **A.** The Fifth Amendment right against double jeopardy.
    - **B.** The Fifth Amendment right against self-incrimination.
    - **C.** The Fourth Amendment right against unreasonable searches.
    - **D.** The Sixth Amendment right against cruel and unusual punishments.

SS.7.CG.2.4

50. Which rationale was offered by government authorities for the forced internment of a large number of Japanese Americans during World War II?
    - **A.** The Bill of Rights did not apply to ethnic minorities.
    - **B.** Japanese Americans would be safer in the internment camps.
    - **C.** Japanese Americans posed an immediate threat to national security.
    - **D.** Not enough Japanese Americans were volunteering for military service.

SS.7.CG.3.6

51. How did passage of the Twenty-sixth Amendment affect the U.S. political process?
    - **A.** Women were guaranteed the right to vote in all states.
    - **B.** Citizens from 18 to 20 years old were given the right to vote.
    - **C.** Poll taxes were no longer permitted for voting in federal elections.
    - **D.** The federal government took over the regulation of statewide elections.

SS.7.CG.2.8

52. What is one method that interest groups use to monitor government?
    - **A.** They file lawsuits on special issues.
    - **B.** They publish editorials in newspapers
    - **C.** They attend legislative committee hearings
    - **D.** They advise candidates on election strategies.

SS.7.CG.4.1

53. Which action is an example of a foreign-policy decision?
    - **A.** The President issued an Executive Order against cyber-bullying.
    - **B.** Congress raised the residency requirement for naturalization to 7 years.
    - **C.** The President signed an executive agreement with the President of Peru.
    - **D.** The Supreme Court upheld the constitutionality of the Affordable Care Act.

SS.7.CG.2.10

54. Maria is very upset that other students at her school are throwing litter on the school grounds. Which step should Maria probably take first to solve this problem?
    - **A.** research how other schools dispose of litter
    - **B.** write a letter to her Florida Representative and Senator
    - **C.** speak to an attorney about filing a lawsuit against her school
    - **D.** hold a peaceful protest meeting with other concerned students

SS.7.CG.3.15

55. The chart below identifies some of the chief characteristics of several economic systems.

Capitalism	Communism	Socialism
?	The government decides production through central planning.	The government owns basic industries and provides free public services. Private enterprise is also permitted.

Which statement completes the chart?

A. There is an absence of freedom of choice

B. Producers and consumers make their own decisions.

C. Government officials instruct private producers what to make

D. The government seizes the wealth of landowners and manufacturers.

SS.7.CG.1.1

56. The chart below shows several characteristics of the American constitutional republic.

- Republicanism
- Representative government
- Separation of powers
- Civic participation

Which influence on America's constitutional republic is reflected in this chart?

A. the ancient Greek *polis*

B. the English Bill of Rights

C. the ancient Roman Republic

D. the Judeo-Christian Tradition

SS.7.CG.1.3

57. How did Magna Carta influence the colonists' views of government?

A. It encouraged them to declare their independence from Great Britain.

B. It gave them the idea that everyone is entitled to certain natural rights.

C. It led them to create a government based on a separation of powers among different branches.

D. It granted them rights as English subjects, including the right to a trial by jury and not to be taxed without consent.

Declaration of Independence

In Congress, July 4, 1776.

The unanimous Declaration of the thirteen united States of America

When in the Course of human events, it becomes necessary for one people to dissolve the political bands which have connected them with another, and to assume among the powers of the earth, the separate and equal station to which the Laws of Nature and of Nature's God entitle them, a decent respect to the opinions of mankind requires that they should declare the causes which impel them to the separation.

We hold these truths to be self-evident, that all men are created equal, that they are endowed by their Creator with certain unalienable Rights, that among these are Life, Liberty and the pursuit of Happiness.--That to secure these rights, Governments are instituted among Men, deriving their just powers from the consent of the governed, --That whenever any Form of Government becomes destructive of these ends, it is the Right of the People to alter or to abolish it, and to institute new Government, laying its foundation on such principles and organizing its powers in such form, as to them shall seem most likely to effect their Safety and Happiness. Prudence, indeed, will dictate that Governments long established should not be changed for light and transient causes; and accordingly all experience hath shewn, that mankind are more disposed to suffer, while evils are sufferable, than to right themselves by abolishing the forms to which they are accustomed. But when a long train of abuses and usurpations, pursuing invariably the same Object evinces a design to reduce them under absolute Despotism, it is their right, it is their duty, to throw off such Government, and to provide new Guards for their future security.--Such has been the patient sufferance of these Colonies; and such is now the necessity which constrains them to alter their former Systems of Government. The history of the present King of Great Britain is a history of repeated injuries and usurpations, all having in direct object the establishment of an absolute Tyranny over these States. To prove this, let Facts be submitted to a candid world.

He has refused his Assent to Laws, the most wholesome and necessary for the public good.

He has forbidden his Governors to pass Laws of immediate and pressing importance, unless suspended in their operation till his Assent should be obtained; and when so suspended, he has utterly neglected to attend to them.

He has refused to pass other Laws for the accommodation of large districts of people, unless those people would relinquish the right of Representation in the Legislature, a right inestimable to them and formidable to tyrants only.

He has called together legislative bodies at places unusual, uncomfortable, and distant from the depository of their public Records, for the sole purpose of fatiguing them into compliance with his measures.

He has dissolved Representative Houses repeatedly, for opposing with manly firmness his invasions on the rights of the people.

He has refused for a long time, after such dissolutions, to cause others to be elected; whereby the Legislative powers, incapable of Annihilation, have returned to the People at large for their exercise; the State remaining in the mean time exposed to all the dangers of invasion from without, and convulsions within.

He has endeavoured to prevent the population of these States; for that purpose obstructing the Laws for Naturalization of Foreigners; refusing to pass others to encourage their migrations hither, and raising the conditions of new Appropriations of Lands.

He has obstructed the Administration of Justice, by refusing his Assent to Laws for establishing Judiciary powers.

He has made Judges dependent on his Will alone, for the tenure of their offices, and the amount and payment of their salaries.

He has erected a multitude of New Offices, and sent hither swarms of Officers to harrass our people, and eat out their substance.

He has kept among us, in times of peace, Standing Armies without the Consent of our legislatures.

He has affected to render the Military independent of and superior to the Civil power.

He has combined with others to subject us to a jurisdiction foreign to our constitution, and unacknowledged by our laws; giving his Assent to their Acts of pretended Legislation:

For Quartering large bodies of armed troops among us:

For protecting them, by a mock Trial, from punishment for any Murders which they should commit on the Inhabitants of these States:

For cutting off our Trade with all parts of the world:

For imposing Taxes on us without our Consent:

For depriving us in many cases, of the benefits of Trial by Jury:

For transporting us beyond Seas to be tried for pretended offences

For abolishing the free System of English Laws in a neighbouring Province, establishing therein an Arbitrary government, and enlarging its Boundaries so as to render it at once an example and fit instrument for introducing the same absolute rule into these Colonies:

For taking away our Charters, abolishing our most valuable Laws, and altering fundamentally the Forms of our Governments:

For suspending our own Legislatures, and declaring themselves invested with power to legislate for us in all cases whatsoever.

He has abdicated Government here, by declaring us out of his Protection and waging War against us.

He has plundered our seas, ravaged our Coasts, burnt our towns, and destroyed the lives of our people.

He is at this time transporting large Armies of foreign Mercenaries to compleat the works of death, desolation and tyranny, already begun with circumstances of Cruelty & perfidy scarcely paralleled in the most barbarous ages, and totally unworthy the Head of a civilized nation.

He has constrained our fellow Citizens taken Captive on the high Seas to bear Arms against their Country, to become the executioners of their friends and Brethren, or to fall themselves by their Hands.

He has excited domestic insurrections amongst us, and has endeavoured to bring on the inhabitants of our frontiers, the merciless Indian Savages, whose known rule of warfare, is an undistinguished destruction of all ages, sexes and conditions.

In every stage of these Oppressions We have Petitioned for Redress in the most humble terms: Our repeated Petitions have been answered only by repeated injury. A Prince whose character is thus marked by every act which may define a Tyrant, is unfit to be the ruler of a free people.

Nor have We been wanting in attentions to our Brittish brethren. We have warned them from time to time of attempts by their legislature to extend an unwarrantable jurisdiction over us. We have reminded them of the circumstances of our emigration and settlement here. We have appealed to their native justice and magnanimity, and we have conjured them by the ties of our common kindred to disavow these usurpations, which, would inevitably interrupt our connections and correspondence. They too have been deaf to the voice of justice and of consanguinity. We must, therefore, acquiesce in the necessity, which denounces our Separation, and hold them, as we hold the rest of mankind, Enemies in War, in Peace Friends.

We, therefore, the Representatives of the united States of America, in General Congress, Assembled, appealing to the Supreme Judge of the world for the rectitude of our intentions, do, in the Name, and by Authority of the good People of these Colonies, solemnly publish and declare, That these United Colonies are, and of Right ought to be Free and Independent States; that they are Absolved from all Allegiance to the British Crown, and that all political connection between them and the State of Great Britain, is and ought to be totally dissolved; and that as Free and Independent States, they have full Power to levy War, conclude Peace, contract Alliances, establish Commerce, and to do all other Acts and Things which Independent States may of right do. And for the support of this Declaration, with a firm reliance on the protection of divine Providence, we mutually pledge to each other our Lives, our Fortunes and our sacred Honor.

Georgia
Button Gwinnett
Lyman Hall
George Walton

North Carolina
William Hooper
Joseph Hewes
John Penn

South Carolina
Edward Rutledge
Thomas Heyward, Jr.
Thomas Lynch, Jr.
Arthur Middleton

Massachusetts
John Hancock
Maryland
Samuel Chase
William Paca
Thomas Stone
Charles Carroll of Carrollton

Virginia
George Wythe
Richard Henry Lee
Thomas Jefferson
Benjamin Harrison
Thomas Nelson, Jr.
Francis Lightfoot Lee
Carter Braxton

Pennsylvania
Robert Morris
Benjamin Rush
Benjamin Franklin
John Morton
George Clymer
James Smith
George Taylor
James Wilson
George Ross

Delaware
Caesar Rodney
George Read
Thomas McKean

New York
William Floyd
Philip Livingston
Francis Lewis
Lewis Morris

New Jersey
Richard Stockton
John Witherspoon
Francis Hopkinson
John Hart
Abraham Clark

New Hampshire
Josiah Bartlett
William Whipple

Massachusetts
Samuel Adams
John Adams
Robert Treat Paine
Elbridge Gerry

Rhode Island
Stephen Hopkins
William Ellery

Connecticut
Roger Sherman
Samuel Huntington
William Williams
Oliver Wolcott

New Hampshire
Matthew Thornton

The Declaration of Independence of the United States of America by Armand-Dumaresq (painted c. 1873).

Scene at the Signing the Constitution by Howard Chandler Christy (painted c. 1940).

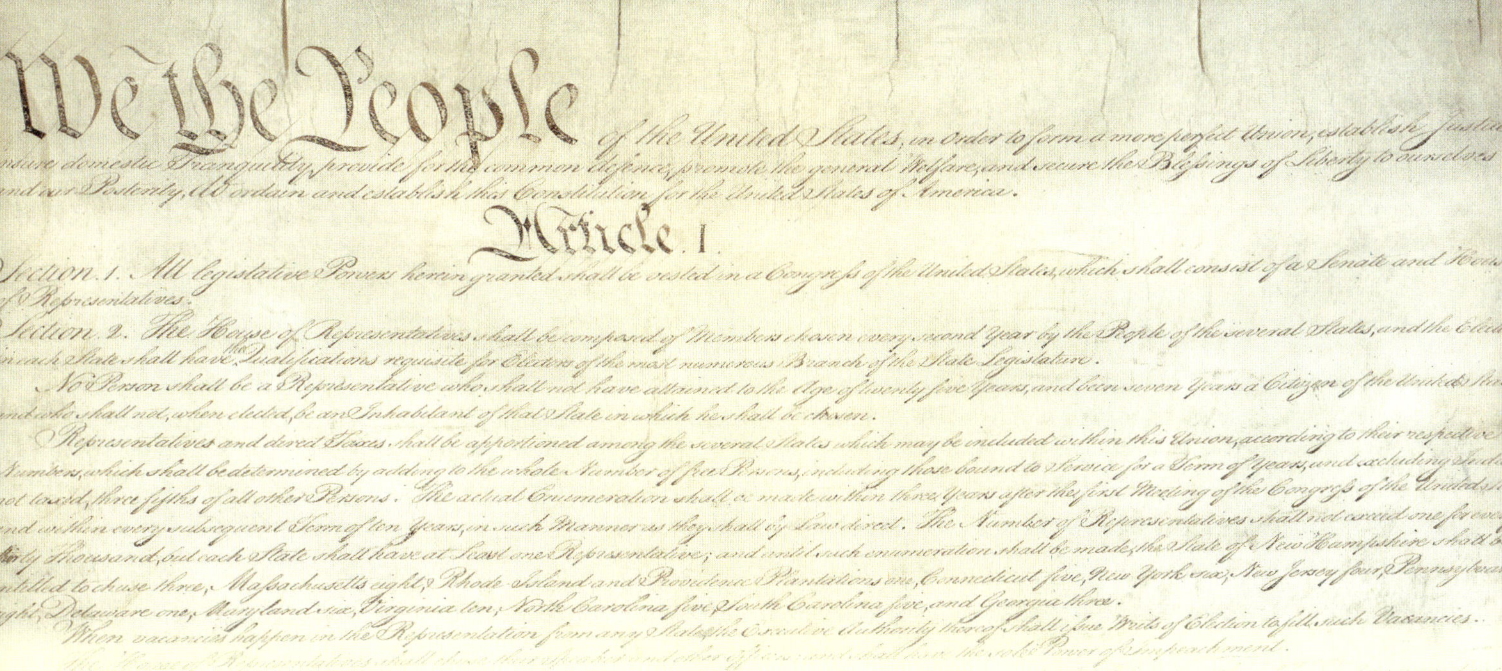

The Constitution of the United States

We the People of the United States, in Order to form a more perfect Union, establish Justice, insure domestic Tranquility, provide for the common defence, promote the general Welfare, and secure the Blessings of Liberty to ourselves and our Posterity, do ordain and establish this Constitution for the United States of America.

Article. I.

Section. 1.

All legislative Powers herein granted shall be vested in a Congress of the United States, which shall consist of a Senate and House of Representatives.

Section. 2.

The House of Representatives shall be composed of Members chosen every second Year by the People of the several States, and the Electors in each State shall have the Qualifications requisite for Electors of the most numerous Branch of the State Legislature.

No Person shall be a Representative who shall not have attained to the Age of twenty five Years, and been seven Years a Citizen of the United States, and who shall not, when elected, be an Inhabitant of that State in which he shall be chosen.

Representatives and direct Taxes shall be apportioned among the several States which may be included within this Union, according to their respective Numbers, which shall be determined by adding to the whole Number of free Persons, including those bound to Service for a Term of Years, and excluding Indians not taxed, three fifths of all other Persons. The actual Enumeration shall be made within three Years after the first Meeting of the Congress of the United States, and within every subsequent Term of ten Years, in such Manner as they shall by Law direct. The Number of Representatives shall not exceed one for every thirty Thousand, but each State shall have at Least one Representative; and until such enumeration shall be made, the State of New Hampshire shall be entitled to chuse three, Massachusetts eight, Rhode-Island and Providence Plantations one, Connecticut five, New-York six, New Jersey four, Pennsylvania eight, Delaware one, Maryland six, Virginia ten, North Carolina five, South Carolina five, and Georgia three.

When vacancies happen in the Representation from any State, the Executive Authority thereof shall issue Writs of Election to fill such Vacancies.

The House of Representatives shall chuse their Speaker and other Officers; and shall have the sole Power of Impeachment.

Section. 3.

The Senate of the United States shall be composed of two Senators from each State, chosen by the Legislature thereof, for six Years; and each Senator shall have one Vote.

Immediately after they shall be assembled in Consequence of the first Election, they shall be divided as equally as may be into three Classes. The Seats of the Senators of the first Class shall be vacated at the Expiration of the second Year, of the second Class at the Expiration of the fourth Year, and of the third Class at the Expiration of the sixth Year, so that one third may be chosen every second Year; and if Vacancies happen by Resignation, or otherwise, during the Recess of the Legislature of any State, the Executive thereof may make temporary Appointments until the next Meeting of the Legislature, which shall then fill such Vacancies.

No Person shall be a Senator who shall not have attained to the Age of thirty Years, and been nine Years a Citizen of the United States, and who shall not, when elected, be an Inhabitant of that State for which he shall be chosen.

The Vice President of the United States shall be President of the Senate, but shall have no Vote, unless they be equally divided.

The Senate shall chuse their other Officers, and also a President pro tempore, in the Absence of the Vice President, or when he shall exercise the Office of President of the United States.

The Senate shall have the sole Power to try all Impeachments. When sitting for that Purpose, they shall be on Oath or Affirmation. When the President of the United States is tried, the Chief Justice shall preside: And no Person shall be convicted without the Concurrence of two thirds of the Members present.

Judgment in Cases of Impeachment shall not extend further than to removal from Office, and disqualification to hold and enjoy any Office of honor, Trust or Profit under the United States: but the Party convicted shall nevertheless be liable and subject to Indictment, Trial, Judgment and Punishment, according to Law.

Section. 4.

The Times, Places and Manner of holding Elections for Senators and Representatives, shall be prescribed in each State by the Legislature thereof; but the Congress may at any time by Law make or alter such Regulations, except as to the Places of chusing Senators.

The Congress shall assemble at least once in every Year, and such Meeting shall be on the first Monday in December, unless they shall by Law appoint a different Day.

Section. 5.

Each House shall be the Judge of the Elections, Returns and Qualifications of its own Members, and a Majority of each shall constitute a Quorum to do Business; but a smaller Number may adjourn from day to day, and may be authorized to compel the Attendance of absent Members, in such Manner, and under such Penalties as each House may provide.

Each House may determine the Rules of its Proceedings, punish its Members for disorderly Behaviour, and, with the Concurrence of two thirds, expel a Member.

Each House shall keep a Journal of its Proceedings, and from time to time publish the same, excepting such Parts as may in their Judgment require Secrecy; and the Yeas and Nays of the Members of either House on any question shall, at the Desire of one fifth of those Present, be entered on the Journal.

Neither House, during the Session of Congress, shall, without the Consent of the other, adjourn for more than three days, nor to any other Place than that in which the two Houses shall be sitting.

Section. 6.

The Senators and Representatives shall receive a Compensation for their Services, to be ascertained by Law, and paid out of the Treasury of the United States. They shall in all Cases, except Treason, Felony and Breach of the Peace, be privileged from Arrest during their Attendance at the Session of their respective Houses, and in going to and returning from the same; and for any Speech or Debate in either House, they shall not be questioned in any other Place.

No Senator or Representative shall, during the Time for which he was elected, be appointed to any civil Office under the Authority of the United States, which shall have been created, or the Emoluments whereof shall have been encreased during such time; and no Person holding any Office under the United States, shall be a Member of either House during his Continuance in Office.

Section. 7.

All Bills for raising Revenue shall originate in the House of Representatives; but the Senate may propose or concur with Amendments as on other Bills.

Every Bill which shall have passed the House of Representatives and the Senate, shall, before it become a Law, be presented to the President of the United States; If he approve he shall sign it, but if not he shall return it, with his Objections to that House in which it shall have originated, who shall enter the Objections at large on their Journal, and proceed to reconsider it. If after such Reconsideration two thirds of that House shall agree to pass the Bill, it shall be sent, together with the Objections, to the other House, by which it shall likewise be reconsidered, and if approved by two thirds of that House, it shall become a Law. But in all such Cases the Votes of both Houses shall be determined by yeas and Nays, and the Names of the Persons voting for and against the Bill shall be entered on the Journal of each House respectively. If any Bill shall not be returned by the President within ten Days (Sundays excepted) after it shall have been presented to him, the Same shall be a Law, in like Manner as if he had signed it, unless the Congress by their Adjournment prevent its Return, in which Case it shall not be a Law.

Every Order, Resolution, or Vote to which the Concurrence of the Senate and House of Representatives may be necessary (except on a question of Adjournment) shall be presented to the President of the United States; and before the Same shall take Effect, shall be approved by him, or being disapproved by him, shall be repassed by two thirds of the Senate and House of Representatives, according to the Rules and Limitations prescribed in the Case of a Bill.

Section. 8.

The Congress shall have Power To lay and collect Taxes, Duties, Imposts and Excises, to pay the Debts and provide for the common Defence and general Welfare of the United States; but all Duties, Imposts and Excises shall be uniform throughout the United States;

To borrow Money on the credit of the United States;

To regulate Commerce with foreign Nations, and among the several States, and with the Indian Tribes;

To establish an uniform Rule of Naturalization, and uniform Laws on the subject of Bankruptcies throughout the United States;

To coin Money, regulate the Value thereof, and of foreign Coin, and fix the Standard of Weights and Measures;

To provide for the Punishment of counterfeiting the Securities and current Coin of the United States;

To establish Post Offices and post Roads;

To promote the Progress of Science and useful Arts, by securing for limited Times to Authors and Inventors the exclusive Right to their respective Writings and Discoveries;

To constitute Tribunals inferior to the supreme Court;

To define and punish Piracies and Felonies committed on the high Seas, and Offences against the Law of Nations;

To declare War, grant Letters of Marque and Reprisal, and make Rules concerning Captures on Land and Water;

To raise and support Armies, but no Appropriation of Money to that Use shall be for a longer Term than two Years;

To provide and maintain a Navy;

To make Rules for the Government and Regulation of the land and naval Forces;

To provide for calling forth the Militia to execute the Laws of the Union, suppress Insurrections and repel Invasions;

To provide for organizing, arming, and disciplining, the Militia, and for governing such Part of them as may be employed in the Service of the United States, reserving to the States respectively, the Appointment of the Officers, and the Authority of training the Militia according to the discipline prescribed by Congress;

To exercise exclusive Legislation in all Cases whatsoever, over such District (not exceeding ten Miles square) as may, by Cession of particular States, and the Acceptance of Congress, become the Seat of the Government of the United States, and to exercise like Authority over all Places purchased by the Consent of the Legislature of the State in which the Same shall be, for the Erection of Forts, Magazines, Arsenals, dock-Yards, and other needful Buildings;—And

To make all Laws which shall be necessary and proper for carrying into Execution the foregoing Powers, and all other Powers vested by this Constitution in the Government of the United States, or in any Department or Officer thereof.

Section. 9.

The Migration or Importation of such Persons as any of the States now existing shall think proper to admit, shall not be prohibited by the Congress prior to the Year one thousand eight hundred and eight, but a Tax or duty may be imposed on such Importation, not exceeding ten dollars for each Person.

The Privilege of the Writ of Habeas Corpus shall not be suspended, unless when in Cases of Rebellion or Invasion the public Safety may require it.

No Bill of Attainder or ex post facto Law shall be passed.

No Capitation, or other direct, Tax shall be laid, unless in Proportion to the Census or enumeration herein before directed to be taken.

No Tax or Duty shall be laid on Articles exported from any State.

No Preference shall be given by any Regulation of Commerce or Revenue to the Ports of one State over those of another: nor shall Vessels bound to, or from, one State, be obliged to enter, clear, or pay Duties in another.

No Money shall be drawn from the Treasury, but in Consequence of Appropriations made by Law; and a regular Statement and Account of the Receipts and Expenditures of all public Money shall be published from time to time.

No Title of Nobility shall be granted by the United States: And no Person holding any Office of Profit or Trust under them, shall, without the Consent of the Congress, accept of any present, Emolument, Office, or Title, of any kind whatever, from any King, Prince, or foreign State.

Section. 10.

No State shall enter into any Treaty, Alliance, or Confederation; grant Letters of Marque and Reprisal; coin Money; emit Bills of Credit; make any Thing but gold and silver Coin a Tender in Payment of Debts; pass any Bill of Attainder, ex post facto Law, or Law impairing the Obligation of Contracts, or grant any Title of Nobility.

No State shall, without the Consent of the Congress, lay any Imposts or Duties on Imports or Exports, except what may be absolutely necessary for executing it's inspection Laws: and the net Produce of all Duties and Imposts, laid by any State on Imports or Exports, shall be for the Use of the Treasury of the United States; and all such Laws shall be subject to the Revision and Controul of the Congress.

No State shall, without the Consent of Congress, lay any Duty of Tonnage, keep Troops, or Ships of War in time of Peace, enter into any Agreement or Compact with another State, or with a foreign Power, or engage in War, unless actually invaded, or in such imminent Danger as will not admit of delay.

Article. II.

Section. 1.

The executive Power shall be vested in a President of the United States of America. He shall hold his Office during the Term of four Years, and, together with the Vice President, chosen for the same Term, be elected, as follows

Each State shall appoint, in such Manner as the Legislature thereof may direct, a Number of Electors, equal to the whole Number of Senators and Representatives to which the State may be entitled in the Congress: but no Senator or Representative, or Person holding an Office of Trust or Profit under the United States, shall be appointed an Elector.

The Electors shall meet in their respective States, and vote by Ballot for two Persons, of whom one at least shall not be an Inhabitant of the same State with themselves. And they shall make a List of all the Persons voted for, and of the Number of Votes for each; which List they shall sign and certify, and transmit sealed to the Seat of the Government of the United States, directed to the President of the Senate. The President of the Senate shall, in the Presence of the Senate and House of Representatives, open all the Certificates, and the Votes shall then be counted. The Person having the greatest Number of Votes shall be the President, if such Number be a Majority of the whole Number of Electors appointed; and if there be more than one who have such Majority, and have an equal Number of Votes, then the House of Representatives shall immediately chuse by Ballot one of them for President; and if no Person have a Majority, then from the five highest on the List the said House shall in like Manner chuse the President. But in chusing the President, the Votes shall be taken by States, the Representation from each State having one Vote; A quorum for this Purpose shall consist of a Member or Members from two thirds of the States, and a Majority of all the States shall be necessary to a Choice. In every Case, after the Choice of the President, the Person having the greatest Number of Votes of the Electors shall be the Vice President. But if there should remain two or more who have equal Votes, the Senate shall chuse from them by Ballot the Vice President.

The Congress may determine the Time of chusing the Electors, and the Day on which they shall give their Votes; which Day shall be the same throughout the United States.

No Person except a natural born Citizen, or a Citizen of the United States, at the time of the Adoption of this Constitution, shall be eligible to the Office of President; neither shall any Person be eligible to that Office who shall not have attained to the Age of thirty five Years, and been fourteen Years a Resident within the United States.

In Case of the Removal of the President from Office, or of his Death, Resignation, or Inability to discharge the Powers and Duties of the said Office, the Same shall devolve on the Vice President, and the Congress may by Law provide for the Case of Removal, Death, Resignation or Inability, both of the President and Vice President, declaring what Officer shall then act as President, and such Officer shall act accordingly, until the Disability be removed, or a President shall be elected.

The President shall, at stated Times, receive for his Services, a Compensation, which shall neither be encreased nor diminished during the Period for which he shall have been elected, and he shall not receive within that Period any other Emolument from the United States, or any of them.

Before he enter on the Execution of his Office, he shall take the following Oath or Affirmation:--"I do solemnly swear (or affirm) that I will faithfully execute the Office of President of the United States, and will to the best of my Ability, preserve, protect and defend the Constitution of the United States."

Section. 2.

The President shall be Commander in Chief of the Army and Navy of the United States, and of the Militia of the several States, when called into the actual Service of the United States; he may require the Opinion, in writing, of the principal Officer in each of the executive Departments, upon any Subject relating to the Duties of their respective Offices, and he shall have Power to grant Reprieves and Pardons for Offences against the United States, except in Cases of Impeachment.

He shall have Power, by and with the Advice and Consent of the Senate, to make Treaties, provided two thirds of the Senators present concur; and he shall nominate, and by and with the Advice and Consent of the Senate, shall appoint Ambassadors, other public Ministers and Consuls, Judges of the supreme Court, and all other Officers of the United States, whose Appointments are not herein otherwise provided for, and which shall be established by Law: but the Congress may by Law vest the Appointment of such inferior Officers, as they think proper, in the President alone, in the Courts of Law, or in the Heads of Departments.

The President shall have Power to fill up all Vacancies that may happen during the Recess of the Senate, by granting Commissions which shall expire at the End of their next Session.

Section. 3.

He shall from time to time give to the Congress Information of the State of the Union, and recommend to their Consideration such Measures as he shall judge necessary and expedient; he may, on extraordinary Occasions, convene both Houses, or either of them, and in Case of Disagreement between them, with Respect to the Time of Adjournment, he may adjourn them to such Time as he shall think proper; he shall receive Ambassadors and other public Ministers; he shall take Care that the Laws be faithfully executed, and shall Commission all the Officers of the United States.

Section. 4.

The President, Vice President and all civil Officers of the United States, shall be removed from Office on Impeachment for, and Conviction of, Treason, Bribery, or other high Crimes and Misdemeanors.

Article III.

Section. 1.

The judicial Power of the United States, shall be vested in one supreme Court, and in such inferior Courts as the Congress may from time to time ordain and establish. The Judges, both of the supreme and inferior Courts, shall hold their Offices during good Behaviour, and shall, at stated Times, receive for their Services, a Compensation, which shall not be diminished during their Continuance in Office.

Section. 2.

The judicial Power shall extend to all Cases, in Law and Equity, arising under this Constitution, the Laws of the United States, and Treaties made, or which shall be made, under their Authority;—to all Cases affecting Ambassadors, other public Ministers and Consuls;—to all Cases of admiralty and maritime Jurisdiction;—to Controversies to which the United States shall be a Party;—to Controversies between two or more States;— between a State and Citizens of another State,—between Citizens of different States,—between Citizens of the same State claiming Lands under Grants of different States, and between a State, or the Citizens thereof, and foreign States, Citizens or Subjects.

In all Cases affecting Ambassadors, other public Ministers and Consuls, and those in which a State shall be Party, the supreme Court shall have original Jurisdiction. In all the other Cases before mentioned, the supreme Court shall have appellate Jurisdiction, both as to Law and Fact, with such Exceptions, and under such Regulations as the Congress shall make.

The Trial of all Crimes, except in Cases of Impeachment, shall be by Jury; and such Trial shall be held in the State where the said Crimes shall have been committed; but when not committed within any State, the Trial shall be at such Place or Places as the Congress may by Law have directed.

Section. 3.

Treason against the United States, shall consist only in levying War against them, or in adhering to their Enemies, giving them Aid and Comfort. No Person shall be convicted of Treason unless on the Testimony of two Witnesses to the same overt Act, or on Confession in open Court.

The Congress shall have Power to declare the Punishment of Treason, but no Attainder of Treason shall work Corruption of Blood, or Forfeiture except during the Life of the Person attainted.

Article. IV.

Section. 1.

Full Faith and Credit shall be given in each State to the public Acts, Records, and judicial Proceedings of every other State. And the Congress may by general Laws prescribe the Manner in which such Acts, Records and Proceedings shall be proved, and the Effect thereof.

Section. 2.

The Citizens of each State shall be entitled to all Privileges and Immunities of Citizens in the several States.

A Person charged in any State with Treason, Felony, or other Crime, who shall flee from Justice, and be found in another State, shall on Demand of the executive Authority of the State from which he fled, be delivered up, to be removed to the State having Jurisdiction of the Crime.

No Person held to Service or Labour in one State, under the Laws thereof, escaping into another, shall, in Consequence of any Law or Regulation therein, be discharged from such Service or Labour, but shall be delivered up on Claim of the Party to whom such Service or Labour may be due.

Section. 3.

New States may be admitted by the Congress into this Union; but no new State shall be formed or erected within the Jurisdiction of any other State; nor any State be formed by the Junction of two or more States, or Parts of States, without the Consent of the Legislatures of the States concerned as well as of the Congress.

The Congress shall have Power to dispose of and make all needful Rules and Regulations respecting the Territory or other Property belonging to the United States; and nothing in this Constitution shall be so construed as to Prejudice any Claims of the United States, or of any particular State.

Section. 4.

The United States shall guarantee to every State in this Union a Republican Form of Government, and shall protect each of them against Invasion; and on Application of the Legislature, or of the Executive (when the Legislature cannot be convened), against domestic Violence.

Article. V.

The Congress, whenever two thirds of both Houses shall deem it necessary, shall propose Amendments to this Constitution, or, on the Application of the Legislatures of two thirds of the several States, shall call a Convention for proposing Amendments, which, in either Case, shall be valid to all Intents and Purposes, as Part of this Constitution, when ratified by the Legislatures of three fourths of the several States, or by Conventions in three fourths thereof, as the one or the other Mode of Ratification may be proposed by the Congress; Provided that no Amendment which may be made prior to the Year One thousand eight hundred and eight shall in any Manner affect the first and fourth Clauses in the Ninth Section of the first Article; and that no State, without its Consent, shall be deprived of its equal Suffrage in the Senate.

Article. VI.

All Debts contracted and Engagements entered into, before the Adoption of this Constitution, shall be as valid against the United States under this Constitution, as under the Confederation.

This Constitution, and the Laws of the United States which shall be made in Pursuance thereof; and all Treaties made, or which shall be made, under the Authority of the United States, shall be the supreme Law of the Land; and the Judges in every State shall be bound thereby, any Thing in the Constitution or Laws of any State to the Contrary notwithstanding.

The Senators and Representatives before mentioned, and the Members of the several State Legislatures, and all executive and judicial Officers, both of the United States and of the several States, shall be bound by Oath or

Affirmation, to support this Constitution; but no religious Test shall ever be required as a Qualification to any Office or public Trust under the United States.

Article. VII.

The Ratification of the Conventions of nine States, shall be sufficient for the Establishment of this Constitution between the States so ratifying the Same.

The Word, "the," being interlined between the seventh and eighth Lines of the first Page, The Word "Thirty" being partly written on an Erazure in the fifteenth Line of the first Page, The Words "is tried" being interlined between the thirty second and thirty third Lines of the first Page and the Word "the" being interlined between the forty third and forty fourth Lines of the second Page.

Attest William Jackson Secretary

done in Convention by the Unanimous Consent of the States present the Seventeenth Day of September in the Year of our Lord one thousand seven hundred and Eighty seven and of the Independance of the United States of America the Twelfth In witness whereof We have hereunto subscribed our Names,

G°. Washington
Presidt and deputy from Virginia

Delaware

Geo: Read
Gunning Bedford jun
John Dickinson
Richard Bassett
Jaco: Broom

Maryland

James McHenry
Dan of St Thos. Jenifer
Danl. Carroll

Virginia

John Blair
James Madison Jr.

North Carolina

Wm. Blount
Richd. Dobbs Spaight
Hu Williamson

South Carolina

J. Rutledge
Charles Cotesworth Pinckney
Charles Pinckney
Pierce Butler

Georgia

William Few
Abr Baldwin

New Hampshire

John Langdon
Nicholas Gilman

Massachusetts

Nathaniel Gorham
Rufus King

Connecticut

Wm. Saml. Johnson
Roger Sherman

New York

Alexander Hamilton

New Jersey

Wil: Livingston
David Brearley
Wm. Paterson
Jona: Dayton

Pennsylvania

B Franklin
Thomas Mifflin
Robt. Morris
Geo. Clymer
Thos. FitzSimons
Jared Ingersoll
James Wilson
Gouv Morris

The Bill of Rights

The First 10 Amendments to the Constitution

I

Congress shall make no law respecting an establishment of religion, or prohibiting the free exercise thereof; or abridging the freedom of speech, or of the press; or the right of the people peaceably to assemble, and to petition the Government for a redress of grievances.

II

A well regulated Militia, being necessary to the security of a free State, the right of the people to keep and bear Arms, shall not be infringed.

III

No Soldier shall, in time of peace be quartered in any house, without the consent of the Owner, nor in time of war, but in a manner to be prescribed by law.

IV

The right of the people to be secure in their persons, houses, papers, and effects, against unreasonable searches and seizures, shall not be violated, and no Warrants shall issue, but upon probable cause, supported by Oath or affirmation, and particularly describing the place to be searched, and the persons or things to be seized.

V

No person shall be held to answer for a capital, or otherwise infamous crime, unless on a presentment or indictment of a Grand Jury, except in cases arising in the land or naval forces, or in the Militia, when in actual service in time of War or public danger; nor shall any person be subject for the same offence to be twice put in jeopardy of life or limb; nor shall be compelled in any criminal case to be a witness against himself, nor be deprived of life, liberty, or property, without due process of law; nor shall private property be taken for public use, without just compensation.

VI

In all criminal prosecutions, the accused shall enjoy the right to a speedy and public trial, by an impartial jury of the State and district wherein the crime shall have been committed, which district shall have been previously ascertained by law, and to be informed of the nature and cause of the accusation; to be confronted with the witnesses against him; to have compulsory process for obtaining witnesses in his favor, and to have the Assistance of Counsel for his defence.

VII

In Suits at common law, where the value in controversy shall exceed twenty dollars, the right of trial by jury shall be preserved, and no fact tried by a jury, shall be otherwise re-examined in any Court of the United States, than according to the rules of the common law.

VIII

Excessive bail shall not be required, nor excessive fines imposed, nor cruel and unusual punishments inflicted.

IX

The enumeration in the Constitution, of certain rights, shall not be construed to deny or disparage others retained by the people.

X

The powers not delegated to the United States by the Constitution, nor prohibited by it to the States, are reserved to the States respectively, or to the people.

INDEX